The Battle of Glorieta

The Battle

# of Glorieta

UNION VICTORY IN THE WEST

Don E. Alberts

Foreword by Donald S. Frazier

Texas A&M University Press
College Station

Manufactured in the United States of America

Fifth Printing, 2010

The paper used in this book meets the minimum requirements
of the American National Standard for Permanence
of paper for Printed Library Materials, Z39.48-1984.
Binding materials have been chosen for durability.

Library of Congress Cataloging-in-Publication Data

Alberts, Don E.
The battle of Glorieta : Union victory in the west / Don E. Alberts ; foreword by Donald S. Frazier. — 1st ed.
p. cm. — (Texas A&M University military history series ; no. 61)
Includes bibliographical references and index.
ISBN 1-58544-100-7 (pbk.)
1. Glorieta Pass (N.M.), Battle of, 1862. I. Title. II. Series: Texas A&M University military history series ; 61.
E473.4.A43 1998
973.7'31—dc21 98-5216
CIP

To

Kip and Beth Siler, of Glorieta,

and

Mildred Kemper and Nancy Best, of Texas,

each of whom made the telling of this story

more important.

Contents

Illustrations

MAPS

Foreword

Unbeknownst to most Americans, the U.S. Civil War was a continental conflict. The usual focus on the East, and the exploits of Robert E. Lee's Army of Northern Virginia in particular, is more a reflection of the way we remember the war than how it was actually prosecuted and pursued at the time. For Americans of 1861, interest in places such as California, New Mexico, Colorado, and Texas far outshone the stale and stodgy settled portions of the nation. The West was the nation's future, the East the nation's past.

When secession shredded the national fabric, the western territories were some of the ripping blades. As Union and Confederate leaders formed their strategic plans in the first months of conflict, the fate of the lands of the Far West shaped their thinking. Southerners especially desired to occupy that real estate which had been the center of so much rhetoric and controversy in the 1850s. They were encouraged in this scheme by rumors of secessionist plots from Oregon to Arizona. To establish a dynamic, viable nation, Southerners argued, the Confederacy would have to advance to the Pacific shore. Confederate armies must seize their nation's share of the inheritance. Southerners must conquer the West.

Thus began an important chain of events that would eventually lead to Glorieta, New Mexico. Union men from across the Great Plains, the Pacific Slope, and the Rocky Mountains gathered at recruiting places to oppose the ambitions of those they considered reckless demagogues married to a labor system both outdated and immoral. They called their enemies "Rebels," insisting that these southerners were simply attempting to overturn the U.S. constitution.

Across the South, but most importantly among the farms and pastures of Texas, other Americans also gathered, with a different view of recent events. Abolitionists had sundered the nation, they argued, ignoring constitutional rights to property and abandoning the manifest destiny of the nation to expand. Simply put, the inhabitants of the north were displaying a latent, Puritan, righteous indignation. Colonel Tom Green, commander of the 5th Texas Mounted Volunteers, referred to his foe as "hadn't oughters" and "self-righteous witch burners" when asked for his reasons to fight. Many southerners believed that the so-called "Yankees" were jealous of their influence in national affairs, and were trying every scheme possible to subvert the prosperity and power of an increasingly affluent and important South.

The leap from such generalizations, stereotypes, posturing, and lecturing to marching and shooting is a long one, and many seemed stunned by the military violence that broke out in the summer of 1861. Once the fighting began, both sides backed up and reevaluated the momentous events. Then with deadly earnestness, they equipped their nations for a deadlier, and decidedly grimmer, future.

Oddly enough, a vestige of the earlier idealistic enthusiasm remained as the effects of combats in Missouri and Virginia dampened with distance, and troops in Denver and San Antonio remained true to their initial patriotic impulse and idealism. Thus, while the war back east evolved into a darker and more sinister beast, these western armies were just getting their campaigns underway. While hundreds of thousands of men gathered in grim array on the Potomac and Tennessee, a few thousand prepared to do their part—months out of sync with the rapidly changing events of the war—on the banks of the Rio Grande and South Platte.

What followed was a year-long episode in the course of the Civil War that still struggles to find its place within the larger context of the war. Robert E. Lee and Ulysses S. Grant were not involved, and its combatants genuinely fretted over missing the spotlight and martial fame that their kinsmen and friends enjoyed on distant battlefields. Many of these worrying soldiers would fill unmarked graves in what remains a remote and lonely place. All of the participants emerged changed. Some never would get over their experiences at places like Valverde and Glorieta, and marked the beginning of their manhood from those early months of 1862.

Lately the Confederate invasion of New Mexico and the war in the Far West has received much attention. Always a curiosity to military enthusiasts, the Confederate invasion of New Mexico has inspired at least one western film and more than a half dozen books of varying quality and insight. Four major campaign studies exists, supplemented by a scattering of published primary accounts, journal articles, magazine pieces, and a growing array of battle treatments.

The climax of the war in the Far West was the Battle of Glorieta, and now this combat has received its fair treatment. No scholar or writer has spent as much time researching this fight, thinking about this fight, or actually covering the ground of this fight, as Don Alberts. He calls this battle the "Gettysburg of the West." Maybe so. Perhaps by reflecting the glow of that more famous and titanic struggle in the East, Glorieta—fought more than a year earlier than the Pennsylvania battle—will receive the attention it has long warranted.

—Donald S. Frazier
Abilene, Texas

Acknowledgments

This history of the most important Civil War battle in the Far West reflects almost twenty years of scholarly and field research, much of that time shared with interested and informed students of the Battle of Glorieta.

Certainly foremost among them were Professor Don Frazier of McMurry University in Abilene, Texas, and Dean Jerry Thompson of Texas A&M International University in Laredo, each an authority on the Civil War in the Far West. Both understood the need for the credible historian to engage in field exploration as well as the more traditional documentary scholarship. They generously shared with me the results of their own experiences and research. In addition, Don Frazier prepared the maps that accompany this text; he was an indispensable helper. I also spent much pleasant and productive time in the field, not only with my family but with Dee Brecheisen of Bosque Farms, New Mexico, and with Dr. Phil Mead, Jake Johnson, and Frank Dean of Albuquerque, locating artifact evidence from which battle positions and movements could be identified. Likewise, Lt. Col. Luke Barnett, III, of the Third Armored Cavalry Regiment, shared with me his own Glorieta field research, simplifying my own efforts considerably.

This book has benefited greatly from the efforts of many members of the Glorieta Battlefield Preservation Society, of which I was president for some time. We engaged in a long and successful campaign to save the sites around Pigeon's Ranch and Johnson's Ranch from development or destruction. Several individuals, as well as descendant and reenactment organizations, played key roles in our preservation efforts. Among other activities, they organized reenactments and other living history events that publicized the need to protect Glorieta. Wess Rogers, Cindy and Dave Wilson, the New Mexico Territorial Volunteers, the New Mexico Sons of Confederate Veterans, the Territorial Brass Band, the Artillery Company of New Mexico, the First Colorado Volunteers, the First New Mexico Volunteers, Battery B of the Fourth Artillery, Company C of the Fourth Texas Mounted Volunteers, and the Fifth Texas Mounted Volunteers all enthusiastically worked to save the battlefields. A former New Mexican, Frances H. Kennedy of the Conservation Fund of Arlington, Virginia, provided national publicity for the need for preservation of Glorieta.

State Senator Steve Stoddard and the New Mexico congressional delegation introduced and supported legislation that ultimately made our preservation effort a success. And in the final stages of the long campaign, two fine Texas women, Mildred Kemper of the Columbus, Texas, United Daughters of the Confederacy, and her daughter, Nancy Best of Dallas, added their enthusiastic support and influence. Our combined efforts succeeded in 1991, as the Glorieta Battlefield became a major component of the nearby Pecos National Historical Park.

The process of protecting Glorieta brought to light much new information about Civil War participants and events that has made my own research for this book considerably more meaningful. Also adding immeasurably to my understanding of the battle was the accidental discovery in 1987 of the mass burial site of those Confederates killed around Pigeon's Ranch. Kip and Beth Siler, on whose property the remains were located, had the knowledge and conscientiousness to recognize the importance of the find and to make the site available for forensic and scholarly study. That added significantly to the body of knowledge relevant to the Battle of Glorieta and made this book considerably richer. Their contributions are greatly appreciated.

Finally, I thank my family for their help and support. I spent many hours afield and in various archives with my wife, Rosemary, and daughter, Jackie, as well as with my son, Marine Capt. Clint Alberts, with whom I located many important positions on the battlefield. I consider them, and all the others who helped so much, to be my coauthors.

I hope this book, in conjunction with the preserved battlefield at Glorieta, will serve to memorialize those brave young soldiers who died there for the causes they held dear.

The Battle of Glorieta

CHAPTER ONE

Confederate Invasion

An army under my command enters New Mexico, to take possession of it in the name of and for the benefit of the Confederate States.

—*Brig. Gen. Henry H. Sibley*

Much indeed has been written about the "War in the West" during recent years. Most works, however, have tended to emphasize the often severe fighting and engagements that took place along the Kansas-Missouri border, within the states of Missouri and Arkansas, and, on a quite disastrous level of guerrilla warfare, in Indian Territory. While battles in the trans-Mississippi theater often involved large opposing forces and important issues and movements, none were more important to the future of the nation than smaller, less well reported military events still farther to the west.

The 1861–62 Confederate invasion of the Federal territory of New Mexico was the westernmost campaign of the Civil War. On its outcome depended the future of what would become the American Southwest. On that outcome also hung the fortunes of Colorado, New Mexico's sister territory to the north, of the transmountain region comprising Utah Territory and, later, Nevada, and of southern California. The key battle of the Civil War in New Mexico occurred at Glorieta, some twenty miles southeast of the territorial capital of Santa Fe, and it marked the farthest advance northward by the Confederacy in the Far West, just as the great encounter at Gettysburg during the following year would define the furthest significant penetration of the North by Confederates in the eastern theater of war.[1]

Although huge, New Mexico Territory was sparsely populated. It con-

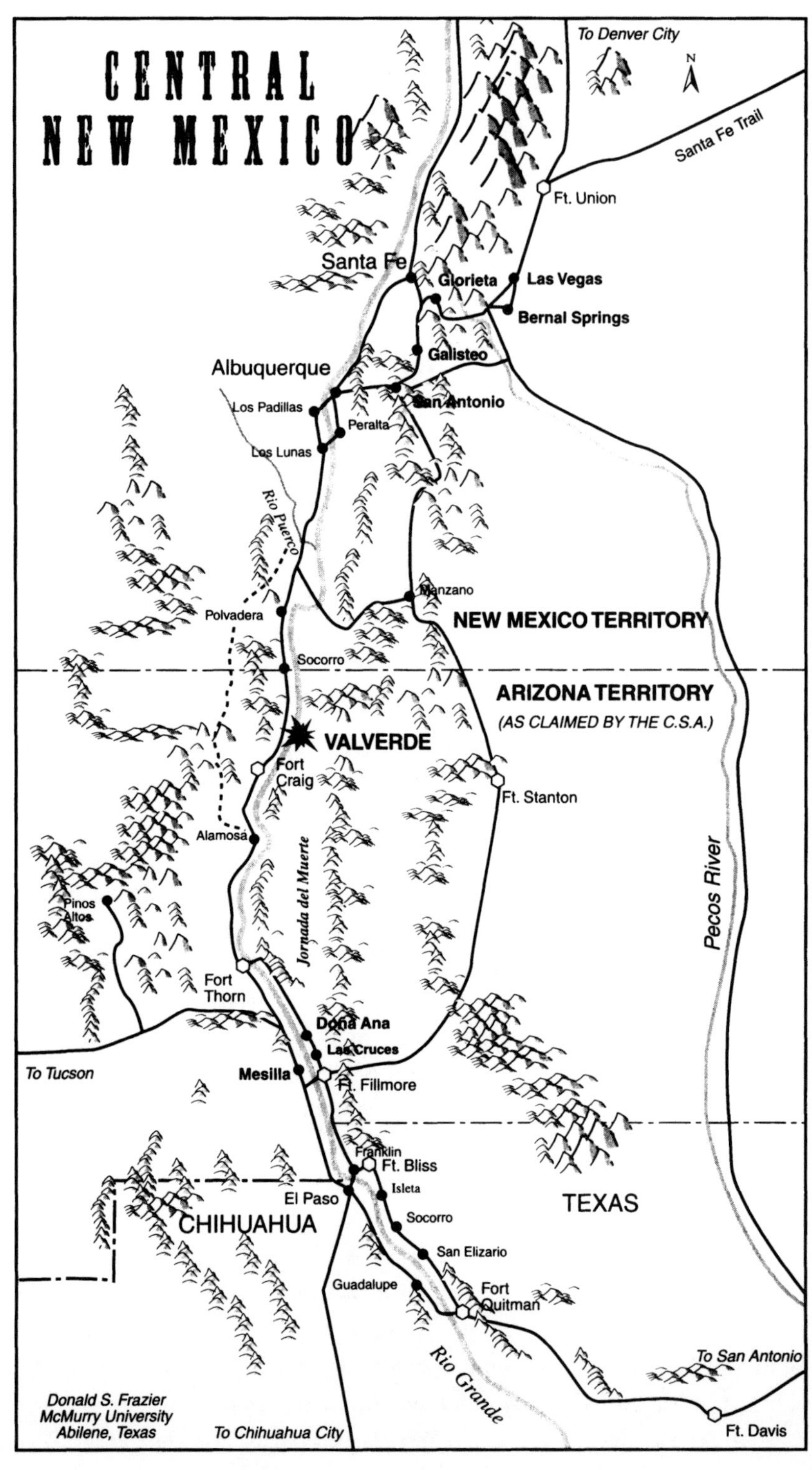

CENTRAL NEW MEXICO
To Denver City
N
Santa Fe Trail
Ft. Union
Santa Fe
Glorieta
Las Vegas
Bernal Springs
Galisteo
Albuquerque
San Antonio
Los Padillas
Peralta
Los Lunas
Rio Puerco
Manzano
Polvadera
NEW MEXICO TERRITORY
Socorro
ARIZONA TERRITORY
(AS CLAIMED BY THE C.S.A.)
VALVERDE
Fort Craig
Ft. Stanton
Alamosa
Jornada del Muerte
Pecos River
Pinos Altos
Fort Thorn
Doña Ana
Las Cruces
To Tucson
Mesilla
Ft. Fillmore
Franklin
Ft. Bliss
Isleta
El Paso
TEXAS
Socorro
CHIHUAHUA
San Elizario
Guadalupe
Fort Quitman
Rio Grande
To San Antonio
Ft. Davis
Donald S. Frazier
McMurry University
Abilene, Texas
To Chihuahua City

sisted of the present states of New Mexico and Arizona, plus the southern tip of Nevada, and was reasonably accessible from the east by only two routes. From the north, specifically Missouri, the Santa Fe Trail crossed Kansas and southern Colorado Territory to enter northeastern New Mexico and continue some two hundred miles to Santa Fe. From the south, the Overland Stage route connected San Antonio, Texas, with the west coast through western Texas and southern New Mexico. Between these two major roads, the old Spanish and Mexican Camino Reál, or Royal Road, came out of Mexico, crossing the Overland Stage line at present day El Paso and continuing northward along the valley of the Rio Grande to meet the Santa Fe Trail at its namesake village. These roads, and the vital water of the Rio Grande, were the physical factors that defined the course of the Civil War in this isolated and arid region.[2]

The people of New Mexico were also significant to the Civil War campaign. The increasingly hostile Comanche, Apache, and Navajo Indians of western Texas and New Mexico played no direct role, but harassed isolated parties of soldiers whenever the opportunity presented itself. The bulk of the native Hispanic population lived in the northern half of New Mexico, which was tied closely to the Union by trade with the northern states through Missouri. A sprinkling of Anglo merchants and government officials also lived in the area, many having married into Hispanic families over the course of the previous two decades. Having been citizens of the United States for only some fourteen years since the Mexican War, the Hispanic natives tended to have minimal loyalty to, or interest in, the Federal government and essentially no interest in the great issue of slavery that had brought on the Civil War.[3] However, while there was no overriding issue uniting them behind the Union effort, they were in agreement on one particular feeling that resulted from prior experiences of invasion and racial insults—they detested Texans. And in New Mexico, Texans comprised the invading Confederate army.

In southern New Mexico—roughly south of the thirty-fourth degree of latitude, or the town of Socorro—the populace was more closely tied to the South through trade and demographic patterns. The major settlement of that region, Mesilla, was a hotbed of secessionist ardor as the Civil War began, an ardor that quickly cooled after the town had been occupied by Confederate soldiers for an extended period.[4]

Texan interest in invading New Mexico Territory began during the early months of the Civil War. On January 28, 1861, a secession convention meeting in Austin passed an ordinance that, when ratified by the voters, made Texas the seventh state to leave the Federal Union. Soon after Texas seceded, the Union departmental commander surrendered all Federal military property to the state and ordered all his troops to withdraw to the Gulf Coast and leave Texas. By the end of March, the garrison of Fort Bliss, near Franklin (now El Paso), Texas, abandoned it to state agents. Soon thereafter, Federal troops at other far western posts—Forts Davis, Quitman, Stockton, Duncan, Lancaster, and Clark—did likewise.[5]

Texan officials were not slow to exploit this military vacuum. During late June and early July, 1861, Lt. Col. John R. Baylor led a battery of artillery and four companies of his Second Texas Mounted Rifles Regiment into Fort Bliss as its new garrison. His immediate objective was capture of still-occupied Fort Fillmore, in the Mesilla Valley of southern New Mexico, some forty miles north of Fort Bliss. By audacious maneuver and aided by almost incredible incompetence or treason on the part of the Federal commander of Fort Fillmore, Baylor was able to force his enemies to abandon the post during late July. He subsequently captured almost the entire garrison as it retreated northeastward farther into New Mexico.[6]

Baylor quickly proclaimed all of New Mexico Territory south of the thirty-fourth parallel to be the Confederate Territory of Arizona with himself as military governor. He kept his small force busy skirmishing with Indians who raided the region around Franklin and into the Mesilla Valley, and the Texans engaged small parties of Federal soldiers from Fort Craig, the principal Union post guarding central New Mexico, some one hundred miles north of the surrendered Fort Fillmore. From Fort Craig, Col. Edward R. S. Canby, commanding the Department of New Mexico, maintained small outposts at strategic points between Fort Craig and Baylor's headquarters at Mesilla. Canby also kept patrols actively in the field to detect any further advance northward by Baylor.[7]

While John Baylor was establishing and maintaining this easy, but tenuous, lodgement in New Mexico, another Confederate officer was preparing the way for a more ambitious and extensive invasion of the territory. Henry Hopkins Sibley, a former regular officer serving in New Mexico, had resigned his commission in the United States Army and traveled to the Confederate capital of Richmond, Virginia. There, he laid his plan to invade and occupy New Mexico before the southern president, Jefferson Davis. Sibley would enlist a mounted force in Texas, live off the land once within New Mexico, easily defeat the Federal forces there, and secure the military supplies, and perhaps natural resources, of the territory.[8] Davis approved of the scheme, which, even if it seemed somewhat farfetched,

Brig. Gen. Henry Hopkins Sibley, commander of the Confederate forces in New Mexico. *Courtesy U.S. Military History Institute, Carlisle Barracks, Pennsylvania.*

held out the possibility of reasonable return compared to the small cost of the expedition to the Confederate treasury. To carry it out, he commissioned Sibley a brigadier general, with authority to raise a brigade of mounted volunteers in southern Texas and pursue the invasion and occupation of New Mexico Territory.[9]

General Sibley actually planned a much more ambitious campaign, the details of which he may or may not have shared with President Davis. According to Sibley's trusted artillery chief, Trevanion T. Teel, the new general intended to march northward after taking New Mexico, capture the rich mines of Colorado Territory, then march westward through Salt

Lake City and across the mountains and deserts, finally to occupy the southern California seaports of San Diego and Los Angeles. By one stroke, with a minimal force and living off the land and its sparse population, Sibley would bring the entire present-day Southwest under Confederate control, along with its highly desirable transcontinental railroad route.[10]

The general believed the native people of New Mexico, as well as recent immigrants to Colorado, Utah, and California, would join his Texans and swell his ranks as he advanced northward and westward. In this he was seriously mistaken. As an experienced serving officer in New Mexico, he should have known that the Hispanic residents of the territory would be unlikely to join Texans in any endeavor; in fact, they later fought with considerable success against the invaders and bushwhacked straggling Rebels at every opportunity.[11] While there were a few Anglo New Mexicans who favored the South, and they tended to be quite vocal, there was little actual support for the Confederacy within the territory. In one spectacular demonstration of that fact, the famous frontiersman "Kit" Carson, a resident of Taos in northern New Mexico, tore down a Rebel flag raised by Confederate sympathizers in that town, nailed the Stars and Stripes to a pole, and hoisted it on the Taos plaza. He then dared anyone to tear down the flag of his country and set a guard to see that it flew day and night—as it does to this day in commemoration of the event.[12] Likewise, in Colorado the miners tended to be fiercely loyal to the old flag, and the Utah Mormons, though undoubtedly caring little for the Federal government, indicated no affection for and never seriously considered alliance with the Confederates. Similarly, a few vocal southern sympathizers in California attracted attention early in 1861, but the vast majority of that state's people were loyal, and in fact rapidly organized military forces to oppose Sibley.

Other aspects of Sibley's plan were equally flawed. The Federal forces within the territory were, with few exceptions, competently led and staunchly loyal; military conquest would not be the pushover represented to Jefferson Davis. The Confederate general also apparently misunderstood or ignored the logistical realities of New Mexico. The Rio Grande Valley would barely support its indigenous population, much less some three thousand mounted soldiers with their associated horses and mules. Even the regular army in New Mexico was not self-supporting, having to import a significant part of its food, fodder, and other military supplies from outside the territory.[13]

The plan was essentially impossible given the logistics, transportation, and communications problems in the Far West. Even if it had been practical, however, there was a final and fatal flaw. Sibley himself was not the man for the job. A native of Louisiana, West Point educated, and a gallant veteran of Mexican War battles at Vera Cruz and Medellin, Sibley was only forty-five years old as he began preparing his force for the invasion of New Mexico. Although he was a reasonably good organizer and the inventor of such military equipment as the Sibley tent and stove used by the Union army throughout the Civil War and afterward, Henry Sibley's army career between the Mexican War and the Civil War was lackluster in the extreme. The onset of war between the states held the prospect of rescuing him from obscurity. Unfortunately for him, he had cultivated or become victim of personal traits that would nullify that prospect. He was a heavy drinker, even more so than the average hard-drinking frontier dragoon officer, being described later by his soldiers as a "walking whiskey keg." He also suffered from some unidentified, recurring illness. Professor Jerry Thompson, Sibley's biographer, has analyzed this illness and drinking syndrome and is unable to determine whether the old soldier drank because he was ill or was ill because he drank.[14] Either way, the effect on his performance during the New Mexico campaign was the same and seriously affected the entire venture and the lives of his men.

In addition, Sibley tended to be a dreamer. In later years, Maj. Trevanion T. Teel, who was close enough to the general to know his character, felt that he was "too prone to let the morrow take care of itself." If that were not enough, his courage was suspect to his men; somehow, he managed to miss every battle fought during the New Mexico campaign. Whiskey rather than cowardice was likely the immediate cause, but the effect on the Texan soldiers of his personal habits and obvious leadership defects was almost universal by the end of the campaign.[15] Henry Hopkins Sibley was, without doubt, one of the Confederacy's worst generals.

The troops he raised, however, were examples of the best volunteers answering the southern call to arms during 1861; with few exceptions, they became excellent soldiers during the New Mexico campaign. Organization of the Sibley Brigade began during August, 1861, as General Sibley established his headquarters in San Antonio, Texas, and advertised for recruits for his upcoming venture. Over the next two months, he created and filled three thousand-man regiments, the Fourth, Fifth, and Seventh Texas Mounted Volunteers, with attached supply and artillery units, a total of approximately 3,200 troops, a brigadier general's normal command. The staff, field, and company officers, NCOs, and privates were a cross section of rural and urban frontier society, with each of ten companies within a regiment tending to be essentially the political structure of the county or town from

Lt. Col. William R. Scurry, Fourth Texas Mounted Volunteers. Commander of Confederate forces at the Battle of Glorieta, he later rose to the rank of brigadier general in the Confederate army. *Courtesy Colorado Historical Society.*

which the recruits came, transferred to a military context. This was an army of neighbors and no "brutal and licentious soldiery," the widely held picture of these Texans as a rowdy, undisciplined crowd coming more from their own accounts of individualistic, open-order tactics in battle rather than from particularly heinous behavior.[16]

To command these regiments, Sibley chose prominent Texans with considerable military experience. Col. James Reily, veteran of the army of the Republic of Texas and former United States consul to Russia, led the Fourth, with Lt. Col. William R. Scurry as his second-in-command. Scurry, known locally as "Dirty Shirt" for his grimy clothes worn during a hard campaign for Texan secession earlier in the year, was also an experienced officer from Republic of Texas days and the Mexican War. In Reily's absence on diplomatic duties to Mexico, the forty-year-old Scurry would later command the Confederates at Glorieta. Another veteran of San Jacinto, numerous interwar Indian campaigns, and the Mexican War, was appointed to command the Fifth Regiment. Tom Green, prominent state hero and politician, served as colonel of the unit throughout the New Mexico campaign and was Sibley's second-in-command, leading the Texans in the Battle of Valverde. The third regiment, the Seventh Texas Mounted Volunteers, was commanded by Col. William Steele, a West Point graduate and veteran of the Seminole Wars in Florida and of the Mexican War, as well as of regular army service during the 1850s.[17] These key officers would serve Sibley well, indeed, during the upcoming year of 1862.

By late October, 1861, Sibley had completed organizing, staffing, and supplying the force that would be his instrument of conquest. The brigade, traveling in detachments to avoid overuse of skimpy water holes and wells, marched westward along the Overland Stage road, through Uvalde, Forts Stockton and Davis, and the Rio Grande Valley, reaching Franklin, Texas, and nearby Fort Bliss just before Christmas. They were hurried on their journey by receipt en route of an urgent message from Colonel Baylor in Mesilla, forecasting an attack by Federal forces and asking for reinforcements.[18]

As his troops began to reach the Fort Bliss area, General Sibley sent them still farther north along the Rio Grande to camp in the vicinity of Mesilla and Fort Thorn, an abandoned Union post near present-day Hatch, New Mexico. As the scattered detachments straggled through Franklin and into southern New Mexico, Sibley proclaimed his invading force to be the "Army of New Mexico" and assured residents of the Federal territory that his Confederate army came "as friends . . . to liberate them from the yoke of military despotism . . . to insure and revere their religion, and to restore their civil and political liberties."[19]

Sibley supplanted Colonel Baylor as commander of all Confederate military forces within New Mexico, adding Baylor's troops to those slowly concentrating around Fort Thorn. By early February, 1862, that concentration was complete. Leaving Colonel Steele and half the Seventh Regiment behind to occupy and guard Confederate claims in the Mesilla Valley and southern New Mexico, Sibley moved northward along the Rio Grande to attack the Union forces in Fort Craig. With approximately 2,500 mounted men, fifteen pieces of artillery, and an extensive supply train, Sibley looked forward to an easy invasion of New Mexico Territory.[20]

With his overall strategic goal of occupation of the entire Southwest intact, the Rebel general's immediate goals were the capture of Fort Craig, opening the way northward to occupation of the Union supply subdepot at Albuquerque and of the territorial capital and its guardian Fort Marcy at Santa Fe. That accomplished, and with the supplies thus acquired, the way would be clear for Sibley's brigade to advance into northeastern New Mexico for an attack on Fort Union, the Federal supply center for the entire Southwest. Capture of the military goods and food in Fort Union was absolutely necessary for continuation of Sibley's plan to invade Colorado Territory and secure the wealth of its booming mining regions for the Confederacy. By February 20, the Texans had approached Fort Craig, skirmished with elements of the post's garrison, and prepared to begin the conquest of the rest of New Mexico.[21] That would not be nearly as easy as Sibley hoped.

As the Confederate invaders spent an inordinate amount of time concentrating and supplying themselves, then sluggishly advanced toward him, the Union departmental commander, Colonel Canby, was extremely active. A forty-four-year-old West Pointer, he had received citations for gal-

Col. Edward R. S. Canby, commanding the Department of New Mexico for the Union. He prudently directed the defeat of the Texans' ambitions in the Southwest. *Courtesy National Archives.*

lant and meritorious conduct at the battles of Contreras, Churubusco, and the Belen Gate during the Mexican War. Highly competent and steady, Canby was also taciturn, keeping his own counsel and often marching along ahead of his men, silent and with an old cigar unlit between his lips; he was labeled the "Prudent Soldier" by his biographer. A better commander for Union forces in New Mexico could hardly be imagined.[22]

Once convinced that the Texans intended to attack him up the Rio Grande Valley and obviously at Fort Craig, rather than along the Pecos River, Canby concentrated his forces. He ordered far-flung outposts abandoned and called in their garrisons to bolster his forces in Fort Craig. In addition, he activated the territory's volunteer and militia units. Adequate supplies of ammunition and food reached the post from Albuquerque and Fort Union, while he put troops to work strengthening the adobe fort's defenses.[23]

Colonel Canby did not rely for the territory's defense solely upon forces available within New Mexico. In the Department of the Pacific, Federal officers were organizing an expeditionary brigade of California volunteers and an artillery company of regulars to march eastward from Fort Yuma, on the Colorado River, to prevent an invasion of southern California by helping Canby expel the Texans from New Mexico. Those forces, however, were still in California preparing for a long desert march as Sibley approached Fort Craig.[24]

The Union commander also requested that the governor of Colorado Territory send to the defense of New Mexico "as large a force of Colorado volunteers as can possibly be spared." Federal officials reacted quickly. The commander of the Department of Kansas, responding to Canby and Acting Governor Lewis L. Weld of Colorado, who was most anxious to provide for the defense of that territory by defending New Mexico, ordered the governor to "send all available forces you can possibly spare to reinforce Colonel Canby." Weld acted at once; one independent company of Colorado volunteers, after a strenuous march, reached Fort Craig as Sibley drew near. Their arrival brought Canby's strength to approximately 3,800 men in and around the post, some 1,200 of them seasoned and trained regulars. Farther north, another independent Colorado company was en route to Fort Craig, and an entire regiment of rugged miners and frontiersmen, the First Colorado Volunteers, prepared to move out of its territory to save New Mexico for the Union.[25]

Upon reaching the vicinity of Fort Craig in mid-February, Sibley realized that the position was too strong to be taken by direct assault.[26] An attempt to lure the Federals out of the fort for a fight on open ground failed when Canby refused to take the bait. The Confederates then decided to bypass the post, threaten the Union supply lines north to Albuquerque and Fort Union, and force the enemy into a major battle to keep those lines open. That plan worked, and the opposing forces met on February 21, 1862, in the first of four Civil War battles in New Mexico, the Battle of Valverde, fought five miles north of Fort Craig in the Rio Grande bottomland. Although General Sibley came onto the field early in the day, he quickly became ill and retired to his camp, turning over command of the battle to Col. Tom Green. The fortunes of war swayed back and forth during the day, but by evening the Rebels had captured one of the two Federal artillery batteries and had driven Canby's forces from the field to shelter behind the walls of Fort Craig. It was an impressive tactical success for the Texans, but it was a Pyrrhic victory. The Union forces were not badly damaged, certainly not destroyed. Fort Craig still stood and was now across the Confederates' own supply line back to the Mesilla Valley, and Sibley had only some five days' rations for men and animals.[27]

The Texans obviously faced a serious dilemma. They could try to retreat back to their scanty supplies left behind in the Mesilla Valley, although a still strong fort and enemy force now lay across their line of retreat; or they could continue northward, leaving that force in their rear, with the hope of capturing Federal supplies at Albuquerque, Santa Fe, and finally Fort Union. Sibley, almost certainly encouraged to do so by his key lieutenants, particularly Colonel Green and Lieutenant Colonel Scurry, chose to press on. Marching along the Camino Reál and the Rio Grande, the Rebels captured the village of Socorro essentially without a fight and established there a hospital to care for their sick and wounded men. Continuing slowly northward along the frontier highway, the brigade finally forded the icy river at Belen and reached their camp on the southern outskirts of the town of Albuquerque by early March. Under command of Maj. Charles L. Pyron, Second Texas Mounted Rifles, Sibley's advance party entered Albuquerque on March 2, only to find that Union forces had removed or destroyed almost all the military supplies and rations in the Post of Albuquerque's subdepot buildings. Nevertheless, they raised the Confederate flag over the plaza while a small band played "Dixie."[28]

Although Sibley badly needed the military supplies he had expected but failed to capture in Albuquerque, his men did manage to secure a forty-day supply of rations and other necessary materials through confiscation and purchase from local merchants and residents, as well as through capture of a small Federal post at Cubero, west of Albuquerque.[29] While that effort was under way and while his main body of troops rested and refitted south of town, Sibley established a comfortable headquarters in Albuquerque and sent his vanguard, still commanded by Major Pyron, farther north to Santa Fe. Pyron's advance element, an irregular unit commanded by Capt. John G. Phillips and known as the "Brigands" or "Company of Santa Fe Gamblers," reached the town on March 10. Pyron himself occupied the territorial capitol on March 13, only to find that its Federal garrison of Fort Marcy, along with the territorial government, had fled to Las Vegas, New Mexico, and the protection of Fort Union.[30]

As soldiers of the main body were doing in and around Albuquerque, over the next two weeks Pyron's men scoured Santa Fe for food and other supplies they badly needed. There were no recorded incidents of violence or serious outrage in either place, but the residents nevertheless were apprehensive and disturbed to see the Rebels in their midst. Mother Magdalen Hayden, mother superior of Santa Fe's Loretto Academy, wrote:

> *Our poor and distant territory has not been spared. The Texans, without any provocation, have sacked and almost ruined the richest portions and have forced the most respectable families to flee from their homes, not precisely by bad treatment, but by obliging them to deliver to them huge sums of money. To avoid handing over their money to these Texans, the heads of families and some others fled. . . . You can imagine better than I can describe what I felt on seeing all our troops, and that banner under whose shadow I had been raised, leave. . . . The terror which I felt is inexpressible.*[31]

The bulk of the Confederate force camped on the grounds of the residence of Judge Spruce M. Baird, on the outskirts of Albuquerque. Baird, the leading southern sympathizer in New Mexico, painted a rosy picture of the welcome the newly arrived troops could expect in northern New Mexico and started several unfounded and erroneous rumors regarding the weakness of the Federal forces they would face, as well as the amount of subsistence to be found. Absorbing these statements for about what they were worth, the Texas soldiers recovered their strength and awaited General Sibley's orders to move against the Federal forces guarding Fort Union.[32]

Many of the brigade officers spent their time enjoying Judge Baird's food and hospitality, while the enlisted men slept, ate, and saw the local sights. Sgt. Alfred B. Peticolas, of the Fourth Regiment, lay about the camp for two days enjoying the rumors and idle time, probably content to do so since he had no way to ride into town; the entire Fourth Texas Mounted Volunteer unit had been dismounted right after the Battle of Valverde. There had been such a high mortality rate among the horses and mules of the brigade that the surviving mounts of the Fourth had been redistributed among the other Texans; grumbling and with sore feet, the unfortunate newly minted foot soldiers served as infantry for the rest of the New Mexico campaign. A luckier Pvt. William Howell, of the Fifth, was able to ride into Albuquerque and "see several things that look a little similar to a civilized country, viz, dry goods, stores, church, frame work about houses, and several American citizens. . . . The Confederate flag is waving on that splendid pole, instead of the old Stars and Stripes."[33]

Sibley spent his time establishing his own brigade headquarters in Albuquerque and in setting up a hospital for the sick, including the many pneumonia cases that soon developed as the weather turned windy and cold. He also established a supply or commissary depot, detailing one company of the Fourth Texas and the San Elizario Spy Company, recruited earlier in southern New Mexico and West Texas, as its guard. By March 8,

Self-portrait of Sgt. Alfred B. Peticolas, Company C, Fourth Texas Mounted Volunteers. Drawn while resting in Texas following the New Mexico campaign. *Courtesy Arizona Historical Society.*

he was ready to start his army toward the immediate goal, the capture of Fort Union, some 150 miles to the northeast, and its absolutely indispensable supplies and munitions.[34]

Having already dispatched his advance party under Major Pyron to Santa Fe, Sibley sent nine companies of the Fourth Texas and the battalion (four companies) of the Seventh into the Sandia Mountains east of Albuquerque, there to find adequate grass and wood so that the men and the Seventh's horses could further recover their strength for the march and battles ahead. Most of the Fifth Regiment temporarily remained in the town, but four of its ten companies were soon detached to reinforce Pyron in Santa Fe.[35]

The beginning of this phase of Sibley's thrust toward Fort Union was far from auspicious. Sergeant Peticolas was in the first unit to march into the Sandia Mountains. "We took up the line of march today in a furious west wind," he wrote, and "the wind increased to almost a hurricane. Clouds of sand came driving against our backs. . . . I put my hat up over my face and thus protected my eyes as much as I could. Fortunately for us, the wind was at our backs and served to help us along." By evening the Fourth Texas had reached Tijeras Canyon, the pass eastward between the Sandia and Manzano mountain ranges, through which ran the most direct road to Fort Union, via the villages of San Antonio, San Antonito, Galisteo, and Glorieta. In bitter cold and driving wind, the troops camped on a slight slope alongside the stream running intermittently through the canyon.[36]

There the shivering soldiers spent two days while the rest of the Confederates joined them from Albuquerque. Peticolas did not waste the time; he had a novel, *The King and the Cobbler,* in his luggage and read it while snow fell in what became a typical New Mexico late-winter storm. One of his friends in Company C, Fourth Texas, had been assigned the duty of historian for the company. Seventeen-year-old Pvt. Ebenezer "Abe" Hanna recorded that they "lay in camps [suffering from] a very cold norther and some snow."[37]

Subsequently the camp was moved a few miles eastward through the canyon to escape the bitter west wind. There, at the village of Tijeras, water and wood were plentiful, but the miserable weather continued. After a night-long snow, Sergeant Peticolas found it "amusing to see the men as they woke and looked around with bewildered expressions, raking the snow out of their hats and shoes, but it was not very pleasant." The young lawyer from Victoria, Texas, weathered the storm by finding a snug place in one of the large supply wagons; with "my feet plunged into a mass of blankets and my overcoat on, I spent the time very comfortably," helped undoubtedly by reading another novel, *The Monk Knight of St. John*.[38]

Still trying to find a more sheltered location, the Fourth Regiment's Lieutenant Colonel Scurry, in command of the force east of Albuquerque, moved the encampment a mile farther north, along the eastern base of the Sandia Mountains, in and around the little village of San Antonio. Pvt. Bill Davidson, of the Fifth Regiment and temporarily posted east of the mountains, later recalled that in this new location it was still "very cold, sleeting and snowing all the time." Many Texans sought refuge with the local Hispanic inhabitants as an alternative to sleeping in the open or in tents. Abe Hanna got "a little protection in the Mexican huts," while Alfred Peticolas stopped "at a Mexican's house and he gives us leave to sleep inside in a room. . . . His lady spread a bed for me for tonight, and there is a warm fire in the hearth. . . . Just now the men are all lying around on the floor, some asleep and some talking. But the coughing is distressing."[39]

In fact, the weather caused many cases of pneumonia and other sickness during the twelve days Scurry's men were immobilized in the Sandia Mountains. The ill soldiers were sent back into Albuquerque to the hospital there, while those remaining loafed about, played cards, drank, danced and sang, or chased after a rumored Union wagon train believed to be near the snowbound Confederate camp. Others saw what could be seen of the nearby scenery.[40]

Sergeant Peticolas took the opportunity to climb a low ridge just east of present-day Cedar Crest, New Mexico, to sketch the Texan camp below. He also had time to complete a sketch of the Battle of Valverde, fought a month earlier, based on his own observations and those related by his companions on other parts of that battlefield. He, along with others, also prepared for the upcoming marches and fights. He traded his knife to another soldier "for a tremendous weapon, about 2 feet long and made of first-rate metal. It is a bowie knife, but more formidable in the hands of a man able to wield it than a sword."[41]

The enforced inactivity began to wear on the men's patience, and there was considerable concern not only with the increasing sickness, but with the death of scarce draft animals needed to pull the column's supply wagons and artillery pieces. Inevitably, there was also considerable griping and dissatisfaction with those in charge of affairs. Private Hanna felt there was no direction or plan. "Headquarters is generally . . . a figure head . . . never having any notion of what is ahead, only going on to see what is ahead of us." Another soldier indicated that whiskey was becoming a problem by recording that "the field officers [are] drunk all the time, unfit for duty—incompetent to attend to their duty." The increasing frustration tended to foster this kind of exaggeration even if the beliefs were somewhat based in fact. Private Davidson later remembered, erroneously, that fifty men were buried in the mountains and felt that "if this weather and exposure continues much longer, we'll have to bury the whole brigade."[42]

The enlisted men were not the only ones who felt the campaign had lost its momentum. Four captains resigned and left the wretched encampment, while others groused over the inaction. Finally, however, the weather moderated, and on March 21, Lieutenant Colonel Scurry led his force northward along the military road toward the village of Galisteo and eventual junction with the Santa Fe Trail east of the territorial capital. Leaving their relatively comfortable quarters behind, the Fourth Texas marched to and through the little village of San Antonito, while the Seventh Regiment's battalion escorted the supply wagon train and two artillery pieces along the slushy, muddy road. As they progressed, Alfred Peticolas reported that they "quartered in an old deserted ranch. . . . We pulled down part of an off room of the ranch and made a good fire in the larger room. I had a magazine to read and did not suffer any inconvenience from being on guard."[43]

The Texan column passed through the village of Golden, a straggling series of gold diggings that did not seem, to the soldiers, to have brought much reward to the miners working nearby. They then turned eastward through a range of low hills known as the Ortiz Mountains. En route, the scattered dwellings displayed white flags to indicate neutrality and in the hope of not being mistreated or robbed by the marching troops. By the evening of March 24, the Rebels reached what appeared to be an outpost of civilization, the village of Reál de Dolorès, the principal feature of which was "a large gold mill for crushing quartz, owned, it is said, by northern men. . . . It is a steam mill and the machinery must have cost a good deal." With a good road on which to march, and good weather and scenery, the Confederates were in high spirits as they got firewood from the village and water from the mill tanks.[44]

Tuesday, March 25, 1862, would mark the last day of the Texans' leisurely advance toward Fort Union. After an early morning start, Scurry's main column took up the line of march eastward from Reál de Dolores. Leaving the wooded Ortiz Mountains behind and coming out on an extensive, high desert plain, Abe Hanna recorded that, though now destitute of timber, the country through which they passed was more level and consequently the marching was easier for the foot soldiers, while "the mountains in the distance, exceedingly white with snow, exhibit quite a picturesque scene."[45]

Along the way, Commissary Sgt. Lucius M. Scott and his men captured a large flock of sheep, undoubtedly Union sympathizers, which supplied the column with fresh meat after they reached the village of Galisteo. There, the Texans were some twenty-five miles south of Santa Fe and twelve miles short of their junction with the Santa Fe Trail, where they expected to join Pyron's column, turn eastward along that road, and advance on Fort Union. The Fourth Regiment had marched afoot at the head of the Confederate column, with the mounted Seventh Texas companies following and still escorting the supply train and artillery. The regiments were reunited at Galisteo when the Seventh and its charges came into camp in late afternoon the next day, March 26.[46]

Just before Scurry's main column moved out toward Galisteo and Glorieta, General Sibley also sent Maj. John S. Shropshire from Albuquerque to join Major Pyron in Santa Fe. Shropshire's command was a four-company battalion of the Fifth Texas Regiment and the San Elizario Spy Company, accompanied by two guns of Major Teel's artillery, approximately two hundred reinforcements for the Confederate advance party. These Rebels left Albuquerque on March 20 and reached the territorial capital two days later, having skirmished with Federal scouting parties en route.[47]

Sibley remained behind in his Albuquerque headquarters, retaining the other six Fifth Texas companies as a mobile force that scouted out to the east of the Sandia and Manzano mountains and held itself ready to intercept any Federal forces moving along the roads between Fort Craig and Fort Union. He believed Colonel Canby might attempt to reach the latter post or to effect a junction with the Fort Union garrison somewhere on the eastern flank of the advancing Confederates. Although he originally entertained such an idea, Canby had no such intentions, and this potent Texan force was subsequently unavailable to reinforce those fighting well to the north of Albuquerque.[48]

Once Shropshire's force arrived, Pyron, the senior major in Santa Fe, acted on information he had received regarding the enemy. Although security is a major component of present-day military planning and movements, during the Civil War, and especially so during the early years of that conflict, security was essentially nonexistent. Civilian travel along the Santa Fe Trail between the territorial capital and Fort Union continued unabated.

Travelers naturally talked freely about the unusual sights they had seen along the route, including numbers, composition, and locations of the opposing armies. The intelligence may not have been very accurate, but it was based in fact.

From such sources, and perhaps from Sibley's headquarters, Pyron learned that Federal forces from Fort Union were approaching Santa Fe. Thereupon, the aggressive commander of Sibley's advance party left the town early on the morning of March 25 and marched to meet his oncoming enemies in the mountains southeast of Santa Fe, where the constricted nature of the terrain along the Santa Fe Trail would neutralize the Federals' anticipated numerical advantage. Pvt. Bill Davidson marched with this vanguard and remembered reaching "an old ranch," and that "the weather was so cold and our covering so light, that we could not sleep much at night."[49]

The Confederates had reached Johnson's Ranch, a minor way station along the only road through the southern end of the Sangre de Cristo mountain range, at the site of the present-day village of Cañoncito. There, the Santa Fe Trail, following the bed of Galisteo Creek westward, emerged through a narrow pass from Apache Canyon, just to the east of Johnson's Ranch. There also, the road coming northward from Albuquerque and Galisteo joined the Santa Fe Trail. The ranch owner, Anthony D. Johnson, known to be a strong Union supporter, had fled with his family into the bitterly cold nearby mountains upon the approach of the Confederate party. He later filed a claim against the Federal government for the losses and damage he experienced from the invading soldiers over the next six days, including a stolen horse and two oxen, twenty bushels of corn, forty gallons of molasses, miscellaneous clothing, and one barrel of whiskey.[50]

Pyron camped in and around Johnson's Ranch, parking supply wagons along Galisteo Creek and corralling his livestock for water and scanty grazing along the bottomland of that creek and Indian Creek, which join at Cañoncito, and quartering the men in the ranch buildings whenever possible. Pyron took the precaution of sending a small number of pickets eastward through the canyon to watch the trail for any sign of the enemy. He was aware that as he prepared to move into the defile and eastward through Apache Canyon, Lieutenant Colonel Scurry's main Confederate column was camped on the same creek, some twelve miles to the south. However, he made no attempt to contact that force or to await junction with it.[51]

CHAPTER TWO

The Union Arms

. . . and then came Colorado and took her by the hand.

—Parody on "The Bonnie Blue Flag"

Although the weather in New Mexico had hampered Confederate operations, the Texans had taken an inordinate amount of time in moving their divided forces northeastward toward Fort Union. Federal officers made good use of the time thus granted them. Colorado responded immediately, as previously noted, to Colonel Canby's plea for reinforcement from that sister territory. One independent company (later Company B, Second Colorado Volunteers), under 1st Lt. Theodore H. Dodd, had completed its recruitment at Cañon City, Colorado, by December 7, 1861. The unit left that mining camp on the same day and marched to Fort Garland, in the San Luis Valley of southern Colorado Territory. There the men and officers were mustered into United States service for three years, with Dodd as captain. Also raised in and around Cañon City, Capt. James H. Ford's independent company soon became Company A of the Second Colorado Regiment. Marching to Fort Garland a week after Dodd, Ford and his volunteers likewise reached the post and were sworn into Federal service on Christmas Eve, 1861, just as Sibley's men concentrated around Fort Thorn, in southern New Mexico, for their thrust northward.[1]

After resting a few days in camp, Dodd's company hurriedly marched southward to Santa Fe, then continued to Fort Craig. These hardy frontiersmen "saw the elephant," the common military term for an initial combat experience, during the Battle of Valverde. They acquitted themselves gallantly, standing firm and blowing to pieces a mounted charge of Texan lancers early in the battle.[2]

Captain Ford's company remained behind at Fort Garland until early February, when it also started for Santa Fe. The men, some of whom were accompanied by their families, encountered great hardship as heavy snows threatened to block their route. Ellen Williams, wife of one of Ford's soldiers, later remembered that "the frost was severe; it broke the lock bolt of one of the heavy freight wagons like it was a pipe-stem. . . . That left part of the company without beds or bedding. . . . We all suffered intensely." The misery continued. "Placing my children (I had two little ones) between my husband and myself, to keep them from perishing . . . I was fatigued enough to sleep soundly myself until reveille in the morning." Eventually, the exhausted company reached the capital and, after resting there one day, marched eastward along the Santa Fe Trail to reach Fort Union on March 11, 1862, just as another wave of winter storm rolled through northern New Mexico, isolating the Confederate main column in the Sandia Mountains.[3]

Colorado's great contribution to the New Mexico campaign was not just these two independent companies, important though they became. At the same time Sibley was recruiting his brigade of Confederates in South Texas, Governor William Gilpin of Colorado and other residents of Denver City and the various outlying mining districts of the territory began organization of a full regiment of volunteers for the Union cause. The governor appointed recruiting officers, who tended thereafter to become the company commanders of the troops they enlisted.[4]

Two active and enthusiastic citizens began the process during late summer, 1861. Samuel H. Cook of the South Clear Creek mining district and Samuel F. Tappan, member of a well-known northern abolitionist family and resident of Central City, Colorado Territory, both quickly raised companies for the new regiment. John P. Slough, a prominent Denver lawyer originally from Ohio, also began recruiting in his frontier city. Slough's unit became Company A of the First Regiment, Colorado Volunteers. Tappan, who set up recruiting centers both at Central City and nearby Black Hawk, had his men designated as Company B of the First Colorado. Subsequently, Governor Gilpin commissioned both to positions within the regiment rather than their original companies. John Slough became colonel of the First Colorado Volunteers, with Sam Tappan as its lieutenant colonel. With these appointments, two other prominent citizens, already enlisted

Lt. Col. Samuel F. Tappan, First Colorado Volunteers. Tappan commanded the Federal left wing during the fighting around Pigeon's Ranch. *Courtesy Colorado Historical Society.*

as lieutenants, were promoted to fill the company command positions: Capt. Edward W. Wynkoop for Company A and Capt. Samuel M. Logan for Company B.[5]

The other eight companies of the regiment also quickly filled during fall, 1861. Capt. Richard Sopris raised Company C in Denver City and in the Buckskin Joe mining district. Also from the city came Company D, with Jacob Downing as its captain. Company E, with Capt. Scott J. Anthony in command, comprised men from the mining towns of Oro City and Laurett and thereabouts.[6] Sam Cook was one of the earliest recruiters. He established his recruiting center in a prominent stone building in Central City and recruited miners from there and throughout the South Clear Creek mining district. His men came from varied backgrounds, many of them down on their luck or disillusioned with mining, which tended at the time to reward their labor with a bare subsistence. The men tended also to be

Col. John P. Slough, First Colorado Volunteers, commanded the Federal forces at Glorieta. The prominent Denver City attorney returned to New Mexico after the war as the territory's chief justice. *Courtesy Colorado Historical Society.*

quite perceptive and aware of the true nature of the mining camp and miners. One, Pvt. Ovando J. Hollister, who left one of the most useful accounts of the atmosphere and activities in Colorado in 1861, decided that Cook and his friends were out to raise a company of volunteers, "thus securing commissions for themselves," an idea that "struck them as a lode, which, once open, might be worked with ease and profit." That attracted, rather than repelled, the young recruits, and Cook's was one of the first companies filled. It was originally intended to be sent to Kansas to assist antislavery forces in that state. However, Governor Gilpin induced the men to stay in Colorado as a mounted company of the First Regiment, promising them that they would be "well mounted, armed and equipped."[7] In fact, they were the only mounted company within the First Colorado and served as cavalry throughout the New Mexico campaign.

Company G, raised in the mining towns of Nevada, Empire City, and other parts of the Clear Creek district, was one of the few units to be photographed before leaving Colorado for New Mexico. Capt. William F. Wilder led its members throughout the upcoming campaign. Central City and its environs contributed recruits for Capt. George L. Sanborn's Company H. Likewise, Company I, which would play a key role in the fighting at Glorieta, came from the same area, with some recruits from Denver City itself. Consisting mostly of German immigrants, the company was commanded by Capt. Charles Maile. Samuel H. Robbins led Company K, which would also soon prove itself in battle, and whose men enlisted in both Denver City and Central City.[8]

With John Slough and Sam Tappan commissioned colonel and lieutenant colonel, respectively, Governor Gilpin made a very unusual appointment as major of the regiment. A true frontier character, Rev. John M. Chivington of Denver City had been a Methodist missionary in Indian Territory and had then served as presiding elder, an administrative and supervisory position, of the Rocky Mountain District of the Methodist

Company G, First Colorado Volunteers, drilling on the main street of Empire, Colorado, during the summer before the New Mexico campaign. This is the only known image of any company of the regiment. *Courtesy Colorado Historical Society.*

Maj. John M. Chivington, First Colorado Volunteers, commanded the Federal forces at Apache Canyon and at the Johnson's Ranch phase of the Battle of Glorieta. *Courtesy Colorado Historical Society.*

Episcopal Church since 1860. A fiery spirit burned within the "Fighting Parson," as his biographer has labeled him, as did all the prejudices nurtured by frontiersmen of the period. Chivington helped in raising the First Colorado, but attributed his appointment as major to being "better acquainted in the territory than any man in it at the time," since he "had been all over it," organizing churches and other related affairs.[9] His position and outgoing, gregarious nature made him popular with the enlisted men and some of the officers of the First Colorado. The pro- and anti-Chivington factions that later developed within the regiment and its successor units were not yet active in New Mexico.

The enlisted men, NCOs, and many of the officers of the First Regiment tended to be "wild, gay, rollicking, tempestuous sons of the frontier, with little respect for formal law but with an innate sense of fundamental justice." Dedicated individualists, they were initially almost completely undisciplined, either by themselves or by their commissioned or noncommissioned officers. They represented perfectly the frontier volunteer soldier. They stole regularly to keep themselves supplied with food and necessities while completing the regimental organization in Denver City. They fought among themselves, with the local police, and with merchants who objected to their informal requisition practices. One officer, Lt. Robert McDonald of Company K, resented the overbearing attitude of a superior officer and "soundly thrashed" him, to the great delight of the privates watching this display of insubordination.[10]

Typical of these military "free spirits" was Capt. Sam Cook's mounted Company F. These men had enlisted for many reasons, but a common feeling of patriotism and affection for "the old flag" motivated them and was fueled by talk of treason and secession that was widely reported (but not really widely supported) during the summer and fall of 1861. After Governor Gilpin and other leading citizens began raising the regiment to quell just such talk and anticipated actions, enlistments quickened. The early companies that responded to this call poured into Denver City faster than the territory could support them. Privates Ben Ferris and Ovando Hollister of Company F were first quartered on Ferry Street in the western part of the city, then moved to larger quarters in the nearby Buffalo House hotel, where they had corral space for their horses across the street. The restless soldiers made themselves so unpopular so quickly that they were soon moved again to a newly established site, Camp Weld, just outside Denver City.[11]

During the autumn and early winter of 1861–62, the mounted company went on expeditions into the Indian country around Fort Laramie, north of Denver City, and to Colorado's Forts Lyon and Wise, but spent a great deal of idle time in unmilitary pursuits. Private Ferris remembered that another member stole a hatful of eggs from a local civilian who had put the hat down to pay for the eggs. The victim chased the soldier the two-and-a-half miles to Camp Weld but was not allowed to pass the guard. At Christmas time, and not having been paid in four months, the men foraged for food. Hollister recounted that "one party worked anxiously and assiduously . . . to pick the lock of a hen-roost door." Pigs also were coaxed and driven to the cookhouse. "A pistol would appear at a knot-hole and piggy would disappear," he reported, while "eggs, hams, oysters, champagne, cheese and vegetables were the results of the night's foraging." These paramilitary operations resulted in a sumptuous Christmas dinner, to which men from other companies were invited. Unfortunately, "by breakfast half a dozen were drunk," resulting in a brawl with the sheriff, city marshal, and a posse of police. One of Hollister's particularly unruly companions was a dedicated drinker and was usually in serious trouble with the law, having to be bailed out by Captain Cook so that he could return to camp and later the New Mexico campaign, where he was killed.[12]

When local merchants tired of supplying the men on government credit, and the territorial quartermaster consequently stopped issuing clothing, Company F members often simply stole what they had to have from stores in Denver City. When theft victims appeared at Camp Weld to complain, Major Chivington knew nothing of the soldiers' unauthorized actions. The bored men sometimes became even more violent. Later, one First Colorado member shot and killed another soldier without provocation. He escaped, and the company to which he belonged raised four hundred dollars to aid his victim's family.[13]

As mentioned, on January 1, 1862, Colonel Canby had called upon Governor Gilpin to organize volunteer reinforcements for the defense of New Mexico Territory. In response to that entreaty and earlier news of the advance of Sibley's Confederates, not only were the two independent Colorado companies sent to Fort Garland, under Canby's jurisdiction, but the Colorado officials agitated to have the First Regiment sent south to the Union commander. After some foot dragging, Maj. Gen. David Hunter, commanding the Department of Kansas and under whose jurisdiction the military affairs of Colorado fell, acted. On February 10, he sent the following order:

> *To His Excellency, Acting Governor of Colorado, Denver City, Colo.:*
> *Send all available forces you can possibly spare to reinforce Colonel Canby, commanding Department of New Mexico, and to keep open his communication through Fort Wise. Act promptly and with all the discretion of your latest information as to what may be necessary and where the troops of Colorado can do most service.*[14]

Governor Gilpin, by this time, had gone to Washington to defend himself against charges of fiscal impropriety in having illegally financed the support of the First Colorado Volunteers in the absence of official authorization, charges that were subsequently dismissed. Acting Governor Lewis L. Weld was equally energetic, however, and prepared the regiment for its move to New Mexico. On February 22, the day after the Confederate victory at

Valverde, the regiment was ready for service in the field. Colonel Slough led the companies then at Camp Weld out of Denver City on the three-hundred-mile march southward to Fort Union. Soon thereafter, Lieutenant Colonel Tappan joined the column with the remaining companies, which had been under his command on temporary detached duty at Fort Wise. Weld informed Canby of the departure from Denver City and expressed his hope that "you will find this regiment . . . a most efficient one and of great support to you. It has had, of course, no experience in the field, but I trust that their enthusiasm and patriotic bravery will make amends, and more than that, for their lack of active service."[15] If some of the residents and merchants of Denver were tired of the First Colorado Volunteers and glad to see them leave, others were not. Territorial officials were especially proud of their efforts in raising the regiment, which by this time had become locally known as the "Pet Lambs of Colorado," a nickname soon—but only briefly—applied derisively by its Texan enemies.

Accompanied by an extensive train of supply wagons, the Colorado soldiers marched steadily southward along the eastern foot of the Rocky Mountains, through "a section of country in which there was scarcely anything worthy the name of a broken wagon road." The scenery was spectacular, of course, as they passed Pike's Peak and the Spanish Peaks off to the west, but the march was hard on men who had spent the past four or five months largely in camp, without field activity to toughen them for such a strenuous expedition. By March 7, the Denver City column and the Fort Wise detachment had united and camped on the Purgatoire River, near present-day Trinidad, Colorado. There they joined the main or Mountain Branch of the Santa Fe Trail, although the roadway was scarcely better than that on which they had been traveling. Ahead of them lay Ratón Pass through the towering Ratón Mountains, on the border between New Mexico and Colorado. The men were in high spirits, notwithstanding their rigorous marches. Private Hollister thought the camp had "the hum and bustle of a small town." Colonel Slough, however, was another matter. The soldiers' disenchantment with their regimental commander began to grow. When they gave him three cheers as he walked through camp, Slough merely raised his cap, but did not speak, causing Hollister to comment that "he had been our colonel six months; had never spoken to us; and on the eve of an important expedition . . . could not see that a few words were indispensable to a good understanding. He has a noble appearance, but the men seem to lack confidence in him." The reason seemed to the Company F trooper to be that "his aristocratic style savors more of eastern society than of the free-and-easy border to which he should have become acclimated."[16]

There was a light covering of snow from earlier storms, but the column made its way slowly up the northern slope of Ratón Pass, camping at the Beaver Dams, halfway to the summit. They continued climbing along the trail where, according to Hollister, "the view from this point [the summit] is magnificent. Mountains meet the eye wherever it turns." South, the men could "imagine, rather than see, the promised land where battles were to be fought and glory achieved." As they reached the summit, several eagles circled above the nearby trail. One private in Company D called out, "Let's shoot them," but Captain Downing intervened by shouting, "These are the birds of Liberty, and they betoken victory to us!" The whole company gave three cheers for the eagles and marched on.[17]

March 9 was a day not to be forgotten by the First Colorado Volunteers. As they were descending the southern slope of Ratón Pass, an army ambulance and an excited messenger coming along the trail from the opposite direction met the column. Although a previous messenger had informed the Colorado officers of the Union defeat at Valverde and of Sibley's northward movement, this information was of a more urgent nature. Col. Gabriel R. Paul, commanding Fort Union, informed Slough and the other field officers of the fall of Albuquerque and Santa Fe, and that the Texans were preparing to march on Fort Union and its depot of supplies. Colonel Paul reported that he had made defensive arrangements for the vital post, but that he had "only some 400 Regulars and about the same number of volunteers, to defend it." He obviously felt immediately and seriously threatened; he needed reinforcements as fast as they could be sent. This was startling news and revived the enthusiasm of the soldiers, who had been toiling up and across Ratón Pass since early that morning.[18]

Although he undoubtedly began planning to move forward more rapidly, Colonel Slough gave no such indication to his officers or men. By late afternoon the command had reached the southern foot of Ratón Pass, and made camp. There, Major Chivington, perhaps at Slough's direction, mustered the regiment and made a stirring appeal. He informed them of the desperate threat to Fort Union, still some one hundred miles away, and the fortunes of the national cause in New Mexico. When he said "All who will make a forced march for the night to save Fort Union, step two paces to the front," every man stepped forward. One of Company A's foot soldiers, Pvt. Charles Gardiner, later wrote to his mother that "here we were ordered to report in *one* hour, for a *force march,* with four days 'grub' and one Blanket." After a brief respite to cook supper and boil coffee, the advance continued. Private Hollister described the frenzied preparations for the forced march. "Leaving everything but our arms and a pair of blankets per man in charge of a Corporal's guard, [we] proceeded with all possible and impossible speed towards our destination, eighty miles distant. The teams, relieved of their loads, took aboard a full complement of passengers, leaving, however, between three and four hundred to foot it." The officers had the men take turns riding in the wagons and walking, and Private Ben Ferris reported that "most of the men rode at least part of the time." Through the darkness, "away into the wee hours of morning did we tramp. . . . The gay song, the gibe, the story, the boisterous cheer, all died a natural death." By the early morning hours, the First Regiment had traveled thirty miles to the Vermejo River, a branch of the Cimarron River, having covered a total of sixty-seven miles since the morning before. There, exhaustion and the death of overworked draft animals forced a brief halt.[19]

Hovering over wretched brush fires and shivering under scanty blankets, the soldiers "nursed their indignation by the most outrageous abuse of everything and everybody." Hollister also observed that Colonel Slough "rode in the coach. That never stops between Red River and Union." With a "crust of hard bread," the march resumed at four o'clock in the morning. Now the column's troubles increased. The same series of snowstorms that had so seriously affected the Confederates near Albuquerque now struck the Colorado volunteers. It "increased in fury till it became a hurricane," remembered one of the suffering soldiers, "which showered and blinded them with driven snow, dust, and sand." Although at a reduced pace, the march continued southward, passing Maxwell's Ranch on the Cimarron River. By nightfall of March 10, Slough's men reached Kit Carson's old ranch at Rayado, New Mexico. They obtained some additional supplies from the ranch's residents, then applied themselves to preparing supper before catching a few hours of sleep. The howling wind made the effort almost impossible; the exhausted soldiers sat around little fires in the swirling smoke, "each with a pound of beef hung on a stick which they were trying to roast but which they were only peppering with dirt and ashes, and smoking beyond all human endurance, cursing and growling as usual while smoky tears rolled down their cheeks."[20] They were still thirty miles from Fort Union.

The march continued early in the morning on March 11. The weather abated somewhat, and mounted Company F, with the wagons, rode and drove ahead of the foot soldiers. By afternoon, the troopers could see Fort

Union ahead in a wide, smooth valley. Hollister observed that the main fortress, a mile from the western side of the valley, was "a simple field-work of moderate size, with bastioned corners surrounded by dirt parapet and ditch. . . . It has bomb-proof quarters in and surrounding it forming part of the works, sufficiently large to accommodate 500 men besides the necessary room for stores." This was the so-called Star Fort or New Fort, recently constructed out in the valley away from the original Fort Union, which was vulnerable to investment by any force equipped with artillery, as Sibley's oncoming brigade was.[21]

Those volunteers arriving first took care of their mounts and helped unload the wagons, awaiting their marching infantry companions, who did not arrive until well after dark. In the meantime, Company F and other early arrivers were formed in column and marched into the post "with drums beating and colors flying," then to the commanding officer's quarters. There Colonel Paul and New Mexico Governor Henry Connelly welcomed the reinforcing troops, commending the zeal with which the regiment had marched to Fort Union's relief, but saying nothing of the current military situation or the prospects for advancing against the enemy. Dissatisfaction among the volunteers set in almost immediately. Private Hollister felt the welcome should certainly have mentioned the local military conditions "that might naturally be supposed to slightly interest us. I thought they might as well have permitted the boys, hungry and tired, to go to their camp near the fortifications as to have perpetrated this farce."[22] Private Ferris was equally exasperated: "Did they tell us to go to bed? NO! Did they tell us to rest? NO! Had they prepared food for us? NO!" Actually, Colonel Paul had made arrangements to feed and shelter the First Colorado Volunteers as they came into the post. According to Pvt. Charles Gardiner of Company A, Colonel Slough "rode ahead and told the Commandant of the post (who was having tents pitched and a supper prepared) that it was entirely unnecessary; for his men were all old mountaineers and accustomed to all kinds of hardships." As a result, most of the men slept in the open, "exposed to a severe, cold March wind," with little or nothing to eat. Company F, however, solved both problems quickly. Its members raided the post sutler's store, stealing champagne, cheese, and crackers, and enjoying these ill-gotten items before going to sleep in the corral with their horses.[23]

For the next week and a half, the First Colorado troops lay around Fort Union with little employment, while their officers and the post's staff discussed and argued over the proper course to be followed. Some good came of the layover. All the men were completely supplied and equipped with regulation uniforms, arms, and accouterments from the adequate stores already at the fort.[24] Generally, though, the idle time was spent in wandering about the post and its environs or in scrounging for food and drink.

In common with most Civil War soldiers, the "Pet Lambs" considered the sutler, a civilian merchant selling scarce goods at whatever price his almost captive customers would pay, to be a legitimate target for robbery and intimidation. Hollister believed "all the sutlers in New Mexico are traitors at heart. . . . Their property is lawful 'loot' to Union soldiers, in my way of thinking." The men acted on that sentiment. One night, "the boys broke into the sutler's cellar and gobbled a lot of whiskey, wine, canned fruit, oysters, etc." Ben Ferris remembered a similar raid, during which the Coloradoans stole other items they did not want, then left them near the tents of sleeping regulars so that the latter would be blamed for the theft.[25]

The volunteers spent a great part of their stay at Fort Union in pursuit of whiskey, which in turn brought on all kinds of discipline problems and much insubordination. The most notorious result of one of these sprees occurred when 1st Lt. Isaac Gray of Company B attempted to arrest Sgt. Darias Philbrook for drunkenness and disorder. The sergeant shot at Lieutenant Gray five times, hitting him once in the face. Other nearby officers emptied their pistols at the assailant, but he escaped, only to be later caught and confined. Gray survived, and Philbrook was in due course tried and executed at Fort Union. The incident, however, got the attention of many of the volunteers. Hollister realized that "it is too much the impression among us that whiskey justifies anything. . . . Such scenes as this . . . are ruinous and disgraceful to the perpetrators not only as soldiers but as men."[26] Some may have learned the lesson from this or previous incidents. After his company had been issued some "rot gut," Private Gardiner wrote that "it availed me nothing, as that is an article I have entirely dispensed with since I have been in the Service, and *hope* to *be able* to say the same when I get out of it."[27]

While the troops thus amused themselves and prepared for the campaign that all anticipated against the Texans, the key officers in Fort Union were quite actively engaged. Gabriel Paul, a long-serving major of infantry and veteran of the regular army in New Mexico, had been promoted to colonel of the Fourth New Mexico Volunteers, a regiment then recruiting in the northern part of the territory. His commission dated from December, 1861, and Canby had later assigned him as commander of the Eastern District of the Department of New Mexico, with Fort Union as his headquarters. As soon as Colonel Slough reached the post, he informed the veteran officer that he, Slough, whose commission dated from August, was now the senior officer at or near Fort Union. Paul immediately protested this revelation directly to Washington, rather than to Canby, who was his immediate superior. "I had the mortification," he wrote, "to discover that his commission was senior to mine, and thus I am deprived of a command. . . . An officer of only six months' service, and without experience, takes precedence over one of many years' service, and who has frequently been in battle." Colonel Paul wrote to army headquarters directly since he also asked to be promoted to the rank of brigadier general of volunteers in order to end that dilemma, an action Canby would be unable to take. However, due to the slowness of message exchange with the East, no action could be taken on his request before active operations in New Mexico intervened.[28]

Colonel Slough's seniority determined subsequent events in northern New Mexico, but only after a sharp clash of the two men's wills and a serious disagreement concerning future operations out of Fort Union. The strategic importance of the post and the absolute necessity of protecting and holding it were, however, never in doubt. Before the First Colorado arrived, Colonel Paul had proposed to leave a small force behind to protect the fort while he took a field column southward to join with Canby's force, which would march northward from Fort Craig; the combined Union column would then attack Sibley's Confederates wherever they were found along the Rio Grande or elsewhere between the two Federal forts.[29]

Canby initially approved that plan, but quickly reconsidered. He conveyed that change of plans to Paul on March 16, explaining his strategic vision in the process. Canby now realized that the Confederates were essentially trapped between two Union posts, both of which were too strong to be easily taken if their garrisons defended them stoutly. Sibley was living off a land that could not long sustain an invading force. Canby, therefore, would remain in Fort Craig to block the Texan's retreat southward should Sibley choose that course of action. The goal was to retain New Mexico Territory for the Union. Even if Fort Garland and Fort Craig should fall, no disaster would occur; they were not strategically important, nor was any other point in New Mexico except Fort Union. Fort Union, however, was critical. Colonel Paul should await reinforcements being organized in Kansas and Colorado for his relief, but "Fort Union must be held and our communications with the East kept open. . . . Do not move from Fort Union to meet me until I advise you of the route and point of junction."[30]

The departmental commander obviously did not know of the arrival of the First Colorado when he sent this March 16 dispatch to Fort Union. By the time he received it, however, Colonel Paul had already organized a field column for the expedition to join Canby, according to the plan he understood as being approved. Since that field column included the First Colorado Volunteer Regiment as well as two artillery batteries and the regular infantry and cavalry units already assigned to the post, Colonel Slough demanded and received command of the column.[31]

Receipt of the March 16 message did not disturb Colonel Paul unduly, since the field column would be kept at Fort Union in accordance with Canby's orders. That complacency was soon shattered, however, by another dispatch from Canby, this time directed to Slough. Dated March 18, the communication indicated that Canby, now aware of the arrival of significant reinforcements, would tolerate a more flexible defense of Fort Union. He had orders and advice for Colonel Slough. "Keep your command prepared to make a junction with this force [from Fort Craig]. I will indicate the time and route. . . . Take no tents. . . . Ammunition, at least 100 cartridges per man and gun. . . . Rely upon the musket, and especially upon the bayonet." Then Canby added, "If you have been joined by a sufficient force to act independently against the enemy, advise me of your plans and movements, that I may cooperate. In this you must be guided by your own judgement and discretion, but nothing must be left to chance." Canby repeated his strategic plan to Slough, and further directed him, while awaiting the expected Kansas reinforcements, to "harass the enemy by partisan operations. . . . Obstruct his movements and cut off his supplies. Use the mounted volunteers for these purposes and keep the regular cavalry in reserve."[32]

There was an element of ambiguity in Canby's instructions to Slough, but there was no order to remain at Fort Union. While he may have been an inexperienced military officer, Slough was a competent and experienced lawyer. He had no trouble interpreting the March 18 dispatch as authorization for his own plan to protect Fort Union. Taking his field column, he would leave the fort with a minimum garrison and advance southward, then westward, along the Santa Fe Trail toward Santa Fe, where the Confederates were reported to be preparing for their own foray against Fort Union. Guided by his "own judgement and discretion," Slough would "act independently against the enemy" and harass, obstruct the movements of, and perhaps cut off the supplies of his foes through what was essentially a reconnaissance in force. His immediate destination was Bernal Springs, some forty-five miles south of Fort Union, where the Santa Fe Trail turned westward toward Glorieta Pass and the capital. By moving his column to that point, he would leave no road unguarded over which any invading force could approach Fort Union. There were few roads in the region to start with, and even those east of Albuquerque that connected with Fort Union joined the Santa Fe Trail west of Bernal Springs, and would thus be blocked.[33]

Colonel Paul was outraged when he learned of Slough's plan. Although the post commander had earlier been perfectly willing to leave Fort Union lightly guarded while he himself led a field column to join Canby, he now claimed that the departmental commander had told Slough not to move from Fort Union "until I advise you of the route and point of junction." Although not true, since that order had been directed to Paul rather than Slough, the statement did emphasize the ambiguity in Canby's March 18 message. Paul argued against what he saw as disobedience of orders by Slough. The old soldier may also have had another serious motivation for opposing the movement. As a regular officer, he was well aware that glory, fame, and promotion resulted from successful field command in any war. He had earlier pointed out in his letter to army headquarters in Washington that Slough's seniority had deprived him of a command "with which I expected to reap laurels." Now that Colonel Slough would lead the field column, any laurels would go to the Colorado commander rather than to himself. That was a completely understandable reaction, in addition to Paul's undoubted dedication to the defense of Fort Union.[34]

The field column that Colonel Paul had organized and Colonel Slough would lead comprised approximately 1,340 men. The First Colorado Volunteers were the main element, and all ten of the regiment's companies were available to take the field, contributing 916 men to the Federal force. All but Company F marched afoot as infantry. A regular army infantry battalion (augmented by one Colorado company) of 191 soldiers was led by Capt. William H. Lewis, Fifth U.S. Infantry. His command had been part of the Fort Union garrison and included Companies A and G of his own regiment, as well as Captain Ford's independent company, which had marched from Fort Garland, through the terrible snowstorms mentioned, to reinforce the garrison before the First Colorado arrived. Each company had approximately 60 enlisted men on strength. The field column also included a squadron of regular cavalry. Capt. George W. Howland of the Third U.S. Cavalry led the squadron (the equivalent of an infantry battalion), consisting of his own fifty-man detachment from various companies of the regiment, the majority of which had remained with Colonel Canby in Fort Craig; a similar detachment of 50 troopers from the First U.S. Cavalry, led by Capt. R. S. C. Lord; and Company E of the Third Cavalry, also with about 50 veteran frontier horsemen and commanded by Capt. Charles J. Walker, Second U.S. Cavalry, who had earlier been detailed to command the company in the absence of an available captain from the Third Regiment.[35]

The column was strengthened by two provisional batteries of artillery accompanying the infantry and cavalry. During early March, Colonel Paul had taken the initial steps to form his field column. He first organized a single artillery battery (a captain's command, equivalent to an infantry company) under the command of Capt. John F. Ritter of the Fifteenth U.S. Infantry. The battery included a section of two 6-pounder guns and another of two 12-pounder field howitzers, commanded by 1st Lt. Ira W. Claflin, Sixth U.S. Cavalry, and 2nd Lt. Robert S. Underhill of the Fourth New Mexico Volunteers. The battery's NCOs and privates were detailed to artillery duty from the Second and Third regular cavalry regiments. Upon arrival of the First Colorado Volunteers at Fort Union, however, either Paul or Slough, probably the latter, decided that more powerful artillery support would be needed, especially since it was known that the Rebels had captured an entire Federal battery at Valverde, which would probably be added to those brought into New Mexico with Sibley. Lieutenant Claflin was ordered to organize a four-piece battery of 12-pounder mountain howitzers, almost all that remained of mobile artillery in northern New Mexico. Claflin would be able to utilize his pieces in sections if he wished, since 1st Lt. John Thompson, Fourth New Mexico Volunteers, was detailed for duty with the battery. All enlisted men manning the howitzers were temporarily assigned to such duty from the Fifth U.S. Infantry. This combination of Ritter's "heavy" battery and Claflin's "light" howitzers would prove to be a highly effective supporting force during the upcoming battle.[36]

By March 22, all was ready for the expedition from Fort Union. Colonel Slough had been anxious to finish organization of the field column; he may not have been entirely convinced that he was complying fully with Canby's orders, and he may have worried that more orders prohibiting his venture might yet arrive. In addition, both Colonel Paul and Governor Connelly were increasingly worried over rumors of the strength and progress of the oncoming Rebels. The governor was almost in a state of panic over the exaggerated stories of Sibley's capabilities and intentions. He repeatedly wrote to Secretary of State William H. Seward, in Washington, requesting reinforcements for New Mexico and updating the secretary on military conditions. One result was that Federal authorities were actually in the process of organizing a powerful reinforcing column in Kansas, approximately five thousand strong and consisting of infantry, cavalry, and artillery, to march westward along the Santa Fe Trail to New Mexico's relief. Another, smaller force was preparing to come to Canby's aid from southern California.[37]

Governor Connelly also supported Slough's plan to march toward the Confederates. He pointed out to Secretary Seward that "this slight difference of opinion [between Slough and Paul] will lead to no unfavorable result, as Colonel Slough will advance upon the road that the enemy will necessarily have to march to reach Union . . . which seems to be the fear entertained by Colonel Paul."[38] John Slough's intentions were neither irrational nor rash. His, and the governor's, analysis of the ability of the field column to advance to seek out and "harass" the enemy while still protecting Fort Union were perfectly valid. In addition, there was reason to believe that the Texans were not nearly as threatening as rumor would have it. Captain Walker had recently come from Santa Fe with his cavalry company and had reported, whether from travelers or from information gathered by sending out small scouting parties to watch the Rebels, on the size and miserable conditions of the Texan force snowbound at San Antonio, on the eastern side of the Sandia Mountains. Slough felt that "if the enemy at San Antonio are no stronger than reported by Captain Walker, the troops under my command will be sufficient to control their action and to defeat them in case of attack."[39]

Colonel Paul was beside himself and misinterpreted this statement as an intention to attack the enemy in his San Antonio camps. Indeed, that would have been unwise and would have left Fort Union vulnerable. He wrote to Slough: "This most certainly is or will be in violation of Colonel Canby's instructions, and, if unsuccessful, must result in the entire loss of the Territory. I must urge upon you to reconsider your decision." Finally, seeing that his reasoning was being ignored, Paul capitulated with, "I protest against this movement of yours . . . in direct disobedience of the orders of Colonel Canby."[40]

Once he realized Slough was going to leave the fort no matter what he said, Paul requested that one section each of Ritter's and Claflin's batteries, along with Lewis's regular infantry battalion, be left behind as "the least force required to garrison this post securely." When Slough refused, Paul could not resist pointing out that "no part of the regular force of this district would have been turned over to you had the instruction of Colonel Canby of the 16th instant been received twelve hours earlier." Two days after Slough left, the post commander wrote to army headquarters in Washington, repeating his objections and pointing out that "I am thus left with a feeble garrison and no suitable artillery for the defense of the principal and most important post in the Territory. . . . My object in this communication," he continued, "is to throw the responsibility of any disaster which may occur on the right shoulders."[41]

Without fanfare, Colonel Slough led the Federal force out of Fort Union during the forenoon of March 22, just as Colonel Scurry was moving his Rebel force northward from the Sandia Mountains, northeast of Albuquerque. Marching orders for the field column had been published the preceding day. A flurry of activity followed as the soldiers prepared their equipment and arms for the expedition. Some took extra precautions. After dark several members of Company F again raided the post sutler, stealing, among other goods, "a lot of whiskey." A party of these scofflaws left early the next morning to hide the liquor somewhere ahead on the line of march, that they might enjoy it again when they camped the first night out of Fort Union. However, this advance party drank, lost, or sold what had been entrusted to them. Even worse, the men stopped about six miles along the way at the notorious Loma Parda, a "small Sodom" established for the recreation of the soldiers at Fort Union. There, while their companions passed the "hog ranch," a dozen or so of these Pet Lambs spent the day "drinking, fighting and carousing with Mexican women." After the column camped on the Sapello River, a couple of miles south of Loma Parda, the miscreants "came in during the night with rough usage painted on their faces." Private Ferris afterward "always regretted the 2ed [second] raid on the poor sutler," and remembered that "some of the boys were in bad plight." His companion Ovando Hollister was also involved, but it was the last binge for the First Colorado during the expedition with Colonel Slough.[42]

The weather was no hindrance to passage down the Santa Fe Trail. The next day saw the column travel southward to camp around the small town of Las Vegas, on the banks of the Gallinas River. There the horsemen camped in or near a large corral in the town itself. They naturally took advantage of the experience and "scattered over it in search of women or plunder." They found little of either; the residents told the soldiers that smallpox was raging in town, which cooled the ardor of most of the sightseers. Private Hollister, however, "having forced myself into several houses and slightly sated my curiosity . . . went home, my life impressions of Mexican character fully confirmed by this first day's experience among them."[43]

Colonel Slough's field column, or at least part of it, was not the only military organization marching south from Fort Union. The day after the Colorado Volunteers had left the post, Captain Lewis's battalion of infantry escorted the two artillery batteries and an extensive quartermaster wagon train along the same route Slough had followed. This supply train was critical to the success of the Federal troops. The Quartermaster Corps was a separate military organization from the line, or combat, units at this time. The post commander of Fort Union, for instance, had no authority over the quartermaster depot located at the post. The practical result was that neither Colonel Paul, still commanding the fort and Eastern Division of the Department of New Mexico, nor Colonel Slough, commanding the field column, could give orders to the quartermaster officers at the depot or accompanying the field force. Fortunately, this potentially disastrous relationship worked well. It did so due in large part to the energy and competence of the quartermaster department.[44]

Capt. John C. McFerran was the chief quartermaster at Fort Union, while his assistant, Capt. Herbert M. Enos, was in charge of the depot itself. Both had worked diligently to prepare the supply train that would accompany Slough and which Enos would command. As Captain Enos later reported, "Great care had been taken that the wagons and harness should be in good repair—none but good mules were taken. The wagon-masters and teamsters were Selected Mechanics and material furnished for any repairs that might be necessary on the march." Supply wagons, baggage wagons, hospital wagons, and ambulances comprised the train.[45]

Leaving Las Vegas early on the morning of March 24, Colonel Slough continued southward along the Santa Fe Trail, sending Captain Howland's battalion of regular cavalry ahead of the column. Pvt. John D. Miller, of Company F, remembered that his unit also left early in the morning. "The cavalry," he reported to his father right after the upcoming action, " were routed out at three o'clock, and after getting a hurried breakfast, we started off in advance." By afternoon, the colonel's main body reached Bernal Springs, some forty-five miles out of Fort Union.[46] This site, which, for whatever reason, he named Camp Paul, was indeed a strategic point. Near present-day Bernal, New Mexico, it was well-known to travelers along the Santa Fe Trail. Here the road abruptly turned westward, toward the villages of San Miguél and San José, then veered northwestward toward Glorieta Pass.

Captain Howland's regular cavalry squadron had continued past Bernal Springs to San José. As Company F, First Colorado Volunteers, reached the springs, it too was sent farther westward. Colonel Slough wanted the volunteer cavalrymen to move fast to join the regulars and ordered that the "Pike's Peakers" leave their excess supplies and equipment in the wagons accompanying the regiment. That accomplished, the volunteer company rode some twelve miles farther, to San José, where the Santa Fe Trail crossed the Pecos River. According to Private Hollister, the Pet Lambs survived the night when, "we borrowed some grub of the regulars, crept into a haymow to sleep, and lived through it."[47]

Toward evening, Captain Enos's supply train came into Camp Paul, where the First Colorado's infantry companies were preparing supper and resting. There he heard what was, to him, startling news. Colonel Slough had ordered that fifteen wagons and teams accompanying his regiment be emptied and prepared to transport troops westward to join the advance cavalry units. Enos was responsible for those wagons and mules, as well as for the civilian quartermaster depot employees acting as wagon masters and teamsters; he was greatly concerned lest something happen to them. His concern is understandable, since safety of the train and its employees, as well as efficient support of the field column's combat units, were his primary duties as commander of the train. Nevertheless, he became something of a bother to Slough, who had more important matters to worry about. Enos protested that if the wagons were detached, the main body of troops would be unable to move from Bernal Springs until they returned. Slough replied that he was responsible for such matters, and that "no other move was contemplated."[48]

He did contemplate more movement, however, and the fifteen wagons were used to transport the infantrymen of what would become Slough's advance guard. Major Chivington would command this vanguard, whose objective, as the colonel explained it, was to advance "toward Santa Fe, with a view of capturing or defeating a force of the enemy reported to be stationed there." Capt. Asa B. Carey of the Fifth U.S. Infantry, which had also just arrived as escort to Enos's wagons, was assigned to muster and lead a battalion of First Colorado infantrymen to join the cavalry already at San José. Slough designated Companies A, D, and E for the purpose. Each volunteer company had an average strength of 90 men with the main column, but the wagons could only carry 180. The respective company commanders, therefore, each selected 60 of their fittest men to join this advance party, leaving the rest behind with the other First Colorado companies to guard baggage and perform fatigue duties. On the morning of March 25, Captain Carey loaded the selected infantrymen into the wagons and, accompanied by Major Chivington, started westward.[49]

At San José, the cavalrymen were ordered to cook two days' rations and "be ready to march at a moment's warning." About an hour before sunset, Company F was overjoyed to see the Colorado major and Captain Carey's wagons pull into their camp. Private Miller remembered that "ten or twelve mule wagons came along, having in them 150 infantry boys of our regiment."[50] At just this same time, Major Pyron's Confederate vanguard was making camp at Johnson's Ranch, near the western entrance to Apache Canyon and Glorieta Pass, while Lieutenant Colonel Scurry's main body of Texans did the same near Galisteo, twelve miles south of Pyron.

Chivington immediately moved his united command, 418 men, farther west along the Santa Fe Trail, toward the Texans. Hollister thought the objective was "to make a sudden dash on Santa Fe." The horsemen and wagon-borne infantry moved rapidly along, even though "the night was verry [sic] dark and still," as Private Ferris remembered.[51] Around eleven o'clock that night, after traveling some seventeen miles, the column arrived at one of the major way stations on the Santa Fe Trail. Kozlowski's Ranch, identified as Gray's Ranch by several of the soldiers, had an excellent spring, wood, and flat, grassy slopes for grazing animals and camping.

There, Chivington learned from some undisclosed source, either a Santa Fe Trail traveler or the ranch inhabitants, that "we were in the vicinity of the enemy's pickets." He decided to stop for the night and send out a patrol of his own to locate the Rebels. Accordingly, the men "got blankets as soon as possible after reaching camp" and went to sleep, cavalrymen picketing their horses nearby. Private Ferris remembered that "having no provisions with us, no cooking was done," and further, "the order on the night ride was not to talk or make any noyes [sic] and that order held good in camp."[52]

Major Chivington chose an energetic officer from Company F, 1st Lt. George Nelson, and a picked party of 20 men, to seek definite information on the Confederates' position.[53] Thus, as the Texan advance party slept near the western exit of the Santa Fe Trail from Glorieta Pass and Apache Canyon, and sent pickets eastward to find the rumored Federals, Chivington's Union vanguard slept at the eastern approaches to the same pass and canyon, having also sent out its own probing scouts. Both forces anticipated a fight on the morrow. If either party or both continued to advance on March 26, such a clash was inevitable.

CHAPTER THREE

Apache Canyon

They were regular demons, that iron and lead had no effect upon, in the shape of Pike's Peakers from the Denver City Gold mines.

—Pvt. George Brown, Fifth Texas

As the early hours of March 26 ticked away, the advance parties of Confederates and Federals slept some eleven miles apart, at each end of Glorieta Pass. Its name was actually somewhat of a misnomer. The pass itself, the highest point on the Santa Fe Trail between Kozlowski's Ranch and Johnson's Ranch, lay midway along the road; common usage, however, lent the name to the entire stretch of trail. Westward five miles from Kozlowski's was the next way station, Pigeon's Ranch. The Santa Fe Trail continued northwestward another two miles, crossed Glorieta Pass proper, then turned southward along the small head of Galisteo Creek and subsequently southwestward to enter Apache Canyon, a small valley of cultivated fields bisected by Apache Creek. South of where the trail crossed its normally dry stream bed, Apache Creek joined the wide, and now deeply eroded Galisteo Creek arroyo (large ditch, or gully), which the roadway paralleled through Apache Canyon. The trail then dropped down into the steep-sided bed of Galisteo Creek as it passed through a narrow defile and out of Apache Canyon to Johnson's Ranch, some four miles from the pass. At that site, the road from Galisteo joined the Santa Fe Trail, which wound around a steep hill guarding the western exit from Apache Canyon and continued to the territorial capital.

Those eleven miles would define the limits of the fighting that was to

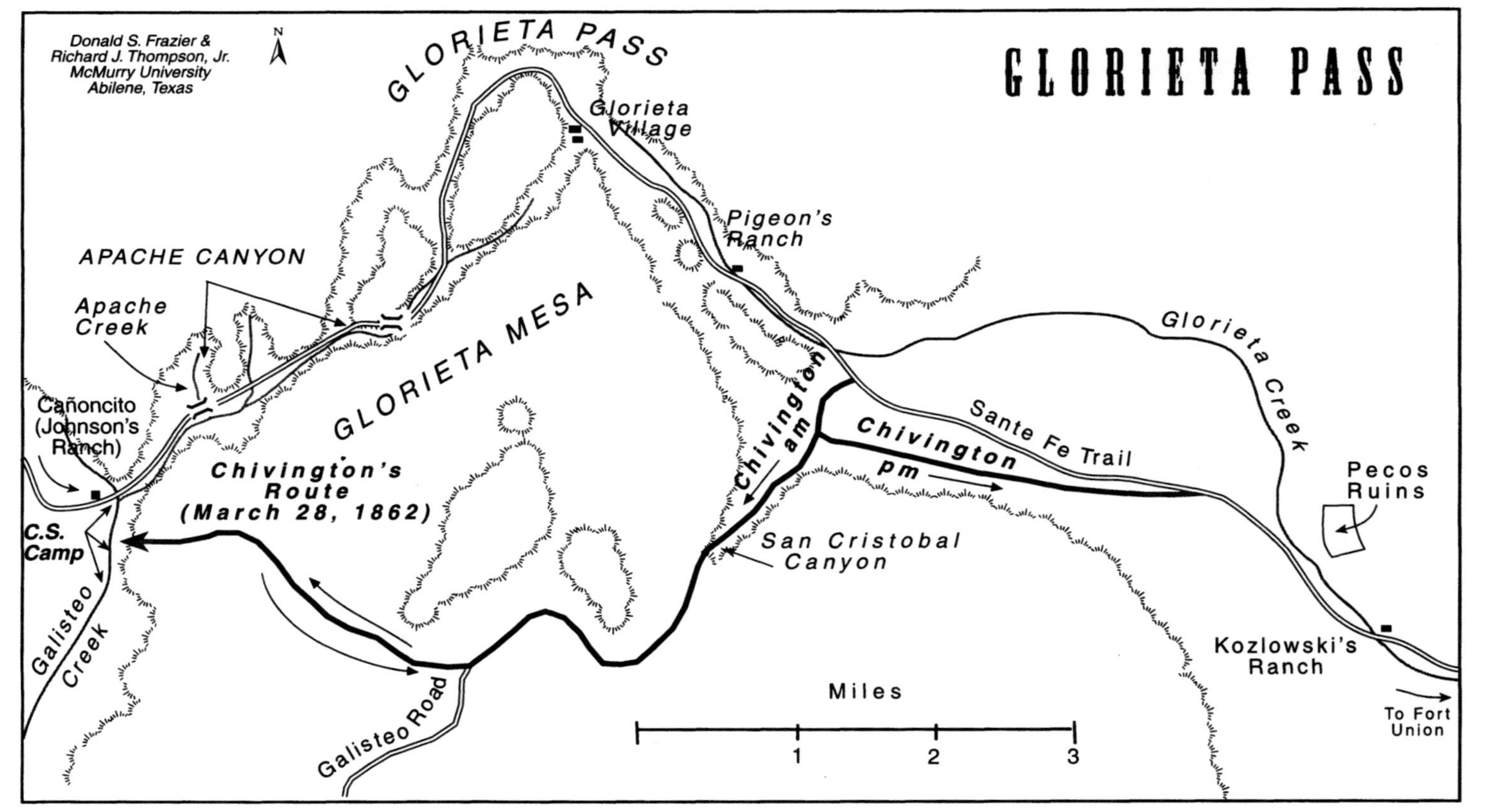
GLORIETA PASS
Donald S. Frazier &
Richard J. Thompson, Jr.
McMurry University
Abilene, Texas
N
GLORIETA PASS
Glorieta
Village
Pigeon's
Ranch
APACHE CANYON
Apache
Creek
Cañoncito
(Johnson's
Ranch)
GLORIETA MESA
Chivington's
Route
(March 28, 1862)
C.S.
Camp
Galisteo
Creek
Galisteo Road
Chivington
am
Chivington
pm
Sante Fe Trail
Glorieta Creek
San Cristobal
Canyon
Pecos
Ruins
Kozlowski's
Ranch
To Fort
Union
Miles
1
2
3

take place during the next few days. Also playing an important role was the topography of the region. Kozlowski's Ranch, with its excellent spring and camping areas, lay in the open valley of the Pecos River. The Santa Fe Trail, however, left the Pecos River to follow westward a small tributary, Glorieta Creek. The valley of Glorieta Creek became increasingly constricted as the road neared Pigeon's Ranch. In fact, a heavily wooded ridge split the valley and ended with a western eminence that later became known as Artillery Hill, directly across the trail from the ranch buildings. The valley in which Pigeon's Ranch stood was therefore very narrow, with only enough flat space for the buildings, corrals, and roadway. On Artillery Hill and north of the road, the rolling valley sides were heavily covered with tall pines as well as thickets of piñon and juniper. To the south, precipitous canyon walls rose to the flat top of Glorieta Mesa, a plateau that extended westward to end just above Johnson's Ranch.

Thus, along the entire Santa Fe Trail between Pigeon's Ranch and Johnson's Ranch, the open areas suitable for maneuver of troops were severely constricted to distances of a few dozen yards to a half-mile from the trail. In addition, the trail itself, which had been reconstructed and well maintained by the military prior to the Civil War, twice crossed the arroyo cut by Galisteo Creek. Traveling south a mile from Glorieta Pass, one crossing, through the five-foot-deep ditch, took the Santa Fe Trail from the north to the south side of the arroyo. Less than a mile farther west, an eighteen-foot wooden bridge recrossed the greatly eroded, deep arroyo to its north side. Farther on, halfway through Apache Canyon, the road crossed the shallow bed of Apache Creek over a second, smaller wooden bridge, one that would play a part in the upcoming conflict, then continued westward to Johnson's Ranch, as previously described.[1]

One other feature of the Glorieta Pass locality would play a key part in the upcoming battles. Pigeon's Ranch was the largest and most important hostelry on the Santa Fe Trail between Fort Union and Santa Fe. With its wellhouse and other outbuildings on both sides of the trail, the main facility and attached corrals provided much needed services and supplies to travelers as well as secure spaces for loaded wagons and draft animals. A "Frenchman" from Missouri, Alexander Pigeon, started building the facility in 1851 or 1852 and operated it continuously through the end of the Civil War. Curiously, he adopted the surname Valle (Spanish for valley) during this period, and the site was also sometimes referred to as Valle's Ranch. Prominent local New Mexican Donaciano Vigil later testified for a claim Valle filed for damages done during the fighting on his property: "I frequently visited his House and Ranch at La Glorietta . . . where he Kept a House of entertainment for travellers and the public, and also Kept and furnished forage and supplies to United States Troops, and trains of transportation; that he also Kept and furnished forage and supplies to all trains requiring the same, whether for Public service, or for private individuals."[2] The thick adobe walls of the buildings and corral enclosures, the latter extending across the narrow valley from the base of Artillery Hill, south of the trail, to a prominent rocky ridge immediately north of the ranch, formed a natural and strong defensive position for military operations that were about to begin.

While their men slept, however fitfully due to the cold, the Confederate and Union vanguard commanders had each sent small parties ahead, along the Santa Fe Trail, during the night of March 25–26. Major Pyron selected members of his Brigands company for the job. They were to determine if possible the strength and location of their enemy and to warn the Texans against any surprise movement, should the Federals actually be advancing toward Santa Fe as rumored. Led by Lt. John McIntire, these four pickets rode eastward during the night, reaching Pigeon's Ranch, where their presence threw a scare into Alexander Valle.[3]

Meanwhile, Colorado lieutenant George Nelson and his party of twenty mounted volunteers had been dispatched by Major Chivington on a similar mission. Pvt. John Miller, a member of this patrol, remembered that "we roamed around all the rest of the night, and about day break came to Pigeon's ranch, five miles beyond Gray's [Kozlowski's] ranch." The proprietor was still awake, and Miller and the other Federal troopers "searched the premises, and after old Pigeon found out who we were, after we told him we were Pike's Peakers . . . he fairly danced, he was delighted." Valle described the recent late-night visit of the Rebel pickets and said they had left in the direction of Kozlowski's Ranch. Somehow, the parties had passed but missed each another in the dark.[4]

Nelson immediately put his men back on the Santa Fe Trail, retracing their route from Chivington's camp. Rounding a turn about a mile east of Pigeon's Ranch, the Federals came upon the four well-mounted and armed Brigands. In the dim predawn light, the latter assumed the approaching party was friendly, since it was coming from the direction of the Confederate camp. Lieutenant McIntire asked if the horsemen were here to relieve him and his men. "Yes," Lieutenant Nelson replied, "we came to relieve you of your arms." The Rebels were too astonished to reply or react as the Federal leader turned to his men and said, "Ready." Private Miller and the others then "cocked our rifles and drew them up to our faces," whereupon Nelson ordered the surprised Brigands to throw down their arms and surrender, which they did without resistance. "We took from the four men nine good Colts revolvers and four splendid Maynard rifles," Miller recalled, "and marched them into camp."[5]

Arriving back at Kozlowski's Ranch, Nelson presented the crestfallen Brigands to Major Chivington, while his men prepared a well-deserved and long-delayed breakfast. The prisoners were a source of great interest to the Federal troops who had just awakened. Two were well known to the Colorado Volunteers. Private Hollister claimed that McIntire had been on Colonel Canby's staff at the Battle of Valverde but had since turned traitor. The other, H. H. Hall, who was wearing the rank insignia of a captain, was well known in Denver. Pvt. Ben Ferris also recognized the pair as "frontier men, men of note," who had been arrested earlier by the Coloradoans, only to escape jail and ride south into New Mexico. Hollister felt that McIntire should "expiate his treason on the scaffold," while Hall, "being a Northern man . . . never should be allowed to taint the fair soil he has disgraced by his silly and despicable treachery."[6]

Putting the prisoners into a wagon with a strong guard, Chivington started them back to the main command, still at Bernal Springs. With this tangible proof of an enemy force nearby, he prepared his men for a march toward Santa Fe. There were some problems; in Company F, an early-morning roll call showed that four of the Colorado cavalrymen had deserted rather than face the expected fight. "They were," Ben Ferris stated, "despised by every living member of our regiment."[7] That was unusual, however, and the regulars and volunteers alike were eager to close with the Texans.

Major Chivington led the column westward from Kozlowski's at about eight o'clock. His force, now reduced by the deserters and those detailed as guards, included about 170 Colorado infantrymen detailed to him by Colonel Slough and 234 cavalrymen, consisting of the squadron of regulars led by Capt. George Howland and the 84 men of Capt. Sam Cook's Company F, First Colorado Volunteers—approximately 404 in all.[8]

The Fighting Parson took the precaution of sending a handful of mounted scouts ahead to locate the enemy or give warning of his foe's approach. The foot soldiers marched at the head of the main column, carrying their knapsacks and rifles, with the cavalry following. Even though they were not encumbered with supply wagons or artillery, all moved at a leisurely pace so that the advance scouts would have sufficient time to warn of any enemy force ahead. The column soon passed the ruins of the old Pecos Mission, a notable sight along the Santa Fe Trail, and by noon Chivington's men had reached and passed Pigeon's Ranch, with Alexander Valle undoubtedly cheering on the boys in blue.[9]

Continuing westward from the ranch for two miles, the Federal force reached Glorieta Pass itself, then turned to the south as the trail gently descended toward Galisteo Creek and Apache Canyon. Here, a long, narrow valley extended along the normally dry headwater arroyo of Galisteo Creek. Today Interstate 25 lies almost parallel to and within one hundred to three hundred yards of that arroyo, which is laced with deep, narrow gullies, some of them the eroded ruts of the Santa Fe Trail. Proceeding down the road for slightly more than a mile and approaching the creek crossing, Chivington's men were excited to see their advance scouts coming in on the run. With Texan prisoners in tow, the pickets yelled that the enemy was just ahead and to "give them hell, boys. Hurrah for the Pike's Peakers."[10]

Indeed, the enemy was just ahead. Earlier, as the dawn had broken on that "bright and lovely day" and Major Pyron's Confederates awakened, many were unrested, having shivered through a very cold night or having sat around fires to seek a semblance of warmth. As the men prepared quick breakfasts and coffee, the pugnacious Pyron decided to move eastward to seek his foe. With no word of the Federals having reached him from the captured Brigands, his force left Johnson's Ranch about the same time Chivington's column moved westward from Kozlowski's.[11]

Pyron had approximately 440 men with whom to oppose Chivington, so the contesting forces would be fairly evenly matched. In addition to his own battalion of the Second Texas Mounted Rifles, some 80 soldiers, he had a battalion of four companies of the Fifth Texas Mounted Volunteers (A, B, C, and D), at least 250 strong by conservative estimate. The competent Maj. John Shropshire, a twenty-eight-year-old lawyer from Columbus, Texas, had been appointed to that rank right after the Battle of Valverde and now commanded the Fifth Regiment's battalion. Although he had suffered a leg wound during the fierce fighting of the preceding month, Shropshire's energy was undiminished as his men marched toward Glorieta Pass. His company commanders were all reliable and experienced officers fresh from their success at Valverde: Capt. Stephen M. Wells of Company A; 2nd Lt. John J. Scott of Company B, the survivors of the suicidal lancer charge at Valverde; Capt. Denman W. Shannon of Company C; and Capt. Daniel H. Ragsdale of Company D.[12]

Pyron also had three small companies of "irregulars." Captain John G. Phillips's Brigands, recently recruited to approximately 30 members from the barrooms and brothels of Santa Fe, was the largest of these units, with another 25 men each from the San Elizario Spy Company and the Arizona Rangers, recruited from the Franklin, Texas, and Mesilla, New Mexico, areas respectively.[13]

The Texan force had the significant advantage of being supported by artillery. Two 6-pounder guns and their associated gun crews and teamsters, members of the Fifth Texas artillery company, were attached to Pyron's command. None of the artillery officers accompanied the section northward from Albuquerque since no major encounter by Pyron's party was contemplated, but the approximately thirty artillerists were ably led by three temporarily promoted NCOs detailed to the artillery from Shropshire's old Company A, Fifth Texas Regiment. Of these, Sgt. Adolphus G. Norman, commanded the section, with Timothy Nettles and Peyton Hume each in charge of one of the pieces. These guns may have been among those originally brought into New Mexico and used at the Battle of Valverde, or they may have been two of the cannon captured there as part of the Federal battery.[14]

A better commander for General Sibley's vanguard could hardly have been found. Charles Pyron, forty-two years old, was a rancher residing near San Antonio, Texas. A veteran of the Mexican War, he had come into New Mexico as a company commander with Colonel Baylor in 1861. Since that time, he had led numerous scouts and forays against Federals and Indians, that experience resulting in promotion to major specifically to lead the battalion of Baylor's men ordered to accompany Sibley northward from the Mesilla Valley. Pyron was a fearless and aggressive officer, perhaps almost too much so. His report of the upcoming action under his command has unfortunately never been located.[15] As a result, much of the detail regarding Confederate numbers, movements, and intentions cannot be analyzed as rigorously as can those of his Federal opponents, more reliance necessarily being placed on Union reports, scanty participant memoirs, and artifact evidence.[16]

Leaving his supply wagons behind in the Johnson's Ranch camp, guarded by a handful of sick or wounded soldiers and a few black servants who had accompanied the Texans, Pyron's column, approximately 420 strong, rode eastward along the Santa Fe Trail.[17] Traveling very slowly even though the road was generally good, by noon the marching Confederates had reached an open, flat shelf north of Galisteo Creek and at the eastern

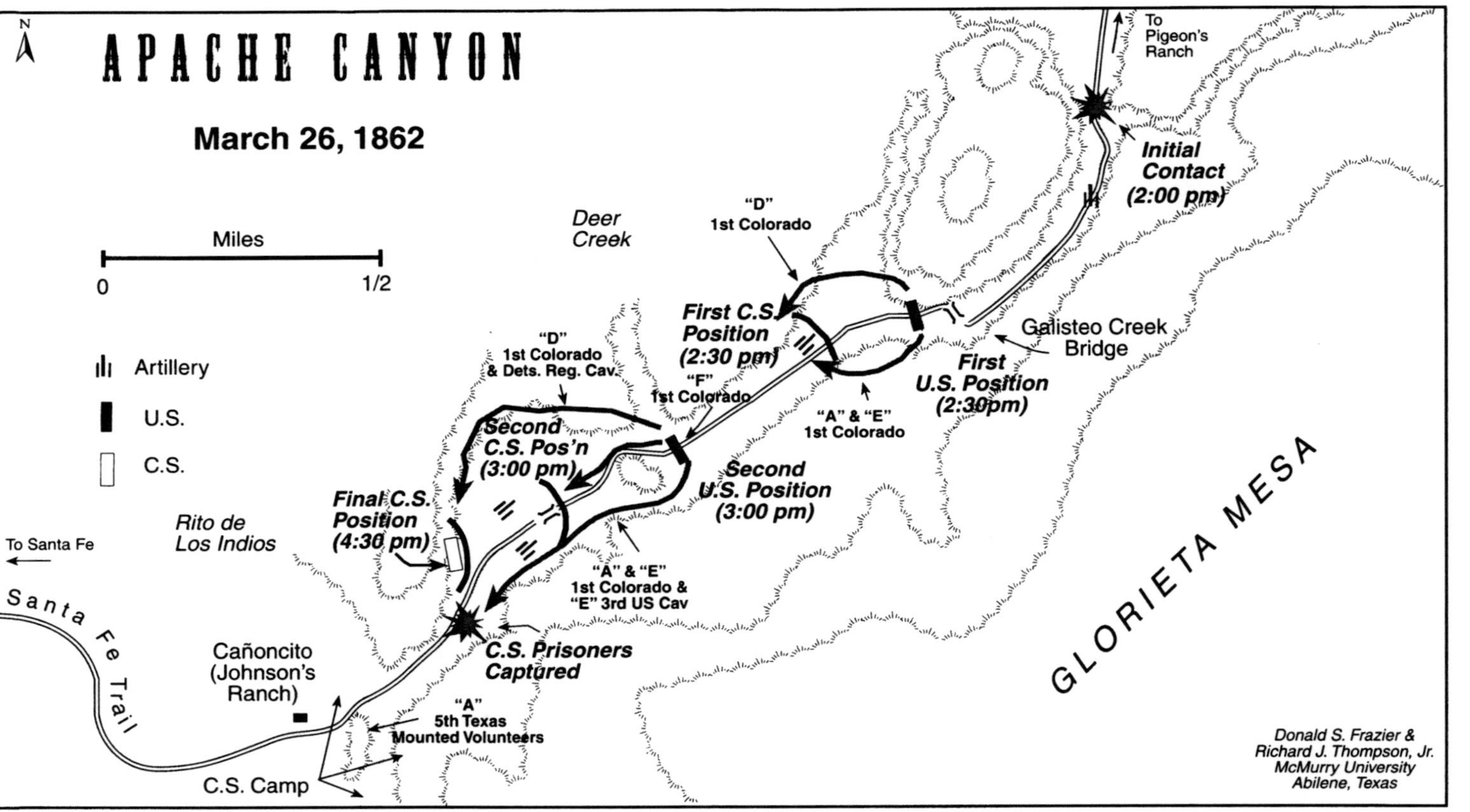
N
APACHE CANYON
March 26, 1862
Miles
0
1/2
Artillery
U.S.
C.S.
To Santa Fe
Santa Fe Trail
Rito de Los Indios
Deer Creek
Cañoncito (Johnson's Ranch)
C.S. Camp
"A" 5th Texas Mounted Volunteers
C.S. Prisoners Captured
Final C.S. Position (4:30 pm)
Second C.S. Pos'n (3:00 pm)
"D" 1st Colorado & Dets. Reg. Cav.
"F" 1st Colorado
"A" & "E" 1st Colorado & "E" 3rd US Cav
Second U.S. Position (3:00 pm)
First C.S. Position (2:30 pm)
"D" 1st Colorado
"A" & "E" 1st Colorado
First U.S. Position (2:30pm)
Galisteo Creek Bridge
Initial Contact (2:00 pm)
To Pigeon's Ranch
GLORIETA MESA
Donald S. Frazier & Richard J. Thompson, Jr. McMurry University Abilene, Texas

limit of Apache Canyon, some two miles east of their camp. Having already crossed the dry Apache Creek, and now finding a long, wooden bridge before him, with a narrow valley beyond, the Texan commander halted his men.[18]

Major Pyron probably hesitated because of an increasing anxiety at not hearing anything whatever from his Brigand pickets. To look for them, he sent forward a party of about 30 men from the remaining Brigands and, strangely, his two artillery pieces. Once this new vanguard left, Pvt. Bill Davidson and his companions of Company A dismounted along the trail and across the flat valley opening, as did the other troopers, still weary from the frigid, sleepless night. "The sun made it warm enough to sleep," he reported, "and we went to sleep trusting everything to our pickets."[19]

That trust was misplaced. The Confederate advance party had gone less than a mile when around a bend in the trail ahead rode the leading scouts of Major Chivington's Federal column. Once again the Texans were taken by surprise. (Davidson and others suspected that they, too, had fallen asleep. Indeed, it is otherwise difficult to imagine why the party had covered so little distance during the intervening two hours.) Those toward the front, including an unidentified first lieutenant, immediately surrendered, the officer being rushed back to Chivington by his captors. Those Brigands further behind rallied to support the two 6-pounders that were quickly unlimbered by their gunners.[20]

Leading the Federal column, the Colorado infantrymen were greatly excited by this turn of events and "knapsacks, canteens, overcoats, and clothing of all kinds were flung along the road as the boys stripped for the encounter. How our hearts beat!" observed Private Hollister. Leaving the cavalry behind in the road, Chivington led his infantry forward along the trail at the double quick. He slowed, however, when coming within sight of the enemy, who indicated their intention of holding their ground by firing two rounds that whistled harmlessly over the Federals' heads. In response, Chivington began to deploy the three infantry companies as skirmishers on either side of the valley, but the Texans rapidly limbered up their cannon and retreated in haste down the Santa Fe Trail.[21]

Less than a mile back down the road, the napping Confederates were rudely awakened. Bill Davidson remembered a "volley of musketry" being fired into their midst, but "in a moment every fellow was on his feet gun in hand to repel the assailants." The officers immediately recognized the peril in which the artillery had been placed, and a mad scramble to save the guns began as "every fellow put out at his best speed for our cannon." Their anxiety was compounded by hearing the report of the guns as Sergeant Norman fired, out of sight up the valley. The running soldiers were soon relieved, however, as the artillery chief retreated toward them at full speed, followed by those Brigands who had not been forced to surrender.[22]

All was confusion in the Texan ranks. Men and horses raced about, the soldiers firing at the enemy force that now came into view some distance up the valley. In addition, one of the wheels of an artillery carriage started to come off, and Davidson's companions helped Sergeant Norman fix the trouble so that both guns would be serviceable. Majors Pyron and Shropshire remained calm, however, and gradually brought order out of the chaos. Pyron withdrew his force slightly, to a point across the Santa Fe Trail near the lower end of the valley shelf, where it narrowed into a good defensive position. In withdrawing, Captain Shannon's Company C "got into a kind of pocket," observed one of the participants, "so that the enemy were on three sides of him." He escaped the potential trap with a few casualties and joined Pyron's new battle line. With Company A anchoring his right and the two 6-pounder cannons in position on the road, the Confederate commander awaited the enemy force, then began to shell the oncoming column.[23]

Now the fight truly opened for most of the Union soldiers. Approaching to within four or five hundred yards of the enemy line, Major Chivington again sent his infantry up the sides of the narrow valley to harass and outflank the Texans. The Coloradoans of Companies A and E, under Captains Wynkoop and Anthony, climbed among the piñons and junipers south of the trail, while Captain Downing's Company D deployed up the slope north of the road and across a broad outcropping of rock to the wooded hillside on the Rebels' left flank.[24]

As these companies began firing on the Confederates, the regular and volunteer cavalry units approached. They had not been able to see the brief encounter just ended, and the first sight of their enemy arrayed before them evoked excitement as well as solemn thoughts. Private Hollister wondered: "Were we worthy of the name we bore? A few minutes would tell." The Rebels had a small red flag "emblazoned with the emblem of which Texas has small reason to be proud," one Colorado trooper observed, while another remembered that it "looked very sausy and wicked at the head of their column of men." A third was less impressed and, upon seeing these "lions in the path," described the banner as "a rag on a pole."[25]

Chivington ordered the cavalry to halt in the road and hold themselves ready to charge the enemy if the opposing line should begin to give way or the cannons retreat. Captain Howland's regular squadron preceded the volunteer horsemen of Company F as it neared the Confederates and crossed over the Galisteo Creek bridge. The Rebels shifted their artillery fire upon seeing this new threat, and the veteran regulars were thrown into confusion by the projectiles screaming over their heads and bursting at their rear. Their officers soon regained control of the situation and led their men back to shelter and regroup behind an outcropping east of the bridge, past the waiting volunteer company.[26]

Some members of Company F had been on the bridge as the cannonading began, but the unit moved forward along the trail and halted. Pvt. John Miller believed that the regulars had "broke ranks and run," while Ovando Hollister was even more convinced of their cowardly behavior as the troopers "parted either way and filed to the rear in confusion, leaving us [Company F] in front."[27] The regulars had not broken and run, of course, such initial confusion being quite understandable under the circumstances, but their behavior was made to order for the Coloradoans' boasting.

Bridge over Galisteo Creek at the upper reach of Apache Canyon. Company F, First Colorado Volunteers, was on this bridge as the Battle of Apache Canyon began.

While the Federal cavalry was being shelled, Major Pyron, leaving his guns in position, slowly advanced his battle line along the Santa Fe Trail, toward the position held by the Union horsemen. Some Colorado cavalrymen crowded together to the side of the road to escape the artillery fire behind another major outcropping. Others, perhaps all, were ordered to dismount to oppose the oncoming Texans. Private Miller remembered that "company F had got a little out of the road and had dismounted to fight on foot," while Ben Ferris recalled that they "marched into a draw on our right and dismounted, every 4th man holding the horses. We deployed and made ready to receive the heretofore invincible Texas Rangers." Seeing this increased activity, the Rebel gun crews increased their fire against the Union center. Private Ferris and Capt. Charles Walker, commanding Company E of the Third U.S. Cavalry, observed that all the shots went wild and did no damage to the Federals.[28]

In the Confederate lines, Bill Davidson saw things differently; the artillery fire appeared to be impressively effective. "Norman, Hume and Nettles," the artillery commanders, were "beginning to preach to them in true war-like style from our 6-pounders," he reported. After slowly advancing some three hundred yards, however, Major Pyron ordered a halt, then a retreat. The Federal infantry companies had succeeded in outflanking the Texan line. Even though their fire was at a fairly long range, especially to the north, since the valley walls diverged as they came even with the Rebels, it was effective. The Texans began to take casualties and found their position in the road to be untenable. Federals (in exaggeration) described them being "shot down like sheep."[29]

As the Confederate line receded, the supporting artillery began to limber up for a withdrawal. Major Chivington reported that "our men from the mountain sides made it too hot for their gunners." He had expected that under such circumstances, when the enemy was most vulnerable, his cavalry would charge down the trail and attack the disorganized foe. It did not happen, and he later blamed Captain Howland for the failure.[30]

That officer, however, was now behind the volunteers of Company F, who were quickly remounting once Rebel firing ceased. Whether Howland was impeded by the volunteer horsemen being in the trail ahead of him or whether he had not yet brought his squadron under complete control, only some ten or fifteen minutes having passed since their earlier fright, is not clear. What is clear, however, is that Captain Cook, whose Company F was soon mounted and unimpeded by any units in front of it, also failed to take the initiative and charge. Private Miller observed that "if we had charged as soon as we had mounted, we could have taken their artillery, but we had no head, no one to go ahead and give orders."[31]

This inaction robbed Chivington of any opportunity of bringing the Apache Canyon fight to a rapid and successful conclusion. His own inexperience in battle was probably more to blame for Federal inertia than any other factor. A veteran commander would have sent another and forceful order to the cavalry, of whichever unit, repeating his earlier directive to charge the retreating enemy. That was apparently too much to expect of a neophyte leader in his first brush with the foe.

Having given the order for a general retreat, Major Pyron galloped westward through Apache Canyon with his men. However, his order to Company A, Fifth Texas, somehow miscarried. That company, fighting dismounted on the right flank of the Confederate battle line, never got the word and watched as their companions began to stream back down the trail. Their immediate attention was drawn to their own predicament, however, as the two Federal infantry companies that had outflanked the Texans south of Galisteo Creek, as well as others now rapidly advancing to surround them, opened an intense fire. Private Davidson and his companions returned the Union fire vigorously, but were about to be completely cut off from their fleeing command when Major Shropshire, keeping an eye on his old company, looked back and saw their serious dilemma.[32]

Already beloved by his men for his fair and considerate behavior, the major now became a hero in their eyes. Shropshire turned his horse and raced back. Considerable confusion reigned. The company commander, Capt. Tom Wright, had been detached the week before for duty with the regimental staff in Albuquerque. In the absence of its familiar leader, the company was fighting that day under its new captain, Stephen Wells, a former private who had only recently been elected to his position and who had never before commanded the unit in battle. Private Davidson was overjoyed to see Shropshire reach them. "Like an avalanche he came to us right through the lines of the enemy," shouting, "Boys, follow me." One of the Company A troopers yelled back that "we are out of cartridges," to which the major replied, "then take your knives and follow me." They did, and broke clear of their trap. In doing so, Bill Davidson reported, "we lost in killed and wounded and missing (captured) twenty-seven of our very best men." He added, however, that "but for Shropshire, the whole company would have been killed or captured."[33]

The Union cavalry took no part in that brief skirmish with the Texans,

Maj. John S. Shropshire, Fifth Texas Mounted Volunteers, led a battalion of his regiment in the Battle of Apache Canyon and was killed commanding the Texan right wing at Glorieta.
Courtesy Archives of Nesbitt Memorial Library, Columbus, Texas.

but stood in the trail watching as the enemy "retired rapidly with their little red clout a mile or so down the canon." Pyron's force looked back, but could see no enemy pursuing them. The major, therefore, formed a second defensive line immediately to the west of Apache Creek, which here was a fairly insignificant dry arroyo, four or five feet deep, spanned by a short, wooden bridge.[34]

The site today is considerably altered, not only by erosion during the intervening century but by the ruins and rubble of an early twentieth-century highway and bridge that followed essentially the same course as the old Santa Fe Trail. Here also, midway through Apache Canyon, the fields north of the trail were gently rolling and sloped gradually southward to the steep banks of Galisteo Creek. Uphill from the roadway, Apache Creek's arroyo was hardly noticeable. South of Galisteo Creek, an abrupt rock wall rose over a hundred feet to a wooded shelf that itself sloped downward to the west to reach the valley floor in rear of the Confederate lines. The position appeared to be favorable for defense, but it soon proved otherwise.[35]

Chivington followed the Texans cautiously. In the absence of any real knowledge of the strength of the enemy, and with the reasonable assumption that the main body of enemy troops was following the advance party just engaged, both Chivington and Pyron were apprehensive of falling into a trap along the narrow canyon and of being attacked by vastly superior numbers. Neither side was sure that it was fighting only an enemy vanguard of essentially equal strength. Nevertheless, the Confederate commander unlimbered his two cannons along the road west of Apache Creek in such a position as to sweep the trail as it approached his line.

Pyron had learned a lesson from the fight just ended; he sent a company up the mountainside on his right, to act as skirmishers and secure that flank from any repeated attempt by the Federals to outflank him. He did the same on the left flank, sending dismounted men northward along Apache Creek, into the hills and fields there. Chivington soon found the Texans "completely covering the sides of the mountains with their skirmishers to support their guns in the canon below them."[36]

Relying on his artillery to halt the oncoming enemy again along the Santa Fe Trail, Major Pyron supported the 6-pounders with most of the balance of his dismounted men. As a precaution, however, he sent the Fifth Regiment's Company A, low on ammunition and cut up by their recent narrow escape, back toward Johnson's Ranch, to cover the camp and supply wagons left there as well as the trail exit through the narrow defile from Apache Canyon. Once back in camp, some three-quarters of a mile behind Pyron's line, the men of Company A replenished their cartridge boxes, formed yet another defensive line on the hillside commanding the exit from Apache Canyon, and awaited events. As an additional precaution, Pyron also sent off a mounted courier to find Colonel Scurry and the main Confederate force, believed to be in the vicinity of Galisteo, urging that officer to come quickly to his aid.[37]

Giving Pyron plenty of time to establish his position, at about three o'clock, the Federal column approached. Before Chivington rose a high hill, separated from either valley side and blocking his view ahead. The Santa Fe Trail passed around the northern base of the hill, approximately three hundred yards in front of the Confederate battle line. It then made an abrupt S-turn southward, directly at the high rocky cliff now guarded by Pyron's flank company, before continuing westward to the Apache Creek bridge. Unsure of what lay ahead, and sending a mounted party to find out, the Federal commander halted his regular and volunteer cavalry in the trail, behind the shelter of the isolated hill. He then spent considerable time waiting for his infantry companies to catch up with the horsemen and contemplating his next move.[38]

Finally receiving a description of the enemy dispositions, Major Chivington decided to repeat essentially his earlier, successful tactics. Again he dispatched the infantrymen of Companies A and E up the mountainside south of the trail, while Downing's Company D filed off to the north to attempt to outflank the Rebel line there. The two Colorado companies' climb to the mountainside shelf, now occupied by enemy skirmishers, was arduous and took considerable time. As a result, the northern flanking party had adequate time to push even with, and ultimately behind, the Confederates. Like Pyron, Chivington had also learned from his recent experience. He again planned a cavalry charge to break the Confederate center in conjunction with the arrival of his flanking parties even with the Confederate line.[39] This time, however, he would not leave its execution to chance.

Pvt. Ben Ferris, waiting with Company F, remembered that the major called out, within hearing of both the regular and volunteer commanders, "Who will charge that battery?" Captain Sam Cook immediately yelled back, "I will," according to Ferris, before the regulars had time to reply. His companion John Miller also recalled the incident but inferred timidity on the part of the regular horsemen: "The other cavalry companies had somewhat recovered from their fright, but not enough to volunteer to make the charge so Captain Cook told the major that Company F would charge the battery when the major was ready for them." Private Hollister, usually alert to discover any flaw in the regulars' behavior and to extol the heroism of the First Colorado, did not overhear or mention such an exchange, nor did Major Chivington mention it in his later reports.[40]

That officer did, however, determine a different employment for the regular cavalry squadron. Company E, Third Cavalry, was sent to support the southern flanking party. The company commander, Capt. Charles Walker, recalled that he "was ordered to dismount and assist Captain Wynkoop's company of Colorado Volunteers in clearing the hills to the left and front of our position." Similarly, leaving their horses held in the shelter of the lone trailside hill, Captains Howland and Lord dismounted their detachments from the First and Third regular regiments and followed

Capt. Samuel F. Cook, Company F, First Colorado Volunteers. Leading his cavalry command at Apache Canyon, Cook was shot twice but survived to return to Colorado. *Courtesy Colorado Historical Society.*

Downing's volunteer Company D to the far right of the Union position.[41]

With great anxiety, John Chivington waited for his plans to be carried out. Private Hollister observed that at this time, the major "seemed burdened with new responsibility, the extent of which he had never before realized, and to have no thought of danger. Of commanding presence, dressed in full regimentals, he was a conspicuous mark for the Texan sharp shooters."[42]

Chivington followed the progress of his flanking parties from his position north of the lone hill, out of sight of the Confederate center below and around a turn in the trail. Reaching the mountainside shelf south of the road and Galisteo Creek, Wynkoop's and Anthony's infantrymen, outnumbering the Rebels significantly, opened fire on the Texan skirmishers already occupying the position. The Texans slowly gave way westward, being supported by shell and case shot fired into the advancing Federals by the 6-pounders below.[43] Soon Walker's dismounted regulars also reached the shelf to reinforce the Coloradoans.

Although they were out of sight off to the north, Chivington could trace the progress of his other party by the sounds of their muskets and carbines as they pushed the Confederate left flank slowly backward. After about an hour, around four o'clock, he was convinced the time for decisive action had arrived.[44]

Then ensued the most dramatic action of the battle. Chivington turned and yelled to the First Colorado's Company F to charge the enemy, since he perceived that the Confederate artillery was preparing to retreat. Some of the cavalrymen had dismounted to rest their horses and perhaps to watch the interesting fight taking place south of the road. "We double quicked to our horses, mounted and were immediately ordered forward," remembered one of these men, Ben Ferris. "As soon as the order to charge left the Major's mouth," another recalled, "we were on the wing, fearful lest our company should win no share of the laurels that were to crown the day."[45]

Drawing their revolvers, and with Captain Cook at their head, the Union cavalrymen formed into a column of four horses abreast and surged forward into a pounding gallop, initially still sheltered by the hill. After two hundred yards or so, Company F rounded the base of the hill and came into full view of the defending Texans up on the shelf before them. Hollister saw "a high, steep, rocky bluff, like the bastion of a fort, square in our front." The Rebels immediately shifted their attention to this oncoming menace. Because of the nature of the ground on either side of the trail at this point, the column was largely confined to the roadway and could not spread out. Here "we received a volley and the man in front of me fell from his horse," reported Pvt. John Miller; "after that the balls fell, thicker and faster all the time." The Texans poured in what seemed to be a devastating hail of bullets, although in fact, few found their marks.[46]

Further back from the dismounted Confederates, Sergeant Norman had the 6-pounders firing now at the oncoming cavalry column. "The cannon was so near that we could feel the hot air from their guns on our faces," claimed Miller with considerable exaggeration. Private Ferris noted that just as they came in sight of the enemy on the shelf above the valley floor, "a rifle shot sounded through the hills and Mort Patterson threw up his hands, high above his head, and fell backwards from his horse." The wounded trooper cried, "Oh boys, don't leave me!" but his comrades raced past him toward the center of the Confederate line.[47]

The trail turned to the right, and the galloping cavalrymen saw for the first time the Texan center and, several hundred yards behind it, the enemy artillery. To the excited troopers, shots seemed to come from every rock and bend in the canyon. The tremendous din and increasing powder smoke had no effect on the charging horsemen, but many of the defending Rebels broke and ran for the rear, jumping across the Apache Creek arroyo on either side of the road or racing down the trail itself. The Texan gunners saw the peril in which they were placed. Hurriedly they limbered up the two cannons, turned, and raced westward through the narrow defile at the west end of Apache Canyon back to their camp and the defensive line already formed there by the Fifth Regiment's Company A.[48]

The First Colorado horsemen found that they were galloping along the Santa Fe Trail parallel to the shelf to their left, from which the Texan skirmishers now increased their fire. John Miller found himself riding right beside one of his lieutenants, through "an awful fire, the balls whistling by our ears." Another cavalryman noted that "we met a redoubled shower of lead, rained on us from the rocks above." Riders began to fall as the column approached the narrow, shallow arroyo of Apache Creek. The Texans may have burned the bridge as an impediment as some historians later claimed, but none of the participants later remembered that being the case. On the column came, its momentum waning as its members fired at scattered Confederates on either side of the trail. The horsemen jumped the little gully or rode through it, continuing the charge.[49]

At or near the arroyo, Captain Cook, at the head of the column, was shot. Some nearby Texan emptied a "buck and ball" charge into the officer's thigh. Cook kept his saddle momentarily, but his horse stumbled, falling on him, and the captain was shot again in the foot as he struggled to free himself from his fallen mount. Finally, he limped to one side and escaped further injury.[50]

Probably the most enduring myth of the Apache Canyon battle is that of a dramatic leap over a chasm by Company F. Long cherished by historians and enthusiasts, this tale has the cavalrymen galloping in "column of twos" down the Santa Fe Trail, and leaping over the burned or burning eighteen-foot bridge at the upper end of Apache Canyon, then continuing into the Texan ranks to win the battle. All made the jump but one, who was crippled for life.

There are, however, several problems with this story. Even if the cavalry horse ever existed that could jump an eighteen-foot gorge, especially while galloping in a column of other horses, there was no such gully to jump. The "burned" bridge, shown in early photographs as the site, was still intact, and in fact was the location of the Federal cavalry as the battle began. Some Colorado horseman may indeed have fallen and injured himself as he crossed the almost insignificant Apache Creek arroyo, but no participant in the fight, Federal or Confederate, mentioned such an incident. Only John Chivington, many years after the war, recalled the event, or what can be interpreted as such an event, in a manuscript memoir that is replete with other serious errors, undoubtedly brought on by the passage of time. The story of the injured horseman and the jump had likely become a favorite among "old soldier stories" around Denver by that time, and Chivington repeated it as fact—perhaps feeling that even if it never happened, it should have![51]

There was, however, genuine drama sufficient to last the Coloradoans a lifetime. Some mounts fell and threw their riders, while other saddles were emptied by the Texans. The loose horses raced among the contending soldiers as scattered groups of Confederates kept up a heavy fire against the Federals. Other cavalrymen found their animals unmanageable, either because of the noise and confusion or as a result of wounds. Private Ferris could not control his horse, "the bridle having been cut on the side of the head letting the bit out of his mouth." Worse still, he soon realized that "my faithful little gray was seriously hurt. I soon found that his color had apparently been his undoing for I found four bullet holes in him." Capturing another "fine horse completely and well equipped, . . . we hastely joined our Co."[52]

As Captain Cook fell, the momentum went out of the charging cavalry column. First Lt. George Nelson, who had captured the Brigand pickets earlier that morning, took command of the company and brought order out of the chaos. He quickly led a group of the troopers on westward in pursuit of the artillery, still visible but rapidly disappearing down the Santa Fe Trail. They charged through more Texans formed along the road, but could not overtake the flying guns and gunners, so turned and charged once more through the enemy ranks, firing their pistols right and left, to rejoin the rest of the Colorado cavalrymen.[53]

While this artillery pursuit was under way, Company F's second lieutenant, William F. Marshall, took charge of the rest of the men and led them in several furious charges through the Texan positions, turning to charge again and again through the scattered throng of Confederates. When Nelson and Marshall reunited, the Colorado cavalrymen turned westward and pushed the Rebels steadily back toward the western exit from Apache Canyon. There, along a narrow ridge running down from the north, across the trail and into the bottom of Galisteo Creek, Pyron formed his straggling men into a final, hastily organized defense line. Private Ferris noted that there the desperate enemy "made quite a fight"; Hollister was more impressed, recalling that the Rebels, "though somewhat confused and scattered by our sudden advent among them, made for cover and stood like a tiger at bay."[54]

Just as the Confederates formed this improvised line, however, disaster struck. With the Federal cavalrymen forcing in the center of the line, Captain Downing reached the Texans' left flank north of the trail. His infantrymen and the dismounted regular troopers under Howland and Lord had driven in the enemy flank guards, and the Federals had crossed the hillsides above the battlefield to descend unexpectedly on Pyron's new line. The Confederates broke under the pressure and streamed toward their right to try to reform in a little side canyon south of the road.[55]

Just as they did so, the Federal flanking party that had been slowly pushing the Texan skirmishers westward down the sloping shelf south of the canyon drove those soldiers into the same small pocket. Now, as Companies A and E, backed by the regulars under Captain Walker, reached the bottom of the shelf, the Colorado infantrymen "came down on them like a parcel of wild Indians, cheering at the top of their lungs, regardless of the shower of bullets raining among them." Downing's Company D did likewise, and "the Texans, terrified at the impetuosity of the attack, broke and fled in every direction," according to Private Hollister.[56]

Some escaped by running or riding quickly back along the trail in the bottom of Galisteo Creek to refuge in the Texan camp, about a half-mile west. Pyron escaped by this means, but many of his men did not. Wynkoop's and Anthony's men captured those who could not escape from the little canyon or who were wounded. "We were obliged to make prisoners of some forty or fifty," Hollister observed; "they forgot that one of them was equal to five of us and insisted on surrendering." One of the captured Texans, Pvt. James McLeary of Company A, Fifth Texas, felt the Confederates "were outflanked, outnumbered, and outgeneralled," causing his companions to "fall back . . . in some disorder."[57]

They were not the only Confederates to have surrendered. Private Miller and Lieutenant Marshall approached a group of still dangerous Rebels who had been shooting at them. "We rode up to five Texans and shot two, Miller recounted. "Three of them threw down their rifles and surrendered." Others did not come in so easily. Union private George Lowe's horse fell with him during the action. He struggled loose from the mount and jumped behind a nearby bank for shelter. He was surprised, however, as "a stalwart Texan captain," who, with a cocked pistol bearing on him, "guessed Lowe was his prisoner." Supposedly, "Lowe sprang on him like a cat, and after a violent struggle disarmed and marched him to the rear."[58]

In another potential capture, Pvt. C. W. Logan of Company F found a wounded Confederate, who called out from behind a rock that he was hurt and wished to surrender. When Logan lowered his gun and came up to disarm and aid the man, the Rebel drew his own pistol and fired, hitting Logan in the arm. "Oh, you son of a bitch. I'll kill you now," the would-be captor exclaimed, and he put a bullet through the man's head.[59]

A few Federals followed the retreating Texans through the narrow defile leading out of Apache Canyon and fired occasionally into the defense line set up in front of the Johnson's Ranch camp. Pvt. Bill Davidson was in that line and remembered that "even after the sun had gone down and until dark-night had come did we continue the struggle. When it became too dark for Mr. Yank to see what he was doing, he withdrew and the fight ended." In Wynkoop's Colorado Company A, Pvt. Charles Gardiner understood that the Texans had "sent in a flag [of truce] requesting time to bury their dead, which was granted until 8 o'clock, next morning," an arrangement later confirmed by Confederate reports.[60]

The fighting had lasted only a half-hour after the Colorado cavalry charge commenced, but by five o'clock or thereabouts, Major Chivington called his advanced troopers back into Apache Canyon and prepared to withdraw. He had successfully accomplished his mission of "advancing toward Santa Fe and capturing or defeating the force rumored to be there." Unsure whether a larger Confederate force might be close behind the Texans he had just fought, and separated beyond supporting distance from Colonel Slough and his own main body of troops, the vanguard commander determined to fall back at least to Pigeon's Ranch.[61]

As the Union infantry companies started back up the Santa Fe Trail, the regular and volunteer cavalrymen prepared to depart also. With a surplus of horses available from the Confederate casualties and those who had fled on foot, Lieutenant Nelson started a mounted column of wounded, from both sides, and prisoners, along with the Federal dead, back on the trail to Pigeon's Ranch.[62]

The battlefield was littered with debris from the fight, including many arms dropped by the departing and surrendering Texans. The Colorado officers ordered the men to carry away whatever guns they could and to destroy all others. Lieutenant Marshall supervised the work of destruction. Private Ferris remembered that Marshall "told them to be careful about breaking guns as some of them might be loaded. Soon after, he [the lieutenant] picked up a gun by the mussel [sic] and hit it against a stump, and it exploded and he got the contents through his stomach." That tragic and unnecessary act was the last shot of the Battle of Apache Canyon.[63]

Hardly even a skirmish when compared with the huge numbers of men involved in eastern Civil War battles, the fight in Apache Canyon was nevertheless impressive in the context of frontier combat. It was the second largest battle ever fought up to that time in New Mexico (Valverde, one month earlier, being the largest). Casualties were surprisingly light considering the prodigious amount of ammunition that had been fired at the enemy by both forces. Five Federals had been killed, four of them from Company F, and fourteen were wounded; no Union soldiers were captured.[64]

Confederate losses cannot be rigorously determined. Union estimates of the enemy casualties were wildly exaggerated, as was normal throughout the Civil War, and Confederate reports ranged from two to thirty-two killed and from three to forty-three wounded. The most reasonable estimate appears to be a Confederate loss of four killed and twenty wounded. What is not controversial, however, is the number of prisoners taken. Including those captured by Chivington's men early in the battle, those taken in the main Texan defense line, and men surrendering in the little side canyon as the fighting ended, seventy-one Confederates were captured out of Pyron's original force of approximately 420 men. It was the greatest loss the Texans would experience during the New Mexico campaign.[65]

Company A, Fifth Texas, suffered particularly heavily at Apache Canyon. Of the prisoners, between twenty and thirty-four were from that unit alone (including their new captain, Stephen Wells), while the Brigands lost about twenty. Captain Shannon's Company C had fourteen men taken prisoner, with the rest coming from the ranks of the other Fifth Regiment companies and the artillery.[66]

Much had been learned during the Battle of Apache Canyon. Major Chivington had commanded in his first combat and had done quite well by sticking with simple but effective tactics and maintaining control over his men and their movements. Pyron had not performed nearly as effectively as his aggressive nature and experience would have indicated. Letting himself be outflanked in his first position was a mistake; choosing a poor defensive position for his second battle line was a disaster, especially considering that less than a half-mile to the rear was a constricted canyon, across the mouth of which even a weak force without artillery could have held off almost any enemy that could reasonably be expected to advance against it.

The soldiers of both sides also learned from their experiences. Private Hollister and his companions found the Texans to be much less fearsome and invincible than their reputation. "Among the conflicting emotions of that evening," he wrote, "not the weakest was one of disappointment in the character of the foe we had met. Why, they ought to have killed the last one of us." The Texans, on the other hand, hitherto having considered themselves ferocious and unbeatable, were more impressed with their northern foe. Private Davidson was surprised at the aggressiveness of the Federals, not having believed that the Yankees had enough enterprise actually to attack them. "We had a great deal to learn yet about what these fellows could do," he concluded.[67]

In the Texan camp, Pyron's men remained in their defensive positions until well after dark, anxiously awaiting the expected arrival of Scurry's main force from Galisteo. "We remained in line under arms," Davidson reported, "as we were every moment expecting another attack." All knew that their reinforcements would put forth every effort to reach them without delay—but could they arrive in time?[68]

As the Confederates worried, the Union column wound its way back along the Santa Fe Trail toward Pigeon's Ranch. The journey was agony for many of the wounded, forced to ride, walk, or be carried along the rough roadway. Captain Cook bore the pain of his thigh and foot wounds with admirable fortitude, according to those carrying him. With the exception of Captain Walker's Company E of the Third regular cavalry, left behind in Apache Canyon to act as a rear guard, by about ten o'clock Chivington's men reached the ranch and soon established a hospital for the wounded in Alexander Valle's main building.[69]

There, some spent the night tending wounded friends. Ben Ferris and Ovando Hollister both took care of their companion Martin Dutro, who had been "shot down obliquely through the head and again through the chest." Hollister was "sick at the wounds of Dutro, and spent the night watching his life ebb away." Ferris claimed that was the most miserable night he had ever spent, as he watched "Mart" Dutro, as well as the suffering Lieutenant Marshall, die just before daybreak. Private Dutro was the company member who had been such a hell-raiser back in Denver City, drinking and fighting with the police so enthusiastically. Captain Cook also suffered all night, likewise attended by Ben Ferris, but he survived to return to Colorado.[70]

The advance parties had met, fought fiercely and in the case of the Federals, effectively, then fallen back to lick their wounds and await reinforcement. Now it would be the turn of the main Federal and Confederate forces to determine the fate of New Mexico Territory.

CHAPTER FOUR

Opening Shots

The sharp report of a gun and sharper whistle of a minie ball warned us that they had come out to meet us.

—*Sgt. Alfred B. Peticolas, Fourth Texas*

As the survivors of the Confederate vanguard awaited reinforcements in their Johnson's Ranch camp, their Federal opponents did the same at Pigeon's Ranch. Major Chivington, however, soon decided to move farther back. As dawn of March 27 broke on the Union encampment and hospital, he decided the water supply at Pigeon's was insufficient to provide for the patients and the column's horses, as well as the large number of Texan prisoners of war. They would move out, but first, the Federals selected a site in an open field "a quarter of a mile down the canon" for burial of their dead from the previous day's fighting. While that sad duty was being performed, better news arrived; a party of Colorado volunteers had located a quantity of flour and corn stored nearby and had confiscated it for use of the troops. With breakfast thus assured, Chivington's men made arrangements to pull out. There being insufficient wheeled transportation to accommodate the number of wounded soldiers of both sides being treated in the makeshift hospital, those unable to walk or ride had to be left behind under the care of one of the First Colorado's surgeons, either Dr. John F. Hamilton or Dr. Lewis C. Tolles.[1]

Guarding their healthy or lightly wounded prisoners, the Federals retraced the five miles along the Santa Fe Trail to their old camp around and on the wooded slope south of the spring at Kozlowski's Ranch. Major Chivington quickly placed the captured Rebels in the charge of Capt. R. S. C. Lord and his detachment of the First Cavalry, for return to and confinement at Fort Union as prisoners of war.[2]

As they rode eastward, Lord's mounted party soon encountered Colonel Slough and the main body of Federals coming toward them. While still at Pigeon's Ranch, Major Chivington had sent off a messenger to the Union commander, informing him of the day's events at Apache Canyon. Receiving this welcome news of his advance party's safety and success, as well as further evidence of the Texans' proximity, Slough saw the need for rapidly marching to his major's relief. That need was emphasized by additional information he received. As soon as the Battle of Apache Canyon was over, travel along the Santa Fe Trail resumed. Whether Slough had sent "spies" or agents ahead to send back information about the enemy force at Johnson's Ranch or whether he got such news from travelers cannot be definitely determined, but from one or another of these sources the Federal colonel learned that the Texans had concentrated "about 1,000 strong."[3]

Around noon, just as Chivington was reaching Kozlowski's Ranch, Slough started his column westward. Captain Enos, with his quartermaster supply train once again almost intact after return of twelve of fifteen wagons by Chivington two days earlier, accompanied the Federal infantry as it left the Bernal Springs camp on a forced march to join the vanguard. Enos was still not happy. "On reaching San Jose," he later reported, "I found that nine mules, belonging to the teams which had been turned over to the mounted Companies, had been taken, to replace broken down horses of Capt. Cook's Volunteer Company." Enos objected to Slough over this misuse of valuable transportation resources, but again the colonel simply replied that "it could not be helped." Allowing only one stop en route for water and rest, Colonel Slough kept the men going through the rest of the day and well into the night. By late evening, he had arrived with the head of his column, which continued to drag into Kozlowski's Ranch until two or three o'clock the next morning, March 28.[4]

Despite the bitter cold, Kozlowski's rang with cheers and greetings as Chivington's men saw their comrades come into camp. Private Hollister remembered that those just arrived "had heard of the engagement yesterday, and could not be restrained." As the excitement wore off, however, officers allowed the weary men to get whatever sleep was left to them, and most dozed off until well after the sun began to warm the camp. Colonel Slough wasted no time, however, calling in his key officers to formulate plans for moving against the Texans as soon as possible.[5]

The Federal commander's strategic goal remained the same as that with which he had previously charged Major Chivington; he would "obstruct the movements of and cut off the supplies of" the Confederate force threatening Fort Union. To do so, Slough would advance against the enemy "with a view of reconnoitering his position at Johnson's Ranch." He would not simply march up the Santa Fe Trail, however, and attack his foes frontally in what could be expected to be a fortified and strong position. Like most volunteer officers early in the Civil War, Colonel Slough was inexperienced in battle but had read military histories and tactics books as preparation for command. Napoleon's tactics were standard fare and highly favored, North and South.

Accordingly, Slough adapted Napoleonic tactics to the situation he believed to be ahead. He would send a strong flanking force under Major Chivington, who had just done so well with an independent command, around to the south of the Santa Fe Trail, across the flat top of Glorieta Mesa. Slough himself would lead the main body westward toward the Rebel position at Johnson's Ranch. Chivington's flanking *manoeuvre sur les derrières* was to be coordinated with Slough's main attack on the Texans with the Federal *masse de decision*. The Fighting Parson's force would descend on the Confederate flank or rear, disrupting and panicking the enemy just as Slough's assault column arrived in front of them. Such tactics looked attractive to inexperienced commanders, but usually amateur officers were unable to execute anything so complex, especially in terrain like the heavily wooded mountains of northern New Mexico.[6]

Colonel Slough originally had approximately 1,340 men with whom to confront the Confederates. However, 50 of those, Lord's cavalry regulars, had now been detached to escort prisoners. The Federal commander decided to assign slightly more than one-third of his remaining force to Major Chivington for the flanking movement. The Colorado major would have the entire provisional infantry battalion, 269 men, of Capt. William Lewis, including Companies A and G, Fifth U.S. Infantry, Jim Ford's independent Colorado company (strengthened by a contingent of New Mexico Volunteers), and Sam Logan's Company B, First Colorado Volunteers. He also organized a battalion of three companies of the First Colorado: A, E, and H, under temporary command of Capt. Ed Wynkoop, who had fought so well two days before at Apache Canyon. Altogether, Chivington would have 488 foot soldiers in his party. In addition, he had along as scouts and guides a small group of native New Mexicans from the First, Second, and Fourth Regiments of New Mexico Volunteers. Heading this unit was Lt.

Col. Manuel Antonio Chaves, Second New Mexico Volunteers, an officer familiar with the local region and experienced in small-unit warfare between Hispanic and Indian parties before the Civil War.[7]

With this detachment, and considering those wounded left in the hospital at Pigeon's Ranch but not counting the noncombatant quartermaster train employees, Colonel Slough had about 800 men with whom to organize his main striking force. He would be in overall command of the field, of course, should a battle develop, and he retained direct control of all the available cavalry as a reserve force. Captain Howland's regular horsemen, 100 strong, and the First Colorado's Company F, about 85 effectives, comprised that strategic reserve. To Lt. Col. Sam Tappan, Slough assigned command of all the available infantry and artillery. Organized as a battalion, Tappan's command consisted of Companies C, D, G, I, and K, First Colorado Volunteers, and both Ritter's and Claflin's cannoneers. The five infantry companies, strengthened by detached men from several regular and New Mexico Volunteer units forming the garrison back at Fort Union, as well as by those soldiers considered unfit to accompany Major Chivington on his arduous flanking movement, contributed some 530 soldiers to Tappan's force, while 85 artillerymen rounded out the 615 men for whom the Federal second-in-command was responsible.[8]

While Colonel Slough made these assignments and briefed his line officers on them and on their roles in any upcoming fight, he neglected to inform Captain Enos, commanding the quartermaster train. Enos's men, as was the case with all the infantry and artillery troops who had recently arrived from Bernal Springs, were dead tired from having marched all night to reach Kozlowski's Ranch. He heard of a planned advance early on March 28. "Between 7 and 8 o'clock of the same morning I discovered that the entire command was preparing to move. After some inquiry, I found that it was a move forward," he reported. He and Slough had a serious confrontation immediately afterward. Captain Enos was "under the impression that each man was to carry two days rations, and a blanket, upon his person." If so, there would be no need for the entire supply train of one hundred wagons to accompany the field column immediately in its advance. That was false information, but believing it so, and considering that "it was known that the Enemy was in the Canon beyond Pigeon's ranch," Captain Enos suggested to Colonel Slough that the entire train, "excepting the Hospital wagons and Ambulances and the ammunition wagons" remain behind at Kozlowski's with a sufficient guard for its protection. "My suggestion was disregarded," the captain noted, and he prepared the supply train to move forward, "in rear of the Command."[9]

Shortly before nine o'clock Colonel Slough was ready to start the Federal column westward to find the Texans. First, he sent a small patrol ahead on the Santa Fe Trail to act as mounted pickets and warn of any enemy they might discover on or near the road. Slough himself rode at the head of the main column with all the cavalry, Company E of the Third Cavalry regulars in the lead. The infantry and artillery followed, with the civilian wagonmasters and teamsters of the supply train bringing up the rear. Major Chivington's flanking party also accompanied the column westward; however, after about three miles, that officer left the Santa Fe Trail and branched off toward the southwest. "At 9:30 A.M.," he reported, "we left the main road and took the trail leading to Gallisteo." As Slough and Chivington understood from Lieutenant Colonel Chaves and other New Mexico Volunteers, that road was a shortcut to the village of Galisteo but would also bring the flanking party to the top of Glorieta Mesa, south of Slough, and eventually near the Confederate encampment at Johnson's Ranch.[10]

A half-hour later, about ten o'clock, the Federal main column arrived at Pigeon's Ranch. There, Colonel Slough was disconcerted to find that the pickets he had earlier sent ahead to watch for the enemy were instead at the hostelry eating. Riding near Slough with Company F, Pvt. Ben Ferris noted that "they had been there all night, and not being relieved at daylight as they should have been, had come back to Pigeon's for breakfast." Colonel Slough soon sent them on westward along the trail to watch for the enemy, as they should have been doing. Meanwhile, the cavalrymen dismounted to join the infantry and artillery soldiers as they arrived. For about an hour the men rested along the trail, many filling canteens from the well across the road from the main building, and others visiting friends in the hospital located in that building. All prepared to continue their march westward in search of the Rebels.[11]

Lieutenant Colonel Scurry was essentially mirroring Slough's actions. As his main Confederate column rested at Galisteo during the day of March 26, some soldiers slept, while members of the Fourth Texas Regiment's Company E buried one of their companions, a twenty-four-year-old private named James M. Rogers. During the afternoon, the four companies of the Seventh Texas came into camp escorting the two artillery pieces accompanying Scurry's force. Those late arrivals began unpacking their personal belongings and taking care of the draft animals while the officers awaited orders for a further advance.[12]

Those orders never arrived. Instead, an hour before sunset, the courier Major Pyron had sent during the fight in Apache Canyon reached Scurry's camp with a frantic request for assistance. All was excitement and activity as rumors of the battle just ended immediately spread through the ranks. Capt. Julius Giesecke, commanding Company G of the Fourth Regiment, believed that "Pyron, with two hundred and fifty men, had been attacked by the Yankees with twelve hundred and fifteen men in Apache Canyon." Sergeant Alfred Peticolas understood that the major "had been attacked by a large body of Pike's Peak men during the day; that they had gotten the best of the engagement and had fallen back to wood and water, which he would hold till we came up to him." The courier bringing the news and Pyron's urgent entreaty knew little of the outcome of the battle, but the note of urgency and the prospect of the entire Union force either having overcome the Rebel vanguard or being about to overcome it spurred Scurry into immediate action. Directing his officers to inform the command of Pyron's plight, he ordered a forced night march to rescue or reinforce "Pyron and his gallant comrades."[13]

The men rushed about collecting and packing personal items in the company wagons, saddling their horses, and preparing the teams for the journey ahead. By sundown Scurry and his officers had the column ready, and the Texans rode and marched northward, generally along Galisteo Creek. Dark came quickly, and with it bitter cold. The men had been told that Pyron's camp was twelve miles away, which was correct, but "before it was walked," related Sergeant Peticolas, "we found it to be at least 15." So it seemed. For the first six miles, the men moved at a "brisk gait," covering the distance in what Peticolas described as "very little time." At that point, however, the trail became rough and diverged from a better road that took a longer, roundabout route to the Santa Fe Trail and Johnson's Ranch. "Consequently," Pvt. Abe Hanna recalled, "the wagons was sent [on] another road, which was some further, with a detail of men to guard them."[14]

The Texans struggled onward along the direct but terrible road after the wagons departed. With no light to guide them, the men stumbled over one another and over obstacles in and near the trail. Soon, even those who had been well rested became fatigued. Private Hanna recorded that "we came to a very steep mountain, and the horses which drew the artillery was wearied. They was not able to draw the artillery to the top of the mountain so they were compelled to be taken up by hand." Actually, the obstacle was a rather low hill rather than a mountain, but it undoubtedly seemed impressive to the tired men and in the dark. With the teams jaded, the Fourth Texas soldiers tied ropes to the cannon carriages and pulled the pieces slowly up the incline, reaching the top after an hour of backbreaking labor. While they did so, those in the column ahead stopped to make "large fires at the foot of the pass and warmed chilled hands and feet," according to Sergeant Peticolas. The necessity to come to Pyron's aid, however, motivated Scurry's men. The sergeant noted that "every man marched bravely along and did not complain at the length of the road, the coldness of the weather, or the necessity that compelled the march." After what seemed an eternity, the Texans reached Johnson's Ranch and Pyron's camp about three o'clock in the morning on March 27.[15]

Regardless of the hour, the men of the advance party were overjoyed to see Scurry's reinforcements arrive. Pvt. Bill Davidson, who had been worrying all night lest the Federals attack later in the morning, described his companions cheering as the new arrivals poured into camp. "What a hand shaking," he remembered. "I tell you I was glad to see them. I thought they were the finest looking men I ever saw in my life." Scurry's officers soon had the weary men scouring nearby hillsides for firewood to warm themselves after the arduous march. The soldiers learned from those already on the site the story of the previous day's battle and of those killed or wounded during the fight. Private Hanna sat around one of the fires for the rest of the night, but others sought sleep. After fixing a meager dinner "of sweetened mush, which we made from meal that we found at this ranch," Sergeant Peticolas and a companion, Pvt. B. A. Jones, who had no blankets with them, decided to seek a place to sleep in one of the buildings of Johnson's Ranch. Succeeding, "he and I slept together on the floor with no bedding, and only a few articles of women's wearing apparel which we found scattered round the house," the young Texas lawyer-turned-sergeant recalled.[16]

As the sun rose over Apache Canyon to the east, Lieutenant Colonel Scurry, having assumed overall command, had every reason to suppose that his enemies would renew their attack on his now-concentrated force as soon as the previously arranged cessation of hostilities ended at eight o'clock. Undoubtedly Major Pyron realized he had fought only the Federal vanguard, and those men would have described accurately the location of the Confederate camp and wagon park to the Union commander. In addition, Santa Fe Trail travelers probably informed the Texans of the location and strength of Slough's and Chivington's units, just as others had done for the Federals concerning Pyron and his camp and force. Scurry decided to defend the Johnson's Ranch site against what he believed was an enemy that greatly outnumbered him. Examining the ground at first light, he found the location to be ideal for defense.[17]

Its most prominent feature was a lone hill or ridge that stood directly west of the exit of the Santa Fe Trail from the defile leading from Apache Canyon. During the Mexican War, New Mexico governor Manuel Armijo had fortified this same hill in anticipated, or feigned, resistance to the westward advance of Gen. Stephen W. Kearny and his invading American army column. As the trail emerged from Apache Canyon, following the bed of Galisteo Creek, it turned abruptly at the base of this hill, passed Johnson's Ranch, and continued northwestward fifteen miles to Santa Fe. On both sides of the defile, the mountains rose abruptly, giving the appearance of being too steep and high for any attacking party to climb. The position was formidable, if not impregnable, and the Texans quickly set about making it even more so.

Along the eastern slope of the hill, Pyron's survivors had dug an earthwork trench protecting their final defensive line of the preceding evening. Now, Scurry's men improved that position. "We halted in line and began to increase the elevation of the bank behind which we were to fight," Peticolas reported. Whether they added logs to the earth embankment is not recorded, but the soldiers soon felt secure behind the work. Captain Giesecke "prepared for an attack," as did the entire force. Scurry planted his four artillery pieces on top of the hill, behind the infantry, and with that arrangement complete, "we layed during the day," according to Abe Hanna. "This very strong position they did not come to attack, and we laid here all day awaiting them," Sergeant Peticolas agreed, including a sketch of the position in his diary.[18]

Pyron's and Shropshire's men spent part of the day in burying their comrades who had been killed during the previous day's battle, and Scurry's troopers did the same for one of their fellow Fourth Regiment members, Pvt. Wayne G. Cave, of Company E, who had died from some undisclosed illness. Company C performed the same sad duty for Pvt. Theodor Schultz, who had been ill for five days with pneumonia and died after reaching the camp. In the last entry of his diary (he would be killed the next day), Pvt. Abe Hanna recorded that "we had the trial of burying the first one of the members of Company C." "Poor boy, a stranger in a strange land, he sleeps the sleep that knows no waking," lamented Alfred Peticolas.[19]

All were relieved in the evening, about dinner time, to see Scurry's

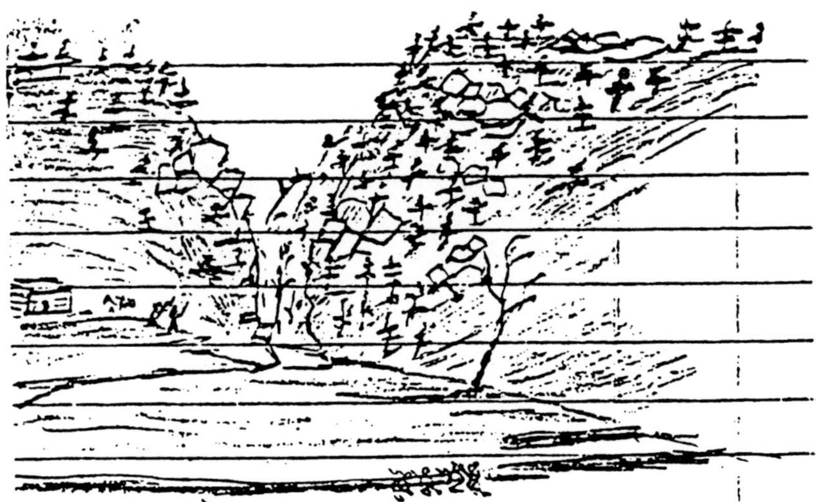

Sergeant Peticolas's sketch of the Texan camp at Cañoncito, with breastworks thrown up to command the Santa Fe Trail. Diary text accompanying sketch: "In our front the road passed through a narrow opening between the mountains; behind us was a considerable hill bristling with our cannon and on the sides of the mountains were placed our sharpshooters. This very strong position they did not come to attack." *Peticolas journal (author's collection).*

supply wagons roll into camp. The men were ravenous; Sergeant Peticolas reported that "we had a good supper," but other Rebels were not so sure. Pvt. Bill Davidson of the Fifth Regiment remembered that "on the night of the 27th some meat was issued to us, the officers said it was dried buffalo, the boys said it was mule steak, no matter what it was, it was the best our officers could do, and really tasted well to hungry men, and we have occupied that position for the past two months." Their appetite for food somewhat satisfied, the men went to sleep with their appetite for a showdown with the Yankees frustrated by the enemy's nonappearance.[20]

If General Sibley had any plan to coordinate the advance of Scurry's force with another column, under Green, that would approach Fort Union from the east of Glorieta Pass, his later report of the campaign fails to mention it, even though some of the Texan soldiers later claimed there was such a plan. The Fifth Regiment companies held back in Albuquerque were apparently intended only as an interdiction force in the event the Federal troops from Fort Craig attempted to reinforce Fort Union by the most direct route, which ran well to the east of Albuquerque and the Sandia

Mountains. Lieutenant Colonel Scurry, therefore, was acting under no constraints to await any other Confederate movements. Consequently, and undoubtedly spurred on by clear recollection of his recent aggressive success at Valverde, Scurry became impatient waiting for the Federal enemy to attack his position at Johnson's Ranch, and during the night of March 27–28, he decided "to march forward and attack them." Formulating plans for such a march, the Confederates prepared to move eastward early in the morning on March 28.[21]

Scurry had approximately 1,285 men available to advance against the enemy, not counting the sick and wounded to be left behind. The Rebel force included nine of the ten companies of the Fourth Texas Mounted Volunteers, marching as infantry soldiers since they had given up their mounts following the Battle of Valverde. The companies were all commanded by captains, with the exception of Company B, led that day by 1st Lt. James Holland due to the illness of Capt. A. J. Scarborough. Company A had been left behind in Albuquerque to guard the Texan supply dump and headquarters there, while other men had been lost to wounds or sickness, leaving a total of about 600 able-bodied members of the regiment ready for action in the Johnson's Ranch camp. Since Lieutenant Colonel Scurry was now leading the entire Texan force north of Albuquerque, command of his Fourth Regiment fell to Maj. Henry W. Raguet. The thirty-five-year-old native of Nacogdoches, Texas, had been shot in the leg while leading a mounted charge at Valverde a month earlier but had healed reasonably well by now.[22]

From the Fifth Texas Regiment, Scurry had the four companies that had fought with Pyron at Apache Canyon two days earlier. Major Shropshire led it as a mounted battalion numbering approximately 250 troopers. Two of its companies, A and B, were led by second lieutenants, John P. Oakes and John J. Scott, respectively, while Denman Shannon and Dan Ragsdale, who had fought well on March 26, commanded their companies, C and D, as captains. Having just arrived with Scurry, Companies B, F, H, and I of the Seventh Texas Mounted Volunteers, all led by their captains, also had 250 men available for action. Maj. Powhatan Jordan, a thirty-three-year-old physician from San Antonio, Texas, had been promoted to that rank after the Battle of Valverde and now led the battalion of the Seventh Regiment into action at Glorieta.[23]

Major Pyron's small battalion of the Second Texas Mounted Rifles, composed of Companies B, D, and E, furnished approximately 80 men for Scurry's force. The Texan column included those members of the "irregular" companies who had not been either wounded or captured during the Apache Canyon battle. In view of the heavy recent loss of men as prisoners, the Brigands, Arizona Rangers, and San Elizario Spy Company contributed about 60 experienced fighters to the Rebel force, all led by Capt. John Phillips of the Brigands.[24]

Lieutenant Colonel Scurry had four pieces of artillery available to accompany his column. Two of these cannons were the 6-pounder guns used by Pyron two days earlier and commanded by Sergeant Norman, with Sgts. Peyton Hume and Tim Nettles each in charge of one gun. Those NCOs and their gun crews were members of the Fifth Texas' artillery company who had come north earlier with Shropshire. The remaining two pieces were both 12-pounder field howitzers, which had accompanied Scurry's main column on the march from the Sandia Mountains through Galisteo to Johnson's Ranch. Both howitzers were served by crews from Major Teel's Company B, First Texas Artillery. Scurry left one of the 6-pounders behind in the charge of Sergeant Nettles, to guard the Texan supply wagon train from any unexpected attack. Second Lt. James Bradford, one of Teel's officers who had brought the howitzers northward, commanded the three-cannon, forty-five-man Confederate battery as it now accompanied Scurry toward the enemy.[25]

Before leaving camp, the Texan commander made arrangements to protect the eighty supply wagons he was leaving behind, along with their horse and mule teams. Sergeant Nettles's 6-pounder remained atop the hill commanding the Santa Fe Trail. To guard it and the wagon train, Scurry detailed not only the gun crew but the wagonmasters and teamsters, as well as his sick and wounded men, some two hundred in all, and all in the charge of the Fourth Texas Regiment's chaplain, Rev. Lucius H. Jones, a thirty-three-year-old Episcopal minister who had accompanied Scurry's men through all their actions so far.[26]

Scurry undoubtedly thought these arrangements for securing his supplies, transportation, and noncombatants were sufficient, given the highly defensible nature of the camp and surrounding mountains. He had not personally experienced the aggressiveness of the Colorado Volunteers two days earlier, and his lack of serious attention to protecting his rear may also have been encouraged by his recent experience capturing the key Union artillery battery at Valverde a month before, when his enemy had apparently retreated without serious fighting. In addition, from the trailside camp, the heights south of Johnson's Ranch appear to be a mountainous ridge or the top of a range of mountains. In fact, this is an illusion; the apparent crest is instead the abrupt western edge of Glorieta Mesa, the flat top of which provides fairly easy passage to a point directly over the Confederate camp site. If Scurry gave little thought to the position's safety, some of his men were worried. Sergeant Peticolas wrote, "Fearing nothing for our train, we left it behind and marched out to give battle," but Pvt. Bill Davidson observed that "at Val Verde, although we were harder pressed . . . yet a continuous guard was kept with the train." Pvt. Henry Wright recalled "leaving our camp, in what we supposed was a secure position."[27]

Scurry evidently intended returning to the supply train that night, since his men took with them in their haversacks or pockets only what little food they had already procured and not eaten. He also sent one company of the Fourth Texas, the "Victoria Invincibles," out toward Apache Canyon early on the morning of March 28, as pickets to warn of and impede any oncoming enemy force. By about eight o'clock, with the 1,285 soldiers in high spirits at the prospect of actually seeking out the Federals, the Texan column moved eastward.[28]

With the Brigands once again acting as an advance guard, despite their dismal performance two days earlier, the mounted battalions of the Second, Fifth, and Seventh regiments, along with other irregulars, led the force eastward along the Santa Fe Trail, the foot soldiers of the Fourth Texas behind, following along the winding road in column. As the Rebel artillery passed, the pickets of Company C fell into line as a rear guard.[29]

Riding or marching eastward, the newly arrived Texans passed through the Apache Canyon battlefield, still littered with debris from that fierce encounter, and were undoubtedly entertained with the personal stories of those who had participated. Crossing the long wooden bridge over Galisteo Creek, then recrossing that dry stream bed to ascend the Santa Fe Trail as it approached Glorieta Pass, Scurry's column reached the pass a little after ten o'clock. Having covered five miles, about half the distance between the two opposing forces' camps, the Confederate leader moved cautiously forward another half-mile, depending upon his pickets to discover any danger ahead. Suddenly they did. Around a bend in the trail ahead came the Brigands, galloping up to announce that the enemy was nearby and in force.[30]

This time, the advance parties of both sides were surprised. Advancing toward each other along the Santa Fe Trail, the Brigands unexpectedly encountered the Federal pickets Colonel Slough had just sent westward from Pigeon's Ranch. One Pike's Peaker shouted out, "Get out of our way you damned sons of bitches, we are going to take dinner in Santa Fe." Pvt. Bill Kirk, one of the Brigands, yelled back, "You'll take dinner in hell," another Brigand reported, and "the jig was on." Both groups raced back to their respective main bodies to report the news, and both commanders reacted swiftly to that news.[31]

Scurry reported, "I hastened in front to examine their position. . . . The mounted men who were marching in front were ordered to retire slowly to the rear, dismount, and come into action on foot." As they proceeded to do so, the Texan commander brought up his three pieces of artillery. The gunners unlimbered in and across the trail, on a slight elevation overlooking a flat, wooded slope about a mile west of Pigeon's Ranch. The foot soldiers of the Fourth Texas also marched forward to the artillery position, where their officers deployed the regiment across the canyon bottom, "from a fence on our left up into the pine forest on our right." In this hasty line, Sergeant Peticolas of Company C remembered, "Cannon were quickly unlimbered and the men aligned, but before they had all gained position, the sharp report of a gun and sharper whistle of a minie ball warned us that they had come out to meet us." Confederate artillery quickly opened fire in reply, as did Scurry's infantrymen. These shots opened the Battle of Glorieta at about eleven o'clock.[32]

Colonel Slough's officers had made further dispositions and organizational arrangements as the Federal force neared and reached Pigeon's Ranch. Quartermaster Herbert Enos continued trying to interest Slough in the welfare of the wagon train. Captain Enos had placed the ammunition wagons for both artillery batteries at the front of the train, followed by the hospital wagons and ambulances, then the baggage wagons and supply wagons in that order. About a mile before reaching Pigeon's Ranch, Enos found a flat, open area alongside the Santa Fe Trail and wanted to park the train there while the fighting force continued westward toward the enemy camp. Colonel Slough agreed the site was acceptable, but refused to allow the quartermaster to stop right then, since no enemy had been encountered and the Texan camp was seven miles farther. Captain Enos was outraged but ordered his teamsters on, the head of the train arriving at Pigeon's Ranch just as the enemy was first sighted.[33]

In effective field command of most of the Federal force, Lieutenant Colonel Tappan made some company assignments among the First Colorado Volunteers that would quickly prove valuable. He assigned Captain Sopris's Company C as infantry support for Captain Ritter's heavy battery of artillery and did the same for Lieutenant Claflin's light battery of mountain howitzers, designating Robbins's Company K as its support unit. Both infantry companies were to accompany their artillerists wherever the cannons were assigned during the upcoming fight, protecting those valuable resources to the best of their ability.[34]

Capt. Charles Walker's regular cavalry company, which had led the Union column to Pigeon's Ranch, was again mounted and riding westward when the startling news arrived from the pickets that the Rebels were nearby, along the trail. To make sure he received accurate information from his advance parties, Slough had sent his acting assistant adjutant general, Capt. Gurden Chapin, with Walker. Walker and Chapin were halted in the trail just to the north of a solitary conical hill today known as Windmill Hill (because of a modern windmill on its crest), a half-mile from the ranch. While Chapin galloped back to inform Slough of this turn of events, Walker immediately rode forward to a point in the curving road from which the enemy cannons could be seen some 250 yards off. Motioning his Third Cavalry troopers forward, the captain reported, "I at once moved into the timber on our left, and dismounted my company and commenced skirmishing on foot." As he did so, Captain Ritter's battery of two 6-pounder guns and two 12-pounder field howitzers arrived, accompanied by Company C. Ritter unlimbered his cannons in and near the road, while Captain Sopris deployed his infantry to the right of the dismounted cavalrymen. Both opened on the enemy. Colonel Slough rode up with his staff just as the firing began and ordered Walker's regulars to mount and follow him as his headquarters escort company, leaving the single Colorado company to support Ritter.[35]

Quartermaster Enos was also quick to act. "I went forward with the batteries," he reported; "they had not been in position over three minutes before the Ammunition wagons were called for. I went back and met them coming up." He helped park them behind Ritter's artillery position, in a small, sheltered side canyon or draw, where they were easily accessible and out of the line of fire from the Texan line. Having parked the ammunition wagons, Captain Enos sent word back to his teamsters at Pigeon's Ranch to turn the train around preparatory to moving it out of harm's way east of the ranch. He went back to supervise that movement, but was soon interrupted by one of his men who had been left with the advanced wagons. The man reported that "an ammunition wagon was stalled and there was no support near it."[36]

That situation was caused by the withdrawal of Ritter's battery and its infantry supports. As they fell back, the Colorado soldiers, in their first battle, were too excited and busy to pay any attention to someone else's problems. They ignored the pleas of the quartermaster employees to help

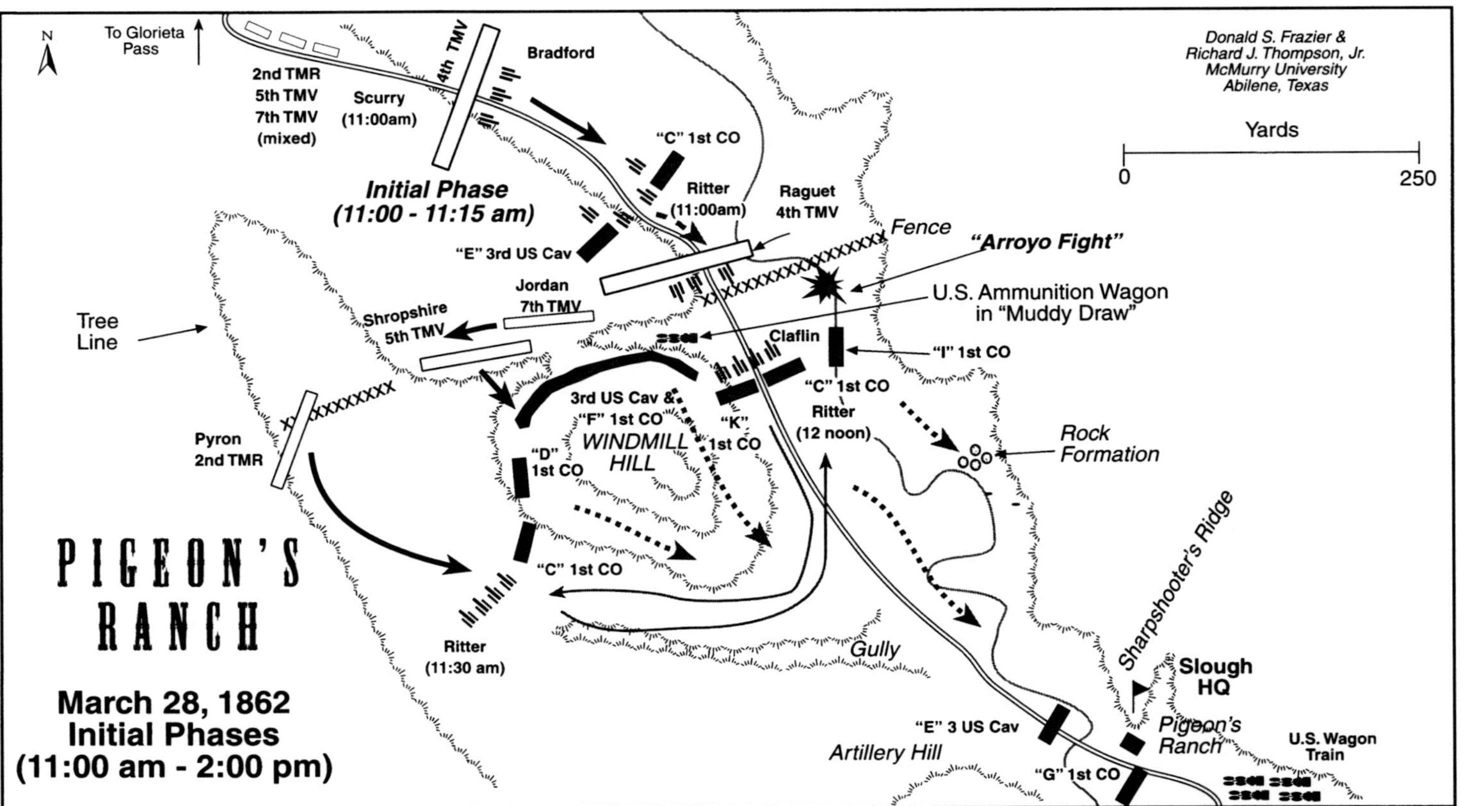

N
To Glorieta Pass
2nd TMR
5th TMV
7th TMV
(mixed)
Scurry
(11:00am)
4th TMV
Bradford
"C" 1st CO
Ritter
(11:00am)
Raguet
4th TMV
Fence
"Arroyo Fight"
U.S. Ammunition Wagon
in "Muddy Draw"
Initial Phase
(11:00 - 11:15 am)
"E" 3rd US Cav
Jordan
7th TMV
Shropshire
5th TMV
Tree
Line
Claflin
"I" 1st CO
"C" 1st CO
Ritter
(12 noon)
3rd US Cav &
"F" 1st CO
"K"
1st CO
WINDMILL
HILL
"D"
1st CO
Pyron
2nd TMR
Rock
Formation
"C" 1st CO
Ritter
(11:30 am)
Gully
Sharpshooter's Ridge
Slough
HQ
Pigeon's
Ranch
"E" 3 US Cav
Artillery Hill
"G" 1st CO
U.S. Wagon
Train
Donald S. Frazier &
Richard J. Thompson, Jr.
McMurry University
Abilene, Texas
Yards
0
250
PIGEON'S
RANCH
March 28, 1862
Initial Phases
(11:00 am - 2:00 pm)

push the ammunition wagon onto the road, so that it could also withdraw. The little draw into which it had been placed was muddy from the melting snows of the past two weeks. Patches of snow lingered under bushes and on the north sides of rocks and trees. The snow was not sufficient to hinder movement of men or animals, but the wagon was stuck.

Enos was frantic. Finding Colonel Slough, he explained the situation, fearing the Rebels would soon capture the vehicle and its valuable contents, and asked for a detail of soldiers to help extricate the wagon. Slough replied that there were no men to send and to "let the wagon get out the best it could." Without realizing that the Union commander, himself in his first battle, was preoccupied with more important matters, the quartermaster took the rebuff as yet another example of the volunteer colonel's ignorance or inability. Left to his own devices, however, Captain Enos quickly sent the messenger and two other employees of the quartermaster department to the wagon to "bring it up or burn it." The three civilians, Morris Bloomfield, Robert Forsythe, and G. G. Brown, were successful, and along with its tired team, heaved the heavy vehicle out of the muddy draw to safety just before advancing Confederates threatened to overrun the position.[37]

This initial phase of the Battle of Glorieta lasted only about ten minutes. During that time, both sides exchanged artillery and infantry fire that was generally ineffective, due both to inexperience and to the thick woods along the Santa Fe Trail. Company C, Fourth Texas, was directly behind the Confederate cannons. Sergeant Peticolas recalled that "as soon as their infantry opened upon us, our Artillery began to play upon them, and we began to fire at intervals with our minie muskets as we could see an object to fire at." Although the enemy fire was light and generally wild, one member of the Fifth Texas was unlucky. Being among the first of the previously mounted men to tie his horse in the rear and run forward to join the fight, Pvt. Bill Davidson was one of the first casualties; he was hit in the leg, reporting that "the Yanks . . . made me very tired on their first fire."[38]

Even before the dismounting Texan horsemen began arriving in his line, Scurry's old regiment greatly outnumbered the lone Union artillery support company guarding Ritter's battery. Slowly, the Fourth Texas began pushing the Federal infantrymen back toward the muddy draw that concealed the stuck ammunition wagon. Their job was made easier as Pyron brought his Second Texas detachment forward after picketing their horses in the rear, just east of the village of Glorieta. Major Shropshire also came forward with his battalion from the Fifth Regiment, as did Powhatan Jordan, leading the Seventh Texas' four companies. Some of Shropshire's troopers spotted their comrade Bill Davidson by the road. The wounded, cursing private had his pipe in his mouth but had taken off his shirt and trousers and "was tearing up his shirt and tieing it around his leg," to stem the flow of blood. Capt. Isaac Adair of the Seventh Regiment was nearby and asked Davidson what was the matter, to which the good-humored casualty replied that "the Yankees had ruined his breeches—tore two big holes in them." The captain and men then quizzed Davidson as to the location of his, and other, units, but he claimed not even to know where he was, much less his company. Adair then asked if he knew the whereabouts of Sgt. Jim Carson, a particular friend of Davidson's, who was leading Company A of the Fifth Texas. Davidson surmised that by now Carson and his companions must be "on top of the enemy's cannon." Tired of this fruitless bluster, Adair and the others moved on, one observing, "seeing that we could get nothing out of him [Davidson] except that Company A was the boss company on earth, and his breeches were torn, we went on further to a gully near an old field, leaving him cursing the Yankees by sections and tearing his shirt."[39]

The arriving Confederates poured into Scurry's advancing line without any order or knowledge of what lay ahead. Almost nothing could be seen by the men. Sergeant Peticolas observed that "you cannot see a man 20 steps unless he is moving." The Texan commander struggled to bring order out of the chaos that had resulted from the sudden outbreak of fighting and the disrupted units. By the time his men pushed to the edge of the slope, west of and above the muddy draw separating it from Windmill Hill, its Union defenders had abandoned the position, and Ritter's heavy battery had limbered up and fallen back to a second position.[40]

As the recently freed ammunition wagon disappeared back around a curve in the trail toward Pigeon's Ranch, Scurry reshuffled his units in the face of increased fire and stiffening resistance from the enemy. He sent Major Pyron and the Second Texas battalion to the far right to check the Federals now extending around the southern base of Windmill Hill. Major Shropshire's Fifth Texas went into line on Pyron's left, behind a series of rock outcroppings on the hillside west of the arroyo separating Windmill Hill from the lower elevation to its west. Bringing the three pieces of artillery forward to the flat ground just west of the draw, and south of and on the Santa Fe Trail, he put Major Raguet's Forth Texas Regiment into line behind the cannons and connecting with Shropshire's left flank. Raguet's six hundred men then formed not only the center of the line but also the Confederate left, extending northward down the wooded slope to and along a fence line surrounding a cultivated field before them. The Texas commander held Major Jordan's battalion of the Seventh Regiment behind the center as a reserve.[41]

As the Confederate field commander made these dispositions, his Federal counterpart was equally active. Neither could see much of the opposing forces or have a firm idea of the numbers he faced. It was obvious to Colonel Slough, however, that his action in splitting his force by detaching over a third of it under Major Chivington had been a serious mistake. Rather than finding the Texans at their Johnson's Ranch camp, as he had planned, he instead found them in great number before him near Pigeon's Ranch and the nearby small village of Glorieta. With some eight hundred men at his command, opposed to almost thirteen hundred Confederates, he was at a considerable disadvantage and was undoubtedly quite anxious. He therefore went on the defensive and formed an effective line, taking advantage of the ground for the purpose, during this second phase of the battle. He also sent off a mounted officer, Lt. Alfred Cobb, to find Chivington, who was supposed to be somewhere south of Pigeon's Ranch on top of Glorieta Mesa, and to direct him to come quickly to the support of the main column.[42]

Even as Ritter's battery and Company C initially resisted the enemy, Slough could see and hear the Confederate fire increase in volume and extend both north and south of the Santa Fe Trail. To secure the trail and his center, he brought Lieutenant Claflin's battery of 12-pounder mountain howitzers forward to a position in and near the road on a small flat at the northern base of Windmill Hill. Colorado Company K followed the howitzers in support and deployed on either side of the artillery, north and south of the trail. Here Claflin, with his short-range pieces, had a clear view across the muddy draw in front of him as Ritter limbered up the heavy battery and withdrew, to be followed quickly by the oncoming Confederate infantry and artillery.[43]

The four small mountain howitzers opened fire on the advancing Rebels, as did Robbins's Colorado infantrymen. That stabilized the Federal center. Soon, however, the Texan gunners were replying to Claflin's fire with counterbattery action of their own, and from a distance of only about a hundred yards. It was generally ineffective, both sides firing wildly and high. None of the opposing gunners was a trained artillerymen; all had been detailed to the batteries from either infantry or cavalry units. They gradually learned from their errors, but it took some time. One nearby Federal soldier, Pvt. Ben Ferris, noted that "both sides opened briskly, all the shots passing over Co. F, cutting through the treetops and making a terrible noise."[44]

Colonel Slough also sent two mounted companies to support Claflin. Captain Howland's improvised company of Third Cavalry regulars and Captain Nelson's Company F volunteers raced westward from Pigeon's Ranch. They had been dismounted and visiting friends as the battle opened. Private Hollister recalled the resulting confusion: as "the bugle sounded assembly, we seized our arms, fell in, and hastened forward perhaps five hundred yards, when their artillery commenced cutting the tree tops over our heads."[45]

The cavalrymen dismounted out of sight of the enemy, behind the projecting northern slope of Windmill Hill, and, leaving their mounts to be held by every fourth trooper, moved forward to extend the infantry support lines already established alongside Claflin's battery. The dismounted men moved off to the south of Company K's line, wrapping around the western and southwestern face of Windmill Hill and remaining in contact with Robbins's infantrymen on their right. Private Ferris remembered "our men dismounting. Went forward until we heard the fight begin. We were on the left of road in a depression"—actually the sides of the gully at the head of the muddy draw.[46]

With his center adequately strengthened, Colonel Slough directed Lieutenant Colonel Tappan to send another force to guard his left flank south of Windmill Hill. Rapid action was called for since the Confederate line curved around that eminence for a considerable distance, as far as the present-day alignment of Interstate 25. Withdrawing Ritter's heavy battery from its exposed position along the Santa Fe Trail, Tappan ordered it to move quickly to the left. "I was ordered to take position further to the rear and south of the road, some distance from it," Ritter reported. He did so, encountering considerable difficulty. The open fields surrounding Windmill Hill on the south, east, and north, had been cultivated and were surrounded by fences. Tearing down the fences was no problem, but the fields were muddy from melting snow and sucked at the narrow wheels of the artillery carriages as Ritter's men drove their teams around the eastern base of the hill to unlimber on a slight ridge within musket range of the Texans. Here he opened fire on the Texan right, hidden in a grove of trees just south of the present-day interstate highway.[47]

As Ritter's assigned supports, Captain Sopris and Company C accompanied the battery commander to the new position on the Federal left. An additional infantry company arrived as Sopris deployed. Tappan had ordered Captain Downing's Company D south to strengthen that flank against what sounded like increasing opposition from the Rebels south and west of Windmill Hill. Downing's line formed around the southern base of the hill and extended along its slopes to connect with the line already formed by the dismounted Union cavalrymen.[48]

Lieutenant Colonel Tappan then turned his attention to the opposite end of the Union line. He assigned the "German" Company I, led by its first lieutenant, Charles Kerber, to the battle line extending northward from the Santa Fe Trail across a small valley below the road and into the rocks and woods beyond. Kerber was to maintain contact with Robbins's Company K, supporting the howitzer battery along and north of the trail. As Company I ran across a large open field north of the road, the Confederate artillery and infantry shifted their attention and fire to this new and exposed target, and the company took several casualties while moving to their assigned flank position. These arrangements completed, Colonel Slough had done an admirable job of preparing a defensive position, assuming a reasonably equitable enemy strength.[49]

Back at Pigeon's Ranch, Captain Enos, having gotten the Federal wagon train turned around in the Santa Fe Trail, again badgered Slough to let him withdraw the train out of any danger of capture. He "asked permission to move it off the ground, but was only allowed to move it a short distance." Enos later claimed that the Federal commander had made no arrangements throughout the day to provide guards for the train, but in that he was mistaken, since Captain Wilder's Company G was kept in the rear, near the ranch, for exactly that purpose.[50]

With both sides well organized by about noon, the volume of fire from artillery and small arms increased, as did the clouds of smoke from the black powder used in all the weapons. With no breeze to disperse it, this "fog of battle" drifted through the trees and hung in the low-lying gullies and the valley, complicating direction of the battle by both Slough and Scurry. Private Hollister vividly described the "deafening roar of artillery, the unceasing rattle of small arms accompanied by all kinds of cheering and yelling from the men," as the second phase of the battle began in earnest.[51]

On the Union left, Captain Ritter's four guns and field howitzers had fired only a few rounds of case shot at the Texans when he realized that his position was becoming untenable. Company C, his battery support, had joined the men of Company D at the base of Windmill Hill, leaving the artillery without much protection from the increasing fire coming from the Rebels' hidden positions in the trees south of the field and behind fences to his right. "Here I was exposed to a galling fire without being able to return it effectively, the enemy being some distance off and entirely sheltered by trees, . . . and I was also some distance from my ammunition wagons," he reported; in addition, "the supports to the battery were all ordered away with the exception of about one platoon of Colorado Volunteers, and I deemed it proper to return to the road." Consequently, Ritter limbered up and retraced his route across the muddy fields to the Santa Fe Trail, again going into action, this time beside Claflin's mountain howitzer battery. His action left the Federal southern flank vulnerable to a determined push by the enemy, but it did add enormous firepower to the Union center. Part of Company C soon joined him along the road, further strengthening that part of Tappan's line.[52]

With this accession, both Union batteries—eight cannons—focused their fire against the three pieces of Rebel artillery across the little draw. Sergeant Peticolas's company began to think they were in the wrong place. "As usual, Co. C was directly in the rear of the cannon," he reported, "On our right was an old field fenced in with pine poles. To this field a good many of us repaired when the firing grew hot." He and his comrades had moved to one of the cultivated fields south of Windmill Hill, where the fence was constructed in a native New Mexican style of vertical posts, rather than rails. The fence served the handful of Fourth Texas soldiers admirably as a shelter from the fury of the dismounted Union cavalrymen.[53]

Lieutenant Colonel Scurry had little time to contemplate his success in stabilizing the center and right of the Confederate line. Off to the north of the road, another emergency immediately arose. After Company I of the First Colorado reached its assigned position on the far right of the Union line, the men realized they could take advantage of that position to outflank the Confederates. They were in the lower reaches of a large, fenced field near an abrupt gully or arroyo cut through the field by the waters of a small stream, Glorieta Creek. The gully ran westward, past the enemy line and into what had become the Texans' rear. Although little water ran through the arroyo during the winter, its banks were sufficiently high to shelter men from the view of the enemy near the Santa Fe Trail, some two hundred yards to the south, or so it seemed. Lieutenant Kerber and the company's other officer, 2nd Lt. John Baker, both former regular army soldiers, decided to take the initiative and attempt to turn the Rebel line. With Baker leading, the ninety Colorado volunteers crouched low and ran up the arroyo.[54]

Unfortunately for Kerber's men, Rebels north of the road spotted the assaulting party, pointing them out to Scurry. The Confederate commander reacted quickly once he saw the danger. Turning over command of the center to Major Raguet, Scurry took the two nearest Fourth Texas companies, C and E, and sword in hand, yelled for them to follow him. His party sprang forward, crossing the fence bordering the Santa Fe Trail and racing across the cleared field with cheers and shouting. Seeing the enemy running toward them, Lieutenant Baker drew his sword and, turning to his men, called: "Let's capture the guns!" As the words left his mouth, he was struck down, seriously wounded in the side. Capt. Charles Buckholts, leading Company E in Scurry's party, jumped into the arroyo with his men, and a short but fierce hand-to-hand fight ensued. The Coloradoans fixed bayonets to repel the larger Confederate force, but they were at a great disadvantage in the bottom of a gully and strung out along it. Scurry later reported that "for a few moments a most desperate and deadly . . . conflict raged along the gulch, when they broke . . . and fled in the wildest disorder and confusion."[55]

The handful of Pike's Peakers defended themselves courageously but were in a hopeless position. After emptying his pistol at them, Captain Buckholts killed one or two with his bowie knife, and his men dispatched more. A young member of Company C, Ben White, fired his double-barreled shotgun down the ravine. Those charges "killed at least ten of them and scarred the balance to death," claimed one of his friends, adding "there were ten or twelve in the gully when we took it, but they all had Ben's mark on them." According to another Texan participant, Pvt. Henry Elliot, except for those in the very front of the Federal column, the enemy turned and fled, leaving only "13 men still remaining. . . . Of these, 6 were killed and 5 taken prisoner." That bloody job completed, Scurry recalled the Confederates and returned them to their places in the main battle line.[56]

The surviving members of Company I, in the meantime, had retreated eastward a hundred yards or so and taken refuge in a large rock formation just north of the gully, up in the trees of the hillside forming the northern boundary of the fenced field. Considerable artifact evidence later indicated the location. Their losses had been even worse than Elliot reported; besides losing one of their two officers, Company I had about fifteen men killed and a like number wounded, as well as five captured—a third of the company out of action at one stroke. Of those wounded, John Baker was subsequently killed; Lieutenant Colonel Tappan reported that the lieutenant was "afterward beaten to death by the enemy with the butt of a musket or club and his body stripped of its clothing." He was likely mistaken; the atrocity was probably committed by local residents who descended on the battlefield after dark to rob the dead and wounded. From behind the boulders, the Colorado survivors opened fire on the left of the Texan line. They remained in that position on the extreme right of the Union line until driven from it later in the battle.[57]

The fighting continued along both battle lines for almost two hours. Although not serious north of the Santa Fe Trail, the contest was fierce in the center and around Windmill Hill. Claflin's and Ritter's Union batteries dueled with the Texan artillery. One of Ritter's section officers, Lt. Peter McGrath of the regular Sixth Cavalry, was mortally wounded during this fighting. Lieutenant Claflin reported that "at this point two of my cannoniers deserted to the enemy—Jones & Miller of the Col. Vols." Such an event seems highly unlikely, and these detailed men may well have been wounded and borne to the rear without the battery commander's knowledge. Gradually, however, the artillery fire slackened as ammunition in the limber boxes started to run low; one of Claflin's mountain howitzers was put out of action with a broken carriage, resulting either from enemy fire or from the heavy use. More ammunition was available in the wagons that Quartermaster Enos had again sent forward to the batteries' support, but the artillery officers were under too heavy a counterfire to send their limbers back to be resupplied.[58]

The firing and fighting steadily increased south of the road. Company F, fighting dismounted in the Union line curving south and eastward along the sides and base of Windmill Hill, saw considerable action. Private Ferris "heard volley after volley at our left and in front," while his fellow volunteer cavalryman John Miller observed that "they had so many more men than ourselves that they could flank us." Private Hollister, remembering the fighting around Windmill Hill, recalled also that the enemy "outnumbering us three to one . . . made the preponderance still greater by flocking thither to avoid our artillery."[59]

With some five hundred more men on the field than his Federal foes, Scurry determined on an obvious tactic. Holding his lines north of and across the Santa Fe Trail steady, he reinforced Major Pyron's battalion on the far right with Powhatan Jordan's battalion of Seventh Texas troopers. Major Raguet's Fourth Texas, about six hundred strong, was quite adequate to oppose the three companies of Colorado Volunteers along and north of the road. With these reinforcements, Major Pyron, commanding the Confederate right, began a steady advance eastward and northeastward against the dismounted regular and volunteer cavalrymen, Colorado Company D, and a part of Company C—Ritter's support company, which had not previously followed the artillery back to the trail and Union center—altogether about 240 men.[60]

Pyron extended his right well into the grove of pine trees marking the southern limits of the battlefield, south of present-day Interstate 25, pivoting on his left to sweep toward the southern and eastern bases of Windmill Hill. The Federals resisted fiercely. Hollister remembered that "in this unequal struggle Lieut. [Clark] Chambers of C, a brave soldier and a gentleman, was severely wounded in the shoulder and thigh while electrifying his men by his voice and example." Similarly, Captain Downing, commanding Company D, stubbornly held his ground, "only yielding, inch by inch, to an overwhelmingly superior fire." Private Hollister observed that "when they [the Federals] were outflanked and nearly surrounded they would deliver a stunning volley and fall back a piece. Thus they were nearly always covered, an advantage which their sparse numbers rendered inestimable."[61]

In the Confederate ranks, Sergeant Peticolas and his Fourth Texas comrade from Company C, eighteen-year-old Pvt. N. B. Lytle, who had been separated from other company members, joined Pyron's advance. Initially, they were partially shielded by the pole fence behind which they had been crouching, and one of their Federal opponents described "a brush fence shielding the Rangers." Along with the other right-flank Confederates, however, the two Texas infantrymen soon approached the base of Windmill Hill, only to watch the enemy melt away into the wooded slopes, then over and around the hill, out of sight.[62]

The Union troops were withdrawing on Colonel Slough's orders. The Federal commander had established his headquarters on the southern point of a steep, rocky ridge immediately north of Pigeon's Ranch, known today as Sharpshooter's Ridge. His mounted escort of Walker's Company E, Third Cavalry, remained below in the Santa Fe Trail, acting as train guards and ready for any further assignment. Slough, Tappan, and adjutant Chapin observed the course of the battle from that vantage point, where almost the entire field was in view.

Although the center was obscured by gunsmoke, the three officers became increasingly worried about events on their flanks. They had seen Company I being attacked on the right and sent running for cover behind the outcropping of boulders that now sheltered those infantrymen. Worse, it was now obvious even to inexperienced commanders that the enemy was in significantly greater force than their own. As Pyron's Texans spread out to the south and began pushing toward Windmill Hill, it was clear that the Union left had been outflanked. Slough decided that an immediate withdrawal was indicated. At about two o'clock he sent mounted couriers to all points of the Federal line with orders to retire to a new line to be established in front of Pigeon's Ranch, a position that appeared ideal for defense.[63]

The Federal infantry on the left quickly retreated, and Pyron's men soon reached Windmill Hill. Sergeant Peticolas noted their success "after taking possession of a little eminence on the right [of the road], commanding the ranch and adobe corralls in the valley." The dismounted Union cavalrymen of Captain Howland's regular company and Lieutenant Nelson's volunteer Company F climbed over to and down the northeastern face of Windmill Hill, where their horses had been held throughout the action. Mounting, they rode eastward to the new Union line. In the center, Ritter's and Claflin's batteries quickly limbered up and followed the retreating cavalry down the Santa Fe Trail, followed in turn by their ammunition wagons and the Colorado companies that had been supporting the artillery and fighting on the right of the Federal line. Captain Robbins and his Company K volunteers manhandled the disabled mountain howitzer back to Colonel Slough's new line. Slough sent Walker's regular cavalry company westward to act as a rear guard and cover the withdrawal of the batteries. That accomplished, the horsemen themselves withdrew, and the Federal forces were once again concentrated and not seriously damaged.[64]

As their enemies evacuated the positions they had successfully held, the Rebels crossed the little muddy draw that had separated the two battle lines and "occupied the positions we had left," Lieutenant Colonel Tappan observed from atop Sharpshooter's Ridge. With those movements, a quiet settled over the battlefield, and a lull in the fighting replaced the furious action of the past hours.[65]

CHAPTER FIVE

Pigeon's Ranch

A flag of truce came from the enemy, and measures were taken by both forces to gather up the dead and take care of the wounded.

—*Col. John P. Slough*

A pause in the fighting was sorely needed by both sides, since units and individuals were intermixed by the confusion of noise, smoke, wooded terrain, and unplanned initial encounter. Captain Enos, beside himself with worry over the safety of the quartermaster train now that the Union forces were falling back to Pigeon's Ranch, again went to Colonel Slough with a request to move the wagons to the rear. Even busier and less interested in Enos's problems than before, the colonel nevertheless gave permission for such a move. "This time I parked the supply train on the ground previously referred to," Captain Enos reported. That position, almost a mile to the rear, was open enough for the quartermaster officer to park his supply wagons off the trail, leaving the more immediately important ambulances and remaining ammunition wagons in the road, ready to roll to the front whenever needed.[1]

As he saw to this, the Federal surgeons moved the hospital wagons just north of the Santa Fe Trail, across from the supply train. There, the doctors set up a field hospital to treat those casualties who had been brought into the Pigeon's Ranch hospital during earlier stages of the battle and who could be moved to the rear. The more seriously wounded, as well as those of both sides previously left behind after the Apache Canyon fight, remained behind the questionable shelter of the ranch buildings' thick adobe

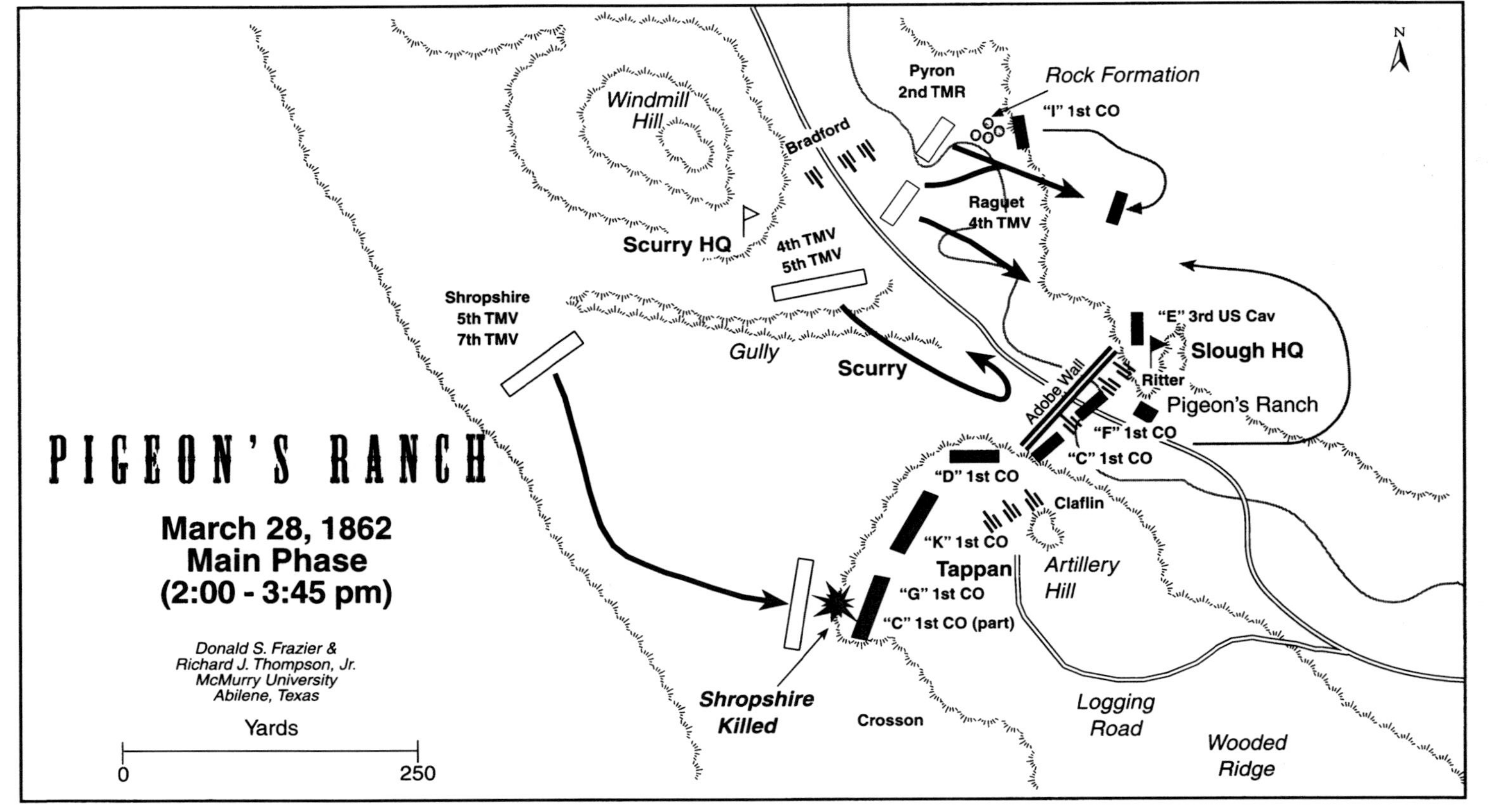
PIGEON'S RANCH
March 28, 1862
Main Phase
(2:00 - 3:45 pm)
Donald S. Frazier &
Richard J. Thompson, Jr.
McMurry University
Abilene, Texas
Yards
0
250
N
Windmill Hill
Scurry HQ
Bradford
Pyron
2nd TMR
Rock Formation
"I" 1st CO
Raguet
4th TMV
4th TMV
5th TMV
Shropshire
5th TMV
7th TMV
Gully
Scurry
"E" 3rd US Cav
Slough HQ
Ritter
Pigeon's Ranch
Adobe Wall
"F" 1st CO
"C" 1st CO
"D" 1st CO
Claflin
"K" 1st CO
Tappan
Artillery
Hill
"G" 1st CO
"C" 1st CO (part)
Shropshire
Killed
Crosson
Logging
Road
Wooded
Ridge

walls. Their mounting anxiety as the firing and noise now approached can well be imagined, though ultimately no harm befell them.[2]

Having given the order for his men to fall back to Pigeon's Ranch, Slough made initial dispositions to hold that line while the Federal force was getting into position. He ordered Captain Walker and Company E, Third Cavalry, onto the crest of Sharpshooter's Ridge, immediately north of the ranch. Those regulars dismounted in the sheltered draw below the eastern slope of the ridge, again leaving their horses held by every fourth trooper, and scrambled up the steep, rocky face to oppose the Rebels with their Sharps carbines. They were to extend northward along the high ground and maintain contact with Lieutenant Kerber's survivors of Company I, who still remained behind their shelter of boulders forming the far right of the new Union line. That was a very thin line indeed.[3]

The Union left flank appeared to be most vulnerable. Lieutenant Colonel Tappan saw the danger to the new Union line if the Rebels should occupy Artillery Hill, across the trail south of Pigeon's Ranch. He and Captain Chapin emphasized that point to Slough as the three planned their next moves from atop Sharpshooter's Ridge. Colonel Slough quickly agreed and dispatched his second-in-command to occupy the hill and prevent the

Pigeon's Ranch. The Santa Fe Trail can be seen in the foreground, passing through a gap in the low adobe corral wall on the left. Windmill Hill is in the left background, and Sharpshooter's Ridge is in the right background. *Courtesy Cultural Properties Review Committee, New Mexico State Records Center and Archives.*

Texans from taking it. As he raced down to the ranch, the nearest soldiers Tappan encountered were about twenty men of Company C, normally assigned to support the heavy battery of artillery. Tappan placed this little party of skirmishers near the top of Artillery Hill, but upon seeing the dispositions being made by the Confederates south of the road, he decided more men were needed. Company G, led by Capt. Bill Wilder, had been guarding the quartermaster trains east of Pigeon's Ranch all morning, but as the wagons moved still farther east and out of immediate danger, Wilder took it upon himself to give up that unpalatable task and bring his men up the trail to join the battle.[4]

As they reached the ranch, Sam Tappan grabbed about seventy men of Company G before they could be assigned anywhere else on the new line. Jumping across the narrow ditch through which ran Glorieta Creek, the infantrymen followed Tappan up the slope of Artillery Hill. There they joined the other skirmishers, providing at least a company-size force with which to defend the key position. Tappan placed them along the western and southern faces of the hill "for nearly three-quarters of a mile in a half circle," he reported. "This position commanded the valley in part, and the irregularities of the surface afforded excellent protection for the men from the fire of the enemy." The position overlooked and extended slightly into the shallow valley that today contains the alignment of Interstate 25 and the Santa Fe railroad. Colonel Slough was also active, sending Downing's infantry Company D, already suffering heavily in defending the Union left flank, to strengthen the left of the new Federal line, this time along the base of Artillery Hill. Four of the five available Colorado infantry companies would soon be under Lieutenant Colonel Tappan's immediate control there.[5]

As Tappan completed his arrangements, the Federal artillery and battery supports began to arrive. With his three mountain howitzers, adjutant Chapin ordered Claflin to take position atop Artillery Hill "directly opposite the Ranch." The animals pulling each little cannon hurried through the throng of soldiers now milling about the Pigeon's Ranch vicinity, across a flat, open area behind the buildings, and climbed a narrow logging road that had been cleared up the side of the ridge just east of Artillery Hill. That road curved around the head of the gully separating the ridge and hill, crossed the crest of the hill, and split into several branches. Lieutenant Claflin followed this road and placed his howitzers on two of its branches, which provided ready-made level positions for his battery, overlooking the Santa Fe Trail and the fields separating Windmill Hill from Artillery Hill.[6]

Commanding the assigned support unit for Claflin, Captain Robbins took a shortcut around the base of Artillery Hill, placing his Company K infantrymen up its western and southwestern slopes. There, behind large pines and rock outcroppings, the Coloradoans found excellent cover from which to oppose the Texans. Robbins's men connected on their left with those previously placed by Tappan and extended toward Company D and Pigeon's Ranch on their right, forming a continuous defensive line around the threatened sectors of Artillery Hill.

Capt. John Ritter brought his battery into the center of the new Union line. His cannoneers unlimbered the two 6-pounder guns in the road just west of Pigeon's Ranch, with the two 12-pounder field howitzers aligned just south of the trail. The battery commander took the opportunity provided by the lull in firing to send his limbers, two at a time, to the rear to have their ammunition chests refilled from Captain Enos's waiting wagons. Soon, all the limbers were back, situated immediately behind each piece, with artillery crews waiting for the Texans to reopen the fight. All the heavy cannons were situated in a corral complex adjacent to the ranch. Enclosing the complex on the west was a low adobe wall that ran from the base of Artillery Hill north to the Santa Fe Trail and thence northward to the base of Sharpshooter's Ridge. It formed an effective breastwork that partially hid the gunners. The wall likewise sheltered Ritter's battery support, that part of Company C not already taken away by Tappan to the far side of Artillery Hill.[7]

Also taking advantage of the adobe corral wall forming the Union center was the volunteer cavalry of Company F. Pvt. Ben Ferris remembered that the unit was ordered to fall back, "which we did slowly until we got to Pidgeons where we took possession of a large adobe corral just west of the house and between the two forces." With his horses sheltered further to the rear, behind the Pigeon's Ranch buildings and held by "number fours," Lieutenant Nelson had his men mixed in with those of Company C directly in front of Ritter's heavy battery. Captain Howland's company of regular cavalry remained at the ranch as a mounted reserve.[8]

With these dispositions for defense ordered, Colonel Slough passed among his men along the Santa Fe Trail and in the corrals west of Pigeon's Ranch, to make sure everything was ready. Even though he was obviously and seriously outnumbered, Slough confidently expected that Major Chivington would have received his message by this time and would be marching to the sound of the guns to reinforce the Federals and fall upon the southern flank or rear of the Rebels.

Meanwhile, Lieutenant Colonel Tappan was still uneasy. From his position atop Artillery Hill, the left wing commander could look westward and see a large body of enemy troops assembling for what he correctly believed would be a direct attack on his men and position and that of the artillery in the Federal center. Tappan left his position briefly and "descended to the valley and communicated my apprehensions to Colonel Slough." Unable immediately to judge the validity of Tappan's worries, the Federal commander sent him back to his hilltop post with a promise to look into the matter.

Slough was as good as his word, and probably now just as worried as Tappan. Climbing back to his headquarters on Sharpshooter's Ridge, John Slough could see for himself the Rebel activity to which Tappan had referred. He quickly sent to Tappan a message confirming the latter's observations and ordering the lieutenant colonel to "hold it [the Artillery Hill position] at all hazards, for all depended upon it; also to be in readiness to advance and attack the enemy's flank when he [Slough] should charge him in front, which he designed doing as soon as Major Chivington should attack him in rear, which he was expecting every moment."[9] This plan and hope led Slough to position the great bulk of his infantry and artillery resources in defense of his left flank and center, distracting him from any serious concern for his right flank, north of Pigeon's Ranch. There, one dismounted regular cavalry company, some thirty-eight effectives, and perhaps sixty surviving infantrymen from Company I, formed along a four-hundred-yard front what was at best a skirmish line.

In the Confederate positions, the early afternoon lull in fighting found the Texans even more mixed together and without direction than the Federals, if for no other reasons than their greater numbers and longer lines. As the enemy evacuated Windmill Hill and its environs, the Texans continued slowly advancing north and south of the hill against desultory fire from positions just established by their enemy atop Artillery Hill and in front of Pigeon's Ranch. An occasional round from one of Ritter's guns exploded among the Rebels south of Windmill Hill, one of which almost killed Major Pyron.

Private Davidson had just brought that officer, commanding the extreme Confederate right, a message from Scurry indicating that an enemy flanking movement was reported on the Texan left. Pyron either imagined that he could see through a break in the drifting gunsmoke that the Federals were attempting such a movement, or remembered seeing Kerber's Company I running toward the northern part of the battlefield earlier. To confirm

Scurry's information, Pyron turned to ride toward his commander. Just as he passed in front of the Seventh Texas battalion, that unit's Cpl. Sharp R. Whitley witnessed a dramatic scene. "Maj. Pyron was galloping from the right down our line . . . when a cannon ball from the enemy cut his horse's head off," Whitley remembered. Horse and rider fell in a bloody heap in front of the men, but Pyron soon extricated himself, removed both his saddle pistols from their holsters, and ran to Scurry on the eastern slope of Windmill Hill.[10]

Upon receiving this information, even though it was incorrect or misinterpreted, Lieutenant Colonel Scurry immediately sent a small party of Fourth Texas men out on the far left of his line, above the scene of the recent fierce hand-to-hand gully fight, to "watch the enemy and report their movements to him." This little group would soon suffer heavily as a result of the assignment.[11]

Scurry and his headquarters staff reached the eastern slope of Windmill Hill just as Major Raguet and the Fourth Texas advanced to a series of open fields that sloped gently downhill toward Pigeon's Ranch and separated the new Confederate line from that thrown up by the Federals. Raguet's left flank was slightly refused, since it was in close proximity to the large boulder outcropping still occupied by the Coloradoans of Company I. The men of the Fourth Regiment were mixed together, many seeking their companies and officers after their last rush through the woods in and around the Santa Fe Trail, their confusion compounded by the thick white smoke drifting through the trees and underbrush and gradually settling in the gullies and low points of the battlefield.[12]

As the Texan infantry moved ahead, so did Lt. James Bradford and the Confederate artillery. Sgt. Adolphus Norman limbered up the 6-pounder, while Bradford's NCOs did the same for his two 12-pounder field howitzers. All drove slowly eastward through the milling Fourth Texas men. The lieutenant selected a new battery position alongside the Santa Fe Trail and at the northeastern base of Windmill Hill, but still in the tree line. The cannoneers unlimbered, withdrawing the teams and limbers a few yards behind the three pieces, and prepared to continue their duel with the Yankee artillery.

In fact, the enemy cannon could not be seen, even though the Rebel gunners faced the open field that would now become the main battleground at Glorieta. Bradford and his men could, however, hear the heavy guns of Ritter's battery firing on the Texan right and see the explosions of his shell and case shot, one of which had just missed Pyron. The gunsmoke

View of the Glorieta battlefield from Lieutenant Colonel Scurry's headquarters position at the base of Windmill Hill. Artillery Hill is just on the right margin of the photo, with Sharpshooter's Ridge to the left of the Pigeon's Ranch Building.

began to disperse as Scurry rode over to Bradford. "We could not see anything in the world to shoot at," one Texan recalled, "but Scurry must have seen them." The Rebel artillery opened fire in the direction of Pigeon's Ranch, only some four hundred yards off.[13]

With that, Captain Ritter shifted his battery to counter the fire of the Texans. With plenty of ammunition in his limber chests and more available just to the rear, his four pieces opened a furious fire on the Confederate cannons, now visible from his corral position. One of his gunners, a Private Kelly of the Fifth Infantry, was almost immediately lucky. Loading a solid shot, Kelly fired and hit one of the Rebel pieces directly on the muzzle, ruining and partially dismounting the weapon.[14]

At the same time, Bradford's artillerymen began to take casualties from this counterbattery fire as well as from the dismounted regular cavalrymen along Sharpshooter's Ridge and the infantry supporting Ritter's pieces. One Texan gunner, nineteen-year-old Pvt. Ed Burrowes of the Fifth Regiment, slumped across the barrel of the 6-pounder, shot through the heart, while Lieutenant Bradford, the battery's only officer, was himself soon wounded and borne from the field. As if things were not already bad enough for the Confederates, Private Kelly's luck still held. He fired a case shot round that exploded near one of the enemy limbers. Ritter and his battery men watched as the limber's ammunition chest blew up, wounding more Texan gunners and damaging another cannon. Panicked by the sight and sound of the explosions, as well as the screams of wounded men and battery horses, one of the artillery NCOs ordered all three cannons withdrawn back up the trail, beyond the range of his enemy's artillery. Out of sight around Windmill Hill, Sergeant Peticolas heard the commotion and later reported that "the firing upon our company and the artillery became so hot that the artillerymen could not stand it, and cutting out our horses that had been shot, they hastily limbered up and departed, leaving one man dead."[15]

The Union infantry near the Santa Fe Trail could see the Confederate gunners struggling to limber up preparatory to this move. Without orders, some surged forward toward the center of Scurry's line. The Texan commander was equal to the emergency. Directing nearby Confederates to repel the charging Yankees, Scurry sent preemptory orders for the two serviceable cannon to be quickly returned to their original positions. Sgt. John W. Patrick, one of Bradford's Rebel artillerymen who had earlier deserted from a regular U.S. Army infantry company in southern New Mexico, brought one of the field howitzers back into action. The other howitzer accompanied it in the charge of Pvt. Bill Kirk, the same Brigand who had earlier exchanged pleasantries with the Union pickets. As the two brass cannon renewed firing, Peticolas noticed that "soon we heard a cheer announcing that the enemy were retiring, as I found out later." Indeed, his Victoria County comrades had forced the unauthorized and reckless Union advance back, and the center of the Texan battle line was stabilized.[16]

Some Confederates thought the whole incident with the retiring cannons was a clever trick by Scurry. They believed he had ordered a phony retreat by the Texan artillery supports in order to draw out the enemy in an attack on the apparently unprotected battery, whereupon hidden Rebels would fall on the exposed and helpless enemy. The perpetrators of this story, participants who were not able to see what actually happened, apparently misinterpreted events. They cherished the story, however, recounting, "This is the first and only time in the annals of history that anybody ever tricked a Yankee, but they were badly tricked, and from that moment they were whipped."[17]

After that violent flurry of action, relative quiet once more settled over the battlefield. Scurry, on the verge of losing control of his force, decided to halt and regroup. Still not sure whether one or both Union batteries were near Pigeon's Ranch, and if so whether they were vulnerable behind the adobe corral walls, he ordered the two Confederate howitzers to keep up a slow fire in an effort to tear down the adobe wall and "to ascertain the locality of the enemy." On his far right, the line stopped. Sergeant Peticolas reported that "Major Pyron then came down to the right and ordered us further on to a little gully in the old field." He and the Fifth and Seventh Regiment men with whom he had been fighting took refuge in a lengthy arroyo that cut diagonally across the new battlefield from the woods on the south, near the present-day railroad, downhill toward Pigeon's Ranch. The position is today under the roadway of Interstate 25. Although the gully was muddy and retained some snow, the weather was mild, and the soldiers were able to rest for a half-hour from what had already been an arduous fight.[18]

The Texan left and center likewise halted as Lieutenant Colonel Scurry called his battalion commanders to his post on Windmill Hill to plan their next moves. He decided on a coordinated three-column attack against the new and obviously strong enemy line. On the right, Maj. John Shropshire would lead his Fifth Texas battalion, as well as Jordan's Seventh Texas, in a flank attack. Shropshire was to keep in the trees bordering the open fields to the south, find the enemy force guarding the southern face of Artillery Hill, and drive them from that position, thereby reaching the vulnerable flank or rear of the Pigeon's Ranch line.[19]

On the left, Maj. Henry Raguet already had the Fourth Texas in line; he was ordered to outflank the Coloradoans located north of Glorieta Creek. They were up among the trees and on the hillside that gradually steepened to form Sharpshooter's Ridge. The rocky western face of that latter position was obviously ideally suited for defense and appeared impregnable. Scurry planned no direct attack against it. Once into the enemy line, Raguet was to push eastward, forcing the Union troops off Sharpshooter's Ridge. Scurry could not tell how many soldiers were on that part of the Union line, so he decided to move Major Pyron and his small Second Texas battalion to the left to reinforce Raguet's flanking force.[20]

Scurry himself would command the center, composed of several companies from the Fourth and Fifth regiments positioned on and near the road. With this force he intended to charge straight down the sloping field, just south of the Santa Fe Trail, and capture the Federal artillery in front of

Pigeon's Ranch. "I informed these gallant officers that as soon as the sound of their guns was heard I would charge in front with the remainder of the command," Scurry reported. That had been the tactic that had won the Battle of Valverde a month earlier, and it should work once again.[21]

Allowing about half an hour for his lieutenants to organize their assault parties, Scurry waited to reopen the ball. The majors worked furiously to unscramble companies and arrange them into the semblance of a military formation. Pyron brought his men trotting down the line to support Raguet, while Shropshire and Jordan struggled to find and sort out their various units, which had become badly mixed together during the earlier phase of the battle. They were not entirely successful, but by three o'clock, late afternoon at that time of year, Shropshire and the others were ready to move.[22]

Having drawn the fire of Ritter's heavy Federal battery and established its location, Scurry signaled his gunners, and the two Confederate howitzers again roared into action, reopening a concentrated fire on the Union center and thereby initiating the Rebel attack.

Raguet and Pyron led their men forward on the left and were almost immediately engaged in a fierce struggle. Major Raguet had sent two or three companies up into the trees north of Glorieta Creek, joining the small party of pickets earlier sent to the area by Scurry. The "Victoria Invincibles" of Company C were among the Texans fighting on the far left and found the going very slow. As the Rebels approached the boulders in which the surviving "Germans" of Lieutenant Kerber's Colorado company were stationed, those Federals opened a furious fire on the Confederates.[23]

When the teenage private Abe Hanna approached to within thirty yards of the rocks, he was shot. A minie ball hit him in the lower torso and pelvis, shattering the nerves to his lower body. Although not in much pain, he was paralyzed from the waist down and began to call for help and for water. Coming behind Hanna, his companion Jake Henson found the boy and knelt over him to pick the stones from under Abe to make him at least a little more comfortable. Jake gave the grateful casualty a drink of water, but Hanna was astonished to see Henson tumble headfirst into the gravel alongside. Another Federal bullet had found its mark, hitting Jake Henson in the shoulder and penetrating to his heart, instantly killing the twenty-year-old Victoria County private as he tended his friend. From Company C alone, another member was killed and three were wounded in this immediate area of the Texan line.[24]

Pyron also brought his battalion to the far northern end of the battle line. With trees and rocks for shelter, the combat degenerated quickly into a series of individual fights. One of his men recalled later that the enemy "made a stand behind some big rocks," and, "here Major Pyron shot six of them with his six-shooter." Such exaggeration was common but reflects the ferocity of the struggle. Another soldier's experience reflects the determination of the participants during the heat of battle. "In going across an opening on the left, Uncle Billy Smith of Co. I, of the 4th, got shot in the stomach and his bowels stuck out," recounted a fellow Texan. "Twice he tried to put them back; finding he could not do it and that he could go no further, he took his gun by the muzzle," and looking at his friends, cried, "Boys, they shan't have it," and broke the piece over a rock.[25]

The Confederate advance on the left slowed perceptibly in the face of such a determined defense by a handful of Colorado infantrymen. Nevertheless, Lieutenant Kerber's men abandoned the boulder formation that had effectively sheltered them and retired eastward. From clear across the battlefield, Sergeant Peticolas "saw the *Abs* run on our left and our men pressing on."[26]

From his command position atop Sharpshooter's Ridge, Colonel Slough could not see the progress of this fighting, due to the heavy woods and the increasing gunsmoke, but he could hear it and recognized the extent to which his previous neglect of that flank now threatened his entire force. There were more men in the Federal center than were needed, so he sent orders for a part of Company C, Ritter's artillery support, and the dismounted cavalrymen of Company F to hurry to the north. The infantrymen left their shelter behind the adobe corral walls, running back past Pigeon's Ranch and filing up the head of the draw behind Sharpshooter's Ridge. Coming out on top, they continued westward along the exposed slopes to reinforce the men of Company I, who were already fighting for their lives. With this accession to the Union line, the regular cavalrymen of Walker's Third Cavalry company were able to draw in slightly, consolidating along the southern reaches of the ridge, adjacent to Slough's headquarters.[27]

Down in the corral, Company F was safe but unhappy. The adobe walls, according to Pvt. Ben Ferris, "afforded ample protection and . . . we had opportunity to empty our carbines at the enemies advance, but our gunners got careless and occasionally dropped grapeshot verry clost to us." Obviously, his position directly in front of Ritter's battery was unpleasant and dangerous, so the order to reinforce the Union right wing was welcome. Lieutenant Nelson yelled for his cavalrymen to follow him out of the corral. Most understood his command, but a few of the volunteer horsemen, scattered south of the corral and mixed in with the infantry, failed to receive the order. One of them, Pvt. John Miller, fought for the rest of the day "on the left of the battery and . . . did good execution." Ben Ferris and Ovando Hollister, however, followed their officer away from the shelter of the adobe wall, where "we became exposed to the enemy and their bullets came thick and fast, but . . . no one was struck." Scrambling up the steep rear face of Sharpshooter's Ridge, the Colorado Volunteers went into line on the right of the regulars, connecting with the newly arrived infantrymen of Company C to stiffen significantly the Federal resistance to the slow advance of Pyron's and Raguet's Rebels.[28]

Meanwhile, fighting raged along the Santa Fe Trail. Hearing Raguet going into action with the Confederate left wing, Scurry ordered his center column to charge the Federal artillery and infantry positions behind the adobe wall. With their company officers yelling and waving their swords and pistols, the men ran down the gently sloping field south of the road to take the enemy guns. Sergeant Peticolas also observed them; he "heard the men in the gully in the old field give a shout and come running down towards the ranch in the valley."[29]

Ritter's 6-pounders and field howitzers reacted with charges of case shot and cannister, and the infantrymen of Company D, along the base of Artillery Hill, fired at the closing mass of Texans. From near the crest of the hill, Lieutenant Claflin's three mountain howitzers now began to blast the Rebels with an enfilading fire as they came to within two hundred to three hundred yards of the Union center. The defense was effective, the Federal center was too strong to be taken by a frontal attack. The charge failed; then the men began to fall back toward Windmill Hill or take cover behind outbuildings and fences, whatever afforded even the most minimal shelter. The Confederate artillery, however, now had a new target. The Texan howitzers began to fire across the field at Claflin's battery. Quickly getting the range, the Rebel cannoneers fired case shot, shell, and even cannister, at their counterparts some four hundred yards distant on the upper slope of Artillery Hill.[30]

With his attack down the center repulsed, Lieutenant Colonel Scurry was greatly disturbed to hear nothing from Major Shropshire's planned assault with the Confederate right wing. Leaving instructions for the center to again charge as soon as Shropshire's fire was heard, the Texan commander rode south to find that things had gone seriously awry.[31]

While Scurry had been directing the charge of his center, the right flanking column had been in action, unheard in the tremendous din created by the booming cannon and crackling small arms volleys. Sergeant Peticolas recorded that "we laid in the gully on the right ½ an hour and then were ordered further on, and rapidly ascended another little eminence where the enemy had their artillery ½ an hour before. . . . We soon passed this hill and began to descend again and to spread out to the right, firing at the enemy whenever visible. This was about 3 o'clock in the evening."[32]

Led by Shropshire and the company officers and NCOs, the men left the shelter of their gully to move off to their front and right, around the southern reaches of the battlefield, to outflank Tappan's Union lines on Artillery Hill. The force quickly reached the little ridge from which Ritter's battery had earlier fired. There, the Rebels were within sight and shot of Claflin's howitzers and Robbins's infantrymen. "A perfect hail of grapeshot came tearing the trees and brushing the brow of the hill and making a tremendous noise," Peticolas remembered, "but without hurting any body." He and his fellow Confederates began to fire on those Coloradoans visible on the extreme southern end of the enemy line, out in the valley ahead of Shropshire's advancing column.[33]

Those Federals soon withdrew into the trees on the southern flank of Artillery Hill, allowing the Texans to continue eastward without serious opposition, to a point where the Confederate leader felt his force had gained the flank, or perhaps rear, of the Federal line. Little or nothing could actually be known for certain due to the thick woods and steep hillside separating Shropshire from Pigeon's Ranch and the Santa Fe Trail, all made even more obscure by the drifting smoke from the rifles and shotguns in his men's hands. Sergeant Peticolas was on the extreme left of Shropshire's force and remembered that "about the time the severest fighting was going on the left and the men were charging in the center, Major Shropshire ordered us to a charge on the right in a right oblique motion so as to get past their left and succeed in driving them back."[34]

That accomplished, Shropshire wheeled to his left for an assault on the southern and southwestern base and slope of Artillery Hill, defended by Colorado Company C, G, and D infantrymen. Those soldiers held their fire as the Rebels prepared to charge. Above them, however, Lt. Ira Claflin could clearly see the Texans preparing to assault the hill. They appeared to be in overwhelming numbers. "Ascertaining that the enemy was preparing to charge my battery in such force as would render the capture certain," he reported, "I retired and joined Captain Ritter in the canon below." Summoning his teams and limbers and attaching the little howitzers, he and his cannoneers retraced their route back across Artillery Hill and down the logging trail to the rear of Pigeon's Ranch. With them went Captain Robbins's Company K in support of the battery.[35] Tappan, more immediately concerned with the assault that was about to be delivered to his line on the southern slopes of the hill, was unaware of the departure of Claflin and Robbins.

That departure, however, had no effect on the fight for Artillery Hill. Major Shropshire led his men forward against what appeared to the Texans to be an impregnable bluff. As the assault party left the tree line and crossed the open ground south of the hill, many of the Texans lost heart and sought shelter behind whatever bush or stunted tree was available. Peticolas observed that "now came the severest fight that we on the right had during the day. We charged up a hill with a wide seam of fair open ground to cross on, towards an enemy who were hidden and invisible . . . and before we had crossed the opening, more than ⅔ rds of the men had stopped, fearing to go into it."[36]

Shropshire, along with Capts. Charles Buckholts and James Odell of the Fourth Texas, yelled to the cowering men to follow their officers toward the hill. The companies were all mixed together after their flanking movement, but Shropshire looked about to see a part of Company A, Fifth Texas, his old command, following him under Sgt. Jim Carson. Some members of the Seventh Texas' Company B were also nearby, as were scattered soldiers from other Fourth and Fifth Regiment companies. Shropshire shouted to the Company B men to "come on and help take that position, or stay back and look at men who would take it!"[37]

At that, the small force of about "35 or 40 brave souls," including Sergeant Peticolas and his few companions from the Victoria Invincibles, charged. "We saw no foe till in twenty yards of them," he reported, "and then they rose from behind their breast works of rocks and poured into us a deadly volley." Corporal Whitley of the Seventh Texas remembered that "they sprang forward, and B, of the 7th, and A, of the 5th, went over the bluff together and routed the Yanks." Sergeant Carson was in the very front of the charge. He recalled that "we . . . got into a gully, shielded ourselves in that, and continued to fire upon the enemy, but in a few moments the firing ceased and the enemy were in full retreat."[38]

The enemy may have appeared routed to the charging Rebels, but in fact Lieutenant Colonel Tappan had withdrawn his line about thirty yards farther up the slope of Artillery Hill. There, the approximately one hundred men reformed their ranks and again awaited a Confederate onslaught. Tappan had waited almost too long to order his men to fire at the Texans. He later explained that he was unsure of the enemy's identity. Many Texans were wearing Federal overcoats and other uniform components either captured a month earlier at Valverde or brought into New Mexico from Federal stores confiscated in Texas. They looked very much like the Colorado Volunteers and U.S. regulars at a distance. Since he had just been warned by Slough to expect Major Chivington's flanking party to join the battle at any time, Tappan was overly cautious, thinking these Rebels might be friendly forces.[39]

Now, about half past three, Tappan could vaguely see what appeared to be a different column approaching Artillery Hill. Unable initially to determine whether it was Chivington's column or the Texans, and he had his men hold their fire until he gave the command. It was the expected assault, and it miscarried. Shropshire, even from horseback, could see nothing of the terrain or enemy on the thick, wooded slope before him. Ordering his men forward, he rode up to the base of the hill, where Carson and his companions had stopped. Seeing and hearing nothing sinister in his front, however, the major dismounted to continue into the woods and raised his hand to order the advance continued. The words never left his lips; a Sharps carbine bullet hit him in the forehead, shattering his skull and killing him instantly.[40]

The fatal shot came from Pvt. George Pierce, one of the dismounted Colorado cavalrymen of Company F, who had attached himself to the infantrymen during the course of the battle. At Tappan's shout, a volley from the line of Federals hardly ten yards away blew the Confederate force apart. In great confusion and with considerable loss, including Capt. Isaac Adair of the Seventh, mortally wounded by a shot to the head, the Texans around Shropshire began to flee. Capt. James M. Crosson of the Fourth Texas was at the front, drew his pistol, and with other surviving company officers tried desperately to stop the rout. The effort succeeded, with the men finally rallying some fifty yards to the rear.[41]

Some were not quick enough. Private Pierce and three of his companions ran to the spot where Major Shropshire's body lay. There they captured Capt. Denman Shannon, commanding the Fifth Texas' Company C, who had lingered nearby. Shropshire had been armed with a pair of ivory-handled, Colt "Navy" pistols. They attracted Pierce's attention, as did the dead officer's watch, so he took them. One Texan, Pvt. J. H. Richardson of the Seventh Texas, was so placed that he saw Pierce's activities. Outraged, he emptied both barrels of his shotgun at the Coloradoans, and "you ought to have seen them git when I opened on them," he later wrote.[42]

The four jubilant cavalrymen took their prisoner all the way back to adjutant Chapin at Pigeon's Ranch. Some of the Confederates remembered that Shannon, as he was escorted up Artillery Hill and apparently realizing how weak were the Union lines, kept motioning to them to follow him and attack the enemy.[43] The Rebels were too disorganized to do so, and Captain Shannon was on his way to Fort Union, one of several Texans actually to complete that advance, although under conditions different from those envisioned.

Captain Crosson assumed command of the dispirited Rebels, again forming them to renew the attack on Artillery Hill. That was the state of affairs as Lieutenant Colonel Scurry came on the scene. He was, of course, saddened to learn why his right wing had not been successful, and directed Bob, Shropshire's servant, who had participated in the charge, to remove his master's body from the battle line. Scurry left a three-company force on the field south of Artillery Hill, under Captains Crosson and Buckholts, with Crosson in overall command. That part of Shropshire's old column was to continue to try to force the enemy off the key hill and reach the Federal artillery and wagons in the rear of Pigeon's Ranch. Scurry himself took the rest of the right wing force and quickly led it back westward, to join the Confederate center. Strangely, he thereafter paid little or no attention to the progress of Crosson's men, whose rapid success might have made a considerable difference in the outcome of the battle.[44]

Captain Crosson, the Polk County lawyer, exhorted his men to make one more assault on Artillery Hill and led them up through the trees against Tappan's line. Again the Texans were driven back, leaving their wounded and dead, the latter including Capt. Charles Buckholts of the Fourth Texas, lying on the south slope of the hill.[45]

Two of Crosson's own Fourth Texas men were also in this charge. Pvt. Henry Wright and his close friend, Cpl. John Poe, had earlier promised each other that if either were wounded, the other would care for him. In the midst of the charge, Poe was "struck by a minie ball . . . just above the heart." The corporal was wearing one of the thick, wool overcoats many Texans had acquired at Valverde, and the bullet, fired at short range, hit one of its large brass buttons, pushing it into his chest and breaking a rib. Sure that his companion was mortally wounded, Private Wright dragged Poe out of the line of fire and propped him up behind a nearby tree, promising to return as soon as possible. "The battle was then practically over,"

Wright recalled, "and I hastened back, but searched in vain, for my friend was gone." Puzzled and worried, Wright later discovered that Poe had somehow found his way to temporary shelter in "some little cabin about a mile from the battlefield," from where he was later transported back to Santa Fe after the fight. Having repelled Crosson, Lieutenant Colonel Tappan also drew back, forming a new line almost on the crest of Artillery Hill, facing southwest, ready to resist from higher, more open ground the next expected Texan assault.[46]

Sgt. Alfred Peticolas knew nothing of these important events, but his actions would soon have an impact on them. The young Victoria lawyer had charged with Shropshire's men in their first assault, but being on the far left of the attacking party, he soon became separated from the rest in the thick brush and undergrowth near the base of Artillery Hill. The major and the main party veered off to Peticolas's right, while he himself tended to go even farther left. After experiencing one volley of rifle fire from the enemy, he heard no more from them. In fact, by the time he reached the base of the hill, firing from in front of him had ceased altogether. He assumed that the Federals had been forced back by Shropshire's attack, since he could hear firing and the noise of battle moving farther away on his right. "So," he related, "not desiring to follow in that direction, but having an excellent chance to fire across in the valley at the artillerymen and on the left, I began to take part in the battle again by walking leisurely along the hill towards where their line was, firing at every opportunity down at the enemy."[47]

The sergeant had by chance simply walked through a gaping hole in the Union defense line. When Claflin's battery had evacuated its position near the hill's crest shortly before, Colorado Company K had dutifully followed. Neither Slough nor Tappan was aware of the gap thus created, and nobody attempted to join Tappan's right flank with the left of Downing's Company D, fighting further north near the Union center. That was a potentially fatal error on the part of the Union commanders, but fortunately for them, no Confederate leader spotted the gap or took advantage of it.

Peticolas continued his adventure in perfect safety, climbing the western face of the hill, past the former position of Claflin's howitzers, and following along the abrupt, rocky rim of Artillery Hill as it overlooked Pigeon's Ranch and the center of the Union line, some 150 yards below. Walking slowly eastward, he would periodically stop to fire into the Federal troops engaged in a fierce defense of the ranch buildings and corrals. No enemy saw him or paid attention to a solitary figure in the trees atop the rocky bluff, and Peticolas continued his stroll, loading and firing his rifle as some particularly fine target attracted his attention.[48]

This pleasant pastime ended abruptly, however, as he happened to look up and to his right while reloading, and was duly astounded: he had walked unknowingly right into Tappan's line along the crest of the hill. "Another glance as I returned ramming convinced me that they were Pike's Peakers," he later recalled, "and in a moment I thought, well, I'm a prisoner after all. Here are the enemy." Peticolas was so surprised that he was speechless, an unusual condition for an attorney, but he had the presence of mind not to look startled. The officer commanding the line, whom Peticolas identified as a major but who was in fact Lieutenant Colonel Tappan, spared him the trouble of having to say anything. "Before I had decided what to do with 50 men looking at me and possessing the power to riddle me with pistol balls or minie balls or plunge a bayonet into me," recorded Peticolas, the enemy officer spoke to him.

"You had better look out, Capt.," Tappan said, "or those fellows will shoot you." Instantly, Peticolas realized that the officer had mistaken him for another Federal soldier, probably because he was wearing a Union overcoat acquired at the Battle of Valverde a month earlier. Keeping his voice steady and noting that apparently none of the Colorado infantrymen "knew me in my true character," Peticolas asked, "Who will?"

"Why, those fellows over yonder," came the reply—Tappan pointing to the south, in the direction of Captain Crosson's stalled flanking party—"there are two or three of them over there shooting at us."

"Is there," Peticolas said. "Then I'll go over that way and take a shot at them." Gathering all the self-control he could muster, the young lawyer and future judge proceeded to bluff his way out of the trap into which he had fallen. He slowly moved away from the enemy line, "with my gun at charge bayonets, walking cautiously, taking advantage of the trees as if advancing on a real foe." Worried that Tappan would catch on and shoot him in the back, Peticolas stole a quick glance to the rear, but was reassured to see no sign of suspicion on the officer's face. "In a dozen steps further," he added, "I was out of sight and over in our own lines once more. I felt joyous that I was not a prisoner and thanking an overriding Providence for my escape." In fact, he felt so good that he turned and emptied his rifle at the enemy he had just eluded.[49]

It was about four o'clock as Sergeant Peticolas walked into Crosson's lines and informed the captain of the location and strength of the enemy infantry he had just encountered. Crosson immediately determined to attack once more and ordered his men up the slope toward the crest. Passing their dead and wounded from the last such attempt, the Confederates soon reached the top, only to discover that their foe had left the field. Artillery Hill was in the hands of the Texans.[50]

Lieutenant Colonel Scurry never lost faith in a frontal attack against the Union center. He tried it again and again. While Crosson engaged in his unimpressive right flank attempts, the Confederate commander added Shropshire's mixed troops from the Fourth, Fifth, and Seventh Regiments as reinforcements for the center column he had already led in one unsuccessful assault. A little before four o'clock, Scurry was prepared to charge again. From atop Sharpshooter's Ridge, Pvt. Ben Ferris noted that "the enemy moved most or all of their forces to the south side of the wagon road. . . . We could see they were preparing for a charge and made arrangements to receive them." Nearby, Private Hollister also observed the movements: "At this juncture about three hundred fresh troops [actually,

The crest of Sharpshooter's Ridge, looking south. Company E, Third Cavalry, and Companies F and C, First Colorado Volunteers, fought along the ridge. The rear of Pigeon's Ranch is visible at left center.

Shropshire's men] came to their assistance, and with this for a charging column they designed to corral our whole command."[51]

Scurry's preparations had not gone unnoticed by the Federal commander. Colonel Slough and Captain Chapin quickly rearranged the lines in front of Pigeon's Ranch. From the rear of the ranch, Lieutenant Claflin came up with his battery and supporting Company K. Slough sent his adjutant down to order Ritter's heavy battery to fall back slightly and cross the road to its north side, to a level stretch of ground near the base of Sharpshooter's Ridge. Lieutenant Claflin unlimbered his three remaining mountain howitzers on the left of the road, in the flat corral just vacated by Ritter. His gunners rammed cannister loads into the short barrels in preparation for close-range action. Captain Robbins led his Company K battery supports forward to the adobe wall in front of Claflin, extending them to the left, south of the road and along the base and lower slopes of Artillery Hill. There, they connected with Company D, whose infantrymen had helped blow the first Texan charge to pieces. There, also, they were joined by Captain Howland's dismounted company of Third Cavalry regulars.[52]

With those arrangements complete, the center of the Federal line was very strong indeed. The ground west, south, and north of Pigeon's Ranch lent itself admirably as a defensive position; Sharpshooter's Ridge was impregnable to attack from the front, and the low adobe wall sheltered infantrymen lying and crouching behind it. Seven pieces of artillery supported the equivalent of three infantry and three dismounted cavalry companies. In addition, the Union commander had an unequaled observation post on the south end of Sharpshooter's Ridge, although he and adjutant Chapin came down onto the ground west of the ranch as the time for action obviously approached. He was well prepared for the Confederates.[53]

Shortly before four o'clock, the two remaining Texan howitzers opened on the Federals, and with a great shout and "rebble yell," the Confederates charged down the Santa Fe Trail and through the field south of it. To the Federals, this was a daunting sight. "The woods were full of them and the situation looked serious to us for a short time," reported Ben Ferris of Company F. Private Hollister remembered that "the bullets came from every point but the rear, showing that this was an effort to close in and capture us." Down in the valley, Captain Ritter opened fire with his 6-pounders and field howitzers, noting that "the enemy here made a desperate charge on our batteries."[54]

The noise grew deafening as blasts from nine cannon echoed off the

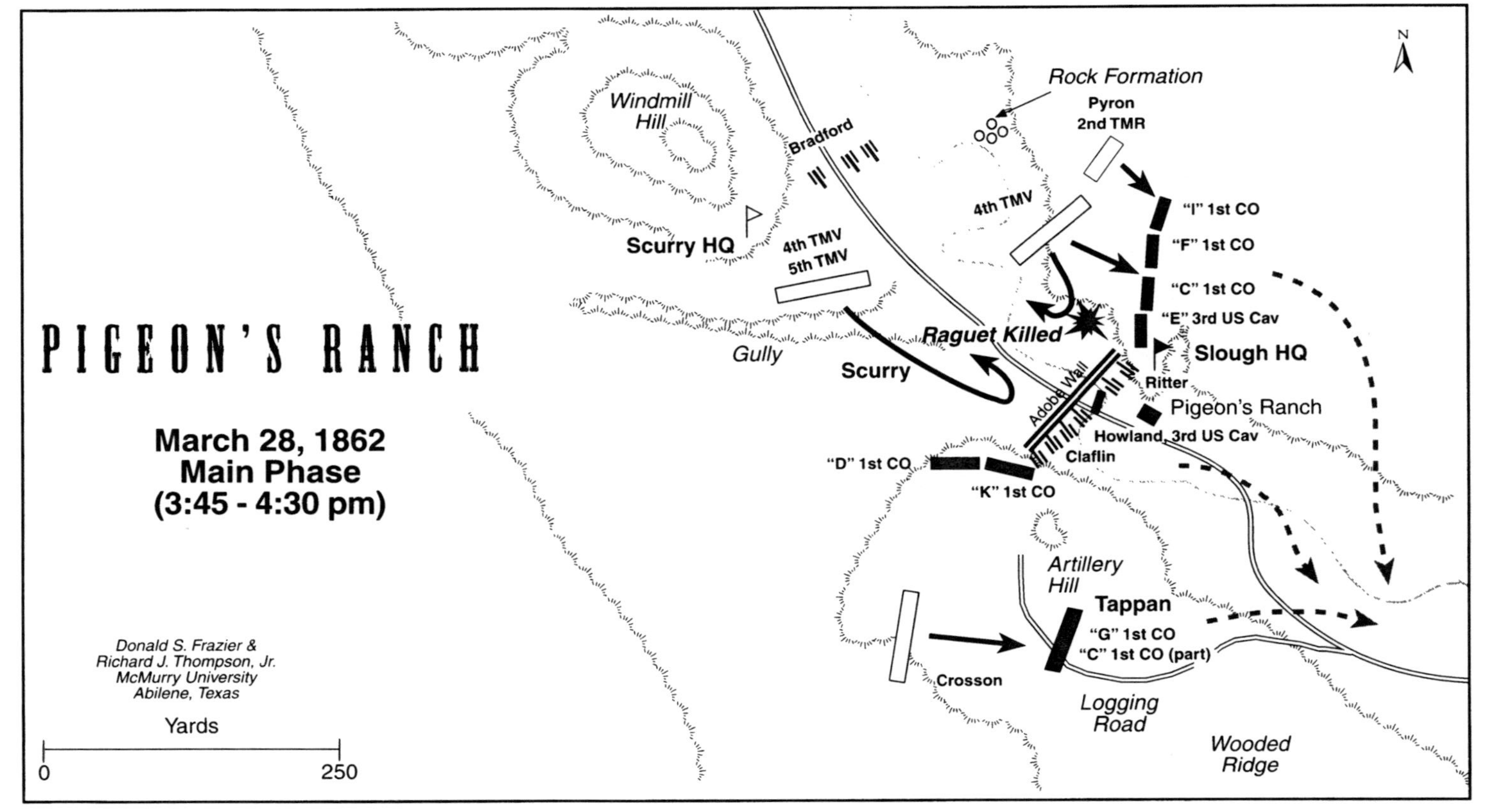
PIGEON'S RANCH
March 28, 1862
Main Phase
(3:45 - 4:30 pm)
Donald S. Frazier &
Richard J. Thompson, Jr.
McMurry University
Abilene, Texas
Yards
0
250
N
Windmill Hill
Scurry HQ
Bradford
4th TMV
5th TMV
Gully
Scurry
Raguet Killed
Rock Formation
Pyron
2nd TMR
4th TMV
"I" 1st CO
"F" 1st CO
"C" 1st CO
"E" 3rd US Cav
Slough HQ
Ritter
Pigeon's Ranch
Howland, 3rd US Cav
Adobe Wall
Claflin
"D" 1st CO
"K" 1st CO
Artillery Hill
Tappan
"G" 1st CO
"C" 1st CO (part)
Crosson
Logging Road
Wooded Ridge

mountainsides north and south of the battlefield. On the right of the Rebel attack column, Pvt. S. L. Cotton, a twenty-year-old married native of Milam County and member of Company E, Fourth Texas, prepared himself for what appeared a desperate undertaking. With grim determination, however, he lunged forward with the rest as the assault began. Scurry and the company officers shouted orders and cheered with the men, swords and pistols waving over their heads, as the Texans ran down the slope toward the adobe wall and the base of Artillery Hill, some four hundred yards away. Above, behind the Federal line and near the crest of the hill, Sergeant Peticolas saw the furious charge and shot down into the defenders.[55]

On rushed the Texans, heedless of the rifle and pistol fire aimed at their ranks. When they got to within fifty yards of the wall, Lieutenant Claflin barked out the order to fire, and the three mountain howitzers "opened on them like a regiment of Mexican dogs roused by the stranger at midnight," wrote Hollister. The iron cannister balls tore through the charging ranks, killing and wounding many. Several ripped into Private Cotton, hitting him in the pelvis and shattering his lower back, excruciating wounds from which he died the following day.[56]

"Claflin's salute appeared to astonish them," one Union soldier recalled. The Texans were indeed stunned by the ferocity of the artillery fire, but worse was yet to come. Both batteries ceased fire, and from in front of them, the supporting infantrymen and dismounted cavalrymen who had been sheltering behind the adobe wall rose and delivered volley after volley of rifle and carbine fire into the faces of the Rebels. Downing's and Robbins's men did the same on the southern flank of the attack. Pvt. John Miller, a volunteer cavalryman fighting dismounted to the left of the batteries, emptied his carbine into the enemy mass and "did good execution. . . . The men stood by the cannon and fought for all that was out," he wrote. But still the Confederates held their ground and fired back, "encouraged and shouted on by as brave officers as live," remembered trooper Hollister, who watched in admiration and fired from Sharpshooter's Ridge. "Our brave soldiers, heedless of the storm, pressed on," Lieutenant Colonel Scurry reported, "determined to take their battery. Here the conflict was terrible."[57]

The Federal infantry fighting south of the road took heavy casualties while stopping the enemy charge. Company D suffered almost a third of the total Union casualties during this phase of the fighting. On Sharpshooter's Ridge, however, the dismounted regular and volunteer cavalrymen were in comparative safety. Capt. Charles Walker later reported that his Third Cavalry company had "some skirmishing with the enemy in small parties," and was "under fire a great part of the day," behaving "handsomely whenever brought under the enemy's fire." The First Colorado troopers, however, remembered playing a much more impressive role. Unable to see through the heavy woods on the hillside to their right, they could see what was happening below them and north of the Santa Fe Trail.[58]

While Scurry had been organizing the fierce charge in the center, Pyron and Raguet had steadily pushed toward Pigeon's Ranch with the Confederate left. Upon hearing Scurry's men cheering and firing, and seeing the staggering resistance put up by the Union center, both majors led their men in a coordinated assault on the Federal right. In the valley bottom below Sharpshooter's Ridge, Raguet led part of the Rebel force curving southward toward the Union batteries. The defending infantrymen of Colorado's Company C, earlier sent to the right to help Company I hold the hillside, spotted the Texans below them and opened fire. At the same time the cavalrymen, lying atop the ridge and firing their breechloading carbines at the main attack, suddenly saw the threat to their positions. "We could see the enemy trying to flank us, advancing along a natural ditch," wrote Ben Ferris. "We could not see much of them but their heads, but we kept up a scattering fire. . . . The dead in this ditch was evidence that we did good execution."[59]

Maj. Henry Raguet was, in fact, leading the Texans forward, along the base of the hill, partially in the gully formed by Glorieta Creek. Shouting and gesturing like his fellow officers further south, he was a conspicuous target, the only mounted man on that part of the battlefield. "The intrepid Ragnet [sic]," reported Scurry, "pushed forward among the rocks until the muzzles of the guns of the opposing forces passed each other." One of the Coloradoans' bullets found him and killed the brave Nacogdoches commander.[60]

Although Major Pyron took command of the Confederate left upon Raguet's death, and led the men on the hillside on toward the Union flank, the attack below Sharpshooter's Ridge came to a halt. In the center, also, Scurry's men, staggered by artillery and rifle fire, hesitated, then turned and ran for whatever cover they could find. Colonel Slough thought any threat from the right was ended as firing there temporarily died down with Raguet's death. He ordered the cavalrymen of Company F down from Sharpshooter's Ridge to their horses being held behind Pigeon's Ranch. Howland's regulars also left the center of the line to retrieve their mounts behind the buildings, with the intention of forming a mounted column to follow up on what then appeared to be a defeat of the Rebels.[61]

Reaching the ranch below, Privates Hollister and Ferris saw the advanced infantrymen pursuing the retreating Texans. Rather than go to their horses, both privates also rushed forward after the Texans on foot and "followed them a ways to see how well they could run." There was no organized pursuit, however, and the Federal soldiers returned to their hillsides and adobe wall as the noise of battle subsided as quickly as it had begun less than a half-hour earlier. Not all made it back safely. Ben Ferris was "following them through the trees on their retreat. Dodging from tree to tree, we kept them going , until ZIP! Something hit my leg. It did not hurt much, but numbed my leg somewhat. . . . I thought best to get back while I could, so, without saying anything to anybody, I walked back to our horses." He then found a mount and "rode alone to the rear where the Dr. had a wagon for a hospital by the side of the road. The ounce ball had entered half way between the knee and foot and passed nearly through. Doc cut a hole in back of my leg and put in a hook and pulled out the flattened ounce ball." Ferris climbed into a nearby ambulance, his role in the Battle of Glorieta finished.[62]

Lieutenant Colonel Scurry's attacks on the right and center had been abject failures so far. Little or nothing could be seen at any distance by either side through the thick smoke from the recent gunfire; however, the main phase of the Battle of Glorieta appeared to be a defeat for the Confederates as they sheltered behind trees, rocks, and outbuildings west of Pigeon's Ranch.

But no! Up among the trees on the hillside north of Sharpshooter's Ridge, firing once again increased, accompanied by cheers and shouts. Major Pyron's men had steadily driven back the hard-fighting Colorado Volunteers of Company I, still under Lieutenant Kerber. The "Germans" gave ground slowly but, too few to stop the Rebels, fell back until they merged with the infantrymen of Company C. Both companies took increasing casualties from the Texans' rifle and shotgun blasts, which grew closer by the moment. Finally, the Colorado men could take it no longer and broke, rushing down the back face of Sharpshooter's Ridge and through the hillside trees behind that ridge, to rally east of the ranch buildings. With their immediate enemies having fled, Major Pyron motioned his mixed force onward, reaching the narrow crest of the rocky ridge, still occupied by Captain Walker's Company E of the Third Cavalry. The regulars turned to fire along the ridge at the oncoming Rebels, alerting Colonel Slough to the immediate danger. The Federal commander abandoned his headquarters position on the ridge and, with the cavalrymen following, left Sharpshooter's Ridge to the Texans.[63]

Walker's men quickly mounted their horses in the ravine behind the ridge and, with the other cavalrymen, escorted Colonel Slough back eastward along the Santa Fe Trail to yet another defensive position the Federal commander had in mind. He planned to withdraw his entire force and reestablish it in a new line, across the large open area where the quartermaster train was parked, almost a mile to the rear. Leaving his adjutant, Captain Chapin, to carry out his orders for withdrawal, Slough soon reached the new position and by half past four, with dusk approaching, began preparations for defense.

While the Federal commander was thus engaged, his infantry and artillery troops still fighting near Pigeon's Ranch were in desperate straits. Major Pyron's Confederate flanking force occupied Sharpshooter's Ridge to its southern extremity overlooking the ranch buildings, the Santa Fe Trail, and the Union artillery and infantry support positions in the corral complex west of the ranch. From there, only some 150 to 200 yards away, and in their enemies' rear, the Texans peered into the fog of battle below them to determine if the soldiers barely visible through the gunsmoke were friends or foes. Private W. Hausman of the Fourth Regiment's Company C, and some sixty of his fellow Victoria Invincibles, led by one of their sergeants, was in the party occupying Sharpshooter's Ridge. The sergeant told them to hold themselves in readiness to charge, while he descended the ridge to identify the force around the ranch. While he did so, the newly arrived Texans took little part in the battle, although they were in a highly advantageous position.[64]

Apparently Scurry could see a little better than the Invincibles. Following the course of Pyron's men on his left, the Texan commander noted the cessation of Federal firing from Sharpshooter's Ridge, and—assuming his major had forced the enemy from that key position, or receiving some information to that effect—Scurry again ordered the Confederate center forward against the adobe wall, corral, and hillside apparently still occupied by the Yankees. This time their task was easier. Captain Downing's Company D and its miscellaneous detached cavalry volunteers had already received Slough's order to withdraw. They quickly abandoned the western base and slope of Artillery Hill and, in good order, filed past the ranch buildings toward the new Federal line well to the rear.

The artillery commanders also got the word to retreat. Captain Ritter's heavy battery north of the trail was in a particularly bad position, however, with Sharpshooter's Ridge close upon his right flank and rear. As his gunners brought up the limbers and teams to withdraw the four cannons, the Rebels atop the ridge spotted the activity and opened fire. Ritter reported that the enemy was "pouring a destructive fire of small-arms in the batteries and killed two horses, so that I deemed it proper to withdraw from my position." Even though his men were highly motivated to cut out the dead animals swiftly and limber up the battery, during the few minutes it took to do this, one of Ritter's cannoneers was killed and two more were wounded.[65]

Lieutenant Claflin's mountain howitzer battery, however, was in an even more precarious position. His men opened fire on the charging Texans now appearing through the smoke, as did his battery support, Company K, in front and to his left. Captain Robbins, however, began to withdraw his infantrymen from the northwestern face and base of Artillery Hill, leaving a lieutenant (probably George H. Hardin of Company G, who had somehow gotten intermixed with Company K) and about forty men to cover Claflin's withdrawal. While the light battery ceased firing and brought up its limbers, Hardin and his men furiously attempted to hold back the oncoming Rebels. "The boys that were supporting the battery," recalled Pvt. John Miller, "determined to die right there, rather than give up the battery." Losing "one man killed, one Sergt. and two privates wounded," Claflin got his howitzers headed back down the road. He later reported: "The conduct of Lieut. Harding and about forty of his men, especially while protecting the batteries before retiring to our last position deserves the highest praise and won for him a reputation with his comrades of which his regiment and company may well be proud." Lieutenant Claflin attributed the safe withdrawal of both batteries to the heroism and desperate stand by this handful of Colorado Volunteers.[66]

With Claflin's departure, covered by Company K's rear guard, the Confederates poured into Pigeon's Ranch. Scurry quickly brought his two field howitzers forward along the Santa Fe Trail. The Fourth Texas sergeant who had come down from Sharpshooter's Ridge to determine the identity of these milling soldiers found them to be friends. After the NCO called to his men waiting above, Private Hausman and his comrades from Company C joined Scurry's force in and around the grounds of the ranch, some visiting gravely wounded friends still lying in the hospital inside the ranch buildings. Scurry soon had the men moving eastward along the trail and on the hillsides north of the road.[67]

Unfortunately, nobody notified Lieutenant Colonel Tappan of the order to fall back from Pigeon's Ranch. His first suspicion that something had gone wrong on the Union right and center came as his little force of men from Companies C, G, and F continued falling back across the crest of Artillery Hill, through a gully separating that hill from the ridge that adjoined it, and onto the side of the ridge. He could hear the ominous slackening of fire from the north side of Artillery Hill and guessed that "our column had fallen back from the valley to my right a considerable distance." Captain Crosson's Texan party found nobody there when it first reached the top of the hill, but spreading out into a regular skirmish line and moving slowly eastward through thick pine woods and large granite boulders, the Rebels soon found Tappan and his company. The Coloradoans were not fifty yards away as the Texans stopped and fired into their perfectly formed line on the old logging trail previously used by Claflin's mountain howitzers. No Federals were hit, however, and they in turn delivered a volley at the Confederates, also apparently without effect.[68]

That outburst of rifle fire brought the fighting on Artillery Hill once more to Scurry's attention. He ordered the two big field howitzers to unlimber in the trail just east of Pigeon's Ranch. The guns fired cannister and at least one round of grape shot up the gully separating the hill and eastern ridge, hitting no one, but convincing Tappan that it was time to leave. His situation was desperate. "Considering it extremely hazardous to remain longer, and thereby enable the enemy to get in my rear and cut me off from support of our battery and protection of our trains," he reported, "I ordered my men to fall back and close in the rear of the retiring column." After delivering their final volley at Crosson's Texans, the Colorado Volunteers turned and ran at top speed down the sloping trail, toward the far rear of Pigeon's Ranch. Now the Confederate artillery had a clear and closer target. The gunners fired at the logging trail and the fleeing foe, cannister balls throwing up sprays of mud and snow on the rocky hillside. Tappan's luck held, however; he and his men ran the gauntlet of iron and lead, reached the road, and rapidly disappeared in the direction of the new Federal line.[69]

The Confederates around Pigeon's Ranch were ecstatic. Scurry saw that the enemy infantry "broke ranks and fled from the field. So precipitate was their flight that they cut loose their teams and set fire to two of their wagons," referring to a pair of Captain Enos's advanced ammunition wagons, which had to be abandoned after their teamsters had been "ordered to carry ammunition to Lieut. Claflin's battery." Pvt. Henry Wright of Austin, still thinking of and worried about his friend left wounded behind a tree on Artillery Hill, remembered that "we had utterly routed them, as they retreated in such disorder." A more realistic Sergeant Peticolas, also reaching the valley behind Pigeon's Ranch, remembered that "they had left the field and were retreating rapidly, having gotten off with Cannon and train. . . . We rallied in force further down on the road and began to follow the retreating foe."[70]

Scurry quickly organized a pursuit. The Texan howitzers limbered up and accompanied the infantry eastward to find the enemy or watch him retreat. Sending parties up on the hillsides north and south of the Santa Fe Trail, the Confederate commander himself kept to the road. Before he had gone a mile, however, Scurry found that the valley had abruptly opened up into a sizable flat area, bounded by steep, rocky, and wooded hillsides. In that open space, the Federals had originally established their field hospital wagons, but those vehicles and their casualties had already been moved farther eastward, out of the way of the oncoming enemy. Here, once again, Scurry faced Slough in a position well suited for defense. "The pursuit was kept up until forced to halt from the extreme exhaustion of the men," the Texan commander later reported, but in fact, although exhaustion undoubtedly played a part, he halted and prepared to attack.[71]

Colonel Slough had again done an excellent job of selecting the ground he would defend. Quartermaster Captain Enos had also taken the initiative. Not waiting for orders to move his train, he had heard the firing drawing near and, believing the Federals were about to be outflanked south of the trail, had gotten the extensive wagon train into the road and moving eastward, back toward Kozlowski's Ranch. He was irate that the soldiers actually fell back to and slightly beyond his rearmost wagons, leaving them so vulnerable that "a few shots were fired upon them from the enemy on the left." As Enos himself rode beside the already retreating wagon train, he noted ironically that "I received an order to move the trains off the ground."[72]

In this final position, Colonel Slough again ordered Claflin's mountain howitzer battery to go into action on the left of the road, with Ritter's heavy guns and howitzers unlimbering on the right. Young James Farmer, who had been acting as a mounted courier for Slough all day, described the artillery position as "a level piece of ground sufficiently for the guns to operate on, that jutted up close to a bluff." Behind and to the left of the artillery was a deep ravine created by Glorieta Creek. It formed a natural trench in which the infantry and dismounted cavalry once more took up positions across and left of the trail. Slough sent his Colorado Volunteers up into the wooded slopes north of Ritter's battery, where many were able to shelter behind huge rock outcroppings. Having reached the Santa Fe Trail well after all the other Federal troops had passed, Lieutenant Colonel Tappan's men formed in the road and marched, "in good order," as he later reported, into Slough's new line.[73]

As they did so, the Texans attacked. Although it was beginning to get cold and dusk was rapidly approaching, Scurry again sent parties onto the hillsides to outflank the Union line. He also tried another charge down the trail and valley floor in an attempt to capture the enemy artillery. Claflin and Ritter opened on the charging Confederate center, while the two Texan howitzers, completely overpowered by the seven opposing cannon, contributed little but noise to the effort.[74]

None of the Rebels had the energy or enthusiasm for more serious fighting. A scattering of rifle fire from the hillsides zipped into the Federal lines, but the undiminished artillery fire discouraged the tired Texans, and the attack withered to a halt, the men falling back out of range of the Union artillery. Jim Farmer claimed that Colonel Slough had ordered the regular cavalry to charge the Texans as they began to fall back, but there is no other evidence of such an intention, and nothing of the kind occurred. The cavalrymen, however, helped in protecting Ritter's battery, "the men assisting in driving the Texans back with their pistols," Farmer remembered. Trooper Hollister recalled only that Company F "took a new position beyond a large open space; our guns thundered as defiantly as ever, but their firing soon ceased. They had no inclination to come out of the woods and fight on open ground."[75]

With neither the energy nor the enthusiasm to continue the battle, the weary Texans retreated to the fields and corrals around Pigeon's Ranch. Search parties spread out over the battlefield and brought in wounded to the hospital, which had been taken over by the Confederate surgeons. Pvt. Henry Wright searched in vain for his friend John Poe. "All that evening and away into the night," he reported, "I wandered over those hills, but failed to find him." Sergeant Peticolas was on a similar mission: "We passed over the battlefield in the evening looking for the wounded," and still wearing the Federal overcoat that had served as his disguise an hour earlier, he "was taken by a wounded Pike's Peak man to whom I stopped to converse with, for one of his own men."[76]

One of the soldiers brought in was Peticolas's young friend Abe Hanna, who had been shot in the groin and paralyzed. The sergeant tried to comfort the mortally wounded teenager and grieved as "Abe Hanna died about an hour in the night very easily. He was shot in the loins and bled inwardly.

He said he felt no pain save that his limbs were numb and dead from his hips down."[77] By nightfall, the Pigeon's Ranch hospital was crowded with the newly wounded and killed, as well as patients from both sides who had been left as the Federals abandoned the ranch in the late afternoon.

Those Texans who had not brought sufficient rations with them spent much of the evening searching for something to eat. The enterprising, or lucky, were successful. Peticolas and fellow Victoria Invincibles did very well. "We got some dried buffalo beef at a ranch a little back where the Abs had it stored and we lined our haversacks pretty bountifully with it," the sergeant reported. In the Fourth Regiment's Company E, however, Sgt. Robert Williams found nothing whatever to eat, though he did locate an empty space in one of the adobe ranch buildings, where he soon went to sleep, regardless of hunger. Cpl. Sharp Whitley's Seventh Texas comrades complained: "Nothing to eat, but we had breakfast this morning, we'll feast on the recollecting of that."[78]

Although darkness would necessarily have put an end to the fighting, some Confederates wondered why Colonel Scurry had stopped their advance when it appeared they again had the enemy on the run. Although the Texan leaders undoubtedly knew better, most of the rank and file believed they had been victorious throughout the day. Private Wright felt that "we had utterly routed them, as they retreated in such disorder," while Sergeant Peticolas claimed that "we gained a complete victory but at the expense of every comfort." Rumors quickly spread through the camp. Some heard that the enemy had attacked the camp they had left that morning, while Peticolas understood that "Col. Green had arrived in the Canion behind us." However, as the fighting ended, many of those left behind at Johnson's Ranch began to reach Pigeon's with tales of disaster in the rear. Conferring in the main ranch building that night, Scurry, Jordan, and Pyron, the surviving senior Texan officers, tried to decide on a course of action for the following day.[79]

The main reason the Confederates could leave the final battlefield position was that their enemies had already begun to do so. Shortly after five o'clock, as night approached, Colonel Slough ordered a general withdrawal of the Federal force to its camp at Kozlowski's Ranch. The men were outraged at the order, thinking, as did the Texans, that they had beaten their enemy. "They vigorously upbraided their commander, for they were eager to move upon the Confederates [the next day] and complete the work . . . either by forcing a surrender or starting them upon a retreat toward Santa Fe," some later remembered. The object of his reconnaissance in force, to annoy and harass the enemy, having been accomplished as far as Slough was concerned, he was glad to have gotten off so lightly and not to have been defeated in this, his first experience as a battle commander.[80]

With Captain Enos and the wagon train leading, the Union batteries limbered up and followed eastward, soon accompanied by the cavalry and infantry. The four-mile march took only slightly more than an hour. Enos and his wagons pulled into Kozlowski's and immediately began unloading the wounded from the ambulances and hospital wagons, while the Colorado surgeons and detailed medical assistants set up what became the new field hospital, south of the road, across from the ranch buildings. Pvt. Ben Ferris, having had his wounded leg treated earlier, was one of the casualties who started to fill the hospital tents. He recalled that two of his companions "got a tent for me and raised it, but as soon as it was up, and while they were staking it, other wounded men got in and filled it, leaving me still on the grass outside. They got another and guarded [it] so well that I was the 1st man in."[81]

Soon the rest of Slough's column reached the welcome spring and camping grounds at Kozlowski's Ranch. Almost immediately, a strange procession approached. Lieutenant Colonel Scurry had realized that his Confederates were too tired and busy with gathering in their own casualties to do the same for the many Union wounded and dead who still lay where they had dropped or crawled during the day's fighting. He took a white scarf from one of his men to make into a flag of truce and sent an officer, probably his acting adjutant, Maj. Alexander Jackson, to follow the Federal column. Jackson was to offer a cease-fire until noon of the following day to allow both sides to retrieve their wounded and dead and to bury the latter. Driving his ambulance eastward along the road, Jackson soon encountered Captains Downing and Ritter riding at the rear of the Federal column. He told the two officers the substance of his mission, but not having the authority to negotiate such a truce, they escorted him on to Kozlowski's Ranch and Colonel Slough. Pvt. John Miller remembered that "before we had been there ten minutes, the Texans came up with a flag of truce." The Union commander readily agreed, and in fact extended the armistice until the morning of March 30, to allow adequate time for the task.[82]

Captain Enos was soon actively arranging for such an expedition. "I had wagons unloaded for the purpose of sending them after the dead and wounded," he reported. He asked Colonel Slough for a detail of men to accompany the wagons back to the battlefield. He was rebuffed and "the detail was not furnished and had it not been for the few teamsters and wagon-masters that I took with me, no wounded would have been brought in on the night of the battle." He was not correct in that assertion, however, as Alfred Peticolas indicated. The Texan was later searching the field for Confederate wounded when he was again mistaken for a Union soldier by "a Sergeant of artillery who came back to look up the wounded and bury the dead." Enos also loaded a number of shovels and picks into the wagons and left, retracing his recent route.[83]

On the field around Pigeon's Ranch, the darkness and rugged terrain greatly hampered both sides' recovery efforts, but some Union casualties were identified and placed in Enos's wagons. Before he called off the operation for the night, the quartermaster captain and the Union surgeons who accompanied him endeared themselves to their adversaries, however. The Rebels had no tools with which to bury their dead, so Enos left his for their use. Corporal Whitley of the Seventh Texas remembered that "we had no spades or pick-axes or anything else, (the Yanks loaned us theirs or give them to us, for we left them there when we fell back to Santa Fe) . . . and their surgeons divided their medical stores and instruments with us."[84]

As Captain Enos brought his wagons of wounded back along the Santa Fe Trail, snow began to fall. In their Kozlowski's Ranch encampment, the Federal soldiers were reasonably comfortable; there were blankets, and food was sufficient. They slept or sat around blazing fires, recounting the day's events and mourning their dead friends. Most were pleased with the day; Private Hollister reflected that "though we were obliged to give ground from the commencement yet considering the disparity of our forces . . . we were well satisfied. The Colorados are willing to fight them, man for man, every day of the year."[85] The only Federals not accounted for were those Enos had missed and prisoners taken during the battle, as well as Major Chivington's party, from whom nothing had been heard. Colonel Slough was decidedly worried over the fate of that third of his force.

The Confederates were worried also. After six straight hours of strenuous fighting, followed by the exertion of locating and bringing in their casualties, the men were naturally exhausted. Not knowing the exact situation behind them, however, Lieutenant Colonel Scurry had no choice but to prepare some kind of defensive line in his rear in case some Union force was coming up the Santa Fe Trail from Johnson's Ranch. He sent men from the Fourth Texas Regiment westward to Glorieta Pass as pickets, to warn of any such approach. Sergeant Peticolas was chosen for this duty, and with his company trudged back "towards our old camp." As the snow began to fall more heavily around his post alongside the famous trail, Peticolas had time to recall his own recent experiences: " I was very thankful that I had no depression of Spirits or many nervous feelings after the battle as I had at *Val Verde,* for I should have been unfit for guard duty if I had felt as I felt that night." However, he had the previously confiscated beef jerky to chew on, and "when my turn was out, I curled up by the fire wrapped up in my overcoat and managed to get a few hours' repose."[86]

In the Confederate camp, as the weather turned colder, many soldiers helped care for the wounded. Pvt. Bill Davidson remembered: "On that night a severe snow storm arose and snow fell to the depth of a foot, and several of our wounded froze to death. . . .We took off our coats and piled them upon them; we built the best fires we could build for them; we rubbed their limbs and bodies but all to no avail, they died in spite of all that we could do." Capt. Julius Giesecke, commanding the Fourth Texas' Company G, after trying to account for his men, "remained on the battlefield without food, near a fire, but froze no little." Others sat around the fires, joking and carrying on as if nothing was the matter. But deep down, many knew better. Pvt. Fred Tremble, one of Pyron's wounded men, whispered confidentially to Bill Davidson that "we were in a hell of a fix." "And I believe he is right," Davidson concluded.[87] Everything considered, it was an anxious and miserable night around Pigeon's Ranch and Johnson's Ranch.

CHAPTER SIX

Johnson's Ranch

The Wagons were all heavily loaded with ammunition, clothing, subsistence, and forage, all of which were burned upon the spot or rendered entirely useless.
—Maj. John M. Chivington

The Confederates shivering around their fires had every reason to be worried. Colonel Slough's flanking party had left the main column on the morning of March 28, as the Federal commander continued toward Johnson's Ranch, intending to find the Rebels still camped and entrenched there. Major Chivington's strong force, over a third of the entire Union command, was to reach that same location and attack the Texans in concert with Slough, as previously mentioned.

Chivington and his men accompanied the other Federals out of their Kozlowski's Ranch camp, but when a little more than three miles along the Santa Fe Trail, the party left the main road and took the shortcut leading to Galisteo. That trail initially crossed the level valley and present alignment of the Santa Fe railroad, then continued southward up what appeared to the soldiers to be an impossibly steep side canyon. Actually, the trail, though indeed steep, was quite passable for infantrymen and their mounted officers. This road ascending San Cristobal Canyon is still used today for access to the top of Glorieta Mesa. An hour's hard climb brought the major's contingent out on the reasonably flat, elevated tableland south of the Santa Fe Trail.[1]

The Fighting Parson's force was as specified by Colonel Slough before leaving camp. Captain Lewis's infantry battalion comprised 269 men, both regulars and New Mexico and Colorado volunteers. Chivington's second battalion of foot soldiers was led in the field by Capt. Ed Wynkoop, of Company A, First Colorado Volunteers, and included that officer's own company and two others from his regiment, another 219 men. Altogether, Chivington had 488 soldiers at his command, a force that appeared to be adequate for his mission of delivering a flank or rear attack on the Rebels.[2]

Once on top of Glorieta Mesa, at about the same time Slough's main force rested around Pigeon's Ranch, Chivington's column marched easily and quickly along the Galisteo trail as it wound southward and westward around forested hills and knolls atop the mesa. Another mile and a half, however, found the Federals at a point where the road continued south toward the village of Galisteo, but where the force was essentially even with, and directly east of, Johnson's Ranch. Now, Chivington had to rely for success on the New Mexicans attached to his column. Two officers of the Second New Mexico Volunteers were familiar with this little-traveled part of the territory. That regiment's Lt. Col. Manuel Chaves and its chaplain, Rev. Alexander Grzelachowski, had traversed the area during the preceding decade. The Roman Catholic chaplain, known affectionately by his parishioners as "Padre Polaco" (the Polish Priest), was assigned to the Archdiocese of Santa Fe but often traveled the back roads around the capital during his ministry. Both Grzelachowski and Chaves habitually conversed in Spanish, and that may have led some accompanying Federals to identify the priest mistakenly as a Hispanic clergyman, "Father Ortiz," who never actually existed.[3]

Shortly before noon, as the first phase of the battle around Pigeon's Ranch raged unexpectedly between the Confederates and Colonel Slough's main column, Chivington was ready to leave the Galisteo road and strike out across country for Johnson's Ranch. He heard nothing of the booming artillery and crackling small-arms fire that were filling the valley below Glorieta Mesa with deafening noise. Although he was only some three miles in straight-line distance from the battlefield, the cannon fire and explosions echoed off the steep cliffs forming the rim of Glorieta Mesa, south of Pigeon's Ranch. The result was that the mesa top, and Chivington's party, were in an "acoustic shadow," keeping the men entirely ignorant of the fighting along the Santa Fe Trail.

Trusting his fortunes to Lieutenant Colonel Chaves and Father Grzelachowski, Chivington left the road and followed his guides across sagebrush flats, along a small dry creek bed, and through the pine and juniper woods atop the mesa. He marched slowly, to give Colonel Slough time to travel the expected eleven miles along the Santa Fe Trail and initiate a frontal attack on the Confederate camp. The major had sent some of his New Mexicans ahead as scouts in case the Rebels had posted pickets on the heights over their camp. These came back to report that the Texans were indeed there. Private Gardiner, one of Wynkoop's Colorado Company A infantrymen with the expedition, recalled that "while we were waiting for the T's to be *drove* to us, our scouts bro't in information that their entire train with a two-gun battery and three hundred men, were only two miles below us, in the mouth of the pass."[4]

With this exciting, if not completely accurate, information, Chivington increased the pace of his march. Tending always westward, after two and a half miles and at about two o'clock, just as the early-afternoon lull in fighting settled upon the field at Pigeon's Ranch, Chivington and his men reached the western rim of Glorieta Mesa. Lieutenant Colonel Chaves proudly announced: "You are right on top of them." The Federal commander had the soldiers march in "perfect silence," one remembered, "until we were almost directly over their heads, on an almost perpendicular mountain, 1500 feet high." Major Chivington later reported he had traveled sixteen miles. The journey undoubtedly seemed that long to a commander unfamiliar with the region and anxious about coordinating his movements with those of Colonel Slough; in fact, he had marched nine miles, in about four and a half hours, a respectable rate considering the difficulty of the terrain. And he was some five hundred feet above the Texan camp, which was plainly visible along the Santa Fe Trail.[5]

Captains Lewis and Wynkoop kept their men quiet and generally out of sight on the high rim above the Confederate camp and its two hundred occupants. Those who could peer below saw the hillside breastworks thrown up during the preceding two days, although nobody seemed to be in them. A hospital area could also be recognized, sheltering approximately 80 casualties and sick who had been wounded at Apache Canyon, around Pigeon's Ranch, or brought northward with Scurry's column. On top of the prominent hill south of the trail and Johnson's Ranch buildings, a single 6-pounder gun pointed eastward toward Apache Canyon. Spread around the hill were the eighty wagons that Lieutenant Colonel Scurry had left behind when he marched eastward earlier that morning. Five hundred or so horses and mules, draft animals for the wagons, were penned into a natural corral at the foot of a slide area on the hillside directly below Chivington, and tethered along Galisteo Creek, where adequate grazing and water were readily available. All seemed serene; Private Gardiner and his comrades of Com-

Johnson's Ranch. Major Chivington's Federal party hiked down the steep mountainside above the campsite to burn the Confederate wagon train parked in the creek bottom. *Courtesy Corbin Haldane.*

pany A spent the time watching with amusement "the unconscious Texans, jumping, running foot races &c."[6]

In fact, the scene was too serene. Having marched two miles less than Colonel Slough's route along a better road, Chivington was puzzled to know why his commander had not already commenced the planned assault on the Rebels. He waited an hour on the mesa rim, but when Slough did not appear, and the force below him did not look formidable, Chivington decided to attack on his own. Immediately in front of him was a precipitous slope, but he ordered the whole party to descend the mountainside and attack the Texans. Still trying to maintain silence, the regulars and Colorado volunteers slipped and slid over halfway down the slope, loosening rocks and gravel in the process, before the enemy spotted them. Reaching a narrow shelf of level ground directly over the slide area, one of the Colorado officers, probably Captain Wynkoop, yelled down: "Who are you below there?" Those Rebels on the hilltop immediately ran for their cannon, as Sgt. Tim Nettles, the NCO commanding the gun crew, shouted back, "Texans god damn you!" The Federal then offered: "We want you," to which the artilleryman replied, "Come and get us god damn you, if you can."[7]

With his enemies alerted, there was no longer any reason to keep quiet or hesitate. Chivington remained on the shelf, from which the entire camp was visible. He detailed Captain Wynkoop and thirty Company A volunteers to remain on the commanding flat ground to provide covering fire for those descending into the Texan camp and to try to pick off the artillerymen, who were preparing to open fire against the men on the slope. Wynkoop's small party immediately fired their rifles down into the confused body of Rebels. They remained on the shelf during the ensuing action, shooting continuously.[8]

Captain Lewis led his battalion of regulars and volunteers, accompanied by the rest of Wynkoop's men, temporarily led by Capt. Asa B. Carey, Fifth Infantry, down the steep slopes before them. Mule trails normally used to bring wood down to Johnson's Ranch from the mesa top ran on either side of the impassable slide area. Down these, and through the trees and rocks nearby, the Federals ran, stumbled, and slid to the bottom of the mountainside, where the valley carried the bed of Galisteo Creek, scarcely deep enough to be noticed. Private Gardiner remembered that he and his companions all raised the "Injun" yell and "all managed to get down." As they did so, Sergeant Nettles and his cannoneers opened on them with the 6-pounder. He got off only two ineffective rounds, however, before he was forced to abandon the gun.[9]

Lewis quickly formed his own command for a charge on the hill and cannon, directing the other battalion to capture the wagon park and its draft animals. That accomplished, he led almost three hundred men up the southern slope of the hill, toward the Rebel gunners. There was little resistance. As soon as the astonished Texans identified the enemy troops descending upon them from what appeared to be an impossibly steep mountain range, many decided flight was their only salvation. Some quickly mounted nearby horses or mules and rode off up the Santa Fe Trail in the direction Scurry had taken that morning. Others decided to trust their legs and ran after their fleeing comrades or back along the trail toward Santa Fe. "But we were too fast for them, and took the most of them prisoner," claimed Gardiner.[10]

Pvt. Bill Davidson, who had been shot in the leg as the Pigeon's Ranch fight began earlier in the day and had had his trousers perforated by the accursed Yankees, was now in the hospital at Johnson's Ranch. As excited as the rest of the Texans, he watched as his friend Sergeant Nettles was attacked. Davidson claimed the 6-pounder had been left behind due to a lack of trained draft animals to pull it and its limber. If so, Nettles had no choice but to abandon the cannon atop the hill. As he did so, however, he spiked the gun by placing a musket ramrod into the touch hole in the breech, then ramming an iron cannonball into the barrel, bending the ramrod internally and disabling the piece for any immediate use by the enemy. The brave sergeant then set fire to the nearby limber and its ammunition chest. The chest blew up before Nettles could run to safety, scorching him so that he appeared to Davidson to be "literally burnt all over." Leaving Davidson behind, however, Nettles quickly "got up behind," on the horse of his fellow sergeant, George H. Little, and both rode off toward Glorieta.[11]

That, at any rate, was the way Davidson remembered events. Private Gardiner of the Federals reported differently in a letter to his mother a month after the battle. He attributed the disabling to Captain Lewis's command, and recalled that "to spike the guns and burn their carriages was but a few minutes work." Dr. William C. Whitford, who later wrote a history of the First Colorado Volunteers, also claimed, as did Private Hollister, that Lewis had not only spiked the cannon but had then "tumbled the carriage on which it was mounted down the eastern side of the knoll, smashing the wheels into pieces."[12] Regardless of who actually destroyed the artillery, it was disabled, and most of the able-bodied cannoneers and teamsters previously left behind to defend the camp either were prisoners or had run away.

About half past three, just as Scurry was launching his most desperate charge against the Federal line before Pigeon's Ranch, the Union officers at Johnson's Ranch received their first information about the battle that had kept Slough from cooperating with them as planned. The five Colorado infantrymen of Company I who had been captured early in the fierce hand-to-hand gully fight west of Pigeon's Ranch had been marched to the rear and were being held captive at Johnson's Ranch. Their views of the course of the battle were naturally quite pessimistic. One informed Captain Lewis that "you had better get away from here quick. The damned Texicans are whipping our men in the canyon like hell, have driven them nearly through the canyon and pretty soon will have them out on the prairie."[13] Although the news was wildly exaggerated, it was the first inkling Lewis had of the ongoing main battle. He could not evaluate the credibility of these freed prisoners but nevertheless decided to complete his operations at the Confederate camp as rapidly as possible.

Lucius H. Jones, the Fourth Texas' chaplain, who had been left behind in charge of the camp, remained to tend the wounded in the Johnson's

Ranch hospital. As some of Captain Lewis's men approached the hospital area, Reverend Jones came out in front, waving a white flag to make sure the Union soldiers knew that part of the camp was a hospital and sheltered no combatants. In the confusion of the moment, someone shot him. The Texans were universally outraged at what they considered an atrocity. Watching the whole episode, Bill Davidson stated that "they fired on our hospital of sick and wounded men. . . . The idea was to leave none to tell the tale, sick or wounded." Later, Lieutenant Colonel Scurry reported the "shooting and dangerous wounding of the Rev. L. H. Jones . . . with a white flag in his hand," and described it as an act "which the most barbarous savage of the plains would blush to own." He also reported that the Yankees had ordered "that the prisoners they had taken be shot in case they were attacked on their retreat" from Johnson's Ranch. The former was, undoubtedly, one of the accidents of war, while the latter was sheer nonsense, but they were both cherished stories in Texas for years after the war.[14]

With the sun rapidly settling in the winter evening, and the enemy perhaps returning to their camp or driving Slough's main force back beyond the reach of the Chivington flanking party, time was of the essence. Captain Lewis detailed a few men to make prisoners of the one hundred or so Confederates still at Johnson's Ranch and to parole those too sick to accompany Chivington back to the Federal camp at Kozlowski's. Seventeen able-bodied prisoners were prepared for the return trip.[15]

At least one of the black servants left behind at Johnson's Ranch also decided to go with the Union soldiers. Mac, Lieutenant Oakes's servant, stayed, but Sgt. Jim Carson's servant had been told that his young master had been killed, so he prepared to leave the camp with its captors. Later, hearing that his information might be wrong, the slave asked one of the Federal officers to write to Lieutenant Colonel Scurry to find out the truth. He wanted to return to Carson if the latter was, in fact, alive. Carson himself replied, and the Union lieutenant let him know that "the negro had gone off with a wagon train, would be back in a few days and that he would send him down under a flag of truce." Unfortunately for Carson, the Confederates retreated before the man returned, and his ultimate fate is unknown.[16]

Captain Lewis's most important job, however, was destroying the supply wagons, a job he assigned to Captain Carey. Most of Carey's men labored to concentrate the supply wagons so that they could be destroyed easily. Still others were ordered to find and free the hundreds of draft animals tethered and penned around the camp. There has long been a belief that the Federals bayoneted or otherwise killed all the Confederate horses and mules, but there is no good evidence that such a slaughter occurred. Private Gardiner reported such an action but probably referred to a few animals penned in the immediate vicinity of the hill, perhaps even those injured in the explosion of a nearby ammunition wagon. With only about half an hour to destroy the wagons and deal with the draft animals, there would not have been time for Lewis's men to have bayoneted such a large number of struggling and thrashing horses and mules, and no rational officer would have wasted his men's limited ammunition supply on such a task. No other Union participant and no Confederate reported the slaughter at the time, so it is likely that perhaps a handful of animals were killed, and the rest were released to deny their use to the Confederates should they return. Besides, Lewis could look around the outskirts of the camp and see groups of local citizens waiting to loot the camp and steal the animals once the Federals left.[17]

Destroying the wagons turned out to be a time-consuming and dangerous task. Gardiner noted that the men "were allowed to ransack and keep whatever valuables they could find." Many were tempted and spent valuable time searching through the vehicles, where there was "a great deal of fine officers clothing, fine Mexican blankets and all kinds of military stores, wines, Brandies, pickles, cand fruit, oysters & Navy Revolvers, double-barrel shot-guns &c&." Some may have taken light articles or guns, but most were daunted by the thought of hauling any heavier loot back up the steep mountainside on their return. Instead, they distributed kegs of powder in each wagon, and as the party began to leave the valley camp and climb to the top of Glorieta Mesa, Captain Carey left men behind to fire the wagons. When the fires reached the powder kegs, each wagon blew up. One, already full of spare ammunition, exploded with unexpected force, severely wounding Pvt. Simon Ritter, of Wynkoop's Company A.[18]

For an hour, Captains Lewis and Carey and their men, along with their prisoners and released comrades and servants, struggled back up the slopes east of Johnson's Ranch, meeting Wynkoop, Chivington, and the New Mexicans on the way. Their labors were made more bearable by the spectacle below them. Private Gardiner recalled that "before we reached the top nearly every wagon had exploded, and sitting to rest upon the top, we witnessed every wagon, with its contents, a smoldering heap of ruins."[19]

The expected coordinated battle at Johnson's Ranch had not taken place, but the part of the Battle of Glorieta that did take place there was the single most important event of the campaign in New Mexico. As even Private Gardiner realized, "*all* their provision, *all* their clothing and nearly all their ammunition was in this train." In fact, everything Scurry's force owned—medicines, private baggage, camp equipment, food, forage, and reserve ammunition—was gone. "Thus ended the severest stroke the Texans ever received at our hands, in this country," wrote Gardiner, and Lieutenant Colonel Scurry's later report reflected the seriousness of his loss. The Confederate wounded left at the ranch had no illusions as to the completeness of their defeat. Bill Davidson understood: "Here we are . . . 1,000 miles from home, not a wagon, not a dust of flour, not a pound of meat."[20]

As Chivington's men rested on the rim of Glorieta Mesa about five o'clock, the major was both pleased with the blow they had struck the enemy and worried about the fate of Colonel Slough, in view of the stories related to him by Captain Lewis and the released Union prisoners. His uncertainty and anxiety were almost immediately compounded as a mounted messenger rode up to Chivington. It was Lieutenant Cobb, the officer sent by Colonel Slough at midday to find and retrieve Chivington's party. The lieutenant had ridden hard, but had had difficulty following the major's trail once it left the road to Galisteo. The dispatch Cobb brought ordered Chivington to come to Slough's immediate relief at Pigeon's Ranch, a relief that the Federal commander had expected all afternoon, not realizing how much time would be involved in getting his message to Chivington and in the major's return. Nevertheless, not knowing that the colonel had retired to Kozlowski's Ranch, Chivington quickly set his column, now a relief force, in motion.[21]

The return march was a nightmare for all involved. Major Chivington had to rely on his New Mexican guides, but Manuel Chaves was not familiar enough with the locale to be confident of his ability to lead the column safely in the dark. He and Father Grzelachowski conferred and decided that since the priest was more familiar with the immediate vicinity, he should lead. Padre Polaco mounted his horse and started eastward as darkness set in. The first two and a half miles across the mesa top were very difficult. From horseback, the Polish chaplain could see well enough to find the way, but the men could see almost nothing. Stumbling over clumps of sagebrush and fallen limbs that were easily avoided by day, the soldiers stepped into ditches and holes, exhausting themselves and often having to hold onto the man ahead just to stay in the column. Even Major Chivington had to dismount to keep his men closed up.[22]

Once the column reached the Galisteo road, marching became easier.

By about eight o'clock Grzelachowski and Chivington were at the head of San Cristobal Canyon, having traveled some four miles. There, Private Gardiner remembered, "we were met by another messenger from Col. S. stating that he had withdrawn his command entirely from the field, that the enemy had discovered his plans, and if we did not proceed by some by-road, we would surely be cut off." This was the first information Chivington had that the Rebels probably occupied some point at or east of Pigeon's Ranch.[23]

Nevertheless, though his men were not now needed as reinforcements, he had little choice but to continue down the steep canyon trail and hope to avoid the enemy wherever they were camped. The snow that began to fall made the descent much more treacherous than the accent had been in the morning. The chaplain led the column slowly down the road, but soon the Confederate campfires could be seen off to the left, around Pigeon's Ranch. Padre Polaco abandoned the road and led the column eastward, through the foothills toward junction with the Santa Fe Trail. Again the men groped through the dark and cold, but "twice came in plain view of the enemies camp-fires . . . all the time the guide . . . protesting that he was not lost." Grzelachowski may have been off the trail, but he was not lost, and the column soon regained the main road back to Kozlowski's Ranch. The end was in sight, but there was one more scare for Chivington's men. Seeing campfires ahead in the night, the major was unsure, from what he knew and what his accompanying messengers knew, whether the camp was Slough's or the enemy's. He had the men fix bayonets and slowly advance on the position, only to come within hailing distance and learn that it was the camp of the Federal force. It was ten o'clock at night, in the middle of a heavy snow storm, but Kozlowski's Ranch never looked so good to the Union infantrymen and their Polish guide.[24]

Colonel Slough's men were overjoyed to see their comrades safely back in camp, and were exuberant as they learned of Chivington's success in destroying the Texan supply train and encampment. Slough's relief was understandable; he reported: "The loss of this train was a most serious disaster to the enemy, destroying his baggage and ammunition, and depriving him of provisions, of which he was short." Major Chivington was pleased with his men's accomplishment. "Captain Lewis had the most dangerous duty assigned him," the major reported, "which he performed with unfaltering heroism. I repeat, all, *all* did well."[25]

As many of the late arrivals, tired, thirsty, and hungry, sat around the fires exchanging accounts of the distant victory, others quickly found fireside spaces and went to sleep. Father Grzelachowski, however, found little comfort upon reaching Kozlowski's Ranch. His horse died, ridden to death in leading Chivington's party throughout the rugged return march. The loss was a serious blow to Padre Polaco, who later wrote to Captain Chapin, acting assistant adjutant general of the Department of New Mexico: "In the engagement between our troops, and the so-called confederate forces, at Canon del Apache, while accompanying Col. Chivington's command, returning from the place where the enemy's train was by us destroyed, the horse I was riding, my private property, died. Will you please inform me if I have a right to claim from the government an indemnification for my horse, and if so, what course must I pursue to receive such an indemnification."[26] Captain Chapin replied to Grzelachowski, explaining that proof of ownership and battle-related death was required for such reimbursement as the priest requested, but final disposition of the application is unknown.[27]

With the return of Chivington's party, the Battle of Glorieta was at an end, and each side could tally its losses. All these figures must be considered approximations due to the lack of rigorous reporting by either commander and lack of follow-up reporting on those who had been mortally wounded and subsequently died. The Confederates had forty-eight men killed and mortally wounded in the fighting around Pigeon's Ranch (thirty-one from the Fourth Texas Regiment alone), with an additional sixty less seriously wounded. Scurry's force also had about twenty-five of its members captured by Slough's and Chivington's forces on March 28.[28]

Strangely, Union losses are less exactly known. Colonel Slough reported twenty-eight men killed and forty wounded, but that figure is too low. Private Hollister could account for forty-six killed and sixty-four wounded just from the ranks of the First Colorado Volunteers (with the majority of those coming from Companies D and I). Adding casualties from the regulars and New Mexico volunteers, the total Union losses at Glorieta were approximately forty-eight killed and mortally wounded, with seventy less seriously wounded, and twenty-one captured and still in the hands of the enemy. The opposing forces, therefore, lost essentially identical numbers, a total of about 133 to 139 men each, in the day's fighting. For both, that was approximately 10 percent of those engaged.[29] Such numbers were small compared to the staggering casualties that would be experienced later in the Civil War, but for the far western frontier, and for such an early period in the war, they were impressive to those who participated in the battle and to those back home.

The day after the Battle of Glorieta brought no rest, but no renewed combat, for the Union troops. Captain Enos was again active. "Early next morning," he reported, "ten wagons and the ambulances were sent back to bring in the remainder of the dead and wounded." The snow made finding additional bodies or casualties, if any had survived lying exposed through the freezing night, very difficult.[30]

Private Gardiner was among the Colorado Volunteers accompanying Enos's wagons and remembered that the enemy "allowed us to go all over their camp with the exception of the back yard of their hospital, which was reported to be *full* of dead bodies." The Union infantryman had time to talk to many of the Confederates in the camp, some of whom related grossly exaggerated stories of their own—and the Federals'—actions and casualties. "They are the most ignorant set of white people I ever came across in my life," he wrote to his mother. "If I was asked once, I was *twenty* times, in *good earnest*, if it was a fact that Abe Lincoln was a *Mulatto*. They are mostly boys from 15 to 20, though there are some very intelligent Germans among them."[31]

Satisfied that no more Federal dead remained unburied on the field, and that all his wounded had been located or accounted for, Captain Enos visited the Confederate hospital. There, several previously wounded Colorado Volunteers, including Pvt. C. W. Logan of Company F, shot in the arm at Apache Canyon, had spent the previous night under the care of the Texan surgeons and attendants. Enos took the Union wounded into his ambulances, consigned additional medical supplies to the Rebels for their own use, and left Pigeon's Ranch to the Confederates.[32]

Slough's men spent the morning at Kozlowski's Ranch burying their dead brought in the previous evening, and in readying themselves for a return to Fort Union. By noon, Enos's wagons were back, only to find that the colonel and the bulk of the command had already left, heading eastward toward the village of San José. Enos unloaded those wounded he had just retrieved and then led the entire quartermaster train along the Santa Fe Trail in Slough's wake. One of his teamsters had been wounded when he became excited, deserted his team, and joined in the battle in support of one of the artillery batteries. With that exception, however, none of his men had been hurt, although he had lost some of the animals when two of his ammunition wagons had been burned as the Federals evacuated Pigeon's Ranch. With the volunteer cavalrymen of Company F providing rear guard protection, the wagons got into camp at San José well after dark. From there, Enos sent a brief preliminary report of the battle ahead by courier to his superior, Captain McFerran, at Fort Union. The quartermaster detachment had served outstandingly at Glorieta, as had Captain Enos. Captain McFerran endorsed the early report by indicating that "the letter of Capt. Enos speaks for itself and shows plainly how well he must have acted and performed his duty."[33]

Back at Kozlowski's Ranch, the wounded remained in the crowded tent hospital, tended by surgeon Joseph C. Bailey and his assistants, as well as comrades left behind as attendants. Since nobody knew what the Texans' remaining strength or intentions really were, and not realizing how badly crippled the Rebels were by having lost their entire supply train, the Federal patients still at Kozlowski's were greatly worried that they might soon become prisoners of war. More of the badly wounded died in the improvised hospital and were buried on the ranch grounds, and all were affected by the cold weather. Pvt. Ben Ferris, after watching his companions of Company F ride out, remembered: "I was left with other wounded . . . and lay in a tent with two other men. Both of them died and I suffered immensely, but I lived. Three or four days after the forces left for Ft. [Union], we were put into freight wagons and started for the same place."[34]

Once arrived at their new encampment at San José, Slough's men received startling news. Their colonel had resigned his commission as commander of the First Colorado Volunteers. They had been griping among themselves as they marched and rode back toward Fort Union, since they considered themselves to be the victors over an overwhelming force of Texans, and to have been deprived of the opportunity to advance again and drive the Rebels back to and through Santa Fe.[35]

At San José—or perhaps before leaving Kozlowski's; the evidence is not clear—Capt. William Nicodemus, adjutant to Colonel Canby in Fort Craig, rode into camp with a message from the departmental commander. The dispatch ordered Slough to return with his column to Fort Union and indicated, or Slough thought it indicated, that the First Colorado colonel had disobeyed previous orders not to leave the fort. Canby's instructions were based on out-of-date information. He had received Slough's preliminary dispatch after the Battle of Apache Canyon reporting that engagement and his "intention to move against the enemy with his entire force." That prospect frightened Colonel Canby, who evidently did not understand the results of the first day's fighting. What should have frightened Canby was not the prospect that Slough would attack the enemy with his entire force but that the inexperienced officer would divide his command and move against the Texans along the critical Santa Fe Trail with a numerically inferior force. That such a maneuver did not result in Federal defeat was due to Slough's considerable tactical skills and Chivington's good fortune, but Canby could not have known or predicted this. He sent Captain Nicodemus northward as rapidly as possible to prevent some catastrophe to Colonel Slough's command, and with it, Fort Union.[36]

Probably, Slough had already begun the move to Fort Union in response to this order. Some of his men, even though they did not like him, believed he had resigned in frustration at having been denied the opportunity to strike the enemy again. Trooper Hollister wrote that "flushed with an honorable and complete victory, his brave troops eager to complete the destruction of the enemy, Col. Slough read the dispatch brought by Capt. Nicodemus in dismay. . . . To obey it was to let the enemy, broken and disheartened, escape; to refuse was to subject himself to court-martial and disgrace."[37]

There is nothing to indicate that Slough was anxious to come to grips with the Confederates again; nor is there much evidence to the contrary. In his preliminary report on the Battle of Glorieta, written the same day he received Canby's dispatch, the Federal commander stated: "Hearing of the success of Major Chivington's command, and the object of our movement being successful, we fell back in order to our camp." He had heard nothing from Chivington before withdrawing to Kozlowski's Ranch, of course, and the statement was obviously intended to give Canby the impression that the battle had gone as planned and had been successful. The fact that it went much better than planned was not yet apparent to Slough, or he would undoubtedly have emphasized that aspect of the results of the battle. Nevertheless, although Slough was an amateur military officer, he was an experienced lawyer. He almost certainly believed that he was vulnerable to censure, perhaps even court-martial. That prospect evidently weighed more heavily on his mind than anything else. Having just won the victory that saved New Mexico for the Union, Slough apparently resigned to preclude any such adverse action being taken against him.[38]

Four days later, on April 2, the Federal column reached Fort Union, bringing to an end the possibility of any further immediate conflict with the Confederates.

While their enemy marched away from Kozlowski's Ranch in relative comfort, the Rebels were in great discomfort back at and west of Pigeon's Ranch. On the day after the battle, many were cold and hungry, but their spirits chilled even more when their officers disclosed that the rumors of Chivington's attack were true. Private Wright remembered that "flushed with the joy of winning the battle, we were suddenly confronted with the fact that after all we had lost the victory." To the wounded Bill Davidson, it seemed "that leaving our train without a heavy guard was a terrible blunder."[39]

Lieutenant Colonel Scurry was faced with a serious dilemma. There was nothing more to eat at Pigeon's Ranch, and his force was low on ammunition after the preceding day's battle. To the east, as far as he knew, the Federals were still across the Santa Fe Trail, and as the battle ended, they had given every indication of continuing fierce resistance to any further advance the Texans might make in that direction. To the west, as Capt. Julius Giesecke heard, Chivington might well still be either in possession of the burned Confederate camp or waiting nearby to strike should Scurry attempt to retreat to Santa Fe.[40]

To resolve at least the latter question, Scurry sent a small force back westward toward Johnson's Ranch to locate any enemy and to occupy the camp should none be nearby. Sergeant Peticolas and the other Fourth Texas men who had spent the night as pickets west of Pigeon's were part of this exploratory party. They had heard the same rumors circulating throughout Scurry's command, but they were soon able to learn the truth for themselves. Marching along the snowy roadway and chewing on beef jerky, Peticolas and his comrades arrived at Johnson's Ranch, where "we learned certainly before noon that our baggage train had been all burnt and that the Mexicans were busy stealing every thing they could lay their hands on."[41]

The paroled Texan wounded still at the desolate site were unable to prevent the vandalism, even if there had been much to protect. It was also obvious that Col. Tom Green had not come with the rest of Sibley's brigade, as rumored. Prowling through the heaps of burnt, snow-covered wreckage, Peticolas was able to verify that his own personal effects, left in one of the wagons, had been destroyed. "I didn't mind losing anything save my watch and journal," he claimed, referring to the first of three Civil War journals he kept; "that I cared much about losing." All was not lost for the others, however, as someone captured a few scrawny sheep that had been hidden nearby, and "we got mutton today for dinner."[42]

When Scurry learned from this outpost party that the road to Santa Fe was clear of the enemy, he began preparing the main Confederate force for a retreat to the territorial capital and food. Some of the men got their first reliable information of their plight. One remembered that "Colonel Scurry made us a little speach and told us our wagons and all supplies had been burned and our sick taken prisoners and the nearest and only place to get any supplies was in Santa Fe."[43]

Meanwhile, some soldiers still sought their missing friends. Private Wright, who had searched the battlefield all night for his friend John Poe, finally heard that the corporal and almost a dozen other wounded Texans had found refuge in a cabin in the nearby village of Glorieta. Going there, Wright found Poe, searched the premises, and found quite a few stored provisions. He hid "a sack of flour and a bale . . . of dried buffalo meat," perhaps the same jerky that had earlier supplied Peticolas and his Company C companions. Wright then found a sitting hen, took her eggs for the wounded men, and "confiscated her for the good of the service, and she made soup enough to feed those sick men for two days." When Scurry's main force left Pigeon's Ranch later the same day, they found and took the provisions Wright had not hidden, but he stayed behind to tend Corporal Poe and the other casualties. "Half of them were dead before the week ended," he later recalled.[44]

Much of the day was spent in burying those Confederates who had been killed outright during the battle of the previous day, or who had been mortally wounded and had since died. The site selected for the mass grave was some three hundred yards east of the Pigeon's Ranch buildings, just south of the Santa Fe Trail and Glorieta Creek. Even digging the grave was difficult. Using the picks and shovels left them by the Federals, Scurry's men could penetrate only about two feet before they reached solidly frozen soil.[45]

As the excavation was in progress, other Texans prepared their comrades' remains for burial. Many of the thirty bodies had stiffened into awkward postures, some having to have limbs strapped together in order to get them into the shallow grave. The men tenderly placed bags of private possessions—combs, pipes, tintypes, needles, tobacco, pencils, etc.—in dead hands folded over chests. One of the Fourth Texas soldiers assigned to the burial detail was Pvt. Brinkley H. Tyler of Company F. He remembered that "we dug a big hole large enough for them and laid them two deep and spread one layer of blankets over them and filled in on them with dirt. It was bad, but the best we could do."[46]

The remains of Captain Buckholts and Majors Shropshire and Raguet were either temporarily buried in the compound behind Pigeon's Ranch or simply laid out under some shelter behind the building, the freezing weather preserving the bodies for later removal or burial. That was very likely the

Mass grave of Confederates killed at Glorieta. These are the remains of those thirty soldiers killed at the battle around Pigeon's Ranch and buried by their comrades the next day, March 29, 1862.

substance behind Union private Gardiner's understanding that the "back yard of their hospital" was "*full* of dead bodies." All were later moved.

The dead buried, Lieutenant Colonel Scurry had little or no transportation available for moving the wounded. His surgeon would remain behind with a detail of hospital attendants, often friends of the wounded, to care for the Confederate casualties in the Pigeon's Ranch hospital until they could be sent for. With little food to leave with them, and only the medical supplies provided by Captain Enos and the Union doctors, the patients faced an uncertain future. Scurry reported that "we remained upon the battle-field during the day of the 29th to bury our dead and provide for the comfort of the wounded, and then marched to Santa Fe, to procure supplies and transportation to replace those destroyed by the enemy." Captain Giesecke of the Fourth Texas was still apprehensive of enemy forces at Johnson's Ranch. "The day passed," he remembered, "and towards evening we had determined to gain Santa Fe by attacking the pass at the risk of our lives; and so we march on right after dark, but found no enemy."[47]

Tramping along the frozen Santa Fe Trail, a twenty-five-mile ordeal began for Scurry's men. Eventually, afoot and on horseback, they came up to their former camp at Johnson's Ranch, where, with no choice but to leave the wounded there, they passed on westward. Sergeant Peticolas, who had been at the ranch all afternoon and evening, saw the head of the main column arrive, and "about 10 P.M. we were ordered to get our guns to march for Santa Fe. . . . We reached a small creek about 4 A.M. and stopped an hour to wait for those that had given out on the road." Indeed, the hungry, freezing, exhausted men who had marched all the way from Pigeon's Ranch began to straggle badly. "The hunger and fatigue of our men was great," observed Captain Giesecke, as he tried to keep the members of Company G, Fourth Texas, together and moving through the dark night. Some soldiers had stopped to build fires alongside the trail. Peticolas found one of these fires irresistible. "I was perfectly worn out and soon fell asleep and slept by the fire till day," he recalled.[48]

The head of the Confederate column reached Santa Fe just at daybreak, and the rest of the soldiers stumbled into town during the morning. Pvt. Robert Williams, another Fourth Texas member, recalled the march and its hardships, but arrived in the early morning. Bells were ringing, and he assumed they were to greet the returning Texans.[49] Actually, it was Sunday morning, and they were the cathedral bells calling parishioners to mass. Watching this procession of dirty, gaunt, footsore invaders from Santa Fe's Loretto Academy, Mother Magdalen Hayden observed:

> *They continued entering until almost noon on Sunday: We could hear them passing all night, our convent being on the street through which they had to pass, but we did not know to which side they belonged until morning when we saw by their clothes that they were Texans. Some came on horseback, others on foot, and others were almost dragged to the city. All were in a most needy and destitute condition in regard to the commonest necessities of life. . . . We hid many of our provisions for fear they would pay us a visit when they found no more in other places.*[50]

Well might the sisters fear for their provisions. The Rebels spent the rest of Sunday searching for food for themselves and their horses. They found very little, Private Tyler recording that at the end of the day he had "received only a half ration." Sergeant Peticolas, a better scrounger than most of the others, "stopped at a store . . . and got some bread and whiskey," for which he and a companion, Pvt. W. T. Davis, traded coffee "that we had gotten at Johnson's Ranch, where our things were burnt."[51]

Finding shelter was also an immediate problem. Scurry and his officers initially quartered the men in abandoned Federal quarters and buildings that had been partially burned as Fort Marcy and other army facilities were evacuated ahead of Major Pyron's previous entry into Santa Fe. Peticolas and his company "found our quarters in a large old ruined building belonging to the government, and about 12 M. got rations and dinner. We slept in this house on hay from the Government Corralls."[52]

Scurry soon found better shelter for his men, but one of his first concerns was to improve morale. Events of the past two days had devastated the enthusiasm of the Texans. Believing they had won a victory at Pigeon's Ranch, they were almost immediately crushed by the news of their defeat at Johnson's Ranch. That reversal of their military fortunes, compounded by the hardships and privations of the retreat into Santa Fe, left most with spirits lower than at any time since they had left South Texas almost seven months earlier. Food and shelter would help restore health and attitudes, of course, but Scurry felt he should do whatever else was needed. He quickly found a printing press still working in Santa Fe and issued to the men what he hoped would be a morale-boosting declaration:

Head-Quarters, Advance Division, Army of New Mexico
Canon Glorieta, March 29, 1862

General Order

No. 4

Soldiers:—You have added another victory to the long list of triumphs won by the confederate armies. By your conduct, you have given another evidence, of the daring courage and heroic endurance, which actuate you in this great struggle for the independence of your country. You have proven your right to stand by the side of those who fought and conquered on the red field of San Jacinto. The battle of Glorieta—where for six long hours you steadily drove before you a foe of twice your numbers—over a field chosen by themselves, and deemed impregnable, will take its place upon the roll of your country's triumphs, and serve to excite your children to imitate the brave deeds of their fathers, in every hour of that country's peril.

—Soldiers—I am proud of you. Go on as you have commenced, and it will not be long until not a single soldier of the United States will be left on the soil of New Mexico. The Territory, relieved of the burdens recently im-

posed upon it by its late oppressors, will once more, throughout its beautiful valleys, "blossom as the rose," beneath the plastic hand of peaceful industry.

By order of Lieut. Colonel W. R. Scurry, Commanding

Ellsberry R. Lane, Adjutant[53]

Although the address contains some obvious exaggerations, it in fact had a positive effect on the soldiers' spirits. Sergeant Peticolas observed that "from what I can hear of San Jacinto, that battle was not near such a hotly contested fight as the battle of Glorieta or Val Verde either. This is the only fault I have to find with the address."[54]

Thus, two days after the Battle of Glorieta, as the Confederates began to recover in Santa Fe and Colonel Slough's Federal force, almost as dispirited, slowly marched back to Fort Union, any resumption of fighting was beyond the foreseeable future, and the results of the battle could be more objectively analyzed.

For the Confederates, capture of Fort Union, with its indispensable supplies, was absolutely necessary, and was the strategic goal of Sibley and Scurry in New Mexico. Preventing such a loss was the strategic goal of Canby, Paul, and Slough. The Texans' tactical objective at Glorieta was to attack successfully the Federal force lying between them and Fort Union, while Colonel Slough's tactical goal was "to obstruct the movements of and disrupt the supplies of" his enemy without subjecting his own force to any catastrophic defeat, which would have laid Fort Union open to capture.[55]

At both the tactical and strategic levels, the Union was successful. At the end of the day on March 28, the soldiers of both sides thought they had been victorious. The Confederate rank and file had seen what appeared to be a rout of their enemy, although actually it was a planned withdrawal at dark to the Federal encampment at Kozlowski's Ranch. The Rebels remained in possession of the battlefield, usually a strong indicator of victory. In this case, however, Scurry's men remained at Pigeon's Ranch through necessity, simply because they had no camp to which to return; it had been burned by Major Chivington's flanking party. The part of the Battle of Glorieta fought at Pigeon's Ranch can easily be seen as a drawn fight. Both sides took essentially the same losses in killed, wounded, and captured. Lieutenant Colonel Scurry's men had pushed a much smaller Federal force back during the day, and had, as a result, "captured" about two miles of the Santa Fe Trail. However, that ground was of no value whatever; their undefeated enemy still stood across the only road to their absolutely vital goal—Fort Union.

As Scurry's men had done on the offensive, Colonel Slough's Union command had fought fiercely and effectively on the defensive. Against an enemy that outnumbered him by about 60 percent, the Union leader had done an outstanding job of keeping his force intact behind good defensive lines, as the enemy was repeatedly able to outflank him. That part of the battle conducted by Chivington at Johnson's Ranch, however, was a resounding Federal victory, undiminished by the fact that it may have been achieved through Lieutenant Colonel Scurry's carelessness in leaving his supply train essentially unguarded. When the Union victory in that phase of the battle is considered in conjunction with the drawn phase at Pigeon's Ranch, the Battle of Glorieta can be seen as a clear Federal tactical victory. Colonel Slough's immediate goals had been attained; he had indeed obstructed the movements of, and disrupted the supply of, the enemy; and his undefeated and reconcentrated force still protected Fort Union.

Logistics played essentially no part in the Federal tactical victory at Glorieta but was the key element in defeat of the Confederate strategic plan for the entire New Mexico campaign. In fact, few if any other Civil War battles or campaigns offer examples of the importance of logistics to compare with Sibley's invasion. There were good reasons for that, of course. The New Mexico campaign was conducted in a frontier wilderness, where living off the land was impossible and there were no navigable waterways or extensive road systems, while much larger campaigns to the east could make use of the nation's produce, rivers, railroads, and road networks.

For the potential guidance of officers planning the New Mexico invasion, however, military history did indeed offer lessons in the importance of logistics to campaigns conducted deep into hostile territory. Not only in Europe but in America, there were prime examples. One, certainly, was the Saratoga campaign conducted by the British Army during the American Revolution. During the summer and fall of 1777, British general John Burgoyne planned to split New England off from the other rebellious colonies by means of a thrust southward from Canada through northern New York to Albany, on the Hudson River. Converging columns would attack northward along the Hudson from New York City and eastward through the Mohawk Valley of western New York. Transporting his army southward up Lake Champlain, then capturing Fort Ticonderoga, Burgoyne found himself at the end of a supply line that was tenuous at best—and faced with traversing some thirty miles of wilderness to reach the Hudson River. To attempt to live off the land, he dispatched a raid eastward to capture supplies and horses, but that force was defeated at the Battle of Bennington in August.

Forced to rely on his logistical trail back to Canada, and in a country where the populace was becoming increasingly hostile, Burgoyne delayed to build up supplies for his further advance southward to Albany. Just as General Sibley delayed for the same purpose in New Mexico, giving his enemies time to strengthen their opposition to him, so also Burgoyne allowed the Americans under Gen. Horatio Gates to fortify a naturally strong position on the west bank of the Hudson, south of Saratoga. That position on Bemis Heights became stronger and more heavily manned as the British force crossed the river and tried unsuccessfully in two separate battles, Freeman's Farm and Bemis Heights (the Battles of Saratoga), to force its way around the Americans. When the other two converging British thrusts miscarried, Burgoyne found that he could not advance, could not defend himself in his position after the battles, could not retreat rapidly, and could not supply his army over a two-hundred-mile route through hostile territory. He was in a position similar to that in which Sibley found himself after the Battle of Glorieta, although Sibley was able, even if barely, to retreat. In October, 1777, Burgoyne surrendered his army to the Americans in what became a turning point of the Revolution, bringing France openly into support of the American colonists.[56]

Napoleon's 1812 invasion of Russia, although of much greater magnitude than the Civil War invasion of New Mexico, saw the French Army at the end of a long and unsupportable supply line in a hostile country. The result was the same as Burgoyne had experienced or worse, with loss of the great majority of Napoleon's troops and the event a significant turning point in European history. As with these two examples, and even if on a much smaller scale, the Texan defeat at Glorieta became a turning point in the future of the American West and Southwest, ensuring that the region would remain loyal to, and a part of, the United States.

Strategically, therefore, Glorieta was also a great Union victory. The Confederates abandoned their advance toward Fort Union and subsequently retreated a thousand miles back to South Texas, never to return. Their defeat cast no shadow on the Rebels' reputations as soldiers. Their accomplishment—marching such a distance across hostile terrain; bringing an army of infantry, cavalry, and artillery into battle after such a journey; and fighting so excellently in each battle—was indeed impressive and was a source of everlasting pride to participants and their descendants alike.

Nevertheless, in the mountains of New Mexico, Union troops had stopped the invading Confederates cold. Glorieta represented the high-water mark of the Confederate invasion of Federal territory in the Far West. As such, many historians over the past forty years have considered Glorieta to be the "Gettysburg of the West."[57] Although the New Mexico engagement was much smaller than the famous eastern theater battle fought a year later, many similarities have become apparent. The frustrating of southern goals and the relatively poor performance of the chief Confederate commanders in both cases come immediately to mind. And in both instances, final retreat out of Union territory began soon after the smoke of battle cleared. Just as the Federal Army of the Potomac first defeated the Rebels and then expelled the Army of Northern Virginia from northern soil in Pennsylvania and Maryland, in this Gettysburg of the West, loyal regular troops, along with the gallant volunteer soldiers of New Mexico and Colorado, defeated the Texans and saved New Mexico Territory for the Union.

CHAPTER SEVEN

Recovery and Retreat

My spies from Santa Fe report that the entire Confederate force left that city. . . . Their preparations indicate the intention of leaving the country.

—Col. Edward R. S. Canby

With the intention of resting and recovering the health and strength of his men in Santa Fe, Lieutenant Colonel Scurry quickly sent his quartermaster and commissary officers scouring the capital city for warm quarters and food for the able-bodied soldiers and their wounded and sick comrades. They were successful in finding usable quarters the day after reaching Santa Fe. Sergeant Peticolas found that "we have gotten quarters in a larger block of buildings belonging to the bishop, who is friendly to us." Indeed, Bishop John B. Lamy gave permission for the Texans to use a series of single-story adobe buildings across the street to the northwest of the Catholic cathedral, the outstanding landmark in town. Each noncommissioned officer was responsible for the supply and well-being of a small number of privates, usually from five to ten, known as a "mess." Sergeant Peticolas secured a space in one of the Bishop's buildings, in which his mess and that of another Fourth Texas NCO occupied "one room with a good floor and fireplace. . . . We are resting," he observed, "but have very poor eating; no bacon nor pork, and very little coffee. I have seen very few American ladies as yet." Obviously, his spirits were beginning to rise.[1]

Food was difficult to locate for such a large number of men, especially since most of the local residents had driven their animals into the hills and mountains surrounding Santa Fe or had hidden what little food they had.

Peticolas found one merchant in town who would trade with the Texans, but after a few days, his mess was still "living on corn meal."[2]

The cold was a serious enemy, especially for the wounded. All their blankets and personal belongings having been burned in the wagons at Johnson's Ranch, the Confederates initially suffered from the late winter weather. Some Santa Fe residents, however, sought relief for them. Louisa Hawkins Canby, wife of the Union departmental commander, soon visited the Texans and saw their plight. She told Lieutenant Colonel Scurry that a large number of blankets and other useful stores had been hidden by Federal officials as they evacuated Santa Fe prior to Major Pyron's entry earlier in the month. Other local residents confirmed her story and some of the Brigands knew of these hidden supplies. Peticolas observed that "the company of Santa Fe Gamblers who joined us since the battle of *Val Verde* and fought gallantly and desperately at Glorietta, is of immense service to us now. They call themselves *brigands* and know everything about Santa Fe."[3]

Either they or Mrs. Canby located the hidden Indian Bureau supplies, and the Confederate quartermasters were able to issue blankets by the first day of April. Sgt. Jim Carson's Fifth Texas company was "supplied with two blankets to every three men," while Capt. Julius Giesecke was able to secure enough for each of his Fourth Texas men to have "at least one blanket." Sergeant Peticolas drew a blanket apiece for members of his mess, making sleeping on the floor of one of the Bishop's rooms much more comfortable.[4]

Although the commissary personnel continued to search for adequate food for men and horses, the most immediate problem was care for the wounded. Louisa Canby had already made some such arrangements. Realizing that there might well be a battle somewhere near Santa Fe when the Texan vanguard under Major Pyron had ridden out to find the Federals on March 25, Mrs. Canby had foreseen that casualties would be coming back into the capital. She had set up beds in the empty rooms of her own "large home," and she urged the other wives of Federal officials living in Santa Fe to do the same. Some protested that it might be Confederates who would need the care, but Louisa Canby replied that "no matter whether friend or foe, our wounded enemy must be cared for . . . ; they are the sons of some dear mother."[5]

Louisa Canby truly became the beloved "Angel of Santa Fe" for the sick and wounded Confederates. To care for the unexpected number of casualties, she found a large building for use as a hospital, and Maj. Powhatan Jordan, who had led the Seventh Texas battalion at Glorieta but who was a physician in civilian life, became its chief surgeon, assisted by Dr. Jacob F. Matchett and other Fourth Texas regimental surgeons who joined him in Santa Fe as the wounded were brought in from Pigeon's Ranch and Johnson's Ranch.[6]

Retrieving the wounded from the battlefield hospitals proved to be a time-consuming operation. The Texans commandeered whatever wagons were available, but found few still in the city. Louisa Canby, however, had canvas sheets stretched across two or three wagon beds, to convert the vehicles into improvised ambulances. Beginning on March 31, the day after the Confederate column reached Santa Fe, Scurry began the recovery process. The ambulances rumbled back and forth between the capital and the field hospitals, a fifty-mile round trip in some cases, throughout the following week.[7]

One of the first patients brought in was Pvt. Bill Davidson, suffering from the wound in his leg and announcing that he was "laid up, undergoing repairs," in the Santa Fe hospital. Toward the end of the week, the Fourth Texas' Henry Wright finally got his badly wounded friend, Cpl. John Poe, into one of the ambulance wagons, where he could appreciate Mrs. Canby's canvas sheet modifications, "forming cots on which the men were lain and rode in comparative ease." Wright felt that "the life of many a poor fellow was saved by this invention." The ambulances also brought in the desperately wounded Capt. Isaac Adair of the Seventh Texas, shot in the head during Shropshire's abortive flank attack.[8]

While the Confederate casualties were being removed to Santa Fe during the week following the Battle of Glorieta, the Texan doctors at Pigeon's Ranch continued to treat those too critical to be moved. With supplies limited to those they had personally brought with them and those left by the Union officers, they were greatly restricted in the care they could give. Shattered arms and legs could, of course, be amputated, the only real treatment for such wounds during the Civil War, but beyond that, little was possible. Between seven and eleven more Rebels, in addition to those already buried in the nearby mass grave, died at the hospital before it was abandoned and were buried on the ranch property, likely in close proximity to the main hospital buildings.[9]

Lieutenant Colonel Scurry and his men also sent for the bodies of their officers left behind at Pigeon's Ranch. They had coffins made in Santa Fe, and on April 2, a detail was dispatched to the ranch to recover the remains. Major Shropshire's servant, Bob, was a member of this party. He and its other members, however, were disappointed to find that the coffin prepared for the six-foot, four-inch Shropshire was too short. They therefore wrapped his body in a blanket and buried him in a shallow, single grave, aligned with the mass grave and ten feet away from the other previously interred Confederates.[10]

Maj. Henry Raguet's and Capt. Charles Buckholts's bodies were brought back to Santa Fe. As Masons, both were buried in the Masonic Cemetery there. Afterward, when Union forces reoccupied the territorial capital, one of the Colorado officers who had fought at Apache Canyon and Glorieta, Edward Wynkoop, by then promoted to major of his regiment, visited Raguet's gravesite. By coincidence, Wynkoop and Raguet were distant relatives. Wynkoop marked the grave so that it could be readily identified. From Fort Craig in central New Mexico, where he was soon stationed, he wrote on June 2, 1862, to Major Raguet's father in Nacogdoches, Texas, identifying himself as a relative who, "although opposed to one another . . . could not help feeling a pang knowing that the same blood ran in our veins." Major Wynkoop described Raguet's gravesite in Santa Fe and offered that "if any time you desire to do anything with his remains and I can be of any service, Command me while in this Territory; you can address me through my mother in Philadelphia."[11] Although it cannot be determined when, Major Raguet's family did utilize Major Wynkoop's information, later removing the remains from Santa Fe and reinterring them in an impressive monument at Nacogdoches.

Boredom and depression soon settled over the Confederate soldiers in Santa Fe. As officers and NCOs worked to feed their men and to find clothing and supplies with which to reequip them, those not on guard duty or otherwise employed had time to acquaint themselves with the town. Sgt. Alfred Peticolas was intrigued with the mores and architecture of Santa Fe. Every day he made in his diary detailed entries and sketches of the buildings and attractions around town. He was especially interested in the enclosed courtyards or patios most larger native adobe homes incorporated, as well as in church architecture. One night, while standing guard duty in the town's fire station, he had time to wonder just "what use a fire company is in a city built of mud." He also spotted a large basket in the fire station, "inscribed both in english and spanish upon every side," with the motto: "George Washington!!!! The father of our country!!!!! First in War!!! First in Peace, and !!!!! First in the hearts of his Countrymen!!!!—at which astounding name and astonishing declaration, strange to say, no one appears surprised."[12]

Other soldiers felt good enough to engage in mischief. The mother superior of the Loretto Academy, whose convent adjoined the cathedral in Santa Fe, was not amused: "The Texans had their quarters all around us. Some of them climbed on the roof of the day school and one entered the school itself through a window which looks out over the street, asking if the room was unoccupied. He opened another window which opens on the court-yard, but as soon as he saw some Sisters he went out the street window. . . . I sent for the Bishop and he notified the commander and so they ceased to molest us."[13] These activities were remembered with much humor once the Rebels returned home. In Victoria, Texas, Pvt. A. Goldman of the Victoria Invincibles later recalled considerable kidding of those involved in looking over the convent wall at the nuns.[14]

These few diversions, however, failed to cheer up the soldiers. Despite better living conditions and Scurry's address praising their success at Glorieta, most of the rank and file knew that they had not been successful after all, even though they considered the battle a victory. They found considerable whiskey around Santa Fe and threw little parties or "fandangos" in their rooms at night. Peticolas looked in on a couple of these sprees but could not get interested. He observed that while he and his mess were comfortably quartered, "there is a sort of gloom resting on the company. We have lost three companions who were very dear to us, and though a soldier's life is calculated to render a man properly callous, it will be long before we forget Henson, Hanna, and Montgomery. . . . We seldom sing now save when liquor abounds," he added, "and the sound of a violin makes me sad."[15]

Confederate spirits rose somewhat on April 3, when Col. Tom Green came into Santa Fe. He and his staff had ridden ahead of the other six companies of his Fifth Texas Regiment, which were en route to the capital to reinforce Scurry. These Texans had been in Albuquerque on March 30, when Scurry's first dispatch describing the Battle of Glorieta and his impending retreat into Santa Fe reached General Sibley at the headquarters of the Army of New Mexico. The men were formed to hear the glorious news, at which they cheered while the brass band struck up "Dixie." However, Sibley, regardless of his other faults, could read between the lines of Scurry's message; he was convinced that the commander of his field column had let himself be surprised, and that the whole future of the campaign in New Mexico was seriously jeopardized.[16]

General Sibley immediately ordered Colonel Green to prepare the six Fifth Texas companies that had been lying idle around Albuquerque for a forced march to reinforce Scurry in Santa Fe. The Confederate supply depot and hospital would be guarded by a handful of men, one company each from the Fourth and Seventh regiments, plus a small artillery battery. The horsemen, along with a section of two mountain howitzers from the Fifth Regiment's artillery company, were ready to march by early morning of March 31. Green led the men northward well before dawn, following the river road through the villages of Bernalillo and Algodones. The day became cloudy, cold, and altogether unpleasant for the Texan riders. One, Pvt. William Henry Smith, felt that "this country is verry disagreeable. . . . If the Lord will spare me to get out of this country I never will come to this country [again]." While his men traveled quite slowly along this good road, camping on their second night out near San Felipe Pueblo, only some twenty-five miles north of Albuquerque, Green decided to ride ahead. By April 3, as mentioned, he was in Santa Fe, making arrangements for the arrival of the reinforcements, who were a day behind him. The Fifth Texas companies rode into the capital after dark on April 4, greeted by their comrades who had fought at Glorieta.[17]

Accompanying the Fifth Texas came General Sibley and his staff. The general had remained behind in Albuquerque after Green's men left, preparing and sending off to his superiors a preliminary report of the actions in New Mexico since the Battle of Valverde, including the latest news from Santa Fe. " I must have re-inforcements," Sibley emphasized to the Confederate high command back in Richmond. Now, after entering the territorial capital, the general again showed how out of touch with reality he was. "On my arrival," he reported, "I found the whole exultant army assembled. The sick and wounded had been comfortably quartered and attended; the loss of clothing and transportation had been made up from the enemy's stores and confiscations, and, indeed, everything done which should have been done."[18] If the statement was intended to recognize that Lieutenant Colonel Scurry had done his best while in Santa Fe, there was some validity to the claim, but as a bombastic cover-up of the real status of the campaign, it was an obvious farce.

The newly arrived Rebels had a chance to see the sights of Santa Fe and to cheer up their comrades. General Sibley brought the brass band with him from Albuquerque, and it played on the town plaza both Saturday and Sunday, April 5 and 6. Other Texans took the opportunity to attend the Catholic services in the cathedral, Sgt. Robert Williams finding "their ceremony picturesque. Candles burning in the daytime." Pvt. Bill Howell was "surprised to see a Catholic nunnery close by my quarters."[19]

On April 7, the same day the great two-day Battle of Shiloh was ending in southern Tennessee, the Confederates in Santa Fe attended a ceremony, with muffled drums, as Major Raguet was buried in the Masonic Cemetery. Some of the new arrivals may also have taken part in an impressive fandango in the quarters of the Fourth Regiment's Company E that same night, although most had already left Santa Fe to return to Albuquerque.[20]

Their withdrawal resulted from Colonel Canby's actions well to the south. On April 1, the Union commander had left Fort Craig with a strong field column, marching northward along the Rio Grande toward a junction with the garrison of Fort Union, which had been ordered south to meet him. His intention was to occupy Albuquerque if he could do so without serious risk or loss, and if not, to threaten the small enemy garrison there, so as to cause the Confederates to evacuate Santa Fe in order to secure their supply depot at Albuquerque. If they did so, no further threat to Fort Union would exist, and the combined Federal force would be able to expel the Texans from New Mexico. He felt that this plan was consistent with his inability to feed and care for large numbers of prisoners should he defeat and capture Sibley's entire brigade.[21]

As Canby neared Albuquerque, he put his plan into action. He would threaten the supply depot there and see whether any serious opposition developed. If the Texans resisted, he would withdraw eastward to join his Fort Union column, and thereafter harry the Confederates southward out of New Mexico. His march toward Albuquerque, by itself, had the desired effect; the Confederates there learned of his approach and sent word to Sibley of this threat to the only remaining Texan supply depot in northern New Mexico. When that desperate message reached Santa Fe, the Confederate general once again ordered Colonel Green and the Fifth Texas to ride, this time retracing their march of three days before. By the evening of April 7, Green's column was ready and rode out of the capital, while Sibley issued orders for the rest of his force to follow as soon as possible.[22]

Sergeant Peticolas noted that they "received orders to leave this evening . . . and we got ready but did not leave. . . . We hear that Canby is approaching Albikirque with a considerable force." By noon the next day, the foot soldiers of the Fourth Texas, along with the troopers of the Second and Seventh regiments and those wounded from the hospital who could travel, also left Santa Fe. Pvt. Bill Davidson, who was still sore and recovering from his leg wound, decided he would rather accompany the column southward than take a chance on becoming a prisoner if left behind at Santa Fe.[23]

Just as the Fourth Texas was evacuating Santa Fe, however, Colonel

Canby arrived before Albuquerque. "I immediately made a demonstration upon the town," he reported, "for the purpose of ascertaining its strength and the position of the enemy batteries. This demonstration was made by Captain Graydon's Spy Company, supported by the regular cavalry." Often referred to as the Battle of Albuquerque, this brief probe at the Confederates brought a fierce response from the Texan artillery and support companies, as well as from many patients in the hospital, who rushed into the lines to help secure the invaluable supply depot. There was only one casualty, Maj. Thomas Duncan, leading the Union cavalry, who was seriously wounded by a bursting artillery shell. The firing ceased when Canby was informed that noncombatants in the town were endangered and were not permitted by the Texans to leave. His objective had been met, however; the Rebels would indeed resist. They also immediately sent for assistance from Sibley and Green.[24]

Tom Green, upon learning of the Union attack, hurried southward with his horsemen. As he did so, Canby remained in his lines southeast of Albuquerque, skirmishing at long range with the enemy throughout the day of April 9. After dark, however, leaving campfires burning to disguise his intentions, he abandoned his positions and withdrew eastward through Tijeras Canyon to the east side of the Sandia Mountains to await his Fort Union troops, who had been ordered to meet him there. Canby's withdrawal would allow the enemy to concentrate in Albuquerque and, he hoped, to move southward on the road back to Texas.[25]

Colonel Green and his men dashed into Albuquerque just as, unbeknownst to the Rebels, Canby was abandoning his encircling lines. Cheers greeted the incoming Confederate horsemen, who prepared to counterattack in the morning. Morning, however, found empty enemy camps and no further fighting in or around the town. General Sibley and the rest of the Confederate column straggled into Albuquerque during April 10 and 11. Sergeant Peticolas, exhausted by the hardships of the forced march south, recalled that "we at last arrived perfectly worn out with our efforts." He could appreciate, however, that "the main plaza of this town is quite neat, and a tall flag staff supports the Confederate flag. . . . The cathedral is a handsomer building than the one in Santa Fe." However, his stay in Albuquerque was short.[26]

Although the Sibley Brigade was now concentrated, supplies for it were meager. Sgt. James F. Starr, assigned to the adjutant general's office in Albuquerque, reported that there was not enough ammunition left for a full day's fight, and rations for only twenty days remained, others noting that ten day's rations were available. Sibley obviously had to leave for the Mesilla Valley in southern New Mexico, where his garrison there could provide some logistical relief. Consequently, beginning on April 12, the Texans abandoned Albuquerque, leaving behind their hospital and its patients as well as eight of their now surplus mountain howitzers, buried near the town plaza. The Confederates were heading for their final clash with the Federal army in New Mexico.[27]

Back in Santa Fe, the town was a much quieter place once the main body of Texans left. Along with the Confederate surgeons, headed by Major Jordan, many able-bodied soldiers remained behind as attendants in the hospital, often to care for wounded friends. Approximately two hundred Rebel patients remained in the hospital, and Pvt. Henry Wright noted that there was "a full supply of attendants, physicians etc., but very few supplies. . . . Fortunately, strong medicines were also lacking and the doctors were forced to practice nature's remedies and use cold water applications, under which treatment the wounded and the fever stricken rapidly recovered." However, it was not cold water that saved some of the quarantined smallpox victims in the hospital, or that saved his friend Cpl. John Poe. As noted, Poe had been brought into Santa Fe having been shot in the chest at close range; the doctors decided to operate. The brass overcoat button that had been driven into his body by the bullet had indeed broken a rib; both were then deflected and "ran around the body to a point just opposite where it entered." The surgeons removed bullet and button, and Poe survived to "preach the Gospel for forty-three years" back in Huntsville, Texas.[28]

Many of the wounded, however, did not recover. Another Fourth Texas member, Sgt. Robert Williams, who remained behind to care for his sick younger brother, reported a high death rate among the wounded. During the week and a half beginning on April 8, he noted at least one death each day. On the ninth, Capt. Isaac Adair, shot in the head at Glorieta and brought back, probably unconscious, to Santa Fe, died. He was buried the next day in the Masonic Cemetery.[29]

Initially, the weather was quite cold and many patients suffered from pneumonia, but the temperatures soon moderated, bringing some relief to the wounded men. Also bringing constant relief through her presence at the hospital was Louisa Canby. One Texan patient remembered "how kindly she stooped over our wounded forms, how soft her touch, how kind her sweet voice." Mrs. Canby brought food and other necessities for the men and organized the other Union women in continually caring for the enemy casualties. They "brought us flowers and fruit, books and papers, and when a number of our patients became convalescent and organized a . . . vaudeville club, attended our entertainments and applauded our efforts," remembered Private Wright. Louisa Canby certainly won the hearts of all, many recalling years later her kindness and remembering the humane acts of "that grand Union woman, the wife of Gen. E. R. S. Canby, the best and bravest general on the Northern side."[30]

On April 11, the Federals reoccupied Santa Fe, Capt. James Ford's company of Colorado Volunteers riding into town escorting eighty-four Texans who had been captured at Apache Canyon and Glorieta. Taken back to Fort Union, four officers and thirty-five enlisted men had been exchanged for Union soldiers of equal rank previously captured and held by the Confederates. Another seven officers and thirty-eight men were released on parole, agreeing not to take up arms against the United States until later exchanged.[31]

The hospital population decreased as some recovered or partially recovered patients and their attendants decided to accompany the released prisoners, who left the following day for Albuquerque and, eventually, Texas, supplied from Federal quartermaster stores. This decrease in size of the Confederate hospital continued as patients either died or recovered and as more paroled prisoners passed through Santa Fe on their way out of New Mexico.[32]

On April 21, Col. Benjamin F. Roberts, Canby's key lieutenant from Fort Craig, now commanding the Northern District of the Department of New Mexico, arrived in Santa Fe to reestablish the Federal military presence in the capital. By that time, even Louisa Canby's efforts to provide food for the Texan patients were insufficient, and the Confederate officers applied to Colonel Roberts for assistance. "Gentlemen," Roberts responded, "I did not intend to molest you in any way, but as you have appealed to me I can consider you as prisoners of war, and issue supplies." All the patients, surgeons, and attendants were then formally "captured" and fed. "Food such as we had not enjoyed for many months was in abundance," recalled Private Wright. "Coffee, sugar and other luxuries . . . made me think that life was again worth living." The prisoners essentially had the freedom of the town until each was eventually released on parole or escorted out of New Mexico.[33]

While the Confederates were thus engaged after the Battle of Glorieta, the Union troops had fewer problems. From their overnight camp at San José on March 29, where they learned of Canby's orders to return to Fort

Union and of Slough's resignation, the Federal column continued eastward toward that post. Passing through Las Vegas, the inclination toward lawlessness of some members of the First Colorado reappeared. James Farmer noted that "the Volunteers gutted several stores, a few Regulars looking on, unable to interfere. . . . They claimed the owners were disloyal." The column continued northward along the Santa Fe Trail, pulling into Fort Union late in the evening of April 2. The First Colorado's infantry companies occupied their former camp sites around the post, while Company F's cavalrymen found quarters in "a log house below the fortification."[34]

The volunteers, tired, sore, and depressed, settled down for a period of rest and recovery at Fort Union. Some, such as Pvt. John Miller, immediately wrote letters to their families describing their adventures of the past eleven days, while others busied themselves reading or playing poker. This pleasant interlude was rudely interrupted on April 5, with orders to pack up and be ready to start on a new campaign in an hour. Major Chivington formed the infantrymen and told them that Colonel Canby had left Fort Craig on April 1, moving north to join his forces with those from Fort Union somewhere between the two posts. With that news, toward evening, most of the First Colorado marched out of Fort Union, accompanied by Lieutenant Claflin's mountain howitzer battery. They traveled only a short distance, camping near the notorious "hog ranch" at Loma Parda, which served as a recreational center for the soldiers garrisoned at Fort Union. That was a mistake.[35]

The next morning, Company F also rode out of the fort and overtook the main column as it reached Las Vegas. There it was discovered that five Colorado volunteers were missing under circumstances that indicated their desertion. Private Hollister noted that they subsequently "sent Corporal Sampson with a squad back to the Lome [Loma Parda] to see if our supposed deserters might not possibly be there on a spree." However, the volunteer cavalrymen had other things to worry about than a few deserters. On the day the move southward was announced, Col. Gabriel Paul, commanding Fort Union, had exchanged and paroled the previously mentioned eighty-four Texan prisoners and prepared them to accompany the column about to leave the post. Company F served as their escort as they marched along the Santa Fe Trail, better clothed and fed than they had been since leaving Albuquerque almost a month earlier.[36]

Colonel Paul now commanded the Federal column moving southward from Fort Union. Ordered by Canby to do so, he made no objection to seeing the post essentially unguarded now that he was in charge of the field column. Leaving behind Capt. Asa Carey—who had been instrumental in destruction of the Texan wagon train—in command of Fort Union, with a handful of men as its garrison, Colonel Paul caught up with his new mobile force on the evening of April 6. As he rode into the camp near Las Vegas, escorted by Captain Lord's company of First Cavalry regulars, Colonel Paul felt he was at last fulfilling his duties as commander of the Eastern District of the Department of New Mexico. Colonel Slough, whose resignation was not effective until April 9, still led the First Colorado Volunteers, assisted by Lieutenant Colonel Tappan and Major Chivington, but now the older, more experienced officer was in command.[37]

By April 9, just as Colonel Canby was engaged in his feint attack against Confederates in Albuquerque, the Fort Union column reached their old camp at Kozlowski's Ranch. The field hospital was still in operation, and not knowing whether there might be Texans about, ready to attack, the soldiers camped on a wooded hill above the ranch and hospital so as not to be constrained by the hospital flag should the enemy be nearby. Toward evening of April 10, Colonel Paul decided to move on toward junction with Canby. He marched westward from Kozlowski's, toward the Glorieta Battlefield and Pigeon's Ranch, but soon left the Santa Fe Trail to take the road to Galisteo, the same road Major Chivington had taken to burn the Confederate supply train.[38]

As he turned southward, Colonel Paul sent the Texan prisoners and their regular cavalry escort on toward Santa Fe, while Colonel Slough, with Captain Howland's regular cavalry company, rode as far as Pigeon's Ranch to determine whether any enemy still occupied that position. Finally reaching the village of Galisteo, Private Hollister was fascinated to think that the Texans had used the site as a campground before their defeat at Glorieta. Their enthusiasm then had been based, he felt, on "the laurels of victory, which had hitherto graced their brows," but were now "withered if not actually torn off."[39]

Continuing southward toward the east side of the Sandia Mountains, retracing the Texans' earlier journey in reverse, the Union column reached the village of San Antonio, where Scurry's men had been snowbound a month before. There, on the evening of April 13, Colonel Canby's and Colonel Paul's commands met. Canby disclosed his information that Sibley's brigade had evacuated Albuquerque, moving down the Rio Grande toward the villages of Los Lunas and Peralta.[40] He planned to march against them but had one important administrative duty to perform before doing so. Since Colonel Slough's resignation was effective as of April 9, on that date Colonel Canby had officially accepted his resignation and discharged the Colorado colonel by special order. Now, Slough called upon Canby to present his resignation in person and to receive from the departmental commander his honorable discharge from United States service. That accomplished, John Slough, the victor of Glorieta, rode northward to Fort Union and thence out of New Mexico for the immediate future.[41]

To replace him at the head of the First Colorado Volunteers, Canby named Major Chivington as the regiment's new colonel. Immensely popular with the men, especially after his successes at Apache Canyon and Glorieta, that officer had presented to Canby a petition, signed by twenty-seven of the unit's officers, asking that Chivington be appointed. Lieutenant Colonel Tappan, who would normally have succeeded to the position, "generously waived his rank," according to Chivington, allowing Canby to make the new appointment, subject to later approval of the governor of Colorado. This was highly unusual, and somewhat ironic in view of Tappan's later bitter hatred of Chivington, but the Fighting Parson nevertheless led the First Colorado during the rest of its active duty in New Mexico.[42]

Colonel Canby quickly put his united command in motion toward the Texans. On April 15, just north of Peralta, he found Colonel Green's Fifth Texas Regiment separated from the rest of Sibley's force by the Rio Grande. Canby attacked Green in what was to be the fourth and last battle of the Civil War in New Mexico. After abandoning Albuquerque, all of the Confederate units except Green's had crossed to the west side of the river and proceeded southward along the Camino Reál. Green chose to follow a parallel route on the east side of the Rio Grande, and by the evening of April 14, he had occupied the mansion and grounds belonging to New Mexico's governor, Henry Connelly. The ensuing Battle of Peralta was one of the least bloody combats on record, with an exchange of artillery fire and desultory musket volleys, all brought to a close by a blinding dust storm that covered Green's withdrawal across the river in late afternoon. Although his troops were infuriated at not being allowed genuinely to attack and defeat the Rebels, Canby's plan was proceeding as he intended, and the battle hurried the Texans out of New Mexico.[43]

After escaping from Peralta, General Sibley and his men continued southward, leaving the Camino Reál near the present-day village of Bernardo for a hundred-mile, eight-day detour along the San Mateo Mountains and around Fort Craig, which was still heavily garrisoned by New Mexico volunteers. Reaching the Rio Grande again, the bedraggled Texans met their

Seventh Texas comrades who had been left at Mesilla guarding the few supplies they could gather in southern New Mexico. Sibley established another hospital for his sick and wounded in Mesilla, then moved farther south, to Franklin (El Paso), Texas. There, during May and June, 1862, the brigade recovered its strength and prepared to abandon the New Mexico campaign.[44]

That decision was emphasized by news that a completely separate Federal force from southern California was rapidly nearing the Rio Grande to reinforce Colonel Canby's units in New Mexico. The knowledge that Canby was already organizing his men in Fort Craig for another push against the Confederates, and that this additional California column would soon arrive, convinced the Texans to evacuate New Mexico and West Texas by July, 1862. The return journey across West Texas during midsummer was arduous indeed, but by late summer and early fall, 1862, the main Sibley Brigade column was back in South Texas.[45]

The New Mexico campaign was barren of tangible results for the Confederacy, although it was a source of lifetime pride for its participants. Of approximately thirty-two hundred soldiers who comprised the Confederate Army of New Mexico as it entered that territory in 1861, some five hundred became Union prisoners due to desertion, straggling, wounds, or combat. As a result of combat and disease, approximately two hundred of the invading Texans died. Many of the prisoners were exchanged or paroled, subsequently rejoining the brigade as it fought through the rest of the Civil War, but the Confederate soldiers nevertheless paid a high price for this unfortunate campaign.[46]

After an extended furlough at their homes, the Sibley Brigade was converted into a cavalry unit, called back into action, and participated in the fighting at Galveston, Texas, during January, 1863. They then marched into southern Louisiana, taking part in the arduous Red River campaigns of 1863 and 1864.[47]

Epilogue

When the hurly-burly's done,
When the battle's lost and won.
—*Shakespeare,* Macbeth

In saving New Mexico Territory for the Union, the regular and volunteer soldiers took severe casualties, as had their Rebel enemies. In dead and mortally wounded, the Federals lost about the same number as their Confederate enemies, approximately two hundred, mostly from combat. The Rebels took no prisoners of war with them as they left New Mexico, so all Federals who had been captured had also been exchanged or paroled if they had not died in captivity as a result of wounds.[1]

Throughout the summer of 1862, the First Colorado Volunteers engaged in numerous patrols and scouting expeditions while assigned to Fort Craig, New Mexico. By August, however, the various companies of the regiment began to move northward to Santa Fe and Fort Union. By the end of the year, they, along with Ford's and Dodd's companies of Colorado volunteers, had all been ordered back to their home territory. The two independent companies became Companies A and B of the Second Colorado Volunteers, while the entire First Colorado Volunteer unit was converted to a mounted regiment, the First Cavalry of Colorado. These two regiments fought Indians within the territory and performed military escort and other duties, with the Second also going farther east to participate in subsequent Civil War campaigns.[2]

The volunteer forces of New Mexico were also reorganized immediately after the Texans withdrew. Realizing that in the Indian campaigns that would inevitably follow, horsemen would be of much greater value than foot soldiers, the territory's military authorities disbanded the First New Mexico Volunteers, who had fought so well at Valverde. During May, 1862, selected officers and companies from the First, Second, Fourth, and Fifth New Mexico Volunteers were incorporated into a single new regiment, the First New Mexico Volunteer Cavalry. Commanded by Col. Kit Carson, the unit served actively within the territory throughout the rest of the Civil War. In 1863, however, increased Indian troubles in the Southwest required additional military attention, and many native veterans of the fighting at Valverde and Glorieta were reenlisted into the First New Mexico Infantry Volunteers for service that lasted until a year after cessation of the Civil War.[3]

Although the Sibley Brigade had left New Mexico, many Confederates remained as prisoners of war, either wounded or as able-bodied attendants of the wounded. The stories of their eventual return to Texas were often remarkable. Cpl. John Poe, scarcely a month after having been operated on for removal of the bullet and button from his back, walked home "through the plains of Texas with a running wound." His friend Henry Wright, who had nursed him to a semblance of health, was still in Santa Fe. Private Wright had a minor altercation with one of the Federal officers over a local girl and was thrown into jail in the capital on some trumped-up charge. When he finally talked his way to freedom, the Union quartermaster furnished him with a new uniform and shoes, as well as haversack and canteen, and he, also, began a perilous journey, mostly alone, through southern New Mexico and West Texas. By late summer, he finally arrived at his home in Moscow, Texas, where he found that "J. T. Poe had reached home two months ahead of me, and pretty well recovered from the effects of his wound had made good use of his time, and persuaded my younger sister to cast in her lot with him in spite of the war."[4]

Other Confederates in Santa Fe got to see more of the enemy's homeland than they expected. First Sgt. Robert Williams had stayed to tend his sick younger brother, Pvt. John Williams, who had recovered by late April. Both soldiers found themselves unexchanged, but signed paroles. Rather than being sent home, however, they were grouped with other similar prisoners and marched up the Santa Fe Trail to Fort Union, thence across Kansas to Fort Leavenworth. Mixed in with other Confederates captured in Arkansas and Indian Territory, the Texans were shipped by steamboat down the Missouri River, then up the Mississippi to Quincy, Illinois, and from there by rail to Camp Douglas, south of Chicago. After two weeks in the prison pen at Camp Douglas, the Williams brothers and other New Mexico captives were exchanged and taken by rail and riverboat back down the Mississippi to Vicksburg. From that Confederate bastion, their odyssey continued after the Texans lingered in camps awaiting orders and transportation; they finally crossed into Louisiana in early October. The two Williams brothers, one now seriously sick, walked across Louisiana and eastern Texas, reaching their home on December 4, 1862, after a journey of more than three thousand miles. "All well," Sergeant Williams noted in his diary. "Meeting with old friends."[5]

Other Confederates reached Texas after difficult but considerably less adventurous journeys. Sgt. Alfred Peticolas of the Victoria Invincibles was promoted to quartermaster sergeant of the Fourth Texas Cavalry (as the regiment was renamed) during the Red River campaigns in Louisiana. After the war, he resumed his legal practice and eventually became one of the most respected and prominent attorneys in South Texas. He subsequently served as a judge in Victoria and wrote his *Index Digest of Civil and Criminal Law of Texas,* which was for many years a standard work in use by the Texas bar. He also served as editor of the *Victoria Advocate,* and lived in that town as a leading citizen until his death in 1915.[6]

Of other Texans' returns, less is known. Bob and Mac, the servants of Major Shropshire and Lieutenant Oakes, respectively, made it back to their homes. Both were at the Battle of Peralta after leaving Albuquerque, but apparently took no part in the fighting there, as Bob had done at Glorieta. One of the Fifth Texas soldiers noted that Mac, "while not such a *mighty* warrior as Bob, . . . goes on every battle field, gets him a good safe place and watches the battle," after which, depending on the outcome of the fight, he either "returns to camp or searches for plunder." Both slaves remained in Texas after being freed at war's end. Mac became a professional gambler, while Bob was a preacher for more than twenty-five years. They remained friends, and Mac later claimed that Bob was not smart enough to be a gambler, while Bob, in turn, decided that Mac would never be devout or honest enough to be a preacher.[7]

General Sibley's key officers went on to play prominent roles in the Civil War in Louisiana and Arkansas. Colonel James Reily, who had not taken part in the New Mexico campaign, resumed command of the Fourth Texas and led his regiment in the initial battles in southern Louisiana at

Bisland and nearby Franklin. On April 14, 1863, as the Fourth Texas held back flanking enemy troops so that the rest of the Confederates could escape through Franklin, Reily was killed in the battle line.[8]

Lt. Col. William R. Scurry, of the Fourth Texas Mounted Volunteers, left the Sibley Brigade while it was still withdrawing from New Mexico. He was promoted to colonel and raised his own regiment in Texas, but was soon made brigadier general, in September, 1862. After leading his brigade in the 1864 Red River campaign, he took the unit north into Arkansas and was mortally wounded at its head during the Battle of Jenkins' Ferry on April 30, 1864. Scurry County, Texas, is named for this hero of Glorieta.[9]

Col. Tom Green of the Fifth Texas was promoted to brigadier general in May, 1863, and placed in command of the First Cavalry Brigade of the Confederate Army in Louisiana, which was thereafter known as Green's Brigade. Soon given command of a cavalry division, he fought through the Red River campaigns, and on April 9, 1864, while leading his cavalry against Union gunboats during the Battle of Pleasant Hill, Louisiana, General Green was killed by Federal artillery. Tom Green County, Texas, is named in his honor.[10]

Col. William Steele commanded the Seventh Texas in New Mexico but remained in the southern part of the territory, guarding supplies. He, also, was promoted to brigadier general during September, 1862, commanding in Indian Territory, then during the Louisiana campaigns. He replaced Tom Green at the head of the cavalry division upon that officer's death and survived the war to engage in private business and become adjutant general of Texas.[11]

Perhaps the most tragic figure among the Confederates was Henry Hopkins Sibley himself. The general led his brigade into southern Louisiana in early 1863, but due to the low esteem in which he was held by Maj. Gen. Richard Taylor, the overall Confederate commander, Sibley was placed in charge of the baggage trains during the retreat of Taylor's men from the Battle of Bisland, while Tom Green led the cavalry force. Sibley blundered in almost every aspect of his duties during that action and the subsequent Battle of Franklin. As a result, General Taylor preferred charges of disobedience of orders and unofficer-like conduct against General Sibley. Those charges resulted in a court-martial that found him not guilty but nevertheless echoed Taylor's low opinion of his generalship. Henry Sibley never held another command during the Civil War. After the war, Sibley found employment as a general in the Khedive of Egypt's army for a few years. However, by 1873, the Khedive, "fed up with his drunken incompetence," dismissed Sibley from his army. Returning to Fredericksburg, Virginia, the old frontier warrior died there in poverty and obscurity in 1886.[12]

Many of the Union officers and men who fought at Glorieta had subsequent careers as varied as those of their Confederate foes. The Colorado Volunteers, of course, were much nearer home as the New Mexico campaign wound down. One of them, Pvt. Ovando Hollister, who had participated in both the Battle of Apache Canyon and the Battle of Glorieta, rode back to Denver City with his Company F, First Colorado Cavalry. By New Year, 1863, the regiment's scattered companies were reunited in the territorial capital. Two months later, however, Hollister left the service to begin writing his *History of the First Regiment of Colorado Volunteers,* published in limited edition in 1863 and later as *Boldly They Rode.* It was the most valuable of his works, although he went on to write several other books over the following twenty-three years. He later moved to Utah, becoming an honored first citizen of Salt Lake City, where he died in 1892 at the age of fifty-seven.[13]

Hollister's fellow trooper in Company F, Pvt. Ben Ferris, probably had a more typical post–New Mexico experience. After having had the bullet that hit him in the leg removed at the Glorieta field hospital during the battle, then lying in the Kozlowski's Ranch hospital after the fight, Ferris was taken by wagon to a new medical facility established a few miles northwest of Las Vegas, New Mexico, at a hot springs location. The enlisted men's hospital room was crowded, but he fortunately found his captain, Sam Cook—badly wounded at Apache Canyon—recuperating in another room and was invited to share the space. He had been in bed about ten days before he "got out on crutches," he remembered, then "took baths in the natural hot water, and loafed and visited those still confined to their beds." After a month, Ferris rejoined his company and left New Mexico with it during late 1862. During autumn, 1864, the three-year enlistments of the First Colorado volunteer soldiers were up, and Ferris was discharged during November.[14]

He stayed around the Denver City area for a time, engaging in the freight business, then, with several companions, traveled south to Mexico, where he fought in the army of Benito Juarez. Returning to the United States, he bought a herd of cattle in Texas and drove them northward to Missouri. Still later, Ben Ferris operated a saloon, a hotel, and a nursery business, finally settling in Iowa, where he occasionally attended reunions of the Grand Army of the Republic and lived until 1929, when he passed away at the age of ninety.[15]

Undoubtedly the most famous of Colorado's volunteer soldiers was Col. John Chivington. After leaving New Mexico and visiting Washington, D.C., to have his regiment converted to a mounted unit, the colonel of the First Colorado Cavalry took over command of the District of Colorado in addition to his regiment.[16] During 1863 and 1864, the Fighting Parson became heavily involved with territorial politics, allied to Governor John Evans in the attempt to achieve statehood for Colorado. That accomplished, Chivington would seek election to the U.S. House of Representatives. An Indian war or campaign appeared to be the most obvious way to gain the publicity and acclaim that would make not only statehood but also election a reality. On November 29, 1864, Colonel Chivington led a force consisting of part of the First Colorado Cavalry and all of the Third Colorado Cavalry against the peaceful Cheyenne village of Black Kettle, on Sand Creek, not far from Fort Lyon in southeastern Colorado.[17]

The massacre that followed Chivington's surprise attack on the sleeping camp was widely acclaimed as heroic back in Denver but quickly brought outraged responses from Congress and the Federal military, including many of his own First Colorado officers such as Lt. Col. Sam Tappan and Maj. Ed Wynkoop, who had fought at Apache Canyon and Glorieta. A military commission to investigate Chivington's actions was called for February, 1865, but he learned of it and quickly applied to be mustered out of the service. Since he was still colonel of the First Colorado Cavalry, whose enlistments had officially expired, his request was granted, and he was discharged during early January, before criticism of his operations could result in any military or congressional actions against him.[18] Thus, the hero of Glorieta became the villain of Sand Creek.

No villain, however, was John P. Slough. Returning to Colorado during the summer of 1862, after Glorieta, he quickly made use of his political connections in the territory. He traveled to Washington and, on August 25, managed to have himself appointed brigadier general of volunteers. With that new rank, Slough served out the balance of the Civil War as the military governor of Alexandria, Virginia. He served with credit in that administrative position, sitting often on courts-martial and various commissions, then serving as a member of the court that convicted Andersonville Prison commander Henry Wirz and sentenced him to death at the end of the war. He was mustered out of Federal military service during August, 1865. A pallbearer at President Abraham Lincoln's funeral, Slough had political connections that continued into the immediate postwar era.[19]

In 1866, he returned to New Mexico as chief justice of the territory's supreme court. One of John Slough's first interests was proper burial of the Union soldiers killed at Apache Canyon and Glorieta. Most, if not all, remains had been exhumed by military parties and reburied in an enclosed space near Kozlowski's Ranch. There, however, vandals had stolen much of the enclosure and the headboards, and only unmarked mounds remained. In December, 1866, Chief Justice Slough petitioned the New Mexico legislature for action to provide for reburial and protection of the remains. "Gentlemen," he wrote, "this is a rightful subject of legislation. . . . I call upon you to act. . . . I, their late commander solicit it. Your sister Territory, Colorado, will rejoice at favorable action." New Mexico's congressional delegate added his support during the following year, but the legislature did not take any decisive action. The campaign, however, eventually succeeded; these efforts of Slough and others were the genesis of the Santa Fe National Cemetery, to which the Union dead were soon transferred, followed in 1895 by reinterment there of the Confederates who had earlier been buried in Santa Fe.[20]

Slough could not, however, remain aloof from territorial politics. During December, 1867, William L. Rynerson, a former Union officer and member of the legislature, introduced a motion of censure of Slough for alleged unprofessional conduct. Slough was infuriated, and when the two men met in the billiard room of Santa Fe's La Fonda Hotel on December 17, they argued violently, whereupon Rynerson shot the unarmed Slough dead. The killer was later acquitted on a plea of self-defense, and the victor of Glorieta would have no further effect on the future of New Mexico Territory.[21]

Col. Gabriel Paul's military career experienced a meteoric rise after the New Mexico campaign. After serving as Canby's southern district commander in Fort Craig for a month after the Battle of Peralta, Paul was released from duties in the territory during late May, 1862. He returned to the eastern theater of battle and was commissioned brigadier general of volunteers during the following September. Compared to those in New Mexico, his responsibilities now became enormous. He led his brigade of the Army of the Potomac in the Battles of Fredericksburg and Chancellorsville. On July 1, 1863, General Paul again led his brigade into the fierce Battle of Gettysburg. Going into action north of the Railroad Cut west of that town, his men fought near the famed Iron Brigade as Confederate attacks became more and more furious. In the heat of battle, a Rebel minie ball hit him in the head, passing through both eyes. The former commander of Fort Union fell and was borne from the battlefield. Blinded,

Gabriel Paul remained on active duty for the rest of the Civil War and retired in 1865. "Though small in stature . . . great in heart and mighty in valor," the old hero lived another twenty years, dying at the age of seventy-five in 1886.[22]

Edward R. S. Canby's subsequent Civil War service was not nearly as active or spectacular as that of Gabriel Paul. However, even as he was leading the New Mexico troops in their final actions against Sibley, Colonel Canby received word that he had been promoted to brigadier general of volunteers effective March 31, 1862. He reorganized the Department of New Mexico in the wake of the Texans' withdrawal, then turned over its command to his successor, Brig. Gen. James Carleton, on September 18, 1862. Riding out of Fort Union at the head of most of the territory's regular soldiers, who had been ordered east, General Canby reported to Washington. There, he served as assistant adjutant general of the army for almost a year, then commanded Federal troops in New York City during the draft riots that followed the Battle of Gettysburg. In 1864, Canby again went west, this time in command of the Military District of West Mississippi, where he was severely wounded by Confederate guerrillas. Late in the war, as a major general of volunteers, he commanded the Army and Department of the Gulf, attacking the fortifications at Mobile, Alabama, just as the Civil War ended.[23] A capable administrator, Canby was promoted after the war to the rank of brigadier general in the regular army. After reconstruction duty, he and Louisa moved to the Pacific Northwest to command the Department of the Columbia. Although Indian affairs during the 1870s were relatively peaceful in that department, compared to others in the West, a minor disturbance involving the Modoc tribe broke out during 1872 and 1873. General Canby accompanied a peace commission into the lava bed region of northern California to attempt to settle the grievances of the Modocs, and during that peace talk, two of the Indians shot and killed Canby with guns they had hidden. Thus fell the "prudent soldier," the only general officer killed during the Indian Wars. Three days after Edward Canby's murder, on April 14, 1873, Gen. William Sherman announced to the army the death of "one of our most illustrious and most honored comrades." Later eulogy found that "he was great in war and good, and equally so in peace." The "Angel of Santa Fe" died sixteen years later and is buried beside him at Indianapolis, Indiana.[24]

The people of New Mexico did not forget to honor those who had sacrificed their lives to save their territory for the Union. In 1867, they erected in the plaza at Santa Fe an impressive monument that includes the following inscriptions:

> *Erected by the People of New Mexico, through their Legislatures of 1866, '7, '8. May the Union be Perpetual.*
>
> *To the Heroes of the Federal Army who fell at the Battle of Valverde, fought with the Rebels, February 21, 1862.*
>
> *To the Heroes of the Federal Army who fell at the Battles in Canon del Apache and Pigeon's Rancho (La Glorieta), fought with the Rebels, March 28, 1862; and to those who fell at the Battle fought with the Rebels at Peralto, April 15, 1862.*

For the cornerstone ceremony, Chief Justice John P. Slough and other territorial officials extended "In behalf . . . of the grateful people of New Mexico . . . to the soldiers of Colorado Regiments, and to the people of Colorado Territory generally, an invitation to be present and participate in the ceremonies of the occasion."[25]

To that enduring monument has now been added another of perhaps even more meaning. After years of effort by its dedicated members, the Glorieta Battlefield Preservation Society, aided in the final stages by the Conservation Fund of Arlington, Virginia, was successful in 1991 in securing the preservation of the Glorieta Battlefield as part of the national park system, so that the story of those who fought and died there for causes they held dear can be understood by generations to come.[26] That story will show the Battle of Glorieta to have been, indeed, the Gettysburg of the West.

Appendix: Order of Battle

Battle of Apache Canyon (March 26, 1862)

United States Force
(Maj. John M. Chivington)

First Colorado Volunteers—Maj. John M. Chivington
- Co. A—Capt. Edward W. Wynkoop
- Co. D—Capt. Jacob Downing
- Co. E—Capt. Scott J. Anthony
- Co. F—Capt. Samuel H. Cook (Cavalry company)
  - strength—170 infantry, 84 cavalry

Regular Cavalry Squadron—Capt. George W. Howland
- First U.S. Cavalry (detachment)—Capt. R. S. C. Lord
- Third U.S. Cavalry (detachment)—Capt. George W. Howland
- Third U.S. Cavalry, Co. E—Capt. Charles J. Walker
  - strength—150 cavalry

Total U.S.—404

Confederate States Force
(Maj. Charles L. Pyron)

Second Texas Mounted Rifles (detachment)—Maj. Charles L. Pyron
- strength—80

Fifth Texas Mounted Volunteers—Maj. John S. Shropshire

Co. A—Capt. Stephen M. Wells

Co. B—2d Lt. John J. Scott

Co. C—Capt. Denman W. Shannon

Co. D—Capt. Daniel H. Ragsdale

strength—250

Independent Attached Units

Arizona Rangers—2d Lt. William Simmons

Brigands (Co. of Santa Fe Gamblers)—Capt. John G. Phillips

San Elizario Spy Co.—1st Lt. J. R. Parsons

strength—80

Artillery Section—Sgt. Adolphus G. Norman

strength—30

Total C.S.—440

Battle of Glorieta (March 28, 1862)

United States Force
(Col. John P. Slough)

FLANKING COLUMN—MAJ. JOHN M. CHIVINGTON

First Battalion (provisional)—Capt. William H. Lewis

Fifth U.S. Infantry, Co. A—Lt. Barr

Co. G—Lt. Norvell

First Colorado Volunteers, Co. B—Capt. Samuel M. Logan

Independent Co. of Colorado Volunteers—Capt. James H. Ford

New Mexico Volunteers (detachment)—Lt. Col. Manuel Chaves

strength—269 infantry and mounted scouts

Second Battalion (provisional)—Capt. Edward W. Wynkoop

First Colorado Volunteers, Co. A—1st Lt. James R. Shaffer

Co. E—Capt. Scott J. Anthony

Co. H—Capt. George L. Sanborn

strength—219 infantry

Total U.S. (Chivington)—488

MAIN COLUMN—COL. JOHN P. SLOUGH

Field Battalion (provisional)—Lt. Col. Samuel F. Tappan

First Colorado Volunteers, Co. C—Capt. Richard Sopris

Co. D—Capt. Jacob Downing

Co. G—Capt. William F. Wilder

Co. I—1st Lt. Charles Kerber

Co. K—Capt. Samuel H. Robbins

Heavy Battery—Capt. John F. Ritter

Light Battery—1st Lt. Ira W. Claflin

strength—615 infantry and artillery

Cavalry Reserve—Col. John P. Slough

Third U.S. Cavalry (detachment)—Capt. George W. Howland

Third U.S. Cavalry, Co. E—Capt. Charles J. Walker

First Colorado Volunteers, Co. F—1st Lt. George Nelson

strength—185 cavalry

Total U.S. (Slough)—800

Confederate States Force (Lt. Col. William R. Scurry)

Second Texas Mounted Rifles (detachment)—Maj. Charles L. Pyron

strength—80

Fourth Texas Mounted Volunteers—Maj. Henry W. Raguet

Co. B—1st Lt. James B. Holland

Co. C—Capt. George J. Hampton

Co. D—Capt. Charles M. Lesueur

Co. E—Capt. Charles B. Buckholts

Co. F—Capt. James M. Crosson

Co. G—Capt. Julius Giesecke

Co. H—Capt. William L. Alexander

Co. I—Capt. James M. Odell

Co. K—Capt. William W. Foard

strength—600

Fifth Texas Mounted Volunteers—Maj. John S. Shropshire
Co. A—2d Lt. John P. Oakes
Co. B—2d Lt. John J. Scott
Co. C—Capt. Denman W. Shannon
Co. D—Capt. Daniel H. Ragsdale
strength—220

Seventh Texas Mounted Volunteers—Maj. Powhatan Jordan
Co. B—Capt. Gustav Hoffman
Co. F—Capt. James F. Wiggins
Co. H—Capt. Isaac Adair
Co. I—Capt. James W. Gardner
strength—280

Independent Attached Units
Arizona Rangers— 2d Lt. William Simmons
Brigands (Co. of Santa Fe Gamblers)—Capt. John G. Phillips
San Elizario Spy Co.—1st Lt. J. R. Parsons
strength—60

Artillery Battery—2d Lt. James Bradford
strength—45

Total C.S.—1,285

Note: Due to factors discussed in the text and notes, many of these figures cannot be precisely determined, especially for the Confederates. They are conservatively estimated, based on existing reports, hospital records, casualties, etc.

Notes

Chapter One. Confederate Invasion

1. Characterization of the Battle of Glorieta as the "Gettysburg of the West" may at first glance seem to exaggerate its importance. Certainly, the New Mexico battle was small in scope when compared to the monumental eastern battles, Gettysburg included, but both were part of Confederate campaigns striking far into Federal territory, with lengthy and tenuous logistical trails, and with specific goals. During the Gettysburg campaign, General Robert E. Lee sought, among other goals, to enhance the Confederacy's chances for foreign recognition as an independent nation. General Henry H. Sibley's goals were only slightly less grand, even if much less likely of accomplishment. He sought conquest of the entire American Southwest and central Rocky Mountain regions, which would bring into the Confederate treasury the wealth of the gold and silver mines of the West, along with such other advantages as the potentially best transcontinental railroad route and room in which the institution of slavery could expand westward.

   Because of its remoteness and the relatively small numbers of people involved, some historians of the Civil War in the Far West tend to discount the importance of the campaign and its key battle. At the time, Texas newspapers tended to do so. That was understandable since other, much larger conflicts, such as the Battle of Shiloh, took place during the same time frame and involved larger numbers of Texan soldiers, and since the New Mexico campaign was a dismal failure for Confederates—as was Gettysburg. The newspapers throughout New Mexico and Colorado, however, tended to emphasize the importance of defeat of the Texans at Glorieta as having saved the West for the Union. Use of the term "Gettysburg of the West," however, seems appropriate, given the importance of both battles as high-water marks of the Confederacy in the east and west.

2. For studies of these overland routes and their importance, see Wayne R. Austerman, *Sharps Rifles and Spanish Mules: The San Antonio–El Paso Mail,*

1851–1881; W. Turrentine Jackson, *Wagon Roads West;* Gabrielle G. Palmer, comp., *El Camino Real de Tierra Adentro;* and Marc Simmons, *Following the Santa Fe Trail.* The Rio Grande and the Pecos rivers, both flowing from north to south through central and eastern New Mexico, respectively, are the only watercourses that could have supported a military expedition through the territory during the 1860s.

3. For a study of native New Mexican attitudes and service, see Darlis A. Miller, "Hispanos and the Civil War in New Mexico: A Reconsideration," *New Mexico Historical* Review 54 (April, 1979): 105–23.
4. Donald W. Frazier, *Blood and Treasure: Confederate Empire in the Southwest,* pp. 101–16. This excellently researched and written recent work provides an overview of the New Mexico campaign and individual Confederate participants. It effectively supersedes the pioneering work done by Martin H. Hall in *Sibley's New Mexico Campaign.* However, the late Dr. Hall's study of the Sibley Brigade itself, *The Confederate Army of New Mexico,* remains an indispensable source of detailed background information on the Texan participants. See also L. Boyd Finch, *Confederate Pathway to the Pacific: Major Sherod Hunter and Arizona Territory, C.S.A.*
5. Ibid., pp. 16–18, 29–30; Don E. Alberts, *Rebels on the Rio Grande: The Civil War Journal of A. B. Peticolas,* p. 10. The last-mentioned work includes the meticulous observations of a young Victoria, Texas, lawyer who served as fifth sergeant of the Fourth Texas Mounted Volunteer regiment throughout the New Mexico campaign.
6. Frazier, *Blood and Treasure,* pp. 48, 57–70; Alberts, *Rebels on the Rio Grande,* p.12. For an excellent treatment of Baylor's activities within southern New Mexico, see Jerry D. Thompson, *Colonel John Robert Baylor: Texas Indian Fighter and Confederate Soldier.* See also James Cooper McKee, *Narrative of the Surrender of U.S. Forces at Fort Fillmore, New Mexico, in July, A.D., 1861.* Major McKee was the Federal surgeon at that post during Baylor's incursion into southern New Mexico.
7. *The War of the Rebellion: A Compilation of the Official Records of the Union and Confederate Armies,* 128 vols., Series I, IV:4–7, 16–21. Hereafter cited as *O.R.,* with all citations to Series I.
8. Hall, *Confederate Army of New Mexico,* pp. 13–14; Thompson, *Henry Hopkins Sibley: Confederate General of the West,* pp. 215–17.
9. Thompson, *Sibley,* pp. 217–18; Frazier, *Blood and Treasure,* pp. 75–76.
10. Trevanion T. Teel, "Sibley's New Mexican Campaign: Its Objects and the Causes of its Failure," *Battles and Leaders of the Civil War,* 4 vols., 2:700.
11. Alberts, *Rebels on the Rio Grande,* pp. 16–17.
12. Thelma S. Guild and Harvey L. Carter, *Kit Carson: A Pattern for Heroes,* p. 218.
13. Darlis A. Miller, "Los Pinos, New Mexico: Civil War Post on the Rio Grande," *New Mexico Historical Review 62* (January, 1987), pp. 1–13, 23–26.
14. Thompson, *Sibley,* pp. 1–32, 49–107, passim.
15. Teel, "Sibley's New Mexican Campaign," p. 700; Alberts, *Rebels on the Rio*

Grande, p. 118; David B. Gracy, II, ed., "New Mexico Campaign Letters of Frank Starr, 1861–1862," *Texas Military History* 4 (Fall,1964), p. 182; Jerry D. Thompson, *Westward the Texans: The Civil War Journal of Private William Randolph Howell,* p. 107. Starr was first sergeant of Co. H, Fourth Texas Mounted Volunteers, while Howell was a member of Co. C, Fifth Texas Mounted Volunteers.

16. Frazier, *Blood and Treasure,* pp. 75–76, 83–90; Hall, *Confederate Army of New Mexico,* pp. 15, 68, 75, 81–82; Alberts, *Rebels on the Rio Grande,* pp. 17–18. A brief word on Civil War military organization may be in order. Army structure was the same in the North and the South. The smallest infantry unit was a company, composed of one hundred enlisted men and three officers, commanded by a captain. These tended to be men recruited from the same town or county or similar geographical region. They were essentially neighbors, often relatives, and elected their company officers from prominent citizens of their locality. Ten companies formed a regiment, the basic unit of identification. Regiments tended to be formed from neighboring companies, and were authorized by each state or territorial governor, who appointed a colonel as regimental commander, with a lieutenant colonel and major as field officers. Each regiment also had a staff organization with officers and noncommissioned officers in charge of quartermaster, commissary, and medical departments. A full-strength regiment had a strength of just over one thousand men. A battalion was an informal grouping of several companies to form a field force for a specific purpose. It could be formed or dissolved at will. Three regiments (sometimes more later in the war) formed a brigade, the command of a brigadier general. Sibley's Brigade was the largest unit organized for the New Mexico campaign, but to the east, larger units were common. Two or three brigades formed a division, commanded by a major general, while three divisions were grouped together as a corps, commanded by a major or lieutenant general. Any number of corps could then be included in the highest level of organization, an army. These were official organizational strengths and commands. In practice, there was much change to these theoretical organizations and rank levels due to battlefield attrition, enlistment expiration, and other factors.

    Cavalry organization was similar, with several companies often being grouped into an informal squadron, similar to an infantry battalion. Artillery, however, was different. The basic unit was a battery of four to eight cannons, commanded by a captain and equivalent to an infantry company. Batteries were subdivided into sections, each with two to four pieces of artillery.

17. Frazier, *Blood and Treasure,* pp. 78–80, 97; Hall, *Confederate Army of New Mexico,* pp. 51–54, 133–34, 217–18. Prof. Frazier's analysis of the characters and abilities of these officers is particularly valuable.

18. *O.R.,* IV:133; Theophilus Noel, *A Campaign from Santa Fe to the Mississippi: Being a History of the Old Sibley Brigade,* p. 16; Oscar Haas, trans., "The Diary of Julius Giesecke, 1861–62," *Texas Military History* 3 (Winter, 1963),

entry for December 23, 1861. Noel served as a private in Co. A and Giesecke as second lieutenant, then captain, of Co. G, Fourth Texas Mounted Volunteers. Noel's work must be used with great care, since he did not personally participate in the actions in northern New Mexico and repeated the stories of those actions later related to him by companions who did participate.

19. *O.R.*, IV:89, 157–58; Haas, "Giesecke Diary," entries for December 17–27, 1861; Alberts, *Rebels on the Rio Grande*, pp. 29–31.

20. Thompson, *Westward the Texans*, p. 85; Hall, *Confederate Army of New Mexico*, pp. 23–25; William A. Faulkner, ed., "With Sibley in New Mexico: The Journal of William Henry Smith," *West Texas Historical Association Yearbook 27* (October, 1951), p. 129. Smith was a private in Co. I, Fifth Texas Mounted Volunteers.

21. Thompson, *Sibley*, p. 243; Frazier, *Blood and Treasure*, pp. 147–56; Alberts, *Rebels on the Rio Grande*, pp. 33–40. For an excellent and comprehensive study of the role of Fort Union in the Southwest, and its importance during the Civil War, see Leo E. Oliva, *Fort Union and the Frontier Army in the Southwest*.

22. Max L. Heyman, Jr., *Prudent Soldier: A Biography of Major General E. R. S. Canby, 1817–1873*, pp. 64, 137–44; Alberts, *Rebels on the Rio Grande*, p. 120.

23. *O.R.*, IV:78–80; Joseph M. Bell, "The Campaign of New Mexico, 1862," *War Papers Read before the Commandery of the State of Wisconsin, Military Order of the Loyal Legion of the United States*, 1:51; Nolie Mumey, ed., *Bloody Trails along the Rio Grande: A Day-by-Day Diary of Alonzo Ferdinand Ickis*, entry for February 15, 1862. Bell was a first lieutenant in the Third U.S. Cavalry, while Ickis was a private in Dodd's Independent Company of Colorado Volunteers.

24. Alvin M. Josephy, Jr., *The Civil War in the American West*, p. 76. This fine, extensive work provides an overall study of the Civil War in all parts of the West, putting the New Mexico campaign into regional context.

25. Ibid.; *O.R.*, IV:82, IX:630; Bell, "The Campaign of New Mexico," pp. 52–54; Josephy, *Civil War in the American West*, p.61; William Clarke Whitford, *Colorado Volunteers in the Civil War: The New Mexico Campaign in 1862*, pp. 44, 75.

26. For a thorough history of Fort Craig and pre- and post-Civil War operations of its garrison, see Marion C. Grinstead, *Life and Death of a Frontier Fort: Fort Craig, New Mexico, 1854–1885*.

27. Frazier, *Blood and Treasure*, pp. 157–82; Alberts, *Rebels on the Rio Grande*, pp. 41–52; Mumey, *Bloody Trails*, entry for February 21, 1862; Bell, "The Campaign of New Mexico," pp. 59–66; Marion C. Grinstead, *Destiny at Valverde: The Life and Death of Alexander McRae*, pp. 31–37.

28. Alberts, *Rebels on the Rio Grande, pp. 52–63; Thompson, Westward the Texans*, pp. 89–93; Giesecke Diary, entry for March 7, 1862; Dr. Harold J. Hunter, "Civil War Diary" (manuscript), entries for February 25–27, 1862. Hereafter cited as Hunter Diary. Dr. Hunter served as assistant surgeon of the Seventh Texas Mounted Volunteers and was left behind in charge of the Socorro hospital.

29. *O.R.*, IX:528–29; Smith Journal, p. 137; William Lott Davidson, "Reminiscences of the Old Brigade—on the March—in the Tent—in the Field—as Witnessed by the Writers during the Rebellion," February 23, 1888. This is a continuous series of articles in *Overton (Texas) Sharp-Shooter* from October, 1887, to March, 1889. Davidson was a private (and sometimes sergeant) in Company A, Fifth Texas Mounted Volunteers. At this short-lived newspaper, he was the primary author of these articles, although he collaborated with Capt. Charles C. Lynn and Lt. Philip Fulcrod, both Sibley Brigade veterans, in some issues. This invaluable source of information on the New Mexico campaign was located by Prof. Don Frazier of Abilene, Texas, and generously shared with the author.
30. Alberts, *Rebels on the Rio Grande*, pp. 67–68; Hall, *Confederate Army of New Mexico*, p. 31.
31. Mary J. Straw, *Loretto: The Sisters and Their Santa Fe Chapel*, pp. 35–36.
32. Alberts, *Rebels on the Rio Grande*, pp. 59–63.
33. Ibid., pp. 61–63; Thompson, *Westward the Texans*, p. 93.
34. *O.R.*, IX:511; Frazier, *Blood and Treasure*, p. 198.
35. Frazier, *Blood and Treasure*, p. 199.
36. Alberts, *Rebels on the Rio Grande*, pp. 66–67. This camp was located on what later became the grounds of my residence in Tijeras Canyon, near the village of Carnuel, and could be identified from artifact evidence.
37. Alberts, *Rebels on the Rio Grande*, p. 66; Ebenezer Hanna, "The Journal of Ebenezer Hanna" (manuscript), Archives Division, Texas State Library, Austin, entry for March 8, 1862. Hereafter cited as Hanna Journal. "Abe" Hanna was a private in Company C of the Fourth Texas Mounted Volunteers.
38. Hanna Journal, entry for March 9, 1862; Alberts *Rebels on the Rio Grande*, pp. 68–69. This camp was located on the grounds of the present-day A. Montoya Elementary School and the nearby post office. I also located this site from artifact evidence of the extensive camp.
39. Hanna Journal, entries for March 13–19, 1862; Alberts, *Rebels on the Rio Grande*, pp. 69–70; Davidson, "Reminiscences of the Old Brigade," February 16, 1888.
40. Thompson, *Westward the Texans*, pp. 93, 95; Hanna Journal, entries for March 14–20, 1862; Alberts, *Rebels on the Rio Grande*, pp. 69–72; Davidson, "Reminiscences of the Old Brigade," February 16, 1888; Connie Sue Ragan O'Donnel, comp., "The Diary of Robert Thomas Williams: Marches, Skirmishes, and Battles of the Fourth Regiment, Texas Militia Volunteers: October 1861 to November 1865," entries for March 12–21, 1862. Williams was a private in Co. E, Fourth Texas Mounted Volunteers.
41. Alberts, *Rebels on the Rio Grande*, pp. 69–72.
42. Davidson, "Reminiscences of the Old Brigade," February 16, 1888; Hanna Journal, entry for March 10, 1862; Faulkner, "Smith Journal," p. 137.
43. *O.R.*, IX:509; Frazier, *Blood and Treasure*, p. 201; Hanna Journal, entries for March 21–23, 1862; Alberts, *Rebels on the Rio Grande*, pp. 72–73.

44. Faulkner, "Smith Journal," p. 135; Hanna Journal, entry for March 24, 1862; Alberts, *Rebels on the Rio Grande,* p. 73.

45. Hanna Journal, entry for March 25, 1862; Giesecke Diary, entry for March 25, 1862; Alberts, *Rebels on the Rio Grande,* pp. 74–75.

46. Alberts, *Rebels on the Rio Grande,* p. 75.

47. Hall, *Confederate Army of New Mexico,* p. 346; Davidson, "Reminiscences of the Old Brigade," February 23, 1888.

48. *O.R.,* IX:509; Frazier, *Blood and Treasure,* pp. 199–200.

49. Davidson, "Reminiscences of the Old Brigade," February 23, 1888; Alberts, *Rebels on the Rio Grande,* p. 75. Unfortunately for historians of this campaign, Major Pyron's reports of his operations after leaving Albuquerque are not in the *Official Records* and have never been located. Either he never wrote any such reports or we have not been diligent enough to uncover them, or perhaps they were lost in the confusion of subsequent events. As a result, some supposition inevitably arises in analyzing Pyron's motives and movements. In turn, that supposition has to be supported by such information as the personal accounts of other participants in his operations, the location and careful analysis of artifact evidence from the sites of his camp and subsequent fight, and the results of personal examination of the areas. This may not result in discovery of every aspect of Pyron's operations, but it is the closest approximation to historical accuracy currently possible.

50. Marc Simmons, "New Light on Johnson's Ranch," *Trail Dust* (October 7, 1992), p. 1.

51. *O.R.,* IX:541–42; Frazier, *Blood and Treasure,* p. 206; Alberts, *Rebels on the Rio Grande,* p. 76.

Chapter Two. The Union Arms

1. Whitford, *Colorado Volunteers,* pp. 43–44.
2. Ibid., p. 44; Mumey, *Bloody Trails,* entry for February 21, 1862.
3. Whitford, *Colorado Volunteers,* p. 44; Ellen Williams, *Three Years and a Half in the Army: or, History of the Second Colorados,* p. 4.
4. For Governor Gilpin's wartime activities, see Thomas L. Karnes, *William Gilpin: Western Nationalist.*
5. Whitford, *Colorado Volunteers,* p. 47.
6. Ibid., p. 48.
7. Ovando J. Hollister, *Boldly They Rode: A History of the First Colorado Regiment of Volunteers,* p. 2; Eugene H. Mallory, comp., "Ben Franklin Ferris' Memoir," (manuscript, no pg.), entries for August, 1861. Hereafter cited as Ferris Memoir. A most valuable and hitherto unpublished source, this memoir was generously shared by Mr. Mallory of Van Nuys, California, great-great-grandson of the Civil War soldier. After many adventures in the goldfields of Colorado, Ferris served as a private in Co. F, First Colorado Volunteers. Private Hollister served in the same company and contributed the best single first-hand account of the First Colorado's participation in the New Mexico campaign.

8. Hollister, *Boldly They Rode,* pp. 49–50.
9. John M. Chivington, "The First Colorado Regiment," *New Mexico Historical Review* 33 (April, 1958), pp. 144–45; Reginald S. Craig, *The Fighting Parson: The Biography of Colonel John M. Chivington,* pp. 23–36. Chivington's memoir was written in 1884, twenty-two years after the events he described. His memory was obviously faulty in several important instances, and self-service may have played a part; nevertheless, his account of the regiment's and his own experiences in New Mexico is a valuable primary source. Union sources are much less numerous for this far western campaign than are Confederate sources. That seems to support the old military history adage that the winners forget and go about their business, while the losers spend the rest of their lives remembering and explaining their, or their ancestors', exploits, motives, and failures. Craig's biography of Chivington is quite dated. His narrative of the New Mexico campaign is not too inaccurate, but his single-minded defense of Chivington during the later period of the Sand Creek massacre and subsequent military and congressional investigations tends to devalue the work to the level of simple propaganda.
10. Hollister, *Boldly They Rode,* preface, pp. 20–25, 31–43.
11. Mallory, "Ferris Memoir," entries for August, 1861; Hollister, *Boldly They Rode,* pp. 3–6.
12. Mallory, "Ferris Memoir," entries for September–December, 1861, and January, 1862; Hollister, *Boldly They Rode,* pp. 34–36; Whitford, *Colorado Volunteers,* p. 50.
13. Hollister, *Boldly They Rode,* preface, pp. 39–43. Although perhaps made more spectacular by the frontier experience, these often humorous and sometimes tragic activities were fairly typical of idle volunteer soldiers during the Civil War. Such behavior tended to moderate once a degree of training and discipline was instilled, especially so after the men experienced active operations and combat.
14. *O.R.,* IX:630; Chivington, "The First Colorado Regiment," p. 146.
15. *O.R.,* IX:631–32; Whitford, *Colorado Volunteers,* pp. 75–76; Chivington, "The First Colorado Regiment," pp. 145–46.
16. Hollister, *Boldly They Rode,* pp. 46–47; Mallory, "Ferris Memoir," entries for February and March, 1862.
17. Whitford, *Colorado Volunteers,* p. 77; Hollister, *Boldly They Rode,* pp. 47–48.
18. *O.R.,* IX:633–40; Whitford, *Colorado Volunteers,* p. 77; Chivington, "The First Colorado Regiment," p. 147.
19. Hollister, *Boldly They Rode,* pp. 48–49; Chivington, "The First Colorado Regiment," p. 147; Mallory, "Ferris Memoir," entries for March, 1862; Donald Gaither, "The Pet Lambs at Glorieta Pass," *Civil War Times Illustrated* 15 (November, 1976), pp. 31–32. This article includes a letter of Charles Gardiner to his mother, May 3, 1862, shortly after his participation in the Battle of Glorieta. Gardiner was a private in Co. A, First Colorado Volunteers.
20. Hollister, *Boldly They Rode,* pp. 49–51.
21. Ibid., pp. 51–52.

22. Ibid., p. 52.

23. Ibid.; Mallory, "Ferris Memoir," entries for March, 1862; Gaither, "Pet Lambs," p. 32.

24. For Co. F, this meant being equipped as were the regular cavalry units in New Mexico. They drew the tight-fitting trousers and short "shell jacket," complete with the yellow piping of that branch of service. Their arms were the short, handy Sharps carbines then being issued to mounted troopers. Although single-shot weapons, they were breechloaders of .52-caliber, highly reliable and effective for the dismounted service the company would soon see. The horsemen also each drew one .44-caliber Colt or Remington pistol and, apparently, one of the heavy Model 1840 Dragoon Sabers, although there is no positive indication that these were either carried or used in action. The other nine volunteer companies were issued the uniforms of the infantry regulars, dark blue frock or fatigue coats, with light blue trousers and black leather cartridge box, cap box, and bayonet scabbard. Their arms were the standard infantry "Springfield Rifled-Musket" used throughout the Civil War. An ungainly but highly reliable and accurate single-shot muzzleloader of .58-caliber, it was a weapon with which the frontier soldier felt comfortable. Officers could draw pistols in the event they did not already have their own personal sidearms. On the Glorieta battlefield, associates and I located many bullets from these types of arms fired into Texan positions, thus confirming this issue of weapons and helping to identify unit positions on an otherwise often confused site. See Don E. Alberts, "Civil War Armaments and Accoutrements Used at the Pigeon's Ranch/Glorieta Battlefield Site," August, 1986. This study, for the Museum of New Mexico's Laboratory of Anthropology, is largely based on my extensive experience locating and identifying artifact evidence on the Glorieta and Apache Canyon battlefields.

25. Hollister, *Boldly They Rode,* pp. 55–56; Mallory, "Ferris Memoir," entries for March, 1862.

26. Hollister, *Boldly They Rode,* pp. 53–55; General Orders No. 25, April 4, 1862, Department of New Mexico (DNM), Record Group (RG) 393, National Archives (NA); Stanley C. Agnew, *Garrisons of the Regular U.S. Army: New Mexico, 1846–1899,* pp. 66–67; James E. Farmer, "J. E. Farmer Diary," p. 21, Adjutant General Files, State Records Center, Santa Fe. Hereafter cited as Farmer Diary. Farmer was a teenage civilian who had accompanied the Seventh U.S. Infantry as part of the regiment was stationed at Fort Union after the evacuation of Fort Marcy in Santa Fe. He attached himself to Capt. Lewis's battalion of the Federal field column. The diary, actually a memoir, was written in Farmer's old age and includes numerous errors.

27. Gaither, "Pet Lambs," p. 32.

28. *O.R.*, IX:645–46; Special Orders No. 210, December 9, 1861, DNM, RG 393, NA.

29. *O.R.*, IX:651–52.

30. Ibid., IX:652–53; Frazier, *Blood and Treasure,* p. 204.

31. *O.R.*, IX:533–34.
32. Ibid., IX:648–50, 653.
33. Ibid., IX:653–54.
34. Ibid., IX:645–46.
35. Ibid., IX:533–34; Hall, *Sibley's New Mexico Campaign*, pp. 129–31. These regular cavalrymen were hardened and experienced veterans. The First and Third Cavalry had long been a major component of the garrison troops of New Mexico Territory. Both had been renamed soon after the Civil War began, the First Dragoons regiment becoming the First Cavalry and the famous old Regiment of Mounted Riflemen being designated as the Third Cavalry, much to their dissatisfaction. Canby had sent Howland and Lord northward around the Confederates a week after the Battle of Valverde to observe the movements of the enemy as well as to bolster the defenses of Fort Union. These regular cavalrymen tended to look with scorn on the volunteer Colorado horsemen of Company F. In return, the Pet Lambs considered the regulars to be "the scum of the earth." Subsequent official reports and unofficial writings must be considered in the light of that mutual antipathy. Hollister, for example, an otherwise quite reliable source, has nothing good to say for the "no account" regulars. Hollister, *Boldly They Rode*, p. 69.
36. *O.R.*, IX:533–34; Special Orders No.4, March 9, and Special Orders No. 10, March 12, 1862, DNM, RG 393, NA; Alberts, "Civil War Armaments," pp. 4–6; interview with Bruce Krohn of Los Lunas, New Mexico, subj: artillery carriages, October 26, 1997. Both the 6-pounder guns and the 12-pounder field howitzers were large, heavy pieces that were pulled by a horse or mule team. Their designations reflected the weight of a solid iron ball that matched the inside diameter, or caliber, of the cannon barrels. The guns were of a smaller caliber, and therefore shot a lighter round, but at a flatter trajectory and longer range than the field howitzers. The latter were short-barreled bronze pieces intended to throw a more effective round over short distances, a characteristic particularly useful in the upcoming combat. Both types of cannons used the same large artillery carriage already standardized within the U.S. Army. The individual piece was towed by a two-wheeled ammunition limber, to the shaft of which the team was harnessed. Standard wheeled caissons, with additional ammunition chests, were not available within the Department of New Mexico, so for the Glorieta expedition, spare ammunition was carried in separate wagons. The heavy pieces could easily travel along the well-maintained roads but could only be used on soft or broken terrain with great exertion on the part of men and animals.

    The 12-pounder mountain howitzers were small, light bronze pieces that could be disassembled for packing on two mules or pulled on a wheeled carriage. By the Civil War, a rugged "prairie carriage" had been designed for the howitzers. Essentially a small-scale version of the carriage used by larger field pieces, each was pulled by a similarly scaled-down ammunition limber drawn by a two-horse team. Since the field column expected to travel along the Santa Fe Trail, and possibly because pack mules may have been unavailable, Claflin's mountain howitzers were pulled on their prairie carriages rather than carried. They were of short range, but they were quite easily maneuvered over rough terrain and were particularly effective at Glorieta.

37. *O.R.*, VIII:633–35, IX:627, 629–30, 637–45.
38. Ibid., IX:650–51.
39. Ibid., IX:654–55.
40. Ibid., IX:655.
41. Ibid., IX:652–55.
42. Mallory, "Ferris Memoir," entry for March, 22, 1862; Hollister, *Boldly They Rode,* pp. 55–56.
43. Hollister, *Boldly They Rode,* pp. 56–58.
44. Report of Capt. H. M. Enos, April 5, 1862, Quartermaster General, Consolidated File, RG 92, NA. This file also contains Enos's initial report written soon after the Battle of Glorieta, on March 31. Both are hereafter cited as Enos Report, with the appropriate date. Captain McFerran's endorsement of Enos's first report is also in this file and is hereafter cited as McFerran Endorsement. I located this valuable source in 1985, but the material has not been previously published.
45. Special Orders No.1, March 8, and Special Orders No.2, March 9, 1862, DNM, RG 393, NA; Enos Report, April 5, 1862, RG 92, NA.
46. Letter, John D. Miller to Father, April 3, 1862, published in the Ithaca (New York) *Chronicle* and in the Pueblo (Colorado) *Chieftan,* n.d., p. 1. Original in the Arrott Collection, New Mexico Highlands University, Las Vegas, New Mexico. Hereafter cited as Miller Letter. Miller served as a private in Company F, First Colorado Volunteers. This account, written soon after the Battle of Glorieta, is generally quite accurate, especially regarding times and distances.
47. Ibid.; Hollister, *Boldly They Rode,* p. 58.
48. Enos Report, April 5, 1862, RG 92, NA.
49. Ibid.
50. Miller Letter, p. 1.
51. Mallory, "Ferris Memoir," entry for March 25, 1862; Hollister, *Boldly They Rode,* pp. 58–59.
52. *O.R.*, IX:530–31; Mallory, "Ferris Memoir," entry for March 25, 1862.
53. *O.R.*, IX:530–31, Miller Letter, p. 1.

Chapter Three. Apache Canyon

1. Jackson, *Wagon Roads West,* pp. 112–13; Mallory, "Ferris Memoir," entries for March 26, 1862.
2. Santa Fe Planning Associates, *Pigeon's Ranch Feasibility Study,* pp. 11–13.
3. Hollister, *Boldly They Rode,* p. 59; Hall, *Confederate Army of New Mexico,* pp. 373–76; Miller Letter, pp. 1–2.
4. Miller Letter, p. 2.
5. Ibid.

6. Ibid.; Mallory, "Ferris Memoir," entries for March 26, 1862; Hollister, *Boldly They Rode,* p. 59.
7. Mallory, "Ferris Memoir," entries for March 26, 1862.
8. Ibid.; *O.R.,* IX:530–31.
9. Miller Letter, p. 2; Hollister, *Boldly They Rode,* p. 61.
10. Miller Letter, p. 2; Hollister, *Boldly They Rode,* p. 61.
11. Hollister, *Boldly They Rode,* p. 59; Davidson, "Reminiscences of the Old Brigade," February 23, 1888.
12. Hall, *Confederate Army of New Mexico,* pp. 138–68, 296–312.
13. Ibid., pp. 345–74. At Apache Canyon and Glorieta, the San Elizario Spy Company was probably led by 1st Lt. J. R. Parsons, while 2d Lt. William Simmons likely commanded the Arizona Rangers. The records provide little information on the participation of these companies.
14. Davidson, "Reminiscences of the Old Brigade," February 23, 1888; Hall, *Confederate Army of New Mexico,* pp. 146–47, 212–13. It is not possible to account rigorously for individual cannon used by either side during this campaign, since individual serial or muzzle numbers were not required to be included on periodic post, ordnance, or battery returns until later in the Civil War. As a result, vague descriptions were often used by reporting officers, sometimes with no differentation whatever as to whether the pieces were guns, field howitzers, or mountain howitzers. That the two guns accompanying Pyron were 6-pounders, however, was not only clearly described by participants but was demonstrated by artifact evidence on the Apache Canyon battlefield. There, all artillery projectile fragments were from Confederate cannon since the Federal force had none on the field. I found many such fragments of exploded shell and case shot rounds, all from 6-pounder guns, none of 12-pounder caliber.
15. Hall, *Sibley's New Mexico Campaign,* p. 131; Hall, *Confederate Army of New Mexico,* pp. 32, 311–12.
16. A word about artifact evidence appears appropriate. Such evidence, collected almost entirely through surface searches and metal detection, plays a major part in my analysis and interpretation of the battles at Apache Canyon and Glorieta. That is necessarily so since the written data is so sparse. Union and Confederate reports of these actions, collected in the *Official Records,* provide only brief narratives and almost no topographical or geographical information. However, actual positions of artillery batteries and battle lines can be located accurately from artifacts; I and others have been working at this since 1976. Artillery positions, for instance, were identified by dropped and fired friction primers and primer components used to fire each round from the cannons. Remnants of the iron strapping used to assemble each artillery round to its wooden sabot, or base, indicated the actual direction of fire from the identified positions. Similarly, musket, pistol, and shotgun projectiles were located, both as dropped ammunition and as a result of firing into opposing lines. An extensive knowledge of ordnance, accoutrements, and other equipment used by the frontier Civil War forces in New Mexico is

a prerequisite for proper use of this artifact evidence. Most of these useful artifacts are subsequently available for battlefield or muesem display.

Use of many of these same sites by Santa Fe Trail travelers before and after the Civil War battles dictates the need for careful and conservative interpretation of this evidence. The task was further complicated by the "salting" of both battlefields with phony artifacts, either imported from other Civil War sites or manufactured, during the 1960s and 1970s, by a notorious New Mexico confidence man. With experience, one can discriminate between such bogus items and the genuine artifacts, but much care is required in doing so. Details of artifact discovery and interpretation on the main battlefield by myself and others are described in my 1986 study for the Museum of New Mexico, "Civil War Armaments and Accoutrements Used at the Pigeon's Ranch/Glorieta Battlefield Site," previously cited. Similar extensive use of metal detecting and artifact evidence on the Mexican War battlefield at Palo Alto, Texas, has recently been successfully undertaken by the National Park Service and is detailed in Charles M. Haecker, "Guns of Palo Alto," *Archaeology* (May–June, 1996):49–53, and in his *A Thunder of Cannon: Archeology of the Mexican-American War Battlefield of Palo Alto,* pp. 4–5, 95–149.

17. Several of the Sibley Brigade officers and a few enlisted men brought their slaves with them as personal servants. Among them, Col. Tom Green, who owned ten slaves, and Capt. Willis Lang, who led the famous lancer charge at Valverde and owned seventy-four slaves back in Texas, brought at least one apiece to assist them during the campaign. Besides Major Shropshire, 1st Lt. Thomas G. Wright, 2nd Lt. John P. Oakes, and 5th Sgt. James Carson, all of Co. A, Fifth Texas Mounted Volunteers, were accompanied by their black servants throughout this campaign. In Co. C, Fourth Texas Mounted Volunteers, Pvt. John Wafford's father, from Victoria, Texas, sent one of his slaves to serve his son in New Mexico (Frazier, *Blood and Treasure,* p. 92).

Shropshire's servant was named Bob, and he often recounted Bob's adventures and shortcomings to his wife back home. At an early date, he commented that "Bob is improving and will soon get to be a very efficient servant." Among other duties, the slave drove a personal wagon carrying officers' belongings, and John Shropshire observed that "Bob is a great Negro, a perfect scamp. . . . When we bought our wagons he asked me if I was going to have a Mexican to drive us. It never occuring to him that he was a suitable person to perform that feat." The officer also noted that "Bob sends his love to all the gals" (Shropshire to Carrie, September 5, November 12, and November 14, 1861. "John Samuel Shropshire Letters," Shropshire-Upton Confederate Museum, Columbus, Texas. Copies in author's collection, courtesy of Mildred Kemper of Houston).

Lieutenant Oakes's servant Mac was not in the Johnson's Ranch camp, since Oakes was temporarily on detached duty away from his company. Although we know less about Mac than about Bob, both later participated in the Battle of Glorieta (Davidson, "Reminiscences of the Old Brigade," December 15, 1887, and February 23, 1888; Interview, author with John Oakes of Albuquerque, New Mexico, December 5, 1996). See also Martin H. Hall, "Negroes with Confederate Troops in West Texas and New Mexico," *Password* 13 (Spring, 1968):11–12.

18. Davidson, "Reminiscences of the Old Brigade," February 23, 1888.
19. Ibid.
20. Ibid.
21. *O.R.*, IX:530–32; Hollister, *Boldly They Rode*, p. 61.
22. Davidson, "Reminiscences of the Old Brigade," February 23, 1888; Hollister, *Boldly They Rode*, p.167. In Hollister's history of the First Colorado Volunteers is included a letter supposedly written to "My Dear Wife" by one of Pyron's Confederates who participated in and was captured at the Battle of Apache Canyon. It is, however, highly suspicious. The letter has the ring of authenticity and is often used as an important source of detail on the Texan operations during that skirmish, naturally so since there are so few other primary sources by Confederate participants. Upon careful scrutiny, however, the letter shows a pattern of errors and bragadoccio, which indicate that it may have been created either by Hollister or by some other Colorado Volunteer after the New Mexico campaign. The letter appears to be accurate in those details that a Federal participant would know or learn and inaccurate in those instances where only a Confederate participant would have firsthand knowledge, e.g., troop units and movements before the encounter. Neither the Rebel author, George M. Brown, nor any other Texans mentioned by him, appear on the muster rolls of Sibley's brigade. Those Union participants mentioned, by contrast, are on the rolls of the First Colorado. The suspicion of creative authorship is further reinforced by lavish praise of the Pike's Peakers' daring heroism and invincibility. I believe it to be a forgery, although it would seem to be more trouble than the propaganda would be worth. If so, the letter is still of value to the historian, since it would accurately reflect the observations and activities of Hollister or whoever else created it, indicating actual events even if displayed from an imaginary opponent's viewpoint. Whenever I have cited the "Brown" material, I have done so in that context. See Thompson, *Westward the Texans*, p. 29, and Hall, *Sibley's New Mexico Campaign*, p. 131, for those authors' interpretations of this material.
23. Davidson, "Reminiscences of the Old Brigade," February 23 and March 8, 1888.
24. *O.R.*, IX:530–32; Chivington, "The First Colorado Regiment," pp. 148–49.
25. Hollister, *Boldly They Rode*, pp. 61–62; Mallory, "Ferris Memoir," entries for March 26, 1862; Miller Letter, p. 2.
26. Miller Letter, pp. 2–3; Hollister, *Boldly They Rode*, p. 62.
27. Miller Letter, pp. 2–3; Hollister, *Boldly They Rode*, p. 62.
28. *O.R.*, IX:531–32; Miller Letter, p. 3; Mallory, "Ferris Memoir," entries for March 26, 1862.
29. Davidson, "Reminiscences of the Old Brigade," February 23, 1888; Hollister, *Boldly They Rode*, p. 167.

30. *O.R.*, IX:530–32; Chivington, "The First Colorado Regiment," p. 149.
31. *O.R.*, IX:530–32; Miller Letter, p. 3.
32. Davidson, "Reminiscences of the Old Brigade," February 23, 1888.
33. Ibid.; Hall, *Confederate Army of New Mexico,* pp. 144, 149.
34. Hollister, *Boldly They Rode,* p. 62.
35. Jackson, *Wagon Roads West,* pp. 112–13. This site description, and all maps and similar descriptions in the present work, are based on appropriate USGS maps and my extensive field surveys of the entire area between Cañoncito and Kozlowski's Ranch during the period 1976–96.
36. *O.R.*, IX:530–31. Although the various Federal descriptions of this second Confederate position are quite clear, I and others, especially Phil Mead and Frank Dean of Albuquerque, have also located it from artifact evidence. Both dropped and fired rifled musket, or "minie," bullets were found on the southern flank of the battle line, at the eastern foot of the mountainside shelf previously mentioned. Few legitimate artifacts of the battle were located in the center, where the Texan guns were placed, due to subsequent disturbance by highway construction. Minie balls (the common .58-caliber, bullet-shaped projectiles), as well as round balls and buckshot (from another musket round, known as "buck and ball," which combined a single round ball and three smaller shot into a close range antipersonnel cartridge), were located in both the Federal and Confederate positions north of the present-day Interstate 25 right-of-way. In addition, some Texans were still armed with 12-gauge shotguns during the battles at Apache Canyon and Glorieta, and the shot fired by these weapons is also frequently found.
37. Davidson, "Reminiscences of the Old Brigade," February 23, 1888.
38. Hollister, *Boldly They Rode,* p. 62; Chivington, "The First Colorado Regiment," p. 149.
39. Chivington, "The First Colorado Regiment," p. 149; *O.R.*, IX:530–31.
40. Miller Letter, p. 3; Mallory, "Ferris Memoir," entries for March 26, 1862.
41. *O.R.*, IX:530–32.
42. Hollister, *Boldly They Rode,* p. 62.
43. *O.R.*, IX:531–32; Alberts, "Civil War Armaments," pp. 17–25. On this shelf I found considerable evidence of the fight between the flanking forces. That evidence included fragments from 6-pounder shells, case shot balls, and a fired .58-caliber round ball from one of the Texans' smoothbore muskets, all fired into the Union positions.

    There were five types of artillery rounds used by the Federal and Confederate forces during the Apache Canyon and Glorieta battles. The best known fired a "solid shot" of either six or twelve pounds (thus determining the size designation of the cannon), useful only against some solid target such as adobe walls. A "shell" was simply a round, hollow ball of the same diameter as the solid shot, filled with powder and exploded by a fuse that was, in turn, ignited by the main powder charge as the shell left the cannon's muzzle. A "case shot" was similar to a shell, except that it had a smaller bursting charge and was filled with lead balls, thus acting as an effective antipersonnel and antianimal shrapnel round. "Cannister" consisted of a tinned can filled with a varying number of iron balls. Upon firing, the can fell away and the balls spread out in a conical pattern, effectively turning the artillery piece into a giant shotgun. The final round was "grape shot." Similar in theory to cannister, nine larger iron balls were fired rather than 27–48 small cannister balls. The round was not very useful in practice, and I have located only two rounds of actual grape shot fired on the Glorieta battlefield. Much confusion arises, however, from the fact that contemporary reports often used the terms "cannister" and "grape shot" interchangeably. All cannons used during this campaign were muzzleloaders, no breechloading, rifled pieces being in New Mexico Territory at the time. For a thorough analysis of Civil War artillery, see Harold L. Peterson, *Round Shot and Rammers,* and Warren Ripley, *Artillery and Ammunition of the Civil War.*

44. *O.R.*, IX:531–32; Miller Letter, p. 3.
45. Mallory, "Ferris Memoir," entries for March 26, 1862; Hollister, *Boldly They Rode,* p. 63.
46. Hollister, *Boldly They Rode,* p. 63; Miller Letter, p. 3.
47. Miller letter, p. 3; Mallory, "Ferris Memoir," entries for March 26, 1862.
48. Hollister, *Boldly They Rode,* p. 63.
49. Ibid.; Miller Letter, p. 3; Mallory, "Ferris Memoir," entries for March 26, 1862.
50. Hollister, *Boldly They Rode,* pp. 63–64. See note 36, this chapter, for description of the buck and ball round.
51. Chivington, "The First Colorado Regiment," p. 149. See also Craig, *The Fighting Parson.*
52. Mallory, "Ferris Memoir," entries for March 26, 1862.
53. Ibid.
54. Ibid.; Hollister, *Boldly They Rode,* p. 64.
55. *O.R.*, IX:530–32.
56. Ibid.; Hollister, *Boldly They Rode,* p. 64.
57. *O.R.*, IX:530–32; Hollister, *Boldly They Rode,* p. 64; James H. McLeary, "History of Green's Brigade," in Dudley G. Wooten, ed., *A Comprehensive History of Texas, 1685–1897,* 2 vols., 2:699, quoted in Thompson, *Westward the Texans,* p. 38.
58. Miller Letter, p. 4; Hollister, *Boldly They Rode,* p. 64.
59. Hollister, *Boldly They Rode,* pp. 64–65.
60. Davidson, "Reminiscences of the Old Brigade," February 23, 1888; Gaither, "Pet Lambs," p. 33.
61. *O.R.*, IX:530–31; Gaither, "Pet Lambs," p. 33.
62. *O.R.*, IX:530–31; Mallory, "Ferris Memoir," entries for March 26, 1862.
63. Mallory, "Ferris Memoir," entries for March 26, 1862.
64. *O.R.*, IX:531–32; Hollister, *Boldly They Rode,* pp. 66–67.
65. *O.R.*, IX:531–32; Hanna Journal, entry for March 26, 1862; Hall, *Confederate Army of New Mexico,* p. 32. This estimate is based heavily on the late Dr. Hall's pioneering work on the Sibley Brigade muster rolls and casualty lists.

66. Hall, *Confederate Army of New Mexico,* pp. 144–72.
67. Hollister, *Boldly They Rode,* p. 67; Davidson, "Reminiscences of the Old Brigade," February 23, 1888.
68. Davidson, "Reminiscences of the Old Brigade," February 23, 1888.
69. *O.R.*, IX:530–32; Mallory, "Ferris Memoir," entries for March 26, 1862; Hollister, *Boldly They Rode,* pp. 66–67.
70. Mallory, "Ferris Memoir," entries for March 26, 1862; Hollister, *Boldly They Rode,* pp. 34, 66–67.

Chapter Four. Opening Shots

1. *O.R.*, IX:531–32; Hollister, *Boldly They Rode,* p. 67; Mallory, "Ferris Memoir," entries for March 27, 1862; Whitford, *Colorado Volunteers,* pp. 96–97. Records do not indicate which surgeon was left behind at Pigeon's Ranch.
2. Hollister, *Boldly They Rode,* p. 67; Whitford, *Colorado Volunteers,* pp. 96–97.
3. *O.R.*, IX:532–33.
4. Ibid., IX:534–35; Enos Report, April 5, 1862, RG 92, NA; Hollister, *Boldly They Rode,* pp. 67–68.
5. Hollister, *Boldly They Rode,* p. 68; Whitford, *Colorado Volunteers,* p. 97.
6. *O.R.*, IX:532–37.
7. Ibid., IX:538–39; Marc Simmons, *The Little Lion of the Southwest: A Life of Manuel Antonio Chaves,* pp. 183–85; Interview with Charles Meketa, December 17, 1996. Charles and Jacqueline Meketa of Corrales, New Mexico, are the leading authorities on New Mexico Volunteers during the Civil War, based on extensive and scholarly research and writing. During my own research, the question arose of why Captain Ford's Independent Company of Colorado Volunteers was so large (approximately 131 men), when almost all other Federal infantry companies in New Mexico were half or two-thirds as large. The answer appears to be provided by Charles Meketa's archival research, which he generously shared with me. As Ford and his Coloradoans passed through Santa Fe enroute to Fort Union, they apparently picked up 20 or 30 members of the First New Mexico Volunteers who had fought at Valverde and then come north with Lieutenant Colonel Chaves, who had been detached on recruiting duty in early March, 1862. Captain Ford also apparently absorbed several members of the Fourth New Mexico regiment, either in Santa Fe or from the garrison of Fort Union. A further complication arose from designation of Ford's Colorado company as a Co. G of the Fourth New Mexico Volunteers after it arrived at Fort Union. Whether or not the mixed Colorado/New Mexico unit ever actually considered itself a component of the New Mexico regiment is not clear; certainly none of the other Coloradoans considered it so. That anomaly is probably the genesis of a consistent belief on the part of some historians and enthusiasts that a unit of the Fourth New Mexico Volunteers fought at Glorieta. It may have, but it was Ford's company nonetheless (Special Orders No. 34, February 25, and General Orders No. 9, March 11, 1862, DNM, RG 393, NA).

8. *O.R.*, IX:532–35.
9. Enos Report, April 5, 1862, RG 92, NA.
10. *O.R.*, IX:531–34, 538–39.
11. *O.R.*, IX:531–32; Mallory, "Ferris Memoir," entries for March 28, 1862; Hollister, *Boldly They Rode*, p. 68.
12. Hanna Journal, entry for March 26, 1862; O'Donnel, "Williams Diary," entry for March 26, 1862.
13. *O.R.*, IX:542–43; Hanna Journal, entry for March 26, 1862; Haas, "Giesecke Diary," entry for March 26, 1862; Alberts, *Rebels on the Rio Grande*, pp. 75–76.
14. Hanna Journal, entry for March 26, 1862; Alberts, *Rebels on the Rio Grande*, p. 76.
15. Hanna Journal, entry for March 26, 1862; Alberts, *Rebels on the Rio Grande*, p. 76; Wess Rogers, "An Evening Stroll in the Company of Iron Men" (manuscript), March, 1987. Copy in author's collection. Recently, a modern Civil War reenactment group representing Company C, Fourth Texas Mounted Volunteers, retraced the route on the anniversary of the march and under similar weather conditions. Even though snow still lingered on the north sides of boulders and trees, mud was no problem since it was frozen. Darkness was, however, and the reenactors were constantly encountering not only ice at creek crossings but low cactus plants, the sharp needles torturing the stumbling men. They experienced a very arduous march, exactly as had their Civil War predecessors.
16. Hanna Journal, entry for March 26, 1862; Alberts, *Rebel on the Rio Grande*, p. 76; Davidson, "Reminiscences of the Old Brigade," February 23, 1888.
17. *O.R.*, IX:542–43.
18. Haas, "Giesecke Diary," entry for March 27, 1862; Hanna Journal, entry for March 27, 1862; Alberts, *Rebels on the Rio Grande*, pp. 76–77.
19. O'Donnel, "Williams Diary," entry for March 27, 1862; Hanna Journal, entry for March 27, 1862; Alberts, *Rebels on the Rio Grande*, p. 77.
20. Davidson, "Reminiscences of the Old Brigade," February 23, 1888; Alberts, *Rebels on the Rio Grande*, p. 77.
21. *O.R.*, IX:509, 542–43. See also Frazier, *Blood and Treasure*, pp. 199–200.
22. *O.R.*, IX:542–43; Hall, *Confederate Army of New Mexico*, pp. 56–130; Service record and commission, Maj. Henry W. Raguet, Fourth Texas Cavalry, Compiled Service Records (Confederate), RG 109, NA. Copies in author's collection.
23. *O.R.*, IX:542–43; Hall, *Confederate Army of New Mexico*, pp. 133–213, 214–92; Service records, Maj. John S. Shropshire, 5th Texas Cavalry, and Maj. Powhatan Jordan, 7th Texas Cavalry, Compiled Service Records (Confederate), RG 109, NA. Copies in author's collection.
24. *O.R.*, IX:542–43; Hall, *Confederate Army of New Mexico*, pp. 295–333, 345–59, 373–76.
25. Davidson, "Reminiscences of the Old Brigade," February 23, 1888; Hall, *Confederate Army of New Mexico*, pp. 211–13, 335–43; Alberts, "Civil War

Armaments," pp. 7–10. Though these were long thought to be additional 6-pounder guns, artifact evidence from the Glorieta battlefield indicates that the pieces were, in fact, the shorter-range but highly effective howitzers. Among other artillery artifacts from the main battlefield around Pigeon's Ranch, I located both 6-pounder and 12-pounder shell fragments and 12-pounder solid shot fired from Confederate cannons into the various Federal positions. Also greatly assisting the analysis of artillery armament was location of an almost-complete round of cannister fired from the Santa Fe Trail immediately in the rear of Pigeon's Ranch, at a range of about 150 yards, into the logging road down which one wing of the Colorado infantrymen retreated from Artillery Hill late in the Battle of Glorieta. The iron base plate from this cannister round was indented from the shock of firing, and the number of indentations (twelve) indicated that the ammunition was indeed that of a 12-pounder field howitzer rather than either a 6-pounder gun or 12-pounder mountain howitzer (Ripley, *Artillery and Ammunition of the Civil War,* pp. 267–68).

In addition, since the Confederates brought no 12-pounder field howitzers into New Mexico and captured none from the Union posts already taken, these two pieces were the two field howitzers captured as part of Capt. Alexander McRae's Federal Battery at the Battle of Valverde.

26. *O.R.,* IX:538–39; Davidson, "Reminiscences of the Old Brigade," February 23, 1888; Hall, *Confederate Army of New Mexico,* p. 57.

27. Davidson, "Reminiscences of the Old Brigade," March 1, 1888; Alberts, *Rebels on the Rio Grande,* p. 77; Henry C. Wright, "Reminiscences of H. C. Wright of Austin," p. 18. Original in Eugene C. Barker History Center, University of Texas at Austin. Private Wright was a member of Co. F, Fourth Texas Mounted Volunteers. This valuable source was located and shared with me by Prof. Don Frazier of Abilene, Texas.

28. Alberts, *Rebels on the Rio Grande,* p. 77. I am well aware of the disputes over many years concerning the strength of the Confederate force that fought the Battle of Glorieta. Some of those disputes have been based on wishful thinking, but much misunderstanding has resulted from Lieutenant Colonel Scurry's own official report written at Santa Fe three days after the battle. Generally accurate, it reports a total force of six hundred men, and that figure has often been accepted at face value. That figure would, however, make no sense. In a state of exhaustion from his exertions during and after the fight, the Confederate commander undoubtedly intended to refer only to the strength of his old regiment, the Fourth Texas, for whose nine companies the number would be reasonable. I have estimated the average strength of the Rebel infantry and mounted companies to be about sixty men actually participating in the March 28 battle. That estimate takes into account the small number of previous Confederate battle casualties, those left behind in hospitals, and those sick and wounded in the field hospital at the Johnson's Ranch camp. Hospital records support such an estimate (at Socorro, Dr. H. J. Hunter reported about 150 wounded Confederates left

for care after the Battle of Valverde, and a similar number were sick at Albuquerque), and even allowing for a number of men absent on various detached duties, my estimate appears reasonable and in line with the more accurately reported greater strengths of corresponding Federal units.

If anything, my estimate errs on the conservative side, and is further supported by the account of one Texan participant, Pvt. Bill Davidson, who reported that for the battle, his Co. A, Fifth Texas, had forty-five men available for duty. Considering that Co. A had suffered a large number of casualties in killed, wounded, and prisoners at Apache Canyon two days earlier, it could be expected to be significantly smaller than the other Confederate companies, especially those just arrived at Johnson's Ranch. Estimates of artillery crew strength are based on knowledge of the number of men required to serve and supply Civil War cannons, supported by similar, reported Federal figures. "Irregular" unit strengths are less reliable but are relatively small and are based on Hall's muster rolls in *Confederate Army of New Mexico*. With all these factors considered, at least 1,285 men accompanied Scurry eastward, and that number could well have been 200 men higher (*O.R.*, IX:541–43; Hunter Diary, entries for February 26 and 27, 1862; Davidson, "Reminiscences of the Old Brigade," March 1, 1888; Hall, *Confederate Army of New Mexico*, pp. 345–59, 373–76).

29. Davidson, "Reminiscences of the Old Brigade," February 23 and March 1, 1888; Alberts, *Rebels on the Rio Grande*, p. 77.
30. *O.R.*, IX:542–43.
31. Davidson, "Reminiscences of the Old Brigade," March 1, 1888.
32. *O.R.*, IX:542–43; Alberts, *Rebels on the Rio Grande*, p. 77.
33. Enos Report, April 5, 1862, RG 92, NA.
34. *O.R.*, IX:535–36.
35. Ibid., IX:531–32, 534–35, 539–40.
36. Enos Report, April 5, 1862, RG 92, NA.
37. Ibid.; McFerran Endorsement, April 6, 1862, RG 92, NA.
38. Davidson, "Reminiscences of the Old Brigade," February 23 and March 8, 1888; Enos Report, April 5, 1862; Alberts, *Rebels on the Rio Grande*, p. 79. This initial battle line defines the western boundary of the Glorieta battlefield and is a quarter-mile west of what has always been considered the opening phase of the Glorieta fight. It lies across New Mexico Highway 50, which here has essentially the same alignment as the Santa Fe Trail, along a fence line just east of a group of modern buildings. I identified the position from written documentation recently located and from artifact evidence. Fragments of artillery shells fired into the Texan positions, along with .58-caliber musket bullets (minie balls), were located by metal detection. That evidence supports the accounts of some limited artillery fire as well as shooting by infantry rather than dismounted cavalry.
39. Davidson, "Reminiscences of the Old Brigade," March 8, 1888.
40. Alberts, *Rebels on the Rio Grande*, pp. 78–79.
41. *O.R.*, IX:542–43; Davidson, "Reminiscences of the Old Brigade," March 1,

1888. This second Confederate artillery position and infantry support line were also located through artifact evidence by myself and Dee Brecheisen of Bosque Farms, New Mexico. The artifacts included a considerable number of artillery projectiles, mainly case shot and shell fragments, fired by the Federals into the opposing Texan cannon sites as counterbattery fire. The exact Confederate piece locations could be determined from piles of friction primer components used to fire each round. In addition, concentrations of .52-caliber Sharps carbine bullets, shot at the Rebel artillery and its supporting infantry by dismounted Union cavalrymen, were embedded in the embankment and hillside west of the little muddy draw and into the cannon positions themselves. The positions behind the rocky projections west of the draw, used by Shropshire's soldiers for shelter, were identifiable by dropped minie balls and dropped and fired percussion caps.

42. *O.R.*, IX:534–35, 538–39.
43. *O.R.*, IX:534–35; Report of 1st Lt. Ira W. Claflin, May 18, 1862, Miscellaneous Records (misc), 1850–66, RG 393, NA. Hereafter cited as Claflin Report. Located after I had written *Rebels on the Rio Grande,* this brief report sheds considerable light on the movements of the Federal artillery at Glorieta.
44. Mallory, "Ferris Memoir," entries for March 28, 1862.
45. Hollister, *Boldly They Rode,* p. 68.
46. Mallory, "Ferris Memoir," entries for March 28, 1862. I was greatly aided in the search for these artifacts and these positions by Dr. Phillip Mead of Albuquerque. Since these horsemen were armed with the short-barreled Sharps carbines rather than the infantry's rifled muskets, their positions could be traced by location of the distinctive Sharps bullets fired at ranges of fifty to one hundred yards into the opposing Rebel lines behind rock outcroppings just west of Windmill Hill.
47. *O.R.*, IX:539–40. This Union artillery position could also be located, if not exactly, through projectiles such as case shot balls and shell fragments fired into the tree line forming the Texan right flank.
48. Ibid., IX:535–36.
49. Ibid., IX:535–37; Hall, *Sibley's New Mexico Campaign,* p. 147–48; Whitford, *Colorado Volunteers,* pp. 106–107.
50. Enos Report, April 5, 1862, RG 92, NA; Hollister, *Boldly They Rode,* p. 68.
51. Hollister, *Boldly They Rode,* pp. 68–69.
52. *O.R.*, IX:539–40.
53. Alberts, *Rebels on the Rio Grande,* p. 79.
54. *O.R.*, IX:542–43; Whitford, *Colorado Volunteers,* p. 107.
55. *O.R.*, IX:542–43; Whitford, *Colorado Volunteers,* p. 107.
56. *O.R.*, IX:542–43; Whitford, *Colorado Volunteers,* p. 107; Davidson, "Reminiscences of the Old Brigade," March 8, 1888; Alberts, *Rebels on the Rio Grande,* p. 79.
57. Hollister, *Boldly They Rode,* pp. 69, 76; Whitford, *Colorado Volunteers,* p. 107. The artifact evidence related to this position to which Co. I retreated included case shot, .58-caliber minie balls shot into the position by Texans

and dropped unfired by some defenders, and .54-caliber bullets fired from the Confederates' Model 1841 "Mississippi Rifles."

58. *O.R.*, IX:539; Claflin Report, May 18, 1862, misc, RG 393, NA.
59. Mallory, "Ferris Memoir," entries for March 28, 1862; Miller Letter, p. 4; Hollister, *Boldly They Rode*, p. 70.
60. *O.R.*, IX:542–43; Hollister, *Boldly They Rode*, pp. 69–70.
61. *O.R.*, IX:542–43; Hollister, *Boldly They Rode*, pp. 69–70.
62. Mallory, "Ferris Memoir," entries for March 28, 1862; Alberts, *Rebels on the Rio Grande*, pp. 79–81.
63. *O.R.*, IX:536–38; Miller Letter, p. 4; Hollister, *Boldly They Rode*, p. 70.
64. *O.R.*, IX:536; Alberts, *Rebels on the Rio Grande*, p. 81.
65. *O.R.*, IX:536.

Chapter Five. Pigeon's Ranch

1. Enos Report, April 5, 1862, RG 92, NA.
2. Mallory, "Ferris Memoir," entries for March 28, 1862; Hollister, *Boldly They Rode*, p. 65. The field hospital site was in a small side canyon that defines the eastern boundary of the battlefield and contains modern memorial markers commemorating those who fought at Glorieta.
3. *O.R.*, IX:531–32; Whitford, *Colorado Volunteers*, p. 109. This dismounted cavalry positon atop Sharpshooter's Ridge was verified by excellent artifact evidence, including dropped, unfired Sharps carbine bullets and a bent but still loaded brass tube of primer pellets used to fire the cavalry carbines.

   I am aware that in the Pigeon's Ranch vicinity, the Santa Fe Trail, from the course of which most directions and distances in this chapter are given, actually runs on a southeast-northwest alignment, rather than east-west. Applicable maps reflect that alignment, but for purposes of simplicity, "north of" and "south of" are used in the narrative rather than "northeast of" and "southwest of." To the battlefield visitor of today, that appears to be the case anyway, and most Civil War participants so reported directions as well.
4. *O.R.*, IX:536–37.
5. Ibid.
6. Claflin Report, May 18, 1862, misc, RG 393, NA; Hollister, *Boldly They Rode*, p. 69. My son, Marine Capt. Clint Alberts, and I located the site of each cannon by metal detecting piles of dropped and fired friction primers and primer components.
7. *O.R.*, IX:540.
8. Mallory, "Ferris Memoir," entries for March 28, 1862; Farmer Diary, p. 22.
9. *O.R.*, IX:536–37.
10. Davidson, "Reminiscences of the Old Brigade," March 1, 1888.
11. Ibid.
12. Ibid.; *O.R.*, IX:543.
13. Davidson, "Reminiscences of the Old Brigade," March 1, 1888.
14. *O.R.*, IX:539–40.

15. Ibid. IX:539–40, 543–49; Hall, *Confederate Army of New Mexico,* p. 212; Alberts, *Rebels on the Rio Grande,* p. 79.
16. *O.R.*, IX:543–44; Hall, *Confederate Army of New Mexico,* p. 341; Alberts, *Rebels on the Rio Grande,* p. 79.
17. Davidson, "Reminiscences of the Old Brigade," March 1, 1888. This is a great story, and once again, even if it is not true, it should have been!
18. *O.R.*, IX:543–44; Alberts, *Rebels on the Rio Grande,* p. 81.
19. *O.R.*, IX:543–44.
20. Ibid.
21. Ibid.
22. Davidson, "Reminiscences of the Old Brigade," March 8, 1888.
23. Alberts, *Rebels on the Rio Grande,* pp. 85–86.
24. Ibid.; Douglas W. Owsley, *Bioarchaeology on a Battlefield: The Abortive Confederate Campaign in New Mexico,* pp. 48–49, 51–52, 59. Owsley's report is the result of an extensive forensic study done for the Museum of New Mexico's Office of Archaeological Studies on thirty-one remains of Confederate soldiers killed at Glorieta. The mass grave containing these remains was discovered by accident in 1987. I was the consulting historian for the two-week disinterment and for later investigation and analysis of the artifacts found with these remains. Owsley, a nationally recognized authority on forensic studies of Civil War and earlier military remains, was later contracted to undertake this particular study. The hope was that such a study, in conjunction with artifact analysis, would identify as many as possible of the Confederate casualties. It did help, identifying Private Hanna's remains with a high degree of probablility, while confirming two others previously identified. The circumstances and details of this spectacular and historically valuable gravesite discovery are discussed later in this work. I have based many statements of soldiers' arms and equipment, as well as wounds, on personal observation of that burial site and its revealed human and nonhuman remains. Where appropriate, that information is hereafter cited as "Author's personal observation and study of artifacts from the Glorieta gravesite, July, 1987."
25. Davidson, "Reminiscences of the Old Brigade," March 8, 1888.
26. Alberts, *Rebels on the Rio Grande,* p. 81. "Abs" was a very unusual, derogatory term, referring to the Union troops as hated abolitionists.
27. *O.R.*, IX:532; Whitford, *Colorado Volunteers,* p. 109.
28. Mallory, "Ferris Memoir," entries for March 28, 1862; Miller Letter, p. 5; Hollister, *Boldly They Rode,* p. 69. As previously mentioned, considerable evidence of firing from Sharps carbines (dropped bullets, brass primer pellet tube, etc.) was discovered along the southern two hundred yards of Sharpshooter's Ridge, indicating the positions of the dismounted cavalry troopers.
29. Alberts, *Rebels on the Rio Grande,* p. 81.
30. Ibid. I located a large amount of Confederate-fired artillery projectiles and shell fragments near Claflin's identified mountain howitzer positions. The

high percentage of case shot balls indicated that to be the favorite round used in this counterbattery fire. The direction of fire from Claflin's battery could be identified by sabot strap pieces located downhill from the Federal howitzers.

31. *O.R.*, IX:543–44.
32. Alberts, *Rebels on the Rio Grande,* p. 81.
33. Ibid. The course of this advance by Shropshire's men is difficult to visualize due to the incursion of Interstate 25, although the tree line forming the southern margin of the Glorieta battlefield is still visible south of that highway.
34. Ibid., pp. 81–82.
35. Claflin Report, May 18, 1862, misc, RG 393, NA.
36. Alberts, *Rebels on the Rio Grande,* p. 82.
37. Davidson, "Reminiscences of the Old Brigade," March 8, 1888.
38. Ibid.; Alberts, *Rebels on the Rio Grande,* p. 82.
39. *O.R.*, IX:536–37.
40. Ibid.; Owsley, *Bioarchaeology,* pp. 45–48; Davidson, "Reminiscences of the Old Brigade," March 8, 1888.
41. *O.R.*, IX:537; Davidson, "Reminiscences of the Old Brigade," March 8, 1888; Letter, Donald W. Healey to author, subj: Capt. Isaac Adair, March 10, 1996. Mr. Healey, of Eugene, Oregon, is the great-great-grandson of Captain Adair and generously shared with me what information he had on his gallant ancestor.
42. Davidson, "Reminiscences of the Old Brigade," February 23 and March 8, 1888. In 1987, while assisting in the disinterment of the Confederate remains at Glorieta, I found a disintegrated box of .36-caliber Colt pistol cartridges unopened in what had been John Shropshire's shirt pocket.
43. Ibid.; *O.R.*, IX:537–38.
44. *O.R.*, IX:543–44; Davidson, "Reminiscences of the Old Brigade," December 22, 1887, and March 8, 1888.
45. *O.R.*, IX:537.
46. Ibid.; Wright, "Reminiscences," p. 20; Alberts, *Rebels on the Rio Grande,* p. 82. Both Wright and Poe were members of Co. F, Fourth Texas Mounted Volunteers.
47. Alberts, *Rebels on the Rio Grande,* p. 82.
48. Ibid., pp. 82–83.
49. Ibid.; Davidson, "Reminiscences of the Old Brigade," March 1, 1888.
50. Alberts, *Rebels on the Rio Grande,* p. 84.
51. Mallory, "Ferris Memoir," entries for March 28, 1862; Hollister, *Boldly They Rode,* p. 70.
52. *O.R.*, IX:539–40; Farmer Diary, p.22; Claflin Report, May 18, 1860, misc, RG 393, NA; Hollister, *Boldly They Rode,* p. 70.
53. Farmer Diary, p. 22.
54. *O.R.*, IX:539–40; Mallory, "Ferris Memoir," entries for March 28, 1862; Hollister *Boldly They Rode,* p. 71.

55. Alberts, *Rebels on the Rio Grande,* p. 82.
56. Owsley, *Bioarchaeology,* p. 49; O'Donnel, "Williams Diary," entry for March 29, 1862; Hollister, *Boldly They Rode,* p. 71; Author's personal observation and study of artifacts from the Glorieta Confederate gravesite, July, 1987. I later identified Cotton's remains from his name, lightly engraved inside his wedding ring.
57. *O.R.,* IX:544; Miller Letter, p. 5; Hollister, *Boldly They Rode,* p. 71.
58. *O.R.,* IX:532.
59. Ibid., IX:544; Mallory, "Ferris Memoir," entries for March 28, 1862.
60. *O.R.,* IX:544–45.
61. Mallory, "Ferris Memoir," entries for March 28, 1862.
62. Ibid.; Farmer Diary, p. 22; Hollister, *Boldly They Rode,* p. 71.
63. *O.R.,* IX:532, 543.
64. Davidson, "Reminiscences of the Old Brigade," March 8, 1888.
65. *O.R.,* IX:539–40.
66. Claflin Report, May 18, 1862, misc, RG 393, NA; Miller Letter, p. 5.
67. Davidson, "Reminiscences of the Old Brigade," March 8, 1888.
68. *O.R.,* IX:537–38; Alberts, *Rebels on the Rio Grande,* p. 84. During 1988, I located these sites by metal detecting two distinct lines of impacted minie balls, each embedded in the Union and Confederate positions.
69. *O.R.,* IX:537–38. I found one of these rounds of 12-pounder field howitzer cannister, comprising balls and iron base plate, fired into the logging trail from the Confederate position on the Santa Fe Trail.
70. Ibid., IX:543–44; Wright, "Reminiscences," p. 19; Enos Report, April 5, 1862, RG 92, NA; Alberts, *Rebels on the Rio Grande,* pp. 84–85.
71. *O.R.,* IX:543–44.
72. Enos Report, April 5, 1862, RG 92, NA.
73. *O.R.,* IX:538–40; Farmer Diary, p. 22; Hollister, *Boldly They Rode,* p. 71.
74. *O.R.,* IX:539–40; Farmer Diary, p. 22.
75. Farmer Diary, p. 22; Hollister, *Boldly They Rode,* p. 71.
76. Wright, "Reminiscences," p. 20; Alberts, *Rebels on the Rio Grande,* p. 86.
77. Alberts, *Rebels on the Rio Grande,* p. 86.
78. Ibid.; O'Donnel, "Williams Diary," entry for March 28, 1862; Davidson, "Reminiscences of the Old Brigade," March 1, 1888.
79. Wright, "Reminiscences," p. 19; Alberts, *Rebels on the Rio Grande,* p. 86.
80. Whitford, *Colorado Volunteers,* p. 114.
81. Enos Report, April 5, 1862, RG 92, NA; Mallory, "Ferris Memoir," entries for March 28, 1862.
82. Lansing B. Bloom, ed., "Confederate Reminiscences of 1862," *New Mexico Historical Review* 5 (July 1930): 318; Miller Letter, p. 5; Whitford, *Colorado Volunteers,* p. 115.
83. Enos Report, April 5, 1862, RG 92, NA; Alberts, *Rebels on the Rio Grande,* p. 86.
84. Davidson, "Reminiscences of the Old Brigade," March 8, 1888.
85. Hollister, *Boldly They Rode,* p. 71.

86. Alberts, *Rebels on the Rio Grande*, p. 86.
87. Haas, "Giesecke Diary," entry for March 28, 1862; Davidson, "Reminiscences of the Old Brigade," March 1, 1888.

Chapter Six. Johnson's Ranch

1. *O.R.*, IX:538–39; Hollister, *Boldly They Rode*, p. 83.
2. *O.R.*, IX:538–39.
3. Francis C. Kajencki, "The Battle of Glorieta Pass: Was the Guide Ortiz or Grzelachowski?" *New Mexico Historical Review* 62 (January, 1987): 47–54; Interviews with Francis Kajencki and Charles Meketa, subj: Padre Polaco, December 18, 1996. See also Kajencki, *Poles in the 19th Century Southwest*. The oft-repeated myth of "Father Ortiz" can finally be put to rest, thanks to the diligent research of Colonel Kajencki of El Paso, Texas, and Charles Meketa of Corrales, New Mexico. They first seriously questioned the story of a miraculously appearing local Hispanic priest (which seemed highly improbable at best) and found documentation leading to the positive identification of Rev. Alexander Grzelachowski. Both contributed the results of their research and shared with me additional information concerning Padre Polaco's subsequent military activities after the Battle of Glorieta.
4. Gaither, "Pet Lambs," p. 33. This route has been identified by the author and by Lt. Col. Luke Barnett, III, of the Third Armored Cavalry regiment. Lieutenant Colonel Barnett identified and mapped, from the air, this dim pathway atop Glorieta Mesa between the present road and Cañoncito (Johnson's Ranch), as part of a drug intervention campaign by his unit during the summer of 1992. An accomplished Civil War historian in his own right, he generously shared his findings with me.
5. Ibid.; *O.R.*, IX:538–39; Whitford, *Colorado Volunteers*, p. 116. The Reverend Dr. Whitford's book is the pioneer work in its field and an undoubted classic. It is of considerable value to the historian of today, but must be used with great caution. Not having been a participant in the Civil War in New Mexico, and doing his research for this book some thirty years after the war, he necessarily relied heavily on the memories of those who had actually participated. His finished product, therefore, is no more reliable than the memories of those Colorado Volunteers who collaborated with him. They misidentified landmarks, repeated cherished but flawed stories, and otherwise unintentionally misled Whitford. One can imagine the condition of such veterans as they accompanied him on the train, past the Glorieta and Apache Canyon battlefields, having ridden all the way from Denver in the club car and feeling no pain. Every tree was "the tree;" every bridge "the bridge," etc. It was great fun, but not necessarily great history.
6. *O.R.*, IX:538–39; Gaither, "Pet Lambs," p. 33.
7. Gaither, "Pet Lambs," p. 34.
8. *O.R.*, IX:538–39. During the 1970s, I located this position from a metal-

detected subsurface line of fired percussion caps discarded by the Colorado Volunteers.

9. Ibid.; Davidson, "Reminiscences of the Old Brigade," March 8, 1888.
10. *O.R.*, IX:538–39; Gaither, "Pet Lambs," p. 34.
11. Davidson, "Reminiscences of the Old Brigade," March 1 and 8, 1888.
12. Gaither, "Pet Lambs," p. 34; Whitford, *Colorado Volunteers,* p. 119.
13. Davidson, "Reminiscences of the Old Brigade," March 8, 1888.
14. Ibid., March 1, 1888; *O.R.*, IX:538–39.
15. Wright, "Reminiscences," p. 19.
16. Davidson, "Reminiscences of the Old Brigade," December 22, 1887, and March 8, 1888.
17. *O.R.*, IX:538–39; Gaither, "Pet Lambs," p. 34; Alberts, *Rebels on the Rio Grande,* pp. 86–87. For an excellent discussion of this animal slaughter story, see Oliva, *Fort Union,* pp. 288–89.
18. Gaither, "Pet Lambs," p. 34.
19. Ibid. I have climbed this hillside many times. It is indeed steep, but a man or horse can accomplish the feat in the time indicated. There was no need for any of the assault party to have let themselves down the slope earlier by using ropes or leather gun slings, as has been reported, unless some rock slide or cliff obstruction was traversed rather than avoided.
20. Ibid.; *O.R.*, IX:541–44; Davidson, "Reminiscences of the Old Brigade," March 1, 1888.
21. *O.R.*, IX:538–39.
22. Gaither, "Pet Lambs," p. 35; Kajencki, "The Battle of Glorieta Pass," p. 52.
23. Gaither, "Pet Lambs," p. 35.
24. Ibid.; *O.R.*, IX:538–39.
25. *O.R.*, IX:534, 538–39; Whitford, *Colorado Volunteers,* p. 123.
26. Letter, Grzelachowski to Chapin, August 4, 1862, Letters Received (LR), DNM, RG 393, NA.
27. Letter, Chapin to Grzelachowski, August 4, 1862, Letters Sent (LS), DNM, RG 393, NA. Interviews with Francis Kajencki and Charles Meketa, subj: Padre Polaco, December 18, 1996.
28. *O.R.*, IX:544–45; Alberts, "Report of Confederates Killed at Glorieta," July, 1987. This report was prepared for the Museum of New Mexico at the time of discovery of the Confederate mass gravesite near Pigeon's Ranch. It includes an estimate of the total number of Texans probably buried at Pigeon's Ranch. Since that total, thirty-eight to forty-two, is greater than the number of people represented by the remains ultimately disinterred—thirty-one—between seven and eleven burials remain undiscovered. None of the thirty-one soldiers whose remains were discovered bore evidence of any kind of surgical procedures, so it is likely that those who died after being operated on in the hospital, or after the initial mass burial, were interred somewhere else on the battlefield, probably close to the ranch buildings. This report and the casualty figures here presented are based upon data compiled by the late Dr. Martin Hall, in the Confederate case, modified by later information from

memoirs, journals, newspaper articles, etc. Federal numbers are based to a great extent on Hollister's list of casualties, again modified by recent data. See Hall, *Confederate Army of New Mexico.*

29. *O.R.*, IX:534–35, 537–40; Hollister, *Boldly They Rode,* pp. 74–76. These Federal loss numbers are based to a great extent on Hollister's list of casualties, again modified by such sources as officers' reports, as well as recent data.
30. Enos Report, April 5, 1862, RG 92, NA.
31. Gaither, "Pet Lambs," pp. 35–36.
32. Enos Report, April 5, 1862, RG 92, NA; Hollister, *Boldly They Rode,* p. 65.
33. Enos Report, March 29, 1862, RG 92, NA; McFerran Endorsement, March 31, 1862, RG 92, NA.
34. Mallory, "Ferris Memoir," entries for March 29–April 2, 1862.
35. Hollister, *Boldly They Rode,* p. 74.
36. *O.R.*, IX:658.
37. Hollister, *Boldly They Rode,* p. 74.
38. *O.R.*, IX:532–33.
39. Wright, "Reminiscences," p. 19; Davidson, "Reminiscences of the Old Brigade," March 1, 1888.
40. *O.R.*, IX:544; Haas, "Giesecke Diary," entry for March 29, 1862.
41. Alberts, *Rebels on the Rio Grande,* pp. 86–87.
42. Ibid.; Davidson, "Reminiscences of the Old Brigade," March 1, 1888.
43. T. L. Greer, "Confederate Reminiscences," *New Mexico Historical Review* 5 (July, 1930), pp. 318–19.
44. Wright, "Reminiscences," pp. 20–21.
45. Author's personal observation and study of artifacts from the Glorieta Confederate gravesite, July, 1987. Even today the Glorieta area is known locally as "Little America" because of its bitter winter weather.
46. Ibid.; Mamie Yeary, comp., *Reminiscences of the Boys in Gray: 1861–1865,* p. 760; Owsley, *Bioarchaeology,* pp. 13, 45–46. The gravesite was still visible near the turn of the century, with Dr. Whitford writing that "a long and slight depression in the ground marks today their resting place—their undisturbed and final bivouac." By the 1980s, however, any surface indication had disappeared under a foot or more of alluvial deposit from periodic flooding of the valley by Glorieta Creek. The site was discovered accidentally in 1987 by local resident Kip Siler, while he was clearing land for his residence. He was both knowledgeable enough to realize what he had discovered and conscientious enough to notify the Museum of New Mexico, whose archaeologists disinterred the remains. I acted as consulting historian during that process. In the grave were the identifiable remains of Pvts. Abe Hanna and S. L. Cotton, the latter having succumbed to his grievous cannister wounds just before being buried. None of the other twenty-eight men could be positively identified. All were subsequently reburied, with impressive ceremony, in the Santa Fe National Cemetery.
47. *O.R.*, IX:545; Wright, "Reminiscences," p. 19; Haas, "Giesecke Diary," entry for March 29, 1862.

48. Haas, "Giesecke Diary," entry for March 29, 1862; Alberts, *Rebels on the Rio Grande,* p. 87.
49. O'Donnel, "Williams Diary," entry for March 30, 1862.
50. Straw, *Loretto,* pp. 35–36.
51. Yeary, *Reminiscences of the Boys in Gray,* p. 761; Alberts, *Rebels on the Rio Grande,* p. 88.
52. Alberts, *Rebels on the Rio Grande,* p. 88.
53. Ibid., p. 90.
54. Ibid.
55. *O.R.,* IX:510, 534–35; Teel, "Sibley's New Mexican Campaign," p. 700.
56. The literature of military operations during the American Revolution is, of course, extensive. For a competent, brief treatment, see Joseph B. Mitchell, *Decisive Battles of the American Revolution,* and for a more thorough history, see Don Higginbottom, *The War of American Independence.*
57. To the best of my knowledge, no participant in the battle of Glorieta made such a comparison. Confederates who participated in the Sibley campaign did not go on to fight in the eastern theater or at Gettysburg, and only a few Union soldiers did so. They tended, therefore, to have little or no personal knowledge of the larger battle from which to form any "big picture" comparisons. Beginning in the late 1950s, however, and recognizing similarities, historians such as Ray C. Colton and Max L. Heyman, Jr., called Glorieta the "Gettysburg of the West," while other pioneer historians of the New Mexico campaign, personified by Martin H. Hall, resisted doing so, apparently being unwilling to recognize any hint of Confederate tactical or strategic defeat during the campaign. During the following four decades, the phrase has become common and is used by most knowledgeable authors and historians (such as Don Frazier, Alvin Josephy, Jerry Thompson, and me) with proper caveats regarding relative size of the engagements, logistical considerations, and other important and obvious differences.

Chapter Seven. Recovery and Retreat

1. Alberts, *Rebels on the Rio Grande,* pp. 88–90. The location of these quarters has been identified by Mary Jean [Straw] Cook of Santa Fe.
2. Ibid.
3. Ibid.; Davidson, "Reminiscences of the Old Brigade," March 15, 1888.
4. Haas, "Giesecke Diary," entry for April 1, 1862; Davidson, "Reminiscences of the Old Brigade," March 15, 1862; O'Donnel, "Williams Diary," entry for April 1, 1862; Alberts, *Rebels on the Rio Grande,* pp. 88, 91.
5. Williams, *History of the Second Colorados,* p. 20.
6. Davidson, "Reminiscences of the Old Brigade," March 15, 1888; O'Donnel, "Williams Diary," entry for March 31, 1862; Wright, "Reminiscences," p. 21.
7. Davidson, "Reminiscences of the Old Brigade," March 15, 1888; Wright, "Reminiscences," p. 21.

8. O'Donnel, "Williams Diary," entries for April 3 and 9, 1862; Wright, "Reminiscences," p. 21.
9. Alberts, "Report of Confederates Killed at Glorieta," July, 1987. The gravesites of these hospital casualties have never been located.
10. Davidson, "Reminiscences of the Old Brigade," March 1 and May 24, 1888; Author's personal observation and study of artifacts from the Glorieta Confederate gravesite, July, 1987. Major Shropshire's grave was the first discovered during that month.
11. Letter, E. W. Wynkoop to H. Raguet, Fort Craig, New Mexico, June 2, 1862; Archives, Museum of New Mexico. Copy in author's collection.
12. Alberts, *Rebels on the Rio Grande,* pp. 92–95.
13. Straw, *Loretto,* p. 38.
14. "Walk Home Long One," *Victoria Advocate,* April 28, 1983.
15. Alberts, *Rebels on the Rio Grande,* pp. 91–92, 96.
16. Faulkner, "Smith Journal," p. 140; Thompson, *Westward the Texans,* p. 96; Davidson, "Reminiscences of the Old Brigade," March 15, 1888.
17. Faulkner, "Smith Journal," pp. 140–41; Alberts, *Rebels on the Rio Grande,* p. 94.
18. *O.R.,* IX:509, 541.
19. O'Donnel, "Williams Diary," entries for April 5 and 6, 1862; Thompson, *Westward the Texans,* p. 97.
20. O'Donnel, "Williams Diary," entry for April 7, 1862; Alberts, *Rebels on the Rio Grande,* p. 96.
21. *O.R.,* IX:658; Farmer Diary, p. 24.
22. *O.R.,* IX:550; O'Donnel, "Williams Diary," entry for April 7, 1862; Thompson, *Westward the Texans,* p. 99; Capt. Jacob Downing and Pvt. John D. Howland, First Colorado Volunteers, "On the Gory Field of Glorieta Heights," *Santa Fe New Mexican,* August 7, 1906.
23. O'Donnel, "Williams Diary," entry for April 8, 1862; Davidson, "Reminiscences of the Old Brigade," March 29, 1888; Alberts, *Rebels on the Rio Grande,* pp. 96–97.
24. *O.R.,* IX:550; Davidson, "Reminiscences of the Old Brigade," March 29, 1888; Jacqueline D. Meketa, *Legacy of Honor: The Life of Rafael Chacon, A Nineteenth-Century New Mexican,* p. 184. Chacon was a captain in the First New Mexico Volunteers.
25. *O.R.,* IX:550; Heyman, *Prudent Soldier,* p. 177.
26. Davidson, "Reminiscences of the Old Brigade," March 29, 1888; Haas, "Giesecke Diary," entry for April 11, 1862; Alberts, *Rebels on the Rio Grande,* pp. 99–101.
27. Gracy, "Campaign Letters," pp. 176, 179; Howard Bryan, "The Man Who Buried the Cannons," *New Mexico Magazine,* 40 (January, 1962): 15; Thompson, *Westward the Texans,* p. 99.
28. Wright, "Reminiscences," pp. 20, 22; O'Donnel, "Williams Diary," entries for March 31 and April 18, 1862; Yeary, *Reminiscences of the Boys in Gray,* p. 612.

29. O'Donnel, "Williams Diary," entries for April 8–18, 1862; Healey Letter, March 10, 1996.
30. Wright, "Reminiscences," p. 24; Davidson, "Reminiscences of the Old Brigade," March 29, 1888.
31. O'Donnel, "Williams Diary," entry for April 11, 1862; Special Orders No. 32, April 5, 1862, DNM, RG 393, NA.
32. O'Donnel, "Williams Diary," entries for April 12 and 20, 1862.
33. Ibid., entries for April 22 and 23, 1862; *O.R.*, IX:552; Wright, "Reminiscences," pp. 22–23; Ruth W. Hord, ed., "The Diary of Lieutenant E. L. Robb, C.S.A., from Santa Fe to Fort Lancaster, 1862," *Permian Historical Annual* 18 (December, 1978): 78. Robb was first lieutenant of Co. K, Fourth Texas Mounted Volunteers.
34. Farmer Diary, p. 23; Miller Letter, p. 1; Hollister, *Boldly They Rode*, pp. 77–78.
35. Miller Letter, p. 1; Hollister, *Boldly They Rode*, pp. 78–79.
36. Special Orders No. 32, April 5, 1862, DNM, RG 393, NA; Hollister, *Boldly They Rode*, p. 79.
37. Special Orders No. 29, April 5, 1862, DNM, RG 393, NA; Post Returns, Fort Union, April, 1862, RG 94, NA; Hollister, *Boldly They Rode*, p. 80.
38. Hollister, *Boldly They Rode*, pp. 81–84.
39. Ibid.
40. *O.R.*, IX:550–51; Gaither, "Pet Lambs," p. 36.
41. Special Orders No. 57, DNM, RG 393, NA; Hollister, *Boldly They Rode*, pp. 86, 89.
42. Chivington, "The First Colorado Regiment," pp. 151–52; Gaither, "Pet Lambs," p. 36; Hollister, *Boldly They Rode*, pp. 86, 89; Compiled Service Record, J. M. Chivington, Adjutant General's Office (AGO), RG 94, NA.
43. *O.R.*, IX:510, 551; Bell, "The Campaign of New Mexico," pp. 69–70; Thompson, *Westward the Texans*, pp. 99–100; Hollister, *Boldly They Rode*, pp. 93–96; Farmer Diary, p. 24. See also Frazier, *Blood and Treasure*, pp. 242–48, and Don E. Alberts, "The Battle of Peralta," *New Mexico Historical Review* 58 (October, 1983): 369–79.
44. Frazier, *Blood and Treasure*, pp. 250–83; Alberts, *Rebels on the Rio Grande*, pp. 107–43.
45. Frazier, *Blood and Treasure*, pp. 272–78; Thompson, *Westward the Texans*, pp. 105–109.
46. Hall, *Confederate Army of New Mexico*, p.37.
47. Frazier, *Blood and Treasure*, pp. 295–96; Thompson, *Sibley*, pp. 309–36; Alberts, *Rebels on the Rio Grande*, pp. 158–64. See also Richard Taylor, *Destruction and Reconstruction: Personal Experiences of the Late War.* This work, by the commander of the Confederate district of Western Louisana, and son of President Zachary Taylor, is an excellent source for the 1863 and 1864 Red River campaigns, in which the Sibley Brigade participated.

Epilogue

1. Hollister, *Boldly They Rode,* pp. 74–76, 189–90; Meketa, *Legacy of Honor,* pp. 173–84.
2. Special Orders No. 36, November 1, 1862; Department of the Missouri (DM), RG 393, NA; Special Orders No. 143, August 12, 1862, DNM, RG 393, NA; Returns, Southern Military District, August, 1862, DNM, RG 393, NA; Hollister, *Boldly They Rode,* pp. 128–48; Chivington, "The First Colorado Regiment," pp. 152–53.
3. Jacqueline D. Meketa, *Louis Felsenthal: Citizen-Soldier of Territorial New Mexico,* pp. 43–44; Charles and Jacqueline D. Meketa, *One Blanket and Ten Days Rations,* p. vii; Guild and Carter, *Kit Carson,* pp. 222–23.
4. Yeary, *Reminiscences of the Boys in Gray,* p. 612; Wright, "Reminiscences," pp. 24–52.
5. O'Donnel, "Williams Diary," entries for April 22–December 4, 1862; Hall, *Confederate Army of New Mexico,* p. 92.
6. Alberts, *Rebels on the Rio Grande,* pp. 158–67.
7. Davidson, "Reminiscences of the Old Brigade," December 22, 1887, and April 5, 1888.
8. Noel, *A Campaign from Santa Fe to the Mississippi,* p. 153; Taylor, *Destruction and Reconstruction,* pp. 158–59.
9. Mark M. Boatner, III, *The Civil War Dictionary,* p. 729; Harold B. Simpson, ed., *Texas in the War: 1861–1865,* pp. 92–93.
10. Boatner, *Civil War Dictionary,* p. 355. See also Odie B. Faulk, *General Tom Green, Fightin' Texan.*
11. Ibid., p. 795; Simpson, *Texas in the War,* p. 93.
12. Thompson, *Sibley,* pp. 326–31, 345–57, 368–69.
13. Hollister, *Boldly They Rode,* pp. 149–52, 162–65; Mallory, "Ferris Memoir," entries for November, 1862.
14. Special Orders No. 77, May 18, and No. 81, May 22, 1862, DNM, RG 393, NA; Mallory, "Ferris Memoir," entries for April–December, 1862, and November, 1864.
15. Mallory, "Ferris Memoir," entries for the years 1865–1927, epilogue.
16. General Orders No. 11, November 2, 1862, DM, RG 393, NA.
17. Robert M. Utley, *The Indian Frontier of the American West, 1846–1890,* pp. 86–93.
18. Special Orders No. 23, February 1, 1865, District of Colorado (DC), RG 393, NA; Letter, Chivington to Dodge, February 15, 1865, Compiled Service Record, RG 94, NA; Special Orders No. 294, December 11, 1869, AGO, RG 94, NA.
19. Letters, Slough to Adjutant General, January 1, 1864, and AGO to Cong. Nicholas Longworth, March 12, 1908, Compiled Service Record, RG 94, NA.
20. John P. Slough, "Petition in favor of the Dead at Kozlowski's," *Santa Fe Weekly Gazette,* December 15, 1866; Article [burial grounds selection], *Santa*

Fe Weekly Gazette, August 17, 1867, p. 2; Letter, with endorsements, J. S. Watts to D. H. Rucker, April 25, 1867, Quartermaster General, Consolidated File, RG 92, NA; Healey Letter, March 10, 1996.

21. William A. Keleher, *Turmoil in New Mexico,* p. 204; Boatner, *Civil War Dictionary,* p. 766.
22. Special Orders No. 89, May 31, 1862, DNM, RG 393, NA; Boatner, *Civil War Dictionary,* p. 624; Alan T. Nolan, *The Iron Brigade,* pp. 224, 247.
23. *O.R.,* XXXVI:329; Heyman, *Prudent Soldier,* pp. 202, 219–20, 228–29, 234–35; Boatner, *Civil War Dictionary,* p. 118.
24. Heyman, *Prudent Soldier,* pp. 349–54, 356–76, 379, 383.
25. Whitford, *Colorado Volunteers,* pp. 155–57.
26. I was president of the Glorieta Battlefield Preservation Society at that time, being succeeded in the position by my wife, Rosemary Alberts. Many New Mexicans, Coloradoans, and Texans contributed to the successful preservation effort.

Bibliography

Archives and Manuscripts

Barnett, Luke J., III. Aerial map of Major Chivington's march to Johnson's Ranch, Summer, 1992. Copy in author's collection.

"Bugler," Co. B, Fifth New Mexico Volunteers. "Reminiscences of the Late War in New Mexico." Arrott Collection, New Mexico Highlands University, Las Vegas, New Mexico.

Chivington, John M. "The First Colorado Regiment." Bancroft Library, University of California, Berkeley.

Confederate Military Affairs, 1861–65. Texas State Library, Archives Division, Austin, Texas.

Hanna, Ebenezer. "The Journal of Ebenezer Hanna." Texas State Library, Archives Division, Austin.

Healey, Donald W. Letters to author, re: Capt. Isaac Adair, March 10, 1996, and January 11, 1997.

Hunter, Harold J. Diary. Smith County Archives, Tyler, Texas.

Kajencki, Francis C. Letter to author, re: Padre Polaco, December 19, 1996.

Mallory, Eugene H., comp. "Ben Franklin Ferris' Memoir." Copy in author's collection.

Miller, John D. Letter to Father, April 3, 1862. Arrott Collection, New Mexico Highlands University, Las Vegas, New Mexico.

National Archives. Records of the Adjutant General's Office, 1780s–1917, RG 94. "Compiled Service Records." "General Orders." "Post Returns." "Special Orders."

National Archives. Records of the Quartermaster General's Office, Consolidated File, RG 92. "Reports."

National Archives. Records of United States Army Continental Commands, 1821–1920, RG 393. "Field Records—New Mexico Volunteers." "General Orders." "Letters Received." "Letters Sent." "Miscellaneous Records, 1850–66." "Records of the Quartermaster." "Returns from U.S. Military Posts, 1800–1916," Mi-

crocopy 617. "Returns from Regular Army Cavalry Regiments, 1833–1916," Microcopy 744. "Special Orders."
National Archives. War Department Collection of Confederate Records, RG 109. "Compiled Service Records." "Records of Texas Troops."
O'Donnel, Connie Sue Ragan, comp. "The Diary of Robert Thomas Williams: Marches, Skirmishes, and Battles of the Fourth Regiment, Texas Militia Volunteers: October 1861 to November 1865." Harold B. Simpson Confederate Research Center, Hill College, Hillsboro, Texas.
Overton Sharp-Shooter. Microfilm collection. The Center for American History, The University of Texas at Austin.
Peticolas, Alfred B. "Journal of A. B. Peticolas, 21 February–15 June 1862." 2 vols. Copies in author's collection.
Rodgers, Wess. "An Evening Stroll in the Company of Iron Men." Copy in author's collection.
Shropshire, John S. "John Samuel Shropshire Letters." Shropshire-Upton Confederate Museum, Columbus, Texas.
State Records Center and Archives, Santa Fe, New Mexico. Adjutant General Files. J. E. Farmer Diary. Militia Description Book. E. W. Wynkoop, letter to H. Raguet, Fort Craig, New Mexico, June 2, 1862.
Williams, Robert Thomas. "The Diary of Robert Thomas Williams: Marches, Skirmishes, and Battles of the Fourth Regiment, Texas Militia Volunteers: October 1861 to November 1865." Harold B. Simpson Confederate Research Center, Hill College, Hillsboro, Texas.
Wright, Henry C. "Reminiscences of H. C. Wright of Austin." Eugene C. Barker Texas History Center, University of Texas, Austin.

Books and Articles

Agnew, Stanley C. *Garrisons of the Regular U.S. Army: New Mexico 1846–1899.* Santa Fe, N.Mex.: Press of the Territorian, 1971.
Alberts, Don E. "The Battle of Glorieta." Paper presented at the Bureau of Land Management Fort Craig Conference, Socorro, N.Mex., 1989.
———. "The Battle of Peralta." *New Mexico Historical Review* 58 (October, 1983): 369–79.
———. "Civil War along the Camino Real." In *El Camino Real de Tierra Adentro,* edited by Gabrielle G. Palmer, 195–203. Santa Fe, N.Mex.: Bureau of Land Management, 1993.
———. "Civil War on the Santa Fe Trail: Preserving the Battlefield at Glorieta Pass." *Civil War Regiments* 2 (1993): 161–68.
———. "Civil War Armaments and Accoutrements Used at the Pigeon's Ranch/ Glorieta Battlefield Site." Unpublished study prepared for the Museum of New Mexico, August, 1986.
———. "Glorieta." In *The Civil War Battlefield Guide,* edited by Frances J. Kennedy. Boston: Houghton Mifflin, 1990.

———. "Glorieta, Battle of." In vol. 3 of *The New Handbook of Texas,* edited by Ron Tyler. Austin: Texas State Historical Association, 1996.

———. *Rebels on the Rio Grande: The Civil War Journal of A. B. Peticolas.* 1984. Reprint, Albuquerque, N.Mex.: Merit Press, 1993.

———. "Report of Confederates Killed at Glorieta." Unpublished study prepared for the Museum of New Mexico, July, 1987.

———. "The Sibley Campaign." In vol. 5 of *The New Handbook of Texas,* edited by Ron Tyler. Austin: Texas State Historical Association, 1996.

Anderson, Hattie M. "With the Confederates in New Mexico during the Civil War: Memoirs of Hank Smith." *Panhandle-Plains Historical Review.* 2 (1929): 65–97.

Anderson, Latham. "Canby's Services in the New Mexico Campaign." In vol. 2 of *Battles and Leaders of the Civil War.* 1884–88. Reprint, New York: Yoseloff, 1956.

Archambeau, Ernest R., Jr. "The New Mexico Campaign of 1861–1862." *Panhandle-Plains Historical Review* 37 (1964): 4–33.

Austerman, Wayne R. *Sharps Rifles and Spanish Mules: The San Antonio–El Paso Mail, 1851–1881.* College Station: Texas A&M University Press, 1985.

Bailey, Lance. "Sibley's Texas Confederate Brigade." *Texas Historian* 43 (May, 1983): 6–10.

Bell, Joseph M. "The Campaign of New Mexico." In vol. 1 of *War Papers Read before the Commandery of the State of Wisconsin, Military Order of the Loyal Legion of the United States.* Milwaukee, Wis.: Burdick, Armitage and Allen, 1891.

Bloom, Lansing B. "Confederate Reminiscences of 1862." *New Mexico Historical Review* 5 (July, 1930): 315–24.

Boatner, Mark M., III. *The Civil War Dictionary.* New York: David McKay, 1959.

Bryan, Howard. "The Man Who Buried the Cannons." *New Mexico Magazine* 40 (January, 1962): 13–15, 35.

Chivington, John M. "The First Colorado Regiment." *New Mexico Historical Review* 33 (April, 1958): 144–54. Published in full from the original in the Bancroft Library, University of California, Berkeley.

Colton, Ray. *The Civil War in the Western Territories.* Norman: University of Oklahoma Press, 1959.

Confederate Congress at Richmond. *Official Reports of Battles.* New York: Charles B. Richardson, 1863.

Craig, Reginald S. *The Fighting Parson: The Biography of Colonel John M. Chivington.* Los Angeles: Westernlore Press, 1959.

Davidson, William L. "Reminiscences of the Old Brigade." *Overton (Texas) Sharp-Shooter,* continuous series from October, 1887, to March, 1889. Microfilm Collection, The Center for American History, The University of Texas at Austin. Copy in author's collection.

Downing, Jacob, and John D. Howland. "On the Gory Field of Glorieta Heights." *Santa Fe New Mexican,* August 7, 1906.

Edwards, William B. *Civil War Guns*. Harrisburg, Penn.: Stackpole, 1962.

Emmett, Chris. *Fort Union and the Winning of the Southwest*. Norman: University of Oklahoma Press, 1965.

Farber, James. *Texas, C.S.A.*. New York: Jackson, 1947.

Faulk, Odie B. *General Tom Green, Fightin' Texan*. Waco, Tex.: Texian Press, 1963.

Faulkner, Walter A., ed. "With Sibley in New Mexico: The Journal of William Henry Smith." *West Texas Historical Association Year Book* 27 (October, 1951): 111–42.

Finch, L. Boyd. *Confederate Pathway to the Pacific: Major Sherod Hunter and Arizona Territory, C.S.A.*. Tucson: Arizona Historical Society, 1996.

Frazier, Donald S. *Blood and Treasure: Confederate Empire in the Southwest*. College Station: Texas A&M University Press, 1995.

Gaither, Donald. "The Pet Lambs at Glorieta Pass." *Civil War Times Illustrated* 15 (November, 1976): 30–38.

Giese, Dale F., ed. *My Life with the Army in the West: The Memoirs of James E. Farmer, 1858–1898*. Santa Fe, N.Mex.: Stagecoach Press, 1967.

Gracy, David B., II, ed. "New Mexico Campaign Letters of Frank Starr, 1861–1862." *Texas Military History* 4 (Fall, 1964): 169–88.

Greer, T. L. "Confederate Reminiscences." *New Mexico Historical Review* 5 (July, 1930): 318–24.

Grinstead, Marion C. *Destiny at Valverde: The Life and Death of Alexander McRae*. Socorro, N.Mex.: Socorro Historical Society, 1992.

———. *Life and Death of a Frontier Fort: Fort Craig, New Mexico, 1854–1885*. Socorro, N.Mex.: Socorro County Historical Society, 1973.

Guild, Thelma S., and Harvey L. Carter. *Kit Carson: A Pattern for Heroes*. Lincoln: University of Nebraska Press, 1984.

Haas, Oscar, trans. "The Diary of Julius Giesecke." *Texas Military History* 3 (Winter, 1963): 228–42.

Haecker, Charles M. "Guns of Palo Alto." *Archaeology* (May–June, 1996): 49–53.

———. *A Thunder of Cannon: Archeology of the Mexican-American War Battlefield of Palo Alto*. Santa Fe, N.Mex.: National Park Service, 1994.

Hall, Martin H. "An Appraisal of the 1862 New Mexico Campaign: A Confederate Officer's Letter to Nacogdoches." *New Mexico Historical Review* 51 (October, 1976): 329–33.

———. "Captain John G. Phillips's Brigands." *Military History of Texas and the Southwest* 11 (1973): 131–35.

———. *The Confederate Army of New Mexico*. Austin, Tex.: Presidial Press, 1978.

———. "The First Colorado Regiment." *New Mexico Historical Review* 33 (April, 1958): 144–54.

———. "The Journal of Ebenezer Hanna." *Password* 3 (January, 1958): 1–29.

———. "Native Mexican Relations in Confederate Arizona, 1861–1862." *Journal of Arizona History* 8 (Autumn, 1967): 171–78.

———. "Negroes with Confederate Troops in West Texas and New Mexico." *Password* 13 (Spring, 1968): 11–12.

———. *Sibley's New Mexico Campaign*. Austin: University of Texas Press, 1960.

Hayes, A. A. "The New Mexico Campaign of 1862." *Magazine of American History* 15 (February, 1886): 171–84.

Heyman, Max L. *Prudent Soldier: A Biography of Major General E. R. S. Canby, 1817–1873*. Glendale, Calif.: Arthur H. Clark, 1959.

Higginbottom, Don. *The War of American Independence*. New York: Macmillan, 1971.

Hollister, Ovando J. *Boldly They Rode: A History of the First Colorado Regiment of Volunteers*. 1863. Reprint, Lakewood, Colo.: Golden Press, 1949.

Hord, Ruth W., ed. "The Diary of Lieutenant E. L. Robb, C.S.A., from Santa Fe to Fort Lancaster, 1862." *Permian Historical Annual* 18 (December, 1978): 59–80.

Jackson, W. Turrentine. *Wagon Roads West*. New Haven, Conn.: Yale University Press, 1952.

Josephy, Alvin M., Jr. *The Civil War in the American West*. New York: Alfred A. Knopf, 1991.

Kajencki, Francis C. "The Battle of Glorieta Pass: Was the Guide Ortiz or Grzelachowski?" *New Mexico Historical Review* 62 (January, 1987): 47–54.

———. *Poles in the 19th Century Southwest*. El Paso, Tex.: Polonia Press, 1990.

Karnes, Thomas L. *William Gilpin: Western Nationalist*. Austin: University of Texas Press, 1970.

Keleher, William A. *Turmoil in New Mexico*. Santa Fe, N.Mex.: Rydal Press, 1952.

Kerby, Robert L. *The Confederate Invasion of New Mexico and Arizona, 1861–1862*. Los Angeles: Westernlore Press, 1958.

Long, E. B. *The Civil War Day by Day: An Almanac, 1861–1865*. Garden City, N.Y.: Doubleday, 1971.

McCoy, Raymond. "The Battle of Glorieta Pass." *United Daughters of the Confederacy Magazine* 15 (February, 1952): 12–13, 23.

McKee, James C. *Narrative of the Surrender of a Command of U.S. Forces at Fort Fillmore, New Mexico, in July, A.D., 1861*. Houston, Tex.: Stagecoach Press, 1960.

McMaster, Richard K, and George Ruhlen. "The Guns of Valverde." *Password* 5 (January, 1960): 20–34.

McPherson, James M. *Images of the Civil War*. New York: Gramercy Books, 1992.

Meketa, Charles, and Jacqueline D. Meketa. *One Blanket and Ten Days Rations*. Globe, Ariz.: Southwest Parks and Monuments Association, 1980.

Meketa, Jacqueline D. *Legacy of Honor: The Life of Rafael Chacon, a Nineteenth-Century New Mexican*. Albuquerque: University of New Mexico Press, 1986.

———. *Louis Felsenthal: Citizen-Soldier of Territorial New Mexico*. Albuquerque: University of New Mexico Press, 1982.

Miller, Darlis A. *The California Column in New Mexico*. Albuquerque: University of New Mexico Press, 1982.

———. "Hispanos and the Civil War in New Mexico: A Reconsideration." *New Mexico Historical Review* 54 (April, 1979): 105–23.

———. "Los Pinos, New Mexico: Civil War Post on the Rio Grande." *New Mexico Historical Review* 62 (January, 1987): 1–13, 23–26.

———. *Soldiers and Settlers: Military Supply in the Southwest, 1861–1885*. Albuquerque: University of New Mexico Press, 1989.

Mitchell, Joseph B. *Decisive Battles of the American Revolution*. New York: G. P. Putnam's Sons, 1962.

Mumey, Nolie, ed. *Bloody Trails along the Rio Grande: A Day-by-Day Diary of Alonzo Ferdinand Ickis*. Denver, Colo.: Fred A. Rosenstock, 1958.

Nankivell, John H. *History of the Military Organizations of the State of Colorado, 1860–1935*. Denver, Colo.: Kestler Stationery, 1935.

Noel, Theophilus. *A Campaign from Santa Fe to the Mississippi: Being a History of the Old Sibley Brigade from Its First Organization to the Present Time; Its Campaigns in New Mexico, Arizona, Texas, Louisiana, and Arkansas in the Years 1861-2-3-4*. 1865. Edited by Martin H. Hall and Edwin A. Davis. Reprint, Houston, Tex.: Stagecoach Press, 1961.

Nolan, Alan T. *The Iron Brigade*. Barrien Springs, Mich.: Hardscrabble Books, 1983.

Oliva, Leo E. *Fort Union and the Frontier Army in the Southwest*. Santa Fe, N.Mex.: National Park Service, 1993.

Owsley, Douglas W. *Bioarchaeology on a Battlefield: The Abortive Confederate Campaign in New Mexico*. Santa Fe: Museum of New Mexico, 1994.

Palmer, Gabrielle G., ed., *El Camino Real de Tierra Adentro*. Santa Fe, N.Mex.: Bureau of Land Management, 1993.

Peterson, Harold L. *Round Shot and Rammers*. New York: Bonanza, 1969.

Ripley, Warren. *Artillery and Ammunition of the Civil War*. Charleston, S.C.: Battery Press, 1984.

Santa Fe Planning Associates. *Pigeon's Ranch Feasibility Study*. Santa Fe, N.Mex.: Santa Fe Planning Associates, 1986.

Santee, J. F. "The Battle of La Glorieta Pass." *New Mexico Historical Review* 6 (January, 1931): 66–75.

Shirley, Mildred, and Jean Mansell. "Henry Clay Wright Leaves Legacy in Texas." *Abilene (Texas) Reporter–News*. May 31 and June 7, 1987.

Simmons, Marc. *Following the Santa Fe Trail: A Guide for Modern Travelers*. Santa Fe, N.Mex.: Ancient City Press, 1984.

———. *The Little Lion of the Southwest: A Life of Manuel Antonio Chaves*. Chicago: Sage Books, 1973.

———. "New Light on Johnson's Ranch." *Trail Dust* (October 7, 1992): 1.

Simpson, Harold B., ed. *Texas in the War, 1861–1865*. Hillsboro, Tex.: Hill Junior College Press, 1965.

Slough, John P. "Petition in Favor of the Dead at Kozlowski's." *Santa Fe Weekly Gazette*, December 15, 1866.

Smith, Duane A. *The Birth of Colorado: A Civil War Perspective*. Norman: University of Oklahoma Press, 1989.

Straw, Mary J. *Loretto: The Sisters and Their Santa Fe Chapel*. Santa Fe, N.Mex.: Loretto Chapel, 1983.

Taylor, Richard. *Destruction and Reconstruction: Personal Experiences of the Late War*. 1879. Reprint, New York: Longmans, Green, 1955.

Teel, Trevanion T. "Sibley's New Mexican Campaign: Its Objects and the Causes of its Failure." In vol. 2 of *Battles and Leaders of the Civil War.* 1884–88. Reprint, New York: Yoseloff, 1956.

Thompson, Jerry D. "The Civil War Diary of Major Charles Emil Wesche." *Password* 39 (Spring, 1994): 37–47.

———. *Colonel John Robert Baylor: Texas Indian Fighter and Confederate Soldier.* Hillsboro, Tex.: Hill Junior College Press, 1971.

———. *Henry Hopkins Sibley: Confederate General of the West.* 1987. Reprint, College Station: Texas A&M University Press, 1996.

———. *Vaqueros in Blue and Gray.* Austin, Tex.: Presidial Press, 1977.

———. *Westward the Texans: The Civil War Journal of Private William Randolph Howell.* El Paso: Texas Western Press, 1990.

Tyler, Ron, ed. *The New Handbook of Texas.* 6 vols. Austin: Texas State Historical Association, 1996.

Utley, Robert M. *Frontiersmen in Blue: The United States Army and the Indian, 1840–1865.* New York: Macmillan, 1967.

———. *The Indian Frontier of the American West, 1846–1890.* Albuquerque: University of New Mexico Press, 1984.

———. *Report on the Integrity of Glorieta Pass Battlefield.* Santa Fe, N.Mex.: National Park Service, 1961.

Wallace, R.B. "My Experiences in the First Colorado Regiment." *Colorado Magazine* 1 (November, 1924): 307–12.

The War of the Rebellion: A Compilation of the Official Records of the Union and Confederate Armies. Four series, 128 vols. Washington, D.C.: Government Printing Office, 1880–1901.

Westphall, David. "The Battle of Glorieta Pass: Its Importance in the Civil War." *New Mexico Historical Review* 44 (February, 1969): 137–51.

Whitford, William C. *Colorado Volunteers in the Civil War: The New Mexico Campaign in 1862.* 1906. Reprint, Glorieta, N.Mex.: Rio Grande Press, 1971.

Williams, Ellen. *Three Years and a Half in the Army: or, History of the Second Colorados.* New York: Fowler and Wells, 1885.

Wilson, John P. *Archaeological Investigations at Pigeon's Ranch, New Mexico.* Report No. 37. Las Cruces, N.Mex.: 1984.

Wilson, Spencer. "The Civil War in New Mexico: Tall Tales and True." *New Mexico Geological Society Guidebook,* 34th Field Conference (1983): 85–87.

Wright, Arthur A. *The Civil War in the Southwest.* Denver, Colo.: Big Mountain Press, 1964.

———. "Colonel John P. Slough and the New Mexico Campaign, 1862." *Colorado Magazine* 39 (April, 1962): 49–52.

Yeary, Mamie, comp. *Reminiscences of the Boys in Gray.* Dayton, Ohio: Morningside, 1986.

Index

CPSIA information can be obtained at www.ICGtesting.com
Printed in the USA
LVOW040415041211

257721LV00002B/9/P

9 781585 441006

To Betty Lee

MOTHER CHARITY

A Big Free Novel

MARTHA B.
BOONE, M.D.

NEW YORK

LONDON • NASHVILLE • MELBOURNE • VANCOUVER

MOTHER CHARITY

A Big Free Novel

Published in New York, New York, by Morgan James Publishing. Morgan James is a trademark of Morgan James, LLC. www.MorganJamesPublishing.com

Proudly distributed by Publishers Group West®

ISBN 9781636982465 paperback
ISBN 9781636982472 ebook
Library of Congress Control Number: 2023939166

Cover Design by:
Rachel Lopez
www.r2cdesign.com

Interior Design by:
Chris Treccani
www.3dogcreative.net

To the many people who worked at Charity Hospital in New Orleans over its sixty-six years at 1532 Tulane Avenue.

It's remembered as one of the largest hospitals for uninsured people in America. We, who were there, lovingly remember it as one of the best trauma centers in America. Charity was a training ground for greatness. We did everything with nothing. If you were there, no one need explain this to you. If you weren't there, nobody can explain it.

These are our stories. May we laugh and cry and remember the joy of a job well done.

"It is obvious that we can no more explain a passion to a person who has never experienced it than we can explain light to the blind."

T. S. ELIOT

1

CHARITY HOSPITAL, NEW ORLEANS

December 24, 1982

Dr. Elizabeth Roberts heard a loud bang as the old emergency room doors swung open and slammed into the wall behind them. Two EMTs came through the doors, running alongside a fast-rolling gurney, screaming, "Gunshot wound to the abdomen! Room Four! Patient stable with blood pressure 130 over 90 and pulse ninety-two! Make way to Room Four! All hands on deck!"

Elizabeth jumped out of the way to allow them to pass and then sprinted behind the rolling gurney into the Room Four trauma suite. Her heart pounded and her hands shook. Her boss, Dr. Norman McSwain, walked into the room behind Livvy, the head nurse. The trauma team surrounded the patient.

Elizabeth assumed the lead position as the surgical intern in charge. She stood at the patient's chest. Dr. McSwain moved to stand close behind her. The patient wore a flowered housedress soaked in blood. The students cut the dress with scissors from neck to knees, revealing the patient's entire body.

Elizabeth performed a quick physical examination and called out her findings to the group as Dr. McSwain, at full attention, listened and watched from over her shoulder.

"Morbidly obese female with blood pressure stable and elevated," Elizabeth began, "Pulse—tachycardic, awake and alert, HEENT normal, airway clear, good bilateral breath sounds, abdomen protuberant, pattern of buckshot with obvious multiple superficial wounds to the abdomen and breasts from the clavicles to the pelvis."

"Who the heck you calling OBESE, missy?" demanded her patient. "I'm plump. I'm *not* OBESE! Just because you a stick, don't mean other folks should be," she said.

Elizabeth heard the head nurse chuckle behind her. Livvy mumbled under her breath, "Four hundred pounds if I ever saw it."

The naked patient tried to sit up as Elizabeth pushed her back onto the gurney. "Please lie down, ma'am," Elizabeth asked. Elizabeth glanced at the chart and saw the patient's name was Viola Johnson.

The patient raised her head to glare at Livvy. "Don't be whispering behind my back, you Creole bi—!Your type thinks you better than everyone else," she said.

Dr. McSwain ignored the patient's comments and addressed the EMTs. "What happened at the scene?"

Rob and Joe faced the mentor they worshipped. Rob spoke first. "Doc, she was walking in front of the Calliope projects on Melpomene around 8:30 this morning, when a drive-by with a shotgun occurred. She wasn't the intended victim. The bystanders told us shot gun pellets bounced everywhere, and some hit her."

Joe continued, "We arrived on the scene within four minutes of the call, and she was lying on the grass crying, rolling around, holding her abdomen and yelling at her brother."

The patient interjected, "You don't know nothing! Da Calliope's the most dangerous project in Louisiana. That place is *full-up* with drug dealers. My little brother done got hisself tangled up in some of that mess, and those boys were driving around looking for him. They was shooting at anybody on the street. Thank Gawd, they a bad shot," she screamed, grabbing her lower abdomen.

Elizabeth fought to palpate the patient's abdomen even as she swatted away the doctor's hands.

Great Christmas Eve here! At least we're too busy to be homesick.

"Dr. McSwain," Elizabeth reported, "Her abdomen's hard as a rock. Even through her adipose tissue, I can feel a hard, large midline mass. The mass extends up to her diaphragm."

Dr. McSwain placed his hand on the patient's arm and said, "Don't be afraid, Miss Johnson. We're going to take good care of you." He pivoted to face Elizabeth and asked, "How much blood do you think she's lost, Dr. Roberts?"

Elizabeth knew when Dr. McSwain called her Dr. Roberts that she had better pay close attention. Her blood pressure rose; she felt a wave of fear, and her senses went on high alert. *Why was he so relaxed? The patient had a gunshot wound to the abdomen!* She felt compassion for the woman, whose naked, obese body was exposed to a dozen staring eyes. Most Room Four patients were unconscious and could not watch the crowd observing them. But until her condition was proved stable, the patient's body remained exposed while the medical team searched for clues.

I'm more nervous than the patient, Elizabeth thought as she answered Dr. McSwain's question.

"Sir, her blood pressure's high and her pulse is strong and steady, with tachycardia at ninety-six beats per minute. Her abdomen is thick and large, so a lot of blood could be contained within, and we couldn't feel it. But her wounds look superficial. I doubt she's lost much blood," said Elizabeth.

Miss Johnson howled again, grabbed her lower abdomen, and begged for pain medicine. "I'm peeing on myself! It hurts so bad that I done peed myself! Ain't you doctors gonna do nothing to help me? I be shot up!"

Livvy patted the patient's other arm and whispered to one of the young nurses, "It's across the hall in L and D . . ."

Elizabeth couldn't hear Livvy's entire list of instructions, but she knew Livvy had already figured out what needed to be done and was sending her nurses to get supplies. Though Elizabeth resented feeling one step behind the head nurse again, her dislike of being bested was mixed with her relief that Livvy was competent and calm.

Dr. McSwain leaned over the patient and asked, "Ma'am, are you pregnant?"

She screamed, "What kind of stupid doctors are you? Of course I ain't pregnant! I been shot! I was just fine till I got shot! Can't you see all them little bleeding holes all over the front of me? I been shot, and you fools think I'm pregnant. Dang! The Big Free done gone to the dogs."

"Livvy, get the nurses to get her up in stirrups for a vaginal exam." He turned to the two EMTs. "Her legs are heavy, so Joe and Rob lend a hand," said Dr. McSwain.

Elizabeth froze. Flabbergasted, her grandfather's words flashed into her mind. "Girl, you look like a cold flounder's been slapped across your face."

Livvy stood close behind Elizabeth and whispered into the back of her head, "It's Mother Charity at her best, Crème Puff. Expect the unexpected. Get ready to deliver a baby."

How many names can one hospital have? Charity, The Big Free, Mother Charity, The Big House, Big Charity.

As Rob and Joe helped the nurses position the patient in the stirrups, clear fluid and blood dripped onto the floor from her vagina.

It's been six months that I've been in this ER, Elizabeth thought. *Am I ever going to be quicker than Livvy in figuring out the patients?*

Elizabeth trembled at the thought of delivering a baby in the trauma room. Here she was, sitting between the patient's legs, which were suspended in stirrups high in the air. Elizabeth didn't like delivering babies. She was more comfortable with gunshot wounds and stab victims. On the family farm, she'd helped deliver cows, horses, mules, goats, cats, dogs, and pigs, and she disliked the way humans made a big fuss about a natural process. The animals moaned a bit, but there was no screaming or cussing. Elizabeth had ruled out obstetrics as a career choice on the first day of her rotation, when a young woman grabbed her around the neck and screamed, "I want an epidural, now!" *At least there's no chest trauma. I'd rather deliver a baby than have to call Dr. White. He's the last person I want to see on Christmas Eve.*

The patient thrashed about, screaming, "Give me some pain medicine! You fools are letting me suffer for no good reason."

Elizabeth parted the patient's labia and saw a head covered in wet hair protruding from the vagina. She massaged the walls with lubricant. The patient groaned as a slime-covered baby girl shot out into Elizabeth's hands.

Elizabeth heard a nursing student sigh and say, "That was so beautiful."

That one will be a labor and delivery nurse, Elizabeth thought

Elizabeth wanted nothing to do with obstetrics, but she could see the young nurse was hooked. Medicine offered something for everyone.

Elizabeth laughed. "Well, that was easy." She surveyed the baby, cut the cord, suctioned the baby's nose and mouth, and handed her off to the cooing nursing student.

Elizabeth breathed a sigh of relief as she waited for the placenta to emerge. The baby was small, and the patient had not torn despite her precipitous delivery. Elizabeth was grateful her job was nearly over, and her mind wandered to food.

The three students filed out the door, headed for more mundane duties. The patient writhed and yelled, "I told you, I'm shot! My belly's killing me!" as she fought to remove herself from the stirrups and get up from the exam table. Livvy gently pushed her shoulders back down on the table and gave her intravenous pain medicine. The head nurse massaged the patient's shoulders and spoke soft reassurances in her ear. Elizabeth was impressed that being called a "Creole b-something" didn't lessen Livvy's sense of duty.

Elizabeth removed her gown and gloves. Dr. McSwain said, "Good job, intern." She heard the newborn crying in the background in the baby bassinet, surrounded by excited medical students. New life thrilled most medical people. Elizabeth wondered what kind of life was ahead for an infant girl whose mom didn't realize she was pregnant. The patient had not asked about the baby or even looked her way.

Elizabeth glanced back at the patient to be certain the bleeding had stopped. As she tossed her gown and gloves into the trash, she heard Dr. McSwain exclaim, "What in the world?"

Elizabeth spun around, saw what Dr. McSwain was seeing, and dove toward the patient, just in time to catch a second baby girl! *Good grief! These things are slippery.*

Elizabeth, Dr. McSwain, Livvy, and two medical students stood frozen in their places.

"What y'all looking at?" asked the patient.

"Ma'am, you've had twins," said Livvy. "You have two healthy girls."

Birth was messy. Elizabeth realized her pearl necklace, scrubs, shoes, hands, and arms were covered in blood, placenta fluid, urine, and even some feces. *Disgusting!* She cut the second baby's cord, handed her to the excited students, and put gloves over her filthy hands to receive the placenta. The patient's bleeding was minimal, and Elizabeth was, once again, grateful. *At last, this is over.*

Livvy questioned the patient softly, trying to get her history. "Did you not notice your period not coming?"

"My periods are not regular," said Miss Johnson. "Sometimes, I didn't get it for months, and then sometimes, it would come and stay for weeks. To tell you the truth, I never thought about it. I was too busy trying to keep my little brother from getting shot by them drug-dealing fools."

While Elizabeth washed up in the sink in the corner of the trauma room, Dr. McSwain pulled his white coat from a hook on the wall and the EMTs loaded up their equipment to return to their ambulance. Elizabeth hoped to get a clean set of scrubs as soon as she rounded on the ER patients again. She'd wash her pearls then too. The nurses took the patient's legs out of stirrups after cleaning her up and applying a clean pad to her perineum. They covered her in a sterile, warm blanket.

Elizabeth's adrenalin rush dissipated, but her job wasn't quite finished. After half the team had left, the patient bellowed.

"HEP, HEP, HEP. The pain's back, and I need some HELP from you fools," said Miss Johnson.

Elizabeth ran to her and felt her abdomen. "Dr. McSwain, her belly's hard as a rock again."

"Well, maybe we missed something. Maybe she does have an injury from a gunshot wound, and it precipitated the births," said Dr. McSwain.

Livvy said, "Get a fresh set of vital signs!"

"Blood pressure 130 over eight-six and pulse ninety-eight," said a nurse.

"Is this pain different from the pain you had a moment ago?" asked Elizabeth.

"No! I told you I was shot in the belly, and you ain't want to believe me," said the patient.

The stirrups had been removed, and the patient was lying flat on the exam room table.

Livvy leaned close to Elizabeth's ear and said, "Frog-leg her legs and look at her vagina again."

Elizabeth noticed this time Dr. McSwain looked like he was the one slapped with the cold flounder. Everyone suspended movement, except Livvy and Elizabeth. The women pulled open the patient's legs and propped her feet together as her knees flopped open to reveal another head covered in soft, wet black hair.

"Good heavens," said Dr. McSwain.

Livvy laughed as she handed Elizabeth clean gloves, saying, "Put these on, Crème Puff."

There were three healthy newborn girls born in Room Four on Christmas Eve. Elizabeth picked up the tiny infant and handed her to Livvy.

Elizabeth cut the cord to the placenta, patted the patient on the thigh, and said, “Good job.”

“Quick, get a cork,” whispered Dr. McSwain to Elizabeth, as he bolted for the door. “I’m headed to Tulane for hospital rounds.”

“Yes, sir,” replied the tired young doctor as the last of the placenta was delivered and the new mother was given a bolus of intravenous pain medicine. The patient was snoring, and her abdomen was finally soft. She looked calm and sweet and peaceful after the bolus of Dilaudid. Elizabeth cleaned and dressed the superficial gunshot wounds, covered the patient’s body with clean sheets, and tucked the sheets around her. *I hope her little brother is OK.*

The student nurses had returned. They were smiling and chattering while cleaning the baby girls and wrapping them for transport to the newborn nursery. Livvy phoned the Obstetrics resident on duty, and Elizabeth heard her say, “You’re not going to believe this one. We got a Christmas Eve surprise in the trauma room—three of them.”

2

"Where's our favorite surgical intern?" said the triage nurse, Aoife.

"The last time I saw our Crème Puff, she was in exam Room Eleven, evaluating a Cajun guy. Poor fellow burned himself racing his cigarette boat on Lake Pontchartrain. That girl gets the strangest cases," said Livvy.

Aoife laughed while her trained eyes looked from gurney to gurney, those lining the walls of the long hall, scanning for signs of distress. There were never enough beds at Charity Hospital, which the locals called The Big Free and many of the staff called Mother Charity.

"Looks like the patients are stable for now. If it's OK with you, Livvy, I'll check on Elizabeth."

Livvy looked at Aoife's chipped orange nail polish and her out-of-a-box dyed red hair. Beneath that poorly groomed elfin appearance was a hard-working nurse. Livvy said, "Sure, go down there and see what's going on. Elizabeth could probably use your help."

Livvy sagged into her chair and reached for her coffee.

The Big Free's shabby emergency room was the busiest trauma center in America, and it provided the toughest and best training for nurses and doctors. The place was more akin to a M.A.S.H. unit than a normal hospital. Though the halls were deceptively quiet at this moment, gunshot wounds, stab wounds, drug deals gone bad, and people being mean to each other provided a constant flow of patients. If you could work at The Big Free, you could make it at any hospital.

Livvy called to Aoife's back, "Who's minding your post at the triage station? I don't want you out helping an intern when Dr. McSwain rolls through the door for afternoon rounds."

"One of the new nurse trainees is sitting at my desk," said Aoife.

"Does she know what she's doing?" asked Livvy.

Aoife paused, tightened the rubber band holding her ponytail, and turned to stare at Livvy. She knew Livvy didn't trust anyone but herself to care for the patients. With a red face and rigid posture, Aoife said, "I made thorough rounds on everyone in the waiting room before coming back to see if I could help you. The student nurse knows to find me the second anything happens," Aoife explained.

"I know they can't learn without having some autonomy. But we're only six months into the new academic year, and everyone's still green. Keep a close eye on your new nurse. Bad things happen quickly down here," said Livvy.

Aoife watched the tired nurse sip her café au lait. "You're right, Livvy. I won't be long. I just want to see how Elizabeth's doing."

As Aoife walked away, Livvy called out, "You know she wants to be called Dr. Roberts now that she made the cut. I heard Tulane Surgery kept sixteen of thirty interns this year. They really culled the herd this time. By some miracle, she made it. I don't think she realizes all that she'll have to give up to be a Tulane surgeon."

"Has being chosen made her more confident?' asked Aoife.

"I wouldn't say that," Livvy replied. She's still scared to death of Dr. White, but she doesn't shake as much when Dr. McSwain talks to her. She twists those blood-stained pearls she wears constantly. She acts like being chosen is a burden. The cut was announced seven days ago, and I don't think she's gone home yet," said Livvy.

"Yes, I heard her grumbling about needing to move. Driving up Airline Highway is dangerous when you're exhausted. I hope she finds something in the French Quarter because then she can walk or ride a bike. The girl's getting as pale and vampire-like as Dr. White. Both could use a good sunning," said Livvy.

"Not all of us were born with warmed caramel for skin. Have some pity on us palefaces," said Aoife.

"Hey, there's much that goes with this color skin that you don't want," said Livvy.

"Let's save that discussion for another day. We've only got six hours left in this shift. I almost forgot to ask; did Elizabeth get any time off for Christmas?" said Aoife.

"No. She drew the short straw and has no time off during the holidays. I think she's getting homesick. She talks about her father more often. I'm trying to convince her to go to the party at Dr. McSwain's for Christmas. I hope she'll go, or maybe he'll change his mind at the last minute and let her drive home. South Carolina's only ten hours away. But I don't know if she could stay awake an hour and that rattle-trap-thing she calls a car might not make the trip again," said Livvy.

"I'll be at the party because being with my family is so crazy. I lied and told them I had to work every holiday shift. I'd much rather be with my hospital family," said Aoife.

"Me too! I'll swing by my mother's house and make an appearance," said Livvy.

"OK, enough! This time I'm really going. No more gossip this shift," laughed Aoife as she turned, winked, and headed down the hall.

Livvy again surveyed the patients in the halls and resumed charting in her nurse's notes. She took several deep breaths and hoped the rest of her shift was quiet.

The closer Aoife got to Room Eleven, the stronger the sulfur smell of the antibiotic cream used on burn patients became. She heard the thick bayou accents of a Cajun man and woman.

Aoife pushed open the exam room door and saw Dr. Elizabeth Roberts bending over a man who was naked except for his cowboy boots and cowboy hat. He seemed in excellent physical condition except for his groin.

Aoife stared at his scrotum and gasped. It was bright red and swollen to the size of a cantaloupe. His inner thighs were red and swollen, and his penis was bright red and swollen to twice its normal size.

Elizabeth stood dressed in a surgical mask, sterile gloves, and a blue surgical gown. Her pearls peeked out from under the blue gown and a wisp of blonde hair escaped her blue scrub cap. The young doctor, laser-focused on her work, did not notice the nurse's entrance. Aoife watched Elizabeth's slow, meticulous, and delicate movements as she cleaned the burns. The patient scowled but didn't move.

"Do what you got to do, Doc," he told her. "I'm the idiot that caused this problem, and I'm just glad you're here to help me. I'm sorry you got to see my manhood in this sorry condition. But I appreciate what you're doing to help me, Cher."

Six months ago, Elizabeth could not have understood what he was saying in his heavily accented Cajun English, but now her ears were more attuned to the dialects of Louisiana.

The exam room door flew open and Dr. McSwain entered. He saw the naked man's exposed red genitals and suppressed a laugh.

"Hello everyone, what do we have here?" he asked.

Elizabeth spun around and stared at him. He also wore cowboy boots. *Norman E. McSwain, Jr., M.D., Chief of Trauma, Tulane Surgery* was displayed above the breast pocket of his white coat. He wore a red cotton turtleneck and a bear claw necklace, and the large brass buckle on his belt displayed the emblem of the New Orleans Police Department. No surgery faculty anywhere dressed like Dr. McSwain. Without his white coat, he could have passed for a forty-year-old rodeo rider.

At the sound of her professor's voice, she froze, her sterile gloves held in midair above the patient's genitals. Her shoulders stiffened when she sniffed his aftershave—a musky odor she detected above the strong sulfur smell of the container of balm she held poised to apply to the patient's burns. His scent caused a surge of fear in Elizabeth.

Elizabeth couldn't speak while her mind ran the protocol for burn care. She was tired, had been working in the ER since early morning, and didn't want to misspeak and receive a lecture from her boss.

While Elizabeth stood frozen, the patient's wife craned her neck to read Dr. McSwain's name on his jacket, and said, "It's nice to meet you, sir. My name is Mrs. Mellette Benoit, and the man on that stretcher is my husband, Mr. Leeodus Benoit. He was the victim of his own stupidity, and this nice lady's trying to help us," said Mellette.

Dr. McSwain and Elizabeth turned together toward Mellette. She was tall and slender, with delicate features and a head of unruly but magnificent red hair. But for her heavy Cajun accent, she could have been a princess from an Irish fairy tale.

"I don't mind so much that he might have fried his eggs with the stupid accident, but I do hope you can preserve his pickle as we find it mighty useful at times," said Mellette. Her husband grinned and nodded in her direction. Their deep affection was obvious. Both Benoits flashed intense bright blue eyes.

Elizabeth thought, *They look related.*

Dr. McSwain leaned in to get a closer look at the patient's injuries and said, "We'll do all possible to help your husband, Mrs. Benoit. Dr. Roberts, why don't you wait a few minutes before applying the cream to his burns? I'd like to hear the entire story and examine Mr. Benoit."

"Yes, sir." Elizabeth knew her professor insisted on formality in front of the patients. She might be Elizabeth when the team was alone, but her professor believed it important to calm the patient by being authoritarian while determining the course of treatment. At some point, Dr. McSwain would leave, and Elizabeth would be this patient's doctor.

"Tell me what happened to you, Mr. Benoit," said Dr. McSwain.

"First of all, please call me Leeodus. Mr. Benoit's my father," said Leeodus. His wife came closer to the bed. Elizabeth noticed her tight jeans, her low-cut T-shirt containing her enormous breasts, and her cowboy boots.

Leeodus did not cover himself as he lay, arms propped behind his head. A long, curly, light brown ponytail escaped from the back of his cowboy hat and draped over the pillow. Mellette twirled the pony tail while her husband talked.

"Well, sir, I have a boat that I race on Lake Pontchartrain," said Leeodus.

"On Thursday afternoon? It's Christmas Eve, son," said Dr. McSwain.

"Yes, sir. The lake's quiet during the weekdays, and I own an Abita beer distributorship and can get off whenever I like. Thursday's my day off, and on Thursdays, me and Mellette and some of our friends like to go out to the lake to race," said Leeodus.

Elizabeth stared at the patient's injury pattern. His inner thighs were getting redder and blisters were forming between his legs. His scrotum enlarged as she watched. The patient's penis was sizable to start and became pinker and more swollen as they waited.

"Dr. McSwain, may I put some cold packs on Mr. Benoit and administer his tetanus shot while you're getting his history?" she asked. Six months ago, Elizabeth would have never interrupted her professor.

"Absolutely. Please proceed with your first aid. I prefer that you not cover the wounds with antibiotic cream until I've heard the mechanism of injury and gotten a good exam. As swollen as his penis is getting, he may need a catheter," said Dr. McSwain.

Both Benoits' eyes widened and their brows furrowed in unison. A catheter didn't sound like anything either wanted for Leeodus.

Mellette patted her husband's shoulder with one long red nail. "Go on. Tell the story, *mi amore*."

"OK, Doc. Here we go. I was a helicopter pilot in the military, and I'm fascinated with gadgets of all types. So my latest gadget was a multipurpose handheld unit similar to a giant flashlight. It's a Taser, flashlight, and emergency alarm, all-in-one. The problem is whoever designed it put the buttons too close together," said Leeodus, waving his arms around and smiling while he explained his toy.

"The doctor's not interested in your gadgets, sweetie," Mellette interrupted. "He wants to know how your balls came to be bright red cantaloupes."

Elizabeth watched Dr. McSwain attempt, without success, to fight back a laugh. Aoife giggled, and Elizabeth realized for the first time the nurse stood behind her.

Leeodus smiled at his wife and said, "Yes, ma'am! So, we were racing on Lake Pontchartrain most of the day, and it was getting to be dusk. We anchored in a little cove, planning to enjoy the sunset. I heard a bump on the back of the boat and took my flashlight to shine into the water to better see what caused the bumping sound on the back of the boat. Mellette was up front getting our picnic together."

Elizabeth positioned cold packs over the patient's genitals while listening to his story. Leeodus grimaced when she touched him but continued his story. Aoife leaned on the wall behind Dr. McSwain, attempting to be invisible. She knew she should return to the triage desk, but couldn't bear to miss the rest of the story.

"Doc," continued Leeodus, "I leaned over to look into the water and pressed the button on the shaft of the flashlight that I thought would turn on the light, and good gawd a-mighty, it was the Taser. I tasered myself! Doc, I fell back into the boat! The dang thing was still on, and it fell right on my crotch and tasered the dawg out of my balls and pecker! I was flopping around like a redfish on my own boat deck. It felt like lightning had struck my crotch."

"I heard him flopping around on the deck, but he didn't call out to me, so I thought he was OK. So I kept making the picnic," said Mellette. A grin tickled the corners of her mouth.

"I couldn't speak, and I couldn't move my hands to remove the Taser from my groin," Leeodus explained. "My body jumped around on the floor of that boat! I fought to keep conscious and tried to yell to my wife." He paused. "Doc, you ever been tasered? It hurts like a mother!"

"Son, I can't say that I've ever been tasered. That must have been an awful experience," said Dr. McSwain as he dressed in a surgical gown and gloves to examine Leeodus.

"How long did you lie on the floor of your boat tasering yourself?" asked Elizabeth.

Mellette leaned closer to the gurney and said, "He was there for a while. I feel just terrible, but I didn't realize there was a problem. Leeodus is always playing jokes on me and everyone else. When I first turned around and saw him out of the corner of my eye, I thought he was faking a seizure. Then I saw him bang his head on the driver's seat, and I knew something was up."

Elizabeth thought, *Faking a seizure? She sure is beautiful but maybe not too smart.*

"Leeodus doesn't drink when he's racing because he needs everything he's got to keep control of that powerful boat, but I do drink a little wine while being a passenger. I was probably a bit drunk, to tell the truth," confessed Mellette.

Dr. McSwain lifted the patient's scrotum to explore between his legs. Leeodus yelped and slapped his hand over his mouth to control a scream.

"I'm sorry to hurt you, son," said Dr. McSwain as he exposed the extent of the burns. "Dr. Roberts, it looks like he has a wide area of first-degree burn, a few centimeters of second-degree burn, and up under his scrotum, near his anus is an area of third-degree burn that might eventually need a skin graft," said Dr. McSwain.

"Oh, *Mi Amore*, I'm so sorry for you. Doc, is his manhood going to work after all of this?" asked Mellette.

"Yes, ma'am. He'll be just fine in a few weeks. But right now, I think he needs to be admitted," said Dr. McSwain.

He pulled off his gown and gloves and turned to Elizabeth. "Give him a dose of Demerol for pain, clean him up well, apply the Silvadene cream thickly, and lay loose sterile gauze over the wounds. That area behind his scrotum will need wet-to-dry dressing changes once he gets on the ward. Remember to look everywhere. You did a good job of cutting all his clothes to expose the entire area. But had we not lifted his scrotum and looked in between his legs, we would've missed the worse part. He'll need to be admitted for a few days," said Dr. McSwain.

I was about to look down there before I was interrupted. But Elizabeth nodded and said, "Yes, sir." She hated to think her mentor thought she didn't explore the entire wound.

Aoife pulled Demerol from her pocket where she kept a small pharmacy and gave it to Leeodus in his intravenous line. He relaxed and giggled. His head fell back on the pillow; he closed his blue eyes and giggled again as his cowboy hat fell onto the pillow.

"Mellette, Leeodus didn't explain how he got out of the boat and how the tasering stopped," said Elizabeth as she cleaned the wounds.

Mellette said, "I ran to the back of the boat once I realized he wasn't joking around. I was taught not to touch anyone struck by lightning, and I thought maybe that stupid Taser was similar. I grabbed a rubber-ended boat hook and pushed the Taser away from his body. It rolled to the back of the boat, and I could see three buttons along the shaft. It was getting dark and I couldn't tell which button was which, so I just pushed until the Taser stopped jiggling. But I pushed one too many buttons and the screaming alarm started. It startled me, and I fell back in the boat and banged my head too. I must have been dazed for a few minutes because, when I became aware, the siren was still blaring and Leeodus was standing in the back of the boat. He picked it up and threw it as far as he could into Lake Pontchartrain. That thing continued to scream out for a few minutes even under water," said Mellette.

Dr. McSwain examined her head with both hands, feeling every area of her scalp. He used his penlight, ever-ready in his top lab coat pocket, to check her pupils.

"She has a tiny lump on her occipital area, but her pupils look normal. I think she's OK," said Dr. McSwain.

While he had her head clasped in his hands, he looked into her eyes and asked, "You guys aren't smuggling drugs in your cigarette boat, are you?"

"Heck, no! I'm Catholic!" said Mellette, as if that absolved them of any possible guilt. "Leeodus is obsessed with speed. He rides his motorcycle, drives his car, and pilots his boat as if the hounds of hell are chasing him. He has too much testosterone, if you want to know the truth. I think all that testosterone has poisoned his brain cells."

While Elizabeth completed the dressing, Aoife sneaked out the exam room door and headed back to the nurses' station. Mellette collapsed on the stool in the corner of the exam room, and Leeodus snored with the peace of intravenous narcotics. Elizabeth draped a clean cotton hospital gown over his body. He looked comical in his askew cowboy hat, pale blue hospital gown, and polished cowboy boots. She chuckled to herself. *This crazy job is never boring, and you meet the most interesting people.*

Bringing her back from her reverie, Dr. McSwain tapped Elizabeth on her shoulder and said, "Good job, intern. Finish up, and I'll see you in the hall for rounds."

Elizabeth stiffened, feeling her usual sense of dread and excitement. *What had she forgotten to do? What would she learn this evening?* As she finished dressing Leeodus's wounds, her mind ran through every patient in every exam room and every patient on every gurney in each hall in the emergency room. She knew being the Tulane Surgery charge intern in the accident room meant carrying the target for every patient seen during her twenty-four-hour shift. Her heart raced and her breath quickened as she wondered what might happen next.

3

Elizabeth continued her tasks in Room Eleven while Dr. McSwain walked the emergency room halls amid the smells of alcohol and blood. His head swiveled from side to side as he evaluated the patients lined along the walls who were awaiting care. The sound of their breathing, the look in their eyes, their position on the gurney, and their stated complaints were valuable clues to their conditions. His years of trauma experience had honed his skills of observation. By the time he arrived at the nurses' station at the end of the hall, he surmised all was well, for the moment. He waited on Elizabeth for rounds.

Livvy saw her boss and smiled. "Good evening, Dr. McSwain. So far, so good. Nothing too big has happened lately."

"Merry Christmas Eve to you, Livvy. What do you and Aoife have planned for Christmas Day? I hope you'll pass by my house for the party tomorrow," said Dr. McSwain.

Aoife stood a few feet away, knowing she should be in the triage area. But it was quiet in the waiting room, and she didn't want to miss out on any action. Dr. McSwain was an excellent teacher, and she learned much by observing him during rounds.

Livvy took a deep breath, gathered her courage and said to her boss, "I was surprised that even though Elizabeth's family lives in South Carolina, she got no time off for Christmas?"

Aoife's body tensed up. She'd never heard Livvy question Dr. McSwain's decisions, and she couldn't remember the head nurse ever inquiring about any intern's welfare.

"Yep, all the residents and interns drew names from a bowl in the surgery department, and she lost. Somebody has to stay and mind the shop and this year, it's her. Livvy, you know all the interns want to go home for Christmas. But somebody has to work besides you, me, and Aoife. You know more people are shot and stabbed on holidays than any other time. It could be quite busy," said Dr. McSwain.

"So, even though most of the other interns are from Louisiana, the out-of-state people are given no preference for Christmas?" asked Livvy. The nurse's head bobbed and her hips swayed. Aoife knew the signs of Livvy trying to get her way. Livvy's hands were not on her hips, so she was only going so far with her inquiry. But still, this was Dr. McSwain she was questioning. Aoife shrunk back as her palms started to sweat.

He stared with cool brown eyes, crossed his arms over his chest, and said, "You know nobody gets preferential treatment at Tulane Surgery, not for any reason! We're putting out surgeons, not debutantes. I suggest you not turn her into some kind of pet, Livvy. She's a good doctor but has a long way to go. She gets treated like every other intern who lost the Christmas lottery."

Looking down at her shoes, Livvy muttered, "Yes, sir. I understand."

"I'm going up to the ward to check on a few patients in the Intensive Care Unit and will be back down after Elizabeth has finished with the burn patient's dressing. That was a nasty mechanism of injury," said Dr. McSwain. The professor laughed, shook his head, and walked away.

The second he was out of hearing distance, Aoife said to Livvy, "We'll get her a nice Christmas gift. I can tell she really misses her family. Everyone likes her. We can all pitch in and get something nice. She's attached to those pearls she's always wearing. They've been doused in blood to the point the string's looking brown. My cousin knows how to restring pearls. Maybe I can get the family rate and get them done in time for Dr. McSwain's party tomorrow."

Livvy said, "Good luck getting those pearls off of her. She can't go longer than fifteen minutes without touching them. They seem to be a combination of a talisman, rosary beads, and a good luck charm. I think her grandmother gave them to her when she was young. I see no way to get them away from her. We'll have to come up with something else."

"There has to be something we can do for her," said Aoife.

Livvy broke out into a mischievous grin. "As a matter of fact, I have a special surprise gift in mind. I've been doing a little research and have decided what that girl needs is a reason to go home to her apartment every now and then. With her poor dating skills, it's unlikely to be a man. I've just the perfect surprise. It'll remind her of me and make her have to go home every couple of days," said the nurse.

"Please tell me! I swear I won't tell," begged Aoife.

"Oh, heck no! You can't keep your mouth shut about anything. I'm keeping this little surprise to myself. I'll get it tonight on my way home. I plan to give it to her at Dr. McSwain's party, in front of everyone, and that way she'll have to take it and act grateful. Her South Carolina manners won't allow her to do anything else," Livvy said. "It's hard to believe now, but five months ago, I wanted her fired."

Aoife wasn't giving up. "Come on, Livvy, give me a hint. I swear I won't tell," she said.

Livvy shook her head from side to side and said, "Aoife Dears Patrick, you're one of the biggest gossips in the hospital. I think that's why you like to work the triage desk at the entrance to the emergency room. You want to know everything first. But not this time! My fun little Christmas gift for our young intern will be a surprise! In fact, it'll be a shock if I'm lucky!"

"OK, be that way. You'll have to find another intern to torment in a week. Elizabeth only has seven more days on this rotation. Where does she go next?" asked Aoife.

The phone rang at the nurses' station, and Livvy gave instructions to the lab. The overhead speakers blasted about a code to West Admit.

Livvy resumed where they'd left off. "I have no idea. She hopes to go out of town to Alexandria to do one of the intern rotations in Northern Louisiana. She heard the interns there have more autonomy and believes the rotations have less major trauma and are more relaxed. She thinks being out in the country will be more to her liking," Livvy said. "But I know the truth. She wants to get as far away from Dr. Harrison White as possible. His intensity scares the wits out of her."

Aoife said, "I feel sad thinking she won't be around. Isn't that a three-month rotation? She's an intern we can trust, and she works hard."

"Tulane doesn't want to move residents and interns four hours away for a month, so out-of-town rotations are usually three months," Livvy replied. "I hate to see my little Crème Puff go away. She provides so much entertainment. I've never met a more naïve grownup. But I think the constant pressure of all this death and dying is wearing on her. She's skinny as can be. She's pinning up the waistband of her khaki skirt with a diaper pin because she's lost so much weight."

"Livvy, she hates when you call her Crème Puff. Stop it! I think any rotation will be fine with her, except cardiothoracic surgery. I think if she had to spend an entire month with Dr. White, she might have a nervous breakdown," said Aoife.

"You're right. I'm thinking she probably won't be assigned to his service. Even after six months, she can't look him in the eye, and he doesn't seem to have warmed to her at all. I thought after she was chosen to stay, he'd be nicer. But so far, not. And as for calling her Crème Puff," Livvy smiled, "anyone who shows up for a trauma rotation wearing a pink hair bow, a pink Izod shirt, a starched khaki skirt, and plaid pink socks with shiny penny loafers deserves to be called Crème Puff. Forever," said Livvy. Both nurses laughed.

Aoife said, "I feel disloyal for laughing, but the nickname certainly describes how she looked that first day."

As they talked, Livvy kept a watchful eye on the medical students and student nurses moving in and out of the examination rooms. She called down the hall to a student named Larry, "You guys OK?"

"Yes, Nurse Robichaud, everything's under control. We're giving tetanus shots, cleaning wounds, and stitching folks up. It's pretty calm so far tonight," said Larry.

"Great! Keep it that way," said Livvy.

Larry Silverstein had been on his first rotation in psychiatry when a young, beautiful woman came to the ER with half of her face shot off after a botched suicide attempt. Elizabeth had helped with the case, and Larry latched onto her as her mentee. He was afraid of blood when Elizabeth first started working with him, but now he was one of her best helpers. He came to the ER to stitch up patients even after his surgery rotation ended.

Aoife moved closer to Livvy and asked, "Is Elizabeth still hoping to move?"

"I think so. Her neighbor, the Polish lady—Mrs. Kaczka—is nice to her. But she has a little yappy Chihuahua that wakes Elizabeth up when she's trying to rest. And between the constant smell of cabbage cooking and Mrs. Kaczka's weekly lectures on 'getting a man,' Elizabeth doesn't feel at home there," said Livvy.

"Growing up on the farm, I guess Elizabeth is used to large working dogs. Her idea of a dog is a German shepherd. She told me she doesn't like little dogs. Buster, the Chihuahua, is a little rat to her," laughed Aoife. "It didn't help that she saved his life after he aspirated a Mardi Gras bead. The little punk tried to bite her afterward and cemented their mutual dislike." Aoife paused, then continued, "I hope she finds a new apartment she likes."

"I know of two guys in the French Quarter, a gay couple, looking to rent out a room. I'm planning to suggest their place to Elizabeth because she loves the quarter, and Ray and John live on Royal Street, Elizabeth's favorite street," Livvy said. "They also have a large dog. I know nothing of dogs, but I think it's a golden retriever? Ray's a hick from Mississippi, and I think they'd get along well."

"Sounds perfect," said Aoife.

"And the price is right," Livvy said. "They own an antiques store on Royal and travel much of the time on buying trips. They want someone to care for the dog and their gorgeous garden when they are out of town. If she lived there, she'd have to go home to feed the dog and water the plants. So, along with my Christmas surprise, we might get her out of the hospital occasionally."

"How would that work if she gets the out-of-town rotation?" asked Aoife.

"Ray and John would keep doing what they do now, hire someone until she gets back," said Livvy.

"Any place in the quarter would be better than her current apartment," said Aoife. "But enough! Time to get back to work."

4

The same evening and an hour later, Dr. McSwain strode through the swinging doors. Standing in the middle of the hall, he made a quick whistling noise and a circling motion above his head with his right arm. It was like a motion a cowboy might make to signal the wagons to circle, and everyone knew he meant, *It's time to round on the patients.*

Livvy leaned toward Aoife's face and asked pointedly, "Don't you have work to do at the triage desk?" Because Livvy's hands were on her wide hips and her head was bobbing, Aoife knew she was serious.

Aoife gave a military salute and stood at full attention. "Yes, ma'am, Head Nurse Lavinia Robichaud, I'm reporting for duty!" Both women laughed as Aoife scurried to the triage desk. Dr. McSwain nodded to Aoife as she passed.

McSwain was handsome in a rugged way, and his red turtleneck was his nod to the Christmas décor. He stood in front of Livvy, broadcasting his thousand-watt smile, rocking back and forth in his cowboy boots, waiting for rounds to start. Just then, Elizabeth exited an exam room, and he again made a circle in the air.

Elizabeth's eyes darted from gurney to gurney, assessing each patient for signs of change.

There are at least thirty patients in this ER . . . how can they expect me to know them all? This is the most unreasonable job. Let's get it over with so he'll go back to Tulane and I can finish my work.

"Hi, Dr. McSwain," Elizabeth greeted him. "You're back quickly. For the moment, there's nobody about to code. We had lots of action earlier from drunken conventioneers. There's a dental convention in town over the holiday, and we've seen six dentists tonight. There've been a few stabbings—all superficial. One needed a chest tube, and the students are transferring him to the floor. His post chest tube placement X-ray is up on the viewing box for you to see."

She paused and took a breath, then continued, "There were two gunshot victims. One was shot in the buttocks and foot trying to escape the bedroom of his best friend's wife. Officer Alois Thibodeaux is taking his statement. Another guy shot himself in the hand while playing with his gun and drinking. Plastic surgery is debriding him in Room Six. There's nobody who needs to go to the operating room right now," concluded Elizabeth.

Dr. McSwain peeked around Elizabeth to see the three medical students hiding behind her. Larry Silverstein, Jalpa Patel, and Sallie Smith were third-year students. None of them were on the surgery rotation, but they were often in the emergency room when Elizabeth was the surgical charge resident. McSwain stared at the group.

"What have you done for the good of mankind today?" Dr. McSwain began rounds with his trademark question. "I'm impressed to see students who want to learn, even on Christmas Eve when you don't have to be here. I hope Dr. Roberts is teaching you well."

He leaned in to read their name tags. "Miss Sallie Smith, what are our concerns with a stab wound victim?" asked Dr. McSwain.

Medical students weren't called doctor until after graduation, when they changed from a short white coat to a long white coat. These three students only got their short coats six months earlier.

Sallie stepped from behind Elizabeth and replied, "We have to worry the injury is deeper than what we can see, and we have to worry about blood vessel injury. The entrance wound only tells part of the story. We have to know every layer beneath the entrance site and what could be injured that we can't see."

Dr. McSwain nodded and smiled in Elizabeth's direction. "Miss Jalpa Patel, what if the patient's stabbed in the chest area?"

Jalpa cowered behind Elizabeth and mumbled into her chest as she looked at the floor and said, "We worry about the lungs, heart, and large vessels in the chest. Our patient who needed the chest tube had a tiny puncture wound in his lung, and it collapsed his lung. Elizabeth showed us his chest X-ray. When Larry got the diagnosis of pneumothorax correct, she let him put in the chest tube." Jalpa beamed.

Students learned at an accelerated pace here. No hospital had the volume of sick and suffering patients. She was called many names, The Big Free, Mother Charity, the Big House, and Charity Hospital-New Orleans. Whatever the honorific, she taught generations of medical professionals. Six months before, Elizabeth was nearly fired for not securing a chest tube properly, an error that almost cost a patient his life. Today, she taught a frightened future psychiatrist how to place a chest tube in the ER. "See one. Do one. Teach one," said Dr. McSwain.

Elizabeth was proud of her trainees.

"Who's going to be a surgeon among you three?" asked Dr. McSwain.

The students looked away from their professor. Larry said, "I want to be a psychiatrist. Elizabeth taught me I should acquire the basic skills all doctors need to help my patients who try to commit suicide. I may be the first doctor they see, and she's made sure I won't faint at the scene."

McSwain fought back a laugh and said, "Great idea, son. That's a great idea. What about you, Sallie?"

Sallie stood tall as she tugged the top of her short afro. "My mother's a nurse practitioner midwife," she said, "and I'm planning to be an obstetrician. I like being in the trauma ER because Elizabeth teaches the entire time she works, and my mom said I should be down here absorbing everything. Mom said 'every bit of knowledge will be useful to me in medicine'."

"Your mother's a sage. At one time or another, you'll use everything you've learned. Pay close attention as lives depend on your knowledge," he admonished them. "What about you, Miss Jalpa Patel?" said Dr. McSwain.

The startled young Indian woman shuffled to the front of the group and said, "I don't know, doctor. I've ruled out urology." The students and Elizabeth chuckled at the inside joke.

Their professor looked on. "How did you rule out urology? You're only halfway through your third year of medical school." said McSwain.

Jalpa's face reddened, and her head bobbed like a metronome. She tried to speak, but words wouldn't come. Elizabeth touched Jalpa's arm and said, "We had a patient at the VA who became upset during our male urologic exam tutorial. Jalpa had a bad experience during the teaching session. It was the first time I'd taught the session, sir, and my inexperience caused poor communication as I'd not prepared the students properly."

The giggling and smirks from the students continued.

Dr. McSwain said, "I imagine there's more to this story. But a good leader always takes responsibility, Dr. Roberts. I'll leave the group to your private moment." He paused and then said, "Jalpa, urology's not for everyone, that's for sure." Jalpa's blush deepened.

Dr. McSwain stepped back and said, "OK, gang, that's enough for this evening's rounds. My Christmas party is tomorrow evening at my house on Bourbon Street in the quarter. Everyone with nowhere better to go is invited. Please tell your fellow students and residents they are welcome to come. There'll be plenty of food and drink, and the New Orleans police will be on horseback to protect everyone. If you walk in a group from the hospital straight down Bourbon Street, you should be safe, and you'll run into my house before you hit Esplanade. Don't veer off into any side streets as crime's been up lately. I hope to see all of you there."

5

Elizabeth left Room Four at 5:00 a.m. It was now Christmas Day. Dr. McSwain stood, coffee in hand, surveying the halls with the intensity of a military sniper. Elizabeth anxiously listened for sounds of trouble coming from the other exam rooms. She knew clanging metal drawers and raised voices meant the staff was grabbing supplies to handle emergencies. The rooms were quiet. She'd lost all sense of time. She was hungry, but food and a shower would have to wait.

Dr. McSwain smiled at her and the students as they huddled in the hall. He said, "Merry Christmas, gang, and what have you done for the good of humanity today?"

His familiar question focused the team. Medical students from Tulane and LSU trained at Charity Hospital for the educational opportunity. Dr. McSwain took advantage of quiet time in the ER to teach and remind his students of their greater purpose—to render service to those in need. Elizabeth felt the familiar cramp in her abdomen. She wished it were only hunger but knew it was fear. Today, she carried the target. In Tulane Surgery parlance, carrying the target meant she was in charge of the activities in the ER, and as the doctor in charge, she carried the blame for anything that went wrong. She'd just slept two hours on the cold table in the radiology area behind Room Four, and she hoped she hadn't missed anything important. Dr. McSwain came early this morning.

He pivoted to Elizabeth and said, "So, Dr. Roberts, tell our students the lessons from yesterday's Room Four experience."

After months under his tutelage, Elizabeth knew every patient encounter brought a teachable moment. But right now, her scrubs were stained with several patients' body fluids. She was twenty-two hours into her twenty-four-hour shift, and she struggled to find the energy to speak. She wondered, *How does Dr. McSwain do it? He never looks tired. He's always bursting with energy and enthusiasm. And he's old! He's at least forty-two.*

"Wake up, Doctor. I asked you a question," said Dr. McSwain.

"Yes, sir," Elizabeth replied. "We learned many lessons from our last Room Four patient. One is to expect the unexpected. Two is to get the history in detail. Three is to examine and re-examine the patient. And four is to always have a high index of suspicion for problems that are not obvious. Her mechanism of injury, the gunshot wound to the abdomen, suggested she might have internal injuries. Her physical examination showed a firm abdomen, suggesting internal bleeding," reported Elizabeth.

"Ok, Doctor. Based on what you've said so far, we should've opened her abdomen in Room Four and looked to compress the bleeding while transfusing her and calling for an operating room to rush her upstairs for major surgery. We did none of that. Why didn't we?" asked Dr. McSwain.

Elizabeth watched the students' tension mirror their professor's increasing tension. *Surgical rounds are like a dance,* thought Elizabeth. *Everyone must be ready for the next move or your toes could get crunched by an unskilled partner.*

"The keys to knowing our patient didn't have a serious abdominal bleed were: at the scene, she did not experience a drop in her blood pressure. We knew that information from the EMTs verbal report. Next, in Room Four, she had high blood pressure, and was only mildly tachycardic. Her blood pressure reading wasn't consistent with major abdominal bleeding." Elizabeth continued, "Her physical exam was confusing but helpful in that she was quite obese and the bullet pattern was buckshot scattered from clavicles to knees instead of one or two high caliber bullet holes."

"What confused you about her abdominal examination?" said Dr. McSwain.

"I couldn't feel much through the ten inches of fat tissue," Elizabeth replied. "But she had a hard abdomen extending above the umbilicus in the midline," said Elizabeth.

"Did the possibility of pregnancy ever enter your mind?" said Dr. McSwain.

Elizabeth stared at the floor. She felt frustrated because she couldn't accept her own ignorance. Wisps of blonde hair escaped her disheveled ponytail and fell around her face as she struggled to answer the question. Even though she knew she was learning her trade, she hated not knowing the correct answers. She shuffled her feet and wrestled with telling the truth and looking bad in front of the team.

"No, Dr. McSwain, it did not," said Elizabeth with a deep sigh. Daddy taught her, *when all else fails, the truth is your best choice, little girl.* Elizabeth looked up into her professor's eyes and prepared herself for the lesson.

"At what point did you realize the patient was not critical?" asked Dr. McSwain.

I can't tell him the truth in front of the students; he'll roast me alive, but . . .

"Honestly, Dr. McSwain, I didn't know what to think. The patient was screaming in pain and her abdomen was hard as a rock, but you and Nurse Robichaud didn't look too concerned. Usually, if something bad is happening with a patient, the two of you stand very close to me and are at full attention. Nurse Robichaud was standing back near the wall, getting instruments from the nonemergency cart, and you had an amused look on your face," said Elizabeth.

Much to her surprise, he laughed, slapping his knees while turning in a circle on the heels of his cowboy boots, as if he were line dancing. Elizabeth and the students were confused, while their professor enjoyed a good belly laugh.

After a few minutes, he was quiet. He stood smiling and looking at the team.

"So the lesson here is to scrutinize your surroundings. If you don't know what in the world's going on, maybe somebody close to you does! That's priceless, Dr. Roberts! One of the reasons you might make a pretty good surgeon one day is your honesty. You're not afraid to say the truth, and that quality serves you well. But, students, just so you know—that is *not* the correct answer for your boards! A palpably firm lower abdomen in a stable female patient should bring to mind a pregnant uterus or a full bladder! A relaxed professor and a quiet nurse do not a diagnosis make. Let's make rounds."

While the team walked the halls, he whispered to Elizabeth, "At this point in your education, it seems you've learned to read me and Nurse Robichaud well. Now, if we can just get you to focus on the patient, your progress will be fast."

What a great Christmas gift, Elizabeth thought, *to be humiliated in front of the students.*

Elizabeth was becoming obsessed with the idea of escaping to a hot shower and some good food. Dr. McSwain liked swift rounds, so he and Elizabeth walked and discussed their patients as she passed each room.

"Exam Room One is Mrs. Green. She's the victim of domestic violence. She was superficially stabbed eleven times by her drunken husband. Jalpa cleaned her wounds, gave her a tetanus shot, and offered the women's shelter," said Dr. Roberts.

The team didn't enter the room but stood at the patient's door, talking in low tones and peeking through the partly open door. Mrs. Green, covered in clean gauze dressings, snored while she clutched the sheets. Her hands were clenched in knots, and she was grinding her teeth between snores. Even in sleep, her furrowed brow made her look afraid.

"Dr. Roberts, did you personally look at all of her wounds?" asked Dr. McSwain. Elizabeth watched Jalpa look indignant and glare at the professor. Education and the honor of a job well done were very important to her. The young Indian woman had made enormous progress in her six months of clinical rotations, and Elizabeth knew English wasn't her primary language.

Jalpa's anger at Dr. McSwain was barely contained. Elizabeth knew their professor's question was no reflection of his trust or regard for Jalpa. Tulane Surgery trusted no student with a patient's life.

"Yes, sir," Elizabeth replied. "Jalpa did an excellent job, and I checked every wound before and after she did her work. Jalpa's meticulous, sir." Jalpa smiled and bowed her head toward Elizabeth.

"Is Mrs. Green going to the women's shelter? Did she press charges against her monstrous husband?" asked Dr. McSwain.

Sallie, the only Black female in this year's third-year medical school class, spoke up, "Dr. McSwain, what's with these women?" she asked. "Her half-drunk husband drives her in here and deposits her on our doorstep, then drives away before the police can nab him. We spend hours cleaning up his handiwork, and then she wants to go right back home to the same jerk who did this to her?" Her bright brown eyes were flashing, and her afro jiggled with every indignant gesture.

Elizabeth thought, *If some man tried that with me, I'd gut him in a minute. Just like a deer. And maybe I'd skin him like a squirrel for good measure.*

Dr. McSwain rubbed his chin in thought. "I can't explain it, Sallie. One reason I chose surgery is because I like immediate gratification. I like to see a problem, know I have the skills to fix it, then fix the problem. I prefer to see a patient come in screaming and go out smiling." He paused and then continued, "The nuances of human behavior fascinate me, but trying to treat them seems fruitless. So I leave all the *whys* and *wherefores* to the psychiatrists, clergy, and social workers. I prefer to cut out problems with cold steel."

"Can we at least consult psychiatry and social work?" asked Sallie. "I can't believe there's nothing we can do to help women like these escape this cycle of abuse. Everyone deserves a peaceful life."

Elizabeth said, "The social worker's already been here, Sallie. Mrs. Green was given information on the women's shelter and offered a ride.

You can see the paperwork's in the trash receptacle by her bed. She didn't even look at the address. I told Mrs. Green that one day, her husband's going to go too far and kill her. Unfortunately, she seems resigned to her plight."

"Yep, one day, they'll bring her in, and we won't be able to patch her up. I wish I had some insight into this behavior to help you students understand, but I don't understand it myself," said Dr. McSwain.

As they walked to the next exam room, Elizabeth heard Sallie mutter under her breath, "Some man might stab me one time, and then they'd be bringing his sorry butt in here in a body bag on his way to the morgue. The women in my family don't put up with that crap, not for one minute."

Sallie came from a single-parent family. Her mother raised Sallie to be independent. She didn't understand someone who wasn't independent like she was, and the situation made her angry. Elizabeth saw her staring at the back of Dr. McSwain's head and thought, *She's willing him to do more, but she doesn't understand that he's a surgeon and has no ability to do more.*

At the next room, Jalpa stepped to the front of the group and said, "In this room we have a nineteen- year-old Tulane undergraduate student. He was drinking at a beer party, imbibed a bit much, and left the party with a few friends to scale the fence surrounding the pool of the nicest home on Audubon Avenue. The family was away, and the students continued their wild party until the neighbors called the police."

"Why's he here, Jalpa?" Elizabeth asked. "Get to the point for our trauma rounds." Elizabeth's bed was calling, and her stomach was dragging on her backbone for lack of sustenance. When hungry, she could be mean-spirited.

Jalpa sighed, gave Elizabeth a side-eyed glare, and said, "After the NOPD arrived, the other students left, and nobody was booked. This young man chose to fight the police in his drunkenness. It was a short fight. He stumbled and hit his lower jaw on the concrete around the pool's edge. The impact cracked his jaw and gave him a huge cut on his chin that bled a great deal, as head wounds do."

Elizabeth nearly laughed out loud. Two months ago, every time Jalpa had to present a patient, she nearly fainted. Now, she was confident nearly to the point of arrogance. Elizabeth felt a surge of pride watching her students perform on rounds.

"Who stitched him up?" asked Dr. McSwain as he entered the exam room and looked down at the sleeping man. The room reeked of alcohol. The student's T-shirt and swim trunks were covered in blood. Asleep, he looked like a boy about twelve, not a college student. Worn out by partying, alcohol, the police encounter, and the emergency room experience, he was heavy with sleep.

"It was a light night down here and plastic surgery had little to do, so the first-year plastics resident did the honors," said Jalpa.

"Are the police going to book him?" asked Dr. McSwain.

Elizabeth said, "No, sir. Officer Alois Thibodeaux was in earlier and decided there was no property damage and thought the student's jaw fracture would be punishment enough. Officer Thibodaux phoned the doctor who owned the home, and he didn't wish to press charges when he learned it was a Tulane student."

The group exited the exam room and turned left. They were greeted with the backside of the Benoit couple, Leeodus and Mellette, headed to the nurses' station. Leeodus clutched his IV pole. He'd been in the ER an entire day getting intravenous antibiotics.

Leeodus's cowboy hat sat cock-eyed on his head. Black socks peeked above his boots. His open hospital gown exposed his nakedness. Neither Benoit seemed to notice. Leeodus had the build of a welterweight boxer, broad in the back and narrow at the hips.

Elizabeth heard Leeodus talking to the male nurse. "Yes, sir. I realize you have rules, and I appreciate all y'all have done for me. But I got to get out to my fish camp and secure my pirogue."

The dressing Elizabeth had placed on his wounds had been reinforced with thick silver duct tape. The couple had been busy.

"Look, nurse, I've taken care of all kinds of farm animals for twenty years, and I ain't never lost one," said Leeodus. He pointed to his wife with his left hand while clutching the IV pole with his right hand. "We've set bones, done minor surgery, and given all kinds of medicines to all kinds of animals. We go to the local feed and seed and buy whatever drugs we need, and what we can't get there, we get from our veterinarian. The same drugs used on animals are used on humans. Everybody knows that. This little crotch burn is nothing to us."

Leeodus leaned over the nurse's desk and propped both forearms on it. The site of a grown man naked except for cowboy boots, cowboy hat, and a thick, white gauze dressing around his genitals, secured with a layer of duct tape, was outrageous. The team wasn't able to contain their laughter.

Mellette and Leeodus turned to look at them. The nurse behind the desk stood at attention when he saw Dr. McSwain.

"Hey, Doc, can you tell this nice man to check me out of The Big Free?" asked Leeodus. He grinned, shrugged his shoulders to shake the hospital gown into place, and walked toward the group, rolling his IV pole with him.

"Mr. Benoit, where'd you find duct tape in the emergency room?" said Dr. McSwain.

"That's easy, Doc. Mellette carries it in her purse at all times. Because I have a fish camp on the bayou and a farm in Houma, I'm always needing to fix something. Duct tape will hold near anything temporarily," said Leeodus.

Elizabeth was frustrated. The longer she worked the emergency room, the more she realized patients were hardheaded and most would do anything to avoid being admitted to the hospital. She felt a quick flash of anger as she thought of the time and energy she'd spent cleaning and dressing Leeodus's wounds and doing the paperwork necessary to admit him to the hospital.

"Mr. Benoit," she said to him, "we want you to be admitted for intravenous antibiotics and for us to watch closely the burns between your scrotum and rectum. Tearing duct tape off of your skin could tear away the skin we'd need for a graft and hinder the healing process. Without proper wound care, you'll get infected."

Leeodus didn't look convinced. He shook his head and looked at the floor. Mellette gave him a nod of encouragement. Leeodus flashed a smile and said, "Even though the idea of a beautiful doctor-lady studying my privates every day is very alluring, I have to get home to feed up. There're chores that can't wait for me to lounge around here and enjoy your attentions, Cher."

Mellette poked her husband in the ribs with her elbow and said, "Don't mind him, Doc. He flirts with everybody, male and female. Shoot, he flirts with our pigs. Don't you worry none about that duct tape. I'll use oil to unglue and tease it off. I promise I won't tear off Leeodus's skin. I'm real good at tending wounds. That's one of my jobs at the farm."

Elizabeth was too tired to coax them to stay. Dr. McSwain's nod gave her the authority to decide.

"OK, we'll discharge you, but only if you promise to come to burn clinic once a week."

Mellette moved to take out her husband's intravenous line. The nurse bolted from behind his desk and escorted them back to their room. "Let me take that out for you," he said. "And I'll give you directions to the burn clinic and your prescriptions."

Elizabeth thought she'd probably not see them again. She knew the Benoits would use whatever home remedy they thought was appropriate. *At least I could give him the tetanus shot while he was too drugged to argue.*

"Why don't people follow our instructions or take our advice?" asked Sallie.

Elizabeth shared Sallie's frustration.

"Well, Sallie," Dr. McSwain reminded her, "that's why I like doing trauma surgery. The patients usually don't argue. They're either unable to argue or they're so scared that they'll do whatever you tell them to do." He continued, "A big difference between surgeons and medical doctors is that surgeons are doctors of action. We like the immediate gratification of finding a problem and repairing it. If I had to spend my life begging diabetics to lose weight, exercise, and take their insulin on schedule, I'd jump off the top of a building and wind up here in Room Four! Or maybe I'd have the good sense to jump from the twentieth floor and be a grease spot for the poor street cleaners to handle," laughed Dr. McSwain.

Elizabeth was surprised to feel grief at the thought of Dr. McSwain not being around. Even though he was tough on her, she realized she respected him and wanted him to continue to teach her. And, maybe one day, they'd share a mutual respect.

"Looks like things are pretty quiet here," concluded Dr. McSwain, signaling the end of rounds. "You kids take a Christmas morning nap and remember that all stragglers are invited to my house later this afternoon." He turned to Elizabeth. "Dr. Roberts, anything else you need to show me?"

"No, sir," said Elizabeth.

The students looked relieved, gathered their books, and dispersed.

Dr. McSwain moved close to Elizabeth until he stood directly in front of her. "I hear from Livvy you're stuck in town for Christmas. Christmas fell on an LSU day this year, and I'm having my Christmas party for everyone left behind. It starts at four o'clock, and I'd like you to come."

Elizabeth wanted nothing but sleep and food. After learning she'd be unable to go home to South Carolina for Christmas, she accepted the idea of spending the day taking a long hot bath, eating takeout Chinese food, and getting twelve hours of uninterrupted sleep.

But Dr. McSwain seemed adamant. "Walk up Bourbon and look for the party between St. Ann Street and Dumaine Street. My house is a couple of blocks from Preservation Hall. You can't miss it. The police block off a couple of blocks of Bourbon Street for me, and we open the entire house and garden, and there's plenty of room for everyone," said Dr. McSwain.

Elizabeth realized this was not an invitation. Her professor was giving her instructions, and Elizabeth saw no way to worm her way out of going to the party.

"Yes, sir. Thanks for including me. I'll be there," said Elizabeth.

"Of course you'll be there! You're a Tulane surgeon and this is New Orleans! We live for our next party! Merry Christmas!" said Dr. McSwain.

It was now six in the morning. Elizabeth walked to the last exam room, the one closest to the nurses' station, and flopped down on a patient gurney. Her last thought was *The LSU charge resident will be here soon,* and she was asleep in thirty seconds.

6

Elizabeth awoke from a deep, dream-laden sleep. She felt a gentle rocking motion and a hand on her shoulder. She opened her eyes and saw the flaking mint green paint of the ER and felt pain in her left hip and shoulder, the result of having fallen asleep on the unpadded metal gurney.

"Elizabeth, wake up. It's Adrien. You're in the ER, and everything's OK."

"Am I late?" said Elizabeth. Her voice was raspy and sounded distant to her. She could smell her slimy teeth and yearned for a shower. In the first few months of her internship, she'd worried about germs and didn't want to sleep on a gurney that had previously held patients. Now, whenever she had a chance, she dove under the stiff yellowed sheets and slept like a drunken conventioneer.

She swung her legs around, sat up, and looked into the weary eyes of the doctor who was her counterpart on the LSU team. Even in her fog, she realized her shift was over if he was here.

"All's well, for now. Nurse Robichaud made rounds with the medical students, and I tagged along. It's quiet for Christmas morning. I'm surprised the knife and gun club aren't in full force trying to kill their relatives by now. Merry Christmas!" said Adrien.

"There aren't any cardiothoracic cases here, are there?" said Elizabeth. Even half asleep, she knew to be wary of any patient who could draw Dr. White. She didn't want to start Christmas morning with a visit from him.

"Nope. No chest trauma in the ER, and it's after turnover time. You're safe from that boogeyman," said Adrien.

Elizabeth's eyes focused. She looked closely at him for the first time and burst out laughing. Adrien had cut tiny holes in his green scrubs all over the front of his shirt and pants. Little flashing colored lights stuck out of each hole. He wore a pair of felt antlers, and his nose was painted bright red.

"Oh, my goodness, you look fabulous!" said Elizabeth as she jumped off the gurney and stood to admire his work.

Adrien turned in a circle to show the small battery pack attached to his scrub pants. "My family has a huge bonfire on the bayou every Christmas day night with hundreds of our relatives. This is the first time in my life I'll miss it. My girlfriend wanted to make sure I had a fun Christmas despite being here. So she helped me rig my costume." He paused, then confided, "She wanted to put lights on my backside, too, but I drew the line," said Adrien. His playful eyes were bright despite the dark bags under them.

Elizabeth hadn't worn a costume since she was ten but loved the playful party attitude that seemed to be ingrained in native Louisiana people. Elizabeth's moment of joy was interrupted when she realized what could be happening outside the doors of the X-ray room where she had crashed.

"Can we make a quick trip around the department to get one last look?" Elizabeth asked.

Adrien shook his antlers from side to side and firmly said, "*No,* we can't. Dr. McSwain is scrubbed at Tulane with Dr. White on a surgery that starts at seven this morning. Nobody's coming to check behind you this morning. Nurse Robichaud said for me to tell you to go home!"

Wow! She used her spy network to be sure my superiors were somewhere else while I slept. This is a first. Maybe 1983 will bring a kinder Nurse Lavinia Robichaud.

"OK, I trust you," Elizabeth said. "I'm headed to the call room for a long shower."

On her way to the lobby elevators, she passed Livvy. "Thanks for helping me. I really needed some rest."

The nurse put her hands on her hips and held her haughty head high. "If you tell a soul, I'll hurt you, Crème Puff! I'm not anybody's nanny. I'm selfish. I want you to be rested up for Dr. McSwain's Christmas party so I can watch how uncomfortable you are in a social situation. Everyone will be there this year. Even Dr. White might stop by after he gets done visiting with his rich uptown folks on St. Charles Avenue. Don't think I'm your friend in the hospital," she warned. "I cut you one break, and that's it until 1984!"

Elizabeth watched her leave and wondered, *Why does everything have to be a barb? I know she likes me. I think she even thinks of me as an odd version of a friend.*

Elizabeth pressed the elevator button, and the doors opened after five minutes. Except for Room Four, the trauma room in the ER, the hospital maintained the slow cadence of life in New Orleans, where it was always hot and humid and nothing moved fast. Elizabeth thought it odd to have warm, muggy weather on Christmas Day. She remembered Adrien telling her stories of his family turning the air conditioner on high and lighting a fire in the fireplace while wearing shorts and flip-flops on Christmas Eve. She chuckled at the thought.

Unfortunately, Miss Albertha was not on duty yet. The elevator operator was one of Elizabeth's favorite people in the hospital. Her soulful gospel singing in the elevator had helped Elizabeth through the toughest of times. Elizabeth sang along with Miss Albertha in the elevator and felt rejuvenated. This morning, with no Miss Albertha, she'd have to be content with her shower.

Elizabeth stepped off the elevator on the twelfth floor and turned toward Call Room #1207. She heard giggling and grunting coming from behind the door. Just like everything in Charity Hospital ran slowly, everything was also old and dated. The giant wooden door to the call room she shared with Dr. Michael LeBlanc and Dr. Anthony Parker was warped and did not seal. Humidity and time had made gaps between the door and the frame where sound easily traveled to the hall. The closer she moved toward the door, the louder the thumping and groaning became.

The on-call room was small, tight, and held little privacy for anyone. The three doctors shared one adjoining bathroom. Elizabeth hated sharing a room with men at first. But extreme fatigue had lowered her standards.

As she put her oversized key in the tarnished brass lock, the noise got louder. *We must have gotten our ancient black-and-white TV fixed. Tony mentioned he had a patient who could fix it,* Elizabeth remembered. Elizabeth was no TV fan, but the male doctors missed watching sports.

She pushed the door open and saw the naked backside and tousled blonde head of her colleague, Dr. Michael LeBlanc, who was thrusting himself vigorously into a squealing woman whose dyed red hair was visible above his right shoulder. Elizabeth stood six inches from their bed. The draft from the hall slammed the door behind her.

Elizabeth diverted her eyes to the floor and saw a trash can half filled with used condoms. *Looks like they've been at this for a while,* she thought as anger and embarrassment collided.

Three things happened at once. A very sweaty and flushed Michael jumped off of his paramour and stood by the bed in full erect glory, his latest condom still attached and waving at Elizabeth. "What are you doing here?" he said.

Elizabeth glanced at the bed as her friend and co-worker jumped from the bed and rolled herself expertly into the top sheet. She stood beside a naked Michael. "Elizabeth, I'm so sorry. I never imagined you'd be finished with ER rounds this early," said the triage nurse. Aoife was flushed from chest to crown. Big tears glistened in her crystal blue eyes.

Elizabeth felt her personal space had been invaded, and in a disturbing way. Her sense of who Aoife was had been torn apart. She was indignant and angry at having been put in this scenario. *And why is Michael not covering himself up?*

He leaned over, ripped off the condom, and threw it in the trash can, then calmly pulled his plaid boxer shorts off the floor and put them on.

Aoife stood frozen in place, looking like a Greek statue in a toga, her bright red hair flying in all directions. Tears were streaming down her face as she looked at the floor.

Elizabeth was speechless. She refused to run from her own room. She'd never imagined this scenario and was ill prepared to react. And she knew she'd never forget this moment.

Michael spoke first. "Why're you standing there staring at us?" he asked defensively. "Sex is a natural act. We're young and healthy and enjoy our bodies. You're the weirdo. You've been at The Big Free for six months and as best I can tell, you've not even kissed anybody. Half the men at Tulane are in love with you, and all you do is study surgery manuals and work. Stop staring at us and look at yourself!"

Elizabeth recalled punching him in the face in this very room a few months ago. She stared down at the trash can full of condoms, clenched and unclenched her fists, and tried to gain control of her emotions.

Aoife spoke in a low whisper, "Michael, please go in the bathroom to shower and dress and leave Elizabeth and me alone."

Michael bolted, and they could hear the shower running thirty seconds later.

Aoife sat—still wrapped in the sheet—on Michael's disheveled bed. She patted the bed across from her and invited Elizabeth to sit too. Elizabeth felt pity for Aoife as they sat knee to knee in the small room.

"I'm sorry you caught us," Aoife began. "I know you don't understand. I'm a nurse from the ninth ward. It's the wrong side of the tracks. I have little time outside of work, and nobody's interested in me. Michael's handsome and smart and quite frankly, good in bed. He's looking for something convenient and quick, and I'm looking for a momentary fantasy and respite from my exhaustion at work and boredom at home. My parents are alcoholics, and my home life's chaotic, Elizabeth," she said by way of explanation. "I've not known the peace, love, and comfort of a good family, like you. I catch snippets of pretending to be loved, where I can get them," said Aoife.

Elizabeth felt deep sadness for Aoife and wondered what life experiences had led her to devalue herself with a man like Michael, who was self-centered and arrogant. Listening to Aoife, Elizabeth was filled with gratitude for her family, and she realized how much she missed them and how their influence had molded her. Strong men made for confident women, she recognized. The men in her family molded her to be the person she had become, and she was glad.

After a while, she spoke. "Aoife, you can do better than him. Don't you know he doesn't care about anyone else? He's selfish with everyone about everything. Don't settle for someone like Michael. You can get a decent man to love you and treat you well."

Aoife looked down and said, "Maybe I don't think I deserve all that, Elizabeth. Maybe I don't want the house, the kids, and the white picket fence. Maybe I only want to have a little fun and pretend to be loved and not have to hassle with the commitment of a real relationship."

In this moment, Elizabeth realized they were very different people. She could not imagine sex without intimacy. Where she came from, people got married, stayed married, raised children, and built lives around one another. She could not imagine any of her people filling a trash can with used condoms from a person they did not love. She longed to have the love she saw in her married family members.

Elizabeth knew Aoife had a hard life. She remembered hearing her father say, "Judging others about anything is wrong, Elizabeth. Most folks are doing the best they can on any given day."

Elizabeth leaned over and patted Aoife on her sheet-covered knee and said, "It's OK, Aoife. This is none of my business. But I'd appreciate your finding a place to hang out with Michael that's not the on-call room I share."

As Elizabeth turned to grab her overnight bag and head for the door, she heard Aoife giggle. "Didn't you find him standing there with his pecker sticking straight up and covered in that condom the least bit funny?" The nurse dissolved into hysterical laughter. Elizabeth didn't know what to say, but she knew she didn't think anything about the situation was funny. "Come on, Elizabeth, seeing him standing there trying to look all indignant was hysterical!" said Aoife, still laughing as she rolled around on Michael's bed, kicking her legs toward the ceiling.

Elizabeth shook her head, heard the shower turn off, and hurried to the door to avoid seeing Michael again. She slammed the door behind her, grateful to be heading to her own apartment.

7

What a crazy Christmas morning. While she waited for the elevator at Charity, Elizabeth realized she was exhausted, nauseated from hunger, disappointed in Aoife, and disoriented by being away from her family on Christmas Day. This year there had been no time for decorating or cooking or sending cards.

She wondered what was happening today at the family farm. The members of her family were probably cooking and laughing. Her cousins were setting up the football game or riding horses or planning to shoot something. She ached with loneliness. She felt unmoored. Her old life seemed like a dream. Surgery was all-encompassing. She'd rarely spoken to Daddy since moving. She'd call her family later, after she ate and slept.

The elevator opened, and once again there was no Miss Albertha. But Mrs. Yolanda Wilson, a hospital housekeeper, stood by her rolling bucket, leaning on her mop. Elizabeth smiled at the sight of the flashing Christmas lights hanging over the neckline of Mrs. Yolanda's uniform.

"Merry Christmas, baby!" said Mrs. Yolanda.

"Merry Christmas, Mrs. Yolanda. You look festive in your flashing lights."

"Thanks, baby. For Christmas this year, I got the duty of cleaning the Big Free for the next twelve hours. You look like you're leaving. What's a sweet young doctor like you doing this fine Christmas day?"

"It's an LSU day, and there're no clinics today, so I'm going home to sleep, wash clothes, call my family, and go to Dr. McSwain's party tonight."

"That sounds real nice, baby. Livvy has to work till seven, but she'll be over to Dr. McSwain's too. I was invited, but I got too much family to tend to. My grands expect a lot of food, and I've been cooking for four days. They come from five states and sit around like Zulu Royalty, expecting my old butt to serve them, and I do. I made those little monsters and, truth be told, I kind of enjoy it." Her smile was wide, and her crinkly eyes gleamed.

Without the emotional support she had received from Miss Albertha and Mrs. Yolanda, Elizabeth knew she might have quit during the last six months. Their many kindnesses had bolstered her during moments of self-doubt.

"I'm sorry I don't have Christmas gifts for you and Miss Albertha. I appreciate all you've done for me," said Elizabeth. She felt inadequate.

Mrs. Yolanda's eyes glistened. "Your smile and courtesy are the only gifts we need. Every day, we pray for your success. Witnessing you being a good doctor is gifting enough for us, baby."

Her words soothed like a grandmother's blessing. Elizabeth had formed an unlikely "family" in Mother Charity. It was a place that was full of hard-working people who didn't get enough credit. Nobody got enough credit at Charity—there was just too much work to do. People let the products of their labor be their reward. In that way, the hospital reminded Elizabeth of her family's farm, where the work was constant and demanding, and there was no time to contemplate.

As the elevator doors opened to the hospital lobby, Mrs. Yolanda asked, "Where's your next rotation?"

Elizabeth tensed at the thought of the unknown and said, "I'm hoping to get an out-of-town rotation. I hear Huey P. Long in Alexandria and Lallie Kemp in Independence are more laid back. I've had a hard time adjusting to the pressure of being here. I want to go out of town. Also, I need to move to get closer to the hospital."

They stepped out of the elevator and stood at the entrance to the hospital.

"If you move out of your apartment, where will you put your things while you're out of town?" asked Mrs. Yolanda.

"That's easy! Everything I own can go in two cardboard boxes and fit in the trunk of my car. The good thing about being a surgery intern is you don't need much. I'm working, eating, sleeping, or driving. Surgery life is simple."

"Well, I hope you get the rotation you want. Merry Christmas!" said Mrs. Yolanda as she guided her mop and pail through the doors of the emergency room. Her lights flashed and formed a multicolor glow around her as she walked away.

Elizabeth trudged to her car with the acrid smell of her dirty clothes seeping from the cracks in the zipper of her overnight bag. She smelled the mold in the underground tunnel that ran from Charity Hospital to Tulane Medical School. The closer she got to Tulane, the cleaner the surroundings became. The private donors to Tulane created a better physical plant than the taxpayers of Louisiana provided to The Big Free. Despite its significance and infamy, Mother Charity was always underfunded and over-utilized. She wondered often how so much was done for so many with so little. Charity was the heartbeat of New Orleans, and it ran on little more than patients' need and staff determination.

She reached her car and threw her bag on the back seat. Charleston's salty climate had rusted the floor of her ten-year-old Corolla, and she knew not to put anything on the floor if it weighed more than four ounces because it would fall through to the road below.

Elizabeth drove up Airline Highway. She was hot and rolled down her car windows. It was odd to be in such balmy weather on Christmas Day. *Santa must be planning to deliver in shorts and a T-shirt; at least he won't have to worry about a fire in the fireplace.*

The closer she got to her apartment, the stronger the smell of cooking cabbage grew. She crept up the stairs stealthily to avoid her nosy neighbor. While digging in the bottom of her on-call bag for her keys, she dropped them on the concrete hall floor. The loud jingle brought her neighbor jogging to her apartment door. Elizabeth knew there was no escape. She resigned herself to smiling and talking with Mrs. Kaczka.

"How ya making it, Docta?" asked Mrs. Kaczka. Her two-toned red hair with brown roots was wrapped around pink foam curlers. She clutched her Chihuahua to her pink and orange floral house dress. A cloud of stinky cabbage wafted around her.

"Merry Christmas, Mrs. Kaczka," said Elizabeth. Buster growled and bared his teeth, squirming to get out of Mrs. Kaczka's arms and stretching his neck to bite Elizabeth. *I shouldn't have extracted the Mardi Gras bead from your trachea, you miniature monster,* thought Elizabeth, forcing herself to smile.

"Please share Christmas dinner with Larry, Buster, and me."

Elizabeth couldn't do it. She had to have some time alone, or she'd be running down Airline Highway screaming at the top of her lungs and might never stop. Forget Southern manners.

"I'm sorry, I can't," said Elizabeth as she reached down for her keys.

"You got a man yet, honey? If you had a man, you'd be able to go over to his people's home for Christmas. A pretty girl like you, ya need a man."

Elizabeth wanted to scream. "I'm exhausted, Mrs. Kaczka. I'm going to bed, and then I'm going to the home of my professor for his party tonight. I appreciate your kindness, but I must decline."

She jammed the key in her door and ran inside, leaving her neighbor standing in the hall. Elizabeth couldn't continue the pretense of being a happy neighbor. She didn't want advice from a woman who wore pink and orange together every day and whose favorite being was a nasty little rat dog. *I have to get out of here. I won't again be so careless in choosing my home.* She couldn't wait to relocate to the French Quarter.

She locked her door as the phone on the wall in her kitchen rang. *What now? Surely, it's not the Tulane operator calling me on my one day completely off this month? They usually call on the beeper first.*

"Hello," said Elizabeth.

"Hey, sis, it's Daddy. Merry Christmas! We miss you."

With the sound of his voice, her problems dissolved. She slumped onto the stained linoleum floor and felt the warm rush of unconditional love. Her father's voice connected her to the love and kindness of her big family clan. Her blood pressure lowered. Her pulse decreased, and her muscles relaxed.

"Oh, Daddy, I miss you-all too!"

At the same moment, both said, "How are you?" They laughed and sighed.

"I'm good, Daddy. There's so much to learn. I wanted to write to everybody, but there's no time. Everyone here's nice to me, and I like New Orleans." Elizabeth knew worrying him on Christmas Day with a recitation of her fears, regrets, and disappointments would serve no purpose. She wanted him to be glad he'd called.

"You sound tired, little girl."

He can always see right through me, but now is not the time.

"How are Mom and Granddaddy and Grandmamma and all the cousins?"

"We're having our usual redneck Christmas celebration. Your cousins were up all night roasting a pig and fighting over the best way to do it. We have many barbecue experts but only one poor pig," said Daddy. His husky laugh comforted her.

God, I would give everything up this minute to have one hug from my daddy.

Her father, Zeke Roberts, and his mother, Granny Roberts, who died when Elizabeth was six, were her anchors. Granny taught Elizabeth the importance of education and humor. Her father's side of the family lived in town and ran a general store. Everyone went to college but died young from heart disease, living short, sweet lives. The members of her mother's family, on the other hand, were hard-working, religious farm people who had little time for education. Elizabeth's mother, Louise Roberts, had a much harder early life than her husband. She wasn't tender like Daddy.

"Oh, Daddy, tell me the details. I want to pretend I'm there with you-all." Elizabeth's South Carolina drawl thickened when she talked with her father.

He was a smoker who coughed in the morning, and she waited for his reply while he coughed for a few minutes. His habit used to irritate Elizabeth. But today, his smoker's cough sounded like home.

"The back field smells like vinegar, tomato paste, blackstrap molasses, and pig. Your cousins are sitting in folding chairs around the pig pit as if they think a resurrection might occur if they don't watch the pig every second. Actually, I think they're guarding against the other relatives starting the pig pick early."

Elizabeth knew there would be more than fifty people gathered at her grandparents' farm. They usually ate around 2:00 p.m., so she knew everyone was hungry by now.

"Tell me more, Daddy."

"The house smells like pecan pie and sweet potato pie. The pecan trees in the front yard produced tons of pecans this year, and your aunts put over two hundred pints in the freezer. Pecan pies are everywhere. The smell is driving me crazy. I might sneak into the kitchen and get a piece while everyone else is distracted guarding the hog."

Elizabeth's mouth watered despite her choked-back tears. She knew a good long cry was well overdue.

"What else?" asked Elizabeth.

"Are you OK? You sound like you're about to cry, sis."

She could hold back no more. Tears ran down her face over the dark circles beneath her blue eyes. *Why am I trying to hide my feelings? This man knows everything about me.*

"I'm happy to hear your voice. And I'm homesick. That's normal, don't you think? This is my first Christmas away from home."

"Are they treating you all right?"

Elizabeth knew she could not explain Tulane Surgery and Charity Hospital to anyone who had not worked there. What she had imagined it to be and what it was bore no resemblance. Worrying her father was nothing she would ever do.

"I'm learning at such a fast rate that it's hard to keep up. Tulane is a place of excellence, and I'm happy and proud to be a part of it. The challenges are great and so are the rewards."

He coughed and chuckled, "Listen to you, with your big city words! You mean it's kicking your butt, little girl?"

Elizabeth felt a sense of relief. In those few words, her daddy let her know he understood her experience. *He knows.*

"I want to hear more about the family. What's everyone doing right now?"

"Like I said, the older boy cousins are guarding the pig in case it tries to resurrect itself. The younger boy cousins are out in the pasture on horseback chasing cows, pretending to be ranchers and playing roundup. Your cousins are not too good at roping. The truth is, the cows look bored, and most of them refuse to move," said Daddy.

Elizabeth burst into laughter, picturing the scene.

"Granddaddy's working with his hunting dogs. His quail pens have all been cleaned, and he's dog training. Nobody can train a hunting dog better than your granddaddy. Your two oldest cousins are standing nearby, watching. They're trying to absorb all of Granddaddy's techniques. Of course, he has a few secrets he'll never share. But they keep trying."

"What are the girls doing?"

"Well, sis, they've made several hundred biscuits since five o'clock this morning. They formed an assembly line in the kitchen and your grandmother has them working. They milked the cows early, and all of us had ham biscuits for breakfast. Now they're cooking the big meal."

Elizabeth pictured her father standing in the long center hall near the front door of her grandparents' farmhouse, talking on the only phone in the house. She relaxed on the floor of her kitchen and released all the angst of the last few months. Suddenly, the sound of an explosion came through the phone.

"Daddy, what in the world is that?"

"Honey, you don't want to know!" She knew from his amused tone nobody was in danger.

"Yes, I do want to know. I want to know everything."

Her father sighed deeply and said, "Do you really want to spend our precious time on the phone talking about your cousins' escapades?"

"Yes, sir, I sure do. I want to talk about things that aren't serious. My life's filled with solving patients' serious problems. Something light and silly is exactly what I want to hear."

"OK, you asked for it. One of the big freezers on the back porch died. Thank heavens your grandmother's a light sleeper and noticed the decrease in noise coming from the back porch. In the middle of the night, they transferred all that food to another freezer. The next day, your cousins attempted to move the freezer and dropped it as they came down the steps. It couldn't be repaired."

"Oh! I bet Granddaddy was not happy about that!"

"I wasn't here, but I heard your grandfather let out one of the two curse words he uses per year. After the cousins got away from your grandfather, they started plotting how they could repurpose the freezer."

Elizabeth heard another explosion in the background. Daddy chuckled.

"You know how your cousins love to shoot at things? How they set up targets and use guns and bows and arrows to destroy them? Well, sis, they upped their game this time. Now they are blowing up that freezer."

"What are you talking about?"

"This year, the boys are having a contest to see who can make the best homemade rocket launcher to blow up that freezer. They used the mule to drag the freezer into the middle of a plowed field and set up their contest. Three are competing. You should hear the third blast any minute."

The image of her smart, athletic, male cousins blowing up a freezer for entertainment was all Elizabeth needed to release her pent-up emotions. She couldn't speak as she laughed while tears and mucous ran down her chin. These same young men had played cowboys and Indians until they dropped. Their football and baseball games were ferocious. But they were raised to be gentle with the girls. The sound of the third explosion blasted through the phone.

"Thank heavens that's over!" exclaimed her father. "This redneck Christmas scene is rowdier than ever. The older they get, the more complex are their plans for wreaking havoc. I'm relieved to hear no humans screaming. As long as they don't harm themselves or the farm animals, your granddaddy tolerates the shenanigans," said Daddy.

Elizabeth knew her father missed his side of the family at Christmas. They usually saw them at Thanksgiving. Elizabeth loved her mother's large family, but she knew Daddy didn't enjoy shooting guns or love working the earth like they did. She was grateful for being exposed to two ways of living in the South. She grew anxious, knowing the call couldn't last much longer.

"Let me get your mother on the phone. She wants to speak to you."

Elizabeth tensed and felt the pain of disconnecting from him. She loved her mother, but their bond was strained by their differences. "OK, Daddy. I love you. Hug everyone for me." She heard the rustling as the phone changed hands.

"Hi, sis, it's Momma. Merry Christmas, sweet girl. We miss you!"

Elizabeth pictured her mother's fair skin, chocolate eyes, and curly dark brown hair. She knew her mother would wear her favorite "Cherries in the Snow" lipstick and nail polish.

"Hi, Momma! I love you and Merry Christmas. How are you?"

"I'm missing my daughter, that's how I am! When are you coming home? It's been what? *Ten* years or more?" laughed Momma.

"No, ma'am. It hasn't been ten years. It's been six months. I miss you too. How are all the girls? I miss seeing everyone."

"Well, nobody made you move to New Orleans, of all places," her mother responded. "You have a whole big state here with tons of boys just waiting to marry you, you know. You're the hard-headed one who had to move to New Orleans and leave the family. I suspect you're about ready to come home by now."

She heard more rustling in the background and heard her father whisper, "Louise, honey, let it rest. Elizabeth's far from home and lonely on Christmas. Say something sweet to her."

"Oh, OK, Zeke Roberts! You always let her have her way. Elizabeth, I love you and hope you'll be home soon. We miss you like crazy, and I'm giving the phone to your daddy."

Elizabeth felt relieved. Her mother was adamant about expressing her dislike of Elizabeth's choices. And the worst part was that, sometimes, Elizabeth thought her mother was correct.

"Time to get back to the pig pick," said her father. "We love you very much and hope you have a great Christmas. Bye, little girl," said Daddy as he hung up.

"I love you too," said Elizabeth to the dial tone. Her family couldn't afford lengthy long-distance calls. She knew the bill would be more than Daddy planned. But she was grateful for the time with him. Imagining her cousins blowing up the old freezer made her smile. She was happy and tired and barely made it to her pull-down bed before she fell asleep.

Elizabeth slept a few hours and awoke to the smell of cabbage and the sounds of polka music and barking from the apartment next door. No matter where she went for her new rotation assignment, she'd get away from the thin walls dividing her from Mrs. Kaczka and Buster. Wherever Tulane Surgery sent her, it would be a welcome change.

As her feet touched the green shag carpet, she was slapped with the dreadful realization that she had to go to Dr. McSwain's Christmas party. Dressing up, driving to the French Quarter, and pretending to celebrate on Christmas seemed like insurmountable tasks. Elizabeth didn't like parties. They seemed artificial to her. Her idea of a party was sitting with her cousins on their grandfather's back porch, churning fresh peach ice cream, and teasing each other mercilessly until tears ran down their faces.

No shoes, no fancy dress, no makeup, and no fussing with her hair—just laughter and good food with the people she loved.

But she had to do her duty. And today, her duty was to keep Dr. McSwain and Livvy happy by going to his party.

The nurses had advised her to dress up, saying people go all out for parties in New Orleans. She still had the black dress she'd borrowed to wear to Commander's Palace with Dr. Caballero. It had cost her a half day's pay to get a dry cleaner to remove the remoulade and crab smell out of the dress. She kept the borrowed black sandals that were a little too big. But, she rationalized, if she didn't drink alcohol, she could navigate for an hour in the shoes without sustaining orthopedic injury. Her grandmother's pearls were stained with the blood of various trauma patients, but Elizabeth wore the stained side in the front on workdays and turned them around to the clean side if she wasn't in the ER. She had tried to clean the string but hadn't been successful. Pearl restringing was not in her budget. She hoped nobody would be bleeding at the party.

After she dressed, she gathered her hair in a knot at the base of her neck. She applied pink lip gloss and a smudge of blush. She was ready. Clinique face soap was her one luxury, and it kept her skin looking nice. Nothing could help the dark, puffy circles under her eyes. She looked at herself in the bathroom mirror and thought the dark circles made her blue eyes look brighter. *What a thought . . . exhaustion as a beauty aid.* She laughed to herself as she left her apartment and headed to the Quarter.

8

Elizabeth liked being in the French Quarter, the oldest part of New Orleans, but she dreaded the party.

Elizabeth loved driving past the old shabby mansions. She crept up North Rampart, looking for the turnoff onto Esplanade. Livvy had instructed her to look for overhanging oak trees covered in moss and Mardi Gras beads.

She turned right onto Esplanade and was greeted by a long street lined with hundred-year-old giant oaks. The tree canopy blocked the sun and dropped the temperature by ten degrees. Elizabeth exited her car and felt a cool breeze. She imagined Esplanade would be an oasis during the oppressive heat of July since the trees provided constant shade and the nearby river offered a breeze.

Elizabeth parked her car, remembering to leave the car doors unlocked because even the worst looking cars in town were subject to broken windows. She also left her glove box open so any would-be robbers could gaze in and know she had no gun. The police officers in the ER had cautioned her to leave her car unlocked, to remove her car radio, and to leave the glove box open. Life here was so different from South Carolina. Her mom's family left their hunting rifles displayed on racks in the back windows of their trucks, and nobody ever touched them.

Her Granny taught her to always take something for the host, and she'd never been to a party without a gift. Aoife had told her The Central Grocery on Decatur was open all day. She decided to walk there and get a gift for Dr. McSwain. The roots of the great old oaks made for cracked and uneven sidewalks. She looked down while walking to avoid tripping.

As she clomped the four blocks in her party dress and loose sandals, she swiveled her head from side to side and looked at the beautiful homes. Most needed paint and window and roof repairs, but the bones of the old homes were magnificent. She stubbed her toe on a root sticking up through the concrete and nearly fell. Her balance wasn't great, even in flat shoes. The exposed roots, cracked and uneven sidewalks, and strappy black sandals challenged her ability to stay upright. She knew she'd never make it back to her car if she added alcohol.

Elizabeth took a right onto Decatur. She felt an intense breeze coming off the Mississippi and saw the Central Grocery for the first time. Livvy told her it had been continuously operating in the same location since 1906. A Sicilian man named Mr. Lupo had made the first muffuletta sandwich on this very spot. Elizabeth had never had a muffuletta. But she was hungry enough to eat two.

The grocery was narrow but deep. The door was warped by the humidity like everything else in New Orleans. It jangled with Christmas bells as she entered and stepped back in time.

Cured meats hung from the ceiling. Pungent cheeses were on display in an open refrigerated cooler. Forgetting her task, she wandered up and down the long narrow aisles and marveled at the imported olive oils, pastas, and anchovies. *This place sure beats the Piggly Wiggly back home.*

The woman at the counter looked to have come with the building. She was every bit of eighty. Her olive skin and wrinkles collided into a warm smile. She said, "Merry Christmas, party girl. You sure are dressed up for making groceries."

Elizabeth smiled and said, "I'm going to a party at my professor's house, and I need a gift. What can you suggest?"

"Our family recipe is a big hit. Italian olive salad is a New Orleans party favorite."

Elizabeth remembered her borrowed dress and thought something less messy might be better. Her wallet was thin from the last time she dry cleaned it.

The woman saw her reticence. "Not a big olive fan, huh?"

"Oh, no. I'm sure it's delicious. I'm looking for something a little more festive for Christmas."

"Well, how about a doberge cake? They're always a big hit."

"I'm sorry, but I'm not familiar with the doo-barge cake," said Elizabeth.

The woman laughed, "No, honey, it's *doberge* . . . the cake has multiple thin layers of yellow or chocolate cake with chocolate or lemon or vanilla pudding between the layers. It's covered with a thin layer of buttercream icing and glaze is poured over the outside. It'll knock their socks off!"

The cake sounded perfect. "How much is it?" asked Elizabeth.

"It's a little pricey at twenty dollars. But they take a long time to make, and the ingredients are expensive," said the woman. As she pointed to the cakes, Elizabeth noticed her sturdy wrinkled hands and ancient dented wedding band.

Elizabeth was disappointed. "I'm sorry, but my budget won't allow a twenty-dollar cake. Is there anything I might get for five dollars?"

With a warm smile, the old woman shuffled to the back of the store and returned with a poinsettia wrapped in red foil. Elizabeth hadn't seen any other plants for sale in the store and wondered if the plant belonged to the woman, not the store.

"This is perfect, and it's just five dollars, even," said the woman.

The kindness in her eyes showed Elizabeth the truth.

"I can't take your plant," said Elizabeth.

"It was the last one. I was hoping someone would come along and take it off my hands before Christmas was over and I couldn't sell it at all," said the woman.

Elizabeth smiled, handed her the five dollars, and left feeling grateful for the kind people of New Orleans.

9

Elizabeth felt the warmth of the last of the afternoon sun on her face as she turned onto Dumaine Street. She loved the iron grillwork, the colorful flowers spilling over the balconies, even in December, the rainbow pastel shades of painted stucco, the cacophony of the street musicians, and the smell of seafood cooking as the doors to some of the best restaurants in town opened and the scent of garlic wafted out.

She walked two blocks and, standing in the center of the intersection, she turned in a slow circle, took deep breaths, and soaked in the beauty of the late afternoon. It was an hour before dark, and the sky's pink glow enhanced her favorite time of day. The closer she got to Bourbon Street, the louder the rock and roll music blasted. Elizabeth couldn't believe Royal, the most charming street she'd ever seen, was one block from Bourbon, the embodiment of debauchery. The rich lived next to the poor. The educated ate lunch at counters with the construction workers. And the best antique district in America was next to a sea of drunks wandering in and out of strip clubs and bars. Civilized and seedy were next-door neighbors in New Orleans.

The poinsettia she held in her hands reminded her of her task. She nearly ran into Officer Alois Thibodeaux on his horse. He and five other New Orleans police officers had cordoned off two blocks of Bourbon Street and sat at attention on horseback, ready to direct party goers.

The calm horse stepped back from Elizabeth, and Officer Thibodeaux said, "Merry Christmas, miss. You headed to Dr. McSwain's?"

"Yes, sir," said Elizabeth.

"Is that you, Dr. Roberts?" said the officer as he leaned forward toward her.

"Yes, sir. It's me." She felt embarrassed as Officer Thibodeaux looked her over from atop his horse.

"Doc, you look gorgeous," he said. "Them scrubs you wear at the Big Free don't do you justice. I might not know it was you if I didn't recognize dem pearls and dat South Carolina drawl." He paused. "I don't mean no harm, but dang, you clean up nice." He pointed to the gate and said, "Dere ya go, dawlin'. Eat sum ersters for me." He sometimes exaggerated his accent for fun.

New Orleans accents, like its neighborhoods, offered stark contrast. The people of uptown spoke in a soft, lilting patois. Elizabeth didn't hear the twang of Arkansas or Mississippi from natives of the city. Officer Thibodeaux spoke with what she'd heard the locals call a *YAT* dialect. YAT was associated with the working-class people of the ninth ward. Elizabeth first thought folks with the YAT accent might be from Brooklyn or New Jersey. She had never visited either but knew students from those areas with similar accents.

"Thanks," said Elizabeth in response to Officer Thibodeaux's compliment. As she bolted for the tall iron gate marking Dr. McSwain's outdoor garden, she heard chuckles from the other policemen. She knew Officer Thibodeaux meant no disrespect, but she preferred to be complimented for her intelligence, not her looks.

There was a short line on the sidewalk to get into the garden. An officer greeted the guests to be certain the drunken tourists from the other end of Bourbon Street were not attempting to crash the party. As Elizabeth got closer to the iron gate, she heard Dr. McSwain's voice. Her heart rate quickened until she remembered she was not at the ER and this was not trauma rounds.

She noticed he used his teaching voice even at his Christmas party. As she advanced, she heard him say, "They've been producing white liquor for over 300 years all over the world. Pretty much wherever they made grain, you'll find moonshine stills."

Elizabeth expected a beautiful flower-filled garden like she'd seen in the Garden District, or at least a big Christmas tree. She stood surprised and frozen in place with her poinsettia. Dr. McSwain lectured a group of students gathered around a giant copper contraption. There were several faces she didn't recognize.

She'd heard about moonshine stills in North Carolina but thought they were illegal, hidden in mountain caves. She didn't expect to find a still openly displayed in the garden of a stately old home in New Orleans. She froze in surprise, realizing the still was tended by her professor.

The students, including Jalpa Patel and Sallie Smith, were paying rapt attention to Dr. McSwain and didn't notice Elizabeth.

Jalpa asked, "Dr. McSwain, can you explain how it works?"

"Sure. There're several types of stills. This is your standard two-chambers still. Everyone knows copper makes for the best flavor. I add sugar, filtered water, cornmeal, and some distillers' yeast in the main pot. It's been fermenting for two weeks."

He pointed to the fire source at the base of the main pot and said, "The propane heater heats the mixture to the perfect temperature, and the alcohol steam is formed. It eventually passes through the chilled coil pipes to cool the steam and release the liquor into the collection device. Keeping ice on the copper wire condenser is the job of the medical students tonight." He laughed and pointed to the students.

Elizabeth stood aghast. Dr. McSwain stood in front of the tall copper still, explaining the making of moonshine as if it were an organic chemistry experiment. He held a blue glass mason jar with *Ball* clearly printed across the jar—the same type of jar her grandmother used for canning. He reached for another jar and gave it to Jalpa, asking her to hold it under the dripping copper pipe as he sipped the white liquid from the other jar for flavor. "Yum, yum! It might be my best batch yet," he said as he passed the nearly full jar to Sallie.

Elizabeth sensed a presence at her shoulder and heard Livvy's voice. "Your mouth's gaping, Crème Puff. Close your jaw before you drool on Vicki's dress."

Elizabeth turned to see Nurse Robichaud, her sometimes friend and sometimes nemesis.

"Isn't that illegal? I heard moonshine is 75 percent alcohol. There're policemen everywhere. I don't want Dr. McSwain to get in trouble," said Elizabeth.

"Don't be so naïve," Livvy admonished her. "He has a permit for that still, and anyway, those policemen adore him. He's their doctor and has saved many of their lives. Norman McSwain would have to kill a couple of people in broad daylight in front of the mayor for the NOPD to arrest him for anything!" said Livvy.

Elizabeth looked from Livvy back to the group in the garden and saw familiar faces. Rob and Joe, the EMTs, were in front of a carved granite water fountain that gurgled in competition with the dripping moonshine still. Mikey Sherman, the nurse from the urology clinic at the VA, laughed and talked to Aoife and her roommate, Vicki. Elizabeth remembered her favorite co-worker, Dr. Anthony Parker, was on vacation. Tony was the lucky one who went home for Christmas. She saw Dr. Ernesto Caballero standing under a Ficus tree that provided shade for half the garden. He chatted with a female medical student and hadn't noticed Elizabeth's entrance. Elizabeth was embarrassed by the memory of their only date. He'd taken her to Commander's Palace for an elegant meal, and she had fallen asleep in her crab remoulade while he was away answering a page to the hospital. He was a nice man and attractive, but dating was awkward for her. *Maybe she can catch his attention and keep it.* Elizabeth had declined two dates from Dr. Caballero since their first one, and she was running out of excuses.

Dr. McSwain looked up, saw her, and smiled. "Well, good evening, Dr. Roberts! Merry Christmas and thanks for coming."

As Elizabeth stepped forward to hand Dr. McSwain the poinsettia, Dr. Harrison Lloyd White III emerged from behind Dr. Caballero and leveled his cool raptor-like stare at Elizabeth.

At the sight of him, she lurched forward and pushed the poinsettia into Dr. McSwain's midsection. Nausea and dread crushed her burgeoning Christmas party spirit. He was the cardiothoracic fellow who had treated her with exceptional disdain and terrified her. She had no prior experience with people who, for no apparent reason, heartily disliked her and desired she fail. Livvy said his perfectionism drove him, but Elizabeth thought he might simply hate women doctors.

"Thanks for the plant," said Dr. McSwain. "Why don't you put it over there on the corner of the bar?" Dr. McSwain pushed the plant back into her hands.

The bar was a foot from where Dr. White was standing. Elizabeth would rather have stepped into a rattlesnake pen. She knew she had to do what Dr. McSwain suggested, but anxiety froze her in place.

"Yes, sir," said Elizabeth. But her feet wouldn't comply.

"You look like a garden statue," Livvy murmured. "He won't bite you, at least not in front of a group," continued Livvy as she touched Elizabeth's elbow and tried to guide her toward the bar.

Elizabeth jerked her elbow out of Livvy's hand and backed up. She'd seen red-tailed hawks look at mice the same way Dr. White was looking at her, and she didn't plan to be on his menu tonight.

"Let me go, Livvy. I'm going inside to the restroom. Where is it?"

"Don't let that man turn you into mush. He's just another guy. Where's your backbone, girl?" Livvy asked. "You look panicked. Go through the double French doors and take a right. The powder room is on the left."

Elizabeth scurried off, still carrying the poinsettia and navigating the uneven pavers of the garden. Her head was down, and she used the plant to screen her face from Dr. White's glare.

She was grateful to find the bathroom empty. She entered, turned, and locked the door, still holding the plant. Her heart raced, and her palms sweated. The tiny bathroom was Tulane green, including a green toilet. She smiled at Dr. McSwain's school spirit. She had never seen a toilet that wasn't white and never imagined one came in such a bright Kelly green. She put the toilet seat down, sat on it, placed the plant on the floor in front of her, and took her own racing pulse. Then she looked around at the walls covered in Tulane memorabilia and realized no woman lived in this house.

She wondered what was wrong with her. Dr. White had brutalized her in conferences and made it clear he did not think she was up to Tulane Surgery standards. But his was only one opinion, and she'd made the cut. Most professors must have thought her worthy. Besides, Dr. White was only the cardiothoracic fellow—not a full-fledged professor. He was handsome in his bright red cashmere sweater. He looked like Elizabeth imagined an 1800s English patrician would look—arrogant, aristocratic, and austere.

You've been in the bathroom long enough. Pick up your plant. Open the door. Hold your head high and walk into the house in the opposite direction of where he is. Livvy's right. He's unlikely to bite in public.

She opened the bathroom door and took an immediate right. In her rush to hide from Dr. White, she missed noticing her surroundings. The room connecting the kitchen and bathroom was filled with glass cases. In the cases were old surgical instruments. Dr. McSwain had a compact version of a surgical museum in his house! Elizabeth put her plant on top of one of the cases and looked around. The walls were covered with famous Tulane surgeons from the 1834 founding of the medical school. The founders, Drs. Hunt, Harrison, and Stone appeared in the oldest pictures. She wondered if Dr. White was named after one of the founders. He acted as if Tulane was his own. She looked down into the glass case and saw surgical instruments she recognized. The saw to amputate legs had not changed much. The forceps used to deliver breech babies were similar. Some of the instruments were rusty, and some appeared to have bits of dried blood and tissue on their edges. She was relieved to be learning surgery during the time of good and predictable anesthesia. She shuddered at the thought of having to cut off the leg of a man while he was awake.

She felt a soft touch at her left shoulder and heard the cultured Spanish accent as she smelled the light, musky aftershave of Dr. Caballero.

"Good evening, Elizabeth. Merry Christmas. You look beautiful," he told her. "May I get you something to drink?"

Even in her borrowed heels, he was three inches taller than she was. She looked up into his soft brown eyes and felt a wave of excitement. His cultured voice and wonderful masculine smell were a sharp and pleasant contrast to the instruments of torture she'd been studying.

"Hi. Merry Christmas to you too. I think I'll stick with a Coke tonight as we both know alcohol doesn't much agree with me." She blushed, thinking of their one date.

"That was a night to remember. Don't be embarrassed. You're an intern. Interns sleep anywhere. I found it endearing." He turned to go to the bar.

Elizabeth saw Aoife and her part-time roommate in the kitchen and moved to join them. Elizabeth knew Aoife's alcoholic family required her to be at home to referee, but she preferred her apartment with Vicki. "Hi, Aoife. Hi, Vicki. Merry Christmas."

Aoife gave Elizabeth a weak shoulder hug. "You'll remember my roommate, Vicki. I think you saw her briefly at Joe's bar one night."

"Of course, I remember Vicki. She's the wonderful soul who loaned me this dress and these shoes, which I am remiss in returning. I'll clean them and have them to you next week." Elizabeth felt awkward wearing the other woman's clothes without her permission for this occasion. Elizabeth realized she'd had the clothes for weeks. In the ER, weeks seemed like days.

Aoife looked pretty. Her roots were the same red color as the rest of her hair, and her orange nails were freshly painted, not chipped. Elizabeth hoped Aoife's efforts weren't for Michael. She deserved better. Her Granny's advice popped into her mind. *Thou shalt mind thine own business.*

Vicki smiled shyly at Elizabeth and said, "You're welcome to keep the dress and shoes. I have a part-time job at Mrs. Yvonne LaFleur's shop uptown, and I have more dresses on layaway than a Mardi Gras queen. Besides," she added, "You look better in the dress than me. Blondes are stunning in black dresses."

Dr. Caballero returned with Elizabeth's Coke. "You ladies look great. It's nice to see you away from the hospital and relaxed." He held up his wineglass and toasted them. "To the lovely ladies of The Big Free."

"Hey, what about me?" Livvy interjected. "Y'all left out the loveliest of the lovelies!" said Livvy. She pushed her way into the circle beside Dr. Caballero. He put his arm around her shoulders and beamed. The new doctors were afraid of the head nurse, but the experienced doctors loved her.

"Nurse Robichaud, you're in a category all by yourself. You, my dear, are the forever reigning queen. These ladies are in your service as your court," said the doctor.

"Well, that title will do for now. I was hoping to be the reigning Queen of Zulu, but Queen of The Big Free will do until my real coronation."

She lowered her glass and directed her eyes to Elizabeth. "Dr. Roberts, why don't you come with me, and I'll show you around Dr. McSwain's house. It's a museum to his life. He's led an interesting one so far, and he doesn't mind if people roam around and enjoy his memorabilia. The others have been here many times, and they don't need the tour. Come with me."

As soon as they were away from the group, Livvy said quietly, "You don't want that man to see you afraid of him. Dr. White's goal is to weed out the weak. He thinks if you're weak, you don't deserve to be a surgeon. You have to stop running from him. I hope you're assigned to an out-of-town rotation next so you can develop a spine and come back with more confidence. Standing and fighting is the only way with that one."

They walked through the kitchen and into the library. Elizabeth felt uncomfortable peering into Dr. McSwain's private world. Where she came from, one did not roam around another person's home without the owner giving the tour. The guests here seemed to think Dr. McSwain's house was somehow theirs as well. Every room was filled with laughing, drinking party goers.

The library walls were lined with medical books. The trauma section included many books Dr. McSwain had authored. There was another surgeon's name Elizabeth didn't know. *Dr. Kenneth Mattox. He must be famous too.* There was a wing-back Tulane-green leather chair with a matching footstool in front of the fireplace. Elizabeth thought it odd there was only one chair in the library. Above the fireplace was a framed floor plan for the original Charity Hospital of New Orleans. May 10th, 1736, *L'Hopital des Pauvres de la Charite* was stamped on the print. She leaned forward to read the street names and realized the original Charity Hospital had been at the corner of Chartres and Bienville in the French Quarter.

Livvy focused on the photos in small frames arranged in front of the books. Elizabeth noticed a small framed picture on the fireplace mantle. It contained a smiling girl of about twelve years old. Her hair was curly and red, and her mouth was full of shiny silver braces. She wore a plaid school uniform.

"Livvy, who's that?" asked Elizabeth.

"That's Dr. McSwain's daughter, Merry. He's divorced from her mom, and they live in Atlanta. That child is his everything. But with his devotion to the world of trauma, no woman could stay married to him. Merry usually comes for holidays and the summer. I guess she's either already left or is coming later this week." Livvy continued, "When she's in town, the nurses at Tulane and Charity take turns watching her. The hospital world seems to suit her as well as it does him. She doesn't seem upset by death and drama, and every police officer and EMT in town knows her. She's been in half the ambulances and police cruisers out there. I'll bet they've done some baby-sitting too," laughed Livvy.

"She sure is cute but doesn't look a thing like Dr. McSwain," said Elizabeth. She didn't hear her professor walk into the room and stand behind her.

"No, thank heavens, she looks just like her beautiful mother," Dr. McSwain said. "But unfortunately, she got my wanderlust. She loves to travel. She's become my favorite dive buddy, and we take dive trips a couple of times a year. Her poor mother hates it when I take her off for adventure. That apple didn't fall far from this tree," said Dr. McSwain.

Elizabeth felt shame akin to having been found going through the man's underwear drawer. *I hate that he has to sacrifice time with his daughter to do his work.* She valued her relationship with him as her boss but felt embarrassed and saddened to learn about his personal life; though she found him less intimidating when she pictured him as a doting father.

"Come into this room, and I'll show you some interesting nonmedical things," said Dr. McSwain.

The trio walked into another small room where the walls were covered with framed pictures of Dr. McSwain and Merry and fish from floor to ceiling. Most of the photos were taken underwater. A few photos without Merry were yellow with age, and Dr. McSwain looked much younger. *He was handsome before he became old.* Cary Grant had nothing over the younger version of her professor. *How can he be so active in his forties?* She thought old professors sat at home smoking pipes and reading journals. Dr. McSwain didn't sit, except at Death and Complications Conferences. Even there, he often paced in the back with the energy of a much younger man.

He escorted Elizabeth and Livvy from picture to picture, telling tales of his many dives. When Merry was not involved, the adventures sounded death defying. He created trauma and drama, even on vacation.

They walked into another small room with a beautiful old wooden desk and multiple guns and sabers and knives suspended from the ceiling. The walls of this room were also covered in framed photos from floor to ceiling. On the wall above the desk was a picture of Dr. McSwain and President Ronald Reagan. Dr. McSwain and President Reagan stood in front of the president's desk in the Oval Office shaking hands. The photo was dated one year prior. Elizabeth was impressed. Until now, she'd known nobody who'd ever been to the White House or met a president.

"Dr. McSwain works with our military to help improve surgical outcomes in the field. The president invited him to the White House to thank him," Livvy proudly explained.

"Oh, Livvy, don't get too excited. The man was probably trying to secure a campaign contribution!" laughed Dr. McSwain.

Livvy whispered, "He's too modest. That photo above the door is the secretary of the Navy. Dr. McSwain also has helped train SEALs to get better outcomes in the field. He gets around."

Elizabeth felt honored to have the opportunity to learn from a surgeon like Dr. McSwain.

"OK, nurse," Dr. McSwain interrupted. "My head's starting to swell. You girls wander around this bachelor pad, and I'll get back to my other guests. Who knows what those medical students might be doing with my moonshine."

10

Elizabeth heard footsteps and turned to see two men enter the room behind Livvy. One was blond and handsome and resembled Dr. White. The other was short, bald, and delicate-looking. Both wore coats and ties and had beautifully manicured nails. They smelled of citrus and sandalwood.

"Oh, great, you found us," said Livvy. She turned to Elizabeth and said, "I was hoping to introduce you to Ray and John. They have an apartment for rent on Royal. It comes with a big sweet poodle that sometimes needs a babysitter."

The men smiled, and each shook Elizabeth's hand. "I'm happy to meet you," she said. "I appreciate your considering me. But the schedule for the next three months hasn't come out yet, so I don't know where I'll be. I might not be available to rent your apartment until April." As she blurted out her concerns, she realized she was desperate to live on Royal Street.

John, the blond, said, "We're waiting for the right tenant. We're in no hurry. We're more concerned about our dog than rent money. You can store your furniture and belongings in the apartment while you're away, then start paying rent in April if that works with your schedule. We'd like a quiet tenant who'll help us care for our dog. She's our child."

"A big fuzzy spoiled child," added Ray. He had a pronounced lisp, and Elizabeth heard the twang of the Deep South, whereas John's voice had a melodic old New Orleans accent.

"Elizabeth grew up on a farm in South Carolina and is good with animals," said Livvy. Elizabeth turned in surprise. Livvy knew nothing of her experience with animals and knew nothing of her competence in caring for them.

"Good!" said John. "Let's get your things moved this week. In the Quarter, it's best to move in early in the morning because the street's blocked off later. We have a truck we use for deliveries for our antiques business, and we could send it to pick up your things. We don't have many deliveries between Christmas and New Year's Day," said John. He looked at Ray for confirmation, and Ray nodded his approval.

Elizabeth realized Livvy had orchestrated this whole move without her knowledge, and she wasn't sure how she felt about that. She was delighted to move to Royal Street; in fact, it was her dream. But Livvy hadn't consulted her at all.

Livvy smiled at Ray and said, "It's decided, then."

Elizabeth felt her face turning red. "Thanks for the offer of the truck, but everything I own fits in one cardboard box. I can move in ten minutes."

The men smiled and looked at each other. "OK, that's fine," said Ray. "The apartment is fully furnished."

"Livvy told us you're at the hospital most of the time, when she vouched for your suitability as a tenant," said John.

So, while we're here, let's chat a few minutes and get to know each other," suggested Ray.

John spoke first. "I'm John Parker. I'm a lawyer, and I have lived in New Orleans my entire life. My family owns the building we call Gaslight Antiques, and Ray runs the business. The store is on the main front area, and our garden and living area are in the back," said John as he turned to Ray.

"I'm Raymond Lee Jones," said Ray. "Everyone calls me Ray except my redneck Arkansas family. They call me Raymond Lee. That won't work in the uppity New Orleans antiques world, so I tell people to call me Ray." He paused. "I grew up on a farm, though mostly, I try to forget all that. I'm what's known in New Orleans as a transplant, a wannabe. I used to think I could pretend to be a native, but my accent betrayed me. Now, I make sure I'm the most knowledgeable antiques expert in town. The locals tolerate me because of John's uptown pedigree and my skills as a decorator," said Ray.

"Ray exaggerates," said John with a chuckle.

Elizabeth liked them. *Mrs. Kaczka and her mean Chihuahua will look best in my rear-view mirror.*

John seemed smart, and Ray was sweet. "Tell me about your dog," said Elizabeth.

Both beamed. Ray said, "She's a big poodle named Bella. She has the IQ of a genius and the most gorgeous coat ever. She's a picky eater, and she loves water. We have quite a time keeping her out of our fountain. She must stay on her leash when we walk by the Mississippi, and she can't be left alone in the garden, or she will try to crawl into the fountain. Other than that, she's God's most perfect creature."

Elizabeth was excited. The prospect of living on Royal Street, having a big dog to walk, and sweet landlords seemed too good to be true.

"I have to warn you," John said. "Ray likes to cook Southern food. He does a passable job with Louisiana cuisine. But he excels in the comfort foods of the Deep South. By the end of our first year together, I'd gained ten pounds!" he confided. "You're thin now, but watch out for Ray, the waistline spoiler. I think he was a fat Italian grandmother in a past life," said John.

"She could use to gain a few pounds," interjected Livvy.

Elizabeth glared at her. Just because she knew Elizabeth had to pin most of her skirts with a giant diaper pin to keep them up didn't mean she should get so personal with people Elizabeth had just met.

"It sounds all settled to me," Livvy continued, ignoring Elizabeth's glare. "This week, Elizabeth will move her one box of worldly possessions to 700 Royal Street before sun up! I think now is the best time to give her my Christmas gift. I want to make sure it meets the approval of her new landlords," said Livvy.

Livvy grinned, winked, put her hands on her hips, and tilted her head from side to side. She looked triumphant.

Elizabeth squirmed. *This can't be good.*

"Aoife and Vicki grab that box from under the counter in the kitchen and bring it in here to the desk," shouted Livvy into the kitchen.

Elizabeth had no gift for Livvy or anyone else. Her one holiday gift purchase was the poinsettia for Dr. McSwain. Livvy looked excited. Elizabeth anticipated embarrassment.

"Put the box on the desk, ladies," said Livvy.

Elizabeth looked at the box. It was covered in gold foil with a red velvet bow. It was about ten inches by eight inches. It didn't look like a candy box. She thought she heard a chirping sound coming from inside. *Surely, she didn't put a live bird in a cardboard box.* The chirping sounds stopped. Elizabeth wondered if she'd imagined the sound. There were two large holes in the top, but the box was too small for a cat or dog. The thought of another responsibility struck a panic in Elizabeth. *Maybe whatever it is just died.*

"I want to give you a reason to go home. You spend too much time at work, and you sleep, eat, and breathe the hospital. I wanted something waiting at home for you. Two tiny reptiles are perfect," said Livvy.

Several of the party-goers gathered around the desk. Elizabeth realized they knew about her gift. *What the heck?* She was grateful Dr. White and Dr. LeBlanc weren't there, presumably still outside in the garden.

Livvy should know better than to do this to me at a professor's party.

"Go ahead and open it, Crème Puff," Livvy instructed. "Be careful not to tilt the box. Untie the bow and open the foil, starting with the holes on the top."

Elizabeth glared at Livvy. They had agreed she would not call her by the nickname or taunt her in public. Elizabeth thought they had a truce.

"Yes, Nurse Robichaud," Elizabeth said. "Whatever you say, Head Nurse Robichaud." *Sarcasm goes both ways.* The chirping sound started up again. This time, she was sure it was not her imagination.

Elizabeth untied the bow and tore the foil off the top. The chirping became louder.

"Don't tip the box," cautioned Livvy.

Elizabeth peered into the torn wrapping paper and saw a clear plastic box with bamboo reaching to the top. There was water in the box. Tiny colored rocks lined the bottom.

"You're going to love this gift," said Aoife.

Elizabeth peeled the foil down one side of the plastic cube and saw two tiny creatures less than one inch each. They were speckled brown with pointed noses, and were attached to the side of the clear container. They stared at Elizabeth and chirped.

Frogs? Elizabeth had never seen frogs like these.

Livvy said, "They're African miniatures. They chirp when they want to mate. Their names are Poseidon and Neptune since they're water frogs."

Elizabeth spun to move close to Livvy. "You know I don't have time to care for anything!" she said in a low voice. "I can't find time to wash my own clothes! Why would you give me something requiring more responsibility?"

"Now, Crème Puff, these frogs are special. They're African to remind you of me. And they only need one food pellet every three days. They're not high maintenance. Don't you love that little song they sing?"

"I think they're hilarious," Aoife chimed in. "Look at the way they have their little webbed palms spread out and stuck to the wall. They're talking to you, Elizabeth. I think they like their new mother," said Aoife.

Elizabeth felt forced to pretend she liked the gift and was pleased at the prospect of caring for frogs. Everyone was looking at her in anticipation, waiting for her to speak. *At least it wasn't a snake or a kitten or a puppy. The frogs will eventually die, and I can flush them down the toilet. In the meantime, the chirping is cute.*

"Thanks, guys," Elizabeth managed to say. "I'll cherish these African miniature frogs, and I'll think of Nurse Robichaud every time I rush home to give them their pellets."

"An instruction sheet and enough food pellets for three years are included," Livvy told her. "Remember, they're reptiles and need to be kept at 70 degrees Fahrenheit. And you have to drain the water and replace it with fresh spring water every few months. See, Elizabeth, easy breezy," said Livvy.

Some of the group dispersed, and Elizabeth picked up the frog container and waved it under Livvy's nose. "You mean there's no special veterinarian for these special African frogs?" she asked, trying to maintain a light, bantering tone. "Surely, they need to make a trip to their homeland every year? Certainly, they need expensive shots and a special diet? Is there an African miniature frog veterinarian that makes house calls, Livvy?" asked Elizabeth. She regretted telling Livvy about her dislike of pets. In her experience on her grandparents' farm, animals stayed in the yard. Pets belonged outside.

She gave me something she knows I don't want . . . and in front of everyone!

"There's no reason for you to get so testy," Livvy countered. "Honestly, you're the only woman on earth who gets a Christmas gift and gets mean about it," said Livvy.

Aoife peeked around the corner at the two. Elizabeth felt cornered and remembered her manners.

"I appreciate the thought, Livvy," she said politely. "But I don't know how I'll get them to Alexandria. My car has no heat, and the floors are rusted and open to the ground. I have no ability to keep their temperature at an even 70 degrees as you instructed," Elizabeth explained. "So unfortunately, the frogs might have to winter with Nurse Robichaud. I'm sure they'd be comfortable at the nurses' station in the ER or at your home, Livvy," Elizabeth said sweetly.

Livvy's eyes flashed with anger. "They're not sterile! They most certainly cannot live at the ER," said Livvy. She and Elizabeth stood close, glaring at each other.

Ray came to the rescue, saying, “Now ladies, it’s Christmas. John and I can give these little guys one food pellet every three days, if Elizabeth doesn’t make it home. The poor girl doesn’t even know where she’ll be for her next rotation. We can help with the frogs.”

Aoife smiled. “Vicki and I can help too. We think they’re adorable and would be happy to frog sit.”

Elizabeth wondered how she was to transport the frogs from location to location while she worked an unknown schedule in an undetermined location. *The gift was a logistical nightmare. With any luck, they’d have a frog vacation somewhere and forget to come home.* She winked at Livvy as she formulated a plan. “Thanks, Nurse Robichaud.”

“Think nothing of it, Crème Puff,” said Livvy. “Those frogs have a life expectancy of six months. But, with your overdeveloped sense of duty, they’ll probably last a decade. A reason to leave the hospital is your real Christmas gift.”

11

Dr. McSwain announced to the group, "Let's eat! We have shrimp jambalaya and red beans and rice with Andouille sausage, crab-stuffed mirliton, duck gumbo, and bread pudding. Chef Paul Prudhomme's folks dropped off the food this afternoon. He's trying to build his new restaurant business, and I'm trying to keep him open. Enjoy the food, and make sure you stop by K-Paul's sometime because his prices are so low, even a medical student can afford to eat there."

A line formed in the kitchen as the food was uncovered. Elizabeth watched while several nurses she recognized from Charity arranged the buffet. The nurses seemed familiar with Dr. McSwain's kitchen. He looked on but did no kitchen duty. *They seem comfortable acting as surrogate wives.*

Dr. White and Dr. Michael LeBlanc stood in line talking. Michael leaned on the glass case that held the antique surgical instruments. Dr. White didn't often chat with interns. When he raised his eyes and saw Elizabeth looking at them, she knew the Christmas spirit wasn't extended to her. Dr. White held his plate as delicately as he held the instruments of surgery. His long pale fingers spread around the plate. He encircled his wineglass with the other hand. No shaky grip on that one.

Michael's sly grin was focused on Elizabeth. He was drinking from a large mason jar of moonshine. Michael's face was red from the alcohol, and he looked unsteady as he leaned over and whispered something to Dr. White. Both men laughed while they continued to look her way. Elizabeth felt a chill. She wished she'd never seen Michael naked, and she despised him for avoiding Aoife at the party.

Elizabeth circled around the table of food, taking small amounts of everything, eventually settling in a corner of the garden to sit on the wall and eat with the medical students. She felt most comfortable with them.

Jalpa said, "I like your frogs. Sallie and I can keep them if you get that out-of-town rotation you want."

With any luck, she'd be rid of Livvy, Dr. White, Michael, Mrs. Kaczka, and the frogs in one day. Since she'd lost the Christmas vacation lottery, maybe she'd get her first choice for the next rotation.

Livvy and Dr. McSwain ate standing under the Ficus tree. They talked and laughed and seemed relaxed. Elizabeth was intrigued as she observed people who were so tense and ready to spring into action at the hospital seeming so relaxed and normal at this party. She wrestled with the transition, but her sense of trepidation persisted. *Whether the sharks are in a roiling ocean or in a backyard swimming pool, they're still sharks.*

Sallie and Jalpa talked about their families. Sallie's mom was on duty in labor and delivery today. She hadn't worked on Thanksgiving but was working on Christmas. Sallie didn't mind being without her mom on the holiday, as she was tired and enjoyed napping most of the day. Jalpa talked about her Hindu family, which didn't celebrate Christmas. She thought Christmas was a nice holiday but said she thought the celebration was over the top. Elizabeth ate the spicy food and enjoyed listening to the students talk.

"How many gods do Hindus have, Jalpa?" said Sallie.

Jalpa looked at her plate and squirmed. "I don't know exactly. We have major gods and demigods. My family's loosey-goosey about the whole thing. Our main god is Brahma, the Creator. We're somewhat monotheistic in that he's the big deal." She ate a bite of bread pudding and tried to change the subject. "I've spent more time learning English than studying religion."

But Sallie was persistent. "I don't understand. I know there're all kinds of Hindu gods' names I've seen in books. How can you say y'all have one god?"

Jalpa sighed. "I'm no religious expert. I go to the temple with my parents if it's required of me. But, on a daily basis, I don't think about it."

"That's kind of what Larry said about being Jewish. To him it's more of a social and family thing than a daily practice. Mom and I are Catholic, and Jesus and Mary are part of our day, every day. Do y'all pray, and if you do, to which god?" asked Sallie.

"Why do you want to talk about this?" Jalpa asked. "Really, I'd much rather talk about medicine." She paused. "But since you insist, we have a bit of a trinity too. Vishnu's the Preserver. Shiva's the Destroyer. Brahma's the Creator. Our religion's personal. We meditate and recite mantras. It might be somewhat similar to your doing your Rosary. Our version of the Bible's written in Sanskrit and is called the Vedas. And now, it's the end of your Hindu religious education for today, Sallie," concluded Jalpa.

"You don't have to be so touchy about it," Sallie replied. "I want to get to know you a little better and talk about something besides the hospital. I love that Tulane accepts all kinds of folks. It makes life more interesting. I understand now that you're a half-assed Hindu," laughed Sallie. "I should have known by the way you gobbled down that duck gumbo. I don't think duck's on the Hindu menu. You and Larry crack me up. He's a bacon-eating Jewish boy. If you get behind him in the Charity food line, there won't be much bacon left. So I don't understand the purpose of the dietary laws. It looks like none of y'all follow them. Not like us Catholics. We're serious about Lent."

Elizabeth sat quietly. *I enjoy the banter if it's not directed at me. It reminds me of my cousins and our constant teasing. I sure do miss them.*

Livvy joined the group. In her hands she carried the clear plastic container, which she handed to Elizabeth. "You forgot your gift in the kitchen," she said. "The frogs miss their new momma."

Elizabeth put her plate on the brick ledge and took the container that held the frogs. She shook her head and looked at Livvy. "Just what I need," she murmured. "Another duty." She knew Livvy's intent was to force her to leave the hospital more often, but Elizabeth resented the prospect of being burdened during the few private minutes she had to herself. The longer she was a surgery intern, the more she craved time alone. Many days, she pretended to be competent, but she often felt insecure. Sometimes, she longed to be away from the constant pressures of performing for her teachers, making life-and-death decisions, and caring for others.

"You have to admit those tiny frogs are cute. I love the way they spread their little webbed feet on the glass and look at you and chirp. It's an unusual sound that they make," said Sallie.

Livvy pulled a glass bottle similar to a salt shaker from her purse. "These are their pellets. Open the container and drop two into the aquarium."

"Nurse Robichaud, I didn't want to correct you in front of the group, but those frogs are amphibians, not reptiles," said Jalpa. She looked down in embarrassment at her boldness.

"Well, aren't you miss smarty pants!" exclaimed Livvy. "Why, just two months ago, you nearly passed out whenever you had to talk, and now you're a frog expert. My, my," laughed the nurse.

"I'm sorry," said Jalpa. "I studied comparative anatomy as an undergraduate. Reptiles have scales, breathe through lungs, and frequently have claws. These little guys can live underwater because they have gills; they have no scales, and they have webbed feet. They also have very slippery skin that can exchange oxygen and carbon dioxide. They're fascinating creatures," said Jalpa.

Jalpa would make a great frog sitter. Maybe she could start today?

"Go ahead and feed them," said Livvy.

Elizabeth opened the container and dropped the tiny brown pellets into the water. The pellets floated. To her surprise, one of the frogs slapped the other, dove at the pellets, and consumed both in one gulp. The less aggressive frog looked disoriented and searched the water's surface for the pellets that had been there one second before.

"Vicious little one-inch slimy critter, isn't he?" Livvy watched, amused.

"He could be a Tulane surgeon," said Sallie.

"How do you feed the other frog?" asked Jalpa.

"I tap on the side of the aquarium to distract the bully, and then I drop the pellet onto the head of the wimpy one. May the best frog win," said Livvy.

"Oh, great! My new frog family is dysfunctional and requires management," said Elizabeth. *This is too much like my cousins fighting over the last biscuit.* She vowed to secretly change the bully's name to Livvy.

"I promise you'll grow to love Poseidon and Neptune. They'll keep you company and make you laugh," said Livvy. "Get that worried frown off your face. They're two cute little frogs to keep you company. Don't act like you have to explain their demise at the Death and Complications conference."

Elizabeth was tired, and she was ready to go home. She wondered how best to leave the party early without being considered rude. She didn't care to talk to some guests and had already spoken to everyone she liked. Fewer guests were gathered around the food and more were standing around the bar and the moonshine still, with eyes glazed and voices loud and slurred. Some of the nurses and doctors were touching each other in ways that made Elizabeth uncomfortable.

Elizabeth knew most wouldn't miss her if she left early, but she knew she must say goodbye to the host. She stood up, smiled at the group, and took her empty paper plate to the trash can near Dr. McSwain. He smiled and held up his glass in a toast. "How're you doing, Dr. Roberts? Did you get enough to eat?"

"Yes, sir," Elizabeth replied. "It was wonderful. Thanks so much for inviting me."

"You're leaving, are you? The drinking games haven't even started yet."

She felt Michael and Dr. White look her way. Elizabeth had not talked to either and planned to keep it that way.

"I'm a lightweight with alcohol, and besides, I live all the way out on Airline Highway and have to drive home," said Elizabeth. Dr. Caballero appeared at her side.

"May I walk you to your car, Elizabeth?" said Dr. Caballero.

"Thanks for the offer, but police officers are lining the street, and I feel safe," said Elizabeth.

"I'd feel better if I saw you to your car," he replied. "The French Quarter can be treacherous, particularly after dark."

Elizabeth felt conflicted. She knew he wanted another date, and even though he was handsome and kind, his fancy car, fine clothes, choice of expensive restaurants, and cultured upbringing intimidated her and made her feel like an imposter.

The few boyfriends she'd had were guys she met and grew to know over time through mutual interests. They shared casual relationships, and she hadn't worried about her looks or her manners. They were low-country kids like her, and she could be genuine, be herself. She also felt she didn't have the time or energy for dating now. While she squirmed and tried to think of a way out of having him walk her to her car, Michael strode over and stood in front of her, blocking her view of Dr. Caballero. He was standing too close, and she could smell his disgusting breath—a mixture of alcohol, seafood, and duck gumbo. Elizabeth stepped back and tottered near the flowers when her heel caught in a crack in the brick. When Michael grabbed her arm, she realized he was unsteady too.

Michael looked over his shoulder and said, "Hey, Caballero, I'll see Elizabeth to her car. We have a few things to discuss. You know, intern stuff."

What's this drunken nut up to? Surely, he's not trying to get a date too? That's one rebuff she could quickly dispense.

"Elizabeth, are you OK?" asked Dr. Caballero.

"Yes, I'm fine. Michael can see me to my car." She'd shake him off at the gate when she saw the police on horseback. *Maybe it's time for our showdown. Although, I'd rather talk when both of us are sober.*

Michael waited in the garden near the moonshine still while Elizabeth gathered the box with the frogs. She noticed Dr. White watching her as she navigated her way through the guests.

"Merry Christmas, Elizabeth," said Dr. McSwain. She waved to her boss and walked quickly past Dr. White without acknowledging him. Then she waved goodbye to the group and held up the frog aquarium so Livvy could see she'd not forgotten her gift.

Michael grinned and swayed while he waited. Elizabeth thought he looked happy for someone who didn't get to go home for Christmas for the first time in his life.

"I got the best Christmas gift ever," said Michael. He stopped Elizabeth in front of the moonshine still. He reached to exchange his half-full jar for an empty one and tried to hand Elizabeth the jar containing moonshine.

"I don't want any, thanks. That moonshine's way too strong." She tried to push past him toward the exit gate.

Michael stepped in front of her, blocking her way, and held the jar under her nose. "After you receive my juicy news, you might change your mind about the moonshine, Dr. Roberts."

Elizabeth tried to push past him again. He was tall and muscular and easily blocked her way. "Michael, move! I have to get home to pack, and I'm exhausted. You've had too much to drink, and you're being rude."

"But Elizabeth, I have a great Christmas gift for you, something you'll cherish forever." Elizabeth felt like a rat being taunted by the barnyard cat. She wanted to flee, but fear of him and his idea of a gift cramped her belly. He looked too satisfied.

"All right, what's so important that you can't wait until we get to my car?" said Elizabeth.

"First, you might want to take a sip of this moonshine," said Michael as he laughed and held the jar to her face again.

"NO!" She realized she'd yelled when several guests turned to look at them. "What is it?" asked Elizabeth, speaking more quietly. Michael leaned close, as if to kiss her, and said, "You, my dear girl, are assigned to Dr. Harrison Lloyd White III on cardiothoracic surgery, and you start

January first. Happy New Year, Elizabeth." He leaned back to revel in her shock and laughed.

The garden faded in and out of view. Her knees weakened. She thought she might see her crab mirliton again. *Oh no, please don't let me faint or vomit—or both!* Her worst nightmare had come true. She'd left her family and home to get this far. How much more would she have to sacrifice?

She transferred the small aquarium to her left hand, snatched the moonshine from Michael's hand, threw it back, and guzzled half of it in one gulp. She squealed, coughed hard, spun around, and ran as best she could at full speed toward the street. She passed through the gate, snatched off her shoes, and sobbed as she ran, barefoot, down Bourbon Street, still holding the Mason jar and the frogs.

She had heard folks talk about hysterical women, but she had never been one . . . until now.

She was shaking all over. She wanted to run to the Mississippi River and let it sweep her away. She was disoriented, and the moonshine burned from her tongue to her belly button. Eventually, she slowed and tried to steady the aquarium in one hand. She eased the Mason jar in her other hand onto the front steps of a stranger's home. *Was that moonshine or drain cleaner that bastard gave me? It probably wasn't drain cleaner. Michael would want me alive to experience the full wrath of Dr. White.* Michael would enjoy observing the slow burn and misery of the month-long rotation.

Officer Thibodeaux approached on his horse. "You OK, Dr. Roberts?"

It took her a moment to remember him. "Yes, sir," she replied. "But I'm a little turned around. I can't remember where I parked my car."

"Are you drunk, cher?" asked the officer.

"No, sir. I'm just tired. I parked on the side of the Quarter away from Tulane. Is that to the right or to the left?"

"It's to the right. I'll follow you on horseback and make sure you make it to your car. What's that you have in your hand?" said Officer Thibodeaux.

She looked at the aquarium and her sandals. Her heart pounded and her face and chest were flushed. Staring at the frogs calmed her. "It's a Christmas gift," she told him as the officer turned his horse. She followed along beside him.

"You gonna hurt your feet walking on this nasty street, Doc. Why don't you sit on the front steps of that house and put on your shoes before we continue," the officer suggested.

Elizabeth was sure she couldn't balance on the high heels and not spill the aquarium. *Livvy and her stupid gift!* And that blasted Michael and his pronouncement. This was her worst Christmas ever!

"Bourbon Street gets cleaned every morning, but people vomit and bleed out here every night. If you don't put on your shoes, I sure hope you've had your tetanus shot, Doc," said the officer.

If I got tetanus, I wouldn't have to do the cardiothoracic rotation, thought Elizabeth as she hobbled toward the end of Bourbon. She kept her eyes glued to the street and stepped where the street lights shined the brightest. After two blocks, she saw her car on the right.

"Thanks, Officer Thibodeaux. I have it from here."

She opened the trunk of her car and placed the aquarium in the center and threw in the sandals. She opened the door, flopped into the driver's seat, fumbled for the key hidden under the seat and sobbed. Dr. White's perfectionism, condescension, elitism, and open hostility triggered her insecurities. She worried that her fear of him would cause her to make insurmountable mistakes. She couldn't imagine a month with that degree of stress, but she knew the only way she could get out of the rotation was to resign. She could barely stand fifteen minutes of his lightning rounds in the ER. How could she be with the man for a month? Tears dripped down her face, almost enough for a puddle to form in her lap.

Thirty minutes passed, but she couldn't stop crying and shaking and trying to bargain with the universe. She'd go home and write her letter of resignation. Life was not meant to be this difficult, and she could not subject herself to Dr. White. He was too mean and too severe and too much of a bully. She didn't fit at Tulane Surgery, anyway. Maybe she'd be a small-town family practice doctor? She could do minor procedures in the office and have a nice day.

The moonshine was gurgling in her stomach, so she quickly opened her car door and threw up on the street. The duck, crab, and crawfish marinated in moonshine splattered the asphalt. She wiped her mouth on her arm and leaned back in her seat. In the rearview mirror, she saw Officer Thibodeaux on his horse, watching her from the intersection of Esplanade and Bourbon.

Elizabeth took a deep breath to steady herself. If she wasn't going to run into the Mississippi, she might as well drive home. After all, those frogs might be getting cold. She cranked her old car and headed out of the Quarter, composing her resignation letter as she headed for her apartment.

12

Elizabeth drove home, feeling unbalanced by the effects of the residual moonshine. She squinted to focus on the road, and her heart raced. She yearned to drive back to South Carolina and the comfort of her family. She knew they'd welcome her back without judgment.

Even though hers was a long line of people who believed in personal responsibility and always doing your duty, being a surgeon was not expected of a girl. She'd already accomplished more than anyone thought imaginable by graduating from college and medical school with honors on a full academic scholarship. After that, she had gotten a very competitive internship. None of her family would care if she failed at Tulane Surgery. Mom would be delighted to have her home again and be marriageable.

She drove north in the dark on Airline Highway, avoiding the potholes while considering her options. One option was to simply not show up at the emergency room tomorrow, even though she was scheduled for six more days of duty in the ER. She could keep driving home.

She felt guilty realizing her choices would not be fair to Tony. Even though he was a second-year surgery resident, they'd make him take all of her ER shifts if she quit with no notice. Tony had been good to her. She owed it to him to finish out her time in the ER. *I can do anything for six days—except work with Dr. White.*

She'd walked, trance-like, halfway to her apartment when she realized she'd forgotten the frogs. When she took them out of the trunk, she saw one was standing on top of the other. *There was a pecking order, even in the frog world.* She imagined the smaller frog was her, and the other alpha frog was Dr. White.

She trudged up the ugly concrete stairs, regretting that she'd picked the ugliest apartment in a nondescript part of town. If she resigned, she'd never get to live on Royal Street. As she ascended the stairs, the smell of burnt cabbage intensified. She tiptoed to avoid her nosey neighbor, crept inside her apartment, and quietly closed the door.

She placed the frogs in front of her coffee pot. She'd be sure not to forget them there. She put the bottle of food pellets beside their aquarium. The big one, Poseidon, chirped. They were cute; she had to admit. She tapped on the side of the aquarium to divert the attention of the more aggressive frog and dropped a pellet on the head of Neptune. He snatched it, but Poseidon bumped him, trying to steal the pellet. Elizabeth wondered how long the trick would work. Did frogs learn? Would she eventually have to come up with a new trick?

She tossed Poseidon a pellet and turned to write on the calendar on her refrigerator. *Gave pellets.* Her exhaustion and fear left her memory undependable. Her anger flared, knowing Livvy was controlling her with this gift.

She pulled her bed down from the wall and sat to undress. As she tugged on her flannel gown, she wondered what Dr. White wore to bed. *He probably has heavy cotton starched sheets with lavender sprayed on the pillow by an adoring housekeeper and starched pajamas with his initials on the chest.* She'd seen pajamas for rich men in a magazine advertisement for Berlin's, a men's store on King Street in Charleston. She realized she had no idea what the men in her family wore to bed. They usually wore work clothes, and she suspected they slept in their underwear and T-shirts. Her mind wandered to foolish things as she tried to calm herself enough to sleep and think about her future.

She'd never owned a typewriter, so she decided after her next shift she'd go to the med school library and type her resignation letter to give to the chairman. She had always given two weeks' notice when she left a job. Her father told her, "Leave every job better than you found it, and leave so they'd be willing to hire you again." If she stayed two weeks at

Tulane Surgery, she'd have to spend at least a week with Dr. White, and that wasn't possible. She tossed about in bed.

Dr. McSwain would not be happy, and her abrupt departure would not bode well for future women surgery applicants. Elizabeth didn't see herself as a trailblazer, but it was important to her to make a good showing for the women who came behind her. She knew there were surgeons who thought women did not belong in surgery and would be happy to see her fail. She hated the idea of lending credence to their beliefs, but Dr. White made her so anxious she was afraid she'd hurt a patient.

She sat up to scribble the letter and wondered if she should lie and say she was leaving due to family illness. Dr. McSwain would understand family illness as a reason to resign, but her father had admonished her not to lie. "Little girl," he'd say, "lying starts a chain of events you cannot control. It's much better to take your licks on the front end and get it over with. Lying ruins your reputation and makes people not trust you on anything."

If she planned to leave New Orleans, what difference did it make? Her anxiety grew as her upbringing battled her fear and the drive for self-preservation. She'd do anything to avoid Dr. White. Daddy would never know she'd lied. If he knew how mean Dr. White had been to her, he might even go along. Her writhing gut told her that wasn't true. Even if her father didn't know, she knew. It was best to admit defeat, go home, and forget about Tulane Surgery.

She wrote: *My resignation is effective January 7, 1983.* Her hands shook, and her eyes watered. Maybe marrying a farmer her mother picked out for her wouldn't be so bad.

Why had she come to New Orleans? What did she want?

She knew she wouldn't sleep and decided she might as well stay up and think about her life. She loved to learn. She smiled, remembering her younger self coming in from school, doing her chores, and going straight to her homework. Many of her cousins were forced to do their homework, but not Elizabeth. She loved school. When adults at church asked, "What's your favorite subject?" it was a difficult question because she loved them all. She'd rather sit with a book than do anything. After she left Tulane, how would she continue to satisfy her desire to learn? Well, she could do what she did as a kid and hide in the library.

What else was important to her? She loved a challenge. She liked to test herself to find her limits. She wasn't competitive with others as much as competitive with herself. She had learned by the first grade she was not strong physically. Nobody chose her for their sports team. She laughed, remembering the time she skinned her knees after falling from a bicycle that wasn't moving. Her future wasn't as an athlete.

Tulane gave her the mental challenge she craved. She'd never before learned at such an accelerated rate. She would miss that part. Most days, she couldn't wait to get to the hospital to see what would happen next.

People were important to her. She respected integrity and hard work and appreciated people who helped others. She admired Livvy, Aoife, Tony, and Dr. McSwain. Even though he was mean to her, she had to admit Dr. White took excellent care of the patients. Leaving the people she'd come to respect would be hard as well.

Her heart rate slowed and her rattled nerves calmed as she completed the resignation letter. Livvy and Dr. McSwain would be disappointed, but she would still be a doctor and be free of her nemesis.

Her decision was made. She'd resign tomorrow.

13

Elizabeth arrived early to work. Livvy and Aoife were already at the nurses' station drinking coffee, and Aoife handed her a cup.

"Michael told us. Did you sleep?" asked Livvy.

"I slept well. I thought about my life and made some decisions." Elizabeth tucked her overnight bag under the counter. She thought it best not to return to the call room until her emotions were under control. She didn't want to risk fighting with Michael. His cruelty was too fresh.

"What's going on down here?" said Elizabeth.

Livvy looked at Elizabeth's downcast eyes. "I know you're trying to act like everything's OK, and I know you're scared to death. It's OK to admit that you had your heart set on going out of town and that Dr. White's the last person you want as your new boss," she told her. "Don't hold it all in because we all know, anyway, Elizabeth."

"Thanks for your concern, but I don't want to start a busy shift speaking about my personal decisions. Let's focus on our patients," said Elizabeth.

Livvy laughed and lowered her head, propping her arm on the counter.

"You must be really upset. You're using tight–lipped, white-people language, and your little stick body's rigid. That's how you act when you're scared. Let's talk about this," said Livvy. "I don't want you getting some crazy notion about quitting. That would be stupid."

"I'm not a child," Elizabeth countered. "I'm a grown woman, and I want to handle this problem in my own way." She knew Livvy would make her resignation as difficult as possible. Her only way to survive this day was to throw herself into her work.

"Have you and Aoife made rounds?" said Elizabeth.

Livvy ignored her question. "Not so fast. Have you told Tony about your next rotation yet?"

Elizabeth felt her ears glowing red and her blood pressure rising as a tight band encircled her brow. She paused, her cup of coffee in midair, and stared at the mint green chipped paint on the walls behind the nurses' desk. She wanted to throw the coffee in the trash and run.

Tony walked up behind her and touched her upper back. "It's OK, Elizabeth. I heard you're assigned to CT surgery. It'll be OK," said Tony.

Tony's touch and soft island voice helped her feel grounded and calmed her fight-or-flight response. She knew Tony had rotated on CT surgery and had survived the scrutiny of Dr. White.

Livvy sipped her coffee and talked with a piece of beignet on her tongue. "I know what you're thinking. I can read your mind. You think you're going to quit. You're planning on going back to South Carolina to that farm. Well, Crème Puff, that ain't gonna happen! You need to get control of your emotions and act like a Tulane surgeon." Livvy's face was flushed, and her voice was loud. Tony stepped back a few feet.

Elizabeth felt cornered. Sweat glistened on her upper lip, and her ears rang. Her hands shook so much she couldn't raise her coffee cup to her mouth.

Tony patted Elizabeth's back again and looked at Livvy. "We can get through this with a little kindness. We don't have to push so hard, do we?" he asked.

Elizabeth leaned closer to him. Maybe he'd understand and help her with her letter of resignation.

Aoife said, "You can't leave. You made the cut. Think of all those poor souls who didn't make the cut. You can't just pick up and leave. That's not right. Some good doctors got cut, Elizabeth." Aoife grabbed another beignet from the bag and powdered sugar drifted to the floor.

Elizabeth moved her stare from the chipping wall paint to the white powder collecting on the yellowed tile floor.

"Yes, you should be looking down," Livvy interjected. "You should be ashamed. They finally start to take women in this field, and you think you're gonna quit because you might have to put up with one intensely perfectionistic cardiac surgeon? I don't think so! Look at me, Elizabeth."

Elizabeth lifted her head and looked into her light brown eyes. Livvy's beauty contrasted with her harsh and unyielding insistence. Fierce and bossy and funny and gorgeous—that was Livvy. Elizabeth felt a wave of affection despite the nurse's bullying.

"Livvy, it's my life," Elizabeth replied. "I get to choose. You can't will me to do what you want. I don't have to carry the torch for all the would-be women surgeons in the world. I can have a life I choose."

Their eyes locked. Livvy put her coffee on the counter and moved closer to Elizabeth.

"You're looking at this all wrong," she told her. "You're only thinking about how it will affect you over the next few weeks. Think about what this time in cardiothoracic surgery will mean to your future patients. It's the rotation that molds young surgeons the quickest. You'll learn about the sickest patients from one of the best doctors I've ever seen. You're allowing your fear to get the best of you, and you're ignoring a great opportunity. Besides," she reasoned, "getting this rotation out of the way early will make you more confident, and we all know you need that," said Livvy.

Elizabeth squirmed. She wished the floor would open up and deliver her back to her family's farm. *This must be what it's like to fight a Komodo dragon.*

Aoife asked, "What do you fear Dr. White might do to you? They're not going to allow him to harm you physically. He can't stab, shoot, choke, or bite you, you know." She giggled.

"I've not heard of him biting anyone yet," said Tony. "Although his resemblance to a vampire gets more progressive as the years go by." His eyes laughed.

"If he bit anyone, Dr. McSwain would surely put a shock collar on him. But he's such an excellent surgeon, they'd probably let him keep working with the collar," said Livvy.

"OK, enough of the foolishness. I don't want to put myself through the torture of dealing with that man for weeks on end. I think I can be a very good doctor without having to work for him. Besides, my family needs me at home," said Elizabeth.

Livvy's face turned scarlet. "Then why in the world did you come to Charity Hospital if you just wanted to be a good doctor? This place is the proving ground for greatness. Why did you waste our time if you just want to be good? You could get that anywhere. Shoot, you could probably get that in South Carolina! This place is for stretching yourself to the limit," said Livvy.

Tony touched Livvy's arm. "Maybe we can talk more about this later," he said.

Livvy snatched her arm away. "Tony, you survived cardiothoracic surgery with Dr. White. You don't look any worse for the wear. How'd you do it?"

Elizabeth looked at Tony, her eyes wide and her brow furrowed. "How was it for you, Tony?" asked Elizabeth in a whisper.

He took a long sip of his café au lait, looked at the floor, and said, "I won't lie. It was hellish. I didn't go home for twenty-eight days of that month. I lived in the hospital. Dr. White will wear you out. He's the biggest perfectionist I've ever met. But he expects no more of you than he expects from himself. Sometimes, he didn't seem human to me. He has a photographic memory. Even if he hasn't slept for days, he remembers every patient's lab values. You have to be on your toes. Honestly, he seems driven by internal demons. He's more committed to his patients' welfare than he is to his own life. He cares little for his own comfort, and you're an extension of him while you're on his rotation. He doesn't coddle himself, and he won't coddle you."

Livvy blew out an exasperated breath. "Wasn't there anything *good* you could tell her about the rotation? Like what you got out of it? Or how you made it through?"

Elizabeth hung on Tony's words like he was a life preserver in the middle of a pitching ocean.

"Elizabeth, honestly, it was the hardest month of my life. I wrote my letter of resignation twice. In fact, I carried it around with me as a coping mechanism. I told myself every day that if it got bad enough, I'd quit. I took it in twenty-four-hour blocks. I told myself I could do anything for twenty-four hours—anything. And, finally, it was over," said Tony. His eyes were sad.

"I didn't hear anything in your comments about what you got out of it, Tony," reminded Livvy.

"Dr. White made me a much better surgeon than I otherwise would be, Elizabeth. He brought me to a higher level of understanding of the very sick patient. I daily saw a master diagnostician combined with the best surgical hands I've witnessed yet. The man can sew with a suture the size of a hair while looking through surgical loops that magnify his world." He paused. "I saw patients that should have died ten times over get snatched back from the abyss by his maniacal will. There's nobody like him. He'll tear you down, but you'll be better for it. I'm happy I'm not him, and I hope I don't have to rotate with him again. I think spending time with him is like boot camp for the Marines. If you make it, you're changed forever . . . for the better," said Tony.

Livvy handed Elizabeth a beignet. "Eat," she commanded. "You're going to need your energy for your cardiothoracic rotation."

"Livvy, stop it. Stop pushing!"

"What scares you so much? It's irrational," said Aoife.

Elizabeth's voice quivered, and she felt shame. She looked at Aoife and said, "I'm afraid I can't make it. I barely survived the accident room. At least down here, we get a few hours off every shift. I can't imagine how I'll hold up psychologically under his criticism every day. I'm afraid I'll crack up or kill a patient because I'm under so much stress."

"That's plain stupid," Livvy replied. "You told me about your two uncles who took part in the landing at Normandy on D-Day. They didn't crack up. Your people are solid. If there's one thing I know about you, it's that you do your duty. It's wired into you. You're more like Dr. White than you realize," said Livvy.

Elizabeth responded, "I'm nothing like him. He's mean-spirited."

To this point, Elizabeth could not think of anything she'd done in her life that caused her shame. They were right; returning home to her hard-working family after quitting was not acceptable. Tony's idea of taking it in twenty-four-hour blocks gave her hope. Aoife was right in saying there would be no physical assault. She'd have to steel her emotions, focus on doing her best, and avoid Dr. White as much as possible. She'd write that letter of resignation and carry it around in her pocket, just as Tony had.

Everyone felt the shift in her attitude. Elizabeth relaxed and chewed. Livvy winked at Tony. Aoife changed the subject.

"It's pretty quiet down here. I think I'll head back to the triage desk," said Aoife. Elizabeth smiled, and so did Livvy. "Let's make rounds, Crème Puff."

"I have to get to clinic," said Tony. "Please call me if you have any further questions about surviving CT surgery." He turned and bumped into Dr. McSwain.

"So, Dr. Parker, how was your island vacation?" asked Dr. McSwain.

Tony grinned and said, "Antigua's gorgeous in December, sir. My family survived this year's hurricane season, and our house only needed minor roof work. There was much to celebrate."

Aoife said, "I'll bet they were glad to see you. It's been a year now, hasn't it? I'll bet you were treated like a returning prince."

Tony laughed and said, "It was eighteen months since I last saw my family. And they saved all of my chores for me. I spent most of the time helping my cousin put a new roof on his house. It was nice to be outside in the sunshine doing manual labor. My brain had a chance to rest. I'm sorry for the residents who had to stay behind, but I sure enjoyed my time off."

Aoife said, "You're at least two shades darker since you left. I was afraid if you stayed in the hospital much longer, you'd be as pale as Dr. White."

Hearing Dr. White's name, Elizabeth felt a jolt through her system. Her left thigh started to itch and twitch. She felt a strong desire to run out the back door. Her instincts animated her body. Her breath became shallow and quick, and she felt numbness and tingling in her hands and feet. She needed to get her letter of resignation finished. Her nerves couldn't take much more.

Dr. McSwain said, "I talked to Livvy earlier, and she assured me all was quiet. If that's the case, I'll head to Tulane, and I'll see you guys later. My phone's not charged at this moment, but you can reach me on the walkie-talkie if anything requires my urgent attention. I mostly came for coffee and beignets."

"You guys are too easy! I could make y'all go anywhere for a little Café du Monde fried dough and chicory coffee," said Livvy.

Dr. McSwain grabbed a cup and headed out the door to clinic.

Aoife dug in the paper bag for another beignet.

Elizabeth said, "Thanks, Livvy."

14

Her twenty-four-hour shift passed in a blur. The trauma area was still except for a drunken conventioneer with a head laceration and another head trauma patient awaiting a neurosurgery consultation. Elizabeth rounded with the students. She inspected their suturing. She overheard Livvy on the phone, saying, "Great, Ray! We'll be over in an hour, and she'll move in tomorrow. She'll be so excited!"

Elizabeth's calm dissolved. She leaned on the wall near the nurses' desk for balance. Her emotions plagued her. One part of her wanted to resign and avoid the scrutiny of Dr. White, while another part of her wanted to live on her favorite street. One week ago, the possibility of renting an apartment on Royal Street would have been a dream come true. She knew she should feel grateful to Livvy. But she felt resentful. Livvy's controlling ways reminded her too much of Mom. Livvy hung up the phone, smiled at Elizabeth, and said, "It's all set. Ray and John are home this morning. We'll walk to their store, and one of them will break free to show us the apartment. You can present yourself to Bella for approval. Don't forget to compliment her beautiful coat." She paused. "This apartment is perfect for you."

Livvy saw Elizabeth's scowl, and her smile faded. "Good gravy! Don't tell me you're mad at me for getting you the best dang apartment in the Quarter at the lowest possible price."

"You don't have to shout," Elizabeth replied. "I appreciate what you're doing. But I'm a grown woman, and I can make my own decisions."

"Well," said Livvy, "your grown woman choices landed you on Airline Highway next to a cabbage-cooking busy-body with the meanest Chihuahua ever born. I'd think you'd be happy to have me improve your life."

Humbled, Elizabeth looked away from Livvy's piercing eyes.

Aoife walked toward the nurses' desk and asked, "When's the big move day? I want to be sure I can trade that shift and help out."

Elizabeth spun around. "You too?" she shouted. "You knew about my move before I did?"

"Stop shouting!" said Livvy.

Aoife stepped back and laughed. She smiled at Livvy and patted Elizabeth on the arm. "Let us help you, Elizabeth. You do everything yourself and refuse to ask for help. That's not the Louisiana way. We help each other around here. And we turn every life event into a party. Death, birth, marriage, divorce, new job, getting fired, moving, starting school, new baby, leaving school, Mardi Gras, St. Patrick's Day—it's all a constant party you share with your friends. Relax and let us help you," said Aoife.

Elizabeth exhaled. *Why am I struggling?* After six months of watching them and working with them, she trusted their integrity and knew they had her best interests at heart. Livvy was being a bully, but moving to the French Quarter was exciting.

Elizabeth threw up her hands in the universal sign of surrender, rolled her eyes, and asked, "What time do we go?"

Livvy clapped her hands, laughed, and grabbed her purse from under the nurses' desk. "Now," she said, "we go now."

"I need to do checkout rounds with Adrien to turn over to LSU. I also need to change into clean clothes before we leave," said Elizabeth.

"I already told Dr. Lambert that nothing's going on. He's reading charts and drinking coffee," Livvy replied. "You're as clean as you ever get. Brush your ponytail and let's go. Ray and John and Bella are waiting."

Elizabeth gave in. She followed the charge nurse through the lobby and out the front door of the Big Free. The smell of pizza from the Fistula

Café hit her nose, and her stomach growled. Yesterday's beignet was long gone.

It was the end of December, but Elizabeth needed no coat. Livvy walked fast, as if she were running to a code. "What's the hurry?" asked Elizabeth.

Livvy wore a heavy, bright-red wool coat and carried her purse stuffed under her left armpit. Elizabeth laughed—everyone from New Orleans pulled out winter clothes anytime the thermometer dipped below seventy degrees. She knew Livvy was walking fast to keep warm, even though the day felt warm to Elizabeth, who enjoyed the sun on her face after being corralled in the hospital for more than a day. She preferred to stand on the sidewalk and soak up the sun but trotted to keep up with the nurse.

"Livvy, can you slow down? I'd like to ask a few questions while we walk."

"These folks are doing us a favor. The least we can do is to be on time," said Livvy.

Elizabeth knew Livvy became nervous around people she believed had money, prominence in the community, or advanced education. She knew Livvy's use of the term "these folks" really meant people Livvy didn't perceive as being part of her group. Elizabeth smiled, knowing Livvy was intimidated by their appointment at 700 Rue Royale, the address of the finest antiques store in New Orleans. As they headed into the Quarter, Elizabeth knew why she wasn't feeling nervous. Her family couldn't afford fancy antiques. If the TV antenna broke, they used aluminum foil for an antenna until they saved money for a new one. Elizabeth's father taught her that all people are equal in the eyes of God, no matter their external packaging; everyone had positive characteristics and negative characteristics. A fish was brilliant at swimming, her father would say, but it couldn't climb a tree. Elizabeth was raised to believe every creature was exceptional in its proper environment.

Even though Livvy talked about equality and was the first to assume prejudice, Elizabeth didn't carry the scorecard in her head that rated people's value or lack of value, a scorecard Livvy kept as second nature. As they walked up Royal, Elizabeth noticed Livvy fussing with her clothes and hair. Ray and John were people Livvy wanted to impress.

As they walked, Elizabeth breathed in the pungent scents of the French Quarter. The river created a wind that pushed the smells of the musty Mississippi, the sweet tea olive, horse manure from the carriages, flowering jasmine, alcohol, and seafood up Royal Street. Delivery trucks filled with fresh vegetables and liquor bottles lined the street. Elizabeth had never been to Louisiana until her Tulane interview a year ago, but the first time she walked the streets of the French Quarter she felt she had come home. She wondered if stories about past lives could be true. Could she have lived here in another life?

Elizabeth wanted to stroll and savor every step, but Livvy hurried along. "Pick it up!" she commanded. "I don't want to be late!"

Royal Street was the main street for the best antiques stores in New Orleans. The famous Brennan's Restaurant was located on Royal too. Eating at fine restaurants was not in her budget, but Elizabeth loved to stand at the gate and admire what she could see of the courtyard. One day she'd have Sunday brunch at Brennan's. *Dr. White probably ate there all the time. His family probably had their own table.*

Elizabeth's reverie was interrupted when she tripped on the cobblestone sidewalk. New Orleans was below sea level and the potholes, uneven sidewalks, and tree roots were hazardous to cars and pedestrians' feet. Livvy grabbed her arm as she teetered. "I hope your hand coordination is better than the rest of your body. Sometimes I think you aren't hooked up too well between your brain and your feet."

Elizabeth knew Livvy liked to make fun of her when Livvy's anxiety was triggered. Teasing Elizabeth calmed her. Elizabeth laughed. She knew it was true. Her brain and hands worked well, but nobody would call her athletic.

They arrived on time at 700 Royal Street. The store's name, Gaslight Antiques, was embedded in royal blue and white tiles on the sidewalk in front of the store. Large gas lamps glowed on either side of the mahogany doors. The old bevel-edged glass was etched with the name of the store in large letters. Ornate furniture covered in gold brocade upholstery shone through the large windows. *Louis XIV must be missing half of his palace furniture at Versailles.* She could see John and Ray standing near the jewelry display case, sipping from small floral-patterned porcelain teacups. Under the display case, on a worn purple velvet cushion, lay a large chocolate poodle with amber eyes. If a dog could be royal, Bella was royal.

Livvy opened the door and allowed Elizabeth to enter first. "Good morning, John and Ray," she greeted them. "You'll remember Dr. Elizabeth Roberts from the Christmas party at Dr. McSwain's house?"

Elizabeth knew Livvy was calling her "doctor" because she relied on formality and etiquette when she was nervous. Ray let John take the lead. John returned his teacup to its saucer and walked over to Elizabeth to shake her hand. His movements were elegant and relaxed. "We're happy you're considering renting our little apartment. I'll warn you; it's tiny but cozy," said John.

Ray, who was shorter than Elizabeth, bubbled with barely controlled energy. Patient no more, Ray lunged in front of John and hugged Livvy. "Don't be silly," Ray said. "She'll have the full run of the place. We're often away at antiques shows, and the garden is a whole world unto itself," he said.

Ray and John stepped back and pointed to the dog. Bella leaned forward and stood under John's left hand at attention. He said, "This is Miss Bella. I'm the father and disciplinarian, and Ray's the mother and spoiler. You'll be the intermediary."

Everyone laughed. Elizabeth knew many gay folks from her time in Charleston but had not been closely acquainted with an openly gay couple. *They seem like any other couple except for their worship of the dog.* As a girl from the country, Elizabeth saw pets as just another animal to feed and tend. But if adoring a spoiled poodle was what she had to do to live in the most beautiful area of New Orleans, she would do it. Bella moved toward her outstretched hand. *No bite or growl. Good so far.*

Livvy stood at the back of the group while the other three conversed about the apartment.

"Our store's in the front of the building. Above us are three floors of antiques. We have a large service elevator that's noisy sometimes. Usually, we move the antiques in and out during the day; you'd likely be at work," explained John.

"John, she doesn't care about the store," said Ray. "It really has nothing to do with why she's here. You can see the girl's tired, and she's likely hungry too. They work the interns to death over at Charity. Let's go outside and show her the apartment and let her get home to her bed," said Ray.

Livvy laughed. "Ray's already mothering you, Elizabeth." She turned to Ray. "Don't spoil her like you have Bella. I have to work with her. No spoiling interns, Ray!"

"He spoils everyone. I think he had twenty kids in a past life," said John.

Ray walked out the front door and held it open for the ladies. Twenty feet to the left of the front of the antiques store stood an ornate iron gate. It was patterned with fleur-de-lis around John's family's name's last initial, *P*, for Parker. When John opened the gate, Elizabeth smelled a light, sweet, intoxicating, citrus odor.

They walked under a dark stucco-lined hallway with gas lights hanging from the ceiling. John said, "Our home was built in 1805 and is representative of the late colonial period. We're standing under a porte cochere, the place where a horse and buggy would pass from the street to the grounds of the home. The street's paved with irregular old red brick. When it rains, it gets very slick, Elizabeth. Take great care if it's wet."

They stepped through the porte cochere and entered the garden. Elizabeth moaned with delight.

"Wow, this is magnificent," said Elizabeth. Her senses were overloaded. The garden was lush, green, and humid. She'd never seen so many types of green and flowering plants in one location. "It's cooler in here than it is outside."

Ray smiled and took over. "Yes, the rest of the country's having winter right now, but in New Orleans, it's a tropical paradise. Our little garden has bougainvillea and begonias nearly year-round. A few plants hate February and must be moved inside, but most live outside through the winter months till the spring."

Elizabeth stood in the center of the garden; her mouth gaped open. Paradise could not be prettier. The entire back wall of the store was lined with plants with lacy leaves and delicate white flowers. She pointed to them, asking, "What's that?"

"It's tea olive. The smell you noticed coming through the porte cochere is the smell it makes nearly year-round. When I smell it, I know I'm home," said Ray.

Livvy trailed behind, eyes wide and nostrils flared. She inhaled deeply and sighed.

While everyone was admiring the cascading flowers and navigating the uneven pavers, Bella snuck over toward the fountain. Ray noticed her movements first and ran to grab her collar. "This is the trouble in paradise. Bella wants to be a water dog, but she can't swim. It's the craziest thing. She's drawn to water. But when she gets in the water, she gets excited and forgets to swim. John and I have had to save her several times. Part of your job, should you choose to accept it, is to keep Miss Bella out of the Mississippi on her walks and out of this fountain every doggone day," said Ray.

The fountain was big enough to contain several large fish and a few aquatic plants. Elizabeth had not seen fish like these large orange and white ones. She saw plants submerged in the fountain with bright purple and yellow flowers. The gurgling waterfall of the fountain, the fast-swimming fish, and the lush water plants were enticing. She understood why Bella wanted to jump in.

Ray hung onto the dog's collar as she gently tugged toward the fountain.

"I've not seen fish like those or flowers like those. What are they?" asked Elizabeth. *They must think I'm an ignorant hick, which isn't far from the truth.*

John said, "Those are koi and are native to Japan. They're a fancy type of carp that can live for over thirty years. The flowers are Louisiana irises. Ray plants them in pots and drops them in the fountain, and they bloom like crazy."

"I had hoped I could crowd the fountain with the pots to make it hard for Bella to enter, but she wedges herself in no matter what I do," admitted Ray. "Please keep an eye out for this sneaky dog and her water fetish."

The garden was magical. Elizabeth couldn't remember being in a more beautiful spot. It felt like a refuge from daily life, and she longed for the peace and tranquility this garden could provide. She was good with animals and knew Bella would pose no problem. She glanced at Livvy. The woman was scowling. *What could be wrong with her? I'm doing everything she wants. What could she possibly have to scowl about?*

Ray noticed Livvy's expression too. "We've wasted enough time admiring my gardening skills; let's get to the apartment to see if Elizabeth will have us."

The group, led by Ray, headed to a pretty black wrought iron spiral staircase. The entire wall behind it was covered with ivy, and the design of the staircase was accentuated by the background of green leaves.

"If you come home drunk, you might have a little trouble with this staircase. But the handrails will help pull you up if your legs are not working too well," said Ray. John chuckled.

"You don't have to worry about that. She's not much of a drinker. She had half a glass of wine at Commander's, and the waiter found her asleep with her face in her crab remoulade," said Livvy.

Elizabeth flushed. Now she knew why Livvy was scowling. Livvy was jealous. She liked to embarrass Elizabeth and bring up her flaws when she was jealous.

Ray and John looked down at the brick pavers and stopped smiling. They realized Elizabeth was embarrassed. Livvy looked triumphant.

"Let's head up," said Ray.

Elizabeth decided to ignore Livvy's embarrassing remarks and focus on her good characteristics. Without Livvy, she wouldn't be here. Elizabeth knew her good heart and forgave her jealousy of Elizabeth's beautiful new home.

As they ascended the curling stairs, Elizabeth saw the entire length of the apartment had a balcony. The balcony was three feet wide and sloped down, giving the feeling it might fall away from the wall at any moment. The ceiling of the balcony was painted haint-blue. Elizabeth had seen many homes in Charleston with similar balconies and blue ceilings. Some folks believed evil spirits could not cross water and used the color to mimic water and keep the "haints" at bay.

"I know it feels odd to stand on a balcony that slopes toward the ground, but you'll get used to it. This balcony's been here for over a hundred years. John has the wood inspected once a year, and it's safe," said Ray.

Elizabeth was mentally arranging a table and a chair to have her coffee on the rare morning she was home. Safety hadn't entered her mind. Bella easily navigated the stairs and stood in front of the door, wagging her tail, impatient to enter.

The tops of the narrow doors held panes of old glass to waist level. Thin white lace curtains over the glass hid the inner rooms. Elizabeth noticed a quarter-inch gap between the doors as Ray turned the old brass knob and pulled them open. Bella bolted inside and jumped on the small couch that was covered in a white linen drape.

A musty odor hit Elizabeth as she followed Ray through the door.

"Bella, you're a bad dog. Get off that couch this minute!" said Ray. Bella didn't move. She wagged her tail, made herself comfortable on the couch, and surveyed the room.

"That's our girl—obedient to a fault," said John, as he tugged at Bella's collar to force her from the couch.

Elizabeth looked around. This apartment was smaller than her current apartment. To the left was an efficiency kitchen with a small refrigerator and a two-eye gas cooktop. A small tabletop microwave oven took up most of the limited counter space. Everything in the kitchen was white and covered in a layer of dust. Filtered light came through the window from the balcony.

In the center of the apartment were a cozy couch and one chair covered in bright yellow floral fabric. Between the two sat a small table with a lamp. Under the window leading to the balcony was a desk and chair. Elizabeth thought it would be a perfect spot for studying.

The wall to the right held a pull-down bed. She'd hoped for a full-size, permanently placed bed but knew it was too much to expect in her price range. A tiny closet for clothes and the door to the small bathroom and shower were straight ahead, just to the right of the couch.

"It's tiny," said Ray. "It needs a good cleaning. Our last tenant left over six months ago, and we've not been up here since. We'll have it deep cleaned if you decide to join our little family," Ray added.

Livvy tapped Elizabeth on her shoulder. "Where will you put your frogs?" She turned to John and Ray. "Is Bella frog-friendly?" Livvy laughed.

Elizabeth rolled her eyes and looked toward John. "Remember, Livvy gave me two miniature frogs for Christmas. They only need six inches of counter space and can easily fit on the refrigerator. There's no rule against pets, is there?" said Elizabeth.

Livvy walked to the desk and looked out the window. "Neptune and Poseidon would be most happy on this desk with a nice view to the garden below."

Elizabeth stiffened with irritation. *I'll decide where to put the frogs.*

"Bella doesn't seem to care about other creatures," John said. "She leaves the fish alone, and she's not interested in the neighbor cat that occasionally finds its way into our garden."

Ray smiled. "Bella's such a narcissist that I'm not sure she believes other creatures exist. Bella is all about Bella. Your frogs should be fine. I'll be happy to feed them if you ever get stuck at the hospital."

Livvy put her hands on her hips and stepped close to Elizabeth. "Oh, no, Ray! I gave this girl those frogs to force her to come home. If she knows those two little frogs are depending on her, she'll leave the hospital a little more."

Elizabeth felt a hot flush and looked at the floor. Bella settled back on the couch, observing the four humans.

John cleared his throat. "We'd really like to have you, if you'd like to have us. The noise from the street is rarely a problem. Even though we back up to Bourbon, our house and another are between you and the street. These old houses have thick stucco and brick and block the sound well. Mostly you'll hear the fountain gurgling and Ray yelling at Bella. You can move in two days from now if you'd like," said John.

Elizabeth twitched with anxiety as she realized her plan to resign was being replaced. She felt fear and excitement. She wanted to live in this place on this street with these people, but she never wanted to see Dr. White again. Her mind whirled as she struggled to decide.

"She'll take it," said Livvy. The other three spun in surprise to look at her. "She's anxious about her next rotation and is a little overwhelmed," Livvy explained. "But she's dreamed of living on Royal Street since the first day we walked through the Quarter to Café du Monde. She'll take it, and she'll move in day after tomorrow," said Livvy.

"Excellent," said Ray.

They turned to leave, and Elizabeth thought of throwing Livvy off the balcony. It seemed reasonable. She should at least kick her wide butt as Livvy followed her new landlords down the stairs. Instead, Elizabeth said nothing and followed behind.

They approached the wrought iron gate, and Ray handed Elizabeth a key. "Move in any time after tomorrow. It will be cleaned by noon. Stop by the antiques store to let us know you're here." He paused. "Unfortunately, parking is not available except in a lot down the street. Most Tulane folks leave their cars in the Tulane lot and walk to the Quarter. You can pull up into the porte cochere to unload," said Ray.

They were back on the street with the key to her new apartment in less than thirty minutes. It had been easy. But Elizabeth felt cranky.

"Come on, let's head to Café du Monde and get some coffee and a beignet," said Livvy. "You can yell at me there."

Elizabeth looked at the ground as she walked behind the nurse. The sun felt good on her skin, and the breeze off the Mississippi lifted her ponytail. When the women were two blocks away and Elizabeth thought Ray and John couldn't hear her, she stopped in the middle of the sidewalk, grabbed Livvy's shoulder, and spun the woman around.

"You must stop bullying me and trying to force me to your will," insisted Elizabeth. She surprised herself by shouting.

"Get your hand off me. You might be grown, but you don't know how to do anything. You are very naïve. This is exactly what you wanted, and I just helped you close the deal. Be grateful, you little brat," said Livvy, striding away.

Elizabeth trotted behind her. "Livvy, it's the way you do things," she said. "You're so bossy, and you act like what I do is your decision. But it's my life. I can quit Tulane Surgery if I want to. You don't control my fate."

Over her shoulder, Livvy said, "Let's get the coffee and food and settle ourselves by the river. If you still want to fight, let's at least do it on a full stomach." She continued walking toward Café du Monde. "Come on, Crème Puff."

15

Elizabeth caught up to Livvy as she turned right into Pirate's Alley and headed for the Mississippi. Elizabeth glanced down Royal Street at the cascading red bougainvillea and purple petunias, knowing she'd soon see this view most days. She was grateful Livvy had found the apartment for her.

The symphony of sounds from the street artists, musicians, and jugglers blended with the sounds of the rumbling river. She loved the quiet of Royal Street but enjoyed it being one block from the intense activity around Jackson Square. Elizabeth let Livvy walk ahead while she took in the square. Sometimes the Quarter seemed the strangest place on earth, and sometimes, she felt she'd always lived there. Her mother would be horrified to see hawkers of all types twenty yards from the front door of a church. Tarot card readers plying their trade in front of St. Louis Cathedral felt normal here.

Livvy waved to rush her, but Elizabeth slowed her pace to savor local artists' paintings hanging on the wrought iron gates surrounding Jackson Square. Most were mediocre. But, every now and then, one of the paintings of the Bayou, or the famous tale of *Evangeline* by Wordsworth, or the homes in the Quarter resonated with her.

Livvy glared at her and said, "Come on, we don't have all day."

"Actually, I do have all day. My shift is over. It's LSU's day, and I am not rushing."

"All right, Miss Lady of Leisure, I'll grab our coffee and beignets and meet you on our bench behind Café du Monde on the river. Your head nurse is happy to serve you, Doctor."

Elizabeth started to laugh but remembered she was aggravated with Livvy for trying to run her life. She pulled out her Day-Timer and handed Livvy five dollars. Livvy sped away toward the coffee shop, and Elizabeth meandered along, looking at the paintings.

A young Black man painted a tourist, a woman who looked intoxicated. She weaved in the chair and spilled some of her colored drink on her Jazz Festival T-shirt. The artist's work was good. His painting captured her debauchery—her weak jaw, droopy eyes, and half-hung head. She looked like her drunken self. Elizabeth thought he was doing a great job but thought it likely that the tourist wouldn't buy it because it looked too realistic.

Elizabeth turned to walk away and looked into the face of a python wrapped around the arm of a man in women's clothes. Too many childhood jokes involving snakes left her unamused. Her knees weakened. She looked at the man and pleaded, "Please get away from me! I'm terrified of snakes!" The person tipped his fancy church-lady hat and stepped back. Elizabeth stumbled and decided it was time to move toward Café du Monde and away from the carnival atmosphere of Jackson Square.

She walked along the back side of Café du Monde, inhaling the sweet combination of coffee and sugar. The French Market was open, and vegetables were on sale, along with crafts and art. Few customers were out in the post-Christmas lull. Elizabeth wondered where the merchants got fresh vegetables in December.

She peeked in the back window of the shop and saw the workers frying the beignets. She smiled and waved at the employees on the assembly line. Her mouth watered. The fried dough covered in powdered sugar was a powerful appetite stimulant. She climbed up the hill of the levee toward Livvy.

The nurse's profile was turned up to the sun. Elizabeth realized that when Livvy wasn't being bossy and controlling, she was queen-like. No women anywhere in the world had the beauty of the women of New Orleans. Elizabeth thought their mix of genetics distinctive, but she knew

Livvy was not cognizant of her beauty. If nobody was watching, Livvy was imperial.

The breeze from the river felt cool. Elizabeth watched tons of muddy water sweep by every second. In front of her was Algiers Point, but it might as well have been Croatia. Elizabeth hadn't visited that side of the river. Her world was the hospital. Container ships, tugboats, and barges shared the wide river in organized chaos. Elizabeth loved to watch the working vessels.

Livvy slid over to make room for Elizabeth on the wooden bench. Powdered sugar puffed up from her lap as she repositioned herself. She handed Elizabeth a paper basket with three beignets. "I put three sugars in your coffee, the way you like it."

"Thanks." The two sat and sipped and chewed in silence. They focused on the river and a barge being pushed by a small tugboat.

After the barge passed, Livvy broke the silence. "I think that tugboat pushing the unyielding and obstinate barge is a nice symbol of what we're experiencing. I'm the tug trying to help you navigate the big curve in the river, and you're fighting me all the way."

Here we go. She's the hero, and I'm the villain. Elizabeth wanted to sit and rest and eat. Her nerves were frazzled from considering her life choices, and she didn't want to argue with Livvy.

"I'm talking to you," said Livvy.

Elizabeth sighed and put her half-eaten beignet back in the bag. She turned toward Livvy. "I appreciate your trying to help me. But sometimes you remind me too much of my mother. She's a person who doesn't know when to stop pushing. There's a difference between helping someone by opening their mind to solutions they might not see and shoving them toward what you think is their destiny. I'm learning who I am and what I want. And what I'm capable of being."

Livvy was poised on the edge of the bench, ready to argue. Elizabeth's calm demeanor threw her off-guard. "I get frustrated with you," Livvy admitted. "You have it all. You're smart and pretty, and you're a good doctor. Yet you seem paralyzed by fear and unable to make decisions. I know you want to live on Royal Street. I know you'll be happier with John and Ray and Bella. Why on earth do you waste so much energy fighting me?" Livvy's voice became louder.

Elizabeth slumped on the bench. "I don't want to fail," she replied. "I'm way out of my league. I'm not a city girl, and I'm afraid I'm not good enough for Tulane Surgery. I'm afraid Dr. White will expose my incompetence. I don't know the rules of New Orleans society, and sometimes, it's all too much for me." She paused. "Sometimes I think Mom's right. Maybe I should go home and marry a farmer and stop trying to be something I'm not."

Livvy patted Elizabeth's leg, leaving a powdered sugar imprint with her warm fingers. "I feel the same way. I was nervous as you know what with John. He's nice as can be, but he's a full-blooded aristocrat. The man went to Tulane undergrad and Tulane Law and his family are hoity-toity and mine are Chalmette ne'er-do-well. They follow a secret set of rules that the rest of us don't know. He's not been anything but kind and polite to me, but I'm as uncomfortable as can be around those people. Everything seems so easy for them."

Those people? Really, Livvy—those people? "Do you mean rich people or educated people or white people?" Elizabeth asked. "Each of those groups seems to pose a problem for you? Why?"

Livvy squirmed on the bench, repositioning herself to face away from the river and toward Elizabeth. Elizabeth knew what was coming and interjected. "Livvy, don't start with your complaints about how you've been done wrong. I don't want to hear it. What I don't understand is you've been in Room Four doing trauma surgery for years, and you know two millimeters beneath the skin of all beings. We're pink. The entire human race is pink! We bleed; we suffer; we die—all of us exactly alike. Why do you persist in lumping people into categories? Does it make it easier for you to judge them?" asked Elizabeth.

As Elizabeth was speaking, they both noticed a homeless man passing in front of them on his way to nap behind the levy. The New Orleans police usually rousted the homeless from the wooden benches along the riverfront around the time the tourists started moving. Today, they missed one.

Elizabeth and Livvy turned to look at his back. His clothes hung on his thin frame and his hair had a few organized plaits, but everything was caked with dirt and grass. His shoulders were stooped, and he dragged his belongings in a Schwegmann's grocery bag.

"You think he believes he's been created equal? You think being pink matters to him?" Livvy's face was hot and red with anger.

Elizabeth sighed. "Livvy, you know most homeless people are either mentally ill or alcoholic. Both diseases touch all races. You also know many homeless people choose to be that way. Think of all the people we send to shelters every day, only to find out they refused to stay. That poor unfortunate fellow doesn't represent a race issue as much as a social issue and a mental health issue. The way you characterize the Black population as having no chances and the white population as having all the chances just isn't accurate. Don't you think poverty and the lack of education are the biggest factors for most folks?"

Livvy's posture was rigid. Her jaw was clenched, and her face was red. With eyes ablaze, she asked, "And who do you think has more poverty and less education, Elizabeth?"

"Try not to get so mad. Try to imagine I might have points you could understand. Try to have a conversation, not a fight. Discussion leads to understanding and understanding might improve race relations, Livvy. Fighting won't."

"You don't get it, you with your little bobbing blonde ponytail and your thin little white girl body. Doors open for you that would not open for me. You're not capable of seeing the world my way."

Elizabeth stared into the sun until she saw orange dots. The cargo containers passing up the great river shimmered in the light and became hazy around the edges. She was exhausted and frustrated. She knew Livvy wouldn't understand that poorer whites in South Carolina felt the same way she did. She could not know people in Elizabeth's farm family felt uncomfortable and inferior to the wealthy, educated, society-conscious Charlestonians. The energy Elizabeth needed to convince Livvy of anything had evaporated. They'd have to agree to disagree. She changed the subject to salvage their morning, but an image popped into clear focus, so she decided to try again.

"Livvy, part of the reason I want so badly to have a career is my mother's mother. She's a wonderful, sweet, loving, God-fearing, hard-working woman. But I never saw her anywhere but at church, in the kitchen, or on the back porch canning or shelling some kind of beans. I didn't see her read anything other than her worn-to-shreds family Bible. She saw nothing of the world outside of her rural town. Her world was making fifty biscuits every morning, frying ten chickens every day, and putting up food from the farm for forty people every day of her life except Sunday. Her idea of travel was walking to the smokehouse to get deer meat. A big trip was going into town, to church, on Wednesday nights. She had eleven children, all delivered at home. Nine survived. She had snow-white hair by the time she was thirty-five. She attended school only to the ninth grade. Had no opportunity. No education. She had white skin and blue eyes. Livvy, I know it's not only Black people who work hard and get little in return. That's why I believe poverty and lack of education are the biggest limiting factors."

Livvy snorted and giggled. "OK, Crème Puff. I guess the new letters behind your name are going to be PWT, after MD."

"What does that mean?" asked Elizabeth.

"Poor White Trash. That's what we call y'all here in New Orleans. PWT for short," said Livvy.

Despite knowing Livvy was trying to get her goat, Elizabeth felt a wave of shame. PWT was a hurtful term because it held an element of truth. She remembered her aunts bringing the cousins' clothes to her grandmother's house the weekend before the school year determined which kids fit into the clothes that had been salvaged from the last school year. Elizabeth was ten before she realized most kids got new clothes at the start of the school year. She'd worn whatever the cousin a few years older than her had not ruined the year before. She hadn't felt poor growing up, but she realized they didn't have things other kids had. Watching her aunts laughing and sorting through the massive pile of clothes warmed her. She was grateful for the community and the love, but shame came with it.

The family bought no new clothes for any of the kids unless they couldn't fit into what was left from last year. Because Elizabeth was skinny, she could always fit, though the clothes hung on her thin frame. By the time she was thirteen, she knew how to make a pattern from newspaper and was working at a fabric shop, negotiating scraps to make her own clothes. Her grandmother, an excellent seamstress, had taught her to sew, and Elizabeth could make a dress or skirt in a weekend. She was proud of her sewing skills and her creativity, but knew PWT, or something equivalent, was likely on the tongues of classmates who saw her homemade dresses.

Elizabeth's first item of clothing bought especially for her was a gift from her dad when she was seventeen. He came home one day carrying a beautiful white crepe blouse with a huge bow that tied at the neck. He had seen it in a store window and splurged. The Sunday she wore it to church, Elizabeth felt like a princess. Now, of course, she had little need of nice clothes. She wore surgical scrubs most of the time.

Livvy called her name, and Elizabeth's childhood memories dissolved. "I didn't mean to insult you."

"Yes, you did. But it's not a problem. Part of me is PWT and proud of it. I can survive on Vienna sausages in a can when the Russians come."

Both laughed. "You're silly, girl," said Livvy. "Let's talk about men. We can't solve our racial differences, but maybe we can get us each a man and have a little more fun."

Race, religion, money, and politics were subjects best avoided to preserve the young friendship. Elizabeth wanted to be Livvy's friend. But men were something else she had no desire to discuss. What was there to say? She sat mute, staring at Algiers's Landing.

Livvy tapped the side of Elizabeth's thigh with the back of her hand. "Wake up. What kind of man do you like? I think you missed the boat with Dr. Caballero. He really seems to like you, and he has the dough to take you to New Orleans' nicest places. I think you should jump on that guy."

Elizabeth looked into Livvy's eyes and saw mirth. She knew Livvy was trying to goad her yet again. "Why go for a senior resident? Why shouldn't I marry a faculty member? I could stop working, live on St. Charles Avenue, and shop at Ms. Yvonne LaFleur' s every week? My whole life could be entertaining other rich folks and going to black-tie events?"

"Right. And I'd never get invited," said Livvy.

"You could be my maid," said Elizabeth as she jumped from the bench, anticipating violence. Livvy was quick. She grabbed Elizabeth's ponytail and stopped her in her tracks.

Livvy growled, tugged lightly on the ponytail, and said, "You'd better take that back right now, little girl. I'll whip your arse right here on the levy in front of that homeless man."

Elizabeth squirmed and laughed. "You're so easy to rile. You know I'm kidding. I'm about as likely to live on St. Charles Avenue as I am to be the president of Tulane. Let go of me, and stop being so sensitive."

Livvy released Elizabeth's ponytail and sat back on the bench. "You made me spill my café au lait. Can I have some of yours? I still have a beignet to finish," said Livvy.

Elizabeth poured half of her cup into Livvy's empty cup. They settled back to enjoy the hum of the river. Elizabeth loved quiet togetherness. She and her father could sit for hours and never talk. Being near each other was enough companionship. Livvy squirmed after five minutes. Quiet time made Livvy anxious.

"What kind of men do you like?" said Livvy. She grinned and cut her eyes to the side to observe Elizabeth.

Now Elizabeth was the one squirming. "I don't know, Livvy. I don't think about it much. I'm so busy with surgery; I don't have time to think about men."

"You know that's not natural. You're in the prime of your life, and you should be hormonal and horny and thinking about men a lot. The way you keep your nose in a surgery textbook just ain't right."

Elizabeth felt her heart beat faster. She had no interest in trying to answer Livvy's questions about men.

Livvy read her mind. "This is what female friends talk about, Elizabeth. Women talk about their jobs, their children, their men, and their dreams. Since we know all about each other's jobs and we have no children, the next natural subject is men. We don't have time for dreams today."

Elizabeth chewed her last beignet, felt the sun on her face, and accepted she had to humor Livvy if they were to have a friendship.

"All right, what do you want to know?"

Livvy laughed. "It's not a tooth extraction with no anesthesia. It's just a conversation to get to know each other better. What type of guy were you attracted to in high school? What would you call 'your type'?"

Elizabeth struggled to remember nine years before. "I like smart men. I like honest people, in general. I also like athletic men. Since I'm not athletic, I admire men who are physical. In my small town, the smart guys who were also athletic were the Jewish guys. My first two boyfriends were Jewish," said Elizabeth.

Livvy's jaw dropped. She looked down and laughed. "Girl, you are full of surprises. I didn't know there were Jewish families in small Southern towns. What percent of the population was Jewish, and how did you end up with the Jewish fellows? I thought their families wanted them to stick with the Jewish girls."

Elizabeth moved down from the bench to sit on the grass, leaned back on her elbows, and looked up at Livvy. She liked surprising the nurse and cracking open her prejudices. Livvy thought she knew everything about how the world worked. Elizabeth enjoyed showing her another side.

"Well, like I said, I like smart guys. I was in the advanced classes in high school and so were many of the Jewish kids. We had around a dozen Jewish families in our town, and most of them were the merchants and business owners. A glamorous Jewish girl in my year took me home with her a few times for dinner, and I met her older brother. He was handsome, an honor student, and did every sport the school offered. He also had a job in the family store and went to Hebrew school. I was interested in him from the start."

"Did the family not want him to date you?"

"No, it was a small town. Everyone knows everyone. This was the ninth grade. Nobody was going to be marrying anyone. Their family became like my second family. I went to all the Jewish services and learned a great deal about the religion. She was my best friend for many years, long after he and I had little contact."

"You're trying to get away from the subject at hand. I want to know what you like about men. You're trying to give me a religion lesson. What did you like about the *men*?" said Livvy.

Elizabeth stared at Livvy. "I like smart jocks, guys who can talk about science and history and art and who have multiple dimensions. I like men who do things. I hate TV, and I hate sitting and staring at sports all the time. I like a man who enjoys going to a museum or out to hear music. I like a man who can carry on a conversation. And I like muscles," said Elizabeth as she felt her face flush.

Livvy laughed, making her body shake. "What was that last part? You like what? Now, we're getting down to the good part."

A tall cargo container progressed up the river and silhouetted Elizabeth's head. She felt the warmth of the sun temporarily eclipsed. "Miss Nosey Livvy! If you must know my deep dark secret, it's that I like a man who looks like he can carry my luggage if I ever get to travel. His biceps must be bigger than mine. Yep, I like big biceps."

Livvy jumped down from the bench and sat very close to Elizabeth on the grass and whispered in her ear. "What else must be big?"

Elizabeth stabbed Livvy in the side with her boney elbow and said, "Enough. I don't tell tales out of school, and I think you know enough about me. This is what you always do. You try to pry everything out of me without giving away anything about you. What do you like in men?" Elizabeth realized she'd not seen Livvy express interest in any man.

Livvy crossed her legs and leaned her elbows onto her knees. With the morning sun behind her, Elizabeth saw Livvy encircled in gold. Her hair, skin, and eyes had a bright golden glow. She knew Livvy was no good at taking a compliment, so she held her thoughts to herself. "Come on, Miss Nosey. Tell all!"

Livvy threw her head back and said up to the sky, "Lord only knows that what I like and what is good for me are two completely different things. I like a hot, sexy, bad boy. I like them wild, and I love the ones that just won't do right. Aoife and I are similar this way." She leveled her gaze, and Elizabeth saw a deep sadness in her golden eyes.

The two were silent. After a while, Elizabeth said, "You deserve better."

"Oh, don't I know it. My mamma says I don't like normal men. She says I'm looking for a temporary freak show instead of a real relationship. So I've decided not to date until I can figure out what's wrong with me." As she started to stand and brush the grass from her backside, she turned to Elizabeth and said, "Too bad you aren't a psychiatrist, Elizabeth."

Elizabeth stood too. She realized Livvy was moving on from her sadness and was headed for humor. She knew not to push. "Well, surgery might let out the evil spirits. You never know. I think me removing your gallbladder might fix you right up."

While they gathered their trash and headed back to Jackson Square, Livvy said, "Maybe so. I've tried everything else. An operation to remove the gris-gris might work."

16

Elizabeth scurried down the steep levy. Without scaling the crest, she'd miss seeing the massive river. She looked back at the levy and wondered how a small hill could contain the mighty Mississippi. Life wasn't always as it appeared. If the river can hide behind a mound of dirt, what could be hiding in plain view in her life?

She heard the clang of Livvy throwing their trash in the bin behind Café du Monde. "Stop daydreaming, Crème Puff. Which street do you want to take out of the Quarter? Let's do something different today."

Elizabeth didn't like doing things differently just for variety. Change for the sake of change wasn't her way.

"Let's walk by the Pontalba Buildings and past the Cabildo," Elizabeth suggested. She loved the history of the Quarter. The Pontalba Buildings were built by Baroness Pontalba in 1850. The elegant red brick buildings were thought to be the oldest continually rented apartments in America. The Cabildo, built around 1797, was the seat of the city council when New Orleans was run by the Spanish and was the site of the signing of the Louisiana Purchase. She thought Livvy wasn't much interested in the history but sought to entice her by saying, "Let's enjoy the chaos of Jackson Square. Then let's cut up Royal Street to Canal."

Livvy shook her head. "You're the only person in the history of the French Quarter to experience only two of its fourteen blocks. Is it stubbornness or laziness or not wanting to do something I want to do that keeps you wandering up and down the same street every time we're here? And why do you need thirty minutes to do a fifteen-minute walk between

Café du Monde and the Tulane parking lot? Some of us have chores to do."

It's always about her. "I'm tired of rushing," Elizabeth explained. "I rush through my entire shift at Charity. There's no time to breathe." She paused. "Besides, it's not safe to walk around after dark, and I get outside in the daylight only once or twice per week. Royal Street is pretty; the rest of the Quarter is beautiful in spots but nasty and stinky in other spots. I get enough nasty and stinky in the emergency room."

Livvy walked rapidly and soon was ten feet ahead of Elizabeth, who refused to speed up. She scanned Jackson Square to avoid the cross-dresser with the snake. She spotted him on the far side of the square and felt relieved.

A line of tourists was queued up in front of the Cabildo. Elizabeth had not been inside. She wondered if Dr. White went to Mardi Gras balls in that historic building. She looked into the windows of the upper floors and noticed the ceilings were high and decorated with sparkling chandeliers. *It's probably magical in there.*

The French Quarter, festively decorated for Christmas, sparkled with lights and greenery in every window. Even the shabbiest buildings were adorned with Christmas cheer. Elizabeth peered into the window of the Petit Theatre and hoped to one day see a play there. She wondered if John and Ray attended.

"You're dilly dallying to irritate me!"

Elizabeth saw Livvy standing in the middle of the street, her hands on her hips and a scowl on her face.

"Livvy, I'm not doing anything to you," Elizabeth retorted. "I'm enjoying my walk. We don't have to walk together. You go the way you want, and I'll go the way I want. Since you're irritated with me, maybe that's the best plan."

Livvy pointed her index finger at Elizabeth and said in a louder-than-necessary voice, "This is why you don't have any relationships.

You have to do it your way. There's this thing called compromise. You might want to attempt it sometimes."

Dang her!

The long line of customers standing in front of the Gumbo Shop stared. Elizabeth was embarrassed. Livvy had no qualms about yelling at Elizabeth in earshot of strangers.

Elizabeth stepped off the sidewalk and walked to the middle of the street. She leaned in, cupped her hands around Livvy's ear, and said, "I may be selfish, but you're a bully. Please stop yelling at me in public."

Livvy laughed. "You look like a crazy kangaroo looking for something to punch. When confronted, you want to fight. But please don't do that. You'd take one swing at me, and I'd take your scrawny, sticklike body out. It might be worth it to see the shock on your face."

Elizabeth sped past her and didn't slow down until she turned the corner onto Royal Street and stood in front of the old courthouse. It was a popular hangout for the homeless and tourists alike. She did not hear footsteps, and she wondered if Livvy had left her. She refused to look back.

She looked at the tourists dressed in Christmas hats. She passed the Court of Two Sisters restaurant and looked through the lobby into the courtyard beyond the entrance. She wondered if Dr. White dined there. *He's probably too refined for the Quarter.* She imagined him eating somewhere in the Garden District where only real New Orleanians ate. *He's popping into my mind because of my anxiety about the rotation.*

She turned right onto Canal, and Livvy walked toward her. "See how slow you are? I walked around the block before you even made it up Royal Street. Is everyone from South Carolina slow like you?"

Elizabeth giggled and did her best Deep South impersonation. "But of course. It's hard carrying around your banjo and your bowl of grits at the same time. And you know our gene pool is shallow. With my low IQ and balancing the banjo and the grits, it makes one quite slow, Miss Fancy Lavinia Robichaud."

Livvy laughed, but the joke was on her. Elizabeth was the only person Livvy had ever met from South Carolina. Livvy had prejudices she didn't even acknowledge.

The two fell in step and arrived at the Tulane parking lot. Livvy gave Elizabeth boxes she'd saved for her move. Without talking, they transferred the boxes from one car to the other. Elizabeth's natural way to part was to hug, but their latest squabble was too fresh for a hug, so Elizabeth smiled and said, "Thanks for the pep talk today."

Livvy said, "See ya, Crème Puff. Thanks to your head nurse, your life's looking up."

Elizabeth agreed, but she wasn't about to say so.

17

Elizabeth drove to her apartment. Even though she was off duty, she thought of the stresses of work.

She looked forward to moving. A nice dog to pet at the end of a long shift might be a good stress reducer. Elizabeth chuckled as she thought of Buster, Mrs. Kaczka's Chihuahua. The miniature monster was like coming home to a crack addict from the ER. He growled and tried to bite her, but at least he wasn't a spitter like the crack addicts often were. She found herself smiling in spite of herself. Elizabeth didn't enjoy gallows humor and thought it tasteless. But coping with the emergency room took her down a path of no return. Dark humor helped her cope.

She parked, pulled the cardboard boxes out of her trunk, and went upstairs. As she ascended the ugly outdoor staircase, she wondered if her mother and Mrs. Kaczka could be right. The thought of enduring Dr. White's reproving scrutiny made her wonder. *Will I ever have a family if I continue down this surgery path?* Self-doubt about her future plagued Elizabeth.

She opened her door and met the smell of rotting food. She'd forgotten to empty her trash again. The fried crawfish tails at Popeye's were on special when she drove by a few days ago. She thought she'd eaten every bite, but the nasty dead fish smell told her she hadn't. She dropped the boxes and ran to the kitchen area to retrieve the trash bag. Then she scampered down the stairs, holding her breath, and dropped the bag in the community trash bin. She'd have to remember to empty her trash regularly at her new apartment. She didn't want to disappoint Ray and John.

Elizabeth crept slowly back up the stairs, aware the slightest noise would arouse her neighbor. She reentered her apartment and heard Neptune and Poseidon chirping. How could two creatures less than one inch long create so much noise? She lifted the top of the frogs' home and tossed in two pellets. Poseidon jumped on top of Neptune and stole his pellet. *Just my luck! I have a bully for a frog.* She giggled. *He must be from Livvy's blood line.* She diverted Poseidon away from Neptune and tossed another pellet directly into the smaller frog's mouth. He swam away and hid under the bamboo stalk. Elizabeth wondered if she'd be hiding from Dr. White like her frog in a few days.

She placed the cardboard boxes on her rented dining table. In six months, she hadn't prepared a meal in the apartment or eaten at the table. Surgical training, she had discovered, was all-consuming. The apartment had little natural light, and everything in it was beige, brown, or stained. Elizabeth had made little effort to convert the space into a home. She ate takeout meals and took speed showers, brushing her teeth and washing her hair simultaneously. If running late, she'd taught herself to drink coffee out of one side of her mouth while brushing her teeth on the other. She fell asleep reading surgery textbooks and awoke at four in the morning to race to Charity. She walked around the efficiency apartment, tossing books and clothes into the boxes. But she took care with the family pictures, wrapping them carefully in newspaper. Mrs. Kaczka tried to draw Elizabeth into the world beyond the hospital by dropping her used newspapers at Elizabeth's door. The large stack of unread sections of the *Times Picayune* came in handy now.

Her apprehension grew with each filled box. The closer she was to moving to the Quarter, the closer she was to her rotation with Dr. White. Anger replaced fear. Her hand shook as she tossed her cheap plastic plates into a box. *How could I let one man make me so crazy? What did he represent? Why could I not see him as just another obstacle to overcome?* She'd overcome so many obstructions already. Her stomach churned as she packed.

Her father would tell her that she was letting her pride get the best of her. He'd tell her that perfection was impossible. He'd remind her that in learning something new, there were mistakes involved. He'd tell her to make sure she learned from each mistake—that was the important part.

But Daddy hadn't stood in front of Dr. White on trauma rounds and seen him dripping with arrogance and self-righteous anger. Daddy had not been in life-or-death situations, where decisions had far-reaching impacts on the lives of others. Daddy had not walked out of the trauma suite and to the family waiting room to tell a child his father was dead. Daddy had not known the guilt of wondering if his actions had contributed to the father's death.

Elizabeth feared her desire to emulate Dr. White. He was the smartest clinician she'd met. Everyone said he was the most gifted surgeon. She wanted his skills, but not his judgmental, pompous tendencies. She longed for his knowledge, but he terrified her. Around him, she felt like an imposter. In front of him, her mind fogged. He was too quick, and the questions he asked felt like a battering ram. Elizabeth thought he saw it as his job to weed out the weak. How could she survive his scrutiny? How could she let her fear of Dr. White's disapproval motivate her? She knew if she could understand why he affected her this way, she could manage her emotions better.

She knew he was wealthy and came from a social class of white Southern privilege to which she didn't belong. She believed Dr. White looked down at everyone beneath him, and that included her. Like Livvy, Elizabeth had always been nervous around rich people. Her people were low-country farmers. She sensed there was a rule book for upper-class rich people that people from the lower classes weren't allowed to read. She imagined how it would feel to know your bills were paid and you didn't have to hustle to eat. She thought it might free up mental energy to be more creative on other fronts. But weren't the rich less resilient? Didn't they fall apart when they didn't get their way?

Elizabeth wasn't bedeviled with envy regarding other people's property, but she wanted to be the smartest in any situation. Being capable meant everything to her.

Elizabeth used her anger to finish packing and drag the boxes down to her car. She'd take the frogs last. *I'm twenty-five years old, and everything I own fits into a few boxes,* she thought as she loaded them into the car. She didn't want to talk to Mrs. Kaczka, but good manners dictated she say goodbye. The woman had cooked for her and tried to be a comfort. After surveying the now-empty apartment, Elizabeth locked the door and dropped the keys into the mailbox marked "Manager." She trudged back up the stairs and knocked on Mrs. Kaczka's door and heard Buster's maniacal barking after the first knock. She pictured him standing in front of the closed door, baring his teeth and barking with all the fury his three pounds could muster.

Mrs. Kaczka cracked the door and peeked out with Buster in her arms. She saw Elizabeth, smiled, and yanked the door open. "Come in, come in," said Mrs. Kaczka. "I'm so glad to see you. I have corned beef and cabbage cooking. Come in and eat."

Elizabeth felt guilt and relief. "Mrs. Kaczka, I've come to say goodbye. I need to live closer to the hospital, and I've gotten an apartment in the French Quarter. I dropped by to thank you."

Mrs. Kaczka started to cry. "Oh, honey, no, no, you can't leave. I'll be lonely without you next door. Who'll be my new neighbor? You know, I didn't like the last fellow who lived there. He made the whole building smell like pot. Please don't move."

Elizabeth felt guilt, then anger. Once again, Mrs. Kaczka reminded her of Mom. Everything was all about her. She didn't consider the move might be advantageous to Elizabeth.

Elizabeth backed out of the door frame and said, "Thanks for the nice meals you shared with me, and thanks for keeping an eye on my place while I was at the hospital. Please tell Mr. Kaczka goodbye and best of luck with Buster."

She turned and bolted down the stairs. By the time she'd reached the third step, she was crying. She used to be sweet. Her old self would have had more compassion for her neighbor. Mother Charity's stress had worn on her heart, and it had hardened. She fulfilled her duty by expressing gratitude, but she recognized she was fleeing to preserve her sanity. Her energy was depleted, and she had nothing left for her neighbor. Whatever unexpected life lessons Royal Street brought, it would likely not involve cabbage, guilt, and a malevolent, barking Chihuahua.

Elizabeth drove to the Quarter under a cloud of relief and anticipation. She pulled into the porte cochere and opened the heavy wrought iron gate. She pulled her car into the brick paved drive, gathered the frogs, ran through the beautiful garden and up the stairs, and placed her pets in her new apartment. The few boxes she had took only two more trips. As she locked the wrought iron gate and backed into the street, she realized she was two days early from the agreed upon move-in date. She hoped the cleaners could work around her boxes. She was happy to be surrounded by the lovely things Ray and John had put in the apartment. She liked nice things; she just didn't own any. The garden was all the decoration she needed.

She parked in the hospital lot and walked toward her new apartment. Her pager squawked. "Please call the Tulane operator for Dr. Norman McSwain holding."

She finally had a day off, was in the middle of moving, and had missed Christmas with her family. Now her boss was calling.

As a surgery intern, she could be fired for not answering her pager. There was really no such thing as being off duty. There was no pay phone nearby, and she had no change.

She jogged to the back door of the Tulane Medical Center Emergency room, picked up a receiver, and dialed zero.

"Hi, it's Dr. Elizabeth Roberts. I'm not on call, but you paged me."

The operator was familiar with whiney interns and residents who hated to be paged. She said, "Dr. McSwain's holding." Elizabeth thought the operator could not be more thrilled if she had said, *God's holding.*

"Hi, how are you?" said Dr. McSwain.

She dreaded the call. "I'm fine, sir."

"I hate to bother you on your day off, but I'm tied up in the OR at Tulane and the surgery charge resident at Charity is in the OR finishing up cases left over from yesterday. A surgery consult needs to be seen in the ER at Tulane hospital, and I hoped you'd do a favor and see the consult? It's a burn patient, and we don't like to keep those waiting."

Elizabeth knew it was no favor he was asking for. Her boss was telling her that her day off was over before it really started. "I'm standing ten feet from the door of the ER," she said, "and I'll be happy to see the consult, sir. Should I call you or the chief resident after I've finished?" asked Elizabeth.

"Thanks. Call me in OR Seven at Tulane," said Dr. McSwain as he hung up.

18

Elizabeth walked through the ER doors and looked at the board on the wall in the hall to locate the exam room for Dr. McSwain's patient.

Room Seven held Leeodus Benoit. *It can't be that crazy Cajun I just saw at Charity.*

She knocked on the exam room door and heard a voice with a heavy Cajun accent say, "Please come in and witness my stupidity."

It was him. His feet, shoved in their cowboy boots, were propped on the hospital bed. He wore a denim shirt, tight Levi's jeans, and a well-worn Western hat. His ponytail hung over his shoulder, and his hands were wrapped to the elbows in thick layers of fluffy white gauze. He was laughing with a policeman as he turned to Elizabeth and winked.

"Well, I'll be dang. If it ain't the prettiest little doctor-lady in Louisiana! How you doing, cher? I thought you were a Charity doctor. You got sick of the Big Free and wandered over to the private world?" said Leeodus as he attempted to stand and remove his hat with his bandaged hands.

The policeman pressed Leeodus back into the gurney and said, "The nurse gave you pain meds. You'd better stay flat for now." The officer tipped his hat to Elizabeth.

Elizabeth couldn't believe it. *How can one guy get into so much trouble in so little time?*

She lifted the metal chart from the foot of his bed and read his record. The nurse had done a brief intake and had wrapped his hands. She flipped to the nurse's notes and read, "Patient burned while removing cat from tailpipe of pickup truck. Patient is intoxicated." Elizabeth chuckled. *Mr. Benoit's never boring.*

"What's the reason for your visit today, Mr. Benoit?" asked Elizabeth, trying not to laugh.

He grinned, showing shiny white bridgework and said, "Doc, I told you at our last meeting that Mr. Benoit's my father, so please, call me Leeodus. And my visit is for the same reason as all my hospital visits—I'm not that smart. When God gave out looks and street smarts and hard work ethic, I was at the front of the line. But when it came to general smarts . . . well, he just passed over this ole Cajun. I suspect God uses me for entertainment."

The policeman was relaxed and laughing. *Whatever brought the officer to the ER with the patient could not be violent or serious. Leeodus isn't handcuffed to the gurney.*

"What happened to you, Leeodus?" said Elizabeth.

"Well, Doc, it's a long story." Elizabeth knew with Mr. Benoit it was frequently a long story. She knew he couldn't be rushed and would eventually get around to explaining the bandaged hands. *My new apartment and my day off will have to wait.*

"Mellette's nuts about her Maine coon cat, Thomasena. She loves that dreadful cat more than me. She's made me promise to be sure I know where the cat is before I back out of the drive in my truck. That cat would taunt me. I swear she's tried to commit suicide for five years just to get me in trouble with my wife. She hides under the hood of my truck. I have to beat on the hood to wake her, and half the time, if I can't find her, I open the hood, and there she is, sitting and grinning at me, daring me to start the motor and chop her up. I was sure she'd scream as cats do and make sure she sounded real pitiful if Mellette heard it. I'd probably never have sex again if I chopped up that cat. Mellette can hold out a long time when angry, Doc," said Leeodus. He looked at the policeman. "It's rough on a guy."

Elizabeth tapped the aluminum chart on the palm of her hand, hoping the quick cadence would get Leeodus to step up the pace of his story.

"How'd the cat lead to your burned hands?" asked Elizabeth as she reached out to unwind the gauze.

"I know you've got a delicate touch from our last encounter, but please, be gentle. My hands hurt like the dickens, cher."

Elizabeth slowly unwound the gauze while she continued to coax the story from Leeodus. "So, Mellette was away at the beach with her sisters for a few days. She didn't take the cat with her. I was in a hurry to get to my job and just plain forgot to check for the demon cat. I think subconsciously, I thought the cat wouldn't mess with me without Mellette as an audience. But I was wrong."

The left hand was exposed, and Elizabeth saw the palm and fingers were blistered, red, and swollen in an even pattern.

"Uh, huh," nodded Elizabeth. "And then what happened?" *I'll get this dressing off while he's distracted. It looks like full-thickness burns in multiple spots. He'll need to stay in the hospital and see the plastic surgery hand team, but, knowing him, he probably won't consent.*

"I jumped in the truck and backed away, and within five seconds, I heard screaming that freaked me out. It was Thomasena. I run over her," said Leeodus.

"I'm so sorry, Leeodus. That's awful," said Elizabeth as she continued to unwrap his other hand.

"I jumped out of my truck and looked under it, and there she was . . . a bloody and mushed mess! Doc, I don't know how that cat was still alive, but she was screaming and just plain pitiful. I knew she could not be saved but wanted to honor Mellette and finish killing the cat as nicely as possible. I drug the screaming cat out from under the truck and put her in a Ziploc bag. Then I duct taped it tightly to the exhaust pipe of the truck and left the motor running. I'd heard carbon monoxide poisoning was an easy way to go. I did my best for that cat, Doc," said Leeodus.

Elizabeth tried hard not to smile. With both of his hands exposed, she could begin her work. "Leeodus, I want to give you some intravenous pain medicine. Then I'll try to clean your wounds and figure out the depth of your burns."

"But Doc, you ain't heard how I got burned yet."

And I also don't know why you're accompanied by the police. Elizabeth paused, took a deep breath, stepped back, and focused on Leeodus's bright blue eyes.

"I'll make it quick. After ten minutes, I figured the cat was dead and at peace. I grabbed the tailpipe of the truck to remove the duct tape. It was scalding hot, and that's how I got burned. I went to screaming worse than the cat. God has a strange system of justice. But in this case, justice was immediate and unforgettable."

"Go on with your story, sir. Doc's got work to do. You're not her only patient today," said the policeman.

"Right, right." Leeodus continued, "Anyway, the cat smelled awful. She smelled like gasoline. Mellette wouldn't believe she'd died in her sleep, which was my planned explanation. I had to wash that dead cat and my scalded hands. I submerged both in water with ice. I figured I'd treat my burns and clean the cat at the same time."

This is crazy!

"In the middle of all of this, Mellette called from Pensacola to say the weather was bad and she and her sisters were nearly home. She was calling to find out if I needed anything from the grocery.

"What a homecoming! Bad weather, dead cat, burned husband. I had to dry Thomasena off real quick if Mellette was going to believe the died-in-her-sleep plan, and I had to clean the blood off the drive and get my hands cleaned up. I knew she'd easily believe I'd burned myself doing something with the truck. But she'd check that cat out good and not miss a thing."

"Tell the doc how I got involved, Leeodus," prompted the officer.

"I taped Thomasena to the windshield of the truck," Leeodus continued, "and I was driving real fast down the Bayou to try to dry out her long hair before my bride hit the door. I guess I was speeding a little and smelled like alcohol. He thought it best to bring me in the police car to the hospital," said Leeodus.

"It was his idea to bury the cat first. He thought Mellette would be less traumatized, and he pointed out that if the cat had been buried this morning, after it 'died in its sleep last night,' Mellette would not know the difference and would not be as traumatized as she would be at seeing Thomasena dead. He also cleaned off the drive while I wrapped up my hands for the trip. The police can be pretty helpful at times," Leeodus concluded. He and the officer laughed together.

Louisiana is the craziest state in the union. Leeodus reminds me of my cousins. I can't help but like this guy.

"I'm injecting the Demerol and Phenergan, Leeodus," said Elizabeth. "Relax and let the drugs work, and we'll begin to work on your hands," said Elizabeth. She stuck her head out of the exam room and called to the nurse. "Please bring a plastics tray, a large jar of sulfa cream, and some hand splints."

Elizabeth strapped Leeodus to the gurney at his chest and hips while he drifted into a deep sleep. He snored while she set up the sterile tray.

The policeman whispered, "That ole boy had himself right sort of worked up. He sure must love his wife. He was trying everything to make up for his mistake. I feel bad for him. The cat was a mess. No way was she going to believe him."

"Are you going to arrest him?" asked Elizabeth while putting on sterile gloves to work on Leeodus's hands.

"Nah, this is Louisiana. Everybody drinks a little while driving. I mostly wanted to know the story of why a man was driving around with a dead cat duct taped to his windshield," said the policeman.

After she'd finished cleaning his wounds and examining him, Elizabeth called Dr. McSwain in the operating room. She explained Mr. Benoit's burned hands to the OR nurse, who explained the situation to Dr. McSwain while he operated.

Later, as Elizabeth expected, the patient refused admission. He showed her his previous burn to the perineum. It was healing much better than she expected. Mrs. Benoit's home remedies must have helped. Elizabeth finished her chart work and walked home.

It was a beautiful walk. She recognized the Neville brothers' funky music coming from a coffee shop and arrived at the entrance to her apartment feeling at home.

In the garden, she was tackled by Bella. The dog licked her face and wound her unattached leash around Elizabeth's ankles. Ray, who was wearing a floral apron and gardener's plastic clogs, ran across the garden swinging a trowel covered in black dirt.

"Are you OK? I thought I'd clean these flower beds out a little before you arrived to see my mess. I'm sorry, but obviously, Bella adores you," said Ray. He dropped his trowel, and it clanged as it hit the brick patio. He unwound the leash from Elizabeth's legs, and as he pulled Bella away, the dog licked the air in Elizabeth's direction.

This place is so much better than my last apartment! It smells great, the dog's an upgrade, and Ray's sweet as pie.

Elizabeth petted Bella's head and said, "I'm fine. Remember, I'm a farm girl. I've wrestled hogs and goats. Chickens are the worst. Bella's a dream compared to a young hog fighting castration."

"You are a farm girl!" laughed Ray. "I lived in the country, too, but I avoided intimacy with the creatures."

"If it's OK, I'll go up and get settled. I accidentally moved in early."

Ray stepped back, bowed, and pointed like a trained courtier to the winding stairs of Elizabeth's new apartment.

At the top of the stairs, she glanced back over the garden paradise. Four inside walls covered in plants, a beautiful trickling fountain in the center, and sweet neighbors. It seemed too good to be true.

She dusted and swept, unpacked her boxes, and pulled down the Murphy bed. She placed her worn sheets on the bed, sat down to take in her surroundings, and was asleep in seconds.

She awoke, crying in her sleep. She'd dreamed Dr. White was accusing her of killing a patient in the ICU. Her pillow was wet. *Screw him! He's even invading my sleep. Livvy's right. I have to pull myself together.*

It was almost daybreak. She'd slept fourteen hours. Elizabeth splashed her face with cold water, fixed a cup of coffee, looked at her clock, and saw she had one hour before her shift. She opened the double French doors and appreciated the garden in the predawn hours. She smelled Ray's flowers. The scent washed away her thoughts of Dr. White. *Just do today, like Tony said.*

She dug a packet of instant grits from a box and placed it in a bowl with tap water, then into the microwave while she dressed for work. Her scrubs were clean enough from the day before, and her Charity meal tickets would feed her for a few days. She never knew how long she'd be at the hospital. *A twenty-four-hour shift can easily become a thirty-six-hour shift.* She gave the frogs extra pellets, just in case.

Royal Street was alive with vendors despite the early hour. The restaurants restocked early. Elizabeth smiled and greeted them as they rushed along the street. She entered the emergency room and felt herself grow tense as she transformed herself into Dr. Roberts. She loved to learn and loved medicine, but every day, she wondered if she was up to the task.

Room Four was empty. *That's a good sign.*

There were only three gurneys in the hall. Patients were sleeping on all three. Everyone was breathing. No blood was dripping from the gurneys. It was thirty minutes until it would change from an LSU day to a Tulane day. Dr. Adrien Lambert was sleeping in the X-ray area, his Christmas lights still flashing three days after Christmas. *He must have never left the hospital.* With the dark circles under his eyes and the blood staining the bottom third of his scrubs, he could have been a patient headed to the psychiatric ward instead of the doctor in charge. Elizabeth circled the halls. All was quiet.

At six-thirty, Livvy popped through the back door of the ER, her arms loaded with containers of food. The smells of seafood and sugar floated behind Livvy as she organized her packages at the nurses' desk. She was humming a Christmas tune.

"Good morning, Livvy. Christmas's over. What's with all the food?" asked Elizabeth.

Livvy looked up and smiled. "New Orleans doesn't celebrate anything for one day. I'm getting this food out of my mother's house to save my girlish figure because Mardi Gras is coming, and king cakes will be everywhere. And I can't resist a good piece of king cake. But I have to get into my best church dress by Ash Wednesday."

Adrien stumbled from his sleep, noticing his lights were still flashing from the holes in his scrubs. He laughed and rubbed his eyes. "Did somebody say king cake? Did you bring king cake?"

Once again, I don't know what in the world they're talking about. New Orleans should be its own country. It even has its own desserts.

"Wake up, LSU!" said Livvy. "You have twenty more minutes in your shift. It's a long time till we get a king cake. This morning, it's left-over deer sausage and chicken gumbo, but you're not getting a bite until after we round. I know you've been asleep, but let's you and me and Elizabeth take a trip around the ER before Dr. McSwain gets here."

Elizabeth watched as Livvy transformed into Nurse Robichaud. She saw the erect posture, the piercing watchful eyes, and the pattern of aggressive speech replace the smiling, food-offering relaxed woman of two minutes ago. *I guess we all have our parts to play.*

The threesome walked the halls and saw nothing surprising, just rooms containing people of every color, shape, size, sex, and state of inebriation. Louisiana was nothing if not a melting pot. Rounds were quick and as they finished, Dr. McSwain came through the door.

"Merry three days after Christmas to you!" he greeted them. "Livvy, I can smell your momma's gumbo. I'm starving. We operated most of the night at Tulane, and I can't remember the last time I ate. Get a bowl of gumbo for me, and we'll do checkout rounds from the nurses' station unless Elizabeth and Adrien have something exciting to report. Oh, I can smell that pecan pie with bourbon. I'll need a small piece of that to chase my gumbo."

How can he look so energized after operating all night? I had a good night's sleep, and I'm tired already.

Livvy served her boss a bowl of gumbo. He ate while he listened to their report. No patient required his attention. He tossed his paper bowl and plastic spoon in the trash, looked at the interns, and said, "We're halfway through the academic year, and you two are coming along. Both of you have scared the crap out of me at times. But it seems Nurse Robichaud has whipped you into shape.

"Adrien, your shift's over. It's time to turn off your flashing lights. Eat some gumbo and go home, son. Elizabeth, let's go into the X-ray area and chat," said Dr. McSwain.

Elizabeth immediately went on high alert. What had she forgotten? Dr. McSwain usually delivered praise in public and criticism in private unless the criticism constituted a teaching moment for the students. His wanting to talk to her in private could only mean one thing—she was in trouble again. Elizabeth noticed Livvy avoided her eyes as the two doctors walked away.

The X-ray area was dark to enable good vision for X-ray reading. Its lead-lined walls made it soundproof. It was the interns' favorite napping spot and was a good place to hide to study. But she and Dr. McSwain weren't reading X-rays today, and she wasn't about to nap. He closed the door and offered her a chair to sit. Her anxiety grew.

"You've done a pretty good job for someone who came from a medical school with minimal trauma training. Your ability to assimilate knowledge from books is exceptional. You have skilled hands, and you learn quickly. But you're more fearful than most interns. I have to hold most interns back because they think they know more than they do. You're reticent and shy. Your next rotation was chosen by the chairman of the surgery department. He's concerned you might not be tough enough for the world of surgery."

Elizabeth felt her face and neck grow hot. She chewed her lip to keep from crying. *There's no crying in surgery.*

"Elizabeth, to date there've been but a few women in surgery," he continued. "Frankly, we don't really know what we're doing yet. We know surgery needs more women, but the transition is slow. I think you'll make it. I think you'll be better than most, and I think intelligence wins out over hubris every time. Please forgive me, but I'm more concerned about you in a fatherly way. Being a surgeon is all-consuming. If you choose to be a professional sports star, or a lawyer, or a doctor, or a military leader, it becomes your life. The best people in every high-stakes job are obsessed with their work." He paused. "I've grown to like you as a person, and I want the best for you. If you stay on this surgery path, you need to realize it gets more and more narrow. Your life will be consumed by your work." He paused again, then said, "Our goal at Tulane is to treat everyone the same. None of us would be in New Orleans if we didn't like all kinds of people. I'd like you, over the next six months, to think about your entire life. If you decide to continue on—and I think you can—you'll make many sacrifices. Your life will forever differ from that of others. Greatness requires it. When an anesthesiologist puts a patient under, that person has given up all control over their life and placed their safety in the surgeon's hands. That patient deserves a team with only one thing on their mind, and that's giving the patient the best operation they can get. Tulane Surgery is about guaranteeing our surgeons give every patient their best. Do you understand what I'm trying to say?" asked Dr. McSwain.

Elizabeth felt nauseated and angry. She knew she was getting this speech because she's a girl. *Did Livvy have anything to do with this? Are they planning to fire me on my cardiothoracic surgery rotation?* She needed time to think, to calm down. She felt afraid to speak despite her professor's intense eye contact and his patience in waiting for her response.

"Yes, sir, I hear you," Elizabeth replied slowly. "I know the life of a surgeon is demanding. I've lived it for six months now, sir. I do have lots of fear. I'm afraid of hurting a patient while I'm learning my trade. It's overwhelming to learn at such a fast pace while life hangs in the balance. I spend all my time reading about surgery, talking about surgery, or doing surgery. Dr. McSwain, I love surgery. I know I'll become less timid as my skills increase." She managed a smile. "I haven't come close to fainting in a good six weeks."

Her mentor couldn't stifle his laugh. "Yes, not fainting does have its advantages," he admitted. Then he got serious again. "As you go through cardiothoracic surgery next month, remember it's the toughest. Everything happens fast, and everything matters. Dr. White's smart as a whip and will hold you to a standard you'll find taxing. But if you really love surgery, you'll leave that rotation tougher and smarter than you can currently imagine. Let your fear motivate you," he suggested. "And Elizabeth, think about your whole life. Is this sacrifice—becoming a surgeon—worth everything you might not be able to have?"

Here we go again! The family and children discussion. At least he's not telling me I cannot have love and family if I continue with surgery. He's trying to softball it, but it's the same message I get from Mom. I know I'd love to have the love and security of a family, but I want more. I want the challenge of learning and having a job that really matters.

"Yes, sir," Elizabeth replied. "I appreciate your honest assessment of me and your time in talking to me about my future. Thank you."

Dr. McSwain's mouth held a mirthless smile, and there was sadness within his eyes. "Best of luck next month, intern," he said as he stood and walked out of the X-ray area.

19

Elizabeth's last few days on the trauma rotation passed quickly. She worked while feeling in a stupor, worn out by her fear and ambivalence.

January first arrived. She couldn't enjoy the New Year's Eve revelry in the French Quarter because of her anxiety. She ushered in 1983 with sleeplessness and apprehension. She fed her frogs, not knowing when she'd be home again, walked to the hospital, and arrived at the door to the cardiac ICU with her stomach contents roiling and her palms sweating.

Elizabeth's senses were on high alert. She smelled the disinfectants, heard the racket of beeping monitors, and watched the deliberate movements of the nurses assigned one-on-one to the sickest patients in the hospital. She was terrified and wanted to run. Instead, she smiled at the ward secretary. His nametag said "Joe," and he had long, red-polished nails.

"Excuse me, sir. Do you know where the new intern is supposed to report for rounds?"

Joe smiled up at Elizabeth and said, "Oh, goody, a girl doctor. This should be fun." Elizabeth took in his short, dyed-blonde hair with dark grey roots and the red lipstick that matched his nail polish. Elizabeth recognized her mom's favorite color, Cherries in the Snow.

"Just stand over there," Joe told her, "and the prince of uptown will appear. You'll know him by his fabulous aftershave and his coat that's starched so heavy, it'll stand up by itself. He'll have an entourage of scared young doctors following him." He smiled. "Don't be afraid, honey pie. He's human, mostly."

Joe seems nice. Maybe there are other nice people working here too. I wonder what's with the lipstick and nail polish? His hair's cut like a man's and his clothes are men's clothes.

Elizabeth looked up as Dr. White walked toward her with the student Sallie Smith, Tony Parker, and Nurse Rose Anders. He ignored Elizabeth but stopped within a foot of her and said, "This is our team for this rotation. I'm Dr. Harrison White." He pointed to Tony and said, "This is Dr. Tony Parker. He's our second-year surgery resident. For reasons nobody understands, he requested at the last minute to be on this rotation again. Nobody has ever requested to be on this rotation twice." He nodded toward a nervous Sallie and said, "This's our overachiever student, Sallie Smith. She doesn't have to start this rotation until Monday, but she came two days early to make sure she learns all she can. I admire a student who gives up two days of holiday time to hit the hospital wards early."

Sallie nodded. Elizabeth had never seen Sallie look so nervous. Dr. White looked past Elizabeth and introduced the OR nurse next. "This's Miss Rose Anders. She's my right hand in the operating room. Anything she tells you to do, you do it. Assume anything she says is coming from me."

Nurse Anders wore a low-cut blouse under her white coat that showed magnificent cleavage. The nurse pushed out her chest and smiled at Dr. White, showing her dazzling, straight white teeth.

Is all that real? Did she come into the world with the white-blonde hair, the enormous chest assets, and the perfect piano key teeth?

Lastly, Dr. White gave a cursory glance to Elizabeth. "Our intern is Dr. Elizabeth Roberts." He didn't make eye contact with her.

Demeaned by an introduction.

"Let's move away from the patient area and go to the nurses' lunch area." Dr. White directed the group as he opened the door for Rose. Sallie and Elizabeth were behind Tony, who held the door for them. Elizabeth watched Dr. White smile and give a warm good morning greeting to Joe.

Dr. White stood, with his spine rigid, in front of a chalkboard, while the team sat around the table. "Welcome to cardiothoracic surgery. This is the place where we stop the human heart, drain it of all its blood, open the chest from neck to abdomen, rearrange the valves and blood vessels, replace what needs replacing, give the patient back their blood, and close them up. It sounds simple, doesn't it? Never forget this is the realm of gods." He paused for effect and then continued.

"Most of you are here to observe. You're expected to know everything, but do little, unless I say so. Nobody, and I repeat *nobody*, Dr. Parker and Dr. Roberts, writes orders in the pediatric cardiac ICU." He glared at them. "I will inform you *if* you ever need to do anything there. You must know everything about those patients but never make a move unless I tell you. The children are particularly sensitive to every change in their metabolism. Dr. Roberts, you'll start out in the adult cardiac ICU and Dr. Parker, since you've had one rotation, you'll be in the pediatric ICU most days."

Elizabeth looked at Tony, feeling grateful he'd sacrificed himself to be with her. She also felt disappointment that they could not be together in the same ICU. His calm demeanor comforted her. Tony was laser-focused on Dr. White's words.

"Super student Sallie, you can float between the two ICUs and the operating room. You can't touch anything in the heart room. But Rose will find a good spot for you to stand on a stool where you can watch without causing too much distraction. Questions are to be held until we round the next day. Once we enter the heart room, there's no talking."

As Sallie nodded, her short afro wiggled. Sallie didn't speak. In fact, she looked like she might never speak again from fear of Dr. White.

"Dr. Roberts and Dr. Parker, your beepers are to be on twenty-four hours a day every day you're on this rotation. Holidays, weekends, LSU days mean nothing here. Every day's a heart day, and you're best advised to answer your pager immediately any time I call. Is that clear?" asked Dr.

White. He leveled his eyes at Elizabeth, looking at her directly for the first time. She suddenly could not speak.

Dr. Parker said, "Yes, sir. We understand, sir."

Dr. White glared at Tony and asked, "You speak for her? I wasn't aware I was training a mute person. Do I need to use sign language with Dr. Roberts?" Rose laughed, and Sallie and Tony looked at the floor.

Elizabeth managed to croak, "I can hear well, Dr. White. I hear very well." Anger filled her and bled out the fear. *I guess this's how it's going to be. He's singling me out for public humiliation in the first thirty minutes of the rotation.*

"OK, team, let's make rounds and get ready for the OR." Dr. White turned and went out the door, and the team followed. Elizabeth's cardio-thoracic rotation had begun.

20

Dr. White led the way to the pediatric ICU. Once there, Elizabeth noticed a young man and woman seated in rocking chairs beside a child in a hospital bed. They had deep, dark circles under their eyes and wore tattered clothing. They were focused on their child and seemed unaware of their surroundings despite the beeping sounds of multiple monitors attached to the other six children in the intensive care room. As the cardiac team approached, the man stood and looked at Dr. White. His eyes were haunted and desperate, darting from the child to the cardiac surgeon.

The child had more tubes coming from him than Elizabeth would have thought possible for so small a being. He had a cleft lip and palate. His face was wider than normal, with low ears and a split in his face from the nose to the chin. A tracheostomy tube protruded from his neck. Despite being on a ventilator, the child looked blue. He had intravenous lines in both sides of his upper chest, a catheter in his small penis, and a gastric tube for feeding coming from his upper left abdomen. His eyes were hooded, and he had no chin. His young mother sat slumped in her chair. She stared without blinking at the child while the father focused on Dr. White.

How can he be alive? Elizabeth glanced at Sallie and saw that her mouth was hanging open, and her eyes were wet. *Sallie's heart is tender. This rotation will be hard on her too.*

Dr. White stepped between the surgery team and the father. He spoke gently. "Good morning, Mr. Trahan. I see you and Mrs. Trahan have been here all night again. Your son's stable. As you know, he has a very long way to go. I'm here with him all the time. If you and your wife want to go home to Plaquemine to eat and rest, I'll keep a close eye on your son for you," said Dr. White.

Mr. Trahan shook his head to indicate "no" and turned to look at his wife, who also shook her head "no." Neither spoke.

Elizabeth watched the cardiac surgeon transform into someone she'd not seen him be. His demeanor was almost sweet. She shook her head to clear her thoughts. She couldn't reconcile the conflicting demeanors of the doctor speaking to this young distraught family with the doctor she'd known for six months.

Dr. White bowed, shook the father's hand, and smiled at the mother. He touched the child's foot—the only area of his body without tape, gauze, or some kind of tube. He said, "I'll be back soon to check on your little guy."

Dr. White signaled the team out into the hall and pointed to a heavy metal door leading to a stairwell. After everyone crowded into the stairwell, Dr. White closed the door tight, turned to the team, and transformed back into the doctor Elizabeth knew.

His raptor eyes settled on Elizabeth. "Intern, what's wrong with the creature we call Baby Boy Trahan?"

Her mouth was dry, and her bowels rumbled. *What to say? He doesn't want the musings of an ignorant intern.* "I'm sorry, but I have no idea, Dr. White," said a panicked Elizabeth.

"Well, let's pretend you're a competent doctor. Why don't you tell me about your scientific observations, and we'll try to piece together a puzzle."

Elizabeth took a deep breath and steadied herself against the cool concrete wall of the stairwell. "If those two people are his parents, they're awfully young and they look very similar; there's a strong family resemblance. If they're his mother and father, I'd worry about some type of near fatal congenital anomaly. And since you're a cardiac surgeon and the child is on our service, I'd imagine that along with all the other problems he has, he has a heart problem too," said Elizabeth. She felt her legs quiver. Sweat was forming on her face despite the coolness of the concrete enclosure.

Dr. White's face reddened, and he stifled a smile. "If this were a game show, you'd be doing well, intern. But it's not. Quit guessing and tell me a few *medical* terms for what you observed."

Sallie and Tony kept their eyes on the concrete floor. Rose beamed at Dr. White.

Elizabeth squirmed and said, "The child's blue. That makes me think despite being on a ventilator; he is not oxygenating his blood well."

"Now we're getting somewhere. Sallie Smith, what's the medical term for 'looking blue'?" asked Dr. White.

Sallie squealed the word, "Cyanosis, sir."

"Good, Sallie. Dr. Roberts, any more astute observations?" said Dr. White.

Elizabeth hated him. She'd seen him capable of kindness and good manners. Why must he direct vitriol at her alone?

That's OK, she thought. *Bully me all you want. I can tell nobody else knows what this child has. It's probably something really rare if he's here at the medical center.*

"The child has a cleft lip and cleft palate. Children with a total defect cannot feed without aspiration, so I assume that's the reason for the feeding tube in his stomach. His facial features are unusual. His ears are low, he has minimal chin, and his eyes are hooded. I'm sorry Dr. White, but I don't recall what heart defect goes along with these findings," said Elizabeth.

The entire team, except Rose and Dr. White, shuffled their feet and squirmed. Dr. White continued to stare at Elizabeth.

Finally, he looked at Tony. "What about you, Dr. Parker?" he asked. "Any ideas?"

"Baby Boy Trahan obviously has multiple congenital defects. I'm running every heart anomaly through my mind and cannot produce one that fits his clinical picture. I'm sorry, Dr. White," said Tony.

Dr. White rocked on his heels. Sallie looked panic-stricken and wondered if she would be next.

He leaned against the heavy metal door and said, “I expect more from you people. Since none of you could come up with one sensible idea, I suggest you not come to the operating room with me today. Dr. Roberts, stay in the adult ICU until I come to get you. Dr. Parker, go to the adult cardiac clinic and take out stitches all day. Student Smith, I’m sorry you have to suffer with the rest. You’ll go with Dr. Parker to clinic. By the end of the day, you’ll be great at removing stitches and start to get a feel for how a wound should heal.” He paused and then continued, “Tomorrow, I expect each of you to know everything there is to know about the congenital anomaly known as tetralogy of Fallot. I’ll give you a few hints. It’s very rare. It involves four heart defects. I repaired all of them two days ago. I’ve been with this child every hour since his surgery. Tetralogy of Fallot is more common in parental consanguinity, which is not rare in Plaquemines parish. It’s a deadly cardiac anomaly.”

Consanguinity means “shared blood,” so it is likely his parents are related.

Dr. White paused, looking at each of them in turn. “This child has little chance to live, but his young parents aren’t ready to accept his fate. And you can’t know; he might live to have his cleft lip and palate repaired. It’s a long road ahead. As you’re reading about this condition, read about what kills them early, what problems kill them during surgery, and what kills them in the early and late post-operative period. I doubt any of you’ll ever care for a child in this condition, but you must know everything about every patient.” He turned to the nurse. “Rose, let’s go do a coronary artery bypass,” said Dr. White as he turned and went through the metal door from the stairwell.

Elizabeth, Tony, and Sallie waited until they were certain Dr. White was not within earshot. Elizabeth looked around the stairwell and said, “Now we know what the devil’s office looks like.”

Her comment broke the tension, and they laughed. Tony said, “He thinks he’s punishing us by sending us to clinic and the ICU, but for once,

I'd rather be in clinic than in the operating room. He's one scary intense dude."

Elizabeth looked at Tony and said, "What do I do in the adult ICU all day? He's given me no instructions, and I've never cared for a heart patient."

"Just be your usual respectful self to the nurses and learn as much as you can from them," suggested Tony. "They do cardiac ICU work every day, and they deal with him all the time. Make sure you're in the ICU if he happens to show up. I don't know why he seems to dislike you, but don't give him any reason. He knows somewhere deep inside that you cannot know anything at this point. For some crazy reason, he seems determined to make an example of you. Focus on learning all you can from the nurses for today, and I'll see you on evening rounds. Good luck."

"Thanks—for everything," she said as they exited the stairwell. Elizabeth returned to the ICU feeling impotent. She smiled at Joe and asked, "What do the interns usually do during their first week here? I've had no experience in this area."

Joe looked up from his desk and opened his mouth to speak, but at the same moment a tall, older nurse approached and said, "Hello, and welcome to our little piece of paradise. I'm the charge nurse for this shift, and Livvy's my buddy. I taught her in nursing school. She's a good one. She called to tell me to keep an eye out for you. Did Dr. White give you any instructions yet?"

Elizabeth saw dark circles under the charge nurse's chocolate brown eyes. She was portly in stature, with graying, wild curly hair. Her nurse's uniform was too tight across her middle, and there was a wide run up the front of one leg of her thick, white support hose. Her voice was pure and clear, and her face was kind. Elizabeth took a deep breath. She knew this nurse and Joe would be her helpers today. She looked at the nurse's name tag and said, "It's nice to meet you, Mrs. Herbert."

The nurse and Joe laughed. She said, "No, honey, it's not pronounced Her-Bert. This is Louisiana, and my name is pronounced Ai-Bear, like Bobby. You've heard of the Cajun Cannon, Bobby Hebert, haven't you?"

Elizabeth had no idea what the nurse was talking about but was desperate for a friend. She smiled and nodded.

Joe said, "Don't let her make you think she actually knows Bobby. Hebert is like Smith in this part of the world. Bobby's the hottest thing to ever come out of Lafourche High. He was named "Most Outstanding Quarterback" in the pro football world at age twenty-three. We're all super proud of him and claim him as our own."

Joe seems masculine when speaking of football.

Elizabeth wasn't a big football fan but had watched Monday Night Football at home with Daddy after she'd finished studying. She didn't remember Mr. Hebert but would be sure to take note in the future. He seemed important to the head nurse and the ward secretary.

"OK, it's obvious football is not your thing. Let's see if we can get you oriented to the ICU and make sure you're ready for Dr. White after he emerges from surgery," said Nancy.

Three hours later, Elizabeth had a piercing frontal headache and seven pages of detailed notes. There was no sign of Dr. White, and she was relieved. She knew every nurse on this shift, knew every lab and ventilator setting on every patient, and was starving. She'd learned each patient had his or her own nurse, respiratory therapist, and nursing assistant. The ICU worked much like the operating room and the trauma ER. There was maximum organization and teamwork.

Everyone seemed to fear and respect Dr. White, except Joe. Everyone was deferential to Joe. The nurses covered for each other so each, in turn, could duck into the staff room and devour their lunch. Elizabeth knew not to leave the area but didn't know how to get food. She felt weak from hunger. Joe watched her slump into a chair by the wall and said, "Come in the staff room for a minute."

On the center of the table was a hospital tray with fried chicken, macaroni and cheese, green peas, and peach cobbler. A glass of iced tea and a buttered biscuit completed the tray. Joe looked at Elizabeth as her mouth filled with saliva and her stomach growled. He pointed with one of his long red lacquered nails to the tray. "Honey," he told her, "I got this for you since you didn't seem to have any food on you."

"Thanks so much, Joe," Elizabeth replied. "I don't have any money on me now, but I can pay you tomorrow if that's acceptable."

Joe laughed and said, "Girl, this food's courtesy of our former patient, the guy in bed five, who passed this morning. We care for the sickest of the sick, and we have deaths most days. The kitchen delivers a few meals before they realize the patient won't be eating anymore. Heck, most patients are intubated and can't eat, anyway. We usually have extra food. Sometimes we feed the families. Sometimes we feed the doctors." He smiled. "But only the nice doctors get fed. I can't believe you haven't learned to steal food from the dearly departed, especially on fried chicken day. I thought every intern knew to pass by the bed of a recent death for a free lunch or dinner."

Despite seeing his eyes sparkle with mirth, Elizabeth was shocked. She looked longingly at the chicken and sat down to eat. "Thanks, Joe. You saved my day." *This rotation might be OK. Nurse Hebert and Joe will help me make it. And this fried chicken's as good as Granny's.*

21

Elizabeth savored the last bit of fried chicken. She sensed Joe standing behind her, staring at the top of her head. Elizabeth felt uncomfortable but didn't want to disturb her new friend. She turned her head slightly to the left and confirmed that he stood mesmerized.

Is he daydreaming or on the verge of a seizure? Maybe his blood sugar's low?

"Joe, what did you have for lunch?" asked Elizabeth, attempting to bring Joe into the present.

Joe moved as if he were startled, stepped back, and said, "I'm sorry. I was marveling at the amazing color of your hair and wondering what kind of color you use. I'm due for a change and thought I might try the product you use. And oh, I had bologna and cheese on white bread for lunch. A girl has to watch her figure."

Joe's face reddened.

Is he calling himself a girl? "God gave me this hair color."

"Oh, honey, you have ten shades of wheat in your hair. God's not that creative," said Joe.

Elizabeth crossed her heart, gave Joe the peace sign, and said, "I promise it's never been colored. Usually, I get sun and my skin's not so pale and my hair's a little lighter. But for the last six months, I've not seen the sun most days."

Joe smiled and reached in to clean up her tray. Elizabeth smelled a strong perfume on his wrist. She thought to give him a compliment as he had her, but the perfume was strong and burned her eyes.

Must be that stuff called Poison. He really shouldn't be wearing that strong odor around patients.

She said, "I like your nail polish color. My mother wears that same color on Sundays. Please leave my tray; I can take care of it. You don't need to wait on me, Joe."

Joe smiled, showing long, nicotine-stained teeth. "I like you," he said. "We're—"

Joe's comment was interrupted by three sounds at once. Nancy burst through the door and said, "Dr. Roberts, you'd better get over to the pediatric cardiac unit immediately."

Elizabeth's pager screeched, and the operator said, "Please report to the pediatric ICU STAT. I repeat. Report to the pediatric ICU STAT."

And from an overhead speaker, the hospital intercom system blasted, "Attention! Any surgeon in the area of the pediatric ICU, please report there immediately."

The blaring cacophony jolted Elizabeth's nervous system. She stood up, turned around, and smacked into Nancy.

"He told me to stay here until he came back to get me," Elizabeth said to Nancy. "He said to not touch any patient in the pediatric ICU. I can't go over there! His orders were explicit."

Nancy turned to the side, opened the door, and said, "You have no choice. The head nurse from Peds called me to say Dr. White just went on by-pass and his patient's not stable. He can't leave the heart room."

Elizabeth's heart raced, and she felt cornered. "What about Dr. Parker?" she asked. "He's in the clinic in this building. He could go."

Nancy grasped Elizabeth by her arm and steered her toward the exit. "There's a multiple gunshot wound patient in Room Four, and Dr. Parker left clinic to help. You must hurry to the Peds ICU. You're needed STAT."

Elizabeth planted her feet and stiffened her body and fought crossing the threshold of the door. The nurse pushed her, and Elizabeth shoved back.

Elizabeth said, "What about other faculty or other residents? Surely somebody can go besides me? He gave me strict instructions. He was clear that I was to stay away from the pediatric cardiac unit."

The nurse was agitated. "You're a doctor. For God's sake, you're a Tulane surgeon. What Dr. White says or doesn't say ever comes before patient care. There's no other doctor available. You have no choice. Get over there. NOW!" The nurse propelled Elizabeth over the threshold, and she ran the twenty yards to the pediatric ICU. She burst through the door, terrified at what she might find.

Dear God, please don't let it be the child with the tetralogy of Fallot. Please don't let me harm anyone, she prayed.

A petite woman in nurse's white, pregnant enough to deliver any day, stood staring at a pediatric chest X-ray. She glared at Elizabeth and asked, "Have you ever put in a chest tube? The boy in bed number one has a tension pneumothorax and can't wait. I've called all over, and nobody is available but you. Please tell me you've done this before," she pleaded.

The nurse's hands shook as she pointed to the X-ray. Her voice trembled as she spoke, and her pregnant belly rubbed against Elizabeth when Elizabeth leaned in to see the details of the Xray.

Holy cow, she's right! The boy's trachea is deviated to one side. This can't wait.

Metal rattled behind Elizabeth as two nurses rushed to set up a procedure tray beside the bed of a little boy with carrot-red hair, azure eyes, and pale skin. The child sat up, leaned forward, and struggled to breathe. All eyes were on Elizabeth. *JEREMY* was the name on the plaque above the head of his bed. Balloons, cards, toy trucks, and flowers covered every surface surrounding his bed.

Elizabeth tasted her fried chicken lunch and gulped to prevent herself from vomiting. "Yes, I know how to do this. How long has it been since you last called Dr. White?"

The nurse setting up the chest tube procedure said, "One minute ago his OR nurse said he couldn't leave. You need to do this now, before this becomes a full code, Doctor."

It's my duty. He won't last much longer. God, help him, and God, guide me.

Elizabeth listened with her stethoscope to his chest to confirm the X-ray findings. He had no breath sounds. He was panting, and his lips were blue. His nostrils flared wide with each attempted breath.

He looks bad. He's working so hard to breathe.

She smiled at the boy to connect with and reassure him. Then she washed her hands and quickly pulled on a sterile gown and gloves. She turned to him, leaned close, and said, "Hi, Jeremy. I'm Dr. Roberts. I see you feel awful. Don't worry; I'm going to help you. You'll get some medicine to make you sleepy, try to relax, and when you come out of your nap, you'll be breathing fine. Nurse, please give him a bolus of IV morphine."

Elizabeth watched the nurse's hands tremble as she pushed the medication into the intravenous tubing.

Jeremy sighed, fell back onto his pillow, and relaxed as the drug ran into his vein. Elizabeth gave him a lidocaine nerve block to diminish his post-procedure pain. She looked around the room, hoping a more senior surgeon had arrived. *There's nobody to help.*

Elizabeth ran through the procedure in her mind before starting and inspected the surgical tray.

All I have to do is avoid the arteries under the rib, don't puncture his lung, aim up to drain the air, and stay out of the abdomen.

She splashed his chest with Betadine, incised the skin she'd numbed, and cut down to the bone of Jeremy's rib. He didn't flinch. She pressed the long steel clamp through muscle and connective tissue into his chest cavity. She knew she'd hit the right spot when an audible rush of air escaped from the wound, and his lung filled his chest while his trachea shifted to its normal midline position. Jeremy winced when she pushed the chest tube deeper. She attached her end of the tube to drainage and was relieved to see minimal blood in the tube. All of them had been holding their breath. Elizabeth and the three nurses let out a loud sigh of relief when the lung inflated. The pregnant nurse flopped into the closest chair and reached for the phone to call radiology for a post-procedure chest X-ray.

Thank you, God. The tube seems to be in the right place, and there's no excessive bleeding.

Elizabeth had learned in the ER to secure a chest tube by taping it in multiple places. She knew that if an adult could accidentally pull out a chest tube, a child was even more likely to pull one out. She finished Jeremy's dressing as he began to rouse. Big tears streamed from his bloodshot eyes. He looked at Elizabeth and said, "I'm so tired. I don't want to do this anymore. I'm never going back to school, am I?"

Elizabeth knew in that moment why she did not want to be a pediatrician. A sick child was the worst thing in the universe to her. As she looked at Jeremy, she realized she didn't know his last name, or his parents' names, or why he was in the ICU, or why he'd had a tension pneumothorax. She'd responded as a trained surgeon should to the problem at hand. She'd done a bedside procedure that saved this child's life. Now she'd have to read his chart and decide whether to speak to his parents or wait on Dr. White.

This poor little guy! I hope the morphine helps him rest.

The pregnant head nurse patted her on the back and said, "Excellent job, Dr. Roberts. I'll speak to Dr. White before I end my shift today."

Elizabeth pored over his chart while she sat in the chair by his bed and waited for the X-ray. At least her fried chicken lunch was now going in the right direction.

22

A few minutes later, the door to the pediatric ICU flew open, and Dr. White stormed through. He snatched the chart from Elizabeth's hands and pushed himself between her chair and Jeremy. He placed his stethoscope on Jeremy's back to check his lungs. Dr. White's eyes were as wide as those of a quarter-horse that had been surprised by a rattlesnake. He wasn't wearing his starched white coat but was dressed in blood-spattered scrubs and white plastic surgical clogs. Elizabeth had never seen him ungroomed or not perfectly attired.

The radiology technician returned with the chest X-ray at the moment Dr. White completed his physical examination. Elizabeth reached for the film to hang it on the X-ray reading box, but Dr. White said, "I'll take that film." He held it up to the overhead light and exhaled deeply. His shoulders relaxed. He turned back to the patient and said, "You OK, little man? I'm sorry I wasn't here when you needed me, but your problem's fixed for now."

Jeremy tried to smile and said, "It's OK. The nice lady helped me. I want to go home. When can I go home?"

Elizabeth's gut tightened, and she fought back tears. She stared at the floor, chewing her bottom lip.

Dr. White said, "Let me go talk to your parents now. We'll talk about your going home another day. I'm sorry, but it won't be today, Jeremy."

Dr. White looks as sad as his patient.

Dr. White patted the child's hand, told the nurse and tech the X-ray was acceptable, and turned to Elizabeth. "Come with me, Dr. Roberts."

Elizabeth trotted behind him into the stairwell. Just as he had done earlier in the day, he slammed the stairwell door closed, stood in front of it, and leaned against the metal door. He crossed his arms in front of his chest and stared at the floor. He was composing his thoughts and preparing his words.

Elizabeth felt afraid. She couldn't decide if his silence or his grooming imperfections were more disturbing. She'd never seen him speechless or blood-splattered. She stared at the top of his head and noticed his crown, which was covered in light chocolate curls. He looked up into her eyes and the rabid emotion she saw pushed her back a step. He grabbed her forearm to prevent her from stepping too far backward and falling down the flight of stairs. His hand was hot, and the strength of his long white fingers surprised her.

He pulled her a few inches closer to him and said, "Dr. Roberts, I don't know what to say to you. You ignored everything I told you. But, in this case, you may have saved Jeremy. I don't allow interns to do procedures on children in the ICU. Lucky for you, it went well. Don't let this go to your head. You got the tube in the right place, and there were no complications. But it could easily have gone another way. Do you know anything about Jeremy?"

Elizabeth sagged as her adrenaline surge subsided. She wanted to be anywhere but in the stairwell, cornered by Dr. White.

"No, sir. I had no time to read his chart. Dr. McSwain taught me that 'a tension pneumothorax is nothing to stand around and ponder.' He said a surgeon 'has to act in some situations with little knowledge.' I tried hard to find someone more senior than me, but everyone was tied up somewhere else. I did the best I could in a critical situation."

"Do you have any idea why Jeremy had the tension pneumothorax to begin with?" Dr. White's cheeks flushed as Elizabeth squirmed.

"I'm sorry. I had no time to read about his condition. I've only seen tension pneumothorax in patients who'd been shot or stabbed or had recently been on a ventilator or recently had a chest tube removed. I also saw it once when radiology did an abdominal biopsy and accidentally entered the chest cavity where the lung comes down low on the flank." Elizabeth's hairline dripped with sweat. Her anxiety mounted. She raced through her memory to find other causes of a tension pneumothorax. She avoided his gaze and looked at his hands. *How can he have such strong hands with such soft white skin?* She almost laughed out loud at her crazy thoughts.

"You hit on the answer, intern, even if by accident. Jeremy has leukemia. The little guy has had a rough two years. He's had multiple rounds of chemotherapy and procedures. It doesn't look good for him. He had an open biopsy of his chest yesterday and was extubated this morning. His parents and grandparents are family friends. We're all members of Rex. I made an error in extubating him too early because they pressured me to get him home. He was extubated too soon after his biopsy, and my poor judgment is why this happened."

What's Rex? Some kind of church or social club?

Elizabeth was flooded with compassion as she watched Dr. White hang his head and look ashamed. His ears turned hot pink. She started to pat his shoulder like she would anyone who looked sad and embarrassed, but her fear kept her glued in place. She wondered how far his contrition would go when he talked to the family. Dr. McSwain had told her to "never lie to any patient's family." He was strict about giving the family all pertinent information delivered in the most compassionate manner. She wondered how the arrogant Dr. White would handle explaining his mistake.

Dr. White regained his composure. "Do you have any questions about this case? I'd like you to present the X-ray on rounds tomorrow. Study the subject tonight and give a few minutes' talk to the team. Now, let's get out of the stairwell and see the family in the waiting room."

She looked at his scrubs and shoes and was about to open her mouth to remind him he had blood on his shoes and clothes when he said, "Stay right here. I have a white coat and clean scrubs tucked in a locker. I'll change and be right back."

As she watched him walk away, she saw through the thin scrubs his strong back and shoulders and wondered what kind of man he really was. *Is he the meanest doctor in America? Or is he the compassionate doctor who speaks with empathy to a suffering family? Is he a snobby uptown aristocrat? Who's the real Dr. White?* Before she could decide, he jogged toward her in clean clothes, combed hair, and shiny shoes.

"Come with me."

She walked behind him, double-stepping to keep up.

He paused outside the packed pediatric surgery family waiting room and took a few deep breaths. He saw the family and headed in their direction. Elizabeth stood back a foot.

An expensively dressed and perfectly coifed woman stood as they neared. A lean and handsome man supported her elbow. "Harrison," she asked, "is my baby OK?"

Dr. White stepped close to the woman and said, "Yes, he's OK for now. Let's step out into the hall."

Everyone in the waiting room was anxious for news of their child. They walked into the hall past the twenty sets of staring eyes. Elizabeth melted into the background. Nobody looked at her. Both parents directed their intensity at Dr. White.

The father put his arm around his wife's shoulders. Both had dark bags under their eyes. Beautiful clothes, immaculate grooming, and spectacular jewelry couldn't hide their chronic fatigue and fear.

"James and Carolyn, I made a mistake this morning. In my hopes of getting Jeremy home as soon as possible, I took his chest tube out earlier than I ordinarily would. His lung collapsed because the hole from his biopsy hadn't had enough time to close. I'm sorry I wasn't there this morning. I was in surgery and couldn't leave my patient on bypass. Fortunately, Dr. Roberts was nearby and replaced the tube in a timely fashion." Dr. White pointed in Elizabeth's direction as he said her name, and the parents glanced at her. The father nodded, and the mother returned her gaze quickly to Dr. White.

"Jeremy's resting," Dr. White continued, "but as you would imagine, he's again disappointed at not being able to go home. I apologize for my haste in removing the tube and for causing him more difficulty."

Carolyn said, "Harrison, of course we forgive you. We wouldn't have made it this far with Jeremy if not for you. But, is my baby ever going to be OK? Is he ever coming home?"

Carolyn's face turned into her husband's chest, and she sobbed. Elizabeth struggled not to sob with her. Dr. White looked at James and said, "Honestly, I don't know. He's fought harder to beat his cancer than any little boy I've ever known, but I'm surprised he's made it this far." He looked into the eyes of the father and patted the mother's back.

"I must get back to the operating room," Dr. White told them. "I checked Jeremy's X-ray. Dr. Roberts placed the tube well. There's nothing else to do at this time. The nurses know to come and get you when he awakens. They know you're anxious to see him. I'll be back to check on him as soon as my case is finished."

Carolyn turned to face Dr. White. Black mascara ran down her cheeks, and red lipstick smeared her chin. She blinked repeatedly to clear her eyes. "Thank you," she said. "This is so hard on all of us."

Both doctors were speechless in the face of the mother's grace. They turned together and headed back to the pediatric ICU. Elizabeth spied Dr. White's lower lip tremble as he turned.

He stared down the hall to avoid making eye contact with her and said, "Go back to the adult ICU. I'll see you later this evening on rounds. Make sure you know everything about all the adult patients for evening rounds. I'll call Dr. Parker to follow up on Jeremy." He walked away and didn't look back.

23

Elizabeth entered the adult ICU wondering why Dr. White couldn't give her a compliment. At least he didn't disparage her in front of the patient's family, and he told them the truth. She knew today's lessons would be valuable in the future. The idea that she'd be a competent surgeon in six years seemed unimaginable. Today, she rejected pediatric surgery as a profession, realizing she couldn't care for critically sick children and survive the experience emotionally intact.

Nancy and Joe smiled as they watched her approach the nurses' desk. The kindness in their eyes informed Elizabeth of the speedy travel of hospital gossip.

How do people perform their jobs yet spread juicy gossip so efficiently?

Nancy said, "Livvy called. She said she'll meet you after your shift to get a muffuletta at the Central Grocery. She'll meet you in the lobby under the painting of Sister Stanislaus Malone." Elizabeth laughed at the thought of Livvy standing under the painting of the famous nun who was raised by the Daughters of Charity, dedicated her life to the poor, and was known as "the nun with a gun." If the stories Elizabeth had heard were true, Livvy and the notorious Sister were similar kinds of women, commanding the world of Charity Hospital ninety years apart.

Elizabeth said, "I don't have time to meet with Livvy. I don't know when Dr. White finishes surgery, and I have to prepare for evening rounds. After rounds, I have to study. Muffulettas can wait."

Nancy said, "Don't always expect this treatment, but today, I'll make rounds with you again and explain everything I know Dr. White's going to ask. We covered much this morning, but the patients' conditions have changed since then. Things happen fast in the ICU. Dr. White has not left the hospital in three days, so he'll want speedy rounds. Understand I'm helping you because you helped my friends today. And please don't tell Dr. White I prepped you."

Joe laughed, shook his head, and said, "I think Dr. Roberts is going to be our pet doctor. You can protest all you want, Nurse Nancy, but she's the sweetest thing we've had in this old ICU in a long time. Even if you declare she's not your pet, I'm declaring her mine!"

Elizabeth was embarrassed but relieved. With Dr. White as her boss, she'd need their friendship.

Elizabeth and Nancy went from room to room for the next two hours. Nancy coached Elizabeth on the top ten questions Dr. White asked every intern. Nancy knew him well. She left an hour after her shift had ended, and Elizabeth was grateful and felt prepared.

Dr. White returned and, as Nancy predicted, rounds were swift. Elizabeth wondered why Nancy was a nurse instead of a doctor. She answered ninety percent of Dr. White's questions correctly and hadn't missed anything important. At the end of rounds, Dr. White looked at Elizabeth and said, "Our head nurse is very knowledgeable, isn't she?" He smirked and walked out.

Of course he knew! I couldn't go from a blabbering idiot to an organized cardiac expert in one day, but I hope he doesn't take it out on her. Today, I learned more from her than I learned from him.

Elizabeth looked through the windows in the ICU and watched the sky turn pink. Her favorite time of day was the hour before dark, when the busy day wound down. Dusk calmed her and gave her a sense of accomplishment. The day was done, and food and sleep were not far away. She had been at the hospital for over fourteen hours. Lunch was seven hours ago, and a muffuletta sounded great. She gathered her books and her purse and headed for the lobby.

Her pager sounded, directing her to call the operator. She dialed and heard Livvy's voice on the other end.

"Where the heck are you, Crème Puff? I saw Dr. White come through the lobby twenty minutes ago. Even Dr. Parker's finished Peds' rounds. I'm starving. Put a move on it, girl. You know I'm mean when hungry."

You must be hungry often.

Elizabeth avoided the unpredictable elevators and scurried down the stairs, wondering why she let Livvy boss her around. Tonight, Elizabeth was tired, and her emotions were raw. She wasn't in the mood for Livvy's bullying, but a muffuletta might make Livvy tolerable.

Elizabeth saw Livvy first. She stood in the art deco lobby of Charity under the old painting of Sister Stanislaus. She stood tall, and her flawless skin glowed in the setting sun, but Elizabeth could see the dark circles under her eyes.

Elizabeth said, "Hi. You look a little tired. I thought nurses got to go home and sleep every now and then."

Livvy scowled. "The Big Free is hopping. We've run a special on gunshot wounds to the chest. The drug dealers are having a war in the projects, and we can't keep up with the casualties. Dr. McSwain's been pulling residents from Tulane and the VA to cover it all. Even the staff doesn't know if it's a Tulane or LSU day." She shook her head. "It's not usually this crazy this close to Mardi Gras. The trauma usually gets worse when it's hottest in late summer, when the heat makes folks crazy. I don't know what's causing the madness this winter. The trauma team was in the OR all day and much of the night before. Enough of Charity!" She smiled. "I hear you're the hero today. You getting less scared of Dr. White already?"

Elizabeth didn't answer. *I'm not going there.*

The two walked toward the Quarter. Few people were on the streets despite the mild sixty-degree weather.

Elizabeth's stomach growled, and Livvy laughed. "You hungry over there, Miss Stick and Bones?"

"Why yes, I am," replied Elizabeth. "I think stress burns more calories than exercise. My heart rate hasn't been below one hundred all day. I was terrified putting that chest tube in that little boy. Livvy, I don't like dealing with sick kids. It's heartbreaking. All the ICU nurses were helpful to me today. I would've had a much harder day if not for them and Joe."

They turned right at Canal. "Let's turn on Royal Street," said Elizabeth.

"No," Livvy told her. "We're not going down the same street. You live on that street now and can walk it anytime. Let's take Decatur to the Central Grocery. I'm too hungry to stop and admire every balcony planting on Royal. I want to see if there are any new artists outside painting Jackson Square."

"Why do you have to be so aggressive?" Elizabeth asked. "All you had to say was 'I prefer to walk up Decatur'."

Livvy stopped, put her hands on her hips, and snorted. "I hate it when you go all proper on me. I'm not being aggressive. I spent my day trying to keep inexperienced new folks from killing people in the trauma room, and I can't turn it off to protect your tender feelings."

Elizabeth ignored Livvy, stepped up her pace, and kept walking. Livvy jogged to catch up.

Elizabeth said, "I think you like being bossy. I think it's your personality. If you wanted to be in charge, why didn't you go to medical school? I think both you and Nancy would make good doctors. Why stop at nursing?"

Livvy looked away and refused to meet Elizabeth's eyes. In the shadows created by the gaslights coming on in the Quarter, Elizabeth caught the glint of tears in Livvy's eyes.

Livvy said, "Not everyone has the same opportunities. Some of us have to do what we can afford. Some of us are not good at test-taking even though our practical knowledge and common sense are strong. Some of us," she paused, then continued, "some of us need to eat, and our families won't or can't provide for us."

Elizabeth realized she'd tread on a tender spot and was torn between speaking the truth and holding her tongue. She sighed and said, "Livvy, nobody helped me get this far. My mother wanted me to marry a farmer and either teach school, be a nurse, or stay home and raise children. She had the handsome farmer picked out. She's still mad at me for moving out at seventeen and going to school and won't forgive me for moving to New Orleans. If it weren't for scholarships and working several part-time jobs, I wouldn't be here. You aren't the only person to endure adversity."

Livvy's face flushed. She stopped in the middle of the sidewalk. "Dang, you tick me off. My family needs me to put food on the table. My father drank most of his paycheck. Not only did I have to pay my own way by the time I was fifteen, I had to help my mother. Nancy's dad was a mean, raging Irish alcoholic. He couldn't keep a job and was frequently in jail. He liked to beat Nancy and her mom between stints in jail. Her mother's idea of protecting Nancy was to take her to Mass more often. Unfortunately, their eating the body and drinking the blood of Jesus didn't decrease her father's drunken attacks. So don't try to tell me your situation was like ours. The worst thing that happened to you was that you had to slop pigs and pick tobacco."

You win! I feel guilty for speaking up.

"OK. I'm sorry," said Elizabeth. "You had it worse than me. Let's drop this conversation and head for food. I think our moods will improve after our stomachs are full."

"I'm not saying you didn't work hard," Livvy continued. "And I'm not saying that you might not be smarter in a book sense. I'm just saying you were loved and treated with respect by the men in your family, and that gives any woman a head start in life."

She's right. The way the men in our family treated me helped create a sense of safety.

Jackson Square came into view. Since it was cool outside, there were no horse-drawn carriages in line to show tourists the French Quarter, and few artists were painting. Elizabeth heard the river churn toward the gulf. She was hungry and walking fast.

Wanting to change the subject, Elizabeth said, "What makes the muffuletta so popular?"

"It's the olive salad and its salty, pungent flavor," Livvy replied. "There's nothing like it. Ya'll have any good food in South Carolina?"

"Nah," said Elizabeth. "We have barbeque and fried chicken. The spicy food obsession people have here isn't a South Carolina thing."

"I can't live without good food and good music," Livvy said. "Why be alive?"

They entered the store and walked to the back counter to order. A dancing stuffed alligator with strings of Mardi Gras beads around its neck greeted the shoppers. An oversized Italian flag hung above the counter where four stools awaited the hungry. A picture of Signor Lupo Salvatore, the supposed inventor of the muffuletta sandwich, hung below the Italian flag.

The store's shelves were close together, uneven, and made of old wood. Every shelf was packed with products from Louisiana and Italy. Elizabeth's mouth watered from the smells of home-baked bread and garlic-laden salami. Livvy ordered for both of them. "Two muffuletta sandwiches to go, please, with extra olive salad on one."

Elizabeth said, "I'd like my bread toasted."

All activity around the counter stopped. Livvy and the server scowled. "Nobody toasts bread on a muffuletta sandwich, girl," she told Elizabeth. "Let me handle this and quit embarrassing me." She laughed and turned back to the server.

Elizabeth wanted to throttle Livvy. *New Orleans people are crazy about their food. They think there's a right way and a wrong way to eat and drink everything.*

"I sure wouldn't want to embarrass you, Miss Livvy, by getting my sandwich the way *I* want it." She tromped away and pretended to shop while Livvy purchased their food.

Livvy appeared a few minutes later with an overpowering garlic smell coming from the bag she waved under Elizabeth's nose. "Let's go, Crème Puff. I'm starving." They headed for Royal Street. Livvy sped up as she neared Elizabeth's apartment.

"You have to understand New Orleans' traditions if you're going to fit in," Livvy explained as they walked. "This sandwich has a history. The market off of Decatur Street used to be full of Sicilians selling their produce. They came to Central Grocery for lunch. They'd buy olive salad, Mortadella cheese, salami, and freshly baked bread. Juggling all that was a challenge. One version of the story says Signor Salvatore combined the olive salad, the cheese, and the salami and added a little ham. He put it on fresh-baked bread, and a New Orleans institution was born."

"That's all fine. But what's wrong with toasting the bread?" Elizabeth opened the gate to the garden entrance and ushered Livvy through.

"You're one hard-headed person! It's just not done. You eat it like Mr. Salvatore designed it, or you take your butt somewhere else to get fast food."

Bella bounded through the garden and jumped on Livvy. Elizabeth laughed when Livvy threw the sandwich bag up in the air and it landed on the brick pavers. Olive oil leaked through the paper bag, and Bella licked the bag. Ray ran to them, grabbed Bella's collar, and apologized. Livvy scooped up the bag, forced a smile at Ray, and headed to Elizabeth's balcony. Elizabeth remembered Livvy was uncomfortable around big dogs.

Elizabeth said to Ray, "I'm sorry. I didn't think to bring you and John a sandwich. Livvy and I are so tired we forgot our manners."

Ray fought to keep Bella at bay. She wrestled to lick her new neighbor. "John won't let me eat those sandwiches because he thinks my breath stinks for days afterward," Ray told her. "He says my garlic breath kills our orchids."

Elizabeth stroked Bella's head, laughed, and headed to the balcony. Over her shoulder she said, "I hope my frogs don't have a great sense of smell, or they might complain too. We'll get muffulettas together the next time John goes out of town."

"Excellent idea," said Ray. He opened the door to the house and pulled Bella inside.

Livvy arranged the food on the balcony table overlooking the garden.

She acts like it's her apartment.

Livvy said, "This garden is beautiful. Ray does a fantastic job. Looking from the street, nobody'd even guess the beauty to be found in this courtyard." She began to eat, though Elizabeth was still standing.

"I'd better check on the frogs. I can't remember if I fed them."

Livvy said, "Oh, come on, sit and eat. Those frogs don't have to be fed but every three days. They can hang out while we eat."

Elizabeth unwrapped her muffuletta. The garlic and olive salad smelled strong and earthy. Olive oil coated her hands and ran between her fingers when she picked up her sandwich. She wouldn't admit untoasted bread was perfect.

Olive oil dripped from Livvy's chin. She wiped her mouth on the corner of the paper that had wrapped her sandwich. They looked down at Ray's gurgling fountain and ate without talking. Elizabeth relaxed and sighed.

Livvy finished first and rose to clean up her place at the table. She went inside to get the trash can and some paper towels. Elizabeth heard her say, "What in the world? One of your frogs is missing, and the water in their aquarium is murky."

Elizabeth ran to the kitchen. She picked up the tiny aquarium with greasy hands and turned it around, looking for the second frog in the gravel. Livvy searched the kitchen and the floor. There was only one frog. The top of the aquarium was secure. There was no spilled water.

Elizabeth looked closely at the remaining frog and said, "There were two frogs when I left this morning. This frog is the one you named Poseidon. He has that little brown fleck on his nose. The missing frog is Neptune."

Livvy said, "That frog looks fatter than he did the last time I saw him. If you haven't been over feeding him, I'd say he ate his roommate."

Elizabeth began to sob. Livvy rushed to her and took the aquarium from Elizabeth and put it on the counter. Livvy put her arms around Elizabeth and patted her back. Elizabeth relaxed into Livvy's full, soft bosom.

"Don't cry, boo. It's just a frog. We can get another one. You didn't really seem to like them that much, anyway." Her voice was soft and kind.

Elizabeth rubbed her eyes, pulled away from Livvy, and said, "This is why I didn't want a pet. I don't have time for myself, much less anything else. You pushed those frogs on me, and this is what happened. Don't you see? I can't take much more responsibility? My *duties* weigh me down."

Livvy turned and stifled a smile. "Honey, you are dog tired. You need to go to bed and forget everything for a while. Frog mortality is nothing to get so jazzed up about. Blame me. I'm the one who picked out this murderous little bastard. I told you I can't pick a man for anything, and I guess that carries over to male frogs! I think we should rename him Charlie, and I think you should take a shower and go to bed."

Elizabeth wiped her face with a kitchen towel and said, "You're probably right. I'm exhausted. I like the name Charlie. It's short and cute and not pretentious like Poseidon. Why'd you choose it?"

Livvy grinned, stepped back a few feet, put her hand on the door, and started to exit. Over her shoulder, she said, "I named him after Charles Manson. That frog is a little murderer, and a cannibal to boot. It must be his African ancestry. See you tomorrow, Crème Puff." Livvy ran down the circular iron stairs to freedom as Elizabeth lunged for her. Elizabeth heard Livvy chuckling as the nurse walked through the garden below.

24

Elizabeth set her alarm for 4:00 a.m. She read about tetralogy of Fallot for an hour. After her studies, she better understood why Dr. White insisted on being meticulous with the pediatric patient. The heart anomaly was complex, and the surgery was challenging. The child had multiple congenital defects, but the condition of his heart would determine whether he lived or died. She had more questions than answers but felt secure in her ability to answer the intern-level questions. She hoped if she answered enough questions correctly, she'd get to scrub in during an open-heart surgery.

She put on her grandmother's pearls for good luck, adjusting the blood-stained section to the back of her neck, and walked to work. Her body was stiff and despite six hours of sleep, she felt she'd never left the hospital.

The night shift was ending in an hour, and the staff reported an uneventful night. Tony peeked out from a patient cubicle and said, "I changed the vent settings on this one. His O2 sat was a little down. I've taken a peek at everyone, and if I were you, I'd start here. I'm running over to Peds ICU as it's been a wild night with the sick kids. Dr. White didn't go home again, and he has two open hearts today. The kid with tetralogy had a rough night too. Dr. White got little sleep, and he's grumpy. Keep your reports simple, stick to important stuff, and good luck." He winked and left.

Elizabeth realized Tony had done part of her work. She appreciated him more as time passed. He was a good leader. She'd be sure to return his favors where she could. Like hers, his was not a competitive spirit.

Elizabeth was ready for rounds in an hour. Dr. White blew through the door. Walking behind him was the ugliest woman Elizabeth had ever seen. She sat in Joe's chair at the ICU secretary's desk. Her hair was an unnatural bright red, and there was too much of it. She was ultrathin and her bright flowered dress hung on her boney frame. Where breasts should have been, there were preposterous sharp points that did not move. Her long press-on nails were red—*Cherries in the Snow red.* She wore glasses similar to Joe's, but her name tag said "Jan." She looked up and smiled. With Joe's voice, she said, "Good morning, Dr. Roberts. Looks like a busy day in here today."

Elizabeth was stunned. Joe's Adam's apple looked huge. It was covered with a thick layer of foundation and was made even more obvious by his enthusiastic attempt to hide it. His foundation makeup was as thick as spackle. She heard her grandmother's voice say, "Don't stare at people; it's rude."

But Elizabeth wasn't the only one. The medical students and nurses were staring too. Joe looked down and busied himself with medical charts. Only Dr. White seemed relaxed, as if he had foreknowledge of Joe's transformation to Jan.

Dr. White said, "Enough hanging around. We've work to do. Hit it, intern!"

Nobody looked in Joe's direction again. Rounds were expeditious and at the end Dr. White said in a voice that seemed louder than necessary, "OK, everyone into the stairwell. We need to discuss the division of duties for the day."

Dr. White normally assigned duties in the staff area. Elizabeth felt anxious. Retreating to the silence of the stairwell usually meant somebody was going to be chastised. Tony met them in the hall as the team moved into the stairwell.

Dr. White was quiet for a moment. He leveled his eyes at each of them and searched their faces before he spoke. "As I'm sure you noticed, our Joe has undergone a little change. He's now Jan. I want each of you to know

Joe's been the best ward clerk in our system for a decade. You must treat him with the utmost respect at this sensitive time. This decision comes straight from the chairman of surgery. Nobody's to ask Joe any questions. I'd better not hear any snickering or gossip. Joe's to be treated exactly as before except he's now a woman, and his name's Jan. I won't pretend to understand his choices. But they are none of our business. The important thing is that Jan's an integral part of our team and is to be treated as such. Any questions?"

Tony said, "No, sir." Everyone else nodded. Nobody smiled or looked at each other.

Elizabeth was proud of Dr. White. She knew he was a strait-laced, proper Southern guy. His loyalty to Joe's work ethic warmed her. New Orleans was quirky like that. You really could come as you are and be completely accepted. After this speech, Elizabeth disliked Dr. White a little less.

"Your assignments today," began Dr. White. "Dr. Parker, you're working the peds clinic. You missed being there yesterday due to the trauma in the ER. So today, plan to be there all day. Dr. Roberts, you've managed to not kill anyone yet, and my *Times-Picayune* horoscope said I was going to have a great day, so you can come to the OR with me. The students will split up. Half go with Dr. Parker and half go with Dr. Roberts. In the OR, remember to hold your questions until after we come off bypass. Stopping the human heart is the realm of the gods, and there are to be no interruptions."

I almost liked him there for a moment, but now he's reverted to being sanctimonious.

Elizabeth felt fear and excitement. Her pulse raced. It was her first heart surgery.

She and Sallie followed Dr. White to the entrance of the operating room. He said, "Ladies, change into fresh scrubs and meet me at the scrub sink. Sallie, you've been taught the proper way to scrub? You won't get to touch anything today. But you'll get a better view if you lean in behind Dr. Roberts to see what's happening."

Sallie bobbed her head up and down. Her eyes were wide. She was breathing fast and was without her usual confidence. She said, "Yes, Dr. White. I've been instructed in sterile technique as much as a new student can be."

"I like your attitude, Sallie. Knowing that you don't know is the best beginning for knowing." They went to separate locker rooms. Elizabeth and Sallie went to the nurses' locker room because there was no locker room for female surgeons.

Sallie said, "I'm excited. I hope I don't faint. Why is there no locker room for female surgeons?"

"Because there are no female surgeons," answered Elizabeth. "Who cares, anyway? Today, we get to see a working human heart. Think how few people ever get the privilege we have today." *This is going to be wonderful. The human body amazes me.* "Remember not to talk until it's over. He was clear on that point. The good part about not talking is we know there'll be a window of time when he's not grilling us."

They dressed, inspected each other, and headed for the scrub sinks.

"Over here, ladies," instructed Dr. White. "Rose's ready for us in the OR and the patient's asleep. The cardiac bypass tech's ready. Today's patient is rather simple. A few still shots from his heart angiogram are hanging on the view box. Take a look at them. He has a ninety percent blockage in the LAD artery. Sallie, do you have any idea what we call that finding?"

Sallie scrubbed her hands and arms, copying Dr. White's every move. She paused and said, "I think it's called the *widow-maker*, sir."

"Correct!" said Dr. White. "Our patient is lucky to have not already had a myocardial infarction. Often with this coronary artery lesion, someone will have one big MI and die with no warning. Our patient reported symptoms similar to indigestion. His internal medicine doctor was a smart Tulane graduate. She knew to have him evaluated for cardiac disease. Our Louisiana diet makes our population rife with heart disease. Also, this man's a diabetic with high blood pressure, and that combination in a fifty-seven-year-old overweight male brings us here."

Elizabeth stared at Dr. White while his attention was on Sallie. She watched the muscles in his forearms, arms, and chest swell at the margins where they met his blue scrub shirt. He scrubbed vigorously, and the muscles bulged and contracted with each stroke. *In street clothes, he didn't look athletic.* He had broad shoulders with the build she associated with runners. She was close enough to inhale his clean, masculine scent. She observed his contagious enthusiasm for teaching Sallie. Elizabeth sensed a deep ache in her pelvis and was mortified to recognize animal longing in her body. Her chest, neck, and face reddened. Terrified he could read her thoughts, she turned her back to them.

How can I be thinking of sex before we're about to do surgery? I'm usually too hungry and sleepy to think of sex.

Dr. White finished his scrub, rinsed his arms, and looked toward Elizabeth. The blue scrub cap he wore accentuated his blue eyes. "Are you OK?" he asked her. "Your face is scarlet. You aren't about to faint, are you? I hope you ate. We could be in there for hours."

I wonder if he cautions the male doctors about fainting. He's mentioned it twice to Sallie and me.

Elizabeth rinsed her arms, wishing she could drop through the floor and away from his piercing eyes. His intensity rattled her. She muttered, "I'm fine. I just got a little hot."

No kidding! I had my biannual lust blowout standing here at the scrub sink.

She and Sallie were the last to enter the heart room. It was freezing, like a meat storage locker. It smelled of alcohol and disinfectant. Elizabeth had never seen so many machines with tubes in one room. Rose and Dr. White stood over the patient's chest. Rose had prepped the patient before Dr. White entered. The patient's inner thigh and chest were shaved, ready for the scalpel's assault.

Dr. White said, "Sallie, why is his left thigh exposed for a heart operation?"

Sallie stuttered. "I—I don't know."

"We're using his great saphenous vein as a graft to bypass the diseased part of his artery." Dr. White looked at Elizabeth and said, "Dr. Roberts, you're observing today. Sometimes I allow Dr. Parker to take the vein, but since you're a green intern, Rose and I will do it today. Pay close attention. One day, you may get to take the vein."

Elizabeth envied Rose's position.

With one quick slice of the scalpel, Dr. White opened the patient's thigh from groin to knee. With no wasted motion, he dissected the vein and tied off all its tributaries. He moved the long vein to another table to fashion it for the bypass graft. As he worked, the surgical instruments seemed to be extensions of Dr. White's long fingers, and Rose anticipated his every move. They worked like four hands from one body. They were instruments playing perfectly together in a complex symphony.

They closed the leg incision and moved in unison to the chest. Dr. White said, "Sallie, what we're about to do is simple but outrageous. The simple part is that we're detouring around a diseased coronary artery with a piece of vein. The complex part is that to do that, we have to drain the patient's body of all its blood, bypass the blood away from the lungs and heart, keep the blood oxygenated and returned to the rest of the body, keep the blood and the bypass machine from clotting off while we work, and then talk his heart into starting back up again in a rhythm that supports life. It usually works—that's the outrageous part. Today, we'll see."

Elizabeth realized she wasn't blinking, and her eyes were dry. She had no saliva in her mouth, and her heart was hammering. Her only duties were to watch and not faint. She hoped she could manage.

Dr. White looked to the technician manning the heart bypass machine and asked, "Bob, is the pump ready?"

Bob said, "All systems are a go, Doc."

In another quick motion, Dr. White pulled the scalpel down the center of the patient's chest. There was no hesitation. Elizabeth recognized the white, glistening sternum. Dr. White scored the bone with electrical cautery and used a noisy sternal saw to open the chest by cutting the breast bone open. The move exposed the beating heart. Elizabeth felt exhilarated and fought back tears.

Dr. White and Rose continued to work, communicating only with eye contact. Despite her jealousy, Elizabeth admired their coordinated dance. Rose's devotion to Dr. White served the patient well. She'd not let him fumble or require him to ask for any instrument. Elizabeth yearned to be the one assisting Dr. White.

The next instrument they used, the sternal retractor, looked like a medieval torture tool. Its large surgical steel edges were positioned to further open the chest cavity. The ribs made a horrible cracking sound as Dr. White cranked the retractor open to further reveal the beating heart. "Now, ladies," he said to Sallie and Elizabeth, "you know why we call it 'cracking the chest'."

Sallie stood riveted behind Elizabeth. Elizabeth felt she should remind her to keep breathing, but feared ignoring Dr. White's instructions to "not talk."

Dr. White looked up and adjusted the OR lights to shine directly on the center of the beating heart. He paused to look at Rose and whined, "Must I operate all alone?" The nurse laughed and shrugged.

Ah . . . an inside joke.

Dr. White sewed the pump cannulas of the bypass machine to the upper and lower heart. He said, "Sallie, these tubes are to bypass the heart and lungs while we do our job and to drain all the blood from the patient and into the bypass machine. Go on bypass, Bob."

Once on bypass, the focus of the operation became smaller, and Sallie and Elizabeth could see little.

Elizabeth recognized names of the greats from the history of cardiothoracic surgery as Dr. White called out to Rose for different instruments named after these heroes of innovation: the Debakey clamp, Ochsner dissector, Satinsky clamp, Babcock, and Mayo. He called for a Castroviejo needle holder, and Elizabeth realized he was sewing the graft with sutures as fine as hair. His movements slowed to match the fragile nature of the work. He could easily make a wrong move, tear the tissue that was as delicate as a spider's web, and ruin the procedure. But he didn't. His focus was sharp. She wondered if he, too, was holding his breath.

With the graft in place, Dr. White said, "Looks good. Rose, you got those internal paddles juiced up just in case our patient doesn't play pretty? Bob, you ready with the protamine? Ladies, we reverse the anticoagulant because we don't want the patient to bleed out."

Dr. White was almost jocular. He didn't talk to Elizabeth that way. He didn't usually talk to anyone that way. *He's jovial.*

He removed the tubes and sewed the holes in the heart closed. He leaned back to allow Sallie and Elizabeth to see the vein graft, and then he said, "Let's wean off the pump, Bob."

Everyone stood still, waiting to see if the heart would restart. It did! That first heartbeat was the most miraculous event Elizabeth had ever witnessed. She was ecstatic for the patient, and she surprised herself by feeling proud of and happy for Dr. White. She had never seen a more skilled surgeon. She wanted that level of skill. *This isn't sexual desire. This is plain, old hero worship.*

Dr. White placed tubes around the man's heart that would drain excess fluid over the next twenty-four hours. Now, it was time to close.

The last part of the surgery was as barbaric as the chest cracking. Long metal wires were used to wrench the sternum closed. Driving the metal sutures through the breastbone took brute force, an act in contradistinction to the delicacy of sewing the great saphenous vein graft to the coronary artery with sutures that were too small to see without magnification.

The surgery was over. Dr. White thanked Rose and Bob for an excellent case and told Elizabeth to make rounds and be ready to discuss the patients in thirty minutes.

Sallie and Elizabeth changed clothes in the nurses' lounge. Sallie said, "That was amazing. I'll never forget that as long as I live! Can you believe what a fantastic surgeon he is? I can see why everyone at Charity treats him like a god."

"Whoa, girl!" said Elizabeth. "Calm down. He's been doing this a while. He's an expert, and we're novices. Maybe there are even better surgeons around here. Let's not get too worked up."

"Well, you can take it any way you want, but I'm in *love*!"

Elizabeth laughed at Sallie's enthusiasm and silently prayed that Sallie was the only one "in love."

25

Sallie and Elizabeth, now dressed, walked toward the adult ICU and saw Dr. White and Tony in the hall, deep in conversation about the child with tetralogy of Fallot.

As Tony talked, he waved his hands. "He doesn't look good to me. I can't explain it. His heart rate's elevated, and his urine output's decreased."

"Let's not get too worked up," Dr. White responded. "He has four tubes, three drains, and two intravenous lines. He might need more pain medication. We don't want to fluid overload him and be forced to give him diuretics later. I decreased his pain meds, hoping to decrease his vent settings and get him breathing on his own." Dr. White noticed Elizabeth and Sallie. "Let's make rounds in the adult ICU," he said to Tony, "and then you and I can sit and go over his chart in more detail." Dr. White turned to Elizabeth.

"I almost forgot. Dr. Roberts, we have a visiting professor coming this week. He's one of Dr. McSwain's closest friends. You'll recognize his name from textbooks and journals. Dr. Ken Mattox will be here, and I need an intern to present a chest trauma case to him and drive him around. Dr. McSwain agreed you can use his car. Plan to get the case from me after we finish rounds, and I'll review it with you. Dr. Mattox is an impressive guy, and we want to make sure he enjoys his time here. It's a tradition that the residents take the visiting professor drinking in the French Quarter after his lectures. It gets rowdy. Somebody has to stay sober to chauffeur Dr. Mattox. That's your job. Dr. Parker will help you with the details of picking him up at the Windsor Court Hotel and delivering him—"

The end of Dr. White's sentence was cut off by the simultaneous STAT paging to him and Dr. Parker.

CODE BLUE PEDIATRIC ICU! REPEAT . . . CODE BLUE PEDIATRIC ICU.

They sped away. As they rounded the corner, the young Cajun couple who were the parents of the child with tetralogy of Fallot was being escorted by a frantic nurse to the family waiting room. Elizabeth didn't know her role in this situation, so she and Sallie followed to observe at the bedside of baby boy Jacques.

Dr. White jerked the curtain so it surrounded Jacques's bed and obscured the view from the other children's beds. He examined the child from head to toe while quizzing the nurses. "He's got no pulse!" he exclaimed. "What happened?"

The head nurse was using an Ambu bag to force ventilation into the boy's lungs. She was working fast and looked over her shoulder, saying, "I don't know what happened. He'd been tachycardic for a couple of hours. Dr. Parker and I checked him every fifteen minutes and found no change except for a slight decrease in his urine output. Then all of his monitors started screaming, and I rushed over to find him with no pulse and turning bluer. I called the code and started hand ventilation to be sure there wasn't something wrong with the ventilator."

Dr. White called out the names of three cardiac drugs to support the child's heart to the other nurses standing by as he frantically examined the child's lungs with his stethoscope and inspected all his tubes. Elizabeth and Sallie and Tony stood to the side, out of his way. Dr. White moved repeatedly over Jacques's body from top to bottom, searching for any sign to guide him.

"Give him a fluid bolus," he ordered. "I don't see how we could have gotten behind in his fluids. I've calculated them very precisely. Push it in through his central line. Everyone, stand back! I'll try to shock his heart."

They moved away from the bed. Dr. White applied pediatric paddles to the boy's little chest. His body contracted and his limbs spasmed, but his heart did not beat. Dr. White called out the names of two more drugs to the nurses. His panicked voice got louder with each order. He shocked the baby again. His eyes flew up to the monitors and down to the baby in rapid succession. The child was dead. Dr. White would not give up.

"Come on, little guy," he entreated. "You can do this. Your parents are pulling for you. Please come back. We can do this. Come on, buddy," said Dr. White.

The nurses looked on with pity in their eyes, poised and ready to follow any order from Dr. White. They knew before Dr. White was willing to admit that little Jacques was gone. Elizabeth felt helpless. Sallie had tears running down her face. Tony stood resolute, staring at the floor.

After forty-five minutes, which seemed more like three hours to Elizabeth, Dr. White looked at the head nurse and said, "This is pointless. I'll bet it was sepsis. With all these blasted tubes running into him, I'm sure one got infected and caused this. We cultured all the lines a day ago, and they were clear. But two cultures haven't come back yet, and I'll bet one of them contains some hospital-acquired bacteria."

Everyone stood with their heads bowed and faces toward the floor. One nurse made the sign of the cross; another clutched the cross around her neck and mumbled prayers. Sallie sobbed. Elizabeth felt disoriented.

Dr. White stood, his arms folded, and stared at the child who'd consumed his life for days. He looked exhausted. Part of his life force had left with the child's, and it left him seemingly defeated.

Without speaking, Dr. White slowly, reverently, and delicately removed every tube. Each action seemed an apology. He sewed closed every gaping hole left by the tube removal. The nurses tried to help him, but he pushed their hands away. He bathed the baby to remove all signs of Betadine, blood, and bodily fluids. The nurse handed him a clean gown and knitted hat.

"No," he told her. These are pink. He's a boy. Get me a blue set." His voice cracked with emotion. He removed the monitors from the bedside and pulled two rocking chairs to the side of the crib. Then he propped up little Jacques's body on a clean white pillow and checked again to be sure no bodily fluids were seeping out from the tube sites. He asked the nurse to put the tape with the lullabies in the cassette player and to keep the volume low when the parents entered. He patted the baby's head on his blue knitted cap and said, "I'm so sorry, little guy. I tried my best."

Dr. White turned to the team, surprised to see them standing there, watching him. He was in a private place of deep grief.

"You guys act busy and stop staring," he instructed. "I'm going to get his parents and tell them the bad news. They are children themselves. This will be their last memory of their first-born. Please let them sit by his bed with him so they will remember something other than tubes, surgeries, and death. Their whole world is in this bed. We failed them. The least we can do is to help their last moments with their child be less horrible."

Dr. White put on a clean white coat, signaled for Tony to stay in the ICU, and went to get the parents.

Elizabeth and Sallie dried their eyes, turned their backs, and sat at the nurses' station desk. They shuffled papers and tried to look busy. Neither had ever seen a child die. Both were shaken. Tony stood at the foot of the crib, trying not to break down. The nurses busied themselves cleaning the floor of any signs of blood. One pulled a cassette of lullabies from a drawer and inserted it in the player. They placed stuffed toys across the head of the child's hospital bed. It seemed Dr. White had been gone for hours.

He returned to the ICU with one hand placed on the mother's back and one placed on the father's. He pushed them gently toward the hospital bed that held their dead son.

"Your boy is at peace now," he told them. "He was the bravest little guy I've ever seen. He fought like an LSU Tiger. You should be proud of him. He got tired, and he went home. He was a good boy, and I'm proud of him. Why don't you sit here in these chairs? We'll pull the curtains and y'all can be alone with him for a little while."

The mother sobbed and touched the baby's hand. "Oh, cher," she said, "you look so peaceful." She turned to look at her husband. "Without all those tubes, he looks asleep. And normal." She stood and stared. The husband pulled her into the rocking chair. Dr. White adjusted the curtains around them and said, "Stay as long as you like." The nurse handed him a fresh box of Kleenex, which he handed to the father through the opening in the curtains.

Elizabeth thought Dr. White had aged five years right before her eyes. He whispered, "Let's go to the adult ICU. There's work to do there."

26

As the team walked to the adult ICU, they tried to shift their focus from the dead to the living and concentrate on what they could accomplish for the patients in the ICU and away from those they could no longer help. The world seemed to be moving in slow motion, and none of them had energy for the next tasks. They were somber.

Dr. White said, "Let's split to conquer rounds so I can get back to the family after they've had time alone with their son. Dr. Parker, you take Dr. Roberts and round on beds one through six. Sallie and the head nurse and I will do beds seven through twelve. If there's anything irregular, come get me. Otherwise, I'll see you in the morning."

Elizabeth felt relief. She hated seeing Dr. White look defeated. She had little understanding of what he must be feeling. As a student and as an intern, she had seen death. She had even experienced the agony of knowing a patient's death was because of her own incompetence. But she'd never experienced the soul-deep battering that must result when one feels responsible for the death of a child. She couldn't wait to get away from Dr. White's oppressive pain.

Tony poured two cups of coffee from the pot at the nurses' station and handed one to Elizabeth. The coffee was nasty and thick and tasted burned, like it had been in the pot for hours. They sipped the black syrup, and Tony said, "At least some things don't change. The ICU has the worst coffee at The Big Free—we can rely on that."

Despite her grief, Elizabeth chuckled, took another sip, and tossed the half-empty Styrofoam cup into the first patient's trash can. She was grateful for Tony's steadfast nature. No matter what he was experiencing, he found the energy to comfort others and lighten the mood.

Making rounds was a welcome task. They knew the well-practiced routine and found the familiarity comforting. The nurses knew of the death of young Jacques in the Peds ICU, and they were quiet and helpful. They knew the young doctors were in pain and distracted.

Elizabeth saw Dr. White and Sallie exit the ICU while she and Tony were working on their next-to-last patient. Dr. White's efficiency impressed her. He did twice the work in half the time it took her and Tony. Elizabeth knew she didn't want to cross paths with the dead boy's grief-stricken parents. She also understood Dr. White was going to perform a task she could not do without losing a bit of her fragile sanity. Elizabeth and Tony slowed their pace while checking on the last two patients to avoid contact with the grieving young couple.

As Elizabeth closed the last patient's chart and moved toward the ICU door, Tony said, "He forgot to give you the case for the visiting professor. I have the films and a copy of the patient's chart in the nurses' lunch area. Come with me, and I'll give it to you. You can study it later tonight after you get some rest. Write any questions you have about the case, and Dr. White and I will discuss them with you tomorrow. I'm going to the call room to change and make rounds for the last time in the Peds ICU. I'll see you tomorrow." After a pause, he added, "I feel like I took a gut punch today. I think I'll stop by the hospital chapel and pray for the soul of little Jacques and for his parents."

Tony's gentleness cracked Elizabeth's resolve. She longed for a hug and to talk with Daddy. Elizabeth rubbed her fingers on her grandmother's pearls at her neck and fought back tears. The closest thing she had to her father's loving presence was to touch her stained pearls and imagine the comfort he'd give. She patted Tony on his shoulder, took the X-rays and chart from his hands, and left to go home.

As she rounded the corner, she heard the sound of sobbing coming from the stairwell. She heard a deep, guttural groan, and the words, "No!

No! No!" came muted through the heavy metal door. She heard pounding on the wall. It was a man's voice, one she thought belonged to the father of baby Jacques. Without further thought, she followed her instinct and jerked open the door, feeling a strong urge to comfort the baby's parents.

She was stunned to see Dr. White alone in the stairwell. When he turned from pounding the wall, Elizabeth saw his puffy red face and bloodshot eyes. The lapels of his white coat were soaked from his tears, and a white handkerchief was wrapped around his bloodied left fist. She realized he must have pounded the wall until his soft hand was scraped. He glared at her. Elizabeth staggered back, shocked by his raw emotional display.

Before she thought otherwise, she moved to encircle him with her arms. At first, he tried to push away from her, but her strong, farm girl embrace tightened around him. He struggled for a second, then bent down and collapsed onto her shoulder and sobbed.

After a few moments, he pulled away and wiped his face. Elizabeth felt embarrassed and awkward, and she struggled for words as she looked around the stairwell, avoiding his eyes.

Dr. White spoke first, asking, "What do you want, Dr. Roberts?" and once again became the Dr. White she knew. "Don't you have work to do?" he demanded.

She backed up to the door, ignored his attempt to change the subject, and said, "Yes, sir. I always have work to do. But I want you to know that I know you did your best. I'm sorry he died. Are the parents OK?"

"They'll *never* be OK," he told her. "When people lose a child, they are never OK again." He paused, then continued, "One thing you'll learn about this job is if you do your duty and truly care about your work, it will break your heart."

He pushed past her and walked out the door into the hall. Elizabeth remained in the stairwell and cried until her coat lapels were also soaked.

As Elizabeth had no handkerchief, she wiped her eyes and nose and face on the inside of her sleeve and stumbled out of the stairwell, feeling anxious and sad. She wondered yet again if she had the toughness required for the life of a surgeon. Tonight, she needed to get home to her bed. She'd reevaluate her career choice for the thousandth time . . . tomorrow.

27

Elizabeth's mind drifted as she walked through the Quarter toward her apartment, feeling emotionally spent, but too agitated to go home. Behind shabby streets, luscious courtyards abounded.

She passed Brennan's and fantasized about dressing up and having Sunday brunch in the garden there. She wondered if Dr. White and his family dined there after church. The young parents and their dead child flashed in her mind, and she felt guilty for her silly thoughts. She chewed her lip to stall the floodgate of tears and made her way to the river. She couldn't settle down.

She climbed the levy and gazed into the murky, swirling waters of the fast-moving Mississippi River. The tightest segment of the bend in the river was near the end of Toulouse, and she watched a tugboat move a barge around the bend. Elizabeth marveled at how the small tug navigated a much longer and larger barge around the turn. She walked along the levy to the old Custom House near Canal. She knew she was going in the wrong direction from her apartment, but walking and watching the industrious tugboat captains soothed her jangled nerves. At the Custom house, she turned around and walked along the levy back in the direction of Jackson Square. She had an irrational urge to swim out to a tugboat for asylum, quit her job, and go somewhere—anywhere.

She didn't want to face her pain or her bizarre attraction to Dr. White or her increasing emotional distance from her family or the fact that her entire being had been taken over by her pursuit of surgical training. She loved her work, and she hated her work. She wanted her old comfortable life on the farm but knew she couldn't return. Her whole life she'd been called "sweet," and she liked being sweet. But neither Dr. White nor Dr. McSwain was sweet. Was she capable of the competence, the greatness she observed in Dr. White and Dr. McSwain? What would remain of her if she continued down this path? Was her mother right? Elizabeth decided these questions were too deep and too many for this day.

She decided to think instead about the trauma case and the X-rays she held in her hands. She'd carried them under her arm on her walk, temporarily forgetting she needed to prepare her presentation to the visiting professor. Dr. Mattox was a close friend of Dr. McSwain's and she didn't want to embarrass her professor in front of his friend. Her anxiety mounted as she approached her apartment. She knew little about chest trauma but had to present a case to the guy who wrote textbooks on the subject.

Her scrubs stuck to her back after her walk, despite the mild winter temperature. She was relieved her neighbors were elsewhere as she rushed through the garden to her apartment. After she closed the door, the tears flooded. She slumped onto her unmade Murphy bed and sobbed. She awoke at two in the morning when the X-ray folder stabbed her in the cheek; she still wore her scrubs and bloodstained shoes and felt both hungry and thirsty. She realized she hadn't studied the case for the visiting professor; she hadn't eaten anything since lunch the day before; she hadn't showered in two days, and her next shift started in three hours. Despite rushing, she was always behind. There never seemed to be time to take care of her daily needs.

Elizabeth took a deep breath, ate a stale bagel, drank some instant coffee, and took a quick shower. She dressed in clean scrubs, silently thanking Livvy for advising her to take home an extra set. She couldn't remember the last time she'd done laundry. Livvy had also suggested she buy packages of cheap underwear and socks to keep everywhere because blood and other body fluids seeped through the scrubs, necessitating lots of changes—another piece of good advice. Elizabeth looked at herself in the bathroom mirror and laughed at her resemblance to her Granny in the cotton "drawers" she was wearing. She couldn't remember the last time she felt pretty or—heaven forbid—sexy. She vowed to clean up her act whenever she had a day off.

For now, she'd settle for sitting in her white cotton baggy underwear and learning the details of her trauma case. But she promptly fell back asleep.

28

Elizabeth bolted out of bed at five in the morning and raced to the hospital with the trauma case records tucked under her arm.

Rounds were uneventful. Tony asked, "Are you ready to discuss the case you're to present to Dr. Mattox later today?"

Elizabeth was too tired to dissemble. "Honestly, Tony, I fell asleep with the films on my chest and haven't had time to study the case. I'm sorry, but I chose to eat and shower instead of study."

Tony laughed and said, "You picked a good day to be a slacker. Dr. White's doing a routine coronary artery bypass and took Sallie with him. We have two free hours if the emergency room remains quiet. Let's go in the nurses' lounge and have some of their delicious coffee and talk about the case."

Elizabeth enjoyed time alone with Tony. She also loved going to the operating room, even if she didn't get to do anything, but she was still emotionally spent from the events of the day before and needed a break. She hung the X-rays on the viewing box in the nurses' lounge to review the films. Then she handed Tony his coffee and sat down with the thick chart to study the patient's case.

Tony sat across from her. Before she could start reading, he touched her hand and said, "What do you know about visiting professor traditions in surgery programs?"

His tone brought her to full attention, and a sense of dread filled her. "I know nothing," she admitted. "In South Carolina, when we had a visiting professor, the students didn't do anything but observe the residents' presentations. The interns and residents dressed up and minded their manners. But I don't know anything else about what goes on, especially here."

"I don't want to make you more nervous than you already are, but I do want to prepare you. At Tulane, we play a stump-the-chump game. We present the most difficult diagnostic dilemma we can find that is within the expertise of the visiting professor. Since Dr. Mattox is a big shot in the world of trauma, you'll try to stump him on a complex trauma case. It's considered bad manners to try to trick the visiting professor, so you don't withhold information. Instead, you present a rare case that he may not have seen before and get him to figure it out in front of the entire faculty, local surgeons, alumni, students, and residents," Tony explained. "Dr. Mattox is brilliant and experienced. We probably have nothing he hasn't seen. But Charity has more trauma cases than ninety percent of programs, and we do see rare problems more frequently than other places do. It's an intellectual game. Be your usual respectful self," Tony advised. "Let's review the case in detail."

"That sounds great," Elizabeth replied. "I appreciate your time in trying to help me. I want to do a good job. I understand that I also have to drive him around. I'll be driving Dr. McSwain's car, and I don't know where the Windsor Court Hotel is located. I'll need detailed directions."

Tony's dark brown face turned pale. He coughed nervously into his hand, stalled for time to think, and said, "That brings up another subject. Has anyone explained our after-hours traditions with visiting surgeons?"

Tony's face signaled to Elizabeth that whatever the tradition was, she wasn't going to like it.

She said, "I know nothing."

Tony stood up and closed the door to the nurses' lounge. He sat down and looked at the table but not at Elizabeth. Her anxiety mounted. Tony usually looked directly into her eyes when he spoke.

"Our tradition is to take the visiting professor to the French Quarter after dinner at a swanky restaurant. After dinner, we go to strip clubs, and there's excessive drinking. Most don't remember much about the evening.

It's the one time a year that raunchy behavior is forgiven. We plan the evening out for an LSU night, and they cover Charity—their faculty and fellows mind the shop at Tulane on this one night. The various visiting professors participate to different degrees, but they all know if they accept the invitation to come here that the rowdy trip to the French Quarter is part of the plan. One intern is chosen to stay sober and see that the visiting professor gets back to his hotel room safely. I guess Dr. McSwain chose you to be the sober driver of Dr. Mattox this year."

Elizabeth's anxiety transformed into exasperation. She said, "OK. What am I supposed to do while the rest of you are at the strip clubs?"

Tony didn't answer. He looked uncomfortable as Elizabeth watched him blushing and squirming in his chair.

He stammered and said, "This year, we're cleaning it up a bit. We're not going to any clubs where the dancers take off their clothes. We're going to New Orleans' most famous burlesque show. Miss Chris Owens is in the Quarter, around the block from where you live, near Dr. McSwain's home. She's a good singer, and her show is respectable. She trained years ago to be a nurse, leads the annual Easter parade through the Quarter, and is an important part of the local economy. Folks come from all over to see her." Tony continued to squirm in his seat, and he looked down into his cup as he sipped his coffee.

He's trying to find words to make this acceptable to me.

Elizabeth searched his face for answers. He didn't look up. "OK," she said. "Tell me how to handle this. I've never been to a burlesque show, and I have *no* idea what I should do."

"It's totally up to you," Tony replied. "If it's reassuring, I'll accompany you and stay with you the entire time. If, at any point, you feel uncomfortable, you let me know. I'll walk you to your apartment and return to get you when the show is over."

Elizabeth felt her hand around her coffee cup shake. "That's not what I asked, Tony," she told him. "I asked what *you* think I should do."

"We've had few women in the surgery department so far," Tony began. "It's hard to thread a path between taking all the guys' fun away and being appropriate and respectful to the female surgeons." He met her eyes. "You'd be best served by going along. You'll benefit from being perceived as a team player. I suggest you go to dinner with the group, and we'll drive the professor to the Quarter. Stick with me, but go everywhere we go, including to the burlesque show. Don't make a big deal out of it. I've seen Miss Owens several times. She shows some cleavage and has long legs and dances and sings. There's nothing raunchy about her shows. The worrisome part is that the guys drink excessively and talk a lot of trash. If you sit between me and Dr. Mattox, you'll be fine. He's a genteel man, and I'm sure Dr. McSwain has made him aware of the situation. After an appropriate amount of time, you and I can drive him back to his hotel, and the evening will be over for us. The boys can continue as they see fit."

Elizabeth felt shocked and angry. She could not imagine most of her colleagues going along with this plan. She wondered how the wives of married residents felt about this "tradition" but quickly decided that since it was only one night, she'd not make a fuss. She imagined Tony had experienced discrimination as a Black professional man with an island accent. He had navigated those murky waters, and she knew he had her best interests at heart. She trusted Tony wouldn't let things go too far.

"One day," Tony continued, "this won't be an issue. Hard to imagine now, but one day there will be a female surgery chair. For reasons I don't understand, all the surgery programs took minority men well before they took any women. Tulane Surgery has always been on the forefront, leading the way in taking the best candidates no matter who they might be. If you look at its history, Tulane has done a great job of integrating everyone, but some old traditions haven't died out yet."

Elizabeth recognized the wisdom of his advice. Resigned, she said, "OK. I'm in. Let's get down to the important part and make sure I know this case inside and out."

Tony chuckled and shook his head. “You’re one tough chick, Elizabeth.”

They spent an hour studying the case and another hour with Tony quizzing Elizabeth.

Dr. White and Sallie returned for afternoon rounds. After those, everyone retired to their on-call rooms to dress for the four o’clock session with Dr. Mattox.

29

Dr. McSwain met Dr. Mattox at the airport and delivered him to the hospital. Elizabeth was grateful to have extra time to review the case alone in the on-call room.

The team gathered in the lobby of Charity at three-thirty. Tulane and LSU students and residents created an ant colony of hustle and bustle, running in a stream through the Art Deco lobby. The Tulane Surgery team formed a group under the *Doctors' Information* sign in the center of the lobby. They entered the elevator together and headed for the Delgado Amphitheatre.

Dr. McSwain teased Dr. Mattox. He said, "Remember, guys, this session is all about stumping the chump. Let's make sure we give our visitor a case to remember."

Dr. Mattox laughed. Elizabeth thought he didn't look the least bit nervous. He seemed calm and thoughtful in the crowded elevator. The conference session was nothing to someone who sliced open someone's chest in the emergency room most days of the week. Elizabeth thought he tolerated Dr. McSwain's ribbing as part of the game of getting the students and residents pumped up for entering the Bull Pen.

Dr. Mattox asked Dr. White, "Who's the lucky guy presenting the case today?"

Dr. White pointed to Elizabeth and said, "That's our cardiothoracic intern this month, Dr. Elizabeth Roberts. She's been an expert in thoracic trauma for all of two days. She'll present the case to you, sir."

Dr. Mattox smiled and nodded in her direction.

The elevator seemed to move slower than usual. The elevator operator, Elizabeth's friend Miss Albertha Simmons, listened to every word of the doctors' conversation and made sure to make a good impression on the visitor. Elizabeth noticed Miss Albertha was particularly well-groomed today and was more deferential to the students and residents than typical.

Dr. Mattox looked at Elizabeth and said, "We might as well start with all of my *why* questions while we're still in the elevator. It's important for a surgeon to know anatomy in detail, but we must also know the history of medicine and surgery. The Spanish philosopher Santayana said, 'Those who cannot remember the past are condemned to repeat it.' So, Dr. Roberts, what is the history of the Delgado Amphitheater and what is its importance?"

Elizabeth's heart hammered. She'd reviewed chest anatomy but never imagined history questions would start in the elevator.

She said, "I'm sorry. I don't know the details of the history. I do know the Delgado Amphitheater is a scary place for Tulane medical students. Every Saturday at 11:00 a.m., they have what's called 'Bull Pen.' The students are brought a patient from the ward. They have thirty minutes to examine and question the patient, and then the faculty and residents arrive to question them. It is an intense form of the Socratic Method. Most students never forget the experience."

Dr. McSwain chuckled. "It is quite unforgettable for most."

Since she couldn't answer his question, Dr. Mattox moved on to the second-year surgery residents. Without being asked, Tony spoke. "Sir, I believe the Delgado Amphitheater was built around the time the hospital opened in 1939. The tradition of the Bull Pen started with Dr. Alton Ochsner. He was the original bull, if I'm not mistaken."

The elevator doors opened, and the team slowly filed out. The staff exited first, with Elizabeth bringing up the rear. As she stepped through the doors, she heard Miss Albertha say, "Good luck, baby." Those few words and her smile calmed Elizabeth.

"Thanks, Miss Albertha," said Elizabeth.

Dr. Mattox paused in the hall and looked at his watch. Seeing it was only 3:45, he continued his questions. "What is Bull Pen?"

Elizabeth knew this one and said, "The philosophy of Bull Pen is to teach third-year Tulane students to think on their feet. The practice of medicine and surgery demands quick decisions, the ability to put together a known set of data, and to use that data to determine a course of action. Our patients' lives depend on our ability to think clearly and accurately and make the best decisions for them—sometimes life and death decisions in a matter of seconds."

Dr. McSwain turned to the students and said, "Bull Pen is emotionally tough on the student undergoing the grilling. Nobody ever forgets the answers they get wrong in Bull Pen. Fear sharpens the senses. I haven't seen a student fall asleep in Bull Pen, but the first student quizzed by Dr. Alton Ochsner did faint."

The team laughed. Elizabeth knew Dr. McSwain was good at saying something to break the tension if it got too high. Dr. White held the door to the old marble amphitheater as everyone streamed in. Elizabeth and Dr. Mattox headed down the steep marble stairs to the floor below. She was shocked to see the amphitheater was standing room only. On her way down to the Pit, she saw students from Tulane, LSU, and the school of nursing, plus professors from both LSU and Tulane and many community doctors and alumni she had only occasionally seen on Saturday surgical grand rounds. Livvy and several other nurses were there too. *Dang if every medical person in town isn't in the room.* Her knees buckled, and she grabbed the railing on the last two steps to keep from stumbling. Dr. Mattox took her elbow and walked her to the middle of the arena.

She arranged her stack of X-rays on the table beside the view box, while Dr. Mattox smiled, nodded and acknowledged many people he knew in the crowd. Dr. McSwain came down to introduce him.

Elizabeth looked up into the crowd, hoping to find someone to ground her and decrease her anxiety. Dr. White sat in the front row. He looked handsome and relaxed. His shining bright blue eyes were accentuated by his starched blue Oxford shirt, red silk tie, and white coat. Elizabeth thought he gazed at her with warmth. She was startled but pleased. His usual raptor-about-to-pounce look was not evident today. She spotted Livvy; Livvy looked nervous. Her eyes darted from Dr. McSwain to Dr. Mattox and back to Elizabeth.

She doesn't know if I can do it or not. How odd! Dr. White thinks I can, but Livvy's not sure.

Dr. McSwain was dressed in his usual red cotton turtleneck, bear claw necklace, cowboy boots, and giant belt buckle with the initials N.O.P.D. proudly displayed. His choice of apparel and athletic stance stood in contrast to Dr. Mattox's solid brown suit, white shirt, brown tie, and wing tip Oxfords. Dr. Mattox's hair had seen a professional barber recently. Dr. McSwain's hair was slick and combed back as if he'd just left the shower. Despite the obvious differences in styles, their warm smiles made the affection between the two evident.

Dr. McSwain took the floor, saying, "I could go on all doggone day about this guy. His accomplishments could keep us here past happy hour. But, suffice it to say, Ken Mattox is the real deal. He works out of Ben Taub Hospital in Houston, and he's the best trauma surgeon I've ever seen. He teaches students, residents, and fellows every day. He's written more surgical articles and trauma textbooks than anyone. Shoot, he knows the president and a few kings too. He's a man of integrity and a really nice guy. If a Tulane student blames me for his low surgery grade and decides to take a shot at me today, for goodness' sake, make Ken operate on me. Even if he doesn't like me all that much, I know he'll do a good job." He paused while the crowd laughed. "Today, our intern is going to present a case he'll never get right. With no further ado, I give you Dr. Mattox and Dr. Roberts."

He winked at Elizabeth as he passed to go to his seat. Dr. Mattox folded his hands in front of his waist and placed his attention on the view box. He and Elizabeth both took deep breaths.

Most of the audience had laughed at Dr. McSwain's introduction, but Elizabeth noticed a few faces stared at their laps as if they were embarrassed. *They probably expected a more professional introduction with the visitor's credentials detailed.*

Elizabeth began the presentation. "Dr. Mattox, thanks for being with us today. I present the first film. This twenty-eight-year-old gentleman was driving at a very high rate of speed in his pickup truck along a country road. His truck struck a large cow, and he was expelled from his vehicle and impaled on a metal fence. The accident was witnessed, and an ambulance team arrived in less than ten minutes. The man was unconscious, draped over the fence post like a rag doll. His blood pressure was ninety over sixty, and his pulse was ninety-six. He was unconscious at the scene.

Elizabeth turned to the first chest X-ray hanging on the view box. As she started to speak and point to the X-ray, Dr. Mattox interrupted her, saying, "Before we move to that very impressive chest film, let's start with first things first. Dr. Roberts. Tell me the details of his physical exam." He rubbed his chin and focused on Elizabeth as if nobody else was in the room.

Elizabeth felt her face flush. *How could I make such a silly mistake? Of course, all clinical evaluations began with taking a history and doing a physical examination!*

She said, "His blood pressure was stable throughout his transport and initial evaluation in Room Four. He couldn't answer any questions, but he was sensitive to deep pain stimuli. His pulse remained high, and his respirations were fast and shallow. He had a fence post sticking straight up into the air above his lateral upper left shoulder. The firemen at the scene had cut part of the fence post near the exit site from the patient's body to allow transport. His heart sounds were fast but not abnormal. He had strong pulses in all extremities, even in the left arm and hand. His pupils were normal and responsive. He had decreased breath sounds at the base of both lungs. He was covered in bruises and minor cuts. His abdomen was soft with normal bowel sounds. On palpation, his skeleton did not suggest broken bones. After a catheter was placed, his urine didn't show gross blood."

Dr. Mattox nodded and asked, "Anything else, Dr. Roberts?"

Elizabeth thought there must be something else or he wouldn't be asking that question. She scanned her memory for the details of her trauma textbooks, but could think of nothing important that she'd left out. Her anxiety grew.

"Dr. Roberts, what do we know from what you have reported so far?" Dr. Mattox continued. "We know much of great importance."

Elizabeth's heart pounded in her ears. She felt dizzy. *I thought I'd be asking the questions.*

"Well, sir," she began, "the information from the scene tells us he was unlikely to have a major vascular injury because he maintained his blood pressure. If he had significant major vessels disrupted in his chest or abdomen, he would have died before getting to Charity. His fast heart rate could be from pain or minor blood loss. But young, healthy people can show great cardiac reserve, so his vital signs don't prove anything conclusive."

"I agree with those statements. Please discuss the importance of the rest of the physical examination."

Dang it! Looks like he's going to quiz me instead of me quizzing him.

Elizabeth continued, "His poor breath sounds on both sides were most likely due to bilateral pneumothoraxes. His trachea was not deviated, so it was doubtful he had a tension pneumothorax. His heart sounds were audible, so cardiac tamponade was unlikely. His abdomen was soft, and there was no tenderness over his liver or spleen. He was transported in a cervical collar and showed no sign of neurological deficits, but we take precautions until we see a normal C-spine film." She paused, then exclaimed, "Oh. I almost forgot! He had crepitation palpable along his right neck and bruising on his right upper chest." She saw Dr. White smile.

Dr. Mattox said, "So I'll summarize, and you correct me where I'm wrong. We have a young man, stable at the scene but impaled on a fence post from being ejected from his vehicle at a high rate of speed. He's in Room Four with a post sticking out of his left upper chest and has little breath sounds on both sides. He also has significant bruising on the opposite chest wall with what is likely air in his tissues in his lower neck. Is that about it?"

Elizabeth nodded and wondered what she had forgotten, but she felt less anxious because she knew they would be quickly getting to the part of the presentation during which she would ask the questions.

"So, Dr. Roberts, what's our trauma algorithm at this point?"

Elizabeth looked out into the crowd while she stalled for time to think. Dr. McSwain and Dr. White stared at her. She had not been present when this patient was brought to the emergency room. All of her information was secondhand. Her mind drifted to the back story on this case. The emergency room that night was manned by a big Texan who came from a long line of trauma surgeons and was confident in his Room Four abilities. His assistant that night was a five-foot–tall, nine-and-one-half-months pregnant nurse who'd worked Room Four under Livvy for five years.

Livvy told her the patient was brought in by EMTs with the fence protruding from his chest, and the intern from Texas had fainted at the sight. His six-foot–four-inch frame was dragged by his cowboy boots into the corner of Room Four by the little pregnant nurse. She told her student nurse, "Call Dr. McSwain and Dr. White and have a student try to wake up our trauma intern. Thank heavens he didn't hit his head. We're too busy for that."

Elizabeth nearly giggled at the memory of Livvy's story, told to her during one of their Café du Monde visits. The intern had recovered quickly and sworn everyone to silence. He wanted a Trauma fellowship with Dr. Mattox more than he wanted a new quarter horse. He talked about how everything was better in the world of trauma west of the Sabine

River. Elizabeth wondered why he wasn't presenting the case. She saw the handsome Texan with his thick handlebar mustache seated in row six of the amphitheater behind Dr. McSwain. She shook her head to clear her mind. Dr. Mattox was staring at her as if she had had a seizure.

"I'm sorry," she said. "I was thinking. In Room Four, we try to decide if it's in the patient's best interest to do something invasive in the emergency room or take the patient straight up to the operating room or get further studies. We had type-specific blood ordered, and his vital signs had been stable for a while, so it seemed the best route was to get more information. We can do a chest X-ray in five minutes from Room Four and the patient doesn't have to be moved, so we did a chest X-ray."

"I agree. We don't want to invoke V.O.M.I.T.," said Dr. Mattox as he turned to the X-ray on the view box. "You know what V.O.M.I.T. stands for, don't you?"

"No, sir," admitted Elizabeth.

Dr. Mattox grinned and said, "It stands for Victim of Modern Imaging Technology. It means don't take the patient to radiology to die instead of going to the operating room. OK. Let's pretend your chief resident, your cardiothoracic fellow, and your Trauma staff are loafing somewhere. You, the surgery intern, are temporarily in charge. Read the film and tell me why we don't get a CAT scan that could give much more information."

"I thought you were supposed to read the film and tell me what it shows," protested Elizabeth. She realized her error at the moment she heard Dr. McSwain loudly clear his throat.

Dr. Mattox spoke. "That's the beauty of surgery!" he exclaimed. "You don't know what's going to happen. You're alone, and the patient's counting on you. You have no backup, and you must decide. Tell me your thought process, Doctor."

Elizabeth turned to the view box, feeling betrayed. Tony hadn't told her she might be the one getting grilled. She pretended the crowd was not there and focused on the film as if the patient's life really did depend on it.

She said, "He has a large foreign body, the fence post, protruding from his left lateral upper chest. On that side, he has a pneumothorax. For the students, a pneumothorax is air trapped between the lung tissue and the chest wall. It can cause lung collapse. On the opposite side, he has multiple broken ribs and another pneumothorax. I see no other bony or soft tissue findings. What I'm able to visualize of his abdomen and cervical spine on the chest X-ray look normal. Our patient has obvious penetrating trauma on his left side and evidence of significant blunt trauma on the right side."

She turned toward Dr. Mattox, searching for clues from his demeanor that she might or might not be on the right path.

He said, "Look more closely at the film. Remember his life depends on you."

She stepped closer to the view box and systematically studied the film. "Ahh," she said. "There's air where it shouldn't be, in the skin and neck tissue on his right. He has subcutaneous air in the skin and around his mediastinum."

"BINGO!" exclaimed Dr. Mattox. "Now we're getting somewhere. The question remains what to do while your superiors are taking their time to get to Room Four. Heck, they're probably having lunch while you struggle to save this man." His smile went all the way to his eyes as he glanced at Dr. McSwain.

"Dr. Mattox, I believe our patient needs bilateral chest tubes placed in the ER. His vascular status is stable for now. The thing most likely to kill him is respiratory distress. We need to get the air out of the pleural spaces so he can fully inflate his lungs."

"OK," said Dr. Mattox. "I'll go along with that move. Let's say the chest tubes were placed without too much trouble. What now?"

Elizabeth shuffled through her stack of X-rays and pulled out the one she'd labeled Post Chest Tube Placement.

Dr. Mattox stepped toward the view box, turning his back to the crowd. After three minutes, he turned to the group and said, "The tubes are in excellent position. But the air in the right pleural space is still there.

I assume you would not show a visiting professor a nonfunctioning chest tube. But if your chest tube is set up properly, I think you have a big air leak on the right. This case is getting interesting."

Elizabeth smiled and nodded to the professor. "What would you do now?"

"Has Dr. McSwain finished his leisurely lunch yet? If he or Dr. White has managed to make it to the emergency room, then I think it's time to take your patient to the operating room. But I'm not finished asking questions yet."

Elizabeth looked at Dr. White. His stare was intense, as if he were trying to send information to her via telepathy.

He looks nervous now too.

She was ready to take her medicine. "Yes, sir."

"What is the differential diagnosis for a persistent large air leak on the right after blunt trauma?" Dr. Mattox asked.

Tony had coached her well on this part, even though she had thought it would be the professor's job to explain it.

"If a properly functioning chest tube can't keep up with removing the air from the chest, there must be a big leak," Elizabeth explained. "There could be an esophageal tear or a large laceration to the lung tissue. Whatever the cause, it's rare. It could be a disrupted right main stem bronchus or an injury to the lower trachea. I see no signs of penetrating trauma on the side opposite the fence post."

Dr. Mattox said, "Your thoughts are good ones. Under what conditions would we open him up, right in the ER? And if we made that choice, what approach would we take and why?"

These are questions for the cardiothoracic fellow, not the intern!

She remembered Dr. McSwain's advice regarding always going back to the anatomy of the body to answer questions of technique. She thought about the details of chest anatomy and said, "Sir, I don't know. But if he's stable, there's really no reason to open his chest in the ER. If he dropped his blood pressure, was not responsive to rigorous fluid resuscitation, and was unstable, we'd consider cracking his chest in Room Four."

Dr. Mattox chuckled, "Cracking his chest? Is that a medical term, Doctor?"

Elizabeth was mortified. "No, sir," she replied. "I'm nervous. We'd consider a median sternotomy in the emergency department."

He said, "We're going to surgery and you're in the elevator. You're planning your case in your mind. I recognize you're an intern and you're not doing this case, but let's pretend for educational purposes that you are the only chance he has. What approach are you using and why?"

Elizabeth felt perspiration running down her neck. Her bra, panties, and pantyhose were stuck to her body. She squirmed but accepted she was the "chump getting stumped." She gave up hope of turning the case explanation over to the professor and took ownership of teaching the students.

"I'd plan to leave the side with the fence post sticking out last. Even though it's the most remarkable finding, it's not causing our patient any immediate distress. When we take it out, we might find major vascular injury, so I'd want to have his lungs and heart functioning as well as possible to handle that stress. I'd address the large air leak on the patient's right side first."

Dr. Mattox said, "Your plan sounds reasonable. What next?"

She said, "Our choices for incision are based on the chest anatomy and what we most think is injured. If we thought he had major vascular injury, we'd go for an anterior thoracotomy. I'm not thinking that at this point. The best approach might be a posterior thoracotomy because the bronchus is posterior. If we need to take out the upper lobe of the lung, it would be the best approach."

She wished she'd studied the operative report more thoroughly. She lamented there was never enough time for all she needed to do. She'd thought Dr. Mattox would be doing all the talking by now. The clock in the back of the amphitheater showed she had ten minutes to go. *No matter what happens, it will be over in ten minutes.*

Elizabeth relaxed a bit, smiled, and asked, “Dr. Mattox, is Dr. White or Dr. McSwain here yet?”

The packed audience burst into uncontrolled laughter, as everyone knew the feeling of waiting for upper-level doctors to show up in a tough situation. Elizabeth could hear Dr. White laughing out loud.

“Nope,” Dr Mattox told her. “They are nowhere to be found, young lady. Lord only knows what they are doing. You have to decide how to position our patient on the operating table. Is there any position that would allow you to take care of all of his possible injuries?”

Once again, Elizabeth felt sweat running down her neck. Her collar was now wet. She had only ever seen any of the incisions she had mentioned in a book. She flashed back to the anatomy of her medical school cadaver, but she could not visualize how all the vital structures could be reached through one incision. She also could not imagine repositioning the patient in the middle of surgery and making another incision if she had been wrong about the injuries. Time seemed to crawl.

“Let me give you a hint. Are there any other tests you could do to get more accurate information about his injuries?” asked Dr. Mattox.

Elizabeth knew CAT scans weren’t readily available at Charity. She also knew the radiology department was not prepared for opening the chest as was routine in Room Four. But she knew a CAT scan might be what he was hinting at.

“If we had a CAT scanner in our trauma area, that would help,” she offered

Dr. Mattox replied, “And if you were Michael DeBakey, that might help too. I’m asking you what is available to you at Charity that might help.”

The audience cackled at the professor’s mention of the most famous heart surgeon at the Houston Medical Center, who was a graduate of Tulane.

Elizabeth’s face flushed. She enjoyed teasing Dr. Mattox but did not enjoy being teased in front of the group.

"Dr. Mattox, I can't think of a thing."

He said, "Dr. McSwain, from Antoine's, is on the phone calling into the OR, and he's screaming, 'Dr. Roberts, do you think it's a tear in his respiratory tract or his esophagus?'"

She felt silly but elated and said, "Oh, my! I forgot about bronchoscopy. We could do bronchoscopy. If the tear was in the right main stem bronchus, we'd move to posterior thoracotomy with confidence. If the bronchoscopy was normal, we'd consider doing an esophagoscopy to look for an esophageal tear."

Dr. Mattox clapped and bowed and said to Elizabeth, "And now your lazy compatriots will swoop in to take all the glory after you have done all the hard work and handed them a rare and exciting case. You did an excellent job, intern. You saved your patient!" He turned to the audience. "For our students, please remember this great case. Your take home points are that the obvious injury is not always the one that will kill your patient. It would have been quite easy to get distracted by the fence post protruding from his chest. Knowledge of anatomy is imperative. Know it well. Your long hours of study are not wasted when your patient needs you most. Remember to do no harm and use all of your available tools. Your patients are counting on you."

The rest of the session wrapped up quickly since their time was up. Elizabeth summarized, "Bronchoscopy revealed a torn main stem bronchus. An upper lobectomy was done, and the bronchus closed. The pneumothorax on the right had resolved. The patient had a team of surgeons working on his left shoulder to remove the fence post. Orthopedics scrubbed in to be sure we did not damage any of the large nerves going to the arm. Dr. White did most of the dissection to be sure the lung was normal and that the major blood vessels were spared. The entire team was amazed to learn the fence post had avoided all major structures. The patient had much soft tissue damage but nothing that wouldn't heal. He was in the ICU for two days and had his chest tubes removed in a week.

He walked out of Charity not remembering anything about the accident three weeks after it happened."

Dr. Mattox said, "Great case. Thanks for having me here today."

The clock showed the hour was up. Her mentors and Livvy were smiling. She had not fainted, and the chump had not been stumped. As she shook his hand, Dr. Mattox said the magic words, "Good job, Dr. Roberts. That case was above the intern level, and you did a good job. Were you there?"

Elizabeth said, "No, sir. I was not there. I was on a different rotation at that time."

He nodded and said, "I see." Dr. McSwain herded Dr. Mattox into the group of waiting colleagues. Dr. McSwain turned to Elizabeth and said, "Dr. Roberts, don't forget to retrieve my car and be at Windsor Court at 7:30 for dinner. After dinner, you'll be his driver." He tossed her his car keys and said, "It's in the Tulane lot by the elevator on the third floor."

Elizabeth glanced at the key and saw the head of a large feline and the word *Jaguar*. She was not a car fan but recognized she'd not be driving a car she knew well. She called after Dr. McSwain, asking, "Sir, what kind of car is it and what color?"

He turned and grinned, "It's a 1972 Jaguar four-door sedan. It's been repainted Tulane Green."

And I have to park that fancy car in the French Quarter at night?

30

Elizabeth located Dr. McSwain's beautiful old Jaguar in the parking lot and drove to her apartment like an eighty-year-old lady on a tractor. She was anxious because she had never driven such an expensive car. It purred like its namesake, and with the tiniest pressure on the accelerator, it lunged forward like a big cat. Cars weren't her thing, but this car drove like a floating cloud. Ray had agreed to open the gate to the porte cochere to allow her to keep the car in their drive until leaving for Windsor Court. Having an elegant car parked beside the antiques store was good for business.

Once in her apartment, Elizabeth lamented her deficient wardrobe. She'd cleaned Aoife's black dress but hadn't returned it. She decided to wear the dress again tonight and vowed to get it cleaned and back to its owner next week. She took a quick cool shower; fearing hot water might induce sleep. Then she arranged her damp hair into a bun at the nape of her neck. She applied mascara and lip gloss and put on her granny's pearls, arranging them to position the worst stains in the back. She still wanted to have the pearls restrung but didn't want to part with them. To Elizabeth, the pearls symbolized the security of home.

Back in the Jaguar, she drove with caution through the French Quarter to the Windsor Court Hotel. Cabs honked at her, attempting to quicken her slow pace. She had no regard for the other drivers' impatience and focused on the preservation of her professor's car.

She drove into the circular brick drive of the hotel. An attendant in a top hat opened her door, put his arm out to assist her from the car, then held out his white-gloved hand for the car key. She froze, realizing she couldn't control what happened to the car for the next several hours. But she couldn't stay with the car, so she handed the key to the attendant and said, "Please take extra care. It belongs to my boss."

He tipped his top hat and said, "Don't worry, miss. I'll put it in the Rolls Royce section."

Elizabeth walked into the lobby, realizing she'd never seen a Rolls Royce, except in a movie.

I really am a hick.

Dr. Mattox stood in the hotel lobby, watching a harpist play. He was wearing the same clothes he'd worn during the afternoon's program, and Elizabeth thought he emanated the peace of a monk. She also knew he must be a man of action. Nobody could run a trauma service and not act decisively. She watched him for a minute, hoping one day she'd be that competent, confident, and kind.

He saw her and made his way over. "Good evening," he said. "Why don't we head up to the dining room? I understand Tulane Surgery has reserved a nice, quiet room for our group's dinner. I love coming to New Orleans because Tulane always feeds its visitors well."

He turned, and they walked toward the elevators. He held the elevator door for her and pushed the button to the third floor. Neither spoke while the elevator ascended.

Elizabeth was stunned by the beauty of the private room. The table setting and candles glowed golden. The back wall was covered in beveled mirrors. Two professional waiters in tuxedos stood at attention beside the table. Drs. McSwain, White, Parker, and LeBlanc chatted while enjoying a drink. They opened their circle to include Elizabeth and Dr. Mattox.

Dr. Mattox addressed Dr. McSwain. "Norman," he asked him, "what are you doing here? This is supposed to be for the residents. Are you a bachelor trying to get a free dinner off the Tulane budget?"

Everyone laughed. Dr. McSwain said, "No, Ken. I'm not trying to crash your party. I came to have a drink and attend to the details of your dinner. I'll be leaving before the gang's seated."

Dr. White asked, "Elizabeth, may I get you a drink?"

It was surreal to have her nemesis treat her so normally in a social setting. Dr. White looked dashing in his royal blue suit. The others' suits likely came off the rack at a chain store, but it was evident Dr. White's was tailored especially for him. Elizabeth thought he looked like British royalty. This was her first departmental dinner with other doctors, and she was the only female. Their lack of formality in using each other's first names was disorienting, but Dr. White's genteel display toward her was the most disorienting of all.

"No, thank you," replied Elizabeth. "I'm not drinking tonight because I'm driving Dr. Mattox."

Dr. White flashed his bright white smile and turned back to his conversation with Dr. McSwain.

When all the residents had arrived and it was time to be seated, Dr. Mattox pulled out Elizabeth's chair and seated her beside him and across from Dr. White. Dr. McSwain waved as he left and said, "Good luck, Ken. Page me if you get in over your head. I might rescue you if the situation sounds entertaining."

Elizabeth was disappointed to be sitting next to the professor. She had spent the entire afternoon being grilled by him and knew she would be driving him around all evening. She had hoped for a relaxing hour of eating and laughing with Tony. Instead, she'd need to be alert under the watchful gaze of Dr. White. She decided to keep quiet and allow Dr. Mattox and Dr. White to converse.

The six delicious courses of the dinner passed with Dr. White and Dr. Mattox talking constantly about chest trauma cases. Elizabeth listened while enjoying the best meal of her life. While she ate, Elizabeth found herself staring at Dr. White's hands. He ate as delicately as he operated. There was no wasted motion.

She had not eaten lamb before, and she enjoyed every bite. The chocolate mousse was delectable, and she fought the urge to moan.

Elizabeth was grateful her granny had stressed the importance of good table manners and had shown her to eat with the proper utensils. Even though their family meals in South Carolina were simple, Granny taught her to use a seafood fork and a dessert spoon, to pace her eating, and to eat with grace. Tonight, Elizabeth forced herself to eat slowly and pause between bites though she was ravenous. Her appetite had become an insatiable monster since coming to Charity. She chuckled as she gazed down the long, elegant table and watched many of her fellow doctors eat like her male cousins—with their elbows on the table, talking with their mouths full, gulping the expensive wine, ordering more than they could comfortably eat.

Elizabeth felt pride to be in the small group with Dr. Mattox, Dr. White, and Tony—people who knew the rules of fine dining. She had been careful to order foods she would be unlikely to spill on her borrowed dress. The dinner took two hours and when the coffee was served, most of the table was tipsy and rowdy. She was grateful she'd had only water.

Dr. White excused himself from the table after he received a page from the Tulane operator, said goodnight to Dr. Mattox, and left. Elizabeth felt a sense of relief until she remembered what was coming next. Dr. Mattox made polite conversation. Elizabeth observed he had only one glass of wine and then asked for coffee. He looked down the table at the assembled residents and seemed resigned to his duties for the rest of the night. He smiled at Elizabeth, folded his napkin, and said, "Shall we proceed?"

Elizabeth thought of her years as a restaurant server and turned to Tony. "What about the bill?" she asked him. "And the tip?"

He laughed and said, "Don't worry. Tulane has an account. It was settled before we arrived. Servers like to work our events because they know the tip will be good. You ready for the Quarter? I'll ride over with you and Dr. Mattox."

They followed several residents, who staggered into the elevator. Michael looked unstable and leaned against the wall. She heard Tony whisper to him, "Man, you'd better slow it down a bit. You've got hours to go, and you're pretty sauced."

Michael said, louder than necessary, "Mind your own business. You're not my daddy, island man. I can't wait to see the look on that prude Elizabeth's face when the dancers start shaking their stuff right in her face."

Dr. Mattox turned to the elevator doors and pretended not to hear. Elizabeth's face flushed and her fists clenched. They waited in line for the Jaguar, and when the car came, Dr. Mattox took the passenger seat and Tony slid into the back seat. Elizabeth drove carefully. The closer they got to Bourbon Street, the louder the noise and music became. Elizabeth stopped the car at the corner of Bourbon and St. Louis. Dr. Mattox got out and stood under the giant poster of Miss Chris Owens. As Tony scrambled out behind him, Dr. Mattox said, "Son, I'd prefer if you stay with her while she parks the car and walk her back. I'll wait here until the guys appear."

Elizabeth was grateful for his gentlemanly behavior. Tony settled into the passenger seat, and she drove away.

She asked, "Where should I park?"

"Dr. McSwain's house is at the end of Bourbon. Let's leave the car there. It's only eight blocks back to the club. You gonna be OK with all this?"

Hearing his island patois soothed her jangled nerves. "We'll see," she replied. "It can't be much worse than gynecology clinic with music."

"You always make silly jokes when you're nervous," Tony reminded her. "I'm asking a serious question. I can drop you at your apartment on Royal, and nobody will think badly of you."

Elizabeth locked the Jaguar, put the keys in her purse, and turned to Tony. "A few days ago, you said it would be best for me to be part of the group. You're the one who said I should buck up and participate. I'm doing what you suggested."

He looked down at the sidewalk, shuffled his big feet, stepped closer to her, and looked into her eyes. "Elizabeth," he began, "I know we're colleagues. But I see you as a little sister. I feel protective. I wanted to slug Michael when he disrespected you in the elevator. Honestly, I don't know what the best thing for you to do is. I want you to be accepted as part of the group, but I don't want you to suffer the foolishness I know some of these clowns are capable of giving out. I truly don't know what's best."

She put her arm through his as they walked in the direction of the club. "Knowing you care about my feelings gives me strength," she told him. "I'm tougher than I look. One of my cousins sealed me in a cardboard box with a green snake and pushed me down a flight of stairs when I was six. This can't be worse than having a snake fall all over me as I tumbled down the stairs." She smiled. "Besides, if it gets to be too much, I'll say good night to Dr. Mattox and signal you to walk me home. You can drive our professor back to his hotel. Let's just see how it goes."

31

Elizabeth and Tony walked the residential lower half of Bourbon Street back to where they had left Dr. Mattox. The houses were stately, and scents of tea olive and jasmine poured from the gardens. Compared to the homes on St. Charles Avenue, they were not as well maintained, but they offered profound contrast to the loud music, smells of alcohol and urine, and screaming crowds crawling down the other end of the street toward Esplanade. Elizabeth wondered how Bourbon Street, the most infamous street in America, known for its unbridled debauchery, ended in a pretty residential area shaded with oak trees and Spanish moss. The Canal side of Bourbon Street always felt on the verge of violence as the sweaty, alcohol-drenched crowds bumped and swayed. One wrong bump and a fight could break out. The Esplanade end of Bourbon was a quiet place where you could string a hammock in your garden and take a nap.

Elizabeth and Tony wound their way through drunken revelers and past the hawkers that leaned from every door hailing passersby. Chris Owens's club was classy compared to the other businesses that made Bourbon Street their home. There were no men screaming from the doorway. Tony held the door, and Elizabeth stepped into the club's interior, which was dark, except for a bright twirling disco ball. The two found their group and chose seats at the end of their front row table as far away from Michael LeBlanc as possible. Dr. Mattox was seated in the middle of the group. He didn't notice their arrival because his eyes were glued to the band on the stage.

Elizabeth looked around the room and was surprised to see many nicely dressed couples and several men in business suits. The crazy Bourbon Street crowd wasn't here. A band on stage played cover songs from the late seventies. There were no scantily clad dancers to be seen.

She followed Tony's stare to a beautiful Black woman sitting at a counter along the wall behind them. Tony wasn't a man who usually gawked at women, but this time, he couldn't pull his gaze away. The woman smiled, lifted her glass to him, and tugged the hem of her wrap dress a small way up her toned thigh.

Oh, no! Looks like I might be losing my protector tonight.

She poked Tony in the ribs and said, "Your jaw's hanging open, and you're drooling. Don't be so obvious."

He forced himself to turn around, laughed, and said, "I'm going to marry that woman. I'm asking her tonight. A woman like that won't be on the market long."

"How many drinks have you had tonight?" Elizabeth asked him.

"Enough to give me false courage," was his reply.

Suddenly the music tempo quickened and blared. The crowd rose to their feet and clapped like thunder. A striking woman with long, jet-black hair, dressed in sequins from head to toe, and with angel wings on her shoulders took the stage. She had the longest legs Elizabeth had ever seen, and she bowed gracefully in her sequined stilettos as she was handed a sequined microphone. In a smoky voice, she said, "Welcome to my show. I'm Chris Owens. I'm glad to see all of you, and tonight we'll have some fun."

She jumped into a series of show tunes. Her voice was sturdy and melodic, and the band was good. She had large breasts and white teeth, and her shiny outfit was no more risqué than a low-cut bathing suit. She moved with grace and poise and seemed to connect to each audience member. Three giant muscular men stood near the stage, watching the crowd. Miss Owens bowed and winked to several audience members Elizabeth thought might be regulars. Elizabeth could feel herself relax. *This will be OK.*

After several songs and another round of drinks, the Tulane residents got more engaged with the show. Michael stood and wolf-whistled after every song. Miss Owens ignored the rowdiest audience members. Her guards did not, as their heads swiveled like secret service agents, surveying the crowd. After the third song, Tony joined the beauty in the back. He took his drink with him and didn't say goodbye. Elizabeth was anxious about losing her backup plan.

The music was too loud and the crowd too chatty for normal conversation. Elizabeth was relieved because she didn't have much to say. Her energy went toward trying to stay awake while drinking lots of water. If she hadn't been so tired, she would have enjoyed the show.

After a short intermission, Miss Owens returned. She looked down from the stage at their group and said, "Tonight we have some very special guests. A group of young surgeons from Tulane are here with their visiting professor, who I understand is quite a big-shot, famous trauma doctor from Texas. I'm happy to see a woman surgeon in the group tonight as well. Don't tell LSU, but Tulane trains some of the best doctors around. Let's give them a big hand."

Most of the audience cheered loudly. A few die-hard LSU fans booed without much enthusiasm. Miss Owens continued, "My neighbor, Dr. Norman McSwain, asked me to bring his good buddy, Dr. Mattox, up on stage for my next number. He told me the doctor loves to dance." She leaned down, displaying her deep cleavage, and beckoned the visiting professor onto the stage. Dr. Mattox's face was bright red, but he forced a big smile as he waved at the crowd and ascended the steps.

Elizabeth was mortified. She knew this must be a nightmare for Dr. Mattox. She wondered how he'd pay back Dr. McSwain for this special moment. The young doctors howled and clapped. Elizabeth crossed her fingers under the table and hoped it would end quickly.

Miss Owens put her arm around Dr. Mattox and launched into a loud rendition of "Proud Mary." She rhythmically bumped her hip into Dr. Mattox's, causing him to sway with the music. She pranced and sang and gyrated her hips toward the professor, while he smiled and tolerated the performance, though he looked very stiff compared to the star. Elizabeth thought the song seemed to go on forever.

Michael slurred his words as he screamed and danced beside his chair. He was unbalanced and bumped into everyone within a foot of him. Tony turned his attention away from his beauty and stared agape when he realized what was happening on stage and at the residents' table.

At the end of the song, Dr. Mattox was assisted off the stage by Miss Owens's guards. She smiled and said, "Thanks for tolerating a big welcome, New Orleans style."

Dr. Mattox looked relieved and made his way back to his seat. He ordered a double bourbon with no ice and seemed to relax, knowing he'd withstood the worst. Elizabeth wondered why this kind of thing was so important to the other residents. As she glanced down the table, she had to admit, she'd not seen her team happier. Whatever male bonding was, it seemed to have happened here.

When her attention came back to Miss Owens and the show on stage, Elizabeth was sure the entertainer looked at her and winked. *Maybe female bonding happens too?*

At midnight, Dr. Mattox left his seat and went to the restroom. On his way back, he leaned over and said to Elizabeth, "I think it's time for me to return to the hotel. Are you ready to go?"

Elizabeth was. She grabbed her purse, jumped up from her chair, and said, "Yes, sir. I'm ready to go, but first, let me speak with Dr. Parker. I want to be certain he has a ride."

Dr. Mattox looked at Tony, who was kissing his new acquaintance with enthusiasm. "I suspect he has a ride," he told Elizabeth. "I'll say goodnight to the group and meet you on the sidewalk."

Elizabeth was sober but felt wobbly in her high-heeled sandals. She'd been sitting for hours, and she wasn't used to sitting so much. Her legs were asleep, and she stumbled as she approached Tony. His lady friend saw her and caught Elizabeth's arm to stabilize her. Elizabeth thought the woman's dark skin felt as soft as butter, and she was surprised by her strength. *In this dark room, she looks like Diana Ross.*

Tony smiled a goofy, lopsided grin. "Are you leaving with me?" Elizabeth asked him.

"I'd like to stay. Are you OK walking the few blocks to get the car with Dr. Mattox? If you park in your driveway after you drop him at Windsor Court, you'll be safe."

"OK. See you tomorrow for rounds."

"Actually, rounds are today," Tony reminded her. "It's after midnight, and we have to be there by five."

Elizabeth smiled at Tony's new friend, waved to the other residents, and left.

Dr. Mattox stood waiting on the sidewalk, watching the crowd of drunken humanity staggering by in waves. "I can't say that I understand this behavior," he said. "I like to have as good a time as the next guy, but getting so drunk I can't walk and weaving up and down Bourbon Street has never appealed to me. I appreciate your driving me, Dr. Roberts. But how will you get home since your accomplice has deserted you?"

"Tony's the best. He always helps me," Elizabeth replied in Tony's defense. "After I drop you at the hotel, I only have to drive a few blocks to reach my apartment. I can park in the driveway, and from there, it's only three feet to my locked iron gate. I'll be fine, but thanks for being concerned."

They walked the eight blocks to Dr. McSwain's house in silence. When they reached the car, Elizabeth walked around the Jaguar to confirm there was no damage. The night was finally almost over. Dr. Mattox sighed and settled into the plush leather. She thought he seemed as relieved as she did.

She was surprised to find the roads were full of cars and partiers so late. They crept along the street, avoiding the drunken crowd and swerving cars. Most people out at this time of night had imbibed. Dr. Mattox watched the crowd but was quiet.

As they passed Jackson Square, Elizabeth remarked she thought it was pretty at night. Folks were crossing the street without looking on their way to Café du Monde. At the corner of St. Louis, she saw a cab near the curb, picking up two passengers. As she got closer, she saw it was Tony and his new woman friend, arm in arm.

Dr. Mattox chuckled, "It looks like your buddy got a ride after all."

Elizabeth worried Tony might not make five o'clock rounds. She had never known him to be late and couldn't imagine him picking up a woman in a bar and going home with her. *Maybe I am the prude Michael claims I am.*

Traffic crept while Elizabeth watched Tony and his new woman kiss and grab at each other in their cab, which had pulled out in front of the Jaguar. Her face reddened, and she felt heat rising in her chest. Dr. Mattox turned his gaze ninety degrees to look out the passenger side window to give the lusty pair privacy. Traffic was at a standstill. After stopping for what seemed a long time to Elizabeth, the cab door flew open, and Tony forcibly tossed his companion out of the cab and onto the sidewalk.

His companion grabbed her purse from the sidewalk and picked up her stiletto that was dangling on the curb. She pulled up the skirt of her wrap dress and ran down the sidewalk, darting deep into the darkness of the French Quarter.

Elizabeth heard Tony howl, "HOW DARE YOU? HOW DARE YOU?"

This Tony bore no resemblance to the man she knew. He looked violent and crazy and drunk.

The cab driver jumped out of the car and yelled at Tony, "Hey man, how about my fare?" Tony pulled his wallet from his back pocket and tossed a pile of crumpled bills at the taxi driver. Elizabeth was frozen. She watched as Tony repetitively wiped his mouth on his coat sleeve, then he bent over and threw up on the sidewalk. He staggered, trying to stay upright. Elizabeth and Dr. Mattox realized Tony hadn't noticed them.

"Dr. Roberts, pull over and let's get him in the car," Dr. Mattox said. "He could be rolled for pulling out his wallet, flashing cash in his drunken state in the Quarter at this hour. If you feel uncomfortable, I'll ride with you to drop him off at his home."

Elizabeth couldn't think. She felt confused. *Is Tony a violent drunk?* She remembered she didn't know where he lived.

She pulled over to the sidewalk as Tony stood up from vomiting. Dr. Mattox rolled down his window and said, "Son, why don't you get in the back seat and let us drive you home?"

Tony reeled around to see who was speaking to him. For a moment, he stood in the middle of the sidewalk, looking confused. Then he staggered a bit, got his bearings, and said, "Yes, sir. That sounds like a plan." He jerked open the back door, got in, and slumped in the back seat.

Elizabeth pulled away from the curb and said, "Tony, roll down your window and hang your head out in case you have to throw up again. I don't want your vomit in Dr. McSwain's car." Her voice sounded cold to her.

He followed instructions. Elizabeth heard him groaning, but nothing else came up.

Dr. Mattox said, "Son, why don't you tell us where you live, and we'll drop you off?"

Tony said, "I'm OK to go with Elizabeth. I can go with her to her apartment and walk to the on-call room from there. I have to be in the pediatric ICU with Dr. White in exactly four hours. I don't have time to go home, Dr. Mattox." Tony sounded dejected.

Dr. Mattox looked at Elizabeth and mouthed the words, "You OK with that plan?"

Elizabeth was pleased to see Tony had left his violence on the sidewalk. "Yes, sir," Elizabeth told Dr. Mattox. "We'll drop you off at your hotel, and I'll head home. Thanks."

At the hotel, Dr. Mattox thanked them for a memorable evening and got out.

Elizabeth hadn't pulled out of the hotel parking lot before she heard a sob from the back seat. Tony was crying. He repeated over and over, "How could I be so stupid?"

Elizabeth couldn't imagine how he could be so upset over an encounter with someone he met a few hours ago. Yes, she was beautiful, but not worth sobbing over. *Could he be one of those violent drunks who cries with remorse afterward?*

Elizabeth decided to ignore the sobs. She said, "I'll drop you at Charity. I don't want you walking through the Quarter at this hour."

Tony continued to sob. Elizabeth was impatient. She'd not as yet cried like that over anyone. Tony wiped his mouth on his sleeve as if he could wipe away the kisses of his temporary paramour.

Elizabeth looked at him through the rearview mirror and asked, "What happened tonight?"

Tony screamed from the back seat, "SHE was a HE, Elizabeth! I sat kissing a man the whole night. I was halfway in love and on my way to the altar with a freakin' man. And if that wasn't bad enough, his erection was bigger than mine! I nearly had a heart attack when my hand touched it."

Elizabeth pulled into a parking space on Canal Street and took a few deep breaths while Tony continued to sob in the back seat. Eventually, he calmed down, and she pulled into traffic and dropped him in front of Charity.

His last words as he exited the Jaguar were, "Please don't ever tell anyone about this."

"Don't worry," she told him. "I'll never tell a soul."

32

The next morning, everyone looked exhausted except Dr. White and Sallie. Tony made no eye contact and kept his hangdog countenance throughout rounds. Shame chastened him.

Dr. White asked, "How was your evening, Dr. Mattox?"

The professor wore the same brown suit with a new starched white shirt and a different tie. To Elizabeth, he looked well rested, though she knew he had gotten little sleep. "It was great," Dr. Mattox replied. "You should have joined us."

"Somebody had to mind the shop," said Dr. White. "I had six years of going to the Quarter with the gang. That was enough for me. I'm such a stick in the mud that I leave town before Fat Tuesday. I go to Rex with my family, but otherwise, I go skiing in Vail when the town gets wild."

What's Rex? Elizabeth realized she couldn't picture Vail, either. Dr. White was casual about both, as if everyone was familiar with Rex and Vail.

Today, Tony didn't present the patients in the pediatric ICU. Dr. White reported the more interesting cases. Dr. Mattox's specialty was trauma, so he didn't bore him with details of children's heart surgeries. Rounds were quick. Dr. White looked at Tony and whispered, "Eat something greasy, drink a liter of water, and go to the call room. Everything's quiet. I'll cover you till noon."

Tony looked startled but grateful. He hurried away.

Dr. White delivered Dr. Mattox to Dr. McSwain's office at the medical school across the street from Mother Charity. Elizabeth returned to the adult cardiac ICU and was grateful it was quiet. She sat in the nurses' station and read her surgery textbook. She was interrupted when the door swung open and Livvy barged in.

Livvy smirked after looking around to be sure they were alone. "How'd it go last night?" she asked. "Anything interesting happen, Crème Puff?"

Elizabeth slapped her textbook shut and glared at her. "Don't you have work to do?"

Livvy pulled out a chair and sat across from her. "My shift starts in an hour and besides, Dr. McSwain's driving Dr. Mattox to the airport, and it's quiet in the ER. I have time to hear all about your adventure."

Elizabeth looked into Livvy's mischievous eyes and knew she'd not be able to get back to studying until Livvy's curiosity was satisfied. "It was fine. Dinner was amazing, and the show was good. I'd not choose it as my favorite entertainment, but it was really not a problem."

"Don't lie! You look away when you lie. You're the worst liar I've ever seen. Dr. Mattox told Dr. McSwain, and Dr. McSwain told me. But I want to hear it from you, Crème Puff." Livvy slapped her palm on the Formica table for emphasis.

Elizabeth folded her hands in front of her on the table, stared into Livvy's eyes, and said, "I'm not stoking the hospital gossip mill, and I'm mad that Dr. McSwain told you. If you say anything to Tony, I'll never talk to you again. I know you live to jab the doctors, but please leave this one alone. Tony deserves our loyalty." She wasn't surprised Dr. Mattox had figured out what had happened. She was grateful he didn't know the full extent of Tony's disaster.

"Oh, girl! You're the worst killjoy ever! New Orleans is full of gorgeous drag queens, transvestites, and people who are a little of this and a little of that. Nobody cares! And this may shock your little South Carolina morals, but it's not unusual for folks to pick up other folks and not know what the package holds till a little later. This is funny as anything else, not something to get so worked up about. You need to loosen up!"

Elizabeth was angry. *She can goad me all she wants. I told Tony I'd not talk about it, and she can't make me.* After a few minutes of staring at each other, Elizabeth said, "Livvy, I have no idea what you're talking about." She stood up and walked out.

Livvy followed her into the ICU. "Tell me or I'm going to ask him."

Elizabeth recognized the statement for the threat it was and replied, "Don't you dare. I mean it, Livvy. He's upset. He knows he made a big mistake in front of a world-famous surgeon. Don't poke this tender spot. Please. He's not laughing about it, and I'm his friend, so I'm not laughing either. Now leave me alone and let me do my work."

Livvy headed for the door and said in passing, "Soon you're back on *my* service in the ER. You'd better remember who your friends are, Crème Puff."

Elizabeth knew Livvy was her friend, and she didn't take her threatening tone seriously. She knew Livvy would help her if she needed help. She also knew Livvy had affection and respect for Tony and wondered why Livvy took such pleasure in the hospital gossip mill. She also wondered why teasing the young doctors gave the nurse such pleasure.

The next three weeks of the cardiothoracic rotation sped by. Tony was subdued. Their jobs became routine; Dr. White operated around the clock. Elizabeth stayed in the nurses' station, studying when she wasn't rounding on the patients. She'd dreaded being on cardiothoracic surgery, but the time sped by. She had learned much—as much from the nurses as she had the doctors—and would miss the ICU staff.

She'd enjoyed having lunch with Jan. Jan's external transformation from Joe was now complete. Elizabeth wondered about Jan's life but was grateful her life was simpler. Elizabeth enjoyed the affection she'd developed for the nurses and for Jan. She knew she'd be less nervous if she rotated back on the service in future years. Somewhere in the middle of this rotation, she'd stopped being terrified. She chuckled to herself. *You can only be just so scared. After a while, your nervous system isn't capable of an adrenaline rush, and you become numb.*

After the last evening rounds of the rotation, Dr. White thanked the team. He told Tony he should consider cardiothoracic surgery as a career.

Then he told Sallie that he'd be willing to write her a letter of recommendation if she insisted on being a gynecologist. He looked at Elizabeth and said, "Dr. Roberts, I appreciate your hard work."

Elizabeth considered his comment a veiled criticism. He didn't invite her back. He didn't suggest she be a heart surgeon. And he didn't offer a letter of recommendation. She thanked him, nonetheless, for teaching her. She wanted his approval and was stung by not getting it, but she realized Tony had been right. She'd learned more from Dr. White than she had from any doctor she'd ever encountered. So she'd have to be satisfied with that.

She thanked Jan and the nurses and wrote detailed notes about the current patients to the next intern, even though she'd heard it would be Michael LeBlanc. She felt sorry for the nurses, as Michael's reputation was fully established as the biggest slacker of her intern year. Despite her distaste for him, she wrote careful notes and planned an informative check-out process.

Dr. White stuck his head in the door of the nurses' station and said, "Dr. LeBlanc's running late for checkout. He called to say he'd be here in a half-hour."

Of course, he's late. He's always late.

Dr. White stepped into the room and closed the door behind him. Elizabeth's pulse raced. She wondered what was coming. She put aside her notes and gave him her full attention. Much to her surprise, he looked nervous.

He pulled out the chair across from her and sat down, bumping her knees under the table. He quickly slid his chair back six inches, and said, "Sorry." The man looked shy and younger. She caught a glimpse of the tow-headed little boy he used to be.

He folded his long pale fingers on the table and said, "I checked the calendar in the resident office at the medical school and found you don't rotate onto cardiothoracic surgery again until after I've finished my fellowship."

Elizabeth's heart rate climbed. *Why is he checking my schedule? Did I do such a bad job that he's hoping he doesn't have to work with me again? What is this about?*

He said, "It's inappropriate for fellows to date students or interns, since the fellow is their boss. But since I won't be in that capacity with you any longer, I was wondering if you'd like to get a hamburger and beer with me after work tonight?"

If the floor had opened and she had fallen to China, Elizabeth could not have been more shocked. She felt dizzy and disoriented. She shook her head, blinked a few times, and wondered if she had heard correctly. She was prepared for a poor performance evaluation but unprepared for his offer of friendship or whatever it was he was offering.

He looks afraid. Her good manners on autopilot, she heard herself say, "That would be fine. Unfortunately, I have no other clothes with me at the hospital."

He smiled and said, "That's not a problem. My favorite burger joint is Audubon Tavern, and people go there dressed in every way imaginable. You're unlikely to be the only one in scrubs. The diners are often runners in tennis shoes and running clothes, sweaty from jogging around Audubon Park."

He stood up, smiled, pushed his chair under the table, and said, "I'll see you in about an hour. I'll meet you here, and we'll head over to the tavern. I look forward to it."

What have I agreed to do? It almost sounds like the man is asking me on a date. Surely not?

Elizabeth fumbled with the notes she was preparing for Dr. LeBlanc, unable to concentrate. One moment, she felt excited, and the next, she felt worried and confused. She hated having dirty hair and wearing wrinkled scrubs. Even if it wasn't a date, she didn't like to go to new places looking shabby.

She checked out the patients to Michael then washed her face in the bathroom and combed her greasy blonde hair into a neat ponytail. She inspected her scrubs for body fluids and chuckled at her big boxy white underwear. She waited in the nurses' lounge and tried to study. Dr. White reappeared dressed in clean, pressed khaki pants and a polo shirt. He looked relaxed and handsome. *We'll probably look like the rich uptown guy taking his gardener out for a burger.*

Dr. White held the door for her. They walked in silence to the parking lot. Elizabeth tried not to fidget. She could not transition her thoughts from the image of the Dr. White who'd been her nemesis for seven months to the man walking beside her. She took a few steadying breaths and got a whiff of his cologne. It smelled light and musky and rich. She wondered if she smelled like a goat.

They reached his car. *Of course, it's a fast red sports car! How could it be anything else? Tulane surgeons like to drive fast.*

The leather seats smelled of saddle soap. She saw the 450SL C across the back trunk. She wondered what the letters and numbers meant. Her old Toyota just said *TOYOTA*—no numbers, no letters.

Dr. White drove from the lot and turned left on Poydras Street. Elizabeth could think of nothing to say. She had spent almost all of her time in New Orleans around Charity Hospital and the French Quarter. Her sense of direction was poor, but she thought they were moving away from the Quarter.

After five minutes of quiet, Dr. White said, "I imagine as a surgery intern, you've had little time to learn your way around the city."

Elizabeth's mouth was dry. Her lips stuck to her teeth. She looked straight ahead and nodded.

"I'm taking you up Tchoupitoulas Street into uptown. We're headed toward Audubon Park. The Tulane undergraduate schools are in what I think is the most beautiful part of New Orleans."

Elizabeth noticed their current street was mostly lined with warehouses and commercial buildings. Her only other drive uptown had been up St. Charles Avenue, in a different sports car, with a different handsome man to a disastrous date last fall. *Well, this can't be as bad as my date to*

Commander's Palace. I'm so afraid of Dr. White that I'm unlikely to fall asleep in my burger like I did in that crab remoulade.

They were quiet. He took a right on Webster and parked beside a shack with uncut grass on the side and a roof that looked like it might fall in at any moment. Elizabeth felt better, sensing she might not be dressed inappropriately after all.

"It doesn't look like much," said Dr. White, "but I promise you the best burgers and fries in town are found at Audubon Tavern."

She followed him across the street, stepped through the rickety door he held open for her, and entered a dark, smelly, low-ceilinged bar. The cracked concrete floor was uneven, and the tables looked sticky. *Perhaps they keep it dark so nobody can see the filth.* At the back of the room was a counter with a place to order food. There were no menus or signs displaying the food choices. *If you don't know what you want, you probably don't belong here.*

Dr. White picked a table near the wall and asked if it was OK with her. She nodded, put her purse on the chair, and followed him to the back counter.

"I'm so sorry," he said apologetically. "I didn't ask you if you eat hamburgers and fries. I should have asked before bringing you here." Again, he sounded nervous.

Elizabeth said, "I eat everything. I love hamburgers and fries." She couldn't imagine anyone who didn't eat hamburgers and fries.

He flashed a big smile and said, "The burgers are on fresh-baked buttered brioche buns. The fries come covered in chili and cheese and onions. Tell them what you want."

She looked at the clerk and said, "Cheeseburger with Duke's mayo, please."

Dr. White flinched. He whispered in her ear, "In New Orleans, we only use Blue Plate mayonnaise."

But of course! New Orleans is the food snob capital of America. How could I hope to order correctly in this town, even in a burger joint?

"No problem. Whatever usually comes on it is fine."

"What do you like on your fries?" asked Dr. White.

She refused to admit she hadn't eaten anything on fries but ketchup. "Get whatever you usually order, and we'll share."

Next, they stopped at the bar. He said, "What would you like to drink?"

She took the safe route and said, "How about something local? What do the locals drink?"

He ordered two Abita beers. Elizabeth remembered her Cajun patients, the Benoits, and smiled to herself. She turned away from the bar while they waited and was surprised to see a table of people from Charity. Her friend Aoife was there with several LSU doctors Elizabeth recognized from the ER. Aoife grinned and waved. Dr. White didn't see them.

Elizabeth felt panic, knowing Livvy would know of her "date" probably before she got home.

She followed Dr. White back to their table. He placed their beers on the table and pulled out her chair for her. It felt weird to be sitting in a dark bar in her scrubs with him. She felt like a fish in an aquarium because everyone at Aoife's table gaped in their direction. Dr. White's chair faced away from the medical group, so he was unaware of their fascinated audience.

He took a sip of his beer from the bottle and said, "I'm a little nervous," he began. "I'm sorry; I forgot to ask you if you preferred a glass with your beer."

She nodded yes. He jumped up and headed back to the bar, returning with a big, frosty mug. He seemed eager to please her, just like men on other dates she'd had.

Elizabeth vowed to sip her beer slowly. Dr. White finished his before the burgers came, and he ordered another. Elizabeth noticed all the workers in the tavern knew him.

They remained quiet and uncomfortable. The food came quickly. Elizabeth was relieved. She didn't know if it was the effect of the beer or having food on which to focus and not having the pressure to talk, but she relaxed.

Dr. White wiped his mouth between bites and paused to make conversation. Elizabeth stared at the big pile of fries covered in thick chili and piled with freshly cut onions. *This can't be a date. Nobody eats piles of onions on a date.*

Suddenly she remembered a question she wanted to ask and blurted out, "What's Rex? You mentioned it to Dr. Mattox."

He stopped with his mouth open and his burger halfway to his face. His arm froze in midair. He sat back in his chair, put his food down, gulped, and said, "Sometimes I forget people not from New Orleans are not used to our crazy world. New Orleans is unlike any city in America. We live for the next celebration. If there's no universally recognized holiday on the calendar, we'll make one up. I've lived my whole life here, and I forget that sometimes, the rest of the world doesn't spend millions of dollars tossing plastic beads into the streets instead of fully funding their schools."

What does throwing plastic have to do with schools?

After she didn't ask any other questions, he continued. "Rex is a social club that hosts a formal ball every year at Mardi Gras time. It's been around since 1872, and my family has always participated. Rex is called a Mardi Gras Krewe. We have a parade and ball and do some philanthropic work. Our floats are handmade. My daddy and granddaddy were Rex in the past."

He seemed proud of his lineage. She had no idea what he was describing. She knew part of the Mardi Gras celebration included parades during the month leading up to it. She'd heard there were balls associated with Mardi Gras, but that was the extent of her knowledge. So she thought it best to remain quiet and let him explain.

"That blank look on your face reminds me of how you look when I ask you questions above your intern level. You look beautiful, even if you're stymied. Think about it like this: Remember when you came out?

Remember shopping for that perfect dress and planning every aspect of the ball you'd attend? It's like that, except we do it every year, and it also has a parade attached."

Panic set in. *Oh, no! He thinks I'm some high society girl. This is horrible. Should I tell him my coming out occurred between the pigpen and the cow pasture? If I do, this will be painful but over quickly.*

Her face turned scarlet, and she fought back tears of embarrassment. He looked puzzled.

She put her hamburger down, took a big sip of her beer, and said, "My family isn't Charleston society. We're farm people. I've never been to a debutante party, and I don't know anybody who has."

He looked confused. "You weren't a debutante?"

She suppressed a near-hysterical laugh and sighed as he looked down at his burger.

"Ah, no. I'm from a different world. My family has the skills required for survival on the land. Coming out is not for our type of folks. I'm sorry to disappoint you, Dr. White."

She was angry at herself for feeling ashamed. Her people were honorable. They had high morals and always did their duty to God and their country. How dare she feel shame?

He took her hand under the table and said, "Please, call me Harrison. I'm very interested in you, Elizabeth. The world of Mardi Gras and balls and parades is silly and superficial. I'm fascinated by your world and how it produced such a forthright, strong, intelligent, determined, and beautiful young woman. I could care less if you had a coming out party. I've lived a spoiled and sheltered life in New Orleans as the son of a family that includes a long line of bank presidents. I don't look down on you. You amaze me."

Upon hearing this, Elizabeth started to cry. Out of the corner of one bleary eye, she saw Aoife staring open-mouthed. She used her napkin to staunch the flow of salty tears down her cheeks. He let go of her hand and patted her knee.

"Maybe we can figure out how to get you to a Mardi Gras event this year. We've only a few short weeks till the ball, but maybe we can think of something."

They changed the subject to medicine, finished their burgers and fries, and got up to leave. She noticed he left a large cash tip on the table. They exited the dark bar, and Elizabeth was grateful it was dark outside. She wanted to melt into the car and avoid scrutiny. Both were quiet on the drive back to the Quarter. Her stomach was full and fatigue took over. She'd been anxious most of the time they were together and felt relief at the prospect of being home alone in her cozy apartment.

When they arrived, he turned into the porte cochere, ran around to her side of the car, and opened the door for her. He extended his hand to help her up from the low-slung vehicle. He pulled her to him and kissed her forehead, and he held her there for a few seconds before saying, "Please call me Harrison if we're not at the hospital, and, yes, Elizabeth, this was our first date."

Elizabeth felt dizzy. His smell, his hot hands, and his body's close proximity overwhelmed her senses. She fumbled for her keys. He took them from her, opened and held the gate for her, and handed the keys through the iron posts, saying, "Good night, and I look forward to next time."

She mumbled, "Thank you," and ran up the stairs to safety.

33

That night, Elizabeth tossed for hours, sleepless and agitated. Eventually, she abandoned sleep and threw on clean scrubs. She walked the streets of the French Quarter, avoiding The Big Free and Livvy the inquisitor. She thought last night might have been a dream and vowed to have no expectations. Dr. White had probably realized by this morning that he didn't need to settle for a country hick. Many uptown girls were probably in love with him and then, well, there was Rose.

She walked through the back door of the emergency room at six-fifteen in the morning to start her new month's rotation. The halls were packed, and the noise level was high. She felt at home. She felt needed. For the charity patients, it was the last house on the block. Nobody came here unless they desperately needed medical care. She was proud to be part of the team that met that need.

Livvy looked up from the nurses' station and pretended she didn't see Elizabeth. Elizabeth found the LSU Surgery charge resident from the last twenty-four-hour shift and approached him. "How's it going?" she asked. "I'm assigned here this month for Tulane days. I've met you before, but I'm sorry . . . I can't remember your name. I'm Elizabeth Roberts."

"I'm John Michaud," he replied. "I can't wait to get out of this hole. It's been completely nuts down here for a week. I want to check out before another disaster shows up. You look pretty clean for an intern. Your scrubs have no bloodstains."

Elizabeth smiled and followed the lanky blond. His glazed eyes and shuffling gait exposed his exhaustion. She said, "I just finished my cardiothoracic surgery rotation."

With her comment, he spun around. "Good night," he said. "You spent a month with Dr. White and lived? That must've been a bit better than facing a firing squad every day. Around shift change, he appears and checks on every chest case, whether it's LSU or Tulane. He's one scary, intense dude. If he was LSU, we'd have smothered him in his call room in his sleep. I hear he's the best surgeon in the system and has a photographic memory. But that level of intensity? Just not worth it."

Elizabeth laughed. *It had been worth it—every knee-shaking moment. I'll forever be a better surgeon for working with him.*

"He's a good teacher," Elizabeth said. "It was intense, yes, but I'm glad I did the rotation. Anybody need to go to the OR down here?"

Dr. Michaud said, "One guy has a swollen hand that might need to be surgically drained. He's a Tulane patient and had both a burn and a cat bite to the area. It's a crazy story, and he's a hot Cajun mess. The LSU guy on call for hands refused to see him because he has a Tulane number. He's in Room Ten waiting for it to be a Tulane day. I'll show you, and you can decide."

Elizabeth knew taking a patient as a holdover from the night before was against the rules. If the patient came in before turnover time at seven in the morning, the last team on call was supposed to take care of the patient. But Dr. Michaud was spent. She'd let it pass this time and hope her chief didn't notice. She pushed open the door and was not surprised to see Mr. Leeodus Benoit. He was without his wife but wore his trademark cowboy hat and boots. His hand was swollen to twice its normal size and red streaks went up his arm. *Cellulitis, for sure.*

Mr. Benoit looked up and said, "Dang, cher! You get around. I'm glad to see you. I told this buddy of yours that I need intravenous antibiotics. Mellette and I've tried everything else. Also, I think there's some pus down deep in this thing. My fingers won't move right and are numb, Doc."

Elizabeth pulled on gloves and took his hand. *He's diagnosed himself well.* "Mr. Benoit, didn't I see you at the Tulane emergency room the last time? Why didn't you go there? If I remember correctly, you have good insurance."

Mr. Benoit rubbed his swollen hand and said, "Well, Doc, it's like this. I'm scared. I need this hand to do my work and take care of my life. Everybody knows if the president of the United States got shot in New Orleans, Louisiana, he'd be brought to Charity. I figure if I got something serious going on, why wouldn't I go where they'd take the president?"

She couldn't argue with his logic. "OK, it's nearly seven now. I'll call the Tulane hand surgeon on call, and we'll get that hand drained. I'll also get the antibiotics started. Where's your wife?"

He looked away and laughed. "Doc, Mellette still don't know I accidentally killed her cat. I didn't want her to come today 'cause I knew I'd have to tell ya'll it was a blasted cat bite to get the right antibiotics, and I didn't want to compound my lying. Thomasena has caused me a world of trouble, even from the grave."

Dr. Michaud said, "Who's Thomasena?"

Elizabeth and Leeodus said at the same time, "Mellette's dead cat."

The two doctors left exam Room Ten, and Dr. Michaud said, "That one's all yours. That's a Tulane monster if I ever saw one. You created that monster, so he's your problem, Doctor. He acts like he's one of your relatives." He waved behind his back as he walked through the back doors of the emergency department and out to temporary freedom.

Elizabeth turned toward the nurses' station to face Livvy. She knew it wouldn't be a fun talk. A tiny dark woman stepped out from an exam room and yelled to nobody in particular, "My baby's guts is in the bed! I done toldt you, my baby's guts is in da bed. Is somebody gone help my baby or not?"

Elizabeth stood six inches taller than the woman who had just spoken. Her braids were disheveled and partially undone. She wore a faded pink shift made from what looked like an old cotton flour sack. She wore no bra, and her breasts hung down like long tubes under the thin dress. Her feet were dirty and her toenails were long, yellow, and curled over the ends of her worn plastic flip-flops.

Elizabeth said, “Ma’am, I’m Dr. Roberts, and I’ll see your child in a few minutes.”

The woman grabbed Elizabeth by the forearm and said, “No, miss, you’ll see her now. If a baby’s guts being in the bed ain’t no dang emergency, then I don’t know what is!”

She pulled Elizabeth through the exam room door. The pretty one-year-old looked clean and well-nourished. A large mass on the baby’s abdomen was covered in wet paper towels. As the mother unwound the paper towels, Elizabeth was appalled to see the entire small intestine was out of the baby’s abdomen and writhing with peristalsis on the exam table and all over the baby’s lower body.

Elizabeth had never seen slimy pink bowels outside of a body. She swallowed hard, and her eyes bulged.

“I told you, Doc,” the baby’s mother continued. “I brought my baby here a month ago because she had a small bump under her belly button. A Dr. LeBlanc told me it was a *onion,* and he could fix it. He operated on my baby two days ago, and now dis is what we got. We exchanged a little *onion* for all her guts being outside her body. Dat ain’t right.”

Elizabeth knew *onion* meant hernia. The child must have had a small umbilical hernia. The sutures had given way or pulled through when the child coughed, and her many feet of small bowel had made their way through the one-inch hole in her abdomen and were trapped outside her body. Once swollen, they could not easily be maneuvered back into the abdomen. The baby needed surgery. The mother moved to hold up the bowels and rewrap them in the moist paper towel. She said, “They turn blue when they get on a stretch. I hold ’em up, and they get back to pink.”

Elizabeth was amazed. The woman had figured out that the blood supply was crimped off if the bowels were pulled from their mesentery. She’d also figured out that the bowels liked to be moist. This mother was not educated, but she was smart and determined to do the best for her baby.

"Ma'am, how long ago did this happen?"

"I found her crying around two this morning. I had nobody to bring me. The cab driver wouldn't take an IOU. So I finally got the head nurse here at Charity, and she told the cab driver to bring me and she'd pay. A tall, light-skinned nurse paid the cab driver his money, and here we are. What you gone do to help my baby?"

Elizabeth realized Livvy was the one who had paid the fare and made sure the baby was seen upon arrival. Livvy liked to gossip and she was bossy, but Elizabeth respected her integrity.

"I'll call Dr. LeBlanc and get him down here to take care of this right away," said Elizabeth.

"Miss, please, I don't want him," said the mother. "He don't care nothing about my baby. He's the one done this to her. Give us a different doctor. Please."

Elizabeth looked at her, ashamed that her colleague had let them down. She vowed to get the problem corrected quickly and avoid calling Dr. LeBlanc if possible.

Elizabeth turned to walk out of the exam room and plowed right into Livvy.

Livvy said, "LeBlanc was sent to Alexandria. He's not in town today. Don't worry, Mom. We'll get you another doctor." She looked at Elizabeth. Elizabeth knew Livvy had been listening through the door. As usual, Livvy was a few steps ahead of the doctors.

Elizabeth stepped into the hall with Livvy and whispered, "I've not seen this before. Who do we call?" She followed Livvy to the nurses' station.

Livvy said, "This was a simple case but something went wrong. It was done by an intern on general surgery, but now that it's a complication, Dr. McSwain told me to call the pediatric surgery doctors and let them do the re-do."

Elizabeth felt a mixture of relief and anger—relief that Livvy had solved the problem and anger that she had gone over Elizabeth's head directly to the boss.

The only thing that matters is that these patients are given excellent care. That's why I came here.

Elizabeth swallowed hard and said, "Thanks, Livvy. I appreciate your making this happen so fast. It's amazing how the mother knew what to do to keep her daughter's bowels from becoming ischemic. A mother's sense of her child's needs is amazing."

Livvy laughed. "Crème Puff, I talked to that lady on the phone, and I told her what to do. To her credit, she followed my instructions. But I'm the one who deserves your admiration." She smiled. "Oh, and I can't wait to hear all about your big hot date with Dr. White. Aoife said you were crying just like on the soaps. Very juicy!"

Elizabeth ignored Livvy and made her way up and down the halls, checking every patient. She hung Mr. Benoit's intravenous antibiotics and formulated a plan with the hand service to get him to the operating room. She talked to the pediatric surgery fellow, and he agreed to take the baby to surgery right away. Everyone else in the emergency department was stable, and her shift whizzed by. Halfway through, Livvy cornered her and said, "We haven't been to Café du Monde in a little while. Let's walk there after your shift ends and reconnect. I'm not working days tomorrow. We'll have all day to catch up."

Elizabeth knew Livvy expected a tell-all. Elizabeth could think of no way to avoid her, and she could use some advice. She knew Livvy would know more about Dr. White than most folks. Elizabeth was hesitant at the thought of spying on him through Livvy but couldn't help herself.

"OK," she replied. "But *no* gossip."

Livvy put her hands on her hips and cocked her head to one side. "Of course not! That would be unprofessional. Let's wrap this up. I'll go home and sleep while you work, and I'll come back to get you in the morning."

Elizabeth longed to have a twelve-hour shift like the nurses did. She hated working for twenty-four hours straight. Livvy couldn't hide the excitement in her voice. Elizabeth was wary. She walked out to the waiting room to survey the area and be sure there were no sick patients the triage nurse had overlooked.

The pediatric surgeons wheeled the baby to the operating room. The mother walked beside the rolling crib. She leaned over to Elizabeth and said, "Thanks, Doc. I appreciate your help. Tell that mulatto lady I said thanks too. Usually, them light-skins don't do nothing for the likes of me. But that one is a good one."

Baffled by the remark, Elizabeth stood in the middle of the hall, watching the gurney pass through the doors toward the elevator. *What could she mean by that? I'll have to ask Livvy later.*

Elizabeth went from room to room, checking the suturing of the medical students, marveling at how proficient they'd become after less than seven months. As a student, she'd only sewn half a dozen simple lacerations in the emergency room before coming to Charity. These students were suturing simple lacerations as well as most full-fledged surgeons by their third year of medical school.

The student from the hand surgery rotation and a student nurse wheeled Mr. Benoit on his gurney to the operating room. He spotted her in the hall and yelled, "Thanks, Doc. Me and Mellette want to have you out to our fish camp on the bayou sometime soon. You're family now. We'll drink some beer, catch and cook some redfish, and listen to my cousin's Cajun band. You'll like it. We'll pass a good time the south Louisiana way. Mellette will call you in a few weeks after it warms up and after Mardi Gras. Thanks, cher."

Elizabeth shook her head and laughed. She felt a tap on her back and turned around to see Livvy.

"Looks quiet. I'm leaving. See you in the morning."

Elizabeth slept a few hours on a gurney in the radiology room in the ER. Her first shift of the month had buzzed by. At six forty-five in the morning, Livvy shook her awake.

"Get up, Crème Puff. Your shift's over."

"I haven't seen Dr. McSwain or the chief surgery resident. I also haven't checked out to the LSU guy yet."

"Dr. McSwain isn't coming this morning. He's helping with a complex colon cancer case at the VA. The chief resident is scrubbed in a vascular surgery case at Tulane. And I walked around with the new LSU guy. He's been down here before, and he knows the drill. You remember Adrien Lambert? He was down here with you the last time."

How dare she check out the patients to a fellow doctor! She's the nurse. Granted, she's the head nurse. But doctor to doctor communication honors the chain of command, and if she makes a mistake, I have to answer for it. I can't believe she can't wait fifteen minutes to drill me for hot gossip. Screw it!

"Why don't you cool your jets over at the *nurses'* station," Elizabeth suggested, "and let me run around with *Doctor* Lambert to be sure he and I are on the same page. I'll come get you as soon as we have finished."

"If you insist," replied Livvy. "He drove all night from some out-of-town rotation, and he's asleep on a gurney in Room Ten. If you don't trust me and want to wake the man up from the only sleep he's likely to get, go ahead and take your little insecure dairy aire in there and wake him up." The nurse stood defiantly.

Elizabeth sighed. Nothing was going on that warranted waking Adrien. She couldn't understand why she felt so angry when Livvy was making everyone's life easier. This morning, she was too tired to fight. "You win," she told Livvy. "Let's go. I'm starving."

"I can tell. You're getting too skinny. And the Lord knows you're mean if you're hungry. Let me grab my purse, and we can get out of here."

34

Elizabeth and Livvy walked their familiar route from Charity to Café du Monde. For most of the way, they were quiet. Elizabeth was tired despite having gotten a few hours of sleep during her shift. Livvy was clean, refreshed, and energized. She pointed out flowers along the way. Though it was winter, variegated purple and white petunias and orange bougainvillea draped over the black wrought iron balconies of the French Quarter.

Both women felt uncomfortable, and neither wanted to discuss the topic hanging between them.

Finally, Livvy said, "I love impatiens and coleus even though they don't have much smell. Jasmine reminds me of the Garden District. Coffee and alcohol remind me of the Quarter."

"Don't forget the smell of urine," Elizabeth interjected. "Between the horses and the drunken tourists, there's always that smell."

Livvy laughed and dove into the deep end. "Did you go on a date with Dr. White or not? Are you calling him 'Harrison' now? Do you think this is a good idea?"

Here we go. She made it ten blocks.

"Livvy, I'm sincere about not wanting to be in the gossip mill. I'd appreciate talking to you in confidence because you're my closest friend in New Orleans. Please keep what we discuss between you and me."

Livvy's bottom lip protruded, and she faked pouting. "You know you ain't really all that interesting, don't you? You act like you're Charles and Diana. Most folks don't care about two Charity doctors. It's not like y'all are celebrities on *Lifestyles of the Rich and Famous* or *The Young and the Restless.*"

Elizabeth had heard of the prince and his wife but wasn't familiar with the other references.

"I know you haven't seen TV in five or six years. You've probably never seen a *People* magazine. You don't know what I'm talking about, do you?"

"No, I don't."

Livvy laughed. "Science nerd! All I'm saying is that you and Dr. White are tired doctors doing doctor stuff and aren't celebrities. So don't get such a big head, thinking you're so important."

They entered Café du Monde and ordered their usual café au laits and two large orders of beignets covered in powdered sugar. Livvy chose a quiet table away from the crowd. She sat and sipped her coffee.

Elizabeth ate her first beignet in two bites. Powdered sugar swirled around them. Livvy continued sipping her coffee as she watched Elizabeth gobble her food. Ten minutes passed in silence. Each tried to get a read on the other. Both wanted something, and neither wanted to speak first.

Elizabeth said, "I need you to help me figure out what's going on, and I need some advice. On the last day of the rotation, Dr. White told me he'd checked my schedule and that he and I wouldn't be on the same service for the rest of his time as the heart fellow. Then he asked me to go get a burger with him. He treated me like we were on a date, but honestly, I'm wondering if I dreamed the whole thing. I remember I cried at the table about something he said. I remember seeing Aoife at a table nearby." She paused. "I'm not sure if I'm to act like we didn't go out for a burger when I see him again, or if I should expect another date with him. To tell you the truth, I was tired and stressed, and I had two beers. I might not have perceived things correctly."

Livvy concentrated hard. She swallowed her bite of beignet, wiped her mouth, and said, "I don't know what to make of it either. Aoife said, 'Dr. White seemed to be fawning all over you.' She said she'd never seen him act like that. She and everyone at her table thought y'all were on a date, except you looked like crap in your dirty scrubs, and he was kind of dressed up. The whole thing scares me. I don't want you to get hurt, Elizabeth."

Oh, no! She's calling me by my name. She must be concerned. "If we go on a few dates, what's the harm in that, Livvy? How would I get hurt?"

Livvy sat back in her chair, took a deep breath, and said, "I don't want to hurt your feelings, but you need to know. Those uptown people are a different breed. They've had money for many generations. They have their own clubs and their own social world. Not many folks who weren't born into it are accepted. There's no snobbery like old-money snobbery." She paused. "You're beautiful and you're smart and you're sweet, but you're too naïve for a grownup."

Elizabeth shrugged. "What could happen? He could decide I'm not for him. I could decide he's not for me. It seems those are the possibilities with any dating situation. And heaven knows Charleston, South Carolina, has its share of old money and cliques. I remember being judged for dating a Jewish guy. He was the cutest, smartest, most athletic guy around, but some people thought it was a bad idea to date outside of our own group. It didn't work out, and both of us are fine. In fact, we're still friends."

"You're a girl. He's a man. You work at the same place. If anything goes sour, you can be sure the wagons will circle around him, not you. I guess you know his daddy's the president of the big bank here and probably donates to the med school. And, Elizabeth, have you ever been in love? Big time in love?"

The waiter refilled their coffee mugs. "I thought I was in love a couple of times, but school was always more important to me. So, I'm not sure." Elizabeth looked out to the street, watched the horse-drawn carriages pass, and made a decision. "Livvy, I hate to ask this because I lecture you about gossip, but what do you know about Dr. White?" She was embarrassed by her need for information.

Livvy brightened. "Don't be silly. Us girls gotta stick together. Dr. White ain't no hound dog, if that's what you're asking. To my knowledge, he hasn't dated around Tulane or Charity, and he's been here fifteen years. Poor guy's probably getting pretty horny, come to think of it."

Elizabeth rolled her eyes and stifled a laugh. "What else?"

Livvy leaned in and opened her mouth to speak as Elizabeth's pager squawked, CALL THE TULANE OPERATOR. DR. WHITE IS HOLDING. PLEASE CALL THE TULANE OPERATOR.

Elizabeth stood and looked around for a phone. The waiter pointed to a pay phone on the street in front of the restaurant. Livvy handed Elizabeth a dime, left a tip on the table, and followed her out to the phone.

Elizabeth's hand shook while dialing. She tried to sound calm. "Yes, operator, this is Dr. Roberts."

Livvy leaned against the pay phone and cocked her head to listen in on the conversation. Elizabeth tried to pull the receiver away, but Livvy grabbed the metal cord on the phone and held tight. Elizabeth quit tugging and let Livvy listen. The Tulane operator connected the call.

"Hi, Elizabeth, it's Harrison. I'm sorry to disturb you after your shift. I hope I caught you before you went to sleep."

Elizabeth felt queasy at the sound of his voice. Her heart raced. "No, this is fine. I'm still awake. How may I help you?" She realized her voice sounded formal and stiff.

He laughed. "You may help me by going to dinner with me tomorrow night. It's your day off this week, and I can get my faculty to cover for a few hours if you don't have other plans. I thought we'd go to Mr. B's. They have good Creole food, and it's near your apartment."

Livvy twirled around and danced on the sidewalk. She covered her mouth so Dr. White couldn't hear her laughter.

"OK. That would be fine. What time?"

"Seven o'clock? I'll park in the Quarter and come to your door. We can walk over, weather permitting."

Elizabeth's mouth was dry. "Sounds good," she said. "See you then." She hung up.

Livvy grabbed her by the shoulders and hugged her. “I think we got our answer. He’s dating you, girl.”

Elizabeth stood in front of the pay phone staring at her friend. “Let’s walk to the river and talk some more. I feel a little overwhelmed.”

Livvy grabbed her hand and pulled her toward the Quarter. “Nope,” she said. We’re going to your apartment, and we’re going to get your checkbook, and we’re going shopping for some new clothes for you. You’re going to need some decent clothes to date an uptown man.”

Elizabeth laughed as Livvy pulled her toward Royal Street. “I don’t have a lot of money. I don’t usually buy new clothes. My cousins and I exchange our Sunday clothes and sometimes loan each other special items.”

“Elizabeth Roberts, this is a new day. You get a tiny paycheck from being an intern. I know you don’t spend it on anything but rent and books. I’m sure you have enough for some new clothes. Run up and get your checkbook. Aoife told me they have a sale going on at Ms. Yvonne LaFleur’s.”

Livvy waited in the courtyard while Elizabeth retrieved her checkbook.

Elizabeth returned and confessed, “Livvy, I’m not a fancy dresser. And I’m not a big spender. Let’s get one simple dress, and we’ll see where it goes from there.”

“This is why you need to be bossed around,” countered Livvy. “We have the entire day off to shop, and we’re going to shop. How long has it been since you’ve felt sexy?”

Elizabeth stopped in the middle of the sidewalk and turned to Livvy. “I can’t remember the last time I felt sexy,” she admitted. “I think about the patients, about learning surgery, and about food. Men seldom enter my thoughts. I wonder more often what’s on special at the Fistula Café in front of the hospital than I think of men.”

Both laughed.

"That's about to change," Livvy told her. "Lucky for you, I know all about sexy."

Livvy paid for them to get on the streetcar, and they rode up St. Charles Avenue toward South Carrollton Avenue.

Livvy said, "We'll ride to the end of the line before it turns. The dress shop is a couple of blocks to the right. I love her store. Everything is so feminine. I'm excited."

Elizabeth was content to listen to the squeal of the brakes on the streetcar and the conductor's voice calling out the names of the stops. She ogled the stately old homes they passed. Today, she didn't mind being bossed by Livvy. She felt drowsy and relaxed and heard the buzzing sound in her head she associated with fighting sleep. Her chin hit her chest at the moment she heard Livvy say, "Wake up. You're sleeping sitting straight up."

Elizabeth decided conversation might discourage somnolence. She didn't want to talk about Dr. White anymore. She felt disloyal for asking personal questions about him. Mentally, she reviewed her last ER shift and remembered something she wanted to know. "Livvy, that lady in the emergency room with her baby, she said the oddest thing. She wanted me to thank you for what you'd done for her daughter. Then she said, 'Tell that mulatto nurse, thanks. Her kind don't usually help my kind.' What'd she mean by that?"

Livvy sat up straight in her seat and looked away. She fumbled with the purse in her lap. After a few minutes, she said, "Crème Puff, you sure know how to ruin a good mood. I've been trying to explain class structure and race in this city. How can someone who grew up in the South be so clueless?"

Elizabeth refused to be offended. "Educate me, then."

"New Orleans has a peculiar history around color," Livvy began. "Have you read about the quadroons?"

"If I did, I don't remember much."

Livvy lowered her voice as others joined them on the streetcar. "In New Orleans, there've always been free people of color. There've also been folks with African and Caribbean blood who chose to pass as white. Because of our mixed heritage, more mixed than many port cities, we have a complex history around color. Quadroons were the most beautiful women from the mixed blood of slave owners who were mostly white and slaves who were mostly not."

Elizabeth interrupted. "We had that in Charleston and all over the country."

Livvy said, "Here, the richest slave owners set up their beautiful quadroons in their own households. The white wives usually knew about the families of the quadroons. To tell you how crazy it was, there were Mardi Gras balls happening on the same nights that husbands attended with both of their women. The old boys would dance with their white wife at one ball and then go over to a quadroon ball and dance with their second woman. Can you imagine the jealousy?"

Elizabeth felt perplexed. "There'd be more than jealousy. There'd be hair pulling and even murder. But what does this story have to do with the woman in the emergency room being surprised you helped her more than one hundred years later? And why have I never heard of this in any history class? Is this truth or myth?"

Livvy laughed. "This is a perfect example of your naiveté, Crème Puff. Just think about it. The men were jealous of each other's quadroon women. The white wife was jealous of the quadroon wife and family. The slaves were jealous of everyone. Quadroons and free people of color frequently looked down on the slaves. Some free people of color actually had slaves. The whole thing was a big mess."

Elizabeth watched the houses go by through the window of the streetcar and thought about Livvy's history lesson. "I still don't see what that has to do with 1983 at The Big Free."

Livvy looked sad and dropped her eyes to her hands. She spoke softly. "Elizabeth, that lady thought that because I'm a light-skinned Creole woman who likely is descended from a quadroon that I wouldn't care about her or help her. The many prejudices that go with skin color are old and deep, and they cause strong emotions that even we locals don't fully understand. Keep your eyes open and pay attention. You'll see it everywhere."

Livvy picked up her purse and tapped Elizabeth on the leg. She pulled the wire for the bell to notify the conductor and nodded toward the doors to signal it was their time to get off at the next stop.

They walked a few blocks and entered the shop of Ms. Yvonne LaFleur. The building was old, with creaking wooden floors. Elegant hats hung on racks at every turn. The aisles were packed with ball gowns, lingerie, and bridal dresses. Glass-fronted counters were filled with flowers, feathers, ribbons, silk scarves, elegant antique jewelry, fans, and purses. Elizabeth smelled an exotic perfume with floral and musky undertones. Her senses were overwhelmed. She'd never been in a shop like this one.

A striking, petite woman with a mound of black hair piled up in a style from the 1800s smiled and walked toward them. She said, "Good morning, ladies. I'm Yvonne. What may I help you find today?"

Livvy's usual arrogance disappeared. She looked star-struck. Elizabeth stood behind Livvy, staring at the gorgeous fashions crushing them in every direction. She couldn't move without touching the expensive merchandise. She was very aware of her ugly, stained scrubs.

Livvy said, "Hello, Ms. LaFleur. We're thrilled to be in your wonderful store. My friend Elizabeth has a special dinner date planned and needs an outfit to wear. Also, she needs to update her lingerie."

Elizabeth jabbed Livvy in the back, nearly sending her sprawling toward Ms. LaFleur. Elizabeth cleared her throat but remained silent.

Ms. LaFleur said, "Wonderful. Do you prefer to walk around by yourselves and see what we have, or do you want guidance?"

Livvy said, "We need guidance," at the moment Elizabeth said, "Alone. We prefer to shop alone."

Ms. LaFleur laughed and said, "I'll give you ladies a few minutes to look around, and then I'll check your progress and see if I might be of assistance. The lingerie is best chosen after the dress to be sure they coordinate. So I'd suggest you start with the dress."

Livvy blurted out, "My good friend Aoife works here, but I don't think she's here today. She loves your store."

Ms. LaFleur surveyed Elizabeth from head to toe, pausing at the wrinkled scrubs. She took at the disheveled hair, stained pearls, and dirty tennis shoes. She said, "We love Aoife. She's the perfect employee. She spends her entire check on merchandise."

The three laughed, and Elizabeth relaxed. Ms. LaFleur continued, "You're a beautiful young woman. You're what I refer to as a fresh palette. With your coloring, the blue family will be quite nice. Do you know where you're going to dinner?"

Livvy said, "They're going to Mr. B's. This is their second date. He's an uptown guy." Livvy beamed. Elizabeth felt embarrassed.

"Keep your dress simple," Ms. LaFleur advised. "A woman shouldn't look as if she's trying too hard. Make sure you're comfortable. You don't want a dress that causes you to fidget all night. Some ladies want to wear something very revealing. I suggest against that, particularly for a dinner date. You don't want to spend the whole evening trying to keep yourself from falling out of your dress. Your clothes should make you feel confident. You'll be most confident in something that suits who you are. Look over there against the wall. I have a collection of nice jersey wrap dresses that would accentuate your svelte curves," said Ms. LaFleur. She left them to answer her ringing telephone in the back of the store.

As soon as they were alone, they started laughing. Livvy said, "I think *svelte curves* is a nice way of saying 'your skinny butt!' And as for dressing you to suit your personality, well, that's exactly what we're trying to get away from. Come on. Let's try on a few of those wrap dresses. What are you? About a size six?"

Elizabeth followed Livvy. "I don't know what size I am. Like I told you on the train, I don't do much shopping. The dress I borrowed from Aoife is a size eight, and it's a little too big. A size six might be a good place to start." Elizabeth stood behind Livvy, while Livvy looked through the rack.

Livvy pulled out two blue-toned dresses and held each against Elizabeth. "Ms. LaFleur's right. The blue makes your eyes look bigger and complements your pale white skin. She knows her business. Try this one, Elizabeth. It even makes your greasy blonde hair look nice."

The dress was made of a clingy jersey fabric and had a V-shaped neckline. Elizabeth thought it was too dressy for church and wondered where she could wear it other than out to dinner with Dr. White.

"Come on," said Livvy. "Try it on. I know you're thinking of ten reasons not to get it. Live a little. Try something new. You're living in New Orleans now. There are no pigs to slop or whatever y'all do back on the farm in South Carolina."

Elizabeth knew Livvy and Ms. LaFleur were trying to help her. She knew dating was not her forte, so she decided to do whatever they suggested this one time. She tried on the dress and exited the dressing room as Ms. LaFleur hurried over to inspect her. The woman handed Elizabeth a pair of black sandals in Elizabeth's size. Livvy whistled and Ms. LaFleur said, "It seems you found the perfect dress on your first try. Put on these sandals, and let's find some undies to compliment the look."

Elizabeth bent to place the sandals on her feet and noticed she had not shaved her legs in a few weeks. The blonde hairs were at least an inch long. She stood erect and gazed at herself in the mirror, surprised by her own reflection. She said, "Except for the hairs on my legs that resemble a Yeti and my baggy underwear causing wrinkles under the dress, I look pretty good. Probably better than I've ever looked in my life."

Livvy said, "Oh, heck, no, girl. You look *hot.* You're gonna knock that man's manliness into the dirt in that dress." Elizabeth was relieved Ms. LaFleur had headed to the lingerie area and couldn't hear Livvy's crass comment.

"Shush, Livvy!" Elizabeth twirled in front of the mirror and tried to remember feeling sexy. She liked how she looked, but she felt tired and worried she was wasting her money.

Ms. LaFleur returned with multiple black lacy garments strung over her arms and hands. She said, "Nothing makes a woman feel sexier than having gorgeous lingerie. Even if nobody sees it but you, knowing what you're wearing under your clothes and how you look in it will give you confidence. Have you ever worn underwired, padded push-up bras, or bikini underwear, or a garter belt with pull-up stockings?"

Elizabeth said, "No, ma'am. My granny wore roll-up stockings and my mom had a garter belt, but I've only ever worn pantyhose, and neither Granny nor Momma had anything that looked like the things you're holding." Elizabeth felt her face and neck flush. She suddenly felt overheated in the close quarters of the store.

Ms. LaFleur smiled. "Not to worry. I suggest you wear the garter belt and stockings to work for a few days before your date and get used to them. They're quite comfortable. Women wore garters and silk stockings forever until the last forty years. I think panty hose are the worst thing that ever happened to women's fashion."

Elizabeth tried to imagine wearing the black bra, panties, garter belt, and silk stockings under her scrubs. Since she didn't have a better idea of how to feel like a woman again, she said, "OK. I'll try that."

Ms. LaFleur folded and packaged the garments with care. Elizabeth didn't want to see the prices. After the bill was totaled, Ms. LaFleur gave her the amount. It was less than she expected.

Ms. LaFleur said, "Since Aoife works here, I gave you the family discount. You got twenty percent off from the sale and an additional thirty percent off for the employee discount." She smiled at Elizabeth. "I hope you have a good date, and I appreciate your hard work at Charity."

Elizabeth didn't know what to say. She took the packages, smiled, and said, "Thank you, ma'am." Livvy led the way out of the store.

Livvy said, "That's New Orleans for ya. She knows what it's like to be a hard-working girl. She's a smart businesswoman. For the rest of your time in New Orleans you'll be a loyal customer, and you'll tell others about her shop. She's no fool. If I'd known she'd give a 50 percent discount, I'd have gotten a dress for myself!"

Elizabeth stopped and said, "Let's go back. We can get something for you too."

"Nah, Crème Puff. I don't want to steal your moment. If you saw all this Creole loveliness poured into one of those dresses, you'd probably cry. Can't no skinny white chick compete with the likes of all this!" Livvy drew her hands in slow motion down the contours of her body and twirled around.

Elizabeth shook her head from side to side and said, "Of course not."

They rode the streetcar back to the Quarter. Livvy got off on Canal and headed to her car, which was parked at the hospital. She yelled to Elizabeth through the streetcar window, "Don't forget to stop and get red nail polish to clean up those hands and feet of yours. They have Cherries in the Snow by Revlon at the pharmacy in the Quarter."

Elizabeth laughed at her controlling friend's advice. She stopped at the pharmacy in the Quarter and bought the nail polish. She smiled, remembering it was her mother's and Joe-Jan's favorite color and hoped it would bring her luck on her date.

When Elizabeth arrived at her apartment, she gobbled a peanut butter sandwich and fell fast asleep without unwrapping her packages.

35

Elizabeth awoke at ten the next morning. She couldn't remember ever having slept fourteen consecutive hours. She moved in slow motion, feeling foggy, stiff, and sore, but also grateful for a day off. After her first cup of coffee, she remembered today was her dinner date with Dr. White. She opened her packages from yesterday's shopping and arranged her new clothes on her bed. Her emotions bounced between excitement and dread.

She spent the day alternately reading her surgery textbook and fantasizing about her date. As she tried to think of interesting topics of conversation, she realized she'd never been this excited about a date.

After putting aside her textbook, she took a long walk through the French Quarter and visited several art galleries. Although she disliked wasting an art dealer's time because art wasn't in her meager budget, she enjoyed studying the art on display and learning about the artists. She wandered into the gallery of George Rodrigue. She read Rodrigue's biography and learned he'd been raised in Cajun country near Bayou Teche, where the Benoits' home was located. She thought his Blue Dog art was fun, and she enjoyed reading the legend of loup-garou. Rodrigue's painting of Evangeline was haunting and beautiful like the poem by Longfellow that Elizabeth remembered from her college English class. She felt homesick looking at the moss-covered oaks in many of the paintings. She thought nowhere on earth had more beautiful trees than the Low Country of South Carolina, but the Louisiana captured by Mr. Rodrigue came close. *Maybe one day, I'll have paid off all my student loans and have extra money for art.*

She wandered the streets of the Quarter, bought an apple for lunch from a vendor in the market near the river, and headed home at two o'clock to begin her beautification process. Unlike many women her age, Elizabeth didn't enjoy primping, but her excitement gave her fortitude for the female ritual she usually avoided.

She took a long shower and shaved her hairy legs. After that, she dried and rolled her long blonde hair, gave herself a manicure and pedicure, and took a nap. She put on her new lingerie and, feeling silly, practiced walking in her new shoes. She admired herself in her mirror after she put on her new dress and made sure her dress didn't fall open too far at the chest when she sat to eat. Then she scrubbed her grandmother's pearls carefully in the sink and left them on her deck to dry, hoping the sun might bleach the bloodstains from the string.

It seemed forever before seven o'clock would arrive. Elizabeth had had so few days off in the last eight months that she didn't know what to do with herself. She used to like to read poetry, she remembered, and pulled out a poetry book from a cardboard box she'd forgotten to unpack. She removed her dress so it wouldn't get wrinkled and settled in a chair in her lingerie to read. She looked down at her scantily clad body and admired the beautiful black lace.

At six-thirty, she combed out her rollers and put on her new dress. She wished she'd thought to buy a bottle of Ms. LaFleur's perfume. The scent of her Prell shampoo would have to do for tonight.

At seven o'clock, she was surprised Dr. White was not on time because he was always impeccable with arrival times at conferences and rounds. By seven-thirty, she thought he might have had trouble finding a parking space. By eight o'clock, she was certain he had car trouble and was stranded. At nine o'clock, she started to cry. Either he'd forgotten, or he had changed his mind, or he got a better offer. Her mascara ran down her face.

She removed her dress, lay on her bed in her black lacy lingerie, and cried for an hour. Some of her tears were for the disappointment of the lost date. But after a few minutes, she shed tears from homesickness, from her inability to please her mother with her life choices, from the horrors she'd seen in the emergency room, and for her loneliness. She thought of calling Livvy and considered calling Daddy. She decided she'd cry for a while longer and not bother anyone else.

At 10:00 p.m., her pager screeched. "Please call the Tulane Operator." Elizabeth bolted upright and dialed. She remembered she'd not given Dr. White her home phone number. She felt a sense of relief, hoping he'd been stranded and was only now able to call. The operator said, "Please hold." A familiar female voice came on the line, saying, "Dr. Roberts, this is Nurse Rose from the cardiothoracic team. Dr. White asked me to call you. He had to take one of our heart patients back to the operating room tonight, and he's having trouble getting the man off bypass. He asked me to explain that he's sorry he missed your conference tonight and will get back with you to reschedule soon."

"Thank you for letting me know," Elizabeth told her. *I guess he didn't want to tell his beautiful scrub nurse that we had a date.* Elizabeth flung her new dress on the floor and cried harder. Before falling asleep, she vowed to never date another doctor.

After six hours of fitful sleep and nasty dreams, Elizabeth awoke. The clock at her bedside showed she was ten minutes late for her pre-shift checkout with the LSU Surgery resident. She looked down at her lacey black lingerie. She had no time for breakfast or a shower or for changing clothes, so she threw her scrubs over the lingerie and jogged to the Charity emergency room.

She burst through the backdoor to find Room Four full of people hovering over the body of a young Black man who was bleeding to death from multiple gunshot wounds.

Livvy greeted her with a cross look and said, "I guess you forgot about your day job in the excitement of your new social life."

Elizabeth surveyed the scene, ignoring Livvy. She saw blood everywhere and on everyone. Adrien Lambert was up to his elbows inside the young man's chest, giving open cardiac massage. One of his hands was in front of the patient's heart and the other was behind it. Sweat poured from Dr. Lambert's head down his neck and back as his scrub shirt clung to his body with every move.

The patient had four venous cut downs, one on each extremity, and students and nurses were squeezing bags of whole blood into every line. The LSU chief surgery resident was hand-ventilating the patient with an Ambu bag through an endotracheal tube. The chief resident said, "That's enough, Adrien. It's time to call it. You've been at this for an hour. He's not coming back."

Adrien's eyes were bloodshot and wide. His voice was raspy and exhausted. He glared at his chief and said, "This is her second son to die tonight! These friggin' crack wars are killing kids faster and faster. His mother teaches my niece in the second grade, and his sister's a new nurse here at Charity. I just got through telling her that her oldest son died in here two hours ago. So, no, I will not stop. He has to come back."

Adrien shook the patient by the shoulders and yelled, "Come back! Please come back. You can do it. Come back for your mother and your sister!" The lifeless, bloody form did not respond.

Livvy walked behind the intern and put her hands on his shoulders. The chief resident put down the ventilation bag and grasped Adrien's bloody forearms and whispered, "Adrien, stop. He can't be saved. You did everything. Bullets severed his retrohepatic vena cava. Nobody survives that injury. *Stop*, now."

It was seven-fifteen in the morning. Everyone in the room looked defeated. Elizabeth moved closer to Adrien and stood between him and the dead young man.

Adrien was sobbing. "Elizabeth," she said, "I don't think I can take this. We had seven gunshot wounds to the chest and abdomen in Room Four in the last nine hours. Two survived. *Two* of the seven. This is bull—" His profanity filled the room. "This town is worse than a war zone."

Elizabeth grabbed him and held him tightly while he sobbed. "I'll go with you to talk to the family," she told him. "Let's get you cleaned up and get some coffee and a little food. This hideous day's almost over, and you can go home and sleep."

Adrien pulled away, looked into her face, and said, "Elizabeth, this day will never be over for this family. They've lost two sons tonight. *Two sons.* Why can't kids see that this crazy crack culture is killing them?"

As Elizabeth pulled him toward the door, she asked Livvy, "Anything else going on down here that can't wait thirty minutes?"

"No," Livvy replied. "Go talk to the family. We're cleaning and setting up Room Four as fast as possible. The retaliation from the war that started in the projects last night will probably come soon. The blood bank's trying to locate more blood. They called all over the city, and AB positive is particularly low."

Elizabeth pushed Adrien through the swinging doors of Room Four. She glanced back and saw the nurses and students loading the young man's body onto a stretcher to go to the morgue. She asked Livvy, "Would it be too much to try to clean him up and put him in an exam room just in case they want to see him? I know his chest and abdomen are open, but we could cover all that up."

"Sure," replied Livvy. "My nurses and I will do what we can. The mother and sister saw the last one and held up pretty well. They'll probably want to see him too. For goodness' sake . . . this job sucks some days."

Adrien changed scrubs and washed his arms, face, and head in the sink near the nurses' station. He drank a cup of coffee and told Elizabeth about the other patients in the emergency room.

His chief resident walked up and said, "I ran around with the students and looked in every room. There's nothing that can't wait." He looked at Elizabeth and said, "Congratulations. It's officially a Tulane day and *tag*, you're it." He walked away.

Adrien couldn't eat. He touched Elizabeth's arm and said, "Let's go get this over with. I hate this part more than anything."

"Me too," she replied. "Let's do it. After you tell them, go home. I'll handle whatever happens after that. You're spent."

The two young surgeons walked into a packed waiting room. The boy's mother and sister stood as they saw the doctors approaching them. They'd been crying and were holding tissues to their faces. They stood out as better dressed and groomed compared to many others in the crowded waiting room.

Dr. Lambert took the mother's hand and said, "I'm sorry. He didn't make it. We did everything we could, and nothing worked."

The daughter said, "You're still talking about my oldest brother, right? You're not talking about my baby brother. Are you? He's OK, isn't he?" Her eyes were pleading. "You must be still thinking about my oldest brother?" She shook as she spoke. Her mother put her arm around her as her eyes darted from Adrien to Elizabeth, begging for a different answer. Adrien stared at his feet as tears dripped from his lashes and splashed the floor below.

Elizabeth spoke then. "I'm very sorry. Both have passed. We did our best." The mother fainted, and the daughter screamed. The screaming froze and distracted the two doctors so nobody grabbed the mother as she fell, hitting her head on the linoleum floor. She began to bleed from the gash that sliced through her eyebrow. The daughter continued to scream as she jumped to the floor to help her mother.

Elizabeth knelt by the woman and used the tail of her white coat to hold pressure on her head wound. "Adrien, get a gurney for the mother." The mother groaned and thrashed about. Elizabeth pulled the daughter into a chair, holding the girl's hand with one hand and keeping pressure on the mother's head with the other. She checked the cut every few minutes, but the bleeding continued, unabated.

The gurney arrived and nurses helped get the mother on it. Elizabeth asked a student to hold pressure on the mother's head wound until they could get her stitched up. The daughter remained on the chair, her arms wrapped around herself, rocking back and forth and making mewing sounds like a young kitten. As the gurney started to roll, she insisted on being with her mother and followed the gurney into the emergency room. As Elizabeth turned to leave, the daughter yelled, "She's gonna want to see him. Please, ma'am, don't take him away until she gets to see her baby for the last time. Please."

"OK," Elizabeth said. "Let's get your momma stitched up first. You take deep breaths and sit in that chair." Elizabeth signaled to the student, Larry, to keep them in the exam room for now. Larry nodded. He was pale and wide-eyed as he watched the scene, more determined than ever to become a psychiatrist.

Livvy sent a student nurse to stay with Larry. Everyone was addled by the back-to-back trauma deaths.

As Elizabeth turned up the hall to start rounds, she heard an EMT pound through the swinging doors behind her and rush down the hall, pushing a gurney with another blood-covered young black man. The EMT screamed, "ROOM FOUR! Multiple gunshot wounds. No blood pressure. Two lines in place."

Elizabeth burst through the doors of Room Four. It was immaculate, fully stocked. All blood splatters were gone, and nurses and doctors stood at attention, ready to start the trauma code all over again. The patient's clothes were cut off from his neck to his groin. A rolled wad of cash, a thick bag of white powder, and a large handgun fell to the floor with his pants. Elizabeth kicked them toward the wall and approached the bed.

Livvy called out, "He has no blood pressure, Dr. Roberts!"

Elizabeth knew the current trauma protocol was to open the chest in Room Four if the patient had visible penetrating trauma and no blood pressure. Cross-clamping the aorta would allow blood to the brain and heart while a surgeon tried to stop the bleeding. It was a shocking and heroic maneuver, but data showed the incidence of death from penetrating trauma if the victim had no blood pressure at the scene was near 100 percent.

Elizabeth said, "Hand me the scalpel. Call my backup. Get the Tulane chief down here, now!" She took the scalpel and cut the entire length of the young man's sternum from his neck to his abdomen in one deep, smooth stroke.

Livvy said, "Dr. Roberts, your backup is scrubbed at Tulane with Dr. McSwain and can't leave."

"Call Tony!" said Elizabeth. "Dr. Parker STAT to Room Four. Leave him no option. I need another surgeon." She grabbed the sternal saw and started to cut. A medical student used a bag and face mask to ventilate. Elizabeth saw the chest rise a small amount with each breath. "Do you know how to intubate?" she asked the student.

The startled student said, "I just finished my anesthesia rotation and intubated a dozen patients with the doctor looking right over my shoulder." He looked terrified.

"Today's your day. Intubate this patient now." She cranked open his sternum and saw his pericardium was full of blood. His heart could not pump blood because it could not fill. Livvy helped the medical student intubate the patient as Elizabeth yelled, "Everyone, cover your eyes! I'm cutting the pericardium to let it drain, and there will be splatter under pressure."

She made a one-centimeter cut in the pericardium, and blood shot a foot into the air. She used her hands to block the blood from hitting Livvy and the medical student. The blood covered her. She'd turned her face to the side to avoid it splashing her eyes, but the side of her face, neck, and chest were covered in the patient's blood. As she suctioned the blood from the pericardium, she felt the disgusting sensation of another person's blood running down her chest and back inside her scrubs.

Livvy said, "The tube's in. We've got blood up and running. I hung O-positive since we don't know his type."

Elizabeth watched the patient's heart and prayed. Tony burst through the doors, wearing a tie and a pressed shirt and khakis. He stood behind Elizabeth. *He must have been working the faculty clinic at Tulane.*

The patient's heart quivered.

Livvy reported, "His blood pressure's eighty over sixty."

Tony whispered in Elizabeth's ear, "Push fluids like crazy. This guy might make it."

The sound of Tony's voice calmed Elizabeth. He took the Ambu bag from the shaking student and told him he'd done a great job.

Elizabeth said, "Call Dr. White and see if he can come. Call the operating room and let them know this patient needs to come up now. He has a torn lung peripherally. Nothing seems to be bleeding much at this time. It looks like the bullet grazed his pericardium, filled it with blood, and caused tamponade. He's looking better every minute. They'll need to close up his chest and repair the lung injury." She heard Livvy on the phone, giving a report to the operating room nurse.

An excited student nurse said, "His blood pressure is ninety over sixty."

Tony said, "Going in the right direction. Get a Foley catheter in him. Are all his lines working? Anesthesia hates for us to send them up with nonfunctioning lines. Flush all of them with heparin. We don't want them to clot off before he gets upstairs."

Elizabeth stood in awe at what had just happened and said a quick prayer. The patient's chest was wide open, and his heart was in full view and beating with force. His bright pink lungs peeked through the incision with each forced breath. Tony attached oxygen from the wall to the bag. Elizabeth was elated.

Dr. White burst through the door in Tulane scrubs with no white coat. He was covered in sweat and looked like he'd run the entire way to Charity. He pulled on sterile gloves and surveyed the situation. Then he looked at Tony and said, "What's going on here?"

"I'm not sure. I just got here. Dr. Roberts handled this code. She can tell you."

Dr. White put his hands in the chest cavity to be sure it was not full of blood. He looked up into Elizabeth's eyes, smiled broadly, and said, "Excellent job, intern. Now help me load this guy on the gurney. Let's get him to the OR. This could be the save of the week."

36

The remainder of Elizabeth's shift was chaotic. The results of one drug gang's vengeance against another kept trauma Room Four riotous and fully occupied. The volume of wounded exceeded their supplies, and blood products had to be rationed. The hospital's stock of cloth scrubs was depleted, and the staff wore paper-thin scrubs instead.

Elizabeth bent over a gurney, using her dwindling strength in a last hard tug to pull a blood-covered patient toward her and onto a gurney headed to the operating room. She heard a ripping sound, felt a blast of cool air on her backside, and realized the flimsy, blood-and-sweat-soaked paper scrubs had split down her back. She heard several staff members laughing. Her fancy black lace underclothes were exposed to the members of the trauma team standing behind her.

Aoife, who had replaced Livvy at the end of Livvy's twelve-hour shift, grabbed a sheet from the stack by the wall and covered Elizabeth's backside. *Thank everything good in this world that Dr. White's not down here now.*

She secured the patient to the gurney, went into the X-ray room, cut a hole in the center of the sheet, and dropped it over her head to cover herself. She ripped a narrow piece of the sheet from the bottom edge and made a belt. Then she strode to the elevator and rode up to the on-call room to change.

She was grateful the on-call room was empty. She threw the sheet in the trash and showered with her undies on, rinsing the caked layers of blood from her body. She peeled off the bra, panties, garter-belt, and hose and tried to rinse the blood from them. She washed her hair with the bar of soap in the shower stall. The water at the bottom of the shower changed from red to rust to rose to clear as she scrubbed. Elizabeth laughed and cried while rinsing herself. She didn't want Tony or Michael to see her wet underwear, so she balled the wet clothes in a dry towel and placed them in the back of her drawer. They wouldn't dare go in her drawer, she reasoned. That was the place where she kept feminine products and clean clothes and hid her Clinique face soap. She was grateful she'd forgotten to wear her pearls, leaving them on her balcony table at home. Once clean, she sped back to the trauma ER.

She stood at the nurses' desk, drank coffee, and steeled herself for rounds. She reflected on the events of the shift and knew no matter her pain, nobody was suffering as much as the family who'd lost two sons. The mother and daughter had cried and screamed at God for taking the only sons in their family. They stayed in the room with the younger son's body for what seemed an eternity. Finally, their wailing subsided. After they left the emergency room, the body was taken to the morgue. Elizabeth had called plastic surgery to suture the mother's face wound. She would not allow that job to be done by a medical student because she wanted the woman's eyebrow to be as straight as possible. She couldn't bring back either of the woman's sons, but she could make sure her face was not deformed.

Every other young man who had died in the last twenty-four hours went unwitnessed except by the people in the emergency room. No family came for them. Nobody sobbed over their bodies for their loss or came to claim their possessions. The police searched their personal items and bagged them, then took them away.

Elizabeth prayed for each one. She prayed the senseless violence would end. She couldn't understand why these young men chose this life that killed so many. As she drank her coffee that morning, she wondered what could be done to stop the killing and clean the community of drugs.

Livvy walked through the door to begin her shift and stood close to Elizabeth. "I hear your fancy underwear was quite a hit in Room Four, Crème Puff." She laughed as she put her purse in a drawer in the nurses' desk.

Elizabeth felt sad and silly and exhausted. She stared at Livvy and said nothing.

"We didn't have a chance to talk about your big date. How'd it go?"

"There was no date. He took a heart surgery patient back to the operating room, and he never made it."

Livvy's mouth dropped open, but she had no words. The two stared at each other. Elizabeth was too exhausted to feel embarrassed.

A bouquet of fresh flowers sat on the top of the nurses' station. Livvy pulled out the card and said, "Well, I'll be dang. They're for you. The card says, *To Dr. Elizabeth Roberts.* Maybe prince charming feels bad for standing you up."

Elizabeth snatched the card from Livvy's hands and stared at the flowers. She felt a surge of excitement and relief. She opened the card and read: *Thanks for taking good care of my Leeodus, cher. We must have you out to our fish camp soon.* It was signed by Mrs. Mellette Benoit. She'd written a telephone number for Elizabeth to call to schedule a visit.

Livvy tried to grab the card to read it, but Elizabeth clutched it to her chest and said, "It's from my *other* admirer."

Livvy tried again to wrestle the card from her, but Elizabeth held tight. She giggled, knowing Livvy hated not knowing the latest gossip. Adrien Lambert, looking less exhausted than the last time Elizabeth saw him, approached and said, "If you two ladies are done with your hair pulling, could we make rounds and get Elizabeth out of here?"

"That's the best thing I've heard in twenty-four hours. Charge on!" said Elizabeth.

Rounds were quick. The knife and gun club were on break for the moment. The medical students stitched lacerations while the student nurses restocked supplies. Adrien and Elizabeth stood in the hall, drank coffee, and talked.

He said, "Thanks for handling the end of my shift the day before yesterday. I've never felt despondent like that. I didn't think I couldn't go on another moment. It tore me up to see the mother and daughter from the family that lost two sons. I don't remember driving home," he confessed. "I slept fifteen hours."

Elizabeth knew how he felt. She often felt lost, unable to understand and process the misery one human caused another. The violence and wasted life baffled her.

Elizabeth said, "When I first came to Charity, I found many of the medical staff to be calloused. When I saw someone wearing a T-shirt that read, *The Life You Save May Take Your Own,* I couldn't believe it. I remember a chief resident checking out a patient to another doctor, and I heard him say of the patient, 'He was an interesting surgery case but a useless human. If I'd been there, I'd have shot him myself.' The dark humor offended me. How could we talk about our patients like that? Now, after less than a year, I sometimes feel hard-hearted too. What's wrong with people?"

Adrien said, "I have no answers to the big questions, but I hope today is quiet. I haven't recovered from my last shift. Sleep alone can't make up for what we see down here. I've decided to ignore the big picture. I'm here to learn to take care of really messed up folks and make sure I'm the best surgeon I can be. Then, one day, I'll move to a small Louisiana town and take care of normal people. I'm leaving the *whys* to God. Only he can clean this city of these drug wars."

The two parted. Elizabeth headed to the call room, and Adrien went to exam Room Ten.

Miss Albertha was running the elevator today. When the doors opened, Elizabeth heard her singing a gospel song, one Elizabeth didn't know.

"When the trumpet of the Lord shall sound and time shall be no more."

When she saw Elizabeth, she stopped singing. She thought the young doctor looked dog-tired. "Hey, babe, how you doing?" she asked. "I missed seeing you last month."

Elizabeth hugged Miss Albertha's shoulders and said, "I missed you too. I came on duty before you got here and left after you got off. What song is that? I don't know that one."

Miss Albertha said, "Sure you do! It's 'When the Roll Is Called Up Yonder.' It's been around a hundred years. I like to sing it to remind myself this life is short, and I'm going somewhere for eternity that is a whole lot better than this." She resumed singing.

Elizabeth savored the rhythmic, soulful, sad a cappella song. She collapsed against the elevator wall, relaxed her muscles, and was taken to the church of her childhood. She felt goosebumps on her arms. Miss Albertha's soothing voice was the antithesis of the emergency room chaos. The doors opened on Elizabeth's floor, and she hated to leave the solace of Miss Albertha's elevator.

"See you soon, babe."

"Thanks for your beautiful song, Miss Albertha."

Elizabeth opened the on-call room door and instantly her good mood was ruined.

Michael sat in the middle of the room, with her black lace bra draped over one of his ears and her lacy garter belt draped over the other. He'd placed her panties over the light shade by the bed and her black stockings hung from the ceiling fan. He was reading the *Times Picayune* and drinking coffee. His feet were propped on the desk; he looked relaxed and smug.

Elizabeth fought the urge to hit him. He grinned and said, "Hi, there. I hear you're considering a new career in modeling ladies' lingerie. I support your career change. I think that would be more appropriate than being a surgeon. I never thought that was such a great idea."

She snatched her bra and panties from his head, making sure his ears got a good tug in the process. She gave him a hard smack on the back of his head and gathered her stockings and panties and crammed them into her overnight bag. "You're the most ill-mannered man I know. What do you think you're doing, going into my drawer and taking my personal items? You're depraved!"

He pushed his chair back to remove himself out of slapping range and took another sip of his coffee. "I was helping you dry them," he said. "You should be grateful for my help." He cackled.

Elizabeth stood over him, trying to control her fury. She clenched and unclenched her fists and took several deep breaths. "What are you doing here?" she asked him. "You're supposed to be out of town. You shouldn't be in New Orleans. I thought I was free of you and your terrible manners for a few days."

He stood up and moved closer. He was tall and muscular, and he flared his chest and said, "That story of you bending over in Room Four and busting out your bloody paper scrubs and exposing your backside in all your black lace is the funniest thing I've ever heard in my life. It's too bad you're so uptight that you can't appreciate the humor in it. It makes me wonder if you're secretly some kind of little slut, Elizabeth." He poked his finger under her chin and raised her face up to his.

She jerked her head away and stepped back. She said, "You disgust me. What are you doing here?"

He sat and resumed sipping his coffee. He said, "Dr. McSwain called me back to discuss that case of the baby whose small intestine popped out through its navel after the umbilical hernia was repaired. He's looking for somebody to roast at Death and Complications Conference this afternoon, and he thinks I'd make a good candidate since I put a couple of the stitches in the little brat. It's ridiculous, of course. I did nothing wrong. It's just McSwain exerting his power over me and trying to make me squirm for no good reason. You've got people dying right and left down there in the trauma area, and he hauls me in from four hours away to discuss a baby with a problem that was fixed in fifteen minutes in the operating room. That kid's mother was dumb as a stick. I'm sure she's the cause of the whole thing." He paused, then smirked again. "So, Elizabeth, who were you trying to impress with your skanky ho outfit?"

Elizabeth grabbed her bag and fled the on-call room before she did something she might regret (or savor). Either way, she needed to prepare for the Death and Complications Conference and couldn't do it with Michael in the room.

She went to the Tulane Surgery Department and changed into her khaki skirt and pink shirt in the women's bathroom. She sat in the library in the department and studied surgery texts, grateful she had no case to present this week, and waited for the conference to begin.

She'd been reading for about an hour when she felt a presence watching her. She looked at the door and saw Dr. White. He smiled, looked behind him to be sure they were alone, and closed the door.

Good grief. He's handsome. I should be mad and say something mean, but I can't.

"I can't begin to tell you how sorry I am about not showing up for our date," he began. "The patient was unstable, and I couldn't leave him for a minute to call. Poor guy didn't make it. Please give me another chance."

Elizabeth saw the black bags under his blue eyes as he moved closer. He'd had a few rough days too.

"It's not a problem," she replied. "Patients first. Isn't that a Tulane Surgery motto?"

He smiled again and said, "This one falls into the category of 'No good deed goes unpunished.' I stupidly volunteered to make rounds for a member of the faculty whose son had a sports event. I was excited about our dinner and trying to kill time while I waited to pick you up. When the patient coded in the ICU, however, my evening plans with you were rearranged."

"Let's forget it," Elizabeth suggested. "What cases are you presenting in the conference today?" He looked sad, and she immediately felt remorse for asking.

"Baby boy Trahan, the little guy with tetralogy."

"I remember him." She choked up, recalling Dr. White's reaction in the stairwell after the child died.

His face flushed red as he sat across from her and opened a textbook to review his notes. Neither spoke again.

Five minutes before the conference was to begin, students, interns, residents, and faculty swarmed into the small library. Elizabeth rose from the table and took her place in the back with the other interns. She noticed Michael had a smirk on his face and showed no signs of remorse about the poor surgical outcome of the baby he had been summoned to discuss.

After everyone was seated, Dr. McSwain stood and said, "We have an unusually long list of complications and deaths this week. Most come from the trauma service. We have reviewed the deaths from gunshot wounds ad nauseam in this conference. Unless any of the faculty objects, I'll summarize to save time: There are too many drugs, too many kids willing to die to sell them, too many illegal guns, and not enough blood. If you get shot too many times from a high-caliber weapon, only God can intervene," he said. "The fact that we save anyone with multiple gunshot wounds is a miracle. The trauma service is doing the best we can in a hideous situation. I have personally reviewed every death from the last two weeks and can find no error we made that could have led to a save. We did save a couple of people who, by all accounts, should have been unsalvageable." He paused. "Anyone else have anything to say before we move onto the death on the pediatric cardiovascular surgery service?"

Elizabeth's heart hammered in her chest. She didn't realize the many deaths in Room Four would be on the list this week. She was horrified to perceive she considered those deaths to be part of the routine of the Charity emergency room. She had not reviewed or prepared even one case and wondered when she had become so calloused. *Is this the life I want? Do I have to give up my humanity to train as a surgeon?*

Nobody spoke, and Dr. White stood. Elizabeth looked down at the floor. He stood tall with perfect posture and looked contrite. He didn't flinch while taking full responsibility for the death. He explained meticulously every step of the patient's care. He recalled in gut-wrenching detail every place where he thought his judgment could have been better. He drilled into the students and residents every error he thought he'd made and how they could avoid the same errors in the future. He was brutal in making an example of himself.

Elizabeth felt queasy and wanted to protest. "You did your best," she wanted to say. "Nobody could have done better." She had not witnessed greater integrity. Dr. White flayed himself for their educational benefit. Her heart ached for the child, his family, and this doctor.

When Dr. White finished presenting his case, nobody spoke. Everyone knew there was nothing anyone could say that Dr. White had not said. He'd done a painful bit of surgery on himself, excising his own ego and getting to the heart of the matter. The baby had died from an infection in his urine. The culture was found to be positive twenty-four hours after his death. Nobody could have made the bacteria in the culture grow quicker. Baby boy Trahan died from a delay in diagnosis of an infection and sepsis. Grim silence followed his discussion.

No doctor's perfect. The work of a surgeon can lead to miraculous lifesaving events, and it can lead to death and horror, sometimes. Small choices have big consequences, and sometimes, there's no good solution. Sometimes, the patient has a problem modern medicine and surgery cannot treat.

Next up was Dr. Leblanc. He grinned and said, "Well, after that happy note, this case should be an easy one. I'd like to thank Dr. McSwain for asking me to present this case. By the way, is Tulane paying my gas money back to Alexandria?" He laughed, but no one else did.

Dr. McSwain said, "Enough of comedy time, Doctor. Please move on with your complication." His face was flushed and his eyes intense. He took the conference seriously, and he expected the residents to do the same. After all, Dr. Leblanc was just an intern.

"Yes, sir. It's pretty simple. A baby had an umbilical hernia repair in which three stitches were placed. The mother of the child was not a smart person. She didn't take care of the wound, and the baby came to Charity with her small bowel extruded through the 1.5-centimeter incision. The baby was taken to the operating room, and the wound was closed in fifteen minutes. The baby and the not-so-smart mother went home the same day. Happy ending for all, I'd say." He bowed, gathered his notes, and started to sit down.

Dr. White glared at him. In a menacing voice, he said, "Not so fast, Doctor. Stitches don't just fall out. If your ridiculous theory was correct, and I'm sure it's not, a dirty wound would take more than forty-eight hours to cause the stitches to *fall out*. Even if the mother had rubbed dirt in the wound, it could not have fallen apart in forty-eight hours, Dr. LeBlanc. Surgeons do not blame their patients or their patients' family members for poor surgical outcomes. Our purpose in this conference is to consider what we might have done better to prevent a problem such as yours in the future. Am I to understand that any patient of ours with uneducated parents is to expect a bad surgical outcome?" His voice got louder with every statement and question.

Dr. McSwain nodded at Dr. White and signaled for him to settle down. Dr. McSwain said, "Dr. LeBlanc is an intern and is not used to presenting at this conference. That having been said, Dr. LeBlanc, Dr. White has some very good points. Even an intern should know the causes of wound dehiscence. I'd appreciate your reviewing them for our students and telling us which of the known causes applied to your patient."

Michael looked frustrated. He took a deep breath and referred to his notes. "The kid didn't have diabetes or obesity, or poor nutrition, and she didn't smoke yet. So I assumed she had an infection. It was the only option that seemed to apply."

Dr. McSwain said, "An infection would certainly be something to consider. Was the little girl febrile?"

"No, sir, she was not."

"Was the wound red and swollen?"

"No, sir, it was not."

"Was there any pus evident when the wound was explored?"

"No, sir." said Leblanc. His eyes were wide and his breathing shallow. He looked panicked. His smirk was gone.

"OK, son. What did the culture of the wound show?"

Dr. Leblanc looked down and said, "It was negative, Dr. McSwain." His eyes pleaded.

"So there were no signs of infection, yet your theory is 'poor wound care and infection' as the cause of the breakdown of this child's wound? Am I understanding your summary correctly?" asked McSwain.

"In all honesty, I have no idea why the wound fell open. It was just three little stitches in a tiny incision. I guess sometimes that just happens," said LeBlanc.

"Son, if you don't want to get fired today, you'd better come clean. I know why it fell apart, and I'm giving you one chance to say it or so help me, you'll never be a Tulane surgeon," said McSwain. He was shaking, and his voice boomed in the small conference room. He looked on the verge of violence.

"The stitches fell apart," said Michael. "They were lying in the incision unwound. There must have been something wrong with the suture material. I didn't want to say that because I couldn't prove it," said LeBlanc.

Dr. White growled. "You tied them incorrectly. Properly placed sutures using the correct knots for the type of suture do not 'fall apart,' They were tied wrong."

Dr. LeBlanc glared at Dr. White and said, "You weren't there. What makes you so certain?"

Dr. McSwain said, "Enough, gentlemen. Dr. White has a point. Students, you can learn from this case. The time we have you spend tying knots repetitively on boards is time well spent. It may seem silly at the time you're doing it, but surgical technique is extremely important. Even the smallest case, three stitches in a 1.5-centimeter incision, can go horribly wrong if not executed perfectly." He pulled three green braided stitches from his pocket and dropped them on the table in front of Dr. LeBlanc.

Dr. McSwain said, "The operating room nurse pulled these sutures out of the trash and gave them to me. The knots had come unraveled. Dr. LeBlanc, please stay after the conference today to speak with me and several of the other faculty. Everyone else may leave. Conference is adjourned for today."

Elizabeth and the herd of students, interns, and residents fled to the door. The palpable anxiety in the room led to their pushing and shoving to escape. Dr. White remained seated with the faculty.

Elizabeth remembered her father's words: *Don't lie, little girl. It's best to take your medicine on the front end.* Michael must have missed that lesson.

37

Elizabeth walked to her apartment, wondering if Michael would be fired following his performance at the conference. It was rare for Dr. McSwain to show his anger.

She entered the garden and saw Ray wearing flower-patterned cotton gloves and a matching apron. He was bent over a bed, pruning plants and digging in the soil while Bella lay at his feet in the late-day sun. Elizabeth smelled gardenias and felt at home. "Hi, Ray," she greeted him and bent to scratch Bella's head. The dog stretched its neck up to meet her hand and licked her with enthusiasm.

"It's good to see you," Ray replied. "John's away buying for our store. Maybe we can grab a muffuletta and eat in the garden tomorrow night."

"That sounds great," Elizabeth replied, "but I have the twenty-four-hour shift at Charity tomorrow. Maybe the next day?"

Ray frowned, wiped sweat from his brow with his elbow, and said, "John will be back then. He can't stand the smell of all that garlic, so maybe we'll do it the next time he goes out of town." He bent to his work.

"Just let me know," Elizabeth told him. She walked up the stairs to her apartment, wondering if she'd ever have time for socializing with friends again. Being a surgeon wasn't conducive to having a normal life. She retrieved her pearls from the table on her deck and realized a day in the sun had done little to lighten the bloodstains. As she put her key in the door, her pager sounded: "Please call the Tulane operator for Dr. White holding."

Elizabeth dialed right away. She wished to know what had happened to Michael.

Dr. White said, "Hello, Elizabeth. I hope I'm not disturbing you. I hate to ask for dates at the last minute, but I saw the calendar and noticed you're working most days for the next week. I'm free tonight. Could I take you to Mr. B's to make up for my poor manners regarding our last date?"

Elizabeth felt uncertain. She was tired and craved sleep, but the sound of his voice excited her. And she was hungry. "What time?"

"I can be there in forty-five minutes. But whatever time works for you is fine."

"Yes. Dinner sounds good. I'll be ready."

"Excellent!" he replied. "I'm excited. I'll be at your door in forty-five minutes."

She laughed and said, "I'll believe it when I see it."

"Nothing will keep me away tonight." And he hung up.

Elizabeth surveyed her apartment. She had no intention of bringing him there tonight, but while she cleaned herself, she also cleaned her space. She picked her new dress off the floor and shook it out. She hung it in the shower area while she showered to allow the steam to help the wrinkles fall out. She made her bed. But then she decided she didn't have the energy or time to do much in the way of primping. She wasn't going to wear her fancy black lace underwear. The humiliation of her ripped scrubs was still too fresh. She wore her ugly old undies instead and noticed her silhouette was not as smooth as it had been when she'd worn the ones she'd bought at Ms. LaFleur's. She laughed at her foolishness.

She put her wet hair up in a neat French twist, dabbed on mascara and lip gloss, and fastened her pearls at her neck. She thought it best she had no time to primp. *He might as well see my poor grooming standards sooner rather than later.*

Her buzzer sounded, and she ran down the stairs and through the garden to the iron gate. As she passed Ray, he said in an exaggerated Southern accent, "Hot damn! You're looking good. I'm glad to see you striking out for someplace besides Charity. Enjoy, sweet girl."

"Thanks, Ray." She hoped Dr. White hadn't heard Ray's remarks as she opened the gate and joined him on the sidewalk. He wore a tailored suit that accentuated his trim, athletic build.

"You look great. True beauty requires little adornment," he told her.

"Good thing," Elizabeth replied. He laughed.

They walked in silence over the rough pavers of the uneven sidewalk, making their way the ten blocks up Royal Street to the restaurant. Elizabeth, wearing her new heels, was forced to catch Dr. White's arm to steady herself. He walked on the traffic side and tucked her hand inside his right elbow. Although she knew he'd do that for any woman he was escorting, whether the woman was his granny or his niece, to her, it felt intimate. Their hips touched every few steps because she couldn't walk in a straight line in her heels. She felt a shock of pleasure every time it happened. He laughed and asked, "Have you been drinking?"

"No. I'm just spasmo," she told him. "I've worn only tennis shoes for months, and I never was all that good at walking in heels, anyway. Sorry."

"I like it. It calms my nerves to focus on stabilizing my date to be sure she makes it to the restaurant."

He opened the door to Mr. B's and a rush of cool air flooded out. *They're running the air conditioner in February.* The place was packed and bustling at 7:00 p.m. on a weeknight. The maître d' hustled their way after he saw Dr. White. He was tall and portly, with a head full of wire-like unruly black hair. His smile was big and welcoming. His name tag said *Ramon.* "We're glad to see you, Harrison. I'm sorry your usual table is tied up."

"No problem. We didn't have a reservation. I'd appreciate your tucking us in—anywhere quiet."

"There's no quiet tonight, Doc. We have several conventions in town, and you know the tourists—they drink too much, eat too much, and yell at everyone around them. Sometimes, I think they think they're at the rodeo, not a fine dining establishment."

Dr. White laughed. "New Orleans would be nowhere without the tourists. Put us near the least rowdy group."

Elizabeth took extra care walking through the crowded room, hoping not to crash into the chair of any patron.

Dr. White pulled out her chair and sat close beside her instead of across from her. His thigh touched hers, and she felt electricity run through the length of her leg. *This is ridiculous! He's just a man.*

Her hands shook as she reached for the menu. Ramon smiled and nodded at her but spoke to Dr. White. "Do you need a little time or shall I bring your usual?"

"Give us some time. We're in no hurry tonight, Ramon."

Ramon bowed and smiled, saying, "As you wish." He headed to another table.

Elizabeth squirmed and tried to focus on the extensive menu.

"Have you been here before?"

"No, I haven't."

"My favorite is their signature dish, barbequed shrimp, but it's messy. I like my new tie too much to eat it tonight. One night, we'll come back in clothes we're willing to ruin and eat my favorite dish."

Elizabeth laughed. She couldn't imagine him—the surgeon with stellar eye-hand coordination—spilling food on himself. "What do you suggest?"

"The food here's mostly upscale Creole cooking. They have a great wood fire grill, and the Trout Meuniere Amandine is superb."

Elizabeth's mouth watered. "Sounds good. I'll have that." She was shocked when she saw the prices on the menu and wondered if they shouldn't share a meal. She stayed quiet and let him lead the way.

"What kind of wine do you like?"

She dreaded that question. She thought it rude to drink only water in a fine restaurant, but she was afraid she'd embarrass herself again if she drank. "I'm not a big drinker," she admitted. "You choose, and I'll enjoy anything."

"I'm on backup call for Tulane. I'll just have one glass."

He ordered a bottle of chardonnay and pronounced the name of the wine with ease. "Latour Puligny-Montrachet."

Elizabeth had never ordered an entire bottle of any kind of wine. The price was half a day's salary for her. This wasn't an iced-tea kind of place. She felt silly and excited. Though she loved new experiences, she hated feeling inadequate. She vowed to have only one glass, even if there was a full bottle at the table.

"Do you like bread pudding?"

She said, "I haven't had it enough to say."

"If it's OK with you, we'll forgo the salad and soup courses and save ourselves for their knock-out dessert. It has an Irish whiskey sauce with dark raisins that you really don't want to miss."

Oh no! More alcohol. "Sounds great."

Ramon, in between his duties at the maître d' station, took their order, and they sat silently looking around at the other diners. Most men wore suits. Most women wore nice dresses. A few sat at the bar and ate in jeans and polo shirts. Elizabeth liked the New Orleans come-as-you-are approach to dressing.

"I hope you like what we have ordered," he said. "New Orleans food is so rich that it's almost sickening. Most of the time, I eat salads and lighter fare. If I ate like this every day, I'd be on the OR schedule to have my gallbladder removed. Since a gallbladder is a second-year resident case. I'll stick with moderation."

They laughed. He brought her attention back to surgery, and she remembered Michael. She said, "What happened to Dr. LeBlanc after we left?"

He looked down and didn't speak for a few seconds. Then he looked into her eyes and said, "Your question brings up a good subject. I'm a fellow now, but in the near future, I may be faculty. You have years to go in your training." He looked serious. "So on that note, I can't tell you anything about what went on with your fellow intern except to say lying regarding patient care is frowned upon by the faculty."

Still looking serious, he continued, "It's important we establish boundaries for the future. I hope you don't mind, but I discussed our dating with Dr. McSwain. He thought as long as I'm not your mentor, advisor, direct teacher, or in any way was responsible for grading you or for your future, it is acceptable for us to date. It's imperative we keep our work and personal relationships separate." He paused again. She hated gossip, didn't usually engage in gossip, and hated being told to mind her own business. *He is chastising me like I'm a child.* She disliked his scrutiny, and she was surprised to learn he thought enough of their dating to discuss it with her mentor, and she hated the fact that he did it without consulting her. Her anger boiled, and she refused to speak.

Their food came, but Elizabeth had lost her appetite. Ramon uncorked the wine. Dr. White tasted it and approved. Ramon filled their glasses. They sat in silence.

"Elizabeth, you look upset," he said. "I'm sorry if I didn't handle things properly with Dr. McSwain. I'm almost through the process of training. But you're just starting out, and you're a girl . . ." his voice trailed off.

Just a girl! She laughed because she thought of throwing her wine in his face. She laughed because she didn't know what to say. His pleading tone told her he thought he was doing the best thing for her, but the disrespect of his talking to her mentor about her personal life enraged her. She looked at her fish, forced a bite into her mouth, and washed it down with a gulp of wine. She couldn't look at him and instead stared at the blurring crowd of raucous patrons.

He leaned in and whispered, "I can tell I've made a big mistake. I'm sorry. I can't not date you. I can't wait until one of us graduates. I've not been in this position before. Elizabeth, you matter to me. I'm very sorry if I've buggered this up before it even got started. Please say something." He put his fork down and leaned closer.

She felt the heat of his body near hers. She didn't want to talk. She was afraid of her own words. What she really wanted was to fight. She longed to drag him outside on the street in front of Mr. B's and throttle him. Her anger needed physical release. The thought of beating him and the look on the faces of the patrons and the passersby brought her back with a laugh. She looked at him and said, "In the future, I suggest you talk to me before you talk to my boss. I was wrong to ask about Michael. That's none of my business. But you were dead wrong to discuss my personal life with Dr. McSwain without my permission."

Dr. White's face glowed red. His ears were scarlet. He was unaccustomed to being scolded. He took a few deep breaths, pulled away, and said, "You're right. I'll speak to you first in the future."

The anger passed. They ate in silence, and Elizabeth avoided her wine. She feared if she lost her inhibitions, she might really try to pummel him.

After she calmed down, she realized the food was some of the best she'd ever tasted. Her fish was moist and lightly seasoned to enhance the delicate flavor. By the time the dessert came, she had relaxed.

"Bread pudding is a New Orleans favorite," Dr. White told her. "I don't know where it got started, but since I was a little guy, we always ordered it at restaurants. Every place in town tries to outdo every other when it comes to bread pudding. I think it's the best at Galatoire's. But this is pretty close. What do you think?"

"I haven't had enough bread pudding to have an opinion. Before coming to New Orleans, my dessert experience was pound cake, peach cobbler, apple pie, brownies, and ice cream. The best dessert I've ever had was fresh-churned peach ice cream on the back porch at my granddaddy's farm."

"What made it so special?"

Elizabeth knew everyone in New Orleans was obsessed with food. If conversation lagged, or if things got awkward, bring up food.

"It was probably the twelve hours we spent working in the fields that made it taste so good."

He nearly choked on his bread pudding. His eyes opened wide, and he said incredulously, "You worked in the fields? What kind of fields?"

"Tobacco, cotton, peanuts, and vegetables of all types. You name it; we grew it. My grandparents' farm was one of the last fully self-sufficient farms in South Carolina. We grew all the food for forty people to eat for most of a year. We had an orchard, pigs, cows, a smokehouse, and chickens, and we grew crops like tobacco and cotton for money to keep it running. All the kids worked every morning before school, every afternoon after school, and all summer. We also canned and froze lots of food for the winter."

His fork dripped with whiskey sauce and hung in midair. His mouth gaped open. He put his fork down, turned to her, and said, "I can't imagine. It must have been very hard. How'd you feel about it?"

She looked at his clean, soft, white hands and wanted to laugh. She was certain he couldn't imagine it as she tried to imagine those hands pouring gentian violet on the scrotum of a squealing piglet and doing a pig pen castration. She looked into his eyes, saw genuine interest, and said, "There was really no time to think about it. As kids, we didn't know anything else. It was pretty wholesome. We worked hard, played hard, went to church on Wednesday and Sunday, and went to school during the year. Everyone did whatever Granddaddy told them to do. He was in charge. You did as you were told."

"It sounds like good preparation for a career in surgery. But how on earth did you make it from there to here?"

She knew nothing of him, but he certainly was learning all about her. She was torn between shifting the conversation to another topic and telling him everything. She thought for a few minutes and decided to tell him the truth.

If this won't run him off, nothing will. "By the time I was an adolescent, I began yearning to spend my time reading, not doing so much physical work. I resented having no time to myself. The guilt and shame I heard about in church didn't seem right to me. Working until I fell into a trance every night seemed no way to spend a lifetime. I became curious about the outside world and restless to explore it. When I was eleven, Mamma gave me a spanking for staying awake reading Marcus Aurelius under the covers with a flashlight. She thought it her duty to get those fancy ideas out of my head and prepare me for a life of being a good wife or maybe a teacher or possibly a nurse. I vowed that night to find a way to read whatever I wanted whenever I wanted."

"Wow. I can't imagine." He'd stopped eating. He sat and stared at her.

"I'm sure you can't. Don't get me wrong. I adore my family. I miss all of them every day. I miss the farm too—though maybe not the chickens. Chickens are the meanest, nastiest creatures on earth. But I started to realize other girls got new clothes every year, and they didn't have to work. I became friends at school with people whose families owned shops, ran car repair places, had beauty salons. I met the kids of doctors and lawyers and realized I wanted more than back-breaking work and church. My father understood. My mother was disappointed." She hated the sad look she saw on Dr. White's face. She didn't mean to sound so negative; she loved her life and was grateful for her family and upbringing.

"Can we change the subject?" she asked. "I've had enough of True Confessions of the Poor White Girl down the Street. Let's talk about something else."

"OK," he told her. "We'll move on. But you do realize New Orleans is as close to the opposite of where you came from as it gets. When you decided to change, you really changed." He laughed.

"Oh, I know. I spent my first three months here in shock. Strangely, it's growing on me. I love the food, the music, the people, and the culture. New Orleans has to be one of the most mixed-up places on earth. There's a kindness and tolerance of others that I love."

"It's mixed up alright," Dr. White agreed. "One day, if you have time to read about something besides surgery, read about the history of New Orleans. It's a port city with all the foibles of ports, but it's more. The French, the Spanish, the Africans, the Indians, plus pirates, Catholics,

Creoles, Cajuns—it's all here in the stew we call New Orleans. There's really no place like it, for better and for worse."

Mr. B's was becoming even nosier with the arrival of more rowdy tourists, and they couldn't hear each other anymore. Elizabeth was grateful. She was not her favorite topic of conversation. They finished splitting the bread pudding. Both had only sipped their wine, and half the bottle remained. He paid the check, thanked Ramon, and left a huge tip.

The Quarter had cooled during their meal. She felt him drop his jacket on her shoulders and put his arm around her as they headed back to her apartment. She felt panicked like she usually did at this point in dating.

I hate this part. I don't know this man—except as a surgeon. I don't want intimacy with someone I don't know. If I'm too cold or hesitant, he'll take it wrong. If I do something I don't want to do, I'll hate myself. She tried to quiet her thoughts. *I need to stop analyzing everything! That's my real problem.*

At her gate, he turned to her and pulled her close. She buried her face in his shoulder. He felt hot and smelled wonderful. He rubbed her back like he might a child's and kissed her head. She felt warm, and her body wanted more. He pushed her back a few inches, pulled her chin up with his forefinger, and kissed her, placing one hand behind her head and trapping her face against his. Her feelings of panic rose, and she fought the urge to squirm away. After a moment, she gave up, relaxed, and went with his lead. She kissed him back. In that small moment, she wanted everything. Her longing for a husband and family crushed her.

Suddenly, he pulled away and groaned. "Whoa!" he said. "I'd better settle down here. Elizabeth, I want a relationship with you. You're beautiful, smart, and interesting. Our lives have been very different up to now, and I'm not the most experienced person at dating. When I was younger, I went to debutante parties and dated girls my family wanted me to date. I've spent most of my time and all of my energy on medicine. I want to go slow with you and do this right."

He took her shoulders and pushed her back a foot. He wiped her lip gloss off his mouth with the back of his hand. She blinked multiple times, trying to dampen the lust he had awakened in her. She was relieved by his retreat. It felt right.

“I know we’ve only had a couple of dates, but we’ve seen each other repetitively under stressful scenarios over the last nine months. I feel we know a great deal about each other.” He looked at the ground, then met her eyes. “My family’s getting together for brunch at Brennan’s in two weeks, and I’d like you to come and meet everyone. It’s carnival season, and I’d like to take you to Rex. Perhaps it sounds crazy, but my mom wants to meet you before the ball if you have any interest in going.”

She felt dizzy. She had been dying to go to Brennan’s. She’d not been to a ball. It seemed too early to meet his family. At this point, she disliked him more than she liked him. He stared at her, waiting for an answer. She knew her mom would approve of him.

“OK,” she said despite her misgivings. “I’ll arrange my schedule to try to make the brunch at Brennan’s. I’ll have to think about the ball.”

He laughed. “You’re something else. I’ve not met anyone willing to turn down an invitation to go to Rex.”

Elizabeth was not impressed. His family, his money, his status in the community meant nothing to her. She wanted to find out what kind of man he was. She wanted to glean his medical knowledge and his surgical skills. And she was still chafing about his having discussed dating her with Dr. McSwain. When she didn’t reply, he said, “I’ll call you with the details.” He walked hastened, leaving her to go up to her empty apartment and unlock her own door.

38

Elizabeth was surprised she slept so well. She munched on a stale bagel as she passed Brennan's on her way to the hospital. She was excited knowing she'd eat there soon with Dr. White's family. *It's unnatural to think of him as Harrison.*

When she entered the bustling hospital, it was still dark outside. She liked being there before shift change so she could enjoy the nurses and observe the goings-on. Charity was a fascinating place if you weren't responsible and could relax and enjoy the circus, but it was terrifying to be in charge. Too many life-threatening events happened simultaneously. It felt out of control because it was.

Gurneys were crowded along the walls. Every exam room except Room Four was full. Today, Room Four was clean and quiet, waiting for the next life-threatening trauma. Elizabeth watched her shell-shocked LSU counterpart, Adrien Lambert, walk from room to room with his students and nurses. Elizabeth savored the few moments before she took the baton of the surgical charge resident. When the clock struck seven, it would be a Tulane day at Mother Charity.

As Adrien finished his rounds, Livvy appeared. She was starting her shift too.

He reported, "It's been another wild night, but right now, it's slow. In Room Eleven there's a young girl I've not had time to evaluate. The medical student thinks she has a tonsillar abscess. The child and the room both smell repulsive. If I were you, Elizabeth, I'd put some menthol on a surgical mask before going in there. If the student's report is correct, the child's been sick for a while. Unfortunately, the mother chose the Voodoo route. It hasn't worked, and now she's here. The kid doesn't have an IV yet." He sighed, then continued, "I've lost sympathy for people who use these quacks and then expect us to bail them out. I figure if the kid's waited weeks, another couple of hours won't matter. Besides, they came in close to turnover time."

I hate seeing Adrien become jaded. I know he's tired, but every patient deserves our best efforts.

Livvy's penetrating eyes stared at Adrien. She waited until he left and said to Elizabeth, "I've been doing this a long time, and I think folks who believe in Voodoo are serious. They don't appreciate a condescending attitude. Many trust their local traiteurs more than they will ever trust us. If we want any chance of getting that mother to do the right thing for her child, we'd better not show any trace of condescension, or they'll be out of here."

"I agree," Elizabeth replied. "Much of what we do as doctors comes from traditional herbal medicine, and it works pretty well. We also know 30 percent of our patients get better no matter what we do, due to the placebo response. The body has amazing healing abilities if given the tincture of patience. I don't judge folks for trying other things, but I hope the mother hasn't waited too long."

"I can smell that hideous anaerobic bacteria smell," Livvy observed. "I'd put my money on a staph infection."

"Tonsillar abscesses can be terrible," Elizabeth agreed. "I think we should start with her, knowing she's likely to need surgery today. Where's that menthol?"

Livvy pulled the jar from under the desk in the nurses' station. "Here you go, Crème Puff."

They rubbed the fronts of their masks with menthol and opened the door to exam Room Eleven. The revolting odor poured out. Elizabeth didn't know if her eyes were watering because of the odor or from the menthol. She fought not to gag.

If it's this foul through a mask impregnated with menthol, how's the mother tolerating it?

A little girl of three years lay on the examination bed, wrapped in a clean blanket. Her neck was covered by a brown piece of cloth. The mother stood holding the child's hand. Both were clean but simply dressed. The mother's worry showed in her furrowed brow. She wore a loose-fitting floral house dress with plastic slides. The baby had immaculate braids with multicolor bobbles attached. Elizabeth touched the mother's back, introduced herself and Livvy, and asked her to tell them what was happening with her child. They did not yet touch the little girl.

In heavy Plaquemines Parish patois, the mother said, "Three weeks ago she started to smell funny. Her head smelled terrible. I brushed her teeth three times every day, and it never got better. I washed her whole body every morning and every night, and the stink got worse every day. I took her to our local healer, and she gave her a gris-gris, did a conjuring, and prescribed nine days of novenas. She rubbed her gums with crawfish tails. Nothing worked. Every day, my babe smelled worse."

The child had visible chills. Livvy took her temperature. It was 103.5. Elizabeth was worried and hoped the child wouldn't seize. Elizabeth asked, "What caused you to come in today?"

The mother said, "Our local traiteur felt she had communicated with the spirit Loa and had been successfully entered. If that and the poultices didn't work, she said we should go to the Big Free."

"May I examine your child?" asked Elizabeth. The mother stepped back a few inches and nodded but held the child's foot. Elizabeth pulled back the blanket and saw an old brown sock wrapped around the child's neck. It felt like it contained the bones of a small animal. The child's chest was covered in a dark stain that had started to crust and peel with the perspiration from her fever.

Elizabeth swallowed her saliva to avoid vomiting. "What's around her neck and on her chest?"

The mother looked at the floor and whispered, "The sock's full of rabbit bones. The traiteur sacrificed a young black chicken and rubbed the blood on her chest. That usually works. This time it didn't."

She's as casual as if she had rubbed her child with Vick's VapoRub and used a humidifier.

The child cried as Elizabeth removed the sock. The odor grew more pungent with her wailing. A string tied with knots and a silver dime was around the child's neck under the sock, and another string was tied around the child's waist. There was white powder on the little girl's neck and back.

"What's the powdery substance?" said Elizabeth.

"Ashes. Those are ashes," said Livvy.

This mother went all out for her little girl. Seems they tried everything. I wonder what was next?

"Livvy, get a medical student in here. Let's get an IV started, get some fluids in her, and get some penicillin going. Whatever is infected will need antibiotics. Mom, at what time did she last eat or drink?"

"She ain't been willing to eat or drink since yesterday. I tell you what, Doc. That scared me more than anything. This little girl's an eater. She'll eat anything."

Elizabeth wished the mother had brought her daughter to the hospital earlier, but she heard Livvy's warning about condescension in her head and squelched her anger about the situation to keep the mother from sensing her emotions.

On examination, Elizabeth didn't find enlarged lymph nodes under the little girl's neck. The child's heart was racing, but her breath sounds were clear. She looked in the child's throat and was shocked to see that her tonsils looked normal. She looked in the child's ears, and they looked normal too. She felt panicked. The typical causes for fever, failure to thrive, poor appetite, and foul-smelling breath were not evident.

"Has she ever had anything like this before?"

"No, ma'am," said the mother.

"Has anyone in the home been sick?"

"My oldest got food poisoning from a bad shrimp, but that was two weeks ago. He's fine now. And he never stunk like her."

"OK, let's get the fluids going and the antibiotics started." Elizabeth and Livvy exited to the hall.

"What the heck is wrong with that child?" Elizabeth asked. "I looked in her mouth for a tooth abscess. Can't see one. Her tonsils look better than mine. Her ears are normal. I feel no enlarged lymph nodes. What could it be, Livvy?"

Livvy put her hands on her hips and sauntered down the hall to the nurses' station. Elizabeth followed. When out of hearing distance from the mother, Livvy said, "I don't know, Crème Puff. Since Miss Marie Laveau, the Queen of Voodoo, is dead, I suggest you call Dr. Parker. He's done a lot of pediatric surgery and can direct you. This is one time I'm glad not to be the doctor. This case is fascinating and all, but I'm glad I don't have to figure it out."

Elizabeth hated to bother Tony. She stood in the hall contemplating every diagnosis possible to explain the smelly, sick, feverish child. She reentered the room and palpated the child's head and neck again to be sure she hadn't missed a skin abscess. The child was clean, and her skin felt smooth and soft.

She screamed when the student started her IV, but the mother held her daughter tight on the table while she cooed and patted the child to reassure her.

Elizabeth walked to the phone and dialed the on-call room number. Tony answered on the first ring.

"It's Elizabeth. I'm sorry to bother you. I'm in the ER with a sick little girl, and I wondered if you have time to discuss the case with me. I can't figure out what's wrong."

"That's what senior residents are for," Tony told her. "We're here to back you up. You call me less often than the other interns, and if you can't figure it out, it must be interesting. I'll be right down, and we'll examine the kid together."

Elizabeth sighed with relief. “I have to warn you. The child has the whole emergency area smelling to the high heavens with an anaerobe.”

“That’s easy. It’s most likely a tonsillar abscess. That’s the only thing that can smell that bad.”

“Dig deeper,” Elizabeth replied. “Her tonsils are totally normal. Mom took her to a Voodoo practitioner, and the child’s been sick for at least two weeks.”

“I’ll be right there. This does sound interesting.” He came through the back door quicker than Elizabeth imagined he could make it.

Livvy handed him a surgical mask and wiped the front with menthol. The three entered exam Room Eleven. Tony staggered back as they opened the door. He coughed, gagged, and took a few shallow breaths. Facing the mother as she bounced the baby on her hip, he said, “I’m Dr. Parker. I work with Dr. Roberts, and she asked me to take a look at your child. Is that okay with you?”

“What’s the matter? Y’all don’t know what’s wrong with my baby? She got something you can’t figure out?” Her eyes were wide, and she clutched the child closer.

Tony paused, put his hand on the mother’s upper back, and said, “We’re certain she has an infection. We want to know the extent of it because sometimes infections only need antibiotics, and sometimes, they need more.”

The mother placed the child back on the exam table but never took her eyes off Tony. “Where you from?” she asked him. “You ain’t no American doctor.”

Elizabeth knew Tony was tired of explaining his accent. She also suspected the mother, having exhausted all resources with the traiteurs, now wanted a white American doctor, not a Black island guy, to treat her child.

He said, “I grew up on an island and still have an accent, but I’m a full-fledged American doctor, ma’am.” He waited for her approval before he touched her child.

Elizabeth twitched with fury. *How dare this woman bring her sick child in here with rags and potions tied on her and not want to see the most competent doctor available?* She tried to maintain her composure and stepped back to allow Tony to handle what was familiar to him. She was afraid of what she might say. She was accustomed to some patients not wanting to see a female doctor. She expected it. But she couldn't understand how anyone could not want Tony.

The mother said, "OK. If you're sure you know what you're doing, go ahead."

Tony swallowed hard while he examined the child's tonsils. He also determined they were normal. He, too, was surprised the ears were normal. He asked the mother to hold the child's head still while he looked in her nose. He turned his head, held his breath, and tried not to throw up. Then he looked over this shoulder at Elizabeth and said, "I've found the problem. Come and look for yourself."

While the little girl thrashed, the mother and Livvy and Tony held her tight. Elizabeth looked inside her nose. "It's a bright purple mass with pus seeping around it. What is that?"

Livvy whispered, "Mardi Gras bead."

Tony said, "It's a Mardi Gras bead. Livvy, get a nasal speculum, and we'll see if we can get it out down here. It looks like it's been in there for a while. She may need to go to the OR to get it removed, but we'll give it a try. Get some morphine and a board to tie her on."

39

Elizabeth and Tony and the mother struggled with the squirming child for fifteen minutes. The swelling had cemented the bead in her nose. Despite using pediatric instruments, they could not dislodge it. The door to the exam room opened, and Dr. McSwain entered without a mask to mitigate the odor. He smiled at the mother, looked at Tony, and said, "That's enough, doctors. I commend your effort to avoid general anesthesia, but now it's time to take her to the operating room, get this thing out, and get her comfortable."

Livvy must have called him when she left the room.

Tony said, "Yes, sir." He let the child go to her mother and put the instruments on the tray.

Dr. McSwain looked at the mother and said, "We'll take good care of your baby. She'll be perfectly fine by tomorrow. You can stay with her until she goes up to the operating room."

The mother said to Dr. McSwain, "You in charge?"

He said, "Yes, I'm in charge."

She looked at Tony and Elizabeth and said, "Good to know it."

Elizabeth and Tony held each other's eyes and followed Dr. McSwain into the hall.

Back at the nurses' station, he said, "Good job. I guess after all the Voodoo, the mother wanted a little gray hair." He pointed to his temples. He'd called the ENT service, and they arrived to take the child to the operating room. Dr. McSwain left the ER to go back to his private practice surgery schedule.

"It could've been the gray hair," Tony said after Dr. McSwain was gone. "But it's most likely that she wanted a white male doctor." He sighed. "Sometimes, I get sick of it. If I'm tired or hungry, it makes me want to scream. Does it bother you?"

Elizabeth said, "When directed at me, not much. But for you, it ticks me off. Dr. McSwain's so confident. I don't know if it's his age or his swagger or his maleness or his being white or a combination of all those things, but I've never seen a patient or family challenge him." She paused then continued, "Honestly, Tony, I try not to think about it. It takes everything I've got to do this job. In the beginning, it bothered me if Livvy called Dr. McSwain. Now, I only want to get the work done and get some rest. I figure when I know what I'm doing, as many patients will want me because I'm a girl as won't want me because I'm a girl."

Tony crossed his arms over his chest in a self-hug and bounced on the balls of his feet. He made a sucking sound with his teeth. "Let's make a pact to stick together. We're smart. We're focused on the work. Let's have each other's backs as much as we can. OK?"

She smiled in warm affection. She didn't need a pact. "Like my daddy says, 'It's a good family that knows we can't all be crazy on the same day.'" Tony chuckled.

Elizabeth watched Tony leave and saw Livvy trying to sneak out behind him. She knew Livvy didn't like to be confronted after having tattled to Dr. McSwain. Elizabeth had many hours to go on this shift and no energy to argue with Livvy. Besides, she realized, *I don't care.* The little girl got what she needed, and right now, what Elizabeth needed was a nap in the radiology room.

The rest of the shift went smoothly. A Tulane student ordered a pizza around midnight. Elizabeth woke up to the smell of garlic, ate a piece of the pizza, checked the students' suturing, called orthopedics to set a couple of broken bones, packed a nosebleed, and slept a few hours in between.

At seven the next morning, Livvy arrived with beignets and café au lait. Elizabeth knew it was Livvy's way of apologizing for summoning the boss. When Livvy's back was turned, Elizabeth punished her by grabbing the largest cup of coffee and the entire bag of beignets and running out the back door before she could be discovered. *Livvy has no idea what she'd face if I ever were to unleash all the revenge tactics I've learned from my cousins.* Hogging the best food was one minor form of revenge.

Her shift completed, Elizabeth jogged through the lobby, past the Fistula fast-food shop and onto the sidewalk, leaving a trail of powdered sugar the entire way. Once outside the hospital, she ran to the corner, laughing out loud while chunks of beignet shot from her mouth. She felt affection for the team, gratitude for training at Mother Charity, and was happy to have a few hours out of the hospital.

On her way home, as she passed Tulane Medical Center. She looked up to the windows of the ICU, knowing Dr. White was probably doing heart surgery there today. She hoped his cases went well and wondered if his patients knew how lucky they were to have him as their surgeon. Her emotions were strong and mixed about him. She had deep respect for him as a doctor and was proud of him. She wanted to be as competent as him. She giggled at the thought of him naked and gobbled up another beignet.

Her plan for the day was to sleep, study her surgery textbooks, and clean the frog's terrarium. There was so much to learn and do and so little time. As she walked, she daydreamed about her upcoming date at Brennan's.

Livvy called a few hours later and asked, "Did you steal my food?"

"Of course not," Elizabeth assured her. "Why would I do that? I know you need all that caffeine and sugar to keep your strength up for gossiping and tattling." She knew Livvy was uncomfortable and that her discomfort usually led to bullying. She didn't mind Livvy being a busybody because she knew Livvy was the biggest patient advocate around.

"I knew y'all couldn't get that bead out of that child," Livvy said. "I've watched surgeons try to get beads out of every orifice, and it seldom works out when there's swelling. I was afraid her mother was going to grab her and leave. Don't be so sensitive. I knew Dr. McSwain was between surgeries and that it was a good time for him to run over."

Elizabeth laughed. "It's not a problem. Six months ago, I would've been upset. Charity has beaten me into a state of reasonableness. Whatever gets the work done is fine by me. I sure did enjoy those beignets, Nurse Robichaud. It's nice the way you take care of us doctors."

"Girl," Livvy began, "I'll get you for this. I had to eat a honey bun from the Fistula Café for breakfast. You will pay." Her tone was playful and light.

They were quiet for a moment. Livvy asked, "How's everything going with Prince Charming?"

"I'd appreciate your keeping this between us," Elizabeth told her. "The hospital gossip mill doesn't need a blow-by-blow account of our dates. I'll tell you, but you have to promise to be discreet."

"Discreet! Discreet! That's a fancy word for an intern, Crème Puff. I told you before that you're not that interesting. I can keep a secret if necessary. What's up?"

"He invited me to brunch at Brennan's with his family on Sunday. He's talked about the ball called Rex but hasn't invited me."

Livvy gasped. "Crème Puff, he's showing you to his family to get their approval to invite you to the biggest Carnival event of the year. This is a big deal. Those uptown types don't stray far from their own flock unless they have good reason. It wasn't that many generations ago that they only married their own cousins."

Elizabeth realized Livvy was probably right.

"I'm scheduled to go to Alexandria for my next rotation," said Elizabeth. "I have no days off that entire month, so no matter what he has in mind, my schedule will make me unavailable." Her sense of relief surprised her.

"Don't be surprised if your schedule miraculously changes."

Elizabeth changed the subject. "I've got to do some laundry, and Ray and John said I could use their washer today. I need to go. I want to be out of their way before they get home from work."

"Run and hide; that's your MO. Sometimes, I think the life of a surgeon is perfect for you. You don't like your feelings, and if anything comes up you don't want to face, you suddenly need to work."

Elizabeth rolled her eyes and sighed. "And you? You're so good with your feelings? I should take lessons from you?"

"I didn't say that," Livvy admitted. "I'm worse than you. I won't even attempt to date. At least you're going on a few dates. I can't stand to think about it."

"We'll use me as the test case. If I go on a few more dates and nothing horrendous happens, then it'll be your turn, and you'll have to go on a date."

"Gotta go!" Livvy said quickly. "Codes everywhere, blood everywhere. Talk to ya soon." And Livvy hung up.

40

Elizabeth worked her assigned shifts and slept on her days off. When the big Sunday arrived, she dressed with care for her brunch date at Brennan's with Dr. White's family.

She had two dressy dresses—the blue one she'd bought at Yvonne LaFleur's, which was the most appropriate for Sunday morning, and the black one she'd borrowed from Aoife. She had worn the blue dress on their date to Mr. B's, though she thought Dr. White probably would not remember what she wore as most guys weren't attentive to girls' wardrobe choices. She felt pretty and relaxed in Aoife's black cocktail dress and decided to wear it. She had borrowed a tin of black shoe polish from Ray, and she used it to polish and buff the worn heels of the borrowed black sandals to a shine. Even though black stockings weren't the best choice for Sunday brunch, Elizabeth thought they were better than wearing her nude pantyhose with a run in one leg.

She washed and rolled her hair. She manicured her nails and applied extra lipstick. She was ready and dressed an hour early. So she played with her pearls and talked to her frog while she waited for Dr. White.

He arrived at ten forty-five on the dot. She answered the buzzer, and he said, "It's me." He sounded as excited as Elizabeth felt.

She ran down the spiral stairs, careful not to slip on the bricks in the garden, and opened the wrought iron gate. He stood smiling with a fresh haircut and his blue eyes sparkling in the morning sun. He wore a grey seersucker summer-weight suit with a starched white shirt and a bright red silk tie. The outfit would have been appropriate for Easter. His only nod to the fact that it was February was his tan shoes. She remembered wealthy men in Charleston wearing white bucks with seersucker suits. She looked down at her black dress and realized the contrast.

Oh, well, nobody really cares what someone's wearing, do they?

"You look gorgeous," Dr White told her. "I'm glad none of my male cousins could make it today, or I'd have serious competition. My sisters, my female cousins, and my parents will be with us this morning. The girls talk nonstop. I apologize in advance."

Elizabeth thought his chatter was odd. He usually only spoke of important matters or about medicine. He looked anxious. She wondered why.

They walked along the familiar route to Brennan's. "It'll be fun to be with a bunch of girls," she told him. "I spend so much time with men at the hospital. Girls will be a welcome change."

He held the heavy glass door at the entrance to the restaurant. The atmosphere inside was festive. As they made their way to the maître d' stand, the hostess looked up and smiled at Dr. White. She walked past three waiting couples and greeted him, saying, "Hi, Harrison. It's good to see you. Your family's gathered in the garden. Follow me."

They walked past an elaborate buffet. Elizabeth's stomach growled. She hadn't seen so many types of food displayed so elegantly. As they walked into the garden, Elizabeth felt like a princess in a fairytale. The garden was lush, with blooming plants everywhere. Coral-colored hibiscuses stood as tall as small trees. Purple bougainvillea spilled from trellises. Several twenty-foot-tall Ficus trees were strung with tiny twinkling white lights. A jazz quartet tucked in the corner of the garden played softly. Elizabeth thought she recognized Louis Armstrong's "Dream a Little Dream of Me." The guests wore their Sunday best. The muted pastel colors of the people's clothing created a blur that reminded Elizabeth of an Impressionist watercolor.

The beauty of nature, the great New Orleans music, the smell of delicious food, and the hope of new relationships filled her with joy. She walked to the table feeling as if she were living in one of her best dreams.

Harrison guided her to a table near the brick wall with steady pressure on her upper back. His hand felt strong and hot. Elizabeth smiled when he introduced her. *They look like movie stars.* The father stood as he saw them approach. He was tall and handsome and dignified. He had the same sparkly blue eyes she loved in her dad and this man's son. He shook her hand and bowed slightly.

Dr. White's mother had perfectly coiffed blonde hair and hazel eyes. She wore a pink tailored suit and kissed her son on the cheek. "Elizabeth, I'm happy to meet you. Harrison has told us many nice things. Thanks for joining us for brunch." Her voice sounded soft and elegant, with a lyrical cadence.

Elizabeth sat beside Dr. White's father and was introduced to the sisters and cousins once everyone was seated. All the girls wore unusual and colorful hats. Elizabeth had only ever seen hats like these on church ladies and Catholics at Easter. The women in her family wore hats at funerals or for sun protection in the fields.

Champagne and mimosas were passed by an attentive server in a tuxedo. Harrison pointed to the beauty across from him and said, "This is my sister, Sarah. She was born after me. I'm the oldest in our family and, of course, the most wise." Everyone laughed. Sarah had wild chocolate-brown curly hair that fell out from under her wide-brimmed, peach-colored hat. She wore a cream-colored suit tailored to fit her curvy body. Sarah smiled and gave Elizabeth a little wave. "Nice to meet you," said Sarah. Elizabeth relaxed.

Dr. White proceeded around the table with introductions while everyone sipped cocktails. "Next to Sarah is my cousin Gay," he continued. "She's older than me and is the smartest of all the cousins. Her dad's my father's older brother. She's engaged to a radiologist at Touro."

Gay laughed easily. She was dressed from head to toe in lavender. Her hat was cocked to one side with netting covering her face. *How does she get food past that netting?* Elizabeth knew if she wore that hat, she'd likely stuff the netting in her mouth when attempting to eat and drink.

Gay said, "Because I could walk and talk before they could, they think I'm a genius." Everyone laughed loudly.

These folks are nice and fun.

Harrison said, "At the end of the table is my baby sister, Kathryn. She's the family black sheep, the one who just won't do right. Dad spoiled her. She refused to go to Sacred Heart, refused to go to Tulane. She's a student at—heaven forbid—LSU. And if that weren't enough, she's interested in the law."

Kathryn stuck out her tongue at Dr. White. Elizabeth saw love in her eyes, and it was evident the brother and sister adored each other. She said, "After him, what could I possibly do to get attention? He's Mr. Perfect. So I pretend to be the spoiled brat and do everything the opposite of him." Kathryn had soft brown eyes and peachy skin with freckles across her nose and cheeks. She was dressed in a sage green suit with a tan straw hat that dipped on one side to show a shiny black feather draped over her neck. She was sitting at the end of the table because her hat required the width of two seats.

Dr. White said, "Kathryn's the baby of the family. Kathryn gets what Kathryn wants if Dad's around."

Mr. White cleared his throat. And Mrs. White said, "Harrison, Elizabeth doesn't need to be bombarded with all our family's laundry before our first trip to the buffet. At least let her have a couple of drinks before telling all."

"Yes, Mother. You're correct," replied her son. "Last, but not least, is my cousin Susan. She's our musical genius. She plays the flute at Sacred Heart and is second chair flute in the New Orleans Symphony. She hopes to go to Julliard."

The petite blonde smiled sweetly and said, "Welcome to our crazy family. You'll get used to us, all except Harrison. He lives at the hospital, so there's little chance of getting used to him. He shows up on holidays and sleeps through most family events."

Elizabeth thought Susan had the elegance of a swan. Her neck was long and her hands delicate. Her skin was milky white. She wore a light blue sheath. Her body was also thin and delicate. Her hat was a tiny pill box with cream-colored netting that covered only her forehead.

Elizabeth felt awkward and a bit like a crow with swans. But Elizabeth liked them. They seemed beautiful, accomplished, and witty. They reminded her of aristocrats from the 1800s about to embark on an Easter egg hunt or a game of croquet on the lawn of a country estate. All of the women wore pearls. Harrison's mother wore the largest, darkest pearls she'd ever seen. When he patted her leg, Elizabeth realized she had been holding her breath during the introductions.

Elizabeth sipped her mimosa and looked around. She thought she could distinguish the locals from the tourists. The tourists' voices were too loud. They ate too much too fast and talked with their mouths full. They were gauche compared to the locals.

Dr. White asked his father about business at the bank. His mother asked Elizabeth how she liked New Orleans. The sisters and cousins joked with each other about men.

Then Mr. White said, "Let's head to the buffet. Elizabeth, as our guest, why don't you lead? Make sure you get ahead of Susan if you want any food. She's little but always ravenous."

The group pushed back their chairs and stood as one. Dr. White assisted Elizabeth, and Mr. White assisted Mrs. White. Elizabeth went first, as requested.

Harrison pointed to the start of the buffet line. Men in tuxedos stood at every station and served. Elizabeth was careful to take small portions even though she'd have liked to pile her plate beyond capacity.

"You must try the shrimp and grits. It's really good here. And don't forget the remoulade for your crab cakes," said Harrison.

They returned to the table, and he pulled out her chair. The server appeared and placed their napkins on their laps.

"Are you doing OK?" asked Harrison.

"Yes. They're lovely. Thanks for inviting me."

"We do a family meal once a month. You'll definitely have to join us at the racetrack when the season starts. We have a nice booth there, and the horse racing is fun."

Elizabeth had never seen a horse race. She thought of the stubborn old mules at the farm and laughed to herself at the thought of them racing. They wouldn't leave the barn for anyone but her granddaddy. *This is a different world, but I like it.*

After everyone was seated and eating, the chatter resumed. The girls talked to each other about art, music, and theater.

Sarah said, "Harrison, your favorite group is going to be at Tipitina's next weekend. The Meters are playing there most Saturday nights for the next month. Maybe we could meet and go?"

Harrison wiped his mouth with his starched white napkin and said, "We're getting into the height of Carnival season. I'll check the calendar and check Elizabeth's on-call schedule. We'll see what we can figure out."

Elizabeth saw a surprised look pass between Harrison's parents. Nobody was more surprised than she was. She felt exhilarated, realizing he was including her in his plans.

The two cousins stared at Harrison but didn't speak. Elizabeth couldn't add to the conversation because her life was in the hospital. She'd never had money for tickets to the theater or the symphony. In college, she'd volunteered as an usher and handed out programs for college productions, so she'd seen many plays and heard many symphonies but had experienced nothing at the professional level.

Still, she felt compelled to join the conversation, asking, "Where do you get your gorgeous hats?" All the women stopped eating and stared at her.

Gay said, "We have them custom made at Fleur de Paris. It's on Royal, near here. Harrison, you should walk by there to show it to her. You'll love it," she told Elizabeth. "They have every imaginable feather, bow, and bobble to suit your whimsy." Elizabeth couldn't imagine herself commissioning a hat. It seemed natural to these young women but absurd to her.

Harrison's mother talked of her charity work and the many organizations she supported. She insisted each girl in the family assist with some aspect of a charity's luncheon. Her son and husband asked polite questions but seemed bored. Elizabeth couldn't remember the last time she'd had a social lunch. Lunch for her was wearing scrubs while standing and gobbling food between patients. Lunch wasn't part of the life of a surgeon. She realized she would probably find ladies' lunches boring, like the men seemed to.

The group returned from the dessert buffet as Elizabeth's pager screamed, *Please call the Tulane Operator. I have a doctor holding. Please call the Tulane operator.*

Harrison helped her with her chair, pointed to the phone near the maître d' station, and said, "I thought you weren't on call?"

"I'm not," Elizabeth replied.

"I hope it's nothing important," said Dr. White. He sat back down at their table but watched her make her way through the doors and into the restaurant.

Elizabeth used the phone near the maître d's station. The Tulane operator said, "Please hold for Dr. LeBlanc."

W*hat the heck is he calling me about?*

Michael said, "Hey, sorry to bother you on Sunday morning. I need to discuss a schedule change with you. I'd like to be at Huey P. Long Memorial next month. You and I were supposed to switch next month with you working Huey P. and me working the trauma emergency room at the Big Free. Dr. McSwain's secretary called me and asked if I'd be willing to switch with you. I'd like to switch because the jerks put me on probation for that stupid complication with the baby. Also, I'm dating a hot nurse there and would like to spend more time with her."

I didn't request a change. I'm looking forward to the slower pace of Alexandria. But I do hate to leave Dr. White for a month. Did he arrange this change so he can ask me to Rex?

"OK," Elizabeth agreed. "I'll do it."

Dr. LeBlanc said, "That was easy. Thanks, Elizabeth. You're all right for a stuck-up little goody two-shoes. I'll let Dr. McSwain's secretary know about our change."

Michael's jab couldn't quell her excitement. She saw a server and asked for directions to the ladies' room. She wanted to reapply her lipstick and be certain there was no food in her teeth.

She walked into an enormous room with chairs upholstered in an ornate brocade tapestry. The tables and lamps sparkled with gold flecks. The toilet area was not visible. She stood in the sitting area and took it all in. The walls were lined with beveled mirrors. The carpet was deep and plush. She heard giggling through the open door of the room beyond.

One voice said, "I can't believe Harrison would bring some hick to brunch and have the nerve to ask Mommy if he could bring her to Rex."

Elizabeth stumbled back toward the entrance. She was stunned.

She recognized the next voice as Harrison's sister, Sarah. "I've never seen anyone more shabbily dressed unless they were homeless. What kind of upbringing did she have to make her think black hose and a black cocktail dress were appropriate for Sunday morning brunch at Brennan's in the garden?"

Susan said, "Y'all are being catty. What would the priest say? What about loving your neighbor?"

Sarah said, "We can love her from afar, Susan. Did you see her scuffed up black shoes? They were too big, and it looked like she'd tried to camouflage the wear with some cheap black polish. Maybe she used a Sharpie."

They all laughed except Susan. She said, "You hens better get over yourselves because Harrison looks smitten. I've not seen him this enthralled with any girl, ever. He's completely taken with her. And y'all had better stop this mean girl mess because if he finds out . . ." Her voice trailed off.

Gay said, "Your mother will never allow this relationship. This girl is smart and pretty enough, but she could not fit into the family. When Harrison said she was a country girl, he wasn't kidding. Did you see those nasty pearls she's wearing? They disgust me."

Susan said, "I don't like any of you right now. She's a surgery resident. That's probably blood on those pearls. I think we should accept her and make cleaning her up our charity project. Each of us can take a part in bringing her up to the family standards. It'll be fun and very Christian of us. I like a good project."

Listening to them, Elizabeth fought conflicting urges. One part of her wanted to run into the room, snatch their fancy hats off their heads, and dunk them in the toilet bowl, then afterward beat them all to a pulp. Another part of her wanted to walk in and smile, touch up her lipstick, and act like nothing happened, leaving them to wonder how much she'd heard. She fought back sobs. She felt insecure and lonely and ashamed and foolish. She felt not good enough. She wanted Livvy and her dad. She turned and tiptoed quietly out the door, trembling as tears ran down her face.

She motioned to their server and said, "Please let Dr. White know I had to leave to go to the hospital. Tell them I said thanks for having me and that I'm sorry I had to leave so abruptly."

The server put his hand on her arm and asked kindly, "Are you alright? Can I get anything for you?"

"Please don't mention my tears. I'm just disappointed to have to leave. Please make sure they know I have left."

She walked out of Brennan's in the direction of the hospital in case anyone saw her. After turning the corner, she ran home as fast as her scuffed up sandals would take her. She sobbed as she ran, hating them all.

Before she got to her apartment, she knew Dr. White was not for her. His family members were not people she could love and respect. She jerked open the wrought iron gate and fled up her staircase to the solace of her tiny apartment. She cried for an hour and then called Livvy.

41

Livvy answered the call and arrived at Elizabeth's apartment in fifteen minutes. She saw the pile of wet tissues, Elizabeth's swollen face and bloodshot eyes, and the tear-soaked front of her old scrub shirt.

Livvy sat and held Elizabeth's hand. "What in the world? Did someone pass? Is your family all right, honey?"

Elizabeth sobbed. She knew she looked pitiful, and Livvy's kindness broke her customary reserve.

As Elizabeth explained, Livvy listened. Saying nothing, she hugged Elizabeth several times and doled out more tissues. As the story progressed, Elizabeth noticed Livvy snatched the tissues from the box with increasing agitation.

When Elizabeth's story ended, Livvy railed, "That's the meanest bunch of witches I've ever heard of. How dare they?" Elizabeth's long white fingers were entwined in Livvy's short plump brown ones. Elizabeth's polished nails covered the backs of Livvy's dimpled hands, which were dry and ashy from washing them thirty times a day. The young doctor yearned to crawl into Livvy's lap, tuck her head under Livvy's chin, and take a nap. She felt raw and stripped. She'd cried until she was dry.

They sat in silence, holding hands for a long time. They stared down at the afternoon sun shining through the French doors and making patterns on the old wooden floor.

Elizabeth was the first to move. She threw her pile of tissues in the trash with one hand, sat up straight, and admitted, "I'm grateful this happened."

Livvy's eyes were wide. She snorted and released Elizabeth's remaining hand. "I wish I'd been in that bathroom. There'd be some fancy uptown girls headed to the emergency room about now."

"No, Livvy," Elizabeth protested. "Let's think about it another way. Most people go for extended periods in a relationship before they find out family secrets and become aware of personality details. Many are married before they come to realize they've married the wrong person. Those girls' meanness was a gift. It was like an amputation. It hurt like the devil, but it was over fast. I couldn't accept being part of a family like his. I'd never fit in. Even the daughter who tried to be nice considered me a 'fixer-upper.' These people are not my people. I'm grateful for this knowledge before things went too far."

"Why don't you sleep on this?" Livvy suggested. "Don't be rash. Pray about it. Harrison White's quite the catch. Most people's families aren't perfect. The relationship is between the two of you. He'll rein them in if he's serious about you."

Elizabeth moved to the stove to make tea. The water in the pot boiled, and she waited with her back to Livvy while the tea steeped. She filled two of her chipped cups full of strong tea and sat across from Livvy.

"I'm done," Elizabeth said. "There's nothing he can say. I can't imagine my family with his family. The thought's too painful to consider. I would never let my sweet, loving family be judged and ridiculed by anyone." She looked at the cup in her hands and said, "I consider a teacup usable if I can drink from it so the chips don't scratch my mouth. Can you imagine those girls' comments if I served them tea in my chipped cups?" She shook her head. "Besides, I came here to learn to be a surgeon, not to get a husband."

Livvy sipped her tea and nodded. "Before meeting you, I thought the only folks plagued with prejudice were people like me. You've taught me that prejudice comes in many forms. You were brave to venture out. I'm not willing to try. I want a perfect man who probably doesn't even exist. And if he did exist, he'd probably not want me." She shook her head. "What will you do now?"

"Fortunately, I have a job that fills one hundred hours a week of my time. So I won't have much time or energy to fret over Harrison White. I'm not good at dating, but I am good at medicine. I'll focus on my strengths. My mom and everyone else will have to accept me as I am." She rummaged through her pile of dirty clothes and pulled out a note.

"These people might be my people. I'm going to call the Cajuns I've seen in the emergency room and take them up on their invitation to visit their fish camp."

Livvy laughed. "You're one crazy chick, Crème Puff. You have considered that you might be going from one brand of crazy to another, haven't you? But one thing about Cajuns is they know how to have a good time. I'd like to go with you if they're open to a tag-along."

"It's four o'clock on Sunday afternoon. Do you think this is a reasonable time to call them?"

"I don't see where you have much to lose. Why not? You already survived a big gut punch today. Ring them up."

Elizabeth pulled the heavy black telephone into her lap and dialed the number. It rang and rang. Finally, an out-of-breath female voice answered. Elizabeth heard laughter and music blasting in the background and wondered if she'd accidentally dialed a bar.

"Hello," said the woman.

"This is Dr. Elizabeth Roberts. I'm trying to reach the Benoits. I may have the wrong number."

"No, cher, you have the right number. Wait just a minute and let me pull the phone in the bathroom. It's quieter in there. This is Mellette," said Mrs. Benoit.

Elizabeth held the phone away from her ear so Livvy could also hear the conversation.

"Leeodus will be delighted you called," Mellette told her. "Come on out to the fish camp. We have a party every weekend unless it's storming. We'd love for you to join us."

Livvy nodded, but Elizabeth felt exhausted from the emotional ups and downs of her day. She needed sleep more than anything.

"I can't come today, but how about next weekend?"

The two held on the line while Mellette gave directions to the camp and confirmed Elizabeth's friends were welcome too. Elizabeth said she wasn't sure of her schedule, but Mellette assured her they would be at the fish camp Friday through Sunday next weekend.

Elizabeth thanked her, returned the receiver to the cradle, and said to Livvy, "I like her."

After they finished their tea, Livvy and Elizabeth walked in the Quarter, avoiding Royal Street and the area around Brennan's. They sat in Jackson Square and watched the local gathering of artists, jugglers, mimes, and drunken tourists. They sat in companionable silence and talked little.

At sunset, Elizabeth returned to her apartment to find her phone ringing. She stared at it for a moment, knowing the caller was Dr. White. She already regretted giving him her number, but she knew he'd keep calling until she answered. After the sixth ring, she picked up.

"I've been worried about you," he said. "I'm sorry you had to leave. I called Charity, and you weren't there. Is everything all right?"

Elizabeth took a few deep breaths. She didn't know what to say.

After a few minutes of silence, he said, "Elizabeth, please talk to me. I'm upset. I hope nothing happened at the luncheon to upset you. Can I come over?"

"Please give me a minute to gather my thoughts, Harrison. Please don't come over. I'm very grateful for the time we've had together, but—"

He interrupted, "*Please* don't tell me you don't want to see me again. Please, Elizabeth, don't."

"I'm very sorry. I realized today that our worlds are simply too far apart. You come from wealth, and I'm a farm girl. It's that simple. It just won't work."

"We knew about our differences from the start. I want this. I want us to work. My feelings have never been this strong for anyone. Please don't give up."

His begging startled her. She clutched the phone and cried silently. *I don't want to marry you. I want to be you.*

"Please tell me what happened," he implored. "Was someone ugly to you? If that was it, I can promise it will *never* happen again. Never." His voice was adamant.

If she told him the truth, she knew it would make no difference in the long run, and it wouldn't fix anything. Elizabeth hated this part of her personality, but after she was done with something she could not go back, only forward. It was her best and worst defense mechanism. When she thought of her career at Tulane, she realized becoming a good surgeon was more important to her than any relationship. She saw no point in causing pain between Dr. White and his family. She couldn't imagine navigating a complex relationship and excelling in the world of surgery at the same time. She chose surgery.

"Dr. White," she began.

"Elizabeth, my name is Harrison."

She said, "Harrison, you're not the one for me. I can't fit into your life. I want to focus fully on my education as a surgeon, and dating you is too big a distraction. I'm sorry." She felt guilty for not telling him the truth.

"Why do I believe there's more to this?" he asked. "Please tell me so I can fix it. Please sleep on this, and let's get a bite tomorrow night after you leave the hospital."

She swallowed hard and said, "No, thank you. I don't want any more dates. There's nothing to discuss. I'm sorry, but I have to go."

She heard him say her name as she gently placed the phone receiver back in the cradle and started, again, to sob.

42

To Elizabeth, the night seemed endless, and she spent it with intermittent sobbing and fitful sleep. When morning came, she headed to the hospital, choosing to walk a different route, avoiding Brennan's because the memories of Sunday's brunch were too painful. She walked fast, focused on work and the day ahead. Determined to forget yesterday, she looked forward to the numbing pace of the emergency room.

Adrien greeted her when she arrived. It was Livvy's day off, and Aoife was the charge nurse today. Elizabeth was relieved nobody working that day knew of her hurt.

Adrien said, "It's been another wild night. But not to worry. The LSU Surgery team has saved the day again. There's nothing left for you to do except manage a guy with a bowel obstruction. It'll take all day in surgery for LSU to clean up what came in over the last six hours. The bowel obstruction guy was last seen by Tulane, so he's yours."

He sounded jovial. Elizabeth wondered why. Adrien usually didn't have the energy to be jocular about the Tulane/LSU rivalry.

He looks good. It must be the right combination of caffeine in his system and sleep in our cubbyhole. "You sound happy. What's up?" she asked him.

"I've been scheduled for an out-of-town rotation next month," he replied. "I can't wait to get out of this pressure cooker. I'll be working twelve-hour shifts instead of twenty-four, and I'll have days off where I don't have to go to the clinic. I plan to take my golf clubs and pretend I'm a radiology resident!"

They laughed. Elizabeth remembered she had canceled her out-of-town rotation to stay in town and not interrupt her dating life. She wondered if it was too late to switch back with Michael. Working out of town sounded great, though she knew she'd miss Livvy and the diversion of visiting the Benoits' fish camp.

Aoife joined them. "Dr. Roberts, I made rounds with the students, and I'd like you to take a look at the guy in Room Seven, please."

Elizabeth appreciated Aoife calling her "doctor" at work. Aoife had been distant since the day Elizabeth surprised her in the on-call room when she was having sex with Michael. Elizabeth hoped they'd eventually get beyond that day.

"Aoife, I know you're tired of hearing this, but I will get your roommate's black cocktail dress and sandals back to her. I'll drop the dress at the dry cleaner's tomorrow." She paused. "Livvy and I are going to a party at a fish camp this weekend. I'd love for you to join us."

Aoife's bright smile and quick hug cleared the slate. "I'd love that! Are any other doctors going?"

"Heavens, no!" said Elizabeth. "The last thing we need is another doctor."

"Excellent! No offense, but I'm a little tired of them myself."

"Let's go to Room Seven."

The patient on the gurney moaned and rolled from side to side as he rubbed his swollen abdomen. His face was flushed, and his eyes were dark and surrounded by purple circles.

Elizabeth studied his chart, introduced herself, and said, "You've had five abdominal surgeries? You seem young for that history."

"Yes. My bowels don't contract right. I have too much colon. It's too big, and I get backed up like this a couple of times a year. It's usually after I eat too much fiber. My guts prefer liquid food."

"I see you refused colostomy the last time you were in. That would solve your problem," said Elizabeth.

"Doc," the patient told her, "I'm only twenty-seven years old. I can't live with a bag filled with poop on my side. I don't even have a wife yet, and I work construction. Can you imagine what the guys at work would say? I know they could smell it. The last time I was in here, they took me to the OR and used some kind of scope to open me up. It was quick and easy, and I didn't miss but one day of work. Can we do that again?"

The operative report from his last visit diagnosed an obstructed colon. His chart said he had a congenital malformation of the colon and a volvulus, or twisting, of the large bowel.

"You know this will happen repetitively until you're forced to have your colon removed, right?"

"I know," he replied. "I'm not ready yet."

"I'll call the resident who is on call for the colorectal service and discuss it with him. I don't have control of his decision, but I'll inform him of your wishes."

She walked to the on-call schedule posted on the wall in the nurses' station and was disappointed to see Dr. Peterson was the senior resident on the colorectal service. She dialed the operator, and while she waited for him to answer, she thought *he really should be a banker and not a surgeon.* She explained the situation to him; he ordered X-rays and said he'd be right down to look at them.

An hour later, while Elizabeth was looking at the films, he arrived. He quizzed her about the findings on the films and noted the obstruction was low in the pelvis.

He said, "This guy should go to surgery, but every operating room is occupied with trauma cases from last night. It's a bit unorthodox, but if you want to try sigmoidoscopy in the emergency room, I'd approve it. You don't need a sterile room to look up the pooper shoot, and after you stick that tube up his rear end with no anesthesia, he might be willing to have surgery. Besides," he said, "I have a tee time scheduled later today." He laughed and walked away.

Aoife echoed what Elizabeth thought. "That guy shouldn't be a surgeon. We can take care of this without him. Lucky for you, I did a rotation in the GI lab. I know how to set up a sigmoidoscopy." She was eager to please Elizabeth.

"I haven't seen this procedure done in the ER," Elizabeth told her. "But if the operating rooms are full, I guess it's OK. That old motto—see one, do one, teach one—will be shortened today to just plain old *do one*."

I've done many colonoscopies. It can't be that hard. "Please get him set up, and I'll meet you in his room in fifteen minutes."

While Aoife prepared the patient, Elizabeth went from room to room with the students, checking their work. She hoped she could treat the patient's problem and get him back to work. She thought about Dr. Peterson's reaction. She didn't respect him, and she disliked his dismissive disregard for the patients. His crass talk was not funny. Many doctors and nurses used dark humor to cope with the stress of the hospital, but Dr. Peterson's scorn for patients seemed different somehow. *I never want to be like him.*

She knew Harrison White and Tony and Dr. McSwain were her role models. Dr. White's handsome face flashed through her mind, and she felt sad and wanted to cry again, but she swallowed her feelings and headed to Room Seven.

The patient was facedown with his buttocks sticking up in the air. Aoife had prepped him and placed drapes all around. She'd given him morphine to relax him. He'd need to cooperate during the procedure and so couldn't be fully sedated.

Elizabeth dilated his anus with a probe and filled his rectum with lidocaine jelly.

He said, "I hate this, but thanks, Doc, for trying to help me. I don't want to lose my good job."

The poor man knelt on all fours, presenting his backside for a painful procedure. To anyone's mind, the scene in Room Seven was barbaric. Many things were done in the emergency room that would ordinarily be done under general anesthesia. Elizabeth justified the attempt to fix the man's problem in the ER because she knew it could be days before he could get on the surgery schedule. The sickest patients came first, but the staff of Mother Charity was known for doing everything with nothing.

Aoife said, "Eliza—I mean, Dr. Roberts—you should wear boots and a thicker gown. Sometimes this can be messy."

The patient looked back over his shoulder at the two women and asked, "Has she done this before? I'm not the first, am I? I heard y'all experiment on folks here."

Aoife patted his back and said, "She's done many in the operating room. We don't do a lot in the Emergency Department. She's very experienced." Aoife winked at Elizabeth.

Elizabeth gently placed the scope in his anus. She was eight inches inside when he started to squirm, and his moaning intensified. Aoife held his hand, patted his head, and whispered reassurances in his ear.

Elizabeth could see a "dead end," a place where the scope ran into a wall of twisted pink inner colon. *Wow! It looks just like the photo in my surgery textbook.* "OK, sir," she told him. "Take a deep breath and try not to move. This is the worst part. It's important we work together here."

"I'll do my best, Doc."

Elizabeth looked through the scope. She hated having her face so close to his anus. She applied steady pressure to push the instrument through the twisted tube of the colon. At the moment she made it through the twist, large volumes of liquid stool shot out around the scope, out his dilated anus, and onto her and the floor and the wall behind her. She held onto the scope despite her disgust. Aoife placed a trash can under the end of the table to catch the remainder of the stool.

"Wow," said Elizabeth. "Aoife, hand me a clean towel."

The patient said, "That hurt like the dickens, but I feel better already."

Dr. Peterson stuck his head in the door and laughed at the scene. "Good job, intern. You've greatly pleased Sterculius, the poop god. This will surely get you an award at the end-of-the-year party. It may not be the 'most likely to succeed,' though."

Elizabeth kept her lips clamped tight for two reasons: she didn't trust herself to speak and she didn't want to ingest any poop. *This is perfect. First, my hopes for a social life are dashed by meeting Dr. White's family. And now I'm covered in poop and that jerk Peterson is here to see it. Yep, just about perfect.*

43

The rest of the week passed quickly. Elizabeth was thrilled about the upcoming trip to the bayou on Saturday. The three met at Elizabeth's apartment.

Livvy looked at what Elizabeth was wearing and said, "You can't wear that khaki skirt and that pink Izod shirt." Still stinging from the brunch debacle, Elizabeth had wondered about appropriate fish camp attire. Livvy wore a loose-fitting sundress, and Aoife wore cut-off denim shorts and a halter top.

Livvy stood in front of Elizabeth's closet and said, "Girl, why don't you have any clothes? What did y'all wear in South Carolina?"

Elizabeth laughed and said, "We had church clothes and work clothes. I have an old pair of jeans. Will they and a scrub shirt work?"

Livvy said, "That'll do."

Elizabeth changed, and they headed to her car. Neither nurse was willing to sit in the front seat of Elizabeth's car because she floor was rusted and open to the road. Elizabeth had placed cardboard over the openings and used duct tape to hold it in place.

Livvy surveyed Elizabeth's car and said, "Your car's worse than Aoife's. If I'd known yours was this bad, I'd have offered to drive."

Elizabeth looked in the rear-view mirror at Livvy and said, "It's not too late to head back."

Livvy said, "If I fall through your rotten car floor, be sure and tell my maw-maw that I love her." They laughed. "Do you know where you're going?"

Elizabeth said, "Not a clue. I knew you'd like a chance to boss me around."

"I hope you're better at driving than sigmoidoscopy," said Livvy. "We're going south to Bayou Barataria. The address you gave me is in Lafitte. Lots of Cajun folks have fishing and duck hunting camps down there."

It feels strange to drive. Elizabeth had walked everywhere since she moved to the French Quarter. After thirty minutes of listening to Aoife and Livvy chatter about the hospital, the surroundings changed to swampy areas with cypress and tupelo. She saw birds and smelled the dense earthy aroma of rotting leaves in areas where the water barely moved. The bayou smelled different from the salt marshes of the South Carolina Low Country. There, the tides at home came and went and stirred the water every few hours. The bayou smelled dark, thick, rich, and dense.

Elizabeth asked, "What's the difference between a bayou and a swamp? Why don't y'all call this a swamp?"

Livvy said, "I'm no biologist, but I think it has to do with water movement. In a swamp, the water doesn't move, and you get that stinky rotten egg smell from the rotting leaves. In the bayou, the water moves out. It moves very slowly, but it moves enough to give a sweet odor."

Livvy, in her role of navigator, gave driving instructions. Elizabeth was grateful to relax and turn when directed to do so. When they came to a narrow dirt road with trees and water on both sides, Livvy instructed, "Turn right here."

Cars lined the narrow road on both sides. Mosquitos pounced as soon as the women exited the car. Aoife and Livvy immediately coated themselves with bug spray. Livvy said, "Crème Puff, come here and let me cover you in bug spray. They have malaria out here." Elizabeth was thankful she was wearing her blue jeans. She lifted her ponytail, and Livvy sprayed her neck.

Elizabeth heard loud music coming from a wooden shack at the end of the road. Aoife started to dance in the middle of the dirt road and said,

"I love zydeco. This song is called 'Don't Mess With My Toot-Toot.' I'm excited."

Elizabeth was unfamiliar with the music blasting from the house, but she thought it sounded playful and fun. As they got closer, she could see the unpainted wooden house was draped in thick moss that grew on the cypress trees. The moss clung to the roof and sides of the house as if the woods were trying to reclaim the house for its own.

The three had started up the stairs to the sloping porch when the screen door burst open and Leeodus walked out. He wore a big grin, jeans, a brown plaid shirt, and his customary cowboy hat and boots.

"Welcome!" he said. "I'm glad to see you, Doc. I remember Nurse Livvy, but who's this beauty? You know I'm partial to redheads!" He looked at Elizabeth. "Don't tell Mellette I was flirting again."

Aoife turned red, shook his hand, and introduced herself.

Leeodus ushered them into the house and pointed to the back. The music was so loud that Elizabeth could hardly hear him talk. "There's beer and a bar back there and boiled shrimp and fried catfish coming out every few minutes. Grab a cold drink and make yourself at home. We've been dancing for hours. Jump right in. If y'all like to fish, there's cane poles and cut bait on the dock, and you're welcome to try your hand. My cousin just caught a big *Poisson rouge* with a *bouchon*. He thinks he's some fancy fisherman, but he's as likely to catch nutria as fish." He cackled with his mouth open and walked off.

Elizabeth stood still and looked around. Aoife ran to the dance floor, ready to join the festivities. Livvy stood close to Elizabeth.

At the back of the house was a giant screened porch hanging over the water. A dock surrounded the entire length of the house and beyond. All the wood was weathered and unpainted. Ceiling fans turned above the musicians, who were crammed in the corner of the screened porch.

"Livvy," Elizabeth asked, "what's that instrument that looks like a washboard?"

"The Cajuns call it a *frottoir.* It's a rubboard. They scratch it with spoons."

Elizabeth had never seen a musical instrument attached to a person like a shirt and played with spoons. She loved the sound of the accordion and liked hearing the fiddle. They watched Aoife dancing with Leeodus.

Livvy said, "This kind of shindig is called a *fais do-do*. Are you going to dance?"

The fiddle player announced the next song, "They Stole My Chicken." Elizabeth giggled. "If someone asks me, I'll dance."

She looked around the walls and saw taxidermy of every type. There were mounted deer heads and ducks and one bobcat. The longest alligator she'd ever seen was stuffed and lying on the floor against one wall. She relaxed. Livvy returned with two bottles of beer.

Someone on the dock screamed and hauled in a giant catfish. Leeodus's wife Mellette danced every dance.

"Livvy, have you ever seen a woman with prettier legs than Mrs. Benoit? She's so graceful. It's fun to watch her," said Elizabeth.

Livvy laughed, "I've never seen shorter cutoff jeans than the ones she's wearing, that's for sure. She's a blur with that red hair flying every time she turns. Yep, she's a beauty."

The accordion, fiddle, triangle, and rubboard players went from song to song, drinking their beers and playing without pausing. At least fifty people were crammed onto the porch and dock. Elizabeth watched small mountains of food being passed from the kitchen area. Someone handed her a bowl of delicious-smelling stew.

"Livvy, what's that in the bowl?" she asked. "It looks like stew with potato salad on it."

Livvy laughed. "That's gumbo. It's made with roux and file powder. Some folks from Louisiana, especially ones from around Houma, put a dollop of potato salad on top of their gumbo. Do me a favor and don't call it stew."

Elizabeth basked happily in the music, food, laughter, and dancing people. She didn't know what most of the French-sounding words meant but felt comfortable anyway. She heard several people address newly arriving folks with the phrase, "How's ya momma an'dem?"

After a while, Leeodus grabbed Elizabeth by the hand and pulled her onto the dance floor. "I waited until you got a beer in you," he told her. "But you can't just stand around. You got to dance, girl."

He pulled her close and gave her a strong lead into a slow waltz, pausing every few minutes to show her the steps. She stepped on his feet, the feet of the people beside them, and her own feet. Nobody cared. Everyone laughed. Many chuckled and called her "sha" and "cher." One man passed them, pointed to Leeodus, and said, "Doc, if you miss a step, it's nothing on you; you trying to dance with a *couyon*, sha!" He waltzed away.

Leeodus said, "Ignore him. That's my brother. He's just jealous." The tempo picked up, and Elizabeth fought to keep up.

Elizabeth passed Livvy, who was dancing with a man who looked to be eighty years old. They danced well together and never missed a step. Livvy smiled broadly and giggled like a child. Elizabeth thought Livvy was the most beautiful woman there. Sweat rolled off everyone in the humid heat.

Elizabeth was out of breath and needed the restroom. Leeodus showed her to the tiny bathroom behind the house. "It's attached to the house and has plumbing, but just barely."

He laughed and trotted back to the dance floor.

Elizabeth looked out the window of the bathroom and saw the start of a magnificent sunset. She watched a small heron land on the shore across from the house. It was her first lavender-colored heron. She stared at the white streak running down its beautiful neck and thought how much she enjoyed learning about new places. She imagined she'd like to travel one day, and resolved to make a mental list of all the places she might go.

She dried her hands and headed back to the screened porch. She wandered into the kitchen, following a nutty aroma. A large woman was stirring a big black skillet. Elizabeth stood beside her.

The woman said, "Baby, don't get too close. This is Cajun napalm, and it'll splatter and burn you bad because it sticks on anything it hits."

Elizabeth stepped back. The woman reminded her of her grandmother. She wore a simple cotton housedress and was barefooted. Her hair was gray and brown and curled out from her bun. Her arms were thick and strong.

"What are you making?"

The woman said, "Roux. I like it dark to go with seafood. The first batch I made was a light roux to go with the chicken and duck gumbo. Now I'm doing crab and shrimp and crawfish gumbo, and I like my roux dark."

Elizabeth loved the smell. "What's in it?"

"Equal parts of fat and flour, about two teaspoons of each per person. Grab that stock pot," she instructed, "and pour some stock in while I keep stirring."

Elizabeth poured the stock, being careful not to splash the cook. She saw a giant pile of shrimp tails and crawfish heads in another pot. She asked, "What's in your stock?"

"I've been boiling them heads and tails all day with some seasoning. Good stock is the key to making a great seafood gumbo."

Leeodus snuck up behind the two and said, "Dang it, Doc. I ain't ever seen Maw-Maw give none of her secrets about her gumbo to anybody. You must have put some kind of spell on her." He laughed. "Next thing you know, she'll be telling you how long to leave the bay leaf in." He laughed again and kissed Maw-Maw on the back of her head before he grabbed Elizabeth by the arm and pulled her toward the dance floor. He said over his shoulder, "You need anything, Maw-Maw? I didn't mean to steal your assistant."

She laughed and said, "No, sha, but be sure she gets some food. She looks a little hungry."

The setting sun turned the water on the bayou into beautiful shades of orange, purple, and red. The tree frogs made a loud racket as the sun sank.

The heron Elizabeth saw earlier reappeared on the shore across from the bayou. The bird hopped around a large turtle, competing for food. Elizabeth thought the bird appeared to be dancing to the beat of the zydeco music.

She and Livvy ate bowls of seafood gumbo and each drank another beer. Aoife danced with every man and woman there. Food held no interest for Aoife. The dance was everything to her.

Some folks started to mumble about having to go to work in the morning and began saying their goodbyes. Elizabeth noticed that nearly all of them cleaned up something before they left. Some people hauled away a bag of trash, others picked up empty beer bottles, and some washed dishes. The men straightened the dock and put away all the fishing paraphernalia. By the time the band played its last song, "Zydeco Gris-Gris," the entire fish camp was clean.

Elizabeth marveled at what she thought was a well-rehearsed family event. Everyone came. Everyone contributed. Everyone cleaned. Nobody was burdened.

As she drove back into the city with Aoife asleep in the back seat and Livvy too tired to talk for once, Elizabeth felt a little buzzed from the beer and her full stomach. *These are my people.*

44

The next morning, back at the emergency room, Elizabeth gave an order for morphine for the kidney stone patient in Room Five. She knew she was writing a prescription for a strong narcotic, but she had deemed it necessary. Livvy peered over her shoulder and said, "I wouldn't do that if I were you."

Elizabeth spun around, looked at Livvy, and said, "The patient has bright red blood in his urine. I saw it myself. What are you trying to say, *Nurse Robichaud*?"

Livvy put her hands on her hips and pointed at the chart. "This guy was here last week on the LSU day. Did you check his fingertips?"

Elizabeth felt frustrated. She wasn't new to the emergency room and didn't like being quizzed by Livvy. *Will she ever trust me?* "What could the patient's fingertips have to do with passing a kidney stone?"

"I'll bet an oyster dinner at Acme Bar that he pricked his fingertips to get the blood for that urine you saw."

"Did you look at his hands?"

"Nope. I haven't been in that room. Call it nurse's intuition."

"I'm not up for games today," Elizabeth said. "I need to study for my end-of-the-year exam. I'd like to get the patients tucked in and get some studying done."

"Should I take Dr. McSwain in there, or do you want to peek?"

Elizabeth closed her eyes, rubbed the bridge of her nose, and counted to ten. *I guess the camaraderie of yesterday is over now that we're back on her turf.* She opened her eyes and glared at Livvy. "OK, Miss Know-It-All, let's go look. But I want twenty-four oysters, not twelve, after I win this bet."

The two entered Room Five. A thin, pale, dark-haired man fidgeted on the exam gurney. He repetitively pulled the sheet on and off and rolled the corners between his fingers. His eyes darted from place to place but couldn't look the two women in their eyes. He said, "Where's my prescription?"

Elizabeth asked, "How's your pain? Remind me, where does it hurt?" He pointed to the opposite side, not the one he indicated in his original complaint. *This doesn't bode well for my winning our bet.* Elizabeth wondered if she had enough money in her checking account to cover the cost of two dozen oysters.

Livvy asked, "May I see your palms, sir?" He held his shaking hands in front of his chest. Elizabeth saw deep scratches on two fingers. The cuts were fresh.

Elizabeth asked, "How'd you get these cuts on your fingers?" The patient dove off the table, throwing the sheet on the floor and pulling out his IV as he ran into the hallway. He was tackled by the security guards and handcuffed quickly, as Livvy had already alerted security, which had stationed the guards nearby.

"I rest my case, Crème Puff." Livvy laughed and walked off. Elizabeth shook her head, knowing the patient soon would be released to hit another ER later that day.

Elizabeth was finishing the paperwork as Dr. White walked through the door of the ER. He looked sad. He looked around to be certain they were alone, then moved close to Elizabeth. He leaned in and was opening his mouth to speak when she said, "Good morning, Dr. White. I wasn't aware we had a consult for cardiothoracic surgery. What can I do for you?" Her heart bounced in her chest.

He stuffed his hands into the pockets of his white coat and looked at his shoes. "There's no consultation. I came to see you. Could we, please, get a bite to eat after work tomorrow?"

Elizabeth's heart raced and tears formed. She blinked, dug her nails into her palms, and swallowed hard. "Please let it go. Please, just let me go. As I told you on the phone, this is not for me. It takes all I have in me to do the work. I have no emotional energy left for relationships." *My mother will have to get over the idea of me married with children.*

He nodded, pivoted like a toy soldier, and left. Elizabeth looked up to see Livvy staring at her. Livvy came over and said, "Are you all right?"

Elizabeth pressed her lips together and nodded. Aoife's red head popped out of Room Eleven and screamed, "I need help in here, NOW!"

Livvy and Elizabeth ran to the room. An elderly gentleman lay pinned between the gurney and the wall. He had a clear plastic bag on his head that was tied around the neck with a blue striped necktie. He was struggling frantically to free himself. He gulped, and the bag filled with moist air. Livvy quickly unlocked the rollers on the gurney. He fell flat on the floor, still clawing at the plastic bag covering his face.

Elizabeth dropped to the floor and helped him untie the necktie. Livvy grabbed a pillow and put it under his head, and Aoife covered him with a blanket. The man was frail and blue around his lips. Livvy attached oxygen from the wall unit to a face mask.

Elizabeth examined his blue nail beds. Tattooed numbers ran half the length of his forearm. He saw her staring at his tattoo. His first words were, "Auschwitz, class of 1943. Doc, please don't tell my wife I tried to off myself; she'd be worse to me than the Nazis." His bright eyes sparkled as he chuckled.

Elizabeth was shocked. *I thought the people who worked in the emergency room displayed dark humor. I can't imagine how this poor guy coped with being in a concentration camp.*

After a few deep breaths, the patient said, "I'm Herb Greenberg. I'm sorry to cause all this drama. I've been told I have incurable pancreatic cancer and that I'll be gone soon. The pain is hideous, and no pill I've been given eases the pain. My wife and daughter brought me here because the Touro emergency room was packed. I thought I'd try to solve the problem myself while I waited. But the arthritis in my shoulders is so bad that I couldn't secure the plastic bag tight enough in the back. That six-inch gap is the reason I'm still here complaining. Doc, you've got to help me," he implored. "Cancer's worse than Auschwitz."

Elizabeth and Livvy helped him stand. He was wobbly at first, but finally managed to sit on the gurney. Elizabeth said, "Livvy, you and Aoife can make rounds. I'll talk to Mr. Greenberg to see what we can figure out." The two nurses left.

Elizabeth sat on a chair beside him and said, "Tell me about you."

His blue eyes filled with tears. "I want to die. There's nothing left but pain and misery. My wife and daughter aren't ready to let me go. They can't understand that enough is enough."

"What if we were able to get some strong intravenous pain medication for you at home? Would that help?"

He reached down and took her hand. "Young lady, I'm eighty-three years old. I've survived a concentration camp. I lived to marry the love of my life and have four wonderful children. I was a physics professor at Tulane for forty-five years. I'm tired. Why does your profession let humans suffer worse than our pets? No veterinarian would let my cat suffer like I'm suffering."

Elizabeth hugged him. She stood beside him, held his hands, and witnessed his pain. "You're right. We don't do death well in this country. We are kinder to our pets than we are to our sickest humans."

"We can't change the system in time for me. Please don't tell my wife I tried to off myself in the emergency room. She looks like a sweet little old lady, but the woman is fierce, and she wouldn't appreciate my independent thinking. Doc, would I have control over the intravenous pain medicine?"

Their eyes locked, and Elizabeth replied, "Yes, sir. You would control the pain medicine."

He patted her on the shoulder and said, "Thank you. Always remember relief of suffering is your duty too. There is no higher calling than the work you've chosen."

She bowed and said, "Yes, sir, I'll remember you and our talk today."

She walked by the nurses' station and said to Aoife, "Please call hospice for Mr. Greenberg. I'll write the orders for him to have as much narcotic as necessary to get him comfortable. Let his wife know he's OK. You can bring her back to see him, but not until after the hospice nurse leaves."

Aoife arranged for hospice while Elizabeth studied for her test in the quiet Radiology room in the back. She looked down at her textbook and saw tears dropping on the page. She thought about her conversation with Dr. White. *This is the life I want. Doing my duty. Using my education. Helping people. This is what I'm meant to do. I can't do what Mom wants.* She wiped away her tears and went back to her book.

An hour later, Tony stuck his head in the door and said, "Hi. Things around here have been so hard lately that I'm planning some fun for us, and you must participate. Everyone's meeting at Joe's on Friday night."

He handed her a piece of paper. "This is a ballot. Vote for the most deserving doctor in each category. I'll announce the winners at Joe's after we've all had a couple of beers. It'll be good for a few laughs. I'll pick up your ballot later. Just so you know, attendance is mandatory per Dr. McSwain. He and a couple of the staff have agreed to cover any emergencies that come up during our awards ceremony."

Elizabeth took the sheet of paper and giggled while she read the categories. "I'll leave my ballot at the nurse's station," she promised, "and I'll be there on Friday night."

Tony left. Elizabeth resumed studying. She hoped Dr. White was one of the staff who'd agreed to cover the emergencies because she wasn't ready to see him again.

45

Work that week sped by in a blur, and Friday night at Joe's came fast. Elizabeth dreaded seeing Dr. White and hoped he wouldn't be attending. She asked Livvy and Aoife to accompany her to Joe's. She hoped exposure to him when in the company of her friends might reduce the hurt and pain she was feeling.

They left the hospital at 7:15 and walked the short distance to Joe's. When they turned the corner on Tulane Avenue, they heard the Rolling Stones' oldie "I Can't Get No Satisfaction," blasting from the small bar.

Elizabeth walked through the door first. The bar was packed, but she spied Dr. White right away. He was propped against the wall with a full beer in his hand. She was disappointed he was present but grateful his gorgeous scrub nurse wasn't with him. She didn't need to add jealousy to her list of raw emotions.

Livvy hugged several nurses she recognized. Aoife avoided Michael LeBlanc and went to the bar to get beers for them.

Tony found Elizabeth and said, "I'm glad you made it. I know you prefer to go home and be alone after a tough week, but I appreciate your coming out. I'm trying to improve our team spirit. Some of the gang are cracking under the pressure and resorting to selfishness to cope. I appreciate those who try to help each other and make the tough life of a surgeon more humane."

Livvy said, "Humane? Really? I'm not sure this gang of drunks is prepared for a philosophy lesson. Let me dummy it down. You think if we're all up on top of one another at Joe's on Friday night, it'll be harder for the a-holes to be a-holes. Am I getting your gist?" She cackled, and they clinked their beer bottles together in a toast.

Elizabeth punched her in the arm and asked, "Livvy, which group do you belong to—the helpers or the selfish?" Elizabeth and Tony laughed.

Livvy said, "Don't start with me, Crème Puff. I came to support you and save you from the big bad blue-eyed wolf. I didn't ask to come to this shindig. You asked me!" Livvy did her best to be indignant, but she was laughing too hard to pull it off.

Each time Elizabeth looked up, she found Dr. White staring at her. He drank little of his beer, and he stood alone, not talking to anyone. His clothes were pressed and clean in contrast to the rest of the crowd, who were guzzling their beer in crumpled and stained scrubs. Livvy steered their group to the wall opposite Dr. White.

Elizabeth was happy to see the medical students Sallie Smith, Jalpa Patel, and Larry Silverstein. She thought back over the year and laughed to herself, remembering their adventures while learning. She took pleasure in their progress and was satisfied with the part she'd played in bringing them along. They had learned so much in a short time. Mother Charity demanded discipline and fortitude.

She saw Dr. Peterson and Michael LeBlanc. She disliked their personalities and paucity of ethics, but she knew she'd learned from both men. She realized some colleagues were shining examples, and others were dire warnings. Good patient care was what mattered to her, and she'd learned to work with all kinds of people to accomplish the goals for her patients.

Aoife hid behind Livvy while Michael's eyes darted from former conquest to potential conquest, seeking what he no doubt hoped would be tonight's delight. Livvy formed a firm wall between him and Aoife, keeping the man at bay.

Dr. McSwain and several other faculty members arrived and stood near Dr. White. Elizabeth felt a surge of anger, remembering when Dr. White told her he had spoken with Dr. McSwain about her private life. She wished she'd never dated anyone within the program and would be sure not to make that mistake again. *Sorry, Mom. I can't be the daughter you desire.*

After an hour of drinking and chatter, Tony took the microphone from the dance floor and asked everyone to settle down. Elizabeth surveyed the crowd and realized most of Tulane and LSU Surgery staff were present.

Tony said, "Thanks for being here tonight. I know it was hard to give up time at the hospital and come over here to drink! I appreciate your sacrifice." The group erupted in laughter and held their beers high to toast Tony and cheer. Most ceased talking and focused on Tony.

Livvy whispered to Elizabeth, "I wonder what 'award' you're getting?"

Elizabeth was panicked. It had not occurred to her she would get anything. Her knees felt weak, and her hands shook. From her mostly untouched glass, a few drops of beer sloshed onto the nasty wooden floor. *I'm too far outside of the group of male surgeons to be considered for any award.* She thought back over the year, recalling the stupid things she'd done, and she wanted to dash for the door. She had "voted" and knew what the categories of awards were but never had considered she might be singled out.

Tony said, "For the non-surgeons present, I'll tell you I passed out ballots to all the surgeons this week. It's the Tulane Surgery version of the Oscars. We're here tonight to make a few people famous."

The raucous laughter made Elizabeth's ears hum, and she grabbed Livvy's arm. "Girl, don't take yourself so dang seriously," Livvy whispered. "This is for fun."

Elizabeth said, "You wouldn't think it's fun if it was happening to you."

Tony took a few sheets of paper out of the front pocket of his scrubs. He motioned for the crowd to quiet and he read, "Our first award is the Assume Award. This award goes to the doctor who has most often made an arse of you and me. It's that one special doctor who always finds a way to laugh at others and make himself look good. This award goes by unanimous vote to the great golfer, Dr. Edward Gregory Peterson."

Elizabeth watched Tony hold up a pink plastic baby butt. She knew the French Quarter was full of trinkets of all types and guessed that was where it came from. Nobody came to claim the award. The crowd clapped and screamed. *He must have snuck out.*

Tony said, "I'll accept this award for Dr. Peterson. I guess he had a late tee time, or maybe he had a board of directors meeting at the bank." Even the LSU gang clapped and hooted.

Elizabeth felt anxious. Seeing the perturbed expression on Elizabeth's face, Livvy said quietly, "You know that's the truth."

Tony said, "Our next award is the Kluver-Bucy Award. For the LSU guys who can't read the big words in those complex medical texts, I'll explain. Kluver-Bucy is a brain injury that causes the patient to be hypersexual and hyper oral. The patient drinks a lot and runs around trying to have sex with anything not moving. This award goes to Dr. Michael LeBlanc."

Aoife's face turned scarlet, and she sank further behind Livvy. Elizabeth felt sorry for her as she watched Michael proudly grab the big beer stein full of foiled condoms and say, "I'm honored to get this award, and I plan to put these to good use but will likely need a refill by tomorrow."

The crowd went crazy. Elizabeth heard Aoife say to Livvy, "That jack—!" The rest of the word was cut off by the whooping of Dr. LeBlanc himself.

Tony said, "Our next award goes to a Tulane *icon*. This guy is the one we call with the toughest cases. He lives in the hospital, and every resident and intern is scared to death of him, but they respect his singleness of purpose. The Surgery Is Better than Sex Award goes to Dr. Harrison Lloyd White III."

Elizabeth was horrified. She was grateful she'd had no more to be embarrassed about than a few ill-fated dates. She was grateful not to be in Aoife's shoes. The award was a plaque with a golden-colored scalpel attached. Dr. White laughed as he took the award. He patted Tony on the shoulder and waved the award around and bowed. He looked uncomfortable and never looked in Elizabeth's direction.

Tony said, "The next award goes to a Tulane faculty member who operated on a patient who caused the residents and interns the most worry and anxiety over the longest period of time. This year's faculty award goes to Dr. Norman McSwain. He had a patient in the ICU for four months, and all the Tulane doctors know who I'm talking about because we all breathed a sigh of relief when this patient walked out. Dr. McSwain gets the coveted Albatross Award."

Dr. McSwain, ever the good sport, crossed the room to much fanfare and got his award. It was a tiny bronze-colored albatross sitting on a small Tulane green marble pedestal.

Dr. McSwain said, "I'm proud to accept this wonderful award. I look forward to passing it on to another faculty member next year. Tony has asked me to keep this beautiful turkey—I mean albatross—on my desk for the entire year until someone else earns it." He walked back to where Dr. White was standing, carrying the award over his head so all could see. He threw back a quick shot of bourbon after re-assuming his position along the wall.

Tony said, "Thanks, Dr. McSwain, for being one of the gang. Our next award goes to a truly deserving person. To my knowledge, this doctor is the only surgeon to ever attempt volvulus reduction in the emergency room. She will be a Tulane legend for many years to come. Let's hear it for Dr. Elizabeth Roberts. She gets the much-coveted BOHICA award. Bend Over Here It Comes Again! In her case, it was the patient that was bent over and the doctor who got *it* with an SH before the IT in the face. Come on up here, Dr. Roberts."

Elizabeth finally knew what the walk of shame felt like. She'd heard sorority girls speak of it in college, but she'd not experienced it. She slowly made her way through the hooting and howling crowd to get her award, a miniature sigmoidoscope attached to a small marble pedestal like Dr.

McSwain's. She hugged Tony and said into his ear, "I'm going to kill you. Even worse; I'm going to get you back."

Livvy laughed so hard tears ran down her face. Even Dr. White was laughing. Elizabeth tried to pull away from Tony and make her way back to the wall opposite Dr. White. Tony grabbed her arm and said, "Stay here a minute, Elizabeth."

She froze. *What could possibly happen now?* She wanted to run to Livvy's protection.

Tony clamped his hand on her upper arm. He reached into a large cardboard box where the awards were housed and pulled out a plaque. He turned the writing to his chest so Elizabeth couldn't see it.

He can't be planning to embarrass me further. No, not Tony.

"We've come to the end of our funny awards. I appreciate everyone's sense of humor. Please know my goal was to build our team. We're a blunt group, and we gig each other regularly, but we're like the military. We stick together to meet our common goal. And, like in the military, we recognize greatness."

Where's he going with this?

The room went quiet.

"As I collected the ballots, I received all kinds of feedback about different people on our medical staff. One thing kept coming up, and that's what this last award is about. Surgeons and staff expressed great respect for one particular member of our team. Over and over again, I heard about integrity and hard work and team spirit and honesty and always, always doing the right thing for the patient. There was indeed a miracle." He paused for effect, then continued. "I must tell you about this miracle: many LSU surgeons complimented a Tulane Surgery intern."

People laughed, acknowledging the LSU and Tulane emergency room relationship was the most contentious and competitive in the system.

Elizabeth wondered why Tony was holding on to her arm. *Does he want me to present this award?*

He said, "Our new award is the Tulane Surgery Intern of the Year, and this year, it goes to my dear friend, Dr. Elizabeth Roberts."

Elizabeth's mouth formed an *O*. She could think of nothing to say. Tony let go of her arm and handed her the plaque. The applause was thunderous. Nobody clapped louder than Dr. White. He smiled and nodded at her.

When the applause subsided, Elizabeth found the words to speak. She said, "Thanks to all of you for this. Nothing happens without a team. It is my honor to do my duty. I'm proud to be part of Tulane Surgery."

Still reeling from surprise, she walked back to the open arms of Livvy and Aoife.

"You deserve that, Crème Puff," Livvy told her. "You're a good soul." Coming from Livvy, that was high praise indeed.

Acknowledgments

I owe my deepest appreciation to the patients and employees of Charity Hospital in New Orleans. I entered her doors a scared naïve South Carolina girl and left them a confident surgeon. I learned from every patient, nurse, technician, doctor, and colleague. We are forever a family.

I owe special thanks to David Hancock and Morgan James publishing for having faith in me. I'd like to thank Gayle West for her help throughout the process and for making our collaboration fun.

My devoted editor, Phyllis Mueller, has made me a better writer than I otherwise would have been. The year 2022 was a particularly challenging year for her, but she never gave up on this project. I thank Cortney Donelson for her copyediting and book organizational skills. The production of a novel is truly a team effort.

Kudos to my beta readers! Nikki Pepper was particularly helpful as she committed many hours to improving the manuscript, despite her demanding corporate job. I am grateful to Joe McKnight, Cathy Cox, Susan Kalota, Ray Atkins, Rich Keegan, Tracie Arnold, Libby Pauley, Mary Anne Walser, and Janet Brumfield. Reading and critiquing an unfinished manuscript is a daunting task, and I appreciate the time and energy involved.

My stories would have never turned into novels without the nudge of Dr. Norman McSwain. He was one of my mentors at Tulane Surgery and a legend in the world of trauma surgery. I thank him posthumously for his support of my work. His daughter, Merry, continues to support my books. His close friend, Dr. Ken Mattox, a living legend in the world of trauma surgery has also been very supportive. I'm forever grateful to my many excellent mentors. Dr. Raju Thomas at Tulane Urology has been very supportive of my work and my entire career. He's one of those teachers that you can call when you have a tough case twenty-five years after you are no longer his student, and he will freely give his help and advice.

My husband, Jesse, is always supporting me. He does one hundred things per day to "move our family forward." I could never ask for a better life partner.

The world of surgery, for me, has always been about the patients. The stories in this novel are fiction. I have written about no specific patient. I honor your trust in me as your surgeon and would never expose private medical information. The stories represent an amalgam of the funny, the horrific, the heartbreakingly brave, and the tragic tails of *Mother Charity.*

My deepest gratitude is for the experiences afforded me at the great Charity Hospital of New Orleans.

About the Author

Martha B. Boone, M.D. was a surgery resident and urology resident at Tulane and trained at Charity Hospital in New Orleans from 1985 to 1991. She retired from the practice of urology after thirty-five years to travel and write. She is the author of *The Big Free* and *The Unfettered Urologist.* Dr. Boone lives in an Atlanta suburb with her husband.

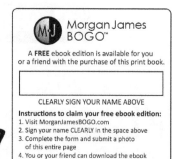

Printed in the USA
CPSIA information can be obtained
at www.ICGtesting.com
JSHW021453130324
59151JS00004B/46